King Cotton in International Trade

World Trade Institute Advanced Studies

Series Editor

Thomas Cottier (*World Trade Institute*)

VOLUME 1

The titles published in this series are listed at *brill.com/wtia*

King Cotton in International Trade

*The Political Economy of
Dispute Resolution at the* WTO

By

Meredith A. Taylor Black

BRILL
NIJHOFF

LEIDEN | BOSTON

Library of Congress Cataloging-in-Publication Data

Names: Taylor Black, Meredith A., author.
Title: King cotton in international trade : the political economy of dispute resolution at the WTO / by Meredith A. Taylor Black.
Description: Leiden ; Boston : Brill Nijhoff, 2016. | Series: World Trade Institute advanced studies ; volume 1 | Based on author's thesis (doctoral - University of Berne, Switzerland), 2010. | Includes bibliographical references and index.
Identifiers: LCCN 2016009518 (print) | LCCN 2016009726 (ebook) | ISBN 9789004313439 (hardback : alk. paper) | ISBN 9789004313446 (e-book) | ISBN 9789004313446 (E-book)
Subjects: LCSH: Cotton trade--Law and legislation. | Foreign trade regulation. | World Trade Organization. | United States--Foreign economic relations.
Classification: LCC K3947.C68 T39 2016 (print) | LCC K3947.C68 (ebook) | DDC 382/.41351--dc23
LC record available at http://lccn.loc.gov/2016009518

Typeface for the Latin, Greek, and Cyrillic scripts: "Brill." See and download: brill.com/brill-typeface.

ISSN 2405-9331
ISBN 978-90-04-31343-9 (hardback)
ISBN 978-90-04-31344-6 (e-book)

Copyright 2016 by Koninklijke Brill NV, Leiden, The Netherlands.
Koninklijke Brill NV incorporates the imprints Brill, Brill Hes & De Graaf, Brill Nijhoff, Brill Rodopi and Hotei Publishing.
All rights reserved. No part of this publication may be reproduced, translated, stored in a retrieval system, or transmitted in any form or by any means, electronic, mechanical, photocopying, recording or otherwise, without prior written permission from the publisher.
Authorization to photocopy items for internal or personal use is granted by Koninklijke Brill NV provided that the appropriate fees are paid directly to The Copyright Clearance Center, 222 Rosewood Drive, Suite 910, Danvers, MA 01923, USA.
Fees are subject to change.

This book is printed on acid-free paper and produced in a sustainable manner.

For your sustained support and faith in me,

thank you

Professor Cottier, Scott, and Pietro;

generous interviewees;

my collaborator in love and life, Geoffrey;

my devoted mother and our family's champion, Nancy;

and 'migrate' and loving father, G. Kent.

And

to my beloved children

Henry, Mary Margaret, and William.

Never give up.

Contents

Preface XI
Abbreviations-A XII
Abbreviations-B XV
Abstract XVIII

Introduction   1

PART 1
Economic and Political Backdrop of US-Upland Cotton

1 Global Trade of Upland Cotton   7
   1.1 Cotton Trading, Supply and Demand Patterns   10
   1.2 Unique Nature of Cotton as Non-Edible Commodity   14
   1.3 US Cotton Production and Its Economic Relation to Total US Agriculture   18
   1.4 Importance of Cotton to Developing/African Countries   22
   1.5 Cotton Cost Comparisons between US and Other Producers   27

2 Political Economy of Agricultural Subsidy Programs   31
   2.1 History of US Cotton Subsidy Programs   31
   2.2 US Cotton Subsidy Programs at Time of Brazil Challenge   44
   2.3 Other Country Subsidy Programs (China, EU)   52
   2.4 Political Power of US Cotton Lobby and US Legislative Process   54

3 WTO Political Environment Prior to *US-Upland Cotton* Case   62
   3.1 Multilateral Agriculture Negotiations and the Formation of the WTO   64
   3.2 Agricultural Reform Efforts Post-Uruguay Round   67
   3.3 Role of African Cotton Producing Countries before Cotton Dispute   78
   3.4 Role of Brazil before Cotton Dispute   86
   3.5 Summary of Part 1   96

PART 2
Anatomy of the US-Upland Cotton *Dispute and Its Jurisprudential Impact on Agricultural Subsidies under* WTO *Rules*

4 Origins of Brazil's *US-Upland Cotton*   103
   4.1 Brazil's Strategic Goals and Relationship with EC Sugar Challenge   103
   4.2 Strong Evidentiary Basis for Brazil's Challenge   118
   4.3 Legal and Economic Assistance to Brazil   121
   4.4 Novel Legal and Evidentiary Issues   129

5 WTO Dispute Settlement: Case Study on *US-Upland Cotton*   132
   5.1 WTO Dispute Settlement Overview   132
   5.2 Relevant WTO Agreements: AoA and SCM Agreements   134
   5.3 Consultation   147
   5.4 Original Panel Proceedings   149
   5.5 Appellate Body Proceedings   180
   5.6 DSU Article 21.5 Compliance Proceedings   214
   5.7 Appellate Body Proceedings under Article 21.5   227
   5.8 Arbitration Proceedings under Article 22.6   237
        Summary of Arbitration Findings   261

6 *US-Upland Cotton:* Key Legal Findings as Precedent for Future WTO Dispute Challenges to Agricultural Subsidies and Lessons Learned from the Involvement of Least Developed Countries   262
   6.1 Key Legal Findings   262
   6.2 Lessons from the Involvement of Chad and Benin   279
   6.3 Summary of Part 2   297

PART 3
Relevance of the US-Upland Cotton *Dispute on the* WTO's *Legislative Mechanism, Agricultural Subsidy Programs of* WTO *Members at Domestic Level, and Sustainability of the World Trade Organization*

7 Impact of *US-Upland Cotton's* Legal Precedent on Negotiation Leverage within the Doha Development Agenda of the WTO   303
   7.1 Brazil   304
   7.2 The C-4, Cotton Initiative and the Creation of the Subcommittee on Cotton   324

CONTENTS

8 **Political Limits on Implementation in the United States** 356
   8.1 Reform in the US and Its Limitations 357
   8.2 Brazil-US Memorandum of Understanding and June Framework 376

9 **Effect of Non-Compliance by the US: Ethical Systematic Considerations** 385
   9.1 Ethical Basis for the Cotton Findings and for Future Reform 385
   9.2 US Threat to the Legitimacy and Sustainability of the WTO 391
   9.3 Summary of Part 3 402

Summation of Findings and Conclusion 403

General References 407
Index 414

Preface

The overall intent of this book is to provide the analytical and evidentiary foundations to support the conclusion that WTO dispute settlement system, coupled with a parallel multilateral negotiation process, can establish, expose, and remedy significant and unethical trade distortions in the area of agricultural subsidies.

The chosen case for study is the *US- Subsidies on Upland Cotton*. Detailed analysis of the jurisprudence, findings, and underlying legal, economic and ethical basis for the findings of the *Cotton* Panel, Appellate Body, and Arbitrators reports are conducted to examine their present and future impact on both the multilateral and domestic reform of agricultural subsidies. The study also required the analysis and evaluation of possible outcomes and limitations of retaliation efforts by Brazil in its efforts to implement US compliance with the WTO trade decisions. The negotiating and political *causatum* related to this dispute are the Cotton Initiative and the ongoing Doha Round negotiations. The interconnectedness of the WTO dispute settlement process and negotiating dynamics of the Doha Round are established based on research and interviews with leading Government negotiators, and government and private sector litigators. Further, the impact of Brazil's challenge on the Cotton Initiative and the strategic interactions of developing and developed countries in the Doha negotiations is examined through the lens of governmental negotiators and NGO representatives.

At a broader level, a study of the *Cotton* case provides a context in which to understand the ethical basis underlying many trade rules, and in particular, those relating to agricultural subsidies and their impact on weaker and smaller WTO Members. The case highlights the key role of WTO dispute settlement decisions in establishing and bringing to light WTO-inconsistent subsidy and trading practices that reflect an unethical application of economic and political power by larger and richer WTO Members. It aims to demonstrate the potential impact of such ethics-based findings on ongoing negotiations and future domestic policy reform by such richer WTO Members.

Abbreviations-A

International Trade – General, Law, Associations, Organizations

General Trade and Legal Terminology

Ad val.	Ad valorem (in proportion to worth)
AD	anti-dumping
AMS	aggregate measure of support
Art.	Article
CVD	countervailing duties
FTA	free trade agreement
GDP	gross domestic product
GM	genetically modified
GMO	genetically modified organism
GNP	gross national product
H(T)S	Harmonized Tariff System
IGO	intergovernmental organization
IP	intellectual property
IPR(s)	intellectual property rights(s)
LDC	least-developed countries
LMG	like-minded group
NGO	non-governmental organization
NTB	non-tariff barrier
QR(s)	quantitative restriction(s)
R&D	research and development
S&D	special and differential treatment
USD	U.S. Dollar

International Organizations

ACWL	Advisory Centre on WTO Law (inter-governmental)
CFC	Common Fund for Commodities
FAO	Food and Agriculture Organization of the United Nations
IBRD	International Bank for Reconstruction and Development (World Bank)
ICAC	International Cotton Advisory Committee
ICC	International Chamber of Commerce
ILO	International Labour Organization (UN)
IMF	International Monetary Fund
IMO	International Maritime Organization
ISO	International Organization for Standardization

ABBREVIATIONS-A   XIII

ITC	International Trade Centre UNCTAD/WTO
ITCSD	International Centre for Trade and Sustainable Development
ITF	International Task Force on Commodity Risk Management in Developing Countries
ITMF	International Textile Manufacturers Federation
OECD	Organization for Economic Co-operation and Development
UN(O)	United Nations (Organization)
UNCITRAL	UN Centre for International Trade Law
UNCTAD	UN Conference on Trade And Development
UNDP	UN Development Program
UNIDO	United Nations Industrial Development Organization
WB	World Bank
WIPO	World Intellectual Property Organization
WTO	World Trade Organization

World Trade Organization

AB	Appellate Body
ABR	Appellate Body Report
AoA	Agreement on Agriculture (WTO)
DDA	Doha Development Agenda
DG	Director General (WTO)
DSB	Dispute Settlement Body (WTO)
DSU	Dispute Settlement Understanding (WTO)
GATT	General Agreement on Tariffs and Trade (WTO)
HOD	Heads of Delegations
ITC	International Trade Commission (U.S.)
ITO	International Trade Organization
LMG	like-minded group
MFA	Multifibre Agreement (GATT 1947)
MFN	most-favoured-nation (clause, principle or treatment)
NAMA	non-agricultural market access NT national treatment (clause or principle)
RP	Reference Paper (WTO)
SPS	(Agreement on) Sanitary and Phytosanitary (Measures) (WTO)
TRIPS	(Agreement on) Trade-Related Aspects of Intellectual Property Rights (WTO)
UR	Uruguay Round
URAA	Uruguay Round Agreement on Agriculture (also: AoA)
WTO	World Trade Organization

Regional Trade Associations and Agreements

CAP	Common Agricultural Policy (EC)
CARICOM	Caribbean Community and Common Market
CCP	Common Commercial Policy
EAGGF	European Agricultural Guidance and Guarantee Fund
EC	European Community European Communities
EU	European Union
EURO	Euro currency
FTAA	Free Trade Area for the Americas
MERCOSUR	Southern Common Market
NAFTA	North American Free Trade Agreement
UK	United Kingdom

Abbreviations-B

Cotton Associations, Merchants, and US-Specific

Cotton Associations

ABRAPA	Brazilian Cotton Producers Association
ACSA	American Cotton Shippers Association
AFCOT	Association francaise cotonniere
A.C.A.	African Cotton & Textile Industries Federation
ACTIF	Alexandria Cotton Exporters Association
ALCOTEXA	Associacoa Mato-grossense dow Produtores de Algodao
AMPA	Brazil's Cotton Exporters Association
ANEA	Association des Producteurs de Coton Africains
APROCA	Australian Cotton Shippers Association
	Bremen Cotton Exchange
CAN	Centro Algodonero Nacional (Barcelona)
CCGA	California Cotton Growers and Ginners Associations
CICCA	Committee for International Co-operation between Cotton Associations
CCA	China Cotton Association The Cotton Corporation of India, Ltd
NCC	National Cotton Council of America
GCA	Gdynia Cotton Association
	Cotton Australia
	Cotton Board (USA)
	Cotton Incorporated
IFCP	International Forum for Cotton Promotion
Cotton SA	Cotton South Africa
CCI	Cotton Council International (USA)
EICA	Cotton Association of India
ICA	The International Cotton Association Ltd (Liverpool)
KCA	The Karachi Cotton Association
SMI-ATI	Federazione Imprese Tessili e Moda Italiene Southern Cotton Association
	Southern Cotton Association
SUPIMA	Supima Association of America
TCB	Tanzania Cotton Board

International Cotton Merchants

	Allenberg Cotton Co.
	America's Cotton Marketing Cooperatives
CALCOT	Calcot, Ltd
	Cargill Cotton
	Cotton Growers Cooperative
	King Cotton Magazine (Weil Brothers Cotton)
DAGRIS	Dagris SA, Companie Cotonniere SA (COPACO) Dunavant Enterprises, Inc.
ECOM	Ecom Agroindustrial Corporation, Ltd
LDCI	Louis Dreyfus Cotton International Olam
PCCA	Plains Cotton Cooperative Association
PCG	Plains Cotton Growers, Inc.
	Plexus Cotton Limited
	Paul Reinhart AG
	Staplcotn

US Legal and Cotton Acronyms

ACTPN	President's Advisory Committee for Trade Policy and Negotiations
APAC	Agricultural Policy Advisory Committee for Trade
Art.	Article
ATAC	Agricultural Technical Advisory Committee for Trade
CCC	Commodity Credit Corporation
CCGC	Carolinas Cotton Growers Cooperative
Cir.	Circuit
CIT	Court of International Trade (U.S.)
CRS	Congressional Research Service
ERS	Economic Research Service
EWG	Environmental Working Group
FAPRI	Food and Agricultural Policy Research Institute
FAS	Foreign Agricultural Service
FCIS	Federal Crop Insurance Corporation
NBER	National Bureau of Economic Research
NEC	National Economic Council
NCC	National Cotton Council of America
PCCA	Plains Cotton Cooperative Association
SWIG	Southwestern Irrigated Cotton Growers
TPRG	Trade Policy Review Group
TPSC	Trade Policy Staff Committee
USDA	United States Department of Agriculture
U.S.C.	U.S. Code

USDA	U.S. Department of Agriculture
USITC	United States International Trade Commission
USTR	United States Trade Representative, Office of the

US Farm Bills, Programs and Related Acronyms

ARP Act of 2000	Agricultural Risk Protection Act of 2000
FACT Act of 1990	Food, Agriculture, Conservation, and Trade Act of 1990
FAIR Act of 1996	Federal Agriculture Improvement and Reform Act of 1996
FSRI Act of 2002	Farm Security and Rural Investment Act of 2002
FCIC	Federal Crop Insurance Corporation
FY	Fiscal Year
FSC	Foreign Sales Corporation
GSM 102	General Sales Manager 102
GSM 103	General Sales Manager 103
ICAC	International Cotton Advisory Committee
LDP	Loan Deficiency payment
MY	Marketing Year
PFC payment	Production Flexibility Contract payment
SCGP	Supplier Credit Guarantee Program

Abstract

This book provides a comprehensive analysis of the *Cotton* dispute and its significant jurisprudential and negotiating effect on disciplining and containing the negative effects of highly trade-distorting agricultural subsidies of developed countries. To that end, this study (1) details the historic, economic, and political background leading up to Brazil's challenge of the US cotton subsidies and the main findings of the five WTO reports that largely upheld that challenge, (2) explores the impact of the initiation and results of that successful challenge in terms of political and negotiating dynamics involving agriculture subsidies and other trade-related issues in the WTO, (3) examines the effects on domestic agriculture subsidy reforms in the United States and the European Union, and (4) sets forth the possible impacts of the *Cotton* challenge on the negotiating end-game of the Doha Development Round.

The nature and effects of the political and economic asymmetries of the WTO Member states are examined throughout the study. It is noted how the *Cotton* decisions have enhanced the negotiating position of developing countries while continuing to highlight significant imbalances within the juridical and legislative functions of the WTO system. Additionally, the study examines the ethical considerations underlying and surrounding the dispute. The Panel and Appellate Body findings of massive price suppression negatively impacting smaller and weaker WTO Members provides a powerful ethical basis for real, long-term reform of trade-distorting agricultural subsidies.

In this light, the study concludes that Brazil's successful *Cotton* challenge enhanced the negotiating position and leverage of both Brazil and the C-4 African countries of Chad, Benin, Burkina Faso, and Mali. It also finds that the *Cotton* decisions were a leading factor in creating a coherent opposition by developing countries in the Doha negotiations, led by Brazil, to United States and EU attempts to maintain trade-distorting agricultural subsidies. It argues that the *Cotton* jurisprudence provides a coherent roadmap for future challenges to such subsidies and guidance for real domestic agricultural policy reform to avoid such challenges.

At the professional developmental level, the research, organization, and drafting of this book have provided the basis to develop the author's expertise within the general field of international trade law. The book has also enhanced the legal and analytical skills necessary to investigate a complex series of legal decisions involving a particular WTO dispute settlement case and its relationship to the negotiating dynamics of long-term reform within the World Trade Organization. At a broader level, this study is conducted to understand and describe the complexities of the international trading regime, the relevant international economic negotiation norms, the incorporation of WTO principles within the negotiation process, and diplomacy management.

It is hoped that the results of this analysis will prove to be a useful resource for future researchers investigating the relationship between the WTO dispute settlement process and domestic and multilateral policy reform.

Introduction

The WTO *Cotton* decisions[1] provide strong evidence about the deleterious effects, both in terms of ethics and consistency with WTO agreements, of developed countries' domestic agricultural policies on developing nations. In addition, it is a compelling case study highlighting the inter-connectedness of the WTO jurisprudence and negotiations. It illustrates the fact that the WTO offers the only realistic potential for developing countries to secure relief from trade-distorting domestic subsidies and additional substantive forms of support through measures such as export credit guarantees. The various Panel, Appellate Body and Arbitrator's decisions generated by the dispute have established important roadmaps for future dispute settlement challenges as well as providing the basis for real reform in ongoing and future multilateral WTO trade negotiations.

This book examines the multiple impacts that Brazil's landmark 2002–2009 challenge to U.S. upland cotton and export credit guarantee subsidies has had on national and world agricultural policy, WTO jurisprudence, and the Doha Trade Round negotiations. The successful WTO challenge by Brazil was the first to target massive domestic agricultural subsidies and export credit guarantees provided by a major developed country. The results of the case established as *fact* the worldwide price-suppressing effects on world cotton prices from the approximately $3 billion in annual U.S. cotton subsidies. The WTO ruled that the subsidies "created an artificial and persisting competitive advantage for US producers over all other operators."[2]

The initiation, prosecution, and results of the *Cotton* dispute have served as a focal point for demands by many WTO Members for real and lasting cuts in trade-distorting agricultural subsidies. Among the WTO Members most actively involved in the negotiations are those most competitively disadvantaged by the US subsidies – the West African cotton-producing countries. These include Benin and Chad, whose involvement in the *Cotton* proceedings constituted the first African involvement in any WTO dispute settlement proceedings. Indeed, their active participation in both the *Cotton* dispute and the later negotiations continues to highlight the ethical dimensions of these US subsidies.

Part 1 provides an economic and political backdrop of the historic as well as contemporary trends of world trade in cotton to highlight the overwhelming

---

[1] WTO *Cotton* dispute refers to five sets of decisions from 2004–2009, entitled *United States Subsidies on Upland Cotton*.
[2] Arbitrator's Report, *U.S.-Subsidies on Upland Cotton*, WT/DS 267/ARB/2, para. 5.221.

export dominance of the United States, despite it being a high-cost producer relative to non-subsidized developing and least developed producers. The subsidized world market power of the United States in cotton – which has existed for decades – reflects the fundamental asymmetries between these two groups of cotton-producing countries. Yet, the Uruguay Round *Agreement on Agriculture* and *Agreement on Subsidies and Countervailing Duties* provided, for the first time, a legal basis to limit such subsidies. Prior to the *Cotton* challenge, no WTO Member had assembled the evidentiary, economic, and legal basis to challenge the subsidy-caused asymmetries in many agricultural markets and *no* WTO Member had been particularly successful in limiting the magnitude of agricultural subsidies available to be used to sustain and even increase world production and export market share by the United States and other developed countries.

Part 2 first describes the dispute settlement process of the WTO and then sets forth a comprehensive study of the five *Cotton* dispute settlement reports. These five *Cotton* reports established a host of groundbreaking jurisprudence under the WTO *Agreement on Subsidies and Countervailing Duties* (SCM) and the *Agreement on Agriculture*. The legal strategy, argumentation and use of experts employed by Brazil established a clear practitioner's and evidentiary roadmap for future successful challenges to agricultural and other forms of trade-distorting subsidies. The comprehensive WTO Panel reports and Appellate Body decisions, as well as the Arbitrators' reports over the period from 2004–2009 created a body of jurisprudence that clarified in detail a number of subsidy-related issues that provides guidance for future challenges. These jurisprudential effects are developed throughout Part 2 of this book.

Of particular ethical and procedural importance is the successful participation by Chad and Benin and the incentive this provided for greater involvement by least-developed countries (LDCs) in future dispute settlement involvement. To this end, a number of lessons learned from *Cotton* are described, regarding the involvement of some countries (Chad and Benin) and non-involvement by other LDCs (Mali and Burkina Faso) in WTO dispute settlement. The *Cotton* dispute also exposes several limitations of the WTO dispute settlement system for LDCs, including the reality that non-participation will result in obtaining only secondary benefits actually secured by others and a limitation of the system as accentuated in *Cotton* in that it offers little short-term implementation benefits to LDCs.

Part 3 describes the primary 'multiplier effect' of *Cotton* – its political relevance and ability to impact the legislative function of the WTO. The underlying unethical nature of the US cotton subsidies that directly damaged developing and least-developed vulnerable cotton producers by lowering their prices was the driving "moral" force behind the *Cotton* decisions. Yet, the *Cotton* dispute also exposed the resistance of well-entrenched political forces within the United States to implement WTO-compliant domestic reform procedures. Evidence and argumentation are presented in this part of the book to demonstrate how *Cotton* allowed Brazil and a variety of G-20 Members to secure a strong presence as major players in the Doha negotiations. Further, the involvement of African countries in the *Cotton* dispute, and the results obtained, established the moral authority of African countries to insist on real reform of cotton trade as an integral part of the WTO Doha negotiations. Organized and empowered by the *Cotton* decisions, African cotton countries have been able to more effectively position themselves through the development and utilization of the *Sub-Committee on Cotton*, in these negotiations. Finally, a link is made between the dispute settlement process and the legislative function of the WTO is established by assessing the changing US and EU positions throughout the Doha negotiations.

In addition, Part 3 extends the analysis beyond the legal and political analyses of the case and provides argumentation for utilizing *Cotton* as a unique and particularly effective case study of the multiplier effects of WTO dispute settlement on policy decisions at the domestic level. This impact was felt not only in the United States but also in other subsidizing WTO Members such as the EU. The rulings by the WTO confirmed the existence of trade distorting effects of price-contingent and export subsidies on world commodity markets. In the case of sugar, the *Cotton* and *EC (EU) Sugar* disputes were important parts of a process of pushing the world's biggest subsidizer, the EU, to change the nature of their subsidies for sugar production and export to less trade-distorting ones. Reforms to the European Community's Common Agricultural Policy can partially be attributable to *Cotton* and its parallel challenge by Brazil in the *EC Sugar* dispute. Further, pursuant to the developments of the *Cotton* case, partial implementation in the United States has occurred, with the elimination of some prohibited domestic and export subsidies particular to cotton. However, the United States continues to provide direct production support in the form of US marketing loan subsidies and the 2008 US Farm Bill established the United States as the world leader in the volume and extent of trade-distorting subsidies.

Another key multiplier effect of the *Cotton* decisions has been the enhanced negotiating strength of Brazil and other developing countries in the Doha negotiations. The decision affirmed Brazil's leadership role in the negotiations as it sought, along with the C-4 African countries and other developing countries to push back against EU and US attempts to roll back certain aspects of the *Cotton* and *Sugar* decisions.

Given the timing of the submission of this book – only a few months after the final Arbitration determination – a number of multiplier effects are expected, but have not yet been realized. Therefore, Part 3 includes a discussion of additional likely outcomes from the final rulings and the state of the Doha negotiations as well as a treatment of ethical considerations and recommendations for the US and similarly-situated developed countries. An assessment of the reactions by the international community to continued non-compliance by the US is undertaken to elucidate why particular outcomes are expected.

Finally, the book closes with a summation of findings as they pertain to WTO jurisprudence and practice, the multilateral negotiations on agricultural subsidies, and domestic agricultural subsidy programs.

> This challenge extends beyond the US cotton program and is a fundamental threat to the conduct of the US domestic agricultural policy.[3]
> NATIONAL COTTON COUNCIL PRESIDENT AND CEO MARK LANGE

---

3 Cline, H., "Brazil Poised to be Major Cotton Player," *Western Farm Press*, (7 January 2004).

PART 1

Economic and Political Backdrop of US-Upland Cotton

∴

Part 1 explores the underlying economic and political backdrop of global trade in cotton. This part of the book provides a reference of understanding of the trade dynamics and economic conditions extant during prior WTO negotiation rounds and at the time of the initiation of the *Cotton* dispute. Such a reference is important to establish in order to properly identify the conditions that existed at the commencement of the dispute resolution process and to recognize the changes that ensued throughout the process and the accompanying negotiations. Finally, and most applicable to the thesis of this book, is the establishment of relevant economic and political factors that were affected and subsequently adjusted at the domestic level during the progression of dispute resolution and negotiations. Therefore, this portion of the book sets forth the importance of cotton within the historical framework and the foundational economic and political asymmetries of WTO cotton producing Members within the international trading system.

Chapter 1 offers an overview of the economic trends of the global trade of upland cotton and its unique characteristics as a non-edible agriculture crop; the patterns and economic trends of upland cotton production and exportation by the United States (US) and other important cotton producing countries with a focus on developing African countries; and production cost comparisons between the US and other producers. Chapter 2 examines extant subsidy programs, generally, with an emphasis on those in the US. Of particular import is the status of US subsidies at the time of Brazil's challenge; how those subsidies compare to other country subsidy programs; and the distinctive and well-entrenched politics of the cotton lobby in the US political system. To that end, this chapter presents USDA studies of the importance of cotton subsidies to the sustainability of US cotton production and exports. Finally, in Chapter 3, the trends and factors discussed in Chapters 1 and 2 are analyzed within the context of the World Trade Organization. First, an evaluation of agricultural reform efforts after the Uruguay Round is made. And second, the role of African cotton producing as well as Brazil and other developing countries before the *Cotton* dispute is described.

CHAPTER 1

Global Trade of Upland Cotton

> Cotton alone, of all the products of our soil or industry, stirs the emotions of whoever contemplates it. Furs, cattle, oil, gold, wheat, corn, railroads – the tale of all these on this continent excites the imagination as one perceives with what courage and adventurousness men have bent the resources of nature to their use. But it is the melancholy distinction of cotton to be the very stuff of high drama and tragedy, of bloody civil war and the unutterable woe of human slavery.
> DAVID L. COHN *The Life and Times of King Cotton* New York, 29 June 1956[4]

Cotton is produced for its soft white fiber, which is universally used as a raw material in textiles and clothing. Cotton is one of the most important textile fibers in the world, accounting for about thirty-five (35) percent of total world fiber use,[5] and is one of the most valuable and widely produced agricultural crops in the world.[6] It is a heavily traded agricultural commodity, nationally and internationally, and is grown in more than one hundred (100) countries and traded among over one hundred and fifty (150) countries. At the time of the initiation of the *Cotton* dispute in September of 2002,[7] approximately twenty (20) million metric tons of cotton was produced annually on approximately eighty (80) million acres worldwide.

Cotton is a tropical plant, although advances in plant breeding and cultivation techniques allow it to be produced in countries from approximately forty-seven (47) degrees North latitude (Ukraine) to thirty-two (32) degrees South (Australia).[8] This is particularly important because within this region lie many of the world's developing and least developed countries (LDCs). Indeed, more than half of the cotton producing countries are classified by the United Nations as developing countries, with about half of those classified as LDCs.[9] Although

---

4 Cohn, D., *The Life and Times of King Cotton*, Oxford University Press, New York © 1956, Forward.
5 From: http://www.ers.usda.gov/Briefing/Cotton/.
6 International Trade Centre: Product and Market Development, "Cotton Exporter's Guide," © International Trade Centre WTO/UNCTAD/WTO 2007, ITC/P218.E/PMD/MDS/07-XI, p. 3.
7 *US-Upland* Cotton, Original Proceedings, Panel Report, Brazil, Exhibit 9, "Cotton: World Statistics." Bulletin of the International Cotton Advisory Committee, September, 2002.
8 UNCTAD website (http://unctad.org/infocomm/anglais/cotton/characteristics.htm).
9 UNCTAD website (http://unctad.org/infocomm/anglais/cotton/characteristics.htm).

cotton's economic value on the world market is not high, in terms of its total percentage value of goods traded, its economic value is significant to those countries in which it is produced, particularly developing and least developed countries. In West and Central Africa, for example, about ten (10) million people depend on cotton production for their incomes.[10]

Cotton is produced in geographically large countries, such as China, India, Brazil and the US as well as several smaller West African and a few countries in the EU.[11] According to the Foreign Agriculture Service of the United States Department of Agriculture, the top exporters of cotton in 2002 were: the United States, the Republic of Uzbekistan, the Francophone African States, Australia, Argentina and Greece. By 2009, the US remained the largest exporter of cotton followed by India, Uzbekistan, Brazil and Australia. In terms of production, the 2002 rankings were: (1) the Peoples Republic of China, (2) the United States, (3) India, (4) Pakistan, and (5) the Republic of Uzbekistan. China remained the highest producer in 2009, followed by India, the US, Pakistan, and Brazil.[12] Figure 1

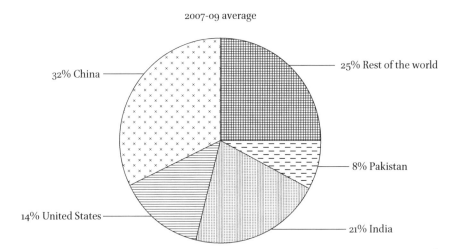

FIGURE 1   *Share of global cotton production by four major producers.*
SOURCE: USDA, ECONOMIC RESEARCH SERVICE USING DATA FROM USDA, WORLD AGRICULTURAL OUTLOOK BOARD, WORLD AGRICULTURAL SUPPLY AND DEMAND ESTIMATES.

---

10   UNCTAD website (http://unctad.org/infocomm/anglais/cotton/characteristics.htm).
11   For a country-specific resource, *see*, Turner, B., *The Statesman's Yearbook: The Politics, Cultures, and Economies of the World: 2007*, 143rd Edition, Palgrave Macmillan, (2006).
12   Rankings were calculated in 480-pound bales. Totals were derived by utilizing USDA information on the National Cotton Council of America's website, last accessed April 24, 2010 at www.cotton.org/econ/cropinfo/cropdata/rankings.

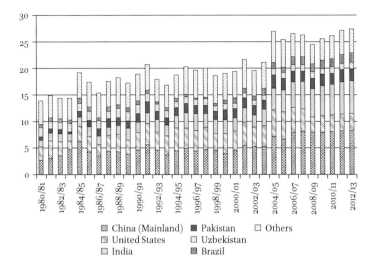

FIGURE 2 *World cotton production (million tonnes), by main countries, 1980/81–2012/13.*
SOURCE: UNCTAD SECRETARIAT, BASED ON INTERNATIONAL COTTON ADVISORY COMMITTEE (ICAC) STATISTICS.

shows the share of total worldwide production by the four major producers in 2007–2009 and Figure 2 shows the historical and projected production of cotton worldwide.

The position of the US as one of the world's largest producers and exporters of cotton is somewhat paradoxical in light of the nature of cotton production in the US. As described in Section 5, production costs in the US are relatively high. Absent significant government intervention, the role of the US in global cotton markets would be markedly different. The economist employed by Brazil on the *Cotton* case, Daniel Sumner of the University of California, Davis, testified that from 2002 to 2005 cotton received twenty-two (22) percent of the total value of government payments for agriculture, yet cotton accounted for only approximately two percent of the total value of US agricultural production.[13] The extent of US subsidization of cotton makes cotton an outlier in the context of total government spending on US agriculture and enables the United States to not only be ranked among the largest cotton-producing countries, but also enables the US to be the leading cotton exporting country, accounting for

---

13   Sumner, Daniel A., "U.S. Farm Policy and the White Commodities: Cotton, Rice, Sugar and Milk," International Food & Agricultural Trade Policy Council (Washington, DC: IPC, 2007). Last visited 26 Apr. 2010<http://www.agritrade.org/Publications/PolicyFocus/Farm_Bill_5_white_commodities.pdf>, p. 1.

over one-third of global trade in raw cotton.[14] Significant domestic cotton production is possible in the US primarily because the strong political ties between the US cotton lobby and the US legislative system allows US producers to exercise their political advantage to the detriment of developing nations. The resulting economic asymmetries between developing and developed countries play a significant role in how and to what extent countries produce and trade cotton.

1.1   Cotton Trading, Supply and Demand Patterns

Cotton is a product that is widely traded internationally. In its raw form, about thirty (30) percent of global cotton fiber consumption crosses international borders, a larger share than for wheat, corn, soybeans, or rice. Much of the world's cotton again crosses international borders after processing into the form of yarn and fabric.[15] As a result, cotton is a commodity whose prices are strongly dependent upon global factors of supply and demand in both pre-processing and post-processing markets. In addition, cotton can be produced and purchased from a variety of sources, rather than a few branded producers, and cotton output is relatively price-sensitive.[16]

Supply is determined, primarily by the total acreage planted and the yield per acre. The total acreage that farmers choose to plant[17] is determined by historical production and perceived demand. Yield is determined by such factors as the quality of seed, soil, topography, and weather conditions. Supply in some countries such as the United States, China, and India, among others, is also influenced during many years by the extent to which governments decide to intervene and provide support to producers. Producers will be more willing to plant cotton where there is government support and an actual or perceived guarantee that the cotton produced will be purchased.[18] American Enterprise Institute Project on Agricultural Policy for the 2007 Farm Bill and

---

14   From: http://www.ers.usda.gov/Briefing/Cotton/.
15   http://www.ers.usda.gov/Briefing/Cotton/background.htm.
16   Statement by Andrew Macdonald, Export Economist of Brazil and International Cotton Markets, 7 October 2003, Oral Statement, Second Meeting, Panel Stage of *US-Upland Cotton.* Later memorialized as a Declaration, signed in May, 2003.
17   Womach, J., "Cotton Production and Support in the United States," US Congressional Research Service, 24 June 2004, p. 7. (26 Apr 2010)<http://www.nationalaglawcenter.org/assets/crs/RL32442.pdf>.
18   *See,* Sumner, D., "Farm Subsidy Tradition and Modern Agricultural Realities," Paper for

GLOBAL TRADE OF UPLAND COTTON

Beyond<http://aic.ucdavis.edu/research/farmbill07/aeibriefs/20070515_sumnerRationalesfinal.pdf>last visited 30 June 2010.

The demand for raw cotton stems primarily from users in the textile and clothing sectors, including ginners, spinners, and the end consumers. It should be noted that many of the leading cotton producers are also major consumers of cotton. The top three consumers, China, India, and Pakistan, are leading mill users of raw cotton and together these three countries account for two-thirds of world consumption, with Turkey, Brazil, and the US following as the next largest consuming countries.[19] Figure 3 shows the global share of mill use cotton demand on the part of the four largest consuming countries.

The importance of international trade in the production and consumption of cotton means that cotton prices are determined at the global level. The basic supply and demand factors of cotton and the functioning of the world cotton markets are important to examine. The cotton market is similar to other commodity markets, wherein price is negotiated between sellers and buyers, based on their perceptions and anticipations of how supply and demand will shift. Previous production and consumption trends dictate how the various actors will make decisions to some extent. Especially important are the links between

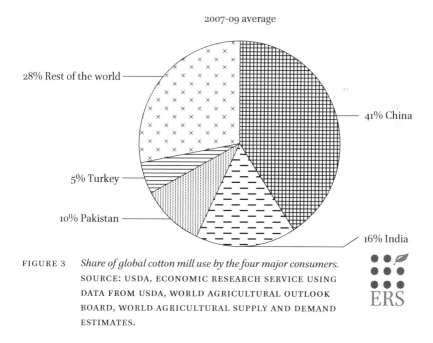

FIGURE 3 *Share of global cotton mill use by the four major consumers.*
SOURCE: USDA, ECONOMIC RESEARCH SERVICE USING DATA FROM USDA, WORLD AGRICULTURAL OUTLOOK BOARD, WORLD AGRICULTURAL SUPPLY AND DEMAND ESTIMATES.

---

19   USDA, "Briefing Rooms: Cotton Background," Economic Research Service, <http://www.ers.usda.gov/Briefing/Cotton/background.htm>last visited 30 June 2010.

how prices are set on the New York Cotton Exchange's (NYCE) futures market from various national 'spot markets,' and the role that the NYCE plays as an indicator of the current price of cotton as well as the ultimate predictor of future prices.[20] In general, the prices determined on the New York Cotton Exchange correspond in large part to market fundamentals in the US. While no single futures market can be considered to be the global benchmark for cotton prices, there are two indices that, together, provide an international cotton price benchmark. The Cotlook A index is the average of the five lowest upland cotton price quotes from nineteen (19) different markets. The Cotlook B index is the average of the lowest three price quotes from lesser grade, coarse count cotton. Cotlook's A-Index and the B-Index are heavily relied upon by traders and consumers of cotton as signaling the world market for cotton. The Cotlook A Index is the most widely used and intended as an *ex post* record of the offering prices on the international raw market. It is used by companies trading in cotton as well as governmental and international organizations such as the United Nations' Centre for Trade & Development (UNCTAD) and the International Cotton Advisory Committee (ICAC).[21]

The Cotlook A and B Indexes, coupled with published contract prices on the NYCE, set the world cotton price and place the US in a position of being the "driver" of the world cotton prices. The most influential market in the world is the US because of the size of its market on both the demand and supply sides. Especially in recent decades, the US produces significantly more than it consumes and, as a result, has a strong need to export its cotton. The resulting cotton price quotes from the US dominate, to a large extent, prices determined from local production in other domestic-use and export markets.[22] Further, the transparency and availability of information regarding US production and consumption, available from the United States Department of Agriculture, signals prices on the New York futures market and communicates to the world the intention of cotton-market players from planters to traders.

Cotton is primarily used for textiles. The overall amount of world cotton production and mill use have increased in the last fifty years.[23] Further, world

---

20 From: http://www.ers.usda.gov/Briefing/Cotton/.
21 Gillson, I., Poulton, C., Balcombe, K., and Page, S., "Understanding the Impact of Cotton Subsidies on Developing Countries," Working Paper, (May, 2004), p. 9. http://www.odi.org.uk/resources/download/3608.pdf last visited 2 June, 2010.
22 From: http://www.ers.usda.gov/Briefing/Cotton/.
23 There has been a noticeable decrease in both, in the past three years due primarily to the global commodity price crisis, the cotton futures market crisis, and the global financial and economic crisis. (Townsend, 2009).

cotton yields have increased considerably in the last twenty-five (25) years with output nearly doubling in terms of kilograms per hectare. Commensurate with the increase in production, average cotton revenue has been on a general decline.[24] Part of this is due to the fact that the general trend of the utilization of cotton in textile production has been steadily diminishing over the last thirty-five years, to about half of its percentage use. Approximately thirty-six percent of world textiles now use cotton fiber.[25] In recent years, the decline in cotton prices has been more pronounced than that of agricultural prices, generally. John Baffes of the World Bank proffered at "The Multilateral Trading System: A US-African Dialogue," sponsored by the iDEAS & Carnegie Endowment in Washington, DC (20 July 2009) that the gap between cotton and agricultural prices is likely to persist as shown below in Figure 4. Further, he commented on the trends of agricultural commodities, noting that the prices many agricultural products increased steadily in the years preceding the price spike in 2008 but that cotton prices generally declined during this period and failed to spike due, in large part, to the presence of cotton subsidies.[26] Further, he noted that a reduction of subsidies during the Doha Development negotiations is a key

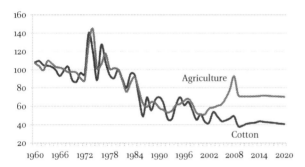

FIGURE 4   *Price indeces for agriculture and cotton real, MUV-deflated. Indices, 1980 = 100.*

---

24   The general revenue decline has seen sporadic spiking but is on a general decline.
25   Townsend, Terry, Executive Director of the International Cotton Advisory Committee (ICAC), "The Multilateral Trading System: A US-African Dialogue," Presentation, sponsored by the iDEAS & Carnegie Endowment in Washington, DC (July 20, 2009).
26   The other rationales Mr. Baffes provided for why cotton prices did not increase during the 2008 boom were: (1) the rapid expansion of Bt cotton in China and India and (2) the fact that, globally, cotton is not substitutable among grains; therefore, the increased demand for maize and edible oils did not affect cotton, similarly. Baffes, John, "The Multilateral Trading System: A US-African Dialogue," Presentation, sponsored by the iDEAS & Carnegie Endowment in Washington, DC (July 20, 2009).

factor to improving the global trade of cotton, particularly African cotton production and producers.[27]

1.2   Unique Nature of Cotton as Non-Edible Commodity

Cotton, unlike the other major agricultural commodities receiving substantial governmental support, is a non-edible commodity. For example, the FSRI Act of 2002 identifies ten crops for benefits such as loan deficiency, production flexibility contract and direct payments. These are wheat, corn, grain sorghum, barley, oats, rice, soybeans, other oilseeds, peanuts, and cotton. In addition, peanuts and soybeans have received important consideration in previous farm bills. Of these, cotton is the only non-edible agricultural commodity. Dr. David Debucquet of the International Food Policy Research Institute (IFPRI) recently argued, in line with an increasing consensus, that food should be defined as all agricultural commodities minus non-edible products.[28] Therefore, there is an explicit separation between food and non-edible products like cotton and, as a result, the rationales often supplied to justify the subsidization of agricultural food products, especially those based on moral arguments, are likely to not be applicable to cotton.

A number of justifications have been used at the domestic level to secure government assistance for agricultural food commodities. These rationales have been recognized and supported at the WTO as well, even to the extent that agriculture is treated separately and differently from non-agricultural products. One of the most compelling justifications for food production support programs is the argument based on the moral imperative of increasing food availability, globally. According to this line of reasoning, allowing some subsidization of food crops enables countries to export surplus agricultural food products to countries that are not able to produce enough or pay for sufficient food to feed their populations. This argument has been used, for

---

27   The other rationales Mr. Baffes provided for why cotton prices did not increase during the 2008 boom were: (1) the rapid expansion of Bt cotton in China and India and (2) the fact that, globally, cotton is not substitutable among grains; therefore, the increased demand for maize and edible oils did not affect cotton, similarly. Baffes, John, "The Multilateral Trading System: A US-African Dialogue," Presentation, sponsored by the iDEAS & Carnegie Endowment in Washington, DC (July 20, 2009).

28   Debucquet, D., "Food and Agricultural Trade Implications for Food Security," WBI Course on Agricultural Trade and Export, Vienna, (April, 2010). < http://www.slideshare.net/DLabordeD/food-and-agricultural-trade-implications-for-food-security>last visited 3 June, 2010.

example, to support agricultural food crop subsidies in order to lower prices, increase production, and export food surpluses from the US to some African countries. However, because of its non-edible nature, this moral imperative argument cannot logically be applied to cotton. In fact, the findings of the *Cotton* dispute demonstrate that subsidizing cotton actually reduces incomes for some African countries, along with the ability to produce and purchase food, and thereby adds to the development problems in many less developed countries.

Another widely used argument for food crop subsidization is one of food security. This line of reasoning is based on the notion that consumer food security promotes national interests. There are two main facets of this general argument. First, policymakers often claim that reliance on local food production will increase food security by reducing supply variability[29] and global market fluctuations. However, it has been shown that decreasing food imports does not increase food security and that emphasizing local food production is "misguided and harmful to the world's poor."[30] Second, concerns about food quality have also been included under the general rubric of food security. Concerns over food quality, especially as related to the emergence of genetically modified (GM) foods and the debated health consequences of consuming such products, is used to defend the separate treatment of agricultural products within the international trade regime, and maintain protectionist measures at the domestic level. Both veins of argumentation cannot be applied to cotton, because cotton is not consumed as food. Therefore, at both the domestic and international levels, negotiators have been hard pressed to effectively justify protectionist measures for cotton based on food security arguments. Nonetheless, the food security argument is widely used, even for cotton. At the international level, a division between agricultural and non-agricultural products has persisted at the WTO due to an on-going consensus that agriculture is 'special.' As a result, agricultural negotiations have been undertaken and rules developed separately from industrial products. One of the main arguments employed by WTO Members is that of food security. At the domestic level, this line of reasoning is employed to justify support for cotton. In the US, for

---

29 Sumner, D., "Food Security, Trade, and Agricultural Commodity Policy" as found in *Agricultural Policy for the 21st Century*, edited by Tweeten, L. and Thompson, S., Iowa State Press (2002), pp. 231–244.

30 Sumner, "Food Security, Trade, and Agricultural Commodity Policy" as found in *Agricultural Policy for the 21st Century*, edited by Tweeten, L. and Thompson, S., Iowa State Press (2002), p. 243.

example, the 1985 Farm Bill, which covered cotton and its related programs, was entitled the "Food Security Act."

A third food-based argument for agricultural subsidies is often presented in a 'scarcity or surplus' framework in which proponents of agricultural subsidies argue that it is better to have a surplus of agricultural products than for a country to find itself in a position of a food shortage. The applicability of this argument to cotton is problematic because, again, cotton is non-edible and therefore cannot be considered a food. In addition, agricultural markets governed by free market forces, without large-scale government intervention, generally thrive where genuine comparative advantage exists. In this light, it is important to note the experiences of New Zealand and Australia, which largely removed farm subsidy and trade restrictive programs and have experienced increased productivity and have not suffered from shortages or disruptions of food supplies.

The above arguments for agricultural support programs, based on agricultural products as food, are not compelling in the case of cotton. However, there are some arguments for agricultural subsidies that do not rely on the edibility of agricultural products. These include national security, open space preservation, rural development, and production variability. In the national security argument, it is claimed that domestic cotton production should be supported because of the potential need to domestically produce cotton military uniforms during times of war. However, this argument is weakened by the fact that, currently, there is not enough domestic textile mill capacity to enable the US to domestically produce enough material to fully supply US troop levels.

Another non-food based argument in support of agricultural subsidy and protection programs is based on the idea that farms provide open space and good land stewardship. These externalities would not be accounted for in a free market and, as a result, need to be promoted by the public sector. While there is an economic argument to support the idea of governmental subsidies to increase the preservation of open space and land stewardship, it is also the case that the incentive provided by subsidies to increase production also leads to increased soil degradation and other negative environmental externalities such as non-point water pollution and the overuse of pesticides and fertilizers.

A third non-food based argument in favor of agricultural support policies is based on the concept of rural community development.[31] It is worth noting that many subsidies were originally designed to be temporary measures aimed at promoting diversity, dynamism, and economic development in rural communities.

---

31 Wright, B., "Goals and Realities for Farm Policy," as found in Sumner, D., *Agricultural Policy Reform in the US*, American Enterprise Press, Washington, D.C., © 1995, p. 17.

On the whole, however, the rural development objectives often discussed in the Farm Bills have not been met because the majority of governmental farm support payments are received by a relatively small number of large farmers and corporate-owned farms.

Another traditional non-food based argument in support of subsidies is based on stabilizing agricultural markets[32] and specifically, farm incomes because of the degree of price and yield variability in these markets due to weather-induced production fluctuations. It is claimed that guaranteed prices and support loan rates increase stability and efficiency because it reduces risk to farmers and encourages them to engage in agricultural production where they might not otherwise be inclined to do so.[33] It is argued that increasing income parity between farmers and non-agricultural producers as well as assisting with the acquisition of land by providing adequate rural credit, makes farming a more attractive career choice for young persons and thereby promotes family farming.[34] In addition, it is claimed that providing support programs to reduce stabilize prices and production in output markets will also lead to greater stability in input markets for factors such as farm implements, fertilizers, seeds, and other inputs. This argument is less compelling in the case of cotton given that the vast majority of the US cotton crop is produced on irrigated land in the southern and western parts of the country. As a result, stochastic weather-based output fluctuations are much smaller for cotton than for many other agricultural products. In addition, futures markets risk stemming from output variability can be hedged against through the use of futures contracts and can be mitigated through private insurance.[35] Further, similar to other sectors of the economy, consumption and production would adjust to price changes,[36] especially with increasingly global markets.

---

32   Goodman, R., "A Five-Point Defense of Farm Subsidies," Alabama Farmers Federation, Member of American Farm Bureau, < http://www.alfafarmers.org/issues/farm_programs.phtml>last visited 3 June, 2010. Dr. Goodman is the Alabama Cooperative Extension System Farm Economist and Auburn University Associate Professor of Agricultural Economics.

33   Gardner, B.D., *Plowing Ground in Washington: The Political Economy of US Agriculture*, Pacific Research Institute, © 1995, pp. 25–30.

34   Wright, B., "Goals and Realities for Farm Policy," as found in Sumner, D., *Agricultural Policy Reform in the US*, American Enterprise Press, Washington, D.C., © 1995, pp. 14–18.

35   Gardner, B.D., *Plowing Ground in Washington: The Political Economy of US Agriculture*, Pacific Research Institute, © 1995, p. 35.

36   Griswold, D., "Should the United States Cut Its Farm Subsidies," Council on Foreign Relations, Debate between Daniel T. Griswold, Director of the Cato Institute and Bob

While it is argued that the provision of support programs for cotton production via the political process may reduce risk for cotton producers and input suppliers, it introduces another type of risk that markets are not designed to accommodate – political risk.[37] Uncertainties about the outcomes from reducing or eliminating trade-distorting subsidies for domestic cotton producers imposes risk on policymakers, such as members of Congress, and thereby reduces the incentive to implement policy changes. Again, the recent experiences of two developed countries, New Zealand and Australia, in successfully largely dismantling their long-standing farm support programs, provide case studies amenable to incentivize similar policy changes in the US.

1.3   US Cotton Production and Its Economic Relation to Total US Agriculture

In the US, American Upland[38] Cotton is the most widely produced variety of the plant belonging to the *Gossypium hirsutum* genus, which accounts for about ninety-seven (97) percent of the annual U.S. cotton crop.[39] Upland cotton is produced across the principal US growing regions comprised of seventeen (17) southern states with Texas, Mississippi, Arkansas, Southern Georgia, California, and the Louisiana Delta.[40] The other principal type of cotton produced is Extra-long Staple (ELS) or 'Pima' cotton, produced primarily in California but also in Texas, New Mexico, and Arizona. ELS cotton is used in high-value products including sewing threads, premium clothing fabrics, and bath towels and rugs.[41]

Young, Chief Economist for the American Farm Bureau, 20–27April, 2007. < http://www.cfr.org/publication/13147/> last visited 3 June, 2010.

37   *See*, Sumner, D., "Farm Subsidy Tradition and Modern Agricultural Realities," Paper for American Enterprise Institute Project on Agricultural Policy for the 2007 Farm Bill and Beyond <http://aic.ucdavis.edu/research/farmbill07/aeibriefs/20070515_sumnerRationalesfinal.pdf>, last visited 30 June 2010.

38   The term 'upland' was derived from the reference to the production of the crop upland from coasts.

39   Starbird, Irving R., United States, Economic Research Service, Department of Agriculture, *The U.S. Cotton Industry*, (June 1987). Last visited 23 Apr. 2010<http://www.eric.ed.gov/ERICDocs/data/ericdocs2sql/content_storage_01/0000019b/80/30/50/c1.pdf>, p. 3.

40   From: http://www.ers.usda.gov/Briefing/Cotton/background.htm.

41   Starbird, Irving R., United States, Economic Research Service, Department of Agriculture, *The U.S. Cotton Industry*, (June 1987). Last visited 23 Apr. 2010<http://www.eric.ed.gov/ERICDocs/data/ericdocs2sql/content_storage_01/0000019b/80/30/50/c1.pdf>, p. 3.

From the 1970s to 2006, cotton acreage in the US rose from about twelve (12) million acres to over 14.5 million acres but has declined since 2006 due, in large part, to changing relative prices which have favored the planting of alternative crops.[42] Figure 5 shows the number of acres planted to cotton and harvested in the US.

As mentioned *supra*, cotton acreage and production has declined in recent years. Coincident with this is a decline in the number of cotton farms in the US. At the time of the initiation of the complaints by Brazil in 2002, there were nearly twenty-five thousand (25,000) cotton farms in the US. That number declined to less than nineteen thousand (19,000) within five (5) years.[43] Although there has been decreases in both cotton acreage and number of farms, there has not been a commensurate decline in US cotton production, which has remained relatively steady...[44] The lack of production declines is due to increased yields per acre due to advances in technology and production practices.[45]

The relatively steady production of US upland cotton has been accompanied by a decline in domestic mill consumption in the US. Consumption of cotton by US textile mills peaked in 1997 and has since plummeted (by 50% in

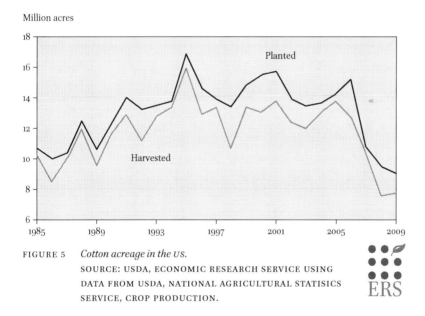

FIGURE 5   *Cotton acreage in the US.*
SOURCE: USDA, ECONOMIC RESEARCH SERVICE USING DATA FROM USDA, NATIONAL AGRICULTURAL STATISICS SERVICE, CROP PRODUCTION.

---

42   From: http://www.ers.usda.gov/Briefing/Cotton/background.htm.
43   From: http://www.ers.usda.gov/Briefing/Cotton/background.htm.
44   See Figure 2 above.
45   From: http://www.ers.usda.gov/Briefing/Cotton/background.htm.

2005 and by 70% in 2009). This was partly due to the end of the Multifibre Arrangment's (MFA) quotas in 2005.[46] However, much of the effects of this agreement were delayed until Phase 4 (Dec 31, 2004), but the reduction in mill use occurred before then and coincided with large increases in capital investment in textile facilities in developing countries. The decline in domestic mill demand and relatively steady cotton production in the US have resulted in increasing export levels over the past decade, as shown in Figure 6.

There are several characteristics related to the production of cotton that differ from other agricultural operations in the US. In the 2007 *Cotton Backgrounder*, an Outlook Report from the Economic Research Service of the United States Department of Agriculture (USDA), several of these characteristics were discussed. As set forth and derived from the 2003 Agricultural Resource Management Survey (ARMS), the primary differentiating characteristics relates to the size of farming operations as well as how cotton production is financed. Generally, the study found that farms growing cotton tend to be larger than other non-cotton growing farms, which is argued to be the reason why gross cotton farm incomes are above-average (net cash income per farm was $127,354 as compared to $11,568 in the same region).[47] Of these gross cash incomes, the US government contributes fourteen (14) percent via support in the forms of direct, countercyclical, and loan deficiency payments as well as

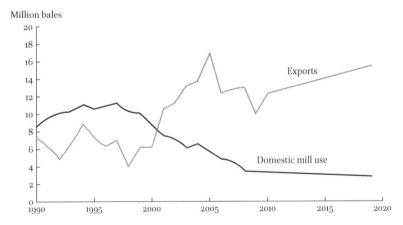

FIGURE 6   *Mill use and cotton exports in the US.*
SOURCE: USDA AGRICULTURAL PROJECTIONS TO 2019, FEBRUARY 2010. USDA, ECONOMIC RESEARCH SERVICE.

---

46   MFA.
47   Meyer, L., MacDonald, S., and Foreman, L., "Cotton Backgrounder," USDA Outlook Report from the Economic Research Service, (March, 2007), p. 12.

others. The total value of this support is an averaged $60,315 per cotton farm compared to $3,121 to non-cotton farms. Applied to household incomes, the resulting averages are $142,463 for cotton producers and $71,447 for non-cotton farmers.[48] Assessed differently, in the 2001–02 year, every acre of cotton farmland in the US received $230.[49]

The above analysis illuminates the following important characteristics of the US cotton market: (1) cotton farms are large relative to other types of agricultural production; (2) there have been declines in the number of farms and cotton acreage while, at the same time, cotton production in the US has remained steady and a commensurate increase in cotton yields; (3) there has been a decline in domestic mill and other types of cotton usage which, along with the relatively steady production levels, has led to increased cotton exportation: and (4) the total value of domestic cotton production accounts for only a small part of the total value of all US agricultural production. These characteristics are crucial to an understanding of the nature of the political and economic implications of cotton subsidy programs in the US.

The value of cotton production relative to the total value of agricultural is especially telling in view of the degree of subsidization of cotton in the US. As mentioned *supra*, during the 2002–2005 period, over twenty (20) percent of all government spending on agricultural programs went to support a crop that makes up less than 1/50th of the value of US agricultural production.[50][2] In 2003, approximately twenty-five thousand (25,000) US cotton farmers were paid approximately $3.8 billion to grow cotton – making the value of the subsidies greater than the value of the crop to the US. The OECD found similar results that the subsidization of upland cotton far exceeds the level of US support to other agricultural crops.[51] The production trends of cotton and their relation to total production in the US illustrates the political influence of the cotton producing sector in the US and the inefficiencies that result from such heavy subsidization. The amount spent on cotton subsidies is even more problematic when consideration is given to the low "transfer efficiency" of the distribution of subsidies because little of the intended monies for support

---

48   Meyer, p. 17.
49   Oxfam, "Cultivating Poverty: The Impact of US Cotton Subsidies on Africa," Briefing Paper 30, London (2002).
50   [2] Sumner, Daniel A., "U.S. Farm Policy and the White Commodities: Cotton, Rice, Sugar and Milk," International Food & Agricultural Trade Policy Council (Washington, DC: IPC, 2007). Last visited 26 Apr. 2010<http://www.agritrade.org/Publications/PolicyFocus/Farm_Bill_5_white_commodities.pdf>, p. 1.
51   OECD, "Agricultural Policies in OECD Countries – Monitoring and Evaluation 2003," (2003), p. 45 (Annex Table 2), as found in Exhibit Bra-5.

ultimately reach farmers. It is estimated that only twenty-five (25) to thirty (30) percent of producer support actually ends up in increasing farm incomes.[52]

Despite these inefficiencies, the average producer support given per farmer had been increasing considerably in almost every OECD country, with the exception of Australia and New Zealand[53] at the time of the commencement of the Doha Development Round and the initiation of the *Cotton* dispute. This trend has continued since that time, with the US providing about $5.1 billion per year in direct payments alone. This estimation does not include additional compensation received such as countercyclical payments (approximately, another $1.1 billion a year) and marketing loan benefits (another $1 billion per year), and crop insurance benefits ($160 million per year) as well as export credit guarantees, which are other significant sources of support for cotton farmers. Moreover, these monies are tied to the historical yield of the acreage base of program commodities – meaning the payments are given, regardless if the farmer decides to plant alternative crops, use the land for livestock grazing, or simply leave the land idle.[54]

1.4 Importance of Cotton to Developing/African Countries

> My understanding of the values of American farm people...is that they are interested not only in the prices of their products, but also in the nutrition of the world's poorer people.
>
> D. GALE JOHNSON Preeminent Agricultural & Development Economist (1916–2003)[55]

The production and trade of cotton is an essential economic dimension of many least developed African countries. Domestic policies to support cotton production by developed nations are often to the detriment of less developed economies and, at the same time, developed country interests are frequently challenged by developing country needs. The subsidization of cotton is one of the most extreme examples of this, is a source of contention between developed and less developed nations and, increasingly, a source of international

---

52 Messerlin, P., "Agriculture in the Doha Agenda," World Bank, (August, 2002), pp. 8–9.
53 Messerlin, p. 5.
54 Sumner, D., "US Farm Policy and the White Commodities: Cotton, Rice, Sugar and Milk," International Food and Agricultural Trade Policy Council, IPC Policy Focus, Farm Bill Series, No. 5 (June, 2007), p. 2.
55 Johnson, D.G., "World Commodity Market," as found in Gardner, B., *US Agricultural Policy*, American Enterprise Institute for Public Policy Research, Washington, D.C., © 1985, p. 24.

indignation. This is well illustrated by the support garnered by the proposals of the principal African cotton producing countries, as part of the Doha Development Agenda (DDA), for accelerated elimination of cotton subsidies by the US and the EU and for financial compensation for losses incurred during the process of subsidy elimination.[56]

Although the value of cotton as a share of total global trade is small, with its estimated annual value of $11.4 billion accounting for only 0.11 percent of the total value of goods traded internationally,[57] its economic value as a cash crop to particular countries, especially developing economies, can be significant. In total, as reported by The World Bank, according to FAO estimates, in 2001 there were approximately one hundred (100) million rural households involved in the production of cotton.[58] The vast majority of these rural households are in developing countries, which are highly dependent on the crop for financial sustainability. Further, there is a strong link between world cotton prices and the rural welfare of cotton-producing African countries.

Several African countries have targeted the production of cotton as a viable crop to increase gross domestic product (GDP), as part of their greater economic development objectives. Cotton is particularly attractive to these countries because traditional production costs are relatively low, given that most African cotton acreage is non-irrigated and fertilizer is generally inexpensive, and cotton is well suited for exporting. It is no surprise, then, that thirty-seven (37) of the fifty-three (53) African countries produce cotton and all but seven (7) are exporters of the commodity.

In this book, the analysis of the effects of domestic cotton policies on least developed countries focuses on the countries of Burkina Faso, Mali, Benin and Chad – designated as the *C-4* countries by the WTO. These are among the world's poorest countries and are particularly vulnerable to the effects of the global price effects stemming from the cotton support policies of the cotton producing developed nations, because of the importance of cotton to their domestic economies and their price-taking role in the global cotton market.

In these countries, cotton is a crucially important part of their economies. In terms of employment, the United Nations' Food and Agriculture Organization estimates that approximately two (2) million workers are employed in the

---

56 Sumner, D., "US Farm Programs and African Cotton," International Food and Agricultural Trade Policy Council, IPC Issues Brief 22, February 2007.
57 UNCTAD export statistics concluded that cotton was ranked 170th on average 2004/05 values. *Id* at 3, p. 17.
58 Baffes, J., "Cotton: Market Setting, Trade Policies, and Issues," The World Bank, Policy Research Working Paper, (February 2004), p. 6.

production of cotton in the *C-4* countries. More specifically, cotton production employs three hundred and eighty thousand (380,000) workers in Burkina Faso (7 percent of total employment), eight hundred thousand (800,000) workers in Mali (17 percent of total employment), four hundred and fifty-five thousand (450,000) workers in Benin (29 percent of total employment), and three hundred and eighty thousand (380,000) workers in Chad (10 percent of total employment).[59] Given household size per worker in these countries, an even greater share of the total population is reliant on cotton, with an estimated ten (10) million people in those countries *directly* dependent on cotton production and many more being indirectly impacted by cotton price variability.

In addition to employment, cotton's importance to economic viability of these countries is particularly striking and illustrated by the fact that cotton ranges from approximately 2.5 to seven (7) percent of the GDPs for the *C-4* countries. The reliance of these countries on the export of cotton as a means of economic development is evidenced by the degree to which cotton comprises total exports: approximately sixty-five (65) (70) percent of exports for Benin, forty (40) percent for Mail, and forty-five (45) to seventy one (71) percent for Burkina Faso.[60, 61] Given their reliance on exporting cotton, it is evident why three of the four *C-4* counties, Burkina Faso, Mali and Benin, lobbied for the establishment of the *Subcommittee on Cotton* within the WTO Doha Development negotiations, as discussed in greater detail in Chapter 8. These countries, along with Cameroon, Central African Republic, Cote d'Ivoire, Senegal, Togo, and Niger comprise the 'Franc Zone,' which is only second to the United States as a leading exporter of cotton.[62]

The importance of cotton to these least-developed countries means that they are particularly vulnerable to the price suppressing and trade distorting

---

[59] Shui, S., "Importance of Cotton Production and Trade and Strategies to Enhance Cotton's Contribution to Economy and Food Security in Africa." FAO Commodity and Trade Division, In WTO African Regional Workshop on Cotton, 23–24 March 2004, WTO Document WT/L/587. Alston, J., Sumner, D., Brunke, H., "Impacts of Reductions in US Cotton Subsidies on West African Cotton Producers," Oxfam America (2007), p. 2.

[60] Gillson, I., Poulton, Co., Balcombe, K., and Page, S., "Understanding the Impact of Cotton Subsidies on Developing Countries," Working Paper (May, 2004), p. 7. <http://www.odi.org.uk/resources/download/3608.pdf>last visited 2 June, 2010.

[61] Gillson, I., Poulton, Co., Balcombe, K., and Page, S., "Understanding the Impact of Cotton Subsidies on Developing Countries," Working Paper (May, 2004), p. 7. <http://www.odi.org.uk/resources/download/3608.pdf>last visited 2 June, 2010.

[62] Meyer, L., MacDonald, S., and Foreman, L., "Cotton Backgrounder," USDA Outlook Report from the Economic Research Service, (March, 2007), World Agricultural Supply and Demand Estimates, WAOB, USDA statistics from 2004–2006 period.

effects of US cotton support policies. The cotton sector is the largest employer in several African countries, including three (3) of the C-4 countries.[63] Further, cotton production is recognized as directly linked to the sustainability of cotton-producing African states. When prices for cotton are low, the effects are felt differently between the US, who can afford to make direct payments to their cotton producers.[64] However, for countries such as those in the C-4, a drop in price significantly affects their GDP and export earnings. This is especially due to the fact that these countries are price-takers in the global cotton market and, therefore, do not affect the prevailing export price of cotton. In a study conducted by Oxfam America, Julian M. Alston, Daniel A. Sumner, and Henrich Brunke concluded that the effects of US cotton policies on the world market are transmitted to the C-4 countries and the degree to which these adverse effects are felt is proportionately greater the poorer the country.[65] For example, it was found that the decline in cotton prices in 2002 resulted in a one (1) percent drop in Burkina Faso's GDP and a twelve (12) percent decline in their export earnings and a 1.7 percent decline in GDP and an eight (8) percent decline in export earnings in Mali.

At the beginning of the *Cotton* dispute, the World Bank, Oxfam, and the International Cotton Advisory Committee conducted studies to examine the connection between cotton subsidies in the US and the incomes of developing cotton-exporting nations. The results of these studies confirmed that there is a direct link between the enormous and detrimental US subsidies and the cotton-earning potential of developing countries. As Daniel Sumner noted, "LDC farmers are significant exporters of cotton and have suffered from price suppression caused by subsidies."[66] Moreover, it was found that the reduction or elimination of subsidies in the US would improve the standard of living in West African nations, particularly the C-4 countries that are especially considered in this book. The World Bank estimated that the removal of subsidies would generate approximately two hundred and fifty (250) million US dollars per year in additional revenue for cotton farmers in these countries. The Oxfam report found that this would amount to a one (1) to two (2) percent increase gross domestic product. In another study, it was estimated that cutting the

---

63 International Cotton Advisory Committee, "The Importance of Cotton in Africa."
64 Sumner, D., "US Farm Programs and African Cotton," International Food and Agricultural Trade Policy Council, IPC Issues Brief 22, February 2007.
65 Alston, J., Sumner, D., Brunke, H., "Impacts of Reductions in US Cotton Subsidies on West African Cotton Producers," Oxfam America (2007), p. 11.
66 Sumner, D. "Farm Programs and the Economics of LDC Cotton," Presentation at the International Conference on Cotton: The Next Steps for Africa, (October, 2006).

$3.8 billion in US subsidies in 2003 would have raised the world cotton price by twenty-six percent (26%), equating to approximately seven (7) to eleven (11) cents for every pound of African cotton.[67] This would have raised incomes to enable the lifting of thousand of African communities out of poverty.

In a 2002 study undertaken for the World Bank, Nicholas Minot and Lisa Daniels analyzed the impact of global cotton markets on rural poverty in Benin.[68] The four objectives of the study were to "(1) describe the living conditions and levels of poverty for cotton growers and other farmers in Benin (2) to estimate the short-run impact (before households adjust) of lower cotton prices on the income of cotton growers on the incidence of poverty in rural Benin (3) to estimate the medium-run, direct impact (after household adjust variable inputs) of lower cotton prices on incomes and poverty in rural Benin; and (4) to estimate the total impact of lower cotton prices including the effect on households that do not grow cotton but are affected indirectly by the reduced demand for labor and the reduced purchasing power of cotton farmers."[69] The results confirm that Benin, like the other C-4 countries, is extremely vulnerable to price changes stemming from the support policies of developed nations. It was found that a forty (40) percent reduction in price – as was occurring at the time of the initiation of the *Cotton* dispute – resulted in a reduction of income per capita of seven (7) percent in the short-run and five (5) to six (6) percent in the long-run, in Benin. Further, poverty was found to rise eight (8) percentage points in the short-run, representing over 330,000 individuals who were directly forced below the poverty line as a direct result to the change in price, with a long run estimate between six (6) and seven (7) percentage points.[70]

In evaluating support policies for cotton producers, it is useful to compare the effects of US cotton policies on the world's poorest countries. For example, at the time of the initiation of Brazil's request for WTO consultations with the US, the annual losses in GDP for Burkina Faso, Mali and Chad due to US cotton price suppression were greater than the development aid that these countries received from the United States. In a study conducted by Oxfam, it was found

---

67 Nankani, G., "Development of the Cotton Sector in West and Central Africa," Presentation at the International Conference on Cotton: The Next Steps for Africa, (October, 2006).

68 Minot, N. and Daniels, L, "Impact of Global Cotton Markets on Rural Poverty in Benin," MSSD Discussion Paper, No. 48, Markets and Structural Studies Division, International Food Policy Research Institute, Washington, (2002).

69 Minot and Daniels, 5.

70 Minot, N. and Daniels, L, "Impact of Global Cotton Markets on Rural Poverty in Benin," MSSD Discussion Paper, No. 48, Markets and Structural Studies Division, International Food Policy Research Institute, Washington, (2002), p. 50.

that US cotton farmers receive *three* (3) *times* more in subsidies than the entire United States Agency for International Development (USAID) budget for Africa's five hundred (500) million people and that the subsidies by US cotton farmers were greater than the entire GDP of Burkina Faso, who has more than two (2) million people depending on the production of cotton, an estimated half of which live in poverty.[71]

While there is widespread agreement that cotton subsidies by the US and EU have caused significant economic harm to some of the world's poorest countries, it is also the case that domestic policies within many African cotton producing countries have added to the plight of cotton farmers. Some of the main issues include: pricing policies that lead to cotton growers often receiving prices significantly below world prices; stabilization funds accumulated during times of high prices being depleted by central governments and being unavailable to support farmers during periods of price declines; inefficient risk management infrastructure; decreased efficiency and technological innovation; panterritorial pricing structures that often reward inefficient growers to the detriment of more efficient ones; and currency used for African cotton being tied to the Euro resulting in increased price volatility and vulnerability to economic conditions beyond the control of African domestic policies.[72] The issues surrounding domestic policy reform within the C-4 and other African cotton producing countries are addressed in Parts Three and Four of this book.

1.5   Cotton Cost Comparisons between US and Other Producers

The cost of cotton production in the US is significantly greater than that in other cotton-producing countries. Relevant to this book, the cost of production for one (1) pound of cotton in the US is three (3) times higher than in the C-4 country of Burkina Faso. It is a similar case with Brazil. It has been economically established that the US does not have a comparative advantage,

---

71   Oxfam, "Cultivating Poverty: The Impact of US Cotton Subsidies on Africa," Briefing Paper 30, London (2002), p. 2.

72   See, for example, Baffes, J., "The 'Cotton Problem' in West and Central Africa: The Case for Domestic Reforms," Cato Institute, Economic Development Bulletin, Washington, D.C. (July 2007); and Lele, U., van de Walle, N., and Gbetiboijo, M., "Cotton in Africa: Analysis of Difference in Performance," Managing Agricultural Development in Africa (MADIA) Discussion Paper, The World Bank (November 1989)<http://www-wds.worldbank.org/external/default/main?pagePK=64193027&piPK=64187937&theSitePK=523679&menuPK=64187510&searchMenuPK=64187283&siteName=WDS&entityID=000178830_98101901372769>last visited 13 June 2010.

or even, capability of producing cotton, economically; however, it does have a comparative advantage of subsidizing production, domestically.

Of the many types of production costs, average variable costs and average total costs are particularly relevant. For cotton production, variable costs include factors of production such as seed, fuel, labor, and chemical fertilizer and pesticides. Total production costs include these costs as well as fixed costs such as land ownership or rental costs, insurance, and depreciation on farm buildings, machinery, and irrigation equipment. Average variable costs are calculated as variable costs divided by units of output and, similarly, average total costs are total costs divided by units of output. In the case of cotton, these costs are commonly calculated on a per-pound of cotton basis.

In order to maintain long-term economic viability, output price has to at least equal average total costs. If output price exceeds average total cost, total revenues exceed total costs and the producer realizes a profit. A price lower than average total costs means that the producer incurs negative profit and, in the long term, will have to exit the industry. In the short term, however, a producer may choose to continue production if the price is below average total cost but above average variable cost. In this case, there will be sufficient revenue to cover operating costs and the producer will be able to cover some, but not all, of the fixed costs of production. Thus, estimates of average variable costs and average total costs per pound of cotton are key indicators of production costs and both short-term and long-term economic viability of cotton production.

Several estimates of production costs for upland cotton indicate that these costs for the US are relatively high. For example, the US Congressional Research Service estimated that, from 1991 to 2004, average variable costs for US upland cotton have averaged $0.50/lb and average total costs have averaged $0.79/lb.[73] These estimates are in line with estimates from the US Department of Agriculture[74] and from agricultural extension service reports in cotton producing states.[75] Over this same period, cotton prices have averaged $0.57/lb.[76] Thus, while revenues were sufficient to cover the variable costs of production,

---

73 Womach, Jasper. CSR Report for Congress, *Cotton Production and Support in the United States*, June 24, 2004.

74 See Commodity Costs and Returns: Data from USDA Economic Research Service at http://www.ers.usda.gov/data/costsandreturns/testpick.htm.

75 For example, production costs in Arkansas by Groves, Robertson and Bryant. (2004) and in Texas by Texas.

76 Womach, Jasper. CSR Report for Congress, *Cotton Production and Support in the United States*, June 24, 2004.

they fell far short of the required revenues to allow cotton farmers to produce cotton at a profit. Moreover, average variable costs exceeded cotton prices from 1999–2002,[77] the years immediately preceding the initiation of the *Cotton* dispute. During those years, cotton producers were, on average, unable to cover even the variable costs of cotton production. As quoted in the CRS Report for Congress, "In the absence of support programs, the data suggest a sizeable proportion of cotton would not be profitable."[78]

International cotton production cost comparisons are provided by the International Cotton Advisory Committee (ICAC), an association of governmental agencies of cotton producing, and consuming countries.[79] The ICAC releases cost comparisons based on survey data supplied by participating Member countries. The production costs data from ICAC indicate that the US is one of the highest cost producing nations in the world for upland cotton and that production costs approach twice those of low cost producers such as Brazil and several African countries.[80] Thus, again, it is clear that the US does not have a comparative advantage in cotton production.

Therefore, in order for the US to remain competitive at the international level, under current production methods, some form of government intervention must take place. Historically, this has been achieved through the distribution of subsidies that increase cotton production and negatively affect international trade of cotton in the short run due to its impacts on world price. In the case of the US, not only is there subsidization of cotton for domestic consumption, but for the exportation of the commodity. In the marketing year 2001, the US dominated the exports in cotton, accounting for nearly forty (40) percent of total world exports. In this situation, of extreme overproduction bolstered by export subsidies, the world market price-setting effects are thereby amplified and damaging to cotton producing countries, especially developing.

China and India
Based on the statistics earlier presented, it is evident that the US is not the only significant player on the world cotton market. However, the US is recognized

---

77 Womach, Jasper. CSR Report for Congress, *Cotton Production and Support in the United States*, June 24, 2004.
78 Womach, Jasper. CSR Report for Congress, *Cotton Production and Support in the United States*, June 24, 2004, p. 14.
79 See http:www.icac.org/general/profile/English.html.
80 International Cotton Advisory Committee (2004). *Survey of the Cost of Production of Raw Cotton* at: http://www.icac.org/cotton_info/research/COP/english.html.

as the primary "driver" of the market. At the time of the *Cotton* dispute's initiation The Peoples Republic of China was the largest producer of cotton. However, it was also the largest consumer and an upward trend in production was coincident with a similar trend in textile manufacturing in the country. The result is that China tends to consume most of what it produces and exports little of the commodity. A similar situation exists in India, another major cotton producer, where domestic production is balanced with internal consumption and there is little reliance on exporting. Further, as noted earlier, the US is relatively transparent and provides large amounts of information to market participants. This is not the case in China, where information is unreliable and incomplete. Therefore, they are both often viewed as 'price followers,' rather than 'drivers' in the international trade of cotton.

Brazil

At the time of the initiation of the dispute, Brazil was the seventh (7th) largest producer of cotton in the world. Although its production is not nearly as large as China and India, it shares the characteristic that domestic consumption is high with the result that Brazil is not a large cotton exporting country.[81] It also shares the feature of being a price-taking country and, because it is open to imports and exports, the prices received by Brazilian cotton growers are exposed to cotton price trends on the world market and subject to both volatility and the global effects of the domestic policies of the US. The overproduction and resulting price suppression effects of US cotton subsidies on world cotton prices get transmitted to Brazilian producers who, unlike US cotton growers, do not receive large-scale government support.

As noted in this chapter, the effects of US cotton subsidies on world markets is significant due to the size of US cotton production and exports, the ways in which cotton prices are calculated, and the price-taking nature of other major producing countries. The effects on Brazil and the African *C-4* countries are especially severe and are the focus of this book. The next chapter provides an overview of the wide variety of support measures in place at the time of the initiation of the *Cotton* dispute that benefitted US cotton growers and exporters.

---

81   In fact, Brazil is often a net importer of cotton.

CHAPTER 2

Political Economy of Agricultural Subsidy Programs

> For cotton is something more than a crop or an industry; it is a dynastic system, with a set of laws and standards always under assault and peculiarly resistant to change. It is map-maker, trouble-maker, history-maker.... It was cotton that made the South into a section.... On cotton.... The South built up a social and political economy essentially different from that prevailing in the rest of the country.
> ANNE O'HARE MCCORMICK, *The New York Times Magazine* 1931

As determined in Chapter 1 there is little economic justification for the scale of US cotton production and exportation, given the amount of subsidization required to ensure that the industry remains competitive at the international level. It is widely recognized that the production of US cotton and large-scale exporting of cotton is, rather, a result of the *political* economy of the US and the lobbying efforts of cotton associations. The cotton industry is comprised of an elaborate fabric of public and private entities, interest groups, and government organizations. This chapter sets forth the history of the US cotton subsidy programs; describes the relevant subsidy programs at the time of the *US-Upland Cotton* dispute; compares those programs to other subsidy programs in China and the EU; describes the political power of the cotton lobby and US within the US legislative process, and concludes with USDA studies that confirm the importance of cotton subsidies for the sustainability of US cotton production and exports.

2.1 History of US Cotton Subsidy Programs

The US government has been interwoven with its cotton industry, nearly since the nation's founding. In the early part of its history, the rise of US cotton production coincided with the rise of the US textile industry. It took considerable time for the US to be able to compete with the dominance of Britain in the world textile industry. However, due to early textile technology transfer to the US as well as the Embargo Act and War of 1812, the developing US was able to grow its infant textile industry sheltered from British imports.[82] It was when

---

[82] Gano, Ambrose, "Feeding King Cotton: American Cotton Associations in WTO Negotiations," Thesis, Pomona College, (April 2008), pp. 20–26.

trade was re-established between the US and Britain in 1815 that US textile manufacturers began to lobby the US government for trade protection. The resulting Tariff Bill of 1816 and Tariff of Abominations of 1828 helped establish the underlying dynamics and inter-connectivity of agriculture, industry, and the US government.[83] Not only did these protect US textile manufacturers from imports, they also increased domestic consumption of US cotton and thereby reduced the reliance of US cotton growers on foreign markets. It was also clear that the federal government could be the source of economic benefits for both cotton users and producers.

While the tariff bills reduced the US reliance on cotton exports, foreign markets were a large source for US produced cotton, the vast majority of which was produced in the southern states. Thus, cotton was a focal point in the economic mêlée between the North and the South during the time of the US Civil War. During that time, cotton exports to Britain from the South were blockaded by the North.[84] The blockade was the instrument by which the South tried to, unsuccessfully, engage Britain in the war.[85] The blockade brought to the fore a long-standing debate on the relative economic strength of the North versus the South. Cotton (along with rice, sugar and tobacco) was critical to the South's argument that they were more favorably positioned economically. It was considered by some that "Cotton was king and could command the world; the South controlled the world's supply of cotton and the manufacturing areas, Northern and European, for all their vaunted wealth, were dependent upon the South for their cotton."[86] This perspective is somewhat understandable, given that cotton constituted forty (40) percent of US exports only ten (10) years before the War. The following statement by an Alabama politician to a British visitor describes when tensions were at their worst, between the North and South, and sets forth how the South used cotton as one of its greatest defenses:

---

83   Rosenbloom, J., "Path Dependence and the Origins of Cotton Textile Manufacturing in New England," National Bureau of Economic Research, Working Paper, Cambridge, MA; NBER, 2002. p. 3.
84   Woodman, H., *King Cotton and His Retainers: Financing and Marketing the Cotton Crop of the South, 1800–1925*, University of South Carolina Press © 1968, 1990, pp. 199–235.
85   Destitution in the cotton-textile industry was acutely experienced in France as well. For excellent insight on the working conditions and 'human experience' of cotton during the Civil War, *See*, Cohn, D., *The Life and Times of King Cotton*, Oxford University Press, New York, © 1956, pp. 119–140.
86   Woodman, H., *King Cotton and His Retainers: Financing and Marketing the Cotton Crop of the South, 1800–1925*, University of South Carolina Press © 1990, p. 144.

We are an agricultural people; we are a primitive but a civilized people. We have no cities – we don't want them. We have no literature – we don't need any yet. We have no press – we are glad of it. We do not require a press, because we go out and discuss all public questions from the stump with our people. We have no commercial marine – no navy – we don't want them. We are better without them. Your ships carry our produce, and you can protect your own vessels. We want no manufactures; we desire no trading, no mechanical or manufacturing classes. As long as we have our rice, our sugar, our tobacco, and our cotton, we can command wealth to purchase all we want from those nations with which we are amity, and to lay up money besides. But with the Yankees we will never trade – never. Not one pound of cotton shall ever go from the South to their accursed cities; not one ounce of their steel or their manufactures shall ever cross our border.[87]

This statement represents the firm conviction of many Southern leaders at the time that the destiny of the South was its own to determine. However, and more in line with reality, it might also be argued that the relationship was one of co-dependency as the North was dependent upon the South for cotton and the South dependent on the financing and marketing of its commodity by the North. As one historian summarized, "cotton was king, but he was a puppet monarch."[88]

The tensions between the North and the South regarding the relative locations of cotton production and textile manufacturing were exacerbated by the financing system that existed at the time and that persisted well after the conclusion of the Civil War. Much of the financing for southern cotton growers was provided by northern financial entities. This system allowed thousands of individuals to move into cash crop production, largely due to the ease of entry into cotton production, even by individuals with few capital resources to invest.[89] This created a vicious cycle of perpetual indebtedness by cotton farmers to more powerful financiers outside the South. This is seen in the developments following the Civil War during which time cotton production grew rapidly in the US and abroad as the demand for the commodity

---

87   William Howard Russell, *My Diary North and South,* Boston, (1863), p. 179 as discovered in: Woodman, H., *King Cotton and His Retainers: Financing and Marketing the Cotton Crop of the South, 1800–1925,* University of South Carolina Press © 1990, p. 145.

88   Woodman, H., *King Cotton and His Retainers: Financing and Marketing the Cotton Crop of the South, 1800–1925,* University of South Carolina Press © 1990, p. 359.

89   Woodman, H., *King Cotton and His Retainers: Financing and Marketing the Cotton Crop of the South, 1800–1925,* University of South Carolina Press © 1990, p. 348.

increased.[90] It was during this time that slave labor ended,[91] the sharecropping system was established in the South,[92] and the "company farm" system began in Texas. Both of these systems were economically favorable to prosperous cotton producers and landowners, but led to undesirable outcomes such as the binding of workers to the farms (paying workers in scrip, rather than money) and the large numbers of farmers being forced into poverty.[93] Although the systems were eventually regarded as socially and morally reprehensible,[94] it is interesting to note that some forms of the systems remain in present day unionized sharecropping and tenant farming.

Though a connection between government, agriculture and industry was established early in American history, it was not until the end of World War I that concerted and coordinated efforts for trade protection and subsidies to cotton farmers began to yield results. Prior to the end of World War I, there had been measures used to protect US agricultural producers from foreign competition and to influence international trade. For example, tariffs had been imposed on many agricultural commodities and institutions such as the Export–Import Bank and its predecessor agencies authorized numerous cotton export loans to China and Europe. Efforts for the federal government to set commodity prices or to provide direct payments to farmers had not met with political success prior to the end of World War I, in large part because farmers enjoyed a period of relative prosperity from the beginning of the twentieth century through the war years.[95] At the end of World War I, however, the prices of most agricultural products fell dramatically in both real and nominal terms.[96] Since that time, US policies have been pulled by the advantages

---

90   Gano, Ambrose, "Feeding King Cotton: American Cotton Associations in WTO Negotiations," Thesis, Pomona College, (April 2008), pp. 20–26.

91   Woodman, H., "The Profitability of Slavery: A Historical Perennial," *Journal of Southern History*, XXIX (August 1963), pp. 303–325.

92   Kester, Howard. *Revolt among the Sharecroppers* (1936). Knoxville: University of Tennessee, (1997).

93   Besanko, D., and Brugess, B., "Subsidies and the Global Cotton Trade," Northwestern University, Kellogg School of Management, Case Study: KEL348, (25 June 2007), p. 2.

94   The Encyclopedia of Arkansas History & Culture, <http://encyclopediaofarkansas.net/encyclopedia/entry-detail.aspx?entryID=2103> last visited 7 June 2010.

95   Gardner, B.D., *Plowing Ground in Washington: The Political Economy of US Agriculture*, Pacific Research Institute, © 1995, pp. 8–11.

96   Hoffman, Elizabeth and Gary Libecap, "Institutional Choice and the Development of U.S. Agricultural Policies in the 1920s," The Journal of Economic History, Vol 51, No. 2 (June 1991), pp. 397–411.

derived from supporting the politically powerful cotton producing industry and the costs of cotton support policies to the national treasury and the distortionary effects of domestic and global markets.

Attempts to not only protect US producers from international trade, but to also have the federal government directly intervene in domestic agricultural markets and provide income support to US producers, are exemplified in the efforts to pass the McNary-Haugen Bill beginning in 1924. The McNary-Haugen legislation included provisions to impose tariffs and to authorize governmental purchases of surpluses for several agricultural products. It is important to note that the repeated attempts to pass this legislation were unsuccessful, until cotton was included in the bill in 1927. It was only then that the bill garnered enough support to pass both houses of Congress. The bill's passage in 1928 was met by a presidential veto. Congress passed the bill again in 1928 and was met by another veto by President Coolidge. Coolidge's veto message at the time is telling:

> I do not believe that upon serious consideration the farmers of America would tolerate the precedent of a body of men chosen solely by one industry who, acting in the name of the Government, shall arrange for contracts which determine prices, secure the buying and selling of commodities, the levying of taxes on that industry, and pay losses on foreign dumping of any surplus. There is no reason why other industries – copper, coal, lumber, textiles, and others – in every occasional difficulty should not receive the same treatment by the Government. Such action would establish bureaucracy on such a scale as to dominate not only the economic life but the moral, social, and political future of our people.[97]

The effect of the attempts to pass the McNary-Haugen Bill was to demonstrate the power of agricultural interests in the political process and to set the stage for successful efforts for government intervention in agricultural markets. The political effectiveness of agricultural interests increased significantly with the advent of the Great Depression and the presidencies of Herbert Hoover and Franklin Roosevelt. The transformation of the federal role in agriculture began during the Hoover administration with the enactment of the Agricultural Marketing Act (AMA) of 1929. There have been more than twenty (20) legislative

---

[97] Coolidge, Calvin. "Coolidge's veto of the McNary-Haugen Bill." Coolidge's Veto of the McNary-Haugen Bill, Academic Search Premier, Accession Number 21213092, 2009, pp. 4771–4778.

acts, since the AMA that have included provisions that affect cotton production whether directly or indirectly. The following describes a few of the more significant laws and their relevant provisions. The AMA of 1929 established the Federal Farm Board (FFB) to provide low-interest loans to farmers and cooperatives and to set price floors for cotton. This proved to be both distortionary to the markets and expensive for the federal government. As a result of the price floors and the resulting overproduction, the federal government bought over ten (10) million bales of cotton.[98]

At the time of the Great Depression, there was a natural concern with the operation of financing agriculture, which threatened the economic health of the US as a whole. In response to the agricultural surpluses generated by the policies of the FFB, policy changes were made during the early years of the Roosevelt administration with the passage of the Agricultural Adjustment Act (AAA) of 1933 and 1938, at a time when "an unprecedented condition call[ed] for the trial of new means to rescue agriculture."[99] The AAA established the Commodity Credit Corporation (CCC) and the Federal Crop Insurance Corporation (FCIC)[100] with the purpose of providing loans to buttress, *inter alia*, cotton prices.[101] While trade barriers had already been put into place for many agricultural commodities, the AAA emphasized reducing production and providing direct payments to farmers to compensate for lower output,[102] rather than creating incentives to overproduce by the use of price supports. This was the first time in history that government had *directly* attempted to control agricultural production in the US.[103] The AAA targeted seven (7) major farm commodities, including cotton. The aim of the AAA was to benefit producers both indirectly, by reducing supply in order to increase prices, and directly by paying farmers to reduce production. The program generated some controversy because cotton farmers had already planted their crops by the

---

98 Folsom, Burton, "The Origin of American Farm Subsidies," The Freeman, April, 2006, p. 35.
99 *Congressional Record*, March 16, 1933, p. 488 as found in: Jacobson, T., and Smith, G., *Cotton's Renaissance: A Study in Market Innovation*, Cambridge University Press, UK © 2001, p. 87.
100 The FCIC is largely independent from the periodically renewed Farm Bills.
101 USDA, "Provisions of the Agricultural Improvement and Reform Act of 1996, Appendix III: Major Agricultural and Trade Legislation, 1933–1996," p. 128.
102 Wheeler, Mark, ed. "The Economics of the Great Depression." Sage Public Administration Abstracts, Vol 27, No. 1 (2000).
103 Jacobson, T., and Smith, G., *Cotton's Renaissance: A Study in Market Innovation*, Cambridge University Press, UK © 2001, p. 87.

time the AAA was put into effect and had to plow under a portion of their crop in order to receive federal payments.[104]

The AAA was declared unconstitutional in 1936 because of its financing provisions included to tax processors in order to pay farmers. The financing mechanisms of the act were changed and it passed again in 1938. Despite its legal and political difficulties, however, the AAA is significant because it created a precedent for the federal government to make direct payments to farmers in addition to its extant policies using price supports and trade barriers. Further, the 1938 Agricultural Adjustment Act, along with the Agricultural Act of 1949 and the Commodity Credit Corporation Charter Act of 1948, makes up the major part of the permanent law that mandates commodity price and farm income support.[105] Thus, while provisions of these acts can be modified by subsequent multiyear farm bills or appropriation acts, the expiration of newer legislation means that the law reverts to the permanent provisions of these acts.

During the thirty (30) years that followed the passage of the AAA, U.S. cotton programs have focused on parity-based price supports, marketing quotas, and acreage allotments.[106] The relatively high support prices effectively established both U.S. and world market prices and encouraged overproduction in the U.S., while leading to increased foreign cotton production and a loss of markets to manmade fibers.[107] The *Agricultural Trade Development and Assistance Act of 1954*, was established to address the problem of marketing US agricultural surplus to recovering economies that did not have the financial resources to pay for goods. Establishing private trade channels for US dollar sales, the US converted proceeds for its products into greater market access for US farm products.[108] As a result, between 1955 and 1963, over eight (8) million bales of cotton were reported to have been shipped abroad, mostly to India, Korea, Poland, and Spain.[109]

---

104 Murray R. Benedict and Oscar C. Stine, *The Agricultural Commodity Programs: Two Decades of Experience,* Twentieth Century Fund, New York, 1956.
105 Womach, Jasper, Agriculture: A Glossary of Terms, Programs, and Laws, 2005 Edition. Congressional Research Service Report for Congress, June 16, 2005, p. 10.
106 Skinner, Robert and Scott Sanford, U.S. Cotton Programs, National Food Review, Vol 13, No. 1 (Jan–March, 1990), pp. 27–32.
107 Skinner, Robert and Scott Sanford, U.S. Cotton Programs, National Food Review, Vol 13, No. 1 (Jan–March, 1990), pp. 27–32.
108 Jacobson, T., and Smith, G., *Cotton's Renaissance: A Study in Market Innovation*, Cambridge University Press, UK © 2001, p. 285.
109 Jacobson, T., and Smith, G., *Cotton's Renaissance: A Study in Market Innovation*, Cambridge University Press, UK © 2001, p. 285.

Recognizing that existing support programs for cotton were leading to increased production and mounting surpluses, a major turning point in cotton policy was instituted with the *Food and Agriculture Act of 1965*. Price supports and income support were clearly separated and cotton price supports were set at ninety (90) percent of the estimated world price, allowing the domestic price to seek world price levels, with payments to producers based on participation in acreage reduction programs.[110] While these changes succeeded in eliminating the huge cotton surpluses by the end of the decade, the cost of the direct payments to producers averaged $847 million annually from 1966 to 1970, amounting to about forty (40) percent of total income from cotton.[111]

The *1965 Food and Agriculture Act* is considered the first 'US Farm Bill.' These bills comprise a series of multi-year omnibus laws that contain federal commodity and farm support policies[112] and other agricultural and natural resource provisions of the US Department of Agriculture. These are renewed approximately every five (5) or six (6) years in order to amend provisions of earlier temporary laws, such as previous farm bills, or permanent law such as the Agricultural Act of 1949. Since 1965, an additional nine (9) farm bills have been signed into law in the US.[113] The farm bills of the 1970s were enacted in dramatically different economic conditions than the 1965 Farm Bill. The demand for domestic cotton was strong due to reduced global production and a relatively weak dollar.[114] These favorable conditions were amenable to efforts to changes in the federal role in supporting prices and income for cotton producers. The *1973 Farm Bill* introduced the target price concept so that deficiency payments

---

110 Stults, Harold, Edward Glade Jr., Scott Sanford, and Leslie Meyer, Cotton: Background for 1990 Farm Legislation. Economic Research Service, U.S. Department of Agriculture, Staff Report No. AGES 89-42, 1989, p. 25.
111 Skinner, Robert and Scott Sanford, U.S. Cotton Programs, National Food Review, Vol 13, No. 1 (Jan–March, 1990), pp. 27–32.
112 Womach, Jasper, Agriculture: A Glossary of Terms, Programs, and Laws, 2005 Edition. Congressional Research Service Report for Congress, June 16, 2005, p. 10.
113 These are the Food and Agriculture Act of 1965, Agricultural Act of 1970, the Agriculture and Consumer Protection Act of 1973, the Food and Agriculture Act of 1977, the Agriculture and Food Act of 1981, the Food Security Act of 1985, the Food, Agriculture, Conservation, and Trade Act of 1990, the Federal Agriculture Improvement and Reform Act of 1996, the Farm Security and Rural Investment Act of 2002, and the Food Conservation and Energy Act of 2008.
114 Skinner, Robert and Scott Sanford, U.S. Cotton Programs, National Food Review, Vol 13, No. 1 (Jan–March, 1990), pp. 27–32.

were made only when average market prices fell below target price levels.[115] A relative rise in production costs after the 1973 Farm Bill resulted in a change in the target price calculation so that production costs were taken into consideration. In addition, payments to farmers based on target prices were based on current cotton acreage planted, rather than the long-standing policy of basing payments on historical allotments. These two changes had important implications in that incorporating current cotton acreage, rather than historical allotments, as well as production costs in determining producer benefits, facilitated a shift in cotton production toward the lower cost regions of the West and Southwest.[116]

Market conditions had changed substantially by the time the *1985 Farm Bill* was being considered.[117] There was significant downward pressure on cotton prices due to historically high domestic production coupled with declining exports and falling domestic textile mill demand. The marketing loan concept was introduced in order to tie the level of producer support more closely to the world price level. Previously, target prices were often above the level of world cotton prices and domestic producers benefitted from effective price floors. However, when world prices dropped below the US support price level, foreign production was encouraged, exports would decline, and US market share would be eroded.[118] The introduction of marketing loans let domestic cotton prices more closely track world prices. In addition, loan prices could be adjusted more rapidly than target prices had been adjusted in the past and, further, the Secretary of Agriculture was given more authority to modify acreage reduction programs in order to reduce surpluses. The 1985 Farm Bill also introduced a new generation of loan deficiency payments (LDPs) along with its novel marketing loan programs, both of which survived through later Farm Bill iterations and were one of a number of programs challenged in the *Cotton* dispute.

---

115 Stults, Harold, Edward Glade Jr., Scott Sanford, and Leslie Meyer, Cotton: Background for 1990 Farm Legislation. Economic Research Service, U.S. Department of Agriculture, Staff Report No. AGES 89-42, 1989, p. 29.

116 Skinner, Robert and Scott Sanford, U.S. Cotton Programs, National Food Review, Vol 13, No. 1 (Jan–March, 1990), pp. 27–32.

117 Gardner, B., *US Agricultural Policy*, American Enterprise Institute for Public Policy Research, Washington, D.C., © 1985.

118 Stults, Harold, Edward Glade Jr., Scott Sanford, and Leslie Meyer, Cotton: Background for 1990 Farm Legislation. Economic Research Service, U.S. Department of Agriculture, Staff Report No. AGES 89-42, 1989, p. 31.

The 1990,[119] 1996[120] and 2002[121] Farm Bills marked an important stage in the development of the US support policies for cotton and set the main channels of support that led to the initiation of Brazil's WTO challenge. The nature as well as structure of the programs under these bills had altered, significantly. As part of its farm legislation overhaul, the US, *inter alia,* increased levels of support for the remaining old programs added new programs, and the methodology for establishing "base" acreages was changed.

The *1990 Farm Bill* incorporated the support programs (with the same loan rate formula and rates in place) from the 1985 Bill with some adjustments. First, the Secretary of Agriculture was given greater discretion to determine the base quality of cotton. Further, Plans A and B, which set the repayment rates for loans under the 1985 Farm Bill when the prevailing world price was below the loan level, were discontinued. Rather, under the 1990 Farm Bill, when the adjusted world price was less than the loan rate, the producer could opt to repay the loan at the pre-established rate or seventy (70) percent of the loan level or another level not less than seventy (70) percent, or the adjusted world price.[122] Further, in line with the 1985 Farm Bill, if the marketing loan provisions failed to make cotton competitive in the world markets and the prevailing world market price was less than the current loan repayment rate, the Secretary was directed to grant negotiable marketing certificates, in the value of the difference between the loan rate and prevailing world price, to cotton buyers. These certificates could then be redeemed for cash or other commodities. Similar to the 1985 Farm Bill, if the national average market price received by farmers was below the established target price, deficiency payments were paid to producers. The computation method remained the same, but the target price was set to no less than $0.729 per pound, down from $0.81 in 1986, for the duration of the Farm Bill.

One of the most notable features of the 1990 Farm Bill was the inception of the three-step competitiveness program. Step One was the marketing loan program, which integrated the discretionary adjusted world price, and included loan deficiency payments. Step Two required payment, in cash or marketing certificates, to be made to domestic users and exporters when the US domestic prices were lower than world prices, essentially compensating US cotton

---

119 Food Agricultural Conservation and Trade Act of 1990, Pub. L. No. 101–624,104 Stat. 3359 (Nov. 28, 1990).
120 Federal Agriculture Reform Improvement and Reform Act of 1996, Pub. L. No. 104–127, 110 Stat. 888 (Apr. 4, 1996).
121 Farm Security and Rural Investment Act of 2002, Pub. L. No. 107–171, 116 Stat. 134 (May 13, 2002).

exporters and domestic users for the higher US prices.[123] 'Exporters' were defined in the regulation as persons regularly engaged in selling eligible cotton from the US who had entered into the marketing certificate program with the US Commodity Credit Corporation. Step Three imposed a special import quota be placed equal to one (1) week of domestic mill consumption, when a consecutive ten (10) week period of US prices exceeded world prices by more than 1.25 cents per pound was experienced – or, in other words, when there was a US shortage in cotton.

The *1996 Farm Bill*[124] marked a particularly significant moment in US farm policy and the WTO as the US did attempt to integrate their Uruguay Round[125] commitments into their domestic agricultural policy. A detailed discussion on the political environment as well as particular commitments made during the time of the Uruguay Round up to the *Cotton* dispute is included in Chapter 3. A greater analysis of the development of the 1996 Farm Bill and its relation to the 2002 Farm Bill, and the initiation of the *Cotton* dispute, is included therein. Important to note here is the fact that the Uruguay Round commitments are reflected in the 1996 Bill and were subsequently reversed and increased levels of support were given to US cotton producers through the adoption of the 2002 Bill.

Most significantly, the 1996 Farm Bill removed the connection between income support payments and farm prices.[126] It was in the 1996 Farm Bill, that the notion of decoupling payments from current production and, alternatively, basing payments on historical production was introduced. The new type of support was given in the form of production flexibility payments, which were the predecessors to the direct payments at the time of Brazil's challenge. The difference is that the production flexibility payments, also called Agricultural

---

122   Willis, B., and O'Brian, D., "Summary and Evolution of US Farm Commodity Titles – Expanded Discussion," National Agricultural Law Center. <http://www.nationalaglawcenter.org/assets/farmbills/commodity-expanded.html#cotton-90> last visited 5 June, 2010.
123   Stults, H. *et al.*, "Cotton Background for 1996 Farm Legislation," at 16, (Economic Research Service, Staff Report No. AGES 89-42 U.S. Dep't. of Agric., 1995).
124   Federal Agriculture Improvement and Reform (FAIR) Act, P.L. 104–127.
125   The Uruguay Round constituted formal multilateral trade negotiations under the GATT and established the WTO. The trade agreements formulated during the Round became the rules for WTO Members, to be implemented at the domestic level, over the 6-year period 1995–2000, and further negotiated after the completion of the Round, pursuant to Article 20. These developments and their relation to US trade policies is included in Chapter 3.
126   USDA, "1996 FAIR Act Frames Farm Policy for 7 Years," Agricultural Outlook Supplement, (April 1996), p. 1.

Market Transition Act or *contract payments*, were fixed in terms of total expenditure per year while similar payments under the 2002 Farm Bill, called *direct payments*, were fixed in terms of the per-unit payment rate.[127] Eligibility was determinant upon a farm's participation in production adjustment programs in any of the years between 1991 and 1995.[128] Extra long staple (ELS) cotton was not eligible for direct payments. Further, the marketing loan gains remained in the 1996 Bill as well as the specified contract payment levels. Therefore, the FAIR Act did not set out to phase out farm subsidy programs. It was still an extension of the policy path from the previous decade. The alterations that constituted change were the moderation of "planting requirements, eliminating price supports and government stockpiles of program crops, and eliminating annual land set-asides."[129]

After the passage of the 1996 legislation, it is important to note that as world prices began to plummet, additional appropriations were granted to prevent US cotton farmers from receiving prices below the targeted level established in the 1996 Farm Bill. By the end of 2000, farm incomes were supplemented by an additional $22 billion and an additional $11.5 billion proposed for 2001.[130]

In the *2002 Farm Bill*, the US took a large 'step back' in terms of the alignment of its agricultural policy with its WTO commitments. Politically, this was facilitated by a general decline in agricultural commodity prices, a decreased emphasis on federal deficit reduction, and a "weakened administration" in the US that chose to curry political favor from farm interests in cotton-producing states where Senate votes were needed.[131] As a result, the US resumed the agricultural policy path it had begun to develop during the time of the Uruguay Round.

---

127 Schmitz, Andrew, Frederick Rossi, and Troy Schmitz, U.S. Cotton Subsidies: Drawing a Fine Line on the Degree of Decoupling, Journal of Agricultural and Applied Economics, Vol 39, No. 1 (April, 2007), pp. 135–149 (p. 137).

128 USDA, "1996 FAIR Act Frames Farm Policy for 7 Years," Agricultural Outlook Supplement, (April 1996), p. 1.

129 Sumner, D., "Farm Subsidy Tradition and Modern Agricultural Realities," Paper for American Enterprise Institute Project on Agricultural Policy for the 2007 Farm Bill and Beyond <http://aic.ucdavis.edu/research/farmbill07/aeibriefs/20070515_sumnerRationalesfinal.pdf> last visited 30 June 2010.

130 Gilson, I., Poulton, C., Balcombe, K., and Page, S., "Understanding the Impact of Cotton Subsidies on Developing Countries," Working Paper, (May, 2004), p. 16.

131 Sumner, D., "Farm Subsidy Tradition and Modern Agricultural Realities," Paper for American Enterprise Institute Project on Agricultural Policy for the 2007 Farm Bill and Beyond <http://aic.ucdavis.edu/research/farmbill07/aeibriefs/20070515_sumnerRationalesfinal.pdf> last visited 30 June 2010.

Practically, the direct payment framework of the 1996 Farm Bill was combined with counter-cyclical payments from the preceding laws. As mentioned, *supra*, the production flexibility contract payments of the 1996 Farm Bill were renamed as direct payments and new counter-cyclical payments were made for the 2002 – 2007 eligible crops.[132] The newly named direct payments differed from the production flexibility contract payments only to the extent that they were fixed for this five-year life of the Act (again, 2002–2007), but were still based on historical acreage and yield.[133] Direct payments were subject to an annual limit of $40,000 per person, although this can be doubled under spouse or three-entity rules. Prior, these payments were based on commodity-specific parameters, but were changed in the 2002 Farm Bill. Also, the 2002 Farm Bill reauthorized the marketing assistance loan program, thereby continuing a long tradition of various price-based loan programs to cotton farmers. The counter-cyclical payments introduced in the 2002 Farm Bill had no official antecedent in the 1996 farm Bill, but replaced the Market Loss Assistance subsidy payments authorized in the 1996 Bill and made during the 1998 – 2001 period.[134] Effectively, the 2002 Farm Bill was a reversion by the US to previous methods and record high levels of domestic agricultural support.

As was argued in the *Cotton* dispute, the United States Department of Agriculture (USDA) carefully tracked the amount of expenditures related to upland cotton production in all three of these Farm Bills. The following are the programs included in the initial submission by Brazil to the first WTO panel for review: production flexibility contract payments; direct payments; market loan assistance; countercyclical payment programs; marketing loan programs; crop insurance subsidies; Step 2 export payments; Step 2 domestic payments; export credit guarantee programs; and cottonseed payments.[135] A brief description of each is herein provided to supplement the historical basis set forth, *supra*, to illuminate the variety of support provided throughout the various stages of cotton production.

---

132   USDA, "Upland Cotton Direct and Counter-cyclical Payment Program and Marketing Assistance Loans," Fact Sheet, Farm Service Agency, (March, 2006), p. 1.
133   Schmitz, Andrew, Frederick Rossi, and Troy Schmitz, U.S. Cotton Subsidies: Drawing a Fine Line on the Degree of Decoupling, Journal of Agricultural and Applied Economics, Vol 39, No. 1 (April, 2007), pp. 135–149 (p. 137).
134   Schmitz, Andrew, Frederick Rossi, and Troy Schmitz, U.S. Cotton Subsidies: Drawing a Fine Line on the Degree of Decoupling, Journal of Agricultural and Applied Economics, Vol 39, No. 1 (April, 2007), pp. 135–149 (p. 137).
135   *United States – Subsidies on Upland Cotton*, "First Submission of Brazil," WT/DS267, (24 June 2003), pp. 21–50.

2.2 US Cotton Subsidy Programs at Time of Brazil Challenge

While a wide variety of subsidy and support regimes for US cotton had been in place for decades, it was not until the establishment of the WTO that there was a dispute settlement process to address the effects of such programs on global markets. The *Cotton* dispute covered various US domestic support measures as well as other externally focused programs such as export guarantees and local content subsidies. Mandated subsidies, such as those legislated for upland cotton at the time of Brazil's WTO challenge, resulted in overproduction and world price suppression. Though efforts and concessions had been made during the Uruguay Round of negotiations as discussed, *infra,* cotton prices had continued to decline and remained suppressed at the historic levels. At the time of the initiation of the dispute, economists from the United States Department of Agriculture predicted that US and world prices (including Brazil prices) were to remain low well into the future.

There were several subsidy programs in place that effectuated these adverse results at the time of Brazil's WTO challenge, several of which were listed in Section 1.1. Although a variety of subsidy and support measures were extant at the time, the vast majority of subsidies can be categorized into: five (5) types of price support programs (marketing loan programs, counter-cyclical payments, direct payments, production flexibility contract and market loss payments, and CCC expenditures for price support); two (2) programs for crop loss assistance (crop insurance subsidies and crop disaster payments); a three (3) step competitiveness scheme (loan repayment rate reduction, payments to domestic mill users and exporters, and special import quotas); and three (3) forms of export assistance (export credit guarantees, foreign market development program, and market access program).[136] Brazil chose not to challenge crop disaster payments, loan repayment rate reduction support, or special import quotas.[137] Therefore, the main channels of support included in the dispute focused on market price payments, decoupled and non-decoupled payments, the imposition of quotas, crop insurance schemes, emergency payments, and export subsidies.

Marketing Loan Program: This program, began in 1986 and re-authorized by the 1996 and 2002 Farm Bills,[138] allows farmers to use their crop as collateral in order to receive immediate and substantial government benefits. In essence,

---

[136] Womach, J., "Cotton Production and Support in the United States," CRS Report for Congress, (24 June 2004), pp. 18–27.

[137] *United States – Subsidies on Upland Cotton,* WT/DS267, First Submission of Brazil, (24 June, 2003), p. 22.

[138] Farm Security and Rural Investment Act of 2002, Title I, Section 1202, p. 24 (Loan rates for nonrecourse marketing assistance loans).

the Program enables farmers to hold their crop at the time of harvest when prices tend to be low, use their crop to secure loan payments from the government, and to subsequently repay their loans when market conditions are more favorable.[139] This program provides for two basic types of payments for cotton producers – marketing assistance loan payments and loan deficiency payments.[140] These were a principal focus of Brazil's *Cotton* case against the US because, as will be discussed in Part 2 of this book, these are among the most trade distorting of the subsidies provided by the US to domestic cotton producers. In essence, these programs dramatically reduce the effects of price variability by ensuring that cotton producers will benefit whether cotton prices are above or below specified loan rate prices.

The 1996 Farm Bill authorized marketing assistance loans for upland cotton for up to ten months. In the case of cotton, the amount of the marketing assistance loan is determined by the difference between the loan rate price and the world price multiplied by the quantity of cotton produced.[141] ELS cotton producers are eligible for assistance under the marketing assistance loan program, but at different loan rate prices than for upland cotton. When market prices are above the loan rate, farmers can sell cotton in order to repay the loan plus interest, usually at below market interest rates. When market prices are below the loan rate, farmers can retain ownership of the cotton to sell it when market prices rise above the loan rate or, in some cases, forfeit the crop. In the latter case, this effectively allows farmers to value their crop at the higher loan rate price rather than the prevailing market price.[142] The loan rates for the 1999 through 2002 were each determined to be 51.92 cents per pound.[143] The 2002 Farm Bill increased the amount of acreage eligible for market assistance loan and increased the loan rate for upland cotton at 52 cents per pound from the 2002 through 2007 crop years.

---

139 *US-Upland Cotton*, Report of the Panel, World Trade Organization, WT/DS267/R, (8 September 2004), p. 70.

140 A third type of payment based on commodity certificates were authorized by a 19999 amendment of the 1996 Farm Bill and were as a means of acquiring crop collateral for commodity loans.

141 Schmitz, Andrew, Frederick Rossi, and Troy Schmitz, U.S. Cotton Subsidies: Drawing a Fine Line on the Degree of Decoupling, Journal of Agricultural and Applied Economics, Vol 39, No. 1 (April, 2007), pp. 135–149.

142 Sumner, D., "US Farm Policy and the White Commodities: Cotton, Rise, Sugar and Milk," International Food & Agricultural Trade Policy Council, Farm Bill Series, No. 5 (June 2007), pp. 1–2.

143 Table 19 in *Agricultural Outlook*, published by USDA, (May, 2002), p. 50 and cited in *US-Upland Cotton*, Report of the Panel, World Trade Organization, WT/DS267/R, (8 September 2004), p. 70.

A producer choosing not to take a marketing assistance loan may instead receive a loan deficiency payment. This is advantageous when cotton prices are low because the payment is equal to the difference between the adjusted world price and the higher loan rate when the world price is below the rate. As Sumner (2003) notes: "The effect on grower planting incentives is to increase the expected net returns per acre for growing cotton and to lower the variability and risk of revenue from cotton production." If eligible producers do not take out a marketing assistance loan, they can still apply for a loan-deficiency payment, which is similar to the marketing assistance payment in that the payment is equal to the difference between the loan rate and the world price. It is important to note that marketing assistance loans are linked to current production levels and, as a result, are tied to current market conditions. Therefore, they are considered to be coupled subsidies[144] with potential trade distorting effects under WTO rules.

Counter-Cyclical Payments (CCC): This payment program, like the Marketing Loan Program, is among the most trade distorting of the US subsidy programs. These payments were introduced in the 2002 Farm Bill and are activated when the market price of cotton is below a specified target price. These payments replaced the emergency market loss assistance program set in 1998–2001 to assist farmers during the commodity crash.[145] Whether counter-cyclical payments may be considered decoupled is still under debate. Producers have the discretion of whether to receive support based on their historic earlier production flexibility contract payment 'base acreage' or update it using average planted acreage during the period.[146] An assessment of the effective price as opposed to target price determines the total amount in counter-cyclical payments made under this program. More specifically, payments are based on historical acreage and yields, and calculated by the counter-cyclical payment rate multiplied by the counter-cyclical payment yield multiplied by .85 times the number of base acres.[147] Therefore, like direct payments, counter-cyclical payments are based on historical production, rather than current production;

---

144 Sumner, Daniel, "Effects of U.S. Upland Cotton Subsidies on Upland Cotton Prices and Quantities," *mimeo*, condensed and edited version of Annex I presented to the 2003 cotton dispute panel, (2006), p. 16.

145 United States, Farm Service Agency, Department of Agriculture, "Upland Cotton Direct and Counter-Cyclical Payment Program and Marketing Assistance Loans Fact Sheet," (28 Mar. 2008) http://www.fsa.usda.gov/Internet/FSA_File/uplandcoto6.pdf, p. 1.

146 The USDA reported on 19 June 2003 that one third of US farms receiving counter-cyclical payments opted to update their base acreage. Exhibit Bra-44, USDA, "Direct Payment and Counter-Cyclical Payment Enrollment Report", (19 June, 2003).

however, they are tied to recent production due to the update option.[148] While the eligible production amounts are based, at least in part, on historical acreage and yields, the CCP payments depend on current prices. As Sumner, *et al.*, has determined, the counter-cyclical payment scheme "effectively provides cotton farmers with cotton price insurance and this provides an additional incentive to plant cotton on cotton base land."[149]

Production Flexibility Contract and Direct Payments: As described above, the direct payments program was authorized by the 1996 Farm Bill and modified slightly by the 2002 Farm Bill. This program pays upland cotton farmers[150] a fixed amount per pound on eighty-five (85) percent (%) of historical cotton production. It is important to note that the direct payments to cotton farmers were not linked to either production or current prices. The decoupling of payments from current production and current market prices, first adopted in the 1996 farm bill and reauthorized in the 2002 Farm Bill, as discussed *supra*, had some important effects. First, it enabled cotton farmers to receive direct payments even without producing cotton. Second, direct payments were capitalized into land values rather than the value of future cotton production.[151] Third, the decoupling of direct payments from current market conditions, either current production or current prices enabled the US to claim that direct payments were non trade distorting under WTO rules.[152]

Between 1998 and 2001, *market loss assistance* was given annually to cotton producers as additional 'emergency' payments for the seven production flexibility contract crops, *inter alia*, cotton. Congress enacted these appropriated payments, after testimony was given that cotton producers were still unable to compete in the world market, even with the marketing loan program, Step 2 payments and production flexibility contract payments from the 1996 Farm

---

147 Monke, J., "Farm Commodity Programs: Direct Payments, Counter-Cyclical Payments, and marketing Loans," (13 Dec. 2004), Last visited 26 Apr. 2010. http://www.nationalaglawcenter.org/assets/crs/RS21779.pdf, p. 3.
148 Sumner, D., "US Farm Programs and African Cotton," International Food & Agricultural Trade Policy Council, IPC Issue Brief 22 (February 2007), p. 12.
149 Sumner, D., "US Farm Programs and African Cotton," International Food & Agricultural Trade Policy Council, IPC Issue Brief 22 (February 2007), p. 12.
150 ELS cotton is not eligible for direct payments.
151 Womach, Jasper, Agriculture: A Glossary of Terms, Programs, and Laws, 2005 Edition. Congressional Research Service Report for Congress, June 16, 2005, p. 19.
152 Womach, Jasper, Agriculture: A Glossary of Terms, Programs, and Laws, 2005 Edition. Congressional Research Service Report for Congress, June 16, 2005, p. 18.

Bill.[153] Payments were determined based on production flexibility contract payments, resulting in a vast majority of producers receiving this additional subsidy in 1999–2001. The value of these payments represented almost eighteen (18) percent of the market value of US upland cotton during this time.[154]

Beyond price support programs, express *crop insurance subsidies* were also being distributed by Federal Crop Insurance Corporation (FCIC)-approved private insurance companies at the time of the *Cotton* dispute, and constituted some of the largest subsidies available for cotton producers. These subsidies effectuate two aims: to provide a direct subsidy on premiums paid for crop insurance as well as subsidy payments made on losses beyond the insurance coverage.[155] Initially, crop insurance was authorized in the AAA of 1938 and the 1996 Farm Bill established the Risk Management Agency of the USDA to oversee the FCIC. Just prior to the establishment of this agency, in 1994, the Federal Crop Insurance Reform Act dramatically increased crop insurance levels to help increase yields and provide greater price protection for producers in down markets. In addition, the Act increased the subsidy for insurance premiums to about fifty (50) percent of premium costs.[156] In 2000, even more extensive crop insurance was provided under the Agricultural Risk Protection (ARP) Act.[157] The types and combinations of policies were unique and offered to only a few commodities, including cotton. Producers were easily able to complete the application process and had various options from which to choose.[158] To further incentivize private insurance companies and bolster cotton producer confidence, the FCIC also offers reinsurance to private companies providing crop insurance policies to domestic cotton producers. Therefore, if losses are

---

153   *United States – Subsidies on Upland Cotton*, WT/DS267, First Submission of Brazil, (24 June 2003), p. 28. Exhibit Bra-41, "The Future of Federal Farm Commodity Programs (Cotton)," Hearing before the House of Representatives Committee on Agriculture. 15 February 2001, p. 2–3.

154   OECD, "Agricultural Policies in OECD Countries – Monitoring and Evaluation 2003," (2003), p. 45, Annex Table 2.

155   Schmitz, Andrew, Frederick Rossi, and Troy Schmitz, U.S. Cotton Subsidies: Drawing a Fine Line on the Degree of Decoupling, Journal of Agricultural and Applied Economics, Vol 39, No. 1 (April, 2007), pp. 135–149 (p. 137).

156   Gardner, B., "American Agriculture in the 20th Century," Cambridge, Harvard University Press, (2002), p. 228.

157   P.L. 107–136. The Agricultural Risk Protection Act of 2000 amends the Federal Crop insurance Act in 7 U.S. Code 1501 et seq.

158   Section 508(c)(1)(B) of the Federal Crop Insurance Act.

sustained by the companies or producers, the federal government would step in and offset their indemnity losses.[159]

The *Step 2 Program* differed from the other three major types of subsidies discussed above and was an integral part of US cotton policy as part of its 1990 three-step competitiveness program,[160] and which was sustained through the 1996 and 2002 Farm Bills. There were two aspects of the Step 2 Program – the export payment side and the domestic support program. Only US producers, exporters (including cooperatives), and domestic users were eligible to benefit from the Step 2 program. The domestic payment program authorizes payments, using the same price mechanism for Step 2 export payments, to any domestic user of US upland cotton.[161]

Collectively, Step 2 subsidies were deemed some of the most egregious subsidies as they directly compensated domestic mill users and US exporters for the difference between their higher domestic and lower world prices. As a result, producers were encouraged to export their higher-priced cotton and the program ensured they remained competitive in the world market. While the other subsidies directly benefitted cotton producers, the Step 2 program was a demand subsidy that made payments to domestic mill users and exporters that indirectly benefited producers. The program allowed for payments to be made to eligible recipients when there was a four consecutive week period where the US domestic price of cotton exceeds the world price by 1.25 centers per pound, and if the adjusted world price did not exceed 134% of the loan rate. Payment rates equaled the difference between the US price minus the world price, minus 1.25 cents per pound. As a result of the successful cotton challenge by Brazil at the WTO, the US ended the Step 2 payments program as of 1 August 2006.[162]

In addition to these various direct and indirect insurance schemes, the US distributed *cottonseed payments* under the Cottonseed Payment Program from 1999 to 2002 to ginners and producers in the US. In the case of ginners, the payments were contingent upon sharing any proceeds with the cotton producer, upon which the payments were based.[163]

---

159   Section 508(k) of the Federal Crop Insurance Act.
160   Brazil did not challenge the Step 1 or Step 3 programs.
161   7 CFR 1427.104(a)(1).
162   Schmitz, Andrew, Frederick Rossi, and Troy Schmitz, U.S. Cotton Subsidies: Drawing a Fine Line on the Degree of Decoupling, Journal of Agricultural and Applied Economics, Vol 39, No. 1 (April, 2007), pp. 135–149 (p. 137).
163   7 CFR, Section 1427.1004(c).

Prior to discussing the export credit guarantee programs, and in an attempt to evaluate the collective levels of subsidization at the commencement of the *Cotton* dispute, it is useful to consider the information in the following table, which summarizes the types and sizes of various cotton support programs:

Program	1999 rate of subsidization	2000 rate of subsidization	2001 rate of subsidization	2002 rate of subsidization[164]
Marketing Loan Gains and LDPs	43.72 percent	13.31 percent	81.36 percent	28.67 percent
Crop Insurance	4.81 percent	3.95 percent	8.54 percent	5.84 percent
Step 2	11.94 percent	5.79 percent	6.36 percent	9.57 percent
Production Flexibility Contract Payments/Direct Payments	17.43 percent	14.12 percent	15.39 percent	15.75 percent
Market Loss Assistance/ Counter-Cyclical Payments	17.35 percent	15.03 percent	21.23 percent	32.43 percent
Cottonseed Payments	2.24 percent	4.54 percent	no payments	1.51 percent
All Programs	97.49 percent	56.74 percent	132.88 percent	93.74 percent
Total Payments	3.445 billion	2.311 billion	4.093 billion	3.113 billion

In terms of the actual amount as well as percentage of market price received by US cotton producers, the table above sets forth the actual value of the subsidies involved. As is evident, the level of US subsidization to the cotton sector is extraordinary. In addition to this assistance, the US also provided cotton exporters with assistance through their export credit guarantee programs.

Export Credit Guarantee (ECG) Programs: These were established in 1978 to assist agricultural commodity exporters in world markets. Cotton exporters

---

164   The value of the MY 2002 crop ($3.321 billion) has been calculated by taking the average price received by U.S. producers during the August 2002–May 2003 period ($0.4193) multiplied by the U.S. production of upland cotton (16.5 million 480-pound bales) as shown in Exhibit Bra-4 ("Fact Sheet: Upland Cotton," USDA, January 2003, p. 4). Data is based on prices published in USDA's Cotton and Wool Outlook. In cases of varying prices, the latest published price quote for a given month has been used.

were among the leading beneficiaries of this legislation. By the time of the commencement of the *Cotton* dispute, cotton exporters were receiving governmental assistance in the form of subsidies from price support, competitiveness, and export credit guarantee (ECG) programs. Of particular concern to Brazil were the three main ECG programs that the USDA's Commodity Credit Corporation operated: the General Sales Manager 102 (GSM 102), General Sales Manager 103 (GSM 103), and the Supplier Credit Guarantee Program (SCGP). Generally, the programs allowed for loans in foreign countries to be created that would not otherwise be economically viable in the marketplace without these US governmental guarantees. For example, both GSM 102 and GSM 103 programs assume virtually all of the credit risk for such loans by guaranteeing ninety-eight (98) percent of the principal and a portion of interest.[165] The difference between the two programs is that the former guarantees short-term bank loans (up to three years) and the latter guarantees repayment of intermediate bank loans (up to ten years).[166] Further, the SCGP provides guarantees on promissory notes between US exporters and foreign purchasers as short-term credit not to exceed one hundred and eighty days. The value of credit amounts to sixty-five (65) percent of the principal, but provides no guarantees for interest payments.[167] In all cases, when a foreign borrower defaults, the US government via the USDA's CCC, assumes the debt.

The US is certainly not the only country that subsidizes its domestic producers; however, the methodology employed and the sheer size of these subsidies are unusual in their scope within global agricultural production. The market power of the US in influencing world cotton prices and the actualized adverse effects of its subsidy programs on the world market are exceptional. These facts, coupled with the recognition and commitment by the US to reduce and/or eliminated a portion of them in the Uruguay Round, have increased international concern about the US domestic regime. The following section, briefly sets forth some of the subsidy regimes in some of the other major cotton producing regions in order to establish a comparative analysis.

---

165   USDA, "Export News and Opportunities," Foreign Agricultural Service, (2002) <www.fas.usda.gov/htp/circular/2002/02-09/gsm.htm> Last visited 6 June, 2010.

166   Womach, J., "Cotton Production and Support in the US," CRS Report for Congress, (24 June 2004), p. 26.

167   Exhibit Bra-72, "Fact Sheet: CCC Export Credit Guarantee Program," *United States – Subsidies on Upland Cotton,* WT/DS267, First Submission to Original Panel, (24 June 2003), p. 48.

168   Zhong, F., and Fang, C., "China's Cotton Policy," Mimeo (2003).

2.3 Other Country Subsidy Programs (China, EU)

China

China is the largest producer of cotton in the world. However, its exports are much smaller than those of the US because China is also the world's largest user of cotton. As a result, China's cotton policies have been formulated with both domestic and external markets as a focus. As China's economy has evolved over the past sixty (60) years, so have its policies on cotton production, use, and global trade.

The early years of China's cotton policies were characterized by governmental control of cotton production and consumption and by trade restrictions designed to shield Chinese cotton from global competition. The first step was the First Five Year Plan[168] of 1953 during which time the government took control of cotton production and use. This included the central government setting production targets and procurement quotas through its public agency, Chinatex.[169] In this regime, farms were state-owned and output was determined by the government, as was the distribution to ginning and milling operations.

These measures remained in place for twenty-five (25) years until major reform efforts began, which aimed at introducing some market incentives into cotton production and use. In 1978, policies aimed at boosting cotton production began with the introduction of price supports for cotton and for increasing the availability of inputs such as fertilizer. Market-based reforms continued in 1980 with the initiation of the Household Responsibility System,[170] in which land-use rights were granted to individual farmers. Private control of farming output decisions and incentives provided by maintaining artificially high domestic prices succeeded and led to cotton surpluses and government stockpiling of cotton.

In 1999, China instituted reforms aimed at reducing excess cotton production and government-owned stockpiles by decreasing the emphasis on support for producers and increasing flexibility in domestic cotton use. As a result of these reforms, prices paid to producers declined and a cotton exchange was formed "to facilitate domestic spot trading."[171] In 2001, additional reforms aimed at increasing domestic cotton trade were undertaken. These included measures to facilitate cross-regional trade, allowing cotton users to buy directly

---

169   Baffes, J., "Cotton: Market Setting, Trade Policies, and Issues," The World Bank (February 2004), p. 14.
170   Baffes, J., "Cotton: Market Setting, Trade Policies, and Issues," The World Bank (February 2004), p. 14.
171   Baffes, J., "Cotton: Market Setting, Trade Policies, and Issues," The World Bank (February 2004), p. 15.

from producers and granting ginning operators more market autonomy. These policies aimed at reducing cotton surpluses in China have been met with success as evidenced by declining stocks and government expenditures on purchasing surplus cotton. In addition, domestic cotton prices in China have declined.

In recent years, China's subsidies to its cotton producers are low, as reported to the WTO.[172] The view is accepted that few, if any, subsidies for cotton remain in China.[173] Instead, the focus has been on China's support of the cotton sector through the imposition of barriers that limit the "transmission of international price signals to growers."[174] This change in emphasis is seen by the fact that China's current governmental assistance to cotton production is not achieved through direct payments to producers, but rather a system of limiting cotton imports and promoting exports. China maintains tariffs, import quotas and licenses designed to restrict trade and keep domestic prices above the world market. In addition, exports are increased through subsidies[175] to exporters of Chinese cotton. China's accession to the WTO resulted in agreements to reduce cotton tariffs and to re-design its quota system.[176]

EU

Cotton output in the EU is comprised almost entirely of production from Greece and Spain and the EU's support policies for cotton began with Greece

---

172 For more information, See, "Annual Report: 2008," World Trade Organization, 2008, p. 34. <http://www.wto.org/english/res_e/booksp_e/anrep_e/anrep08_e.pdf> last visited 30 June 2010.

173 Sumner, D., "US Farm Programs and African Cotton," IPC Publications, International Food and Agricultural Trade Policy Council (February 2007), Brief 22, p. 11.; Shui, S., "Policies toward the Chinese Cotton Industry: the Commodity Chain Analysis Approach," Draft paper, Commodities and Trade Division, FAO of the United Nations, (February 2005).

174 Sumner, D., "US Farm Programs and African Cotton," IPC Publications, International Food and Agricultural Trade Policy Council (February 2007), Brief 22 p. 11.; Shui, S., "Policies toward the Chinese Cotton Industry: the Commodity Chain Analysis Approach," Draft paper, Commodities and Trade Division, FAO of the United Nations, (February 2005).

175 The value China subsidizes its cotton sector is comparable to the US – US$0.17 per pound of production (approximately, $1.92 billion) to China's $0.16 per pound (or, $2 billion). The differentiation is the amount to which it subsidizes for domestic consumption versus exportation of the commodity. In terms of the global trade of cotton and the ability to affect global market prices, is more significant in the case of the latter than the former.

176 Gale, F., Lohmar, B., and Tuan, F., "China's New Farm Subsidies," USDA Outlook, WRS-05-01, (February 2005), p. 2. <http://chinese.hongkong.usconsulate.gov/uploads/images/G3YqRBpWgqBIVXoef2Kqvg/uscn_t_usda_2005wrs0501.pdf> last visited 7 June 2010.

and Spain joining the EU's Common Agricultural Policy (CAP) in 1981. Under this policy, price supports were offered based on the difference between the world market price and the EU specified support price. The subsidies were not given directly to producers but, instead, were provided indirectly by paying ginners the specified price differential so that they could, in turn, offer higher prices to cotton producers. The EU's CAP reduced the amount of these payments for cotton production in excess of specified production limits in a policy designed to control overproduction. Nevertheless, it is estimated that EU cotton producers received, on average, more than twice the world price of cotton during the years between 1995 and 2000.[177]

In 1999, the EU reformed its cotton support program to further penalize production over the quantity limits. Under these reforms, for each one (1) percent of excess production, subsidy levels are reduced by 0.6 percent of the support price, as compared with 0.5 percent previously. As a result of this change, Greece received a support price twenty-eight percent lower than Spain because of the degree to which Greece exceeded its production limits.[178] In addition to output subsidies, EU cotton producers also receive subsidies on inputs such as credit for machinery purchase, insurance and publicly financed irrigation. A more detailed analysis and discussion of the subsidy regimes of the EU as well as its CAP reforms, with regards to cotton and general agricultural policies will be discussed throughout this book.

2.4 Political Power of US Cotton Lobby and US Legislative Process

> Cotton seems to have cast a wizard's spell not only over political leaders, firebrands, and fiscally innocent merchants, but also over hard headed businessmen and economists.
> DAVID L. COHN *The Life and Times of King Cotton* [179]

The sustainability of US cotton subsidies in a world where, economically, the domestic production of the crop is problematic, speaks to the political import of cotton. It is difficult to proffer explanations for the continued US support for

---

177 Baffes, J., "Cotton: Market Setting, Trade Policies, and Issues," The World Bank, Policy Research Working Paper, (February 2004), pp. 13.
178 Baffes, J., "Cotton: Market Setting, Trade Policies, and Issues," The World Bank, Policy Research Working Paper, (February 2004), pp. 15.
179 Cohn, D., *The Life and Times of King Cotton*, Oxford University Press, New York, © 1956, p. 123.

the production (or over-production) of US cotton and its role in world markets other than the strength, political fortitude and effectiveness of the US cotton lobby. Much of the strength of the cotton lobby is concerted in the South, due to the traditional import and political nature of cotton there, and shared more recently with some Western states due to their increasing levels of cotton production. This section will describe the structure and strategic choices of the US cotton lobby, its strengths at the association level and how it has developed to be effective at influencing government, so to ensure the passage of Farm Bills that benefit their industry; and the relationship between the cotton lobby and USTR, in defending its perceived interests at the WTO. The analysis will illuminate egregious political corruption legitimized through the passage of US legislation protecting the economically unsustainable production of cotton in the US.

It is impressive how US cotton farmers have been able to establish a system whereby they may effectively defend the continuation of cotton subsidies in the face of domestic fiscal concerns as well as global dismay and condemnation. This is especially noteworthy in light of the US cotton sector's ability to maintain governmental relationships and secure high levels of subsidies in direct competition with several national interests. In addition, it is important to note that this level of influence has persisted even as the US has increased its involvement within the international trade forum of the World Trade Organization.

As described in some detail in Section 2.1, the production of cotton and the relationship between business and government has been strong since the inception of the United States. The significance of cotton producers and their representative associations in policy formation can be illustrated through the development of the first attempt to establish an agricultural price support program in the US. In 1851, cotton producers were experiencing a sharp drop in the price of cotton. In order to ensure that specified prices would be met, Florida planters designed a concept at a Cotton Planters' Convention wherein a Cotton Planters' Association would be chartered by the States of South Carolina, Georgia, Alabama, Louisiana and Florida.[180] The plan was to create a cotton monopoly whereby the Association would control the storage and sale of all US cotton, by setting a minimum price and buying cotton from farmers who could not sell their cotton on the open market at that price. The Association could then hold the cotton until the minimum price could be received. Thus, the Association would be able to monitor the supply and create an artificial

---

180   Woodman, H., *King Cotton and His Retainers: Financing and Marketing the Cotton Crop of the South, 1800–1925,* University of South Carolina Press © 1990, p. 147.

demand. Though the plan did not materialize at that time, it is important to note that the present day public price support schemes operate much the same when they were first designed in 1851, as a public-private undertaking.

Throughout its history, the lobbying methodology employed by cotton interests has often proven to be more effective than those of other agricultural commodities.[181] The unique and over-riding strategic choice the US cotton lobby has employed is to differentiate itself from other agricultural interests. Rather than joining broader coalitions, it has historically chosen to remain independent and approach Congressional legislators, bureaucracies and administrations independently.[182] Although active since the nation's inception, the past seventy (70) years has demonstrated the effectiveness of the cotton lobby.

The main political actors in the cotton sector include: the National Cotton Council (NCC), the Cotton Board, and Cotton, Incorporated.[183] Arguably the most prominent and influential is the National Cotton Council, founded in 1938. This was the first commodity organization in the US formed to promote a single crop.[184] The NCC has been utilized to mitigate intra-market disputes and promote sector interests through collective action.[185] Comprised of elected delegates and interest organizations, the NCC predominantly engages in political activism. Six committees[186] of the NCC develop cotton policies favorable to

---

181 Browne, W., *Private Interests, Public Policy, and American Agriculture*, University Press of Kansas, Lawrence, Kansas, p. 91 (1988, 2007).

182 This approach most likely was developed by the first chairman of the NCC, Oscar Johnson, who utilized his Washington, DC experience as a New Dealer, to bring together divergent interests into one cohesive mission – speak as one voice, build solidarity, in order to receive the greatest gains possible.

183 Hutson, A., Biravadolu, M. and Gereffi, G., "Value Chain for the U.S. Cotton Industry," Report prepared for Oxfam America, (March, 2005), pp. 56–62. <http://www.unc.edu/~hutson/oxfamamerica_cotton_vc%20_combined%20documentv3(8march05).pdf> last visited 3 June, 2010.

184 Hutson, A., Biravadolu, M. and Gereffi, G., "Value Chain for the U.S. Cotton Industry," Report prepared for Oxfam America, (March, 2005), p. 59. <http://www.unc.edu/~hutson/oxfamamerica_cotton_vc%20_combined%20documentv3(8march05).pdf> last visited 3 June, 2010.

185 Hutson, A., Biravadolu, M. and Gereffi, G., "Value Chain for the U.S. Cotton Industry," Report prepared for Oxfam America, (March, 2005), p. 51. <http://www.unc.edu/~hutson/oxfamamerica_cotton_vc%20_combined%20documentv3(8march05).pdf> last visited 3 June, 2010.

186 The six committees are: Farm Program & Economic Policy, Health, Safety and Environmental Quality, Packaging and Distribution, Public Relations and International Market Development, International Trade Policy, and Research & Education.

the 340,000 identified persons employed in industry and lobby extensively on their behalf oin the seventeen (17) states in which they reside.[187] It has been recognized that "no other industry organization needs to be considered when assessing the politics of cotton."[188] The NCC works with the USDA and USITC to promote cotton consumption within the US and abroad. The NCC reaches international markets through the Cotton Council International (CCI), which is the international division of the NCC, funded by the USDA's Foreign Market Development Program.[189] The CCI is a subsidiary of NCC, created to "shield the NCC from tax liability in foreign countries arising from agreements with local industry associations."[190]

The Cotton Board is a derivation of the 1966 Cotton Research and Promotion Act[191] put into place as a quasi-public entity, in response to the decreased demand of cotton due to substitution in favor of synthetic materials. The group of thirty-four (34) Members and one consumer advisor, nominated by the Secretary of Agriculture, form the Cotton Board. The Board is a related, but separate organization, from the NCC and was established for the primary task of providing assistance to the Secretary of Agriculture. Specifically, the Cotton Board oversees a program to improve the quality and production costs of cotton, which is developed through the policy committee it maintains. It receives, investigates, and reports violations of production or quality standards to the Secretary of Agriculture.[192] Further, it serves as an educational resource by informing producers and importers about various cotton program initiatives.[193] The membership dues of the NCC and private support are transferred through the association to the pay for consultants, make campaign donations, pay for lobbying expenses, and facilitate forums for intra-market conflicts to be resolved.

---

187   NCC, "United for Profits," <http://www.nationalcottoncouncil.com/about/upload/United-for-Profits.pdf> last visited 7 June, 2010.

188   Hutson, A., Biravadolu, M., and Gereffi, G., "Value Chain for the US Cotton Industry," Report Prepared for Oxfam America, (4 March 2005), p. 57.

189   This is also known as the cooperator program.

190   Jacobson, T. and Smith, G., *Cotton's Renaissance: A Study in Market Innovation*, Cambridge University Press, © 2001, p. 286.

191   In 1990, the Food, Agriculture, Trade, and Conservation Act amended the Cotton Research and Promotion Act of 1966. The Cotton Board remains an effective organ of the legislation.

192   Hutson, A., Biravadolu, M., and Gereffi, G., "Value Chain for the US Cotton Industry," Report Prepared for Oxfam America, (4 March 2005), p. 60.

193   USDA, "Cotton Research and Promotion Program: History," <http://www.ams.usda.gov/cotton/ctnR&P.htm> last visited 7 June, 2010.

Closely relational to the NCC, but organizationally and politically independent, is *Cotton, Incorporated*.[194] This is a quasi-public company devoted to developing markets for cotton by providing 'profit-supporting' services to the "entire chain of cotton production and distribution."[195] The organization effectuates this through marketing campaigns designed to attract new consumers while maintaining existing ones, principally in apparel and home furnishing products. In addition, the organization attempts to implement competitive advantage strategies to increase mill production through improved technologies and marketing services.[196] The organization was also established to promote US cotton by taking a broader approach when implementing marketing strategies by promoting cotton in general, rather than US cotton, specifically. Like the Cotton Board, the choice of Cotton, Incorporated to create a broader strategy for the promotion of cotton was a response to the breadth of individuals in the sector affected by the decline in market share due to the success of synthetic fibers, which has accounted for an estimated fifty percent loss of market share.[197] A total of fifty-four (54) directors, all of whom are cotton producers, comprise the leadership of Cotton, Incorporated. Buttressed by the preeminent consulting firm of Booz, Allen and their advertizing agency Ogilvy & Mather, the group influenced substantial scientific, technological and managerial improvements as well as branded the industry with the trademarked 'cotton seal,' recognized today as one of the most influential industry brands,[198] as shown below.

---

194 For a detailed history of the creation of Cotton, Incorporated and its role in reshaping the image of cotton in the world, see, Jacobson and Smith's, *Cotton's Renaissance: A Study in Market Innovation*, Cambridge University Press, © 2001.

195 Jacobson, T., and Smith, G., *Cotton's Renaissance: A Study in Market Innovation*, Cambridge University Press, UK © 2001, p. 154.

196 Hutson, A., Biravadolu, M., and Gereffi, G., "Value Chain for the US Cotton Industry," Report Prepared for Oxfam America, (4 March 2005), p. 61.

197 Jacobson, T., and Smith, G., *Cotton's Renaissance: A Study in Market Innovation*, Cambridge University Press, United Kingdom, © 2001.

198 Jacobson, T., and Smith, G., *Cotton's Renaissance: A Study in Market Innovation*, Cambridge University Press, © 2001, pp. 142–165.

In addition, *political action committees* (PACs) are recognized political actors in the US political process. The cotton PACs consist of large organizations, including Calcot (a cooperative cotton marketing organization, owned by US growers of Far Western cotton and involved in promotion and export activities[199]), J. G Boswell (one of the largest Californian cotton growers), the primary associations for textiles, and shippers, and those organizations already described.[200]

Collectively, the NCC and related associations exert political influence on members of the US Congress and a number of agencies in order to assist in the formulation of legislation and competitiveness programs to protect the interests of domestic producers and exporters. For example, the cotton lobby takes an active role in Farm Bills. They provide information, drafts of proposed legislation, and work with USDA personnel responsible for finalizing the pertinent language in relevant legislations, including a series of fifty two (52) farm bill forums.[201] NCC representatives meet with influential members of Congress and the USDA to garner support for their proposals. Further, members of the NCC (which comprises nearly all members of the industry) are able to send thousands of letters on short notice as well as publish marketing materials to support their positions. Other governmental entities involved include the House Committee on Agriculture and the Senate Agriculture, Nutrition, and Forestry Committee as well as the Senate Agricultural Production and Stabilization of Prices Subcommittee, which is responsible for price and income support policies.

As concerns international trade, negotiating platforms for the US on agriculture, including cotton, is represented through the executive branch by the Office of the United States Trade Representative (USTR). It is the USTR that negotiates trade agreements (bilateral, regional, and multilateral). The domestic influence of the NCC extends, internationally, through this governmental agency, which is primary responsible for, and mandated to, negotiate trade agreements. It is important to note that the close relationship between the NCC and USDA is politically influential since the USDA coordinates with the USTR to develop both domestic policies as well as set terms for international trade agreements. Further, given the USDA advises the USTR through its Foreign Agriculture Service (FAS) agency, the involvement by the NCC in FAS affairs can be highly influential through the USDA to the USTR to ensure that future trade agreements are in line with their interests.

---

199   <www.calcot.com> last visited 7 June 2010.
200   Gardner, B.D., *Plowing Ground in Washington: The Political Economy of the US Agriculture*, Pacific Research Institute, San Francisco, © 1995.
201   Johnson, R., "Farm Bill Legislative Action in the 110th Congress," United States Congressional Research Service, 31 January 2008.

In addition to the relationship between the USDA and the USTR, another domestic nexus of political influence lies within the executive branch with the National Economic Council (NEC). The NEC is chaired by the US President and works with a number of committees and government agencies to formulate negotiating positions. Therefore, it may be concluded that where power is exerted at one point of the power triangle, it might be effective throughout. In addition, private interest groups like the NCC are directly tied to the USTR (and hence the executive branch) through public input channel of the US President's Advisory Committee for Trade Policy and Negotiations (ACTPN). This has two (2) important committees dedicated to agriculture issues: the Agricultural Policy Advisory Committee for Trade (APAC) and the Agricultural Technical Advisory Committees for Trade (ATACs), with one specifically including cotton. It is through these two channels that associations such as the NCC and Cotton, Inc. directly influence US trade negotiation policy.

The political loop is closed when the USTR of the executive branch returns to the Congressional Oversight Group of the legislative branch. There, the primary relationships and efforts with Congressional representatives are again utilized in the interactions between the USTR and representatives from both the House and Senate who comprise the Congressional Oversight Group. An examination of the World Trade Organization and the role of cotton associations in relation to the legislative and judicial functions of the institution will be exemplified through an analysis of the *Cotton* dispute and Cotton Initiative. However, it can briefly be noted that, beyond the process described above, similar methodology is employed, internationally, in the forms described herein. The only significant difference is that the targets of their efforts are foreign diplomats and international organizations as well as, it is questioned, even the WTO secretariat.

Upon review of the highly structured system of the cotton lobby, it becomes apparent that a perverse cycle exists where the interest groups pay money to a group that exerts power on the US legislative system to be able to receive monies that then go back to those individuals paying for the support in the first place. Although the process of lobbying for cotton does not breach any laws – in fact, the actions of the NCC are exactly those proscribed by the founders of the Constitution in terms of public engagement – it does, however, raise the issue of the appropriateness of the extensiveness of support and the entrenchment of government in the sector.[202] Whether the process or outcomes are fair and equitable or the intended objectives met line up with the messages dissemination as part of the interest group's marketing and

---

202   *See*, generally, Gardner, B.D., *Plowing Ground in Washington: The Political Economy of US Agriculture*, Pacific Research Institute for Public Policy © 1995.

politicians' political campaign should be examined. In his book, *Plowing Ground in Washington: The Political Economy of US Agriculture*, Dr. Delworth Gardner argued using economic studies how, antithetical to the messages propagated by politicians and interest groups, that US agricultural policy wastes resources and reduces standards of living.[203] He then set forth the stakes at risk for the US as agricultural trade is liberalized worldwide, and concluded with a quote that is included as a summary:

> The income transfers associated with protection of agriculture in the industrial countries appear to go on more or less indefinitely, largely without analysis of what groups are adversely affected or of what net social gains, if any, are achieved. It would appear, that after such protection has been maintained for a period of time, the main argument for continuation is that the substantial losses would be imposed upon resource-owners in the protected sector. In the case of agricultural protection, there would be large losses in the capital value of land and other relatively long-life assets and the readjustment in the labor supply would be painful and serious. It is difficult for governments who have misled a significant and vocal fraction of their citizens to admit that the policies they have been following have been of relatively modest benefit, that most of the net benefits go to relatively high-income groups and that the continuation of the present high transfer costs, or even higher costs, is necessary merely to maintain the status quo with respect to real product prices.[204]

This chapter has set forth the dynamics and influence of cotton interests in the continuance of a host of programs aimed to benefit US cotton producers and exporters. As is seen, the amount of support received by cotton interests in the US is as substantial as it is difficult to justify on grounds other than political influence. While these stem primarily from domestic influences with the economic and political system of the US, the effects of these policies are felt globally. With the advent of the WTO, the effects of these and similar types of domestic policies on world markets are the subject of international concern. The following chapter elucidates the mechanisms by which the global community can incorporate the effects of domestic policies by WTO Member states.

---

203   Gardner, B.D., *Plowing Ground in Washington: The Political Economy of US Agriculture*, Pacific Research Institute for Public Policy © 1995, p. 15.
204   Johnson, D.G., *World Agriculture in Disarray*, University of Chicago, London: Fontana/Collins (1973), p. 247; Gardner, B.D., *Plowing Ground in Washington: The Political Economy of US Agriculture*, Pacific Research Institute for Public Policy © 1995, p. 49.

CHAPTER 3

WTO Political Environment Prior to *US-Upland Cotton* Case

The *Cotton* dispute significantly altered the political environment of the WTO. One of the greatest achievements of *Cotton* was its ability to effectuate change in the negotiating dynamics and to rebalance trade relations among countries. This was especially true in the interactions between the developed countries of the US and EU[205] and the developing and least developed countries of Brazil, Burkina Faso, Benin, Chad and Mali. This chapter focuses on the impact that *Cotton* had on the political environment of the WTO by reviewing the historical positioning of these countries prior to the case and the Doha Development Round. To that aim, Chapter 3 begins with a short history of the multilateral negotiations of the WTO in order to establish the context in which agriculture was incorporated into these negotiations and to describe the country/region-specific negotiating positions and perspectives of Brazil and Africa prior to the *Cotton* dispute.

There were several key conditions extant prior to the *Cotton* dispute that are of particular relevance. First, it should be noted that the US and EU were clearly the primary political drivers of agriculture negotiations and, consequently, the principal authors of the relevant agricultural trade agreements in effect prior to the *Cotton* case. Second, it is important to note that Brazil was a newly-emerging economic and political force whose influence in the global trading system had not been exercised to any significant degree prior to the dispute. Third, the relevant African countries lacked the requisite internal coordination mechanisms and degree of economic development to enable them to effectively influence international trade negotiations and were, as discussed in the previous chapter, especially vulnerable to the global effects of the domestic agricultural policies of the developed countries. Fourth, the legal agreements of the Uruguay Round that were later used by Brazil in the *Cotton* dispute had yet to be applied and interpreted by the DSU, and the extant disciplines for agricultural subsidies were perceived to be rather weak and their efficacy unknown prior to the dispute.

---

205 For a detailed discussion on US-EU agricultural trade relations in the Uruguay Round, *see*, Josling, T., "Agricultural Trade Issues in Transatlantic Trade Relations," *The World Economy*, Vol. 16, Issue 5, (1993), pp. 553–573.

Given these conditions, it is important to elucidate the process by which the system of multinational agricultural trade agreement and conflict resolution evolved from one of negotiation to litigated dispute resolution. To that end, this chapter describes the various reform efforts made within the WTO's multilateral negotiation framework after the Uruguay Round (1995) until the initiation of the 2002 Cotton dispute. During this time, the WTO was formed and the negotiation framework for global agricultural policy was better established, as exemplified by the Doha Development Agenda (DDA). This chapter also describes the context in which these developments were constructed in order to provide a basis for determining the consequences of them on the international trading system. Critical to note is the fact that it was during this time that a rules-based dispute settlement mechanism was incorporated into the trading system. In addition to allowing the *Cotton* dispute to be adjudicated, this constituted a major change in the international trading system and fundamentally altered the bargaining power of the developed, developing, and least developed countries. In this light, this chapter provides a review of the role of African cotton producing countries and Brazil in the political system of the WTO during this process of fundamental change and before the initiation of the *Cotton* dispute with the aim of setting forth a marker whereby these Member states started to advance their interests and, in so doing, began to bolster the argument that such actions by states can be effective in the greater international trade system.

For the past several years, as a result of the emphasis on cotton during the DDA, developments in the cotton markets and domestic subsidy regimes have been given considerable attention. This has resulted in two significant cotton-specific developments achieved within the international agricultural trade regime. The first is the WTO dispute settlement case brought by Brazil in 2002, *US-Upland Cotton*, which challenged the compliance of US subsidy programs with its WTO obligations. The second is the Cotton Initiative and its eventual formation of the *Subcommittee on Cotton* within the present Doha Development Agenda negotiations. As a result of these two developments, the US has been compelled to reassess its Farm Security and Rural Investment Act of 2002 and Food, Conservation, and Energy Act of 2008, commonly referred to as the US 2002 and 2008 Farm Bills, in order to come into international compliance.

Several economic and political factors were drivers for these developments. These are reviewed both in the previous chapters of this book and are detailed in subsequent portions. Specifically, the historical development and country comparative analysis of the US Farm Bill was detailed in Chapter 2, *supra*. This described why and to what extent the cotton lobby in the US is entrenched in the national political system and how enormous subsidies are awarded, disproportionately, as compared to other US commodities and differently than other subsidy regimes in the world. However, it is also important to this book to describe the political environment, which existed prior to the *US-Upland Cotton* case and the Cotton Initiative, at the World Trade Organization. This chapter is especially important as a foundational groundwork for Parts 2 and 3 of this book, wherein the *Cotton* case and Cotton Initiative are analyzed to determine the nature and efficacy of their *political* effects on the WTO.

3.1 Multilateral Agriculture Negotiations and the Formation of the WTO

Multilateral negotiations on agriculture have played a considerable role in the formation and sustainability of the World Trade Organization (WTO), and its predecessor, the General Agreement on Tariffs and Trade (GATT),[206] for the past several decades.[207] From its inception in 1948, the GATT provided a framework for provisional negotiated agreements on global trade but, to a large extent, domestic agricultural policies were based primarily on domestic considerations and not meaningfully negotiated at the multilateral level. The first time domestic agricultural policies began to be debated and integrated into a multilateral trading regime was during the Uruguay Round. This marked a crucial step in the development of international agricultural trade relations in that it was the first time that internal agricultural support policies, rather than external border measures such as tariffs, were in Table 1. By the time of the Uruguay Round, significant progress had been made on reducing tariffs and

---

206 For a detailed history on the GATT, *see*, Irwin, D., Mavroidis, P. and Sykes, A., *The Genesis of the GATT*, Cambridge University Press, © The American Law Institute (2008). Of particular relevance to this book is the development of the subsidy provisions through the *London, New York, Geneva* (no change), and *Havana Conferences* for the drafting of the International Trade Organization (ITO) Charter as discussed in pp. 156–159. It should be noted that the ITO never came into existence; however, the GATT was ratified and was in effect for forty-seven (47) years.

207 For a primer on the world trading system, *see*, Jackson, J., *The World Trading System: Law and Policy of International Economic Relations, 2nd Ed.*, © The MIT Press, Cambridge, Massachusetts, (2007). Discussion on the development and dynamics of agricultural negotiations in the Uruguay Round through the formation of the WTO, *see*, pp. 313–316. Specifically, clarification of the common misperception of agriculture within the GATT framework is provided. This issue is discussed further in the section, *infra*.

other trade barriers and, as a result, domestic support policies were more trade distorting to farm production and trade.[208]

At the completion of the Uruguay Round, international trade negotiations and agreements had a direct impact on the formation of domestic agricultural policy. This has especially been the case as it relates to developed versus developing country relations and the greater issue of trade liberalization.[209] Following the Uruguay Round, the US made a concerted effort to bring its 1996 Farm Bill into conformity with the commitments made during Uruguay as part of the greater twenty-nine (29) agreements reached in the round.[210]

Moving toward a more market-oriented agricultural policy regime, the US strongly advocated for the inclusion of disciplines on domestic policies that distorted trade and that would develop such disciplines into international rules.[211] During this time, developing countries also took steps to implement domestic policy reforms that would further liberalize trade. Although some least developed and developing countries began adopting such policies, there were incidences of other Members falling short in honoring their international commitments. To many, this was not surprising given that the eight (8) rounds of multilateral negotiations that took place during GATT had, in many ways, failed to alleviate trade woes for the developing world. The widely held perception was that the rules and structure of the trading regime were designed by and favored the developed countries[212] and, as a result, many countries in the developing world chose not to actively participate in the multilateral negotiations process.[213]

---

208 Thompson, R., "The US Farm Bill and the Doha Negotiations: On Parallel Tracks or a Collision Course?" International Policy Council, Issue Brief 15, (September 2005), p. 1.
209 A division among the developed and developing world was consistently an issue throughout Uruguay Round negotiations. For an example, see, Raghavan, C., "North–South Divisions Surface at Uruguay Round Group of Negotiations on Goods Meeting," Geneva, (11 April 1990). <www.sunsonline.org/trade/areas/commodit/04110090.htm> last visited 13 June, 2010.
210 A detailed description of the commitments made by the US is included in Part 2 of this book, as part of the legal analysis.
211 Thompson, R., "The US Farm Bill and the Doha Negotiations: On Parallel Tracks or a Collision Course?" Food and Agricultural Trade, International Policy Council Issue Brief 15, (September 2005), p. 1.
212 For a greater discussion on the history and criticism of the WTO and the lack of participation by developing countries in its design, see, Stiglitz, J., and Charlton, A., *Fair Trade for All: How Trade Can Promote Development*, Oxford University Press, © 2005, p. 43. As Stiglitz describes, it was not until the multilateral trading system was nearly developed and trade expanded to the developing world that participation by developing countries began to increase.
213 Krueger, A., *Trade Policies and Developing Nations*, The Brookings Institution, Washington, DC, © 1995.

At the time of the commencement of the Uruguay Round, there was significant debate as to whether a more static, rules-based system should be designed and adopted to the evolving trade system, thereby incorporating a dispute settlement process; or whether the traditional 'discretionary equilibria' approach, based on continuous negotiations, should be maintained.[214] It was assumed, that relatively small or economically weak countries would prefer the former, under the assumption that the rules would be protective of the weak even though, as experienced in the Uruguay Round, the more economically powerful Member states would be the principal drivers in crafting the rules. Therefore, there was significant concern that these rules would actually further the interests of developed countries, to the detriment of developing nations. In the end, a rules-based system with an enforcement mechanism was added.

Surprisingly, the US was one of the greatest proponents of the rules-based approach. As one scholar noted at the time, "Many ideas for tightening up and constructing rules, and indeed for constructing complex legalistic systems, seem to have come from the United States because, for various historical reasons, this is a legalistic country and, above all, a country that always thinks in terms of constitutions and rules because it is held together by a constitution."[215] Though the US was instrumental in the design of the rules that are the foundation of the WTO, it is important to note that they were not the only nation participating in their construct and that the histories, customs, and legal systems of other nations also influenced the development of the WTO rules and procedures. What seems to be the consensus, however, is that developing countries by-and-large were not among the dominant players in developing the rules that support the system. Nonetheless, as demonstrated by Brazil's use of the WTO trade dispute process, the rules and procedures designed in large part by developed countries could be effectively used by less developed nations.[216]

Of importance in the context of the development of the multilateral trading system is the fact that, prior to the Uruguay Round and the subsequent creation of the dispute resolution process in the WTO, subsidies could not be

---

214 Corden, W.M., "On Making Rules for the International Trading System," as found in Stern, R.M., *US Trade Policies in a Changing World Economy*, The MIT Press, Massachusetts, (1987), p. 414.

215 Corden, W.M., "On Making Rules for the International Trading System," as found in Stern, R.M., *US Trade Policies in a Changing World Economy*, The MIT Press, Massachusetts, (1987), p. 415.

216 The use of these rules by Brazil to try to enforce compliance on the part of the US will be discussed in Parts 3 and 4.

prohibited by international rules or used as a justification by countries for imposing trade restrictions.[217] Overall, the Uruguay Round was deemed a success for the developed world and for the redesigning of the international trade system through the establishment of the WTO. However, the developing world was in large part underwhelmed by the minimal progress, and in many cases, adverse results post-Uruguay, especially in light of the promises that had been made. Consequently, a subsequent round of formal negotiations, the Doha Development Agenda (DDA), commenced with the aim to address development issues and to create a trading system more likely to be equitable to developing and least developed countries. In this context, there is no better poster child for the DDA than cotton and, as a result, the global effects of domestic cotton policies loomed large during the DDA.

3.2 Agricultural Reform Efforts Post-Uruguay Round

As a result of the GATT and establishment of the DSU of the WTO, world farm trade is becoming freer and fairer, and the multilateral trade system supporting it is becoming more sophisticated.[218] Simultaneously, it is important to acknowledge that developing countries have experienced a long history of unequal integration into the world market and have been somewhat marginalized in the development of the system managing the global economy. Further, those imbalances persist and alternative approaches to address these imbalances, such as building greater South-South coalitions and increasing trade relations, have proven somewhat unsuccessful. Rather, in the coming decades, the "management of trade relations between the high-income North and the emerging high-growth centers in the developing world and the economies in transition to a market economy is likely to become an increasingly central issue."[219]

---

217 Corden, W.M., "On Making Rules for the International Trading System," as found in Stern, R.M., *US Trade Policies in a Changing World Economy*, The MIT Press, Massachusetts, (1987), p. 423.

218 It is important to distinguish that this book focuses primarily on the globalization or cross-border economic relationship development as it affects trade in agricultural products as opposed to the internationalization or market regionalization of the agri-business sector. *See*, Coleman, W. and Skogstad, G., "Agricultural Policy: Regionalization and Internationalization," as found in Stubbs, R., and Underhill, G., *Political Economy and the Changing Global Order, Second Ed.*, © Oxford University Press (2000), pp. 310–319.

219 Hoekman, B. and Kostecki, M., *The Political Economy of the World Trading System*, Oxford University Press, Oxford, © 1995, p. 244.

The linkage between the developing to the developed world is ever more strong and the sheer importance of agriculture to developing countries, as well as to the global trade of agricultural products (two-thirds of which are from developing countries), have become more pronounced as an integral issue to be addressed in an evolving trade regime.[220] One solution has been an increase in trade agreements that facilitate trade and infuse stability into an ever-increasing system of interdependence. From the inception of the GATT to the present World Trade Organization, several developments have been made to effectuate increased standards of living around the world. Most relevant to this book are the efforts made during the round of negotiations preceding the *Cotton* dispute and the continuing Doha Development Agenda negotiations. An analysis of the precursor to the dispute settlement mechanism as well as the present negotiation dynamics is fundamental to gauging future developments.

As discussed *supra*, the Uruguay Round resulted in agricultural policies being brought into the greater multilateral trading regime of the World Trade Organization, in large part because previous GATT rules had proven ineffective in disciplining key facets of agricultural trade.[221] Article 20 of the Uruguay Agreement on Agriculture (URAA) required negotiations to recommence in 2000, after the completion of the Round, as incorporated into the 2001 Doha Development Agenda (DDA) as stated in Article 20:

> Recognizing that the long-term objective of substantial progressive reductions in support and protection resulting in fundamental reform is an ongoing process, Members agree that negotiations for continuing the process will be initiated one year before the end of the implementation period, taking into account: (a) the experience to that date from implementing the reduction commitments; (b) the effects of the reduction commitments on world trade in agriculture; (c) non-trade concerns, special and differential treatment to developing country Members, and the objective to establish a fair and market-oriented agricultural trading system, and the other objectives and concerns mentioned in the preamble

---

220 DeRosa, D., "Modeling the Effects on Agriculture of Protection in Developing Countries," as found in Ingco, M. and Winters, A., *Agriculture and the New Trade Agenda: Creating a Global Trading Environment for Development,* Cambridge University Press, © 2004, p. 248.

221 John H. Jackson clarified in his key WTO primer, *The World Trading System: Law and Policy of International Economic Relations,* that agriculture was not exempt from GATT; rather, it was an area especially difficult to bring under the discipline of the GATT. It was during the Uruguay Round through the Agreement on Agriculture, that this was finally achieved. Jackson, J., *The World Trading System: Law and Policy of International Economic Relations, Second Edition,* MIT Press, © 1997, pp.313–316.

to this Agreement; and (d) what further commitments are necessary to achieve the above mentioned long-term objectives.[222]

Agriculture has always been one of the key dimensions of the DDA and the primary objectives of negotiations in agriculture are to (1) substantially improve market access for agricultural products, (2) reduce and phase out export subsidies, and (3) substantially reduce trade-distorting domestic support measures that result in over-production and price suppression.[223] These three areas of *market access*, *export subsidies*, and *domestic support* are often referred to as the 'tripod' or 'pillars' of agricultural negotiations within the WTO.[224]

One of the principal reasons for the importance placed on the treatment of agricultural domestic and trade policies post-Uruguay is the adoption of the *Agreement on Agriculture* (AoA)[225] during the Uruguay Round. The AoA set forth customized rules and disciplines for agricultural products and converted non-tariff barriers to agricultural imports into bound tariffs. The singling out of agricultural issues during the Uruguay Round was a significant step, especially in light of the long-standing debate on whether agricultural products should be treated similarly to non-agricultural products.[226] As Brazilian governmental representative Pedro de Camargo Neto[227] stated:

> Agricultural trade rules should never have been left behind in international agreements in the first place. The only reason it took more than half a century to include agriculture in the multilateral trading system

---

[222] World Trade Organization, Agreement on Agriculture, The Legal Texts: The Results of the Uruguay Round of Multilateral Trade Negotiations, Cambridge University Press, © 1999, p. 46.

[223] *Id.*, at 28, *Preamble of the AoA*, wherein sets forth the long-term objectives to create a market-oriented agricultural trading system and commitment to achieve binding commitments in the areas of (1) market access (2) domestic support and (3) export competition, p. 33. Womach, J., "Cotton Production and Support in the United States," CRS Report for Congress, Congressional Research Service, (2004), p. 15, last visited 1 May, 2010 <http://www.nationalaglawcenter.org/assets/crs/RL32442.pdf>.

[224] These issues have also been conceptually expanded and discussed as a 'pentangle' to include non-trade and special and differential treatment concerns, separately.

[225] World Trade Organization, The Legal Texts: Results of the Uruguay Round of Multilateral Trade Negotiations 231, Cambridge University Press (1994) [hereinafter *AoA*], Article 20, (referring to ANNEX IA: *The Agreement on Agriculture (AoA)*).

[226] Desta, M.G., *The Law of International Trade in Agricultural Products: from GATT 1947 to the WTO Agreement on Agriculture*, Kluwer Law International, Dordrecht, The Netherlands, © 2002, pp. 5–7.

[227] The role of this representative is discussed further in Section 3.3.

was that developed countries preferred to ignore the broader consequences of their domestic policies. They could afford to postpone the political difficulties that adjustments would bring at home.[228]

This statement is one indication of the impending shift that was beginning to take place at the time of Uruguay and thereafter, and a hopeful foreshadowing of potential future developments.

Prior to the AoA, the treatment of agriculture under the GATT was minimal because countries were not willing to allow their domestic agricultural policies to be scrutinized or subjected to international discipline. Even those scholars who maintained that agriculture was not left outside the GATT agreed that fundamental changes occurred in the Uruguay Round under the AoA and that, previously, only relatively weak rules existed for agricultural products or policies.[229] The fact that, through the Doha Development Agenda, a new round of agricultural negotiations was underway was a strong indication that agricultural trade affairs were evolving and improving.

One of the major changes in the focus of multilateral negotiations was a shift from an almost exclusive concentration on tariffs to the inclusion of domestic subsidies. During the long series of GATT negotiations, tariff bindings, or commitments by Members to maximum tariff rates, covered nearly all agriculture products. During the Uruguay Round, Members agreed to phased reductions of tariff rates for developed countries over the 1995 – 2000 period. For the first time, however, subsidies and other domestic support measures were included in the negotiations. The AoA contained language prohibiting subsidies that exceeded negotiated limits for specific products, and set forth reduction phase-outs for domestic support determined to be trade-distorting.

More specifically, changes proposed in the Uruguay Round fell into two categories, amber-box and green box subsidies, based on their trade-distorting effects.[230] Amber-box support measures, those subsidies that were found to distort trade, were agreed to be reduced as determined in part by to the overall support given to agricultural producers, referred to aggregate measures of support (AMS). Decoupled subsidies, such as direct payments not contingent upon historical production or prices, were categorized as "green-box" and were not subject to spending caps under the AoA because they were deemed to be

---

228   Pedro de Camargo Neto, "International Conference on Cotton: The Next Steps for Africa," Washington, DC, (26 October 2006), p. 2.
229   Tangermann, S., "Has the Uruguay Round Agreement on Agriculture Worked Well?" International Agricultural Trade Research Consortium, Working Paper, 01-1, (October 2001).
230   These subsidy categories will be discussed in greater detail in Part 2.

TABLE 1   *Subsidy and protection reductions*

	Developed countries	Developing countries
	6 years: 1995–2000	10 years: 1995–2004
Tariffs		
Average cut for all agricultural products	–36%	–24%
Minimum cut per product	–15%	–10%
Domestic support		
Cuts in total ("AMS") support for the sector	–20%	–13%
Exports		
Value of subsidies (outlays)	–36%	–24%
Subsidized quantities	–21%	–14%

Notes: Least-developed countries do not have to reduce tariffs or subsidies. The base level for tariff cuts was the bound rate before 1 January 1995; or, for unbound tariffs, the actual rate charged in September 1986 when the Uruguay Round began.

Only the figures for cutting export subsidies appear in the agreement. The other figures were targets used to calculate countries' legally binding "schedules" of commitments. Each country's specific commitments vary according to the outcome of negotiations. As a result of those negotiations, several developing countries chose to set fixed bound tariff ceilings that do not decline over the years.

Source: World Trade Organization, "WTO Agriculture Negotiations: The issues, and where we are now."

less trade distorting. Table 1 sets forth the agreed upon targets for cuts to subsidies and protection in the Uruguay Round as published by the WTO:[231]

Finally, and importantly, the AoA required Members to re-commence agricultural negotiations by 2000[232] and, as a result, these negotiations have become a critical component of the Doha Development Round of negotiations.

---

231   "WTO Agriculture Negotiations: The Issues, and where we are now," World Trade Organization (updated 1 December, 2004), p. 5.

232   *Id.*, at 28, p. 46. In accordance with Article 20 of the Uruguay Agreement on Agriculture (URAA), negotiations on agriculture recommenced shortly after the riots at the Seattle Ministerial Conference. This signified the durability of the trading regime and import of agricultural negotiations for WTO Members.

Though significant steps were taken during the Uruguay Round to further agricultural reform at the international level, it is widely recognized that these developments were inadequate[233] and that more action by developed countries was needed. Though the Uruguay Round's Agreement on Agriculture established a framework to address trade barriers and distortions in the three prescribed pillars of agricultural policy and set forth operationally effective rules, protection rates remained high in developed countries (with some agricultural product rates exceeding 500%), and the use of "dirty" tariffication[234] prevented meaningful policy reform to meet intended objectives. The provisions of the AoA were further undermined[235] by the use of measures to sidestep AoA agreements, including the use of specific, rather than *ad valorem*, tariffs as a means for keeping quota fill rates at low levels, manipulating subsidies as "unused," and relaxing or simply not conforming to export subsidy disciplines. Further, over sixty (60) percent of domestic agricultural support in OECD countries was excluded from domestic reduction commitments during the Uruguay Round.[236] The adverse effect of these actions was especially felt in developing countries, where agriculture plays a substantial role in their economies.

Politically, despite the fact that the Agreement on Agriculture was formed and objectives for greater agricultural trade liberalization were set during the Uruguay Round, a number of difficulties arose thereafter. Unfortunately, these have often been cast as perceived failures and have tainted the current negotiations and efforts made in the present Doha talks. As Patrick A. Messerlin argued at a World Bank Roundtable on Policy Research[237] in preparation for the 5th WTO Ministerial Conference in Cairo, in 2003, the association of the post-Uruguay difficulties with the system of multilateral trade negotiations is incorrect and the moderate quantitative effects realized shortly after the Uruguay Round are more properly attributable to the domestic farm policies. Unfortunately, there have continued to be adverse political effects as a result of these misperceptions where Doha negotiators and their constituents are

---

233 See, Anderson, 2004; Messerlin, 2002.
234 "Dirty" tariffication refers to the process of setting bound tariff rates well above applied tariff rates. Anderson, K., "Agriculture, Developing Countries, and the Doha Development Agenda," as found in Ingco, M. and Winter, A. *Agriculture and the New Trade Agenda: Creating a Global Trading Environment for Development*, Cambridge University Press, World Bank (2004), pp. 113–135.
235 OECD, "The Uruguay Round Agreement on Agriculture: An Evaluation of its Implementation in OECD Countries," Paris: OECD (2001), p. 6.
236 Cite.
237 Messerlin, P., "Agriculture in the Doha Agenda," The World Bank, (August, 2002), p. 2.

attempting "to launch a liberalization, whereas many people believe that there has already been a welfare-deteriorating liberalization – the worst situation possible from a political perspective."[238] More specifically, at the commencement of the Doha Round and at the initiation of the *Cotton* dispute, the legacy of the Uruguay Round was that widespread support for agricultural policy reform remained unchanged to a large degree and that there was recognition that such reform efforts post-Uruguay were, for the most part, undesirable and ineffective.

Negotiators at the Uruguay Round had hoped that the sheer fact that the publication of the amounts of support through the new 'tariffication' process would increase transparency regarding the level of farm protection in several of the most developed countries. As Messerlin commented, "the magic of transparency did not work."[239] Dirty tariffication (described, *supra*) coupled with sustained domestic support hindered actual trade liberalization.[240] Therefore, when the Doha talks commenced, negotiators found themselves faced with a post-Uruguay world in which protectionist measures remained, new instruments of protection were being adopted, and the average support to farmers had increased. Although this was perceived to be related to the Uruguay Round negotiations and the resulting *Agreement on Agriculture*, the underlying cause was more attributable to entrenched political support in the form of government intervention for domestic industry protection.

Therefore, the agreements reached during the present negotiations on agriculture, the results of the *Cotton* dispute, and outcomes in other sectors will significantly affect domestic regimes. The significance of post-Uruguay Round reform efforts is critical to the stabilization of international food markets and a great number of developing countries. It has been suggested that reform efforts post Uruguay Round should have included: (1) a complete ban on farm export subsidies; (2) a gradual reform of domestic subsidies by the US and EU; (3) an elimination of the "blue box" category of support programs currently subject to reform measures stemming from the negotiation positions of the US and EU; and (4) the tightening of "green box" loopholes, which exempt certain measures for policy reforms from the scrutiny of the WTO.[241] The analyses

---

238 Messerlin, p. 2.
239 Messerlin, p. 2.
240 Messerlin, p. 3. Another trend was the sharp decrease in support by Australia and New Zealand with a simultaneous dramatic increase in support in the low-income OECD countries of Hungary, Poland, Mexico and Turkey.
241 Anderson, K., "Agriculture, Developing Countries, and the Doha Development Agenda," as found in Ingco, M. and Winter, A. *Agriculture and the New Trade Agenda: Creating a*

completed in Part 3 of this book, will examine to what extent these changes have been made and to what degree they still need to be implemented.

As a result of their effects on the results from multilateral trade negotiations on agriculture, there has been increased criticism of domestic subsidy regimes. After the Uruguay Round, the US did eliminate market management and tried to reduce the effects of their subsidies. However, only a few years later, alternative programs were added to ameliorate the effects of plummeting commodity prices and the Asian Financial Crisis. By the time of the next Farm Bill (2002), these emergency payments were made permanent and additional measures brought out of alignment with Uruguay Round commitments.[242] Further, these farm subsidies, as applied in the US and EU for the benefit of their domestic cotton industries, are recognized as having been one of the primary disruptions in early Uruguay negotiations and continuing into the Doha Development Round. This is exemplified by the eruption of Doha's September 2003 Cancun Ministerial Conference due to the inability of Members to agree on a negotiation framework that would meaningfully liberalize trade in agricultural products. During this time, developing countries demanded further reductions in domestic support by the US and EU which, however, were not forthcoming.

Phases One and Two of Agricultural Negotiations, Post-Uruguay and under the Doha Development Agenda

In March of 2000, only a few months after rioters in Seattle, Washington took to the streets in protest of the Ministerial Conference, Member states recommenced agricultural negotiations. The outcome of these negotiations, derived from forty-five (45) proposals submitted by over one hundred twenty (120) countries, resulted in two paragraphs of the 2001 Doha Ministerial Declaration, specifically on the three earlier-described negotiation pillars on agriculture. There were two particular phases of negotiations prior to this development.

Global Trading Environment for Development, Cambridge University Press, World Bank (2004), pp. 117–118. Ms. Anderson also emphasized that, with regards to the reformation of domestic subsidies, that further decoupling of farm income support from production , as proscribed by the US FAIR Act of 1996, would be helpful.

242 In the *Cotton* case, the initiation of the dispute was due to the fact that the US – though committed to reducing such bound tariffs after the Uruguay Round – had not actually implemented domestic law or policy reforms to achieve those international commitments. Furthermore, WTO non-compliant support was proven to have actually increased in subsequent Farm Bills. Therefore, the US and EU have become increasingly scrutinized and pressured in the last ten (10) years by the international trade community through the use of the WTO rules and negotiation system.

Phase One (2000–2001) was a time, during which countries set forth – whether in comprehensive or subject-specific proposals – their starting negotiation positions. Six (6) "Special Sessions" of the Agriculture Committee were held where these proposals were discussed. An additional six (6) meetings occurred during the second year, consisting of informal discussions and special sessions. These are considered Phase Two (2001–2002) of the negotiations (WTO, 2005 and Messerlin, 2002). During this time, Members commenced talks on specific, rather than general, topics and began to discuss technical details. Framing issues and the technical viability of proposals helped negotiators representing developed and developing countries better frame and amend proposals. These also began establishing a common basis of interests from which to determine a potential consensus.

Despite these developments, however, several factors negatively impacted progress during this time. Of primary importance was the passage of the 2002 Farm Bill by the US only six (6) months after the formal commencement of the Doha Development Round. Two months later, the French opposed the European Commission's (EC) proposal for reforming the EC's Common Agricultural Policy (CAP). Both of these developments signaled to negotiators that there would be less opportunity for these economic giants to negotiate with much flexibility. Regardless, midway through Phase Two, the Doha Ministerial Declaration finalized mandating:

> 13. We recognize the work already undertaken in the negotiations initiated in early 2000 under Article 20 of the Agreement on Agriculture, including the large number of negotiating proposals submitted on behalf of a total of 121 members. We recall the long-term objective referred to in the Agreement to establish a fair and market-oriented trading system through a programme of fundamental reform encompassing strengthened rules and specific commitments on support and protection in order to correct and prevent restrictions and distortions in world agricultural markets. We reconfirm our commitment to this programme. Building on the work carried out to date and without prejudging the outcome of the negotiations we commit ourselves to comprehensive negotiations aimed at: substantial improvements in market access; reductions of, with a view to phasing out, all forms of export subsidies; and substantial reductions in trade-distorting domestic support. We agree that special and differential treatment for developing countries shall be an integral part of all elements of the negotiations and shall be embodied in the schedules of concessions and commitments and as appropriate in the rules and disciplines to be negotiated, so as to be operationally effective and to enable

developing countries to effectively take account of their development needs, including food security and rural development. We take note of the non-trade concerns reflected in the negotiating proposals submitted by Members and confirm that non-trade concerns will be taken into account in the negotiations as provided for in the Agreement on Agriculture.

14. Modalities for the further commitments, including provisions for special and differential treatment, shall be established no later than 31 March 2003. Participants shall submit their comprehensive draft Schedules based on these modalities no later than the date of the Fifth Session of the Ministerial Conference. The negotiations, including with respect to rules and disciplines and related legal texts, shall be concluded as part and at the date of conclusion of the negotiating agenda as a whole.[243]

An important part of the Phase Two developments was a process of analysis and clarification of the effects of subsidy regimes on Member countries. The first of these took place during the initiation of the *Cotton* dispute wherein agriculture negotiators were faced with the task of preparing analyses for each of the proscribed areas of the *Agreement on Agriculture*. Negotiators moved from the export side to the issue of market access and finally to domestic support. After nine (9) sessions over the course of several months, this process resulted in "The First Draft of Modalities for the Further Commitments,"[244] a ninety (90) page document encapsulating the comprehensive positions by negotiators on the three areas.[245] Another study was conducted at the time, intended for use in the commencement of the Doha negotiations, by the Organization for Economic Co-operation and Development (OECD). This study, *Uruguay Round Agreement on Agriculture: An Evaluation of Its Implementation in OECD Countries*[246] was initiated by the adoption of a set of goals by Agriculture Ministers of the OECD to assess whether, and to what extent, the agricultural sector should be incorporated into the multilateral trading system. The OECD study not only encompassed OECD countries but non-OECD WTO Members as well. Key parts of the study included analyses of (1)

---

243 WTO, "Ministerial Declaration," WT/MIN(01)/DEC/1, (November, 2001), http://www.wto.org/english/thewto_e/minist_e/min01_e/mindecl_e.htm last visited 2 June, 2010.
244 "First Draft of Modalities for the Further Commitments," World Trade Organization, TN/AG/W/1, (12 February, 2003). A month later a revised draft was issued, the Revised Draft, World Trade Organization, TN/AG/W/1/Rev.1, (18 March, 2003).
245 "Overview Document," World Trade Organization, TN/AG/6, (18 December, 2002).
246 Diakosavvas, D., Guillot, S., "The Uruguay Round Agreement on Agriculture: An Evaluation of its Implementation in OECD Countries," OECD, Paris, France (April, 2001).

how better to liberalize agricultural trade in a multilateral forum and (2) the effects of domestic policies on international trade.[247] Included in the latter analysis was an important discussion of the effects of domestic agricultural support policies on the part of developed countries on developing and least developed nations.

These studies furthered the recognition of the global effects of domestic policies and helped to assess and shed light on the positions of developing and least developed nations, specifically Brazil and the African Member states, prior to the *Cotton* dispute and Cotton Initiative. Therefore, the remainder of this chapter focuses on the positions and perspectives of the Cotton Four African countries and Brazil in order to distinguish the interests and context within which strategies for each party were developed. Each analysis sets forth the distinctive history, positions, associations, and individuals who participated in the process to more successfully address the effects of agricultural policies on developing countries than occurred during the Uruguay Round.

The recognition that the negotiations of the Uruguay Round were differentially advantageous to developed nations increased the incentive on the part of developing countries involved in agricultural production to seek meaningful change through future negotiations and WTO involvement. In their book, *Behind the Scenes at the WTO: the Real World of International Trade Negotiations*, Fatoumata Jawara and Aileen Kwa summarize the position as:

> The Agreement on Agriculture (AoA) is widely seen as one of the most iniquitous agreements in the WTO, in effect providing special and differential treatment to developed rather than developing countries. Developing countries accepted the Uruguay Round Agreements as a whole largely because they believed that they would benefit from agricultural liberalization and subsidy reduction in the OECD countries under the AoA. These promises were not fulfilled, however.[248]

The view that the Uruguay negotiations were disadvantageous to non-developed nations and that these nations were not well-represented is not universal. For example, Bernard Hoekman and Michel Kostecki argue that the developing countries "participated actively" in the Uruguay round and were "strongly involved in shaping the WTO agreements."[249] Specifically delineated

---

247   *Id.* at 64, p. 4.
248   Jawara, F. and Kwa, A., *Behind the Scenes at the WTO: the Real World of International Trade Negotiations*, Zed Books, London, © 2004, pp. 26–27.
249   Hoekman, B., and Kostecki, M., *The Political Economy of the World Trading System: from GATT to WTO*, Oxford University Press, Oxford, © 1995, pp. 240–241. Will Martin and Alan

in this study was the role of non-developed nations in international interest organizations (i.e. Cairns Group) and novel North–South coalition building (i.e. the Swiss-Colombian coalition).[250] Further, Anne Krueger concluded in *Trade Policies and Developing Nations* that the Uruguay Round was "largely a success for developing countries." She counts the agreements on agriculture and the Multifiber Arrangement as a net gain, with the TRIPs agreement posing only short-term costs to the lower-income countries. Most of the other 'concessions' (such as the increased tariff bindings and the TRIMS agreement) are, according to Krueger, "good policy to begin with."[251]

In contrast to these views, as will be illustrated, *infra*, are the internal perceptions of the African region and Brazil. Rather than actively engaged, they described their respective roles as passive and their interests not integrally considered or meaningfully reflected in the resulting agreements, including the Agreement on Agriculture. Regardless of the perceptions of the role of, and effects on, the non-developed nations at the time, there is now widespread recognition that developing countries are no longer "second-class Members of the GATT-based trading system" and significantly more participation by them is needed and expected in the future. As is widely recognized, agricultural negotiations are what make the Doha Round a "development" round.

3.3 Role of African Cotton Producing Countries before Cotton Dispute

Cotton is now generally considered the litmus test for the success of the Doha Development Round of negotiations, especially in light of the favorable rulings in the *Cotton* dispute and the permanent addition of the *Sub-Committee on Cotton* within the agricultural negotiation framework. However, cotton was

---

Winters also argue that the developing countries fully engaged in the negotiations for the formulation of the resulting Legal Texts of the WTO. *See,* Martin, W. and Winters, A., "The Uruguay Round and the Developing Countries," Cambridge University Press, UK, © 1996. *See* also, Martin, W. and Winters, A., "The Uruguay Round and the Developing Economies," World Bank Discussion Paper, Volume 307, World Bank Discussion Papers, Washington, DC, © 1995: Hathaway, D., and Ingco, M., "Agricultural Liberalization and the Uruguay Round," and Goldin, I. and van der Mensbrugghe, D., "The Uruguay Round: An Assessment of Economywide and Agricultural Reforms."

250   Tussie, D., "The Policy Harmonization Debate: What Can Developing Countries Gain from Multilateral Negotiations?" as found in Anderson, K. and Hoekman, B., *The Global Trading System*, I.B. Tauris, London, © 2002, p. 359.

251   Rodrik, D., "Comments," Kreuger, A., *Trade Policies and Developing Nations*, The Brookings Institution, p. 105.

not always considered one of the critical issues needing to be addressed throughout the Uruguay Round and thereafter. The *C-4* African cotton producing countries of Benin, Burkina Faso, Chad, and Mali had to strategically expend scarce resources in order to coordinate and promote their interests via the multilateral trading system.[252] With over a third of the region's gross domestic product (GDP) comprised of agriculture, the importance of the region's improvement of its agricultural and trade performance was widely recognized.[253] However, in order to fully engage in and benefit from the new world order, comprised of an evolving multilateral trading regime, Africa[254] needed to overcome the barriers of its comparatively weak political and economic positions. Several factors and considerations prevented any meaningful participation in the Uruguay Round, some of which remained through the *Cotton* dispute. These are considered herein.

Prior to the *Cotton* dispute, many African countries were opposed to the new round of negotiations under the Doha Development Agenda.[255] Accounting for less than two (2) percent (%) of world trade in 1994,[256] Africa was the only major region that walked away from the negotiating tables of the Uruguay Round in an arguably worse position.[257] They failed to liberalize imports and, based on GATT agreements as least developed nations, were already exempt from most trade barriers due to preferential agreements between their trading

---

252 Many of the development issues, asymmetries and disadvantages are felt similarly by Brazil and the African region. However, in terms of the World Trade Organization and the approaches taken by Brazil and Africa to engage in the system, Africa varies significantly from Brazil and is thus treated separately in this chapter. These commonalities and similarities will be addressed in greater detail in various sections of this book as well. In this section, specifically, cotton – producing countries of Africa will be given significant consideration, but within the greater historical context of the WTO, and as Member states of a greater region fraught with many similar adversities.

253 Trueblood, M., and Shapouri, S., "Trade Liberalization and the Sub-Saharan African Countries," USDA, Economic Research Service, Food Security Assessment/GFA-11, (December 1999), pp. 29–36.

254 Africa refers primarily to Sub-Saharan or Northern Africa, since South Africa is not a recognized cotton producing country and tends to have a vastly different economic and political position than the other countries, especially those mostly considered in this book.

255 Mutume, G., "Africa Opposes New Round of Trade Talks: Leaders Instead Urge Full Implementation of Earlier WTO Agreements," Africa Recovery, Vol. 15 # 3, (October 2001), p. 7.

256 Kappel, R., " Africa's Marginalisation in World Trade: A Result of the Uruguay Round Agreements," International Trade, INTERECONOMICS, (January/February 1996), p. 34.

257 Hertel, T., Masters, W., and Elbehri, A., "The Uruguay Round and Africa: A Global, General Equilibrium Analysis," *Journal of African Economies*, Vol.7, No.2, pp. 208–234.

partners.[258] Scholars in the area of international economic law expressed concerns about moving from the GATT to the WTO without first addressing implementation issues associated with the Uruguay Round. Though some preeminent scholars recommended moving straight into the WTO system, including John Jackson of Georgetown University, others in the developing world disagreed. As Jagdish Bhagwati noted in his book, *The World Trading System at Risk,* at the dusk of the Uruguay Round, "our hands are already full and our backs overburdened enough by the difficulty of bringing the Uruguay Round to a successful conclusion; the grandiose WTO task could prove diversionary and threaten the chances of the Round's success."[259] Therefore, after the completion of Uruguay, there were differing views on the advisability of Members expeditiously beginning a new negotiation round and trying to commence the dispute settlement system of the WTO.

There are a number of reasons why African WTO Member states were hesitant to aggressively participate in the initial stages of the trade liberalization operations of the newly formed WTO. First, for many African nations, trade liberalization and the reduction of agricultural subsidies is a two-edged sword. Domestic agricultural support and subsidy systems often lead to the lowering of global prices for many agricultural commodities. While the elimination of such support programs and the consequent increase in world prices are favorable to African states for those commodities that they export, such as cotton, the higher prices are unfavorable for those commodities that are imported. In terms of exports, as described in Chapters 1 and 2, Africa depends to an inordinate degree on agriculture, with approximately 35 percent of Africa's GDP and two-thirds of its population depending on agricultural production, and the exporting of agricultural commodities. Reductions in trade-distorting subsidies by the US and the EU and a resultant rise in global prices would greatly benefit African agricultural exporters. For example, the EU's Common Agriculture Policy (CAP) would have indirect effects on Africa in terms of significant reductions in trade-distorting subsidies and import restrictions. Thus, as a result of some agricultural trade liberalization measures, Africa would arguably not suffer the consequences of international dumping and receive higher prices for its exported commodities such as cotton.

On the other hand, reduction in agricultural food products subsidies by the developed nations and a consequent increase in food prices will harm the

---

258 For a greater analysis of the results of the Uruguay Round as it affected Africa, *see*, Harrold, P., "The Impact of the Uruguay Round on Africa," World Bank Discussion Papers, Washington, DC, © 1995.

259 Bhagwati, J., *The World Trading System at Risk*, Princeton University Press, © 1991, p. 97.

majority of African countries because of their reliance on food imports. As assessed by the Food and Agriculture Association (FAO), price increases of upwards of ten percent could result from agricultural export subsidies by developed nations being effectively disciplined by the market effects of the URAA. Increases in the price of imported goods, especially food commodities, would have severe negative consequences for many African states. As a result, there was concern that post-Uruguay trade liberalization might increase agricultural export activity, with associated higher incomes and welfare gains, but be a loss to Africa due to higher food prices.[260] While the Uruguay Round AoA did recognize the need to assist less developed food-deficit African countries with measures to increase food aid, provide technical assistance to increase agricultural productivity, and other measures prior to the commencement of the DDA, none of these proposed measures had been implemented.[261] As a result, African countries were understandably wary of the disciplines on agricultural subsidies from the Uruguay Round's Agreement on Agriculture being implemented on a widespread basis.

A second area of concern for the African nations stems from their relatively weak bargaining positions. Specifically, there was widespread concern within African countries about their negotiating power with the US. Africa was in a vulnerable position due to its high level of dependence on the US for aid[262] and debt relief. An illustrative example is the Africa Growth and Opportunity Act (AGOA),[263] a piece of domestic US legislation aimed at promoting market development in Africa. Under this act, those Sub-Saharan African nations

---

260 Kappel, R., "Africa's Marginalisation in World Trade: A Result of the Uruguay Round Agreements," International Trade, INTERECONOMICS, (January/February 1996), p. 40.
261 For greater detail, see (Inco, M. and Winters, L.A.), "Agricultural Trade Liberalization in a New Trade Round: Perspective of Developing Countries and Transition Economies." World Bank Discussion Paper No. 418, Washington DC, 2001, pp. 11–23.
262 Aid as recognized today became an accepted practice in the 1950s and 1960s, after a number of international institutions were created in reaction to the global economic conditions after two World Wars and the Cold War. Prior to this, aid was first designed as an aftermath to British and French colonial orders. For a brief history on the genesis of foreign aid, see, Fieldhouse, D.K., *The West and the Third World*, Blackwell Publishers, Oxford, UK © 1999, pp. 230–235. The nexus between aid and development is generally agreed to achieve three objectives: moral, political and economic whereby (1) the rich have an obligation to help the poor (2) it is in a nations interest to keep or recruit 3rd world states and (3) injecting capital in countries may allow them to overcome obstacles and head down a road to sustained development. Fieldhouse, p. 235.
263 Africa Growth and Opportunity Act, Title I, Trade and Development Act of 2000; P.L. 106-200. The legislation was extended to 2014 by the AGOA Acceleration Act of 2004.

demonstrating that they are making progress toward the objectives of trade liberalization, as set forth in the AGOA, were eligible to receive duty-free and quota-free treatment for eligible products.[264] Distressed African states were cognizant that this access to US markets (specifically, clothing) could be withdrawn unilaterally. Further, traditional bilateral aid was often coupled with economic obligations, such as conditions that part of the monies provided by the US had to buy US goods or be used for specified purposes.[265] Ostensibly, this was not the case with the AGOA. However, there was a clear concern that if a complaint was filed at the WTO about US subsidies, the Secretary of Agriculture could withdraw foreign aid and food support.

A third cause for caution in the pursuit of African countries for trade liberalization on the part of the US was concern about debt relief for African states. The influence that the US had on the policies of the International Monetary Fund (IMF) and World Bank successfully intimidated a number of African Members of the WTO to not initially engage in legislative actions or litigation against the US on the subject of agricultural trade. Therefore, the US would use capital investment in agriculture (much of which was derived from the government), allowing the US to achieve competitive advantage in agricultural production, which would diminish the comparative advantage held by Africa, in the form of low land and labor costs At the same time, foreign aid lending would allow eligible food-deficit countries to obtain products from the US, while World Bank lending would divert actual agricultural investment towards "the production of plantation export crops."[266] This continued long-standing dependence by the Africa (South) on the US (North).

A fourth concern on the part of many African states stemmed from the fact that the markets for much of their agricultural exports are developed nations. This reliance places them in a position in which actions with the potential to be viewed as contrary to the interests of developed nations must be seriously evaluated. In addition, some trade liberalization measures affecting African

---

264 For a more detailed analysis of the AGOA and its applicability to Africa, *see*, Walmsley, T., and River, S., "The Impact of ROO on Africa's Textiles and Clothing Trade under AGOA," 7th Annual Conference on Global Economic Analysis, Washington, DC (17–19 June 2004) as well as their 2003 study, which gave considerably explanation of how the AGOA affects the welfare of particular African regions absent rules of origin (ROO) considerations.

265 Fieldhouse, D.K., *The West and the Third World*, Blackwell Publishers, Oxford, UK © 1999, p. 233.

266 Hudson, M., "Technical Progress and Obsolescence of Capital and Skills: Theoretical Foundations of Nineteenth-Century US Industrial and Trade Policy," as found in Rienert, E., *Globalization, Economic Development and Inequality: An Alternative Perspective*, Edward Elgar, UK, (2004), p. 101.

agricultural exports to markets in developed nations had already yielded adverse results for the Africans. For example, with the conclusion of the Uruguay Round and the establishment of the WTO, the Lomé Conventions of 1975 would no longer be effective. These had traditionally provided Africa with preferential treatment with regards to their largest trading partner, the European Union.[267] Under Lomé, almost one hundred (100) percent (%) of African goods were able to enter the EU without being required to pay any customs duty. The erosion of these types of trade preferences would lead to net reductions in African exports.[268] The computed value of the losses stemming from trade preference erosion in the EU market, as well as the US and Japan, was estimated to be on the order of twenty-five (25) percent of export revenues for African nations.[269] Therefore, as a result of the Uruguay Round agreements, Africa was faced with the reality that it would lose part of its export share of the EU market. In the end, these considerations coupled with the trend of greater liberalization via the Uruguay Round and the close of the Lomé Convention preferential treatment given to Africa placed the countries, such as the C-4, in a precarious situation where it feared that the EU might lose interest in maintaining historical trade patterns.

A peripheral concern regarding the optimal strategy for African Member states to pursue their interests via multilateral trade negotiations was the emergent and difficult relationship between developing African states and large US-based multinationals. The politics of this relationship influenced WTO relations and later, encouraged certain countries to defend themselves, through the legal and political frameworks of the WTO. For example, after the Uruguay Round, although cotton farmers were experiencing record low prices, there were efforts on the part of US-based agricultural biotechnology companies to increase sales of cotton inputs to African producers.[270] On the belief that investing in cotton production was an economically sound decision, many regions within Africa shifted to cotton. During this process, however, African cotton producers experienced increased costs due to the increased use of US produced inputs,

---

267 The treaties granted preferences to Africa as well as the Caribbean and Pacific group of countries, referred to the ACP states.
268 Kappel, R., "Africa's Marginalisation in World Trade: A Result of the Uruguay Round Agreements," International Trade, INTERECONOMICS, (January/February 1996), p. 33.
269 Yamazaki, F., "Potential Erosion of Trade Preferences in Agricultural Products," *Food Policy*, vol. 21, (1996), pp. 409–418.
270 For discussion on the role of multinational businesses within the WTO system, *see*, Sell, S.K., "Big Business and the New Trade Agreements: The Future of the WTO?" as found in Stubbs, R., and Underhill, G., *Political Economy and the Changing Global Order, Second Ed.*, © Oxford University Press (2000), p. 174.

such as seeds, chemicals, and production equipment. Further, the use of these inputs and new production technologies increased the reliance of African cotton producers on US input suppliers. As a result of these structural changes during the 1990s, many African cotton producers found themselves faced with low cotton prices and high levels of debt owed to US multinationals. To the horror of the region, over five hundred (500) farmers chose to take their own lives in 1999, as a means to escape unpayable debt,[271] and similar instances continue to be reported.[272]

Given the number and complexity of concerns, as well as recognition of their economic and political weakness, the idea of promoting national interests by exerting pressure through confrontation with developed countries was problematic prior to the *Cotton* dispute and the Doha negotiations. The African experience was that it had been marginalized in previous rounds of negotiations. For example, the US had taken a detached approach to negotiating with Africa in previous negotiations, preferring to advance their interests through more active engagement with developed markets. In addition, Africa's experience often included the result that its developed trading partners had not lived up to their agreements. In spite of these concerns, the region was struggling to engage in the changing world economy and perceived that positive external trading relations would be of considerable benefit. Even the USDA recognized that Africa had a tremendous amount to gain from increasing their participation in the proposed subsequent round of negotiations from the Uruguay Round.[273]

---

271   It should be noted that debt to multinational companies is not the only source of conflict as regards Africa. External debt, including loan arrangements with governments and international institutions such as the International Monetary Fund (IMF) and World Bank are primary contributors to the growing trend towards encumbering Africa with additional debt towards the aim of providing development assistance. Whether, the role and to what extent these relationships should be formed is heatedly debated. For an introductory overview of the topic, *see*, Clapp, J., "The Global Economy and Environmental Change in Africa," as found in Stubbs, R., and Underhill, G., *Political Economy and the Changing Global Order, Second Ed.,* © Oxford University Press (2000), p. 209. Prior to the *Cotton* dispute, it was estimated that such external debt constituted approximately twenty-five (25) percent of total African debt, contributing to the vulnerability of Africans to such lending agencies.

272   Shiva, V., "War Against Nature and the People of the South," as found in Anderson, S., *Views from the South: The Effects of Globalization and the WTO on Third World Countries,* Institute for Food and Development Policy, Chicago, IL USA © 2000, pp. 94–95.

273   Trueblood, M., and Shapouri, S., "Trade Liberalization and the Sub-Saharan African Countries," USDA, Economic Research Service, Food Security Assessment/GFA-11, (December 1999), pp. 29–36.

Although the importance of more successfully integrating within the multilateral trading regime was recognized, there was also increased recognition that, given their own internal challenges and the often difficult dynamics between the developed countries and Africa, Africa needed to develop new internal and external strategies in order to do so. In terms of creating an internal strategy, a study conducted at Purdue University found that Africa could gain in the long run if it were to design domestic policies toward optimizing its comparative advantage in agriculture and increase trade with Asia.[274] Prioritizing agriculture, therefore was a strategy employed by Africa as it prepared for the continued negotiations required under the Uruguay Round, as part of a new 'Development' Round, or in other negotiations. To that end, at the commencement of the *Cotton* dispute, it was recognized by Oxfam that the negotiation stance of the relevant African Members needed to focus on prioritizing the following four agendas regarding agricultural issues: (1) pursue a ban on agricultural export dumping[275] (2) develop a binding timetable before the Cancun Ministerial Conference to eliminate all export support, (3) remove green box subsidies recognized to be generating over-production and (4) restructure domestic support programs in developed countries to enhance the welfare of small farmers rather than large-scale corporate agriculture.[276] In order to pursue these strategies at the time of the *Cotton* dispute, there was increased recognition that the positions of the African states needed to be more unified and a coalition built.

To this end, in July of 2001, prior to the formal initiation of the DDA and before Brazil requested consultations with the US regarding their subsidy regime, twenty five (25) least developed countries in Africa met in Zanzibar, Tanzania, and developed an agenda for the upcoming WTO meeting in Doha, Qatar. Their agenda included, *inter alia*: (1) the implementation of all Uruguay Round commitments; (2) increased market access through the elimination of subsidies and the creation of duty and quota-free areas; and (3) continued negotiations on the Agreement on Agriculture with the aim to eliminate all export subsidies in developed countries on goods produced in the developing countries. In addition, it is important to note that Africa was also engaged in several regional trade agreements involving agriculture, including the Common Market for East and Southern Africa (COMESA) and the Southern African

---

274   Hertel, T., Masters, W., and Elbehri, A., "The Uruguay Round and Africa: a Global, General Equilibrium Analysis," *Journal of African Economies*, Vol.7, No.2, pp. 208–234.
275   Export dumping is the sale of products at prices below the costs of production.
276   Oxfam, "Cultivating Poverty: The Impact of US Cotton Subsidies on Africa," Briefing Paper 30, London, (2002), p. 27.

Development Community (SADC). Therefore, it should be recognized that, after Uruguay, Africa was developing domestic policies, re-negotiating regional trade agreements, as well as trying to position themselves with their primary interest in agriculture in a good negotiating position in the multilateral sphere, appreciating their limits and strategizing for a more positive outcome. This was a prime time for Africa to become more engaged in trade reform at every level.

3.4 Role of Brazil before Cotton Dispute

Brazil's position prior to the Cotton dispute was demonstrably different than that of the African cotton producing countries. Many of the rationales for Africa's reluctance to aggressively engage the developed world in negotiating and litigating agricultural trade issues were not applicable to the economic or political position of Brazil. Unlike Africa, Brazil is one political entity rather than a group of sovereign states and did not face the coordination problems that plagued the African countries. Further, Brazil was not heavily dependent on foreign aid, debt relief, or food imports from developed countries, nor did it have a similar history of complicated relations with multinational corporations.[277] In addition, Brazil's economic position was much stronger relative to that of Africa, as evidenced by the fact that the C-4 countries are all officially designated as least developed countries,[278] and Brazil is an emerging developing country.[279] While agricultural production comprises a vitally important component of GDP in Brazil and the C-4 nations, Brazil's agricultural output and diversity far outdistances that of the African states. While both Africa and Brazil took on peripheral roles during GATT negotiations, their respective roles post-Uruguay differed dramatically. This distinction is significant in terms of how, and to what extent, each engaged other WTO Members.

Now well recognized as the 'B' of the large emerging economies of BRIC (Brazil, Russia, India, and China), Brazil is a unique success story of a developing country engaged in the world trading system. Over the last fifteen years,

---

277 However, it is important to note that multinational corporations came to Brazil to take advantage of some of its protected markets and have profited as a result.
278 "Least developed country" is a legal designation given to a state by the United Nations, based on a determination of factors that include: low income, weak human assets, and economic vulnerability. At this time, there are forty-nine (49) designated least developed countries, thirty-two (32) of which are Members of the WTO.
279 Developed or developing country designations are self-imposed and are not given by the United Nations or legally applied in the WTO system.

Brazil has been able to effectively carve out a reputable position in the world trade forum, exert political pressures on some dominant economies of the world, and use its economic capacity to stand among the traditional giants of international trade. This has been achieved by strategically reforming domestic policies and utilizing international institutions.

Change in the Southern force was underway long before the *Cotton* dispute;[280] however, Brazil's role after the initiation of the dispute changed dramatically from its prior position within the WTO. As described in this section, Brazil's participation in the Uruguay Round was nominal; however, its early political alignments and the associations established during that period of time and through the commencement of the DDA added significantly to the development of strategies later employed to promote its interests in the WTO. This can now be measured in terms of Brazil's ability to influence negotiations within the DDA, its experience using the dispute settlement mechanism, and the bilateral engagements with the US in connection to the political and legal effects of the *Cotton* dispute and its precedential meaning to the global trading order.[281] In order to establish the foundations of that assessment, this section describes the economic potential of Brazil at the time of the Uruguay Round, Brazil's involvement in that round, and the political associations, initiatives and persons influencing the formulation of strategies that consequently altered its positioning within the WTO.

During the latter part of the GATT (early 1970s) through the beginning of the Uruguay Round (1986), Brazil's emerging influence on the global economy received considerable attention. Brazil was referred to as a "world power" and placed on the roster of "new influentials" by the Carter Administration. Its designation as an emerging or advanced developing country was heavily discussed in the world trading environment.[282] Brazil's influence was primarily a derivation of its agricultural production both in terms of the quantity and diversity of its output. Second only to the US, Brazil held the reputation as being one of the most important food exporters in the world. Further, there was considerable recognized potential for Brazil to further increase its production, given less than ten (10) percent of the country was cultivated at the time. Indeed,

---

280 *See,* Selcher, W., *Brazil in the International System: The Rise of a Middle Power*, Westview Press, Boulder, Colorado, © 1981.

281 These assessments are presented in Parts 2 through 4 of this book.

282 Selcher, W., "Brazil in the World: A Ranking Analysis of Capability and Status Measures," as found in *Brazil in the International System: the Rise of a Middle Power*, Westview Press, Boulder, CO, © 1981, p. 26.

throughout the period of the Uruguay Round, Brazilian agricultural production significantly increased.

In spite of its emerging status, Brazil took an arguably passive approach to negotiations during the Uruguay Round.[283] Although Brazil was moderately engaged in negotiations on services,[284] its role in negotiations on agricultural products consisted to a large extent of continued appeals for special and differential treatment for developing countries.[285] This raises the question of why was Brazil not more actively involved. There were a number of potential reasons. One line of thought revolves around the idea that Brazil did not fully appreciate the importance of international trade as a means of its economic development. According to Nobel Laureate Joseph Stiglitz, this was mostly due to the fact that, like the other BRIC countries of China, and India, these economies did not recognize trade as a "primary engine of growth" until the 1980s.[286] Rather, they had been pursuing 'import substitution,'[287] which created greater isolation between those countries and the rest of the global economy by protecting new domestic industries.[288,289,290]

283　To the extent that both Africa and Brazil took on peripheral roles during GATT negotiations is similar. However, it is important to emphasize that the domestic mechanisms and potential internal growth differed to a great extent. Where the C-4 countries are all officially designated as least developed countries, Brazil is an emerging developing country. This distinction is significant in terms of the how and to what extent each engaged other WTO Members, as will be further discussed in the remainder of this book.

284　*See*, Caldas, R.W., *Brazil in the Uruguay Round of the GATT: the Evolution of Brazil's Position in the Uruguay Round with an Emphasis on the Issue of Services: Strategies and Policies for the Global Political Economy,* Ashgate Publishing (March 1998).

285　WTO, "Communication from Brazil to Uruguay Round Negotiating Group on Dispute Settlement," MTN.GNG/NG13/W/24, (2 March 1988) <http://www.worldtradelaw.net/history/urdsu/urdsu.htm> last visited 13 June, 2010.

286　Stiglitz, J., *Fair Trade for All: How Trade Can Promote Development*, Oxford University Press, © 2005, p. 43.

287　Import substitution refers to the adoption of a multiple exchange rate system, wherein priority imports are brought in at favorable rates, while imports of goods deemed domestically producible were hit with higher exchange rates. Stiglitz, p. 19.

288　Stiglitz, J., *Fair Trade for All: How Trade Can Promote Development*, Oxford University Press, © 2005, p. 43.

289　"Least developed country" is a legal designation given to a state by the United Nations, based on a determination of factors that include: low income, weak human assets, and economic vulnerability. At this time, there are forty-nine (49) designated least developed countries, thirty-two (32) of which are Members of the WTO.

290　Developed or developing country designations are self-imposed and are not given by the United Nations or legally applied in the WTO system.

Brazil was also an active Member of the Group of Fifteen (G15)[291] which was established to promote developing country interests and primarily attempted to gain greater special and differential treatment both during and after the Uruguay Round.,[292,293] The position of the G15 a few months prior to the commencement of the Doha Development Agenda and the *Cotton* dispute is best captured in the following statement issued by the Heads of State and Government of the Group of Fifteen at their Eleventh Summit held in Jakarta, Indonesia, 30–31 in May, 2001:[294]

> 16. We reaffirm that a rule-based, open, just, equitable and non-discriminatory multilateral trading system is a prerequisite for a sound and balanced international economy and the credibility of the multilateral trading system. In this context, greater inclusiveness, internal transparency and effective participation of all members in the decision making process in the World Trade Organization (WTO) should be enhanced in order to accommodate the legitimate requirements and priorities of developing countries. We stress that the development dimension should constitute an overarching theme in the WTO agenda. We have sustained our efforts to open our markets, strengthen our institutions and orient our economies to the challenges of the new global economy. We note, however, that tariff peaks, tariff escalations and non-tariff barriers, including new restrictions under the pretext of sanitary and phytosanitary measures, persisting in industrial countries on products of export interest to developing countries, have adversely impacted on the

---

[291] The G15 was actually comprised of seventeen countries: Algeria, Argentina, Brazil, Chile, Egypt, India, Indonesia, Jamaica, Kenya, Malaysia, Mexico, Nigeria, Peru, Senegal, Sri Lanka, Venezuela, and Zimbabwe.

[292] Gibbs, M., "Special and Differential Treatment in the Context of Globalization," Proceedings of the G15 Symposium on Special and Differential Treatment in the WTO Agreements in New Delhi, India, on 10 December 1998, <www.wto.org/english/tratop_e/devel_e/semo1_e/gibbs_e.doc> last visited 9 June 2010; Page, S., and Kleen, P., *Special and Differential Treatment of Developing Countries in the World Trade Organization*, London: Overseas Development Institute (2004).

[293] A number of African countries were also Members, and though the C-4 countries are not officially part of the group, their interests are similarly aligned.

[294] G15, "International Conference on Financing for Development," Joint Communique, G15, XI Summit of the Heads of State and Government of the Group of Fifteen, Jakarta, Indonesia, 30–31 May 2001, <http://www.un.org/esa/ffd/themes/g15-2.htm> last visited 10 June 2010.

export performance of these products and growth in developing countries.

17. We are against the use of subsidies, anti-dumping and safeguards provisions as protectionist and trade distorting measures by developed countries. It is also regrettable to observe that while negotiations in the WTO have significantly led to the liberalization of trade in many sectors, equal attention has not been given to those sectors of particular importance to developing countries, such as textiles and agriculture. We urge the developed countries to demonstrate their true commitment to free trade by promoting substantial liberalization in agriculture and textiles and in other sectors and modes of supply of services of export interest to developing countries, in particular the movement of natural persons, as envisaged in the General Agreement on Trade in Services. Real progress in mandated negotiations and review are essential to the future of a fair and free trading system. We also stress the importance of commodities exports for the development of developing countries. In this regard, we call upon UNCTAD and other relevant organizations, as well as the Common Fund for Commodities, to identify measures aimed at promoting stability in prices of commodities and the transformation, value addition and diversification of such products in the countries in which they are produced. We also strongly reiterate that non-trade issues such as labour standards and environmental conditionalities should not be included in the WTO agenda.

18. We strongly stress the need for a meaningful solution to the Implementation Issues pertaining to the Uruguay Round Agreements and Decisions by the IV Ministerial Conference in Doha, Qatar, in accordance with the decision of the General Council of the WTO, and for the operationalization of the special and differential provisions in favour of developing countries as a binding commitment.

19. We urge developed countries to address development concerns of developing countries in international fora, and in particular, in the forthcoming Ministerial Conference of WTO. We emphasize the need to preserve a flexible policy space in which developing countries could pursue policies oriented to promote and sustain competitiveness and dynamism within their goods and services sectors.

It is clear from this excerpt that the G15, representing a significant portion of the developing world, recognized the importance of the multilateral trading system and the need for greater participation by developing countries in the forthcoming round of negotiations. At the same time, however, there were a number of concerns. As is apparent from the preceding quote, the developing countries perceived that, although they had worked towards opening their markets and implementing measures to further their commitments made during the Uruguay Round, the developed nations had not reciprocated. Instead, many of the protectionist policies remained in place in the developed world. As a result, there was genuine concern about the implementation of Uruguay Round agreements and related commitments and the high levels of subsidies maintained in developed countries. As stated at the August, 1999 G-15 Ministerial Meeting held in Bangalore, India in preparation for the WTO Seattle conference:

> The delegates recognized three facets of implementational issues and concerns. The first is the removal of inequities in the existing agreements to restore the balance of rights and obligations forged in the Uruguay Round. Second is the non-realization of benefits by many developing countries in areas of interest to them, such as agriculture and textile and clothing sectors, because of the failure of developed countries to fulfill their obligations in spirit. Third is the special and differential provisions in the Uruguay Round Agreements, which have remained unimplemented. These provisions, including those of a best endeavor nature, have to be operationalized if the developing countries are to derive the intended benefits of these provisions.[295]

Further, there was concern about the number of domestic measures in place in developed countries that adversely affected market growth and the exportation of commodities from developing nations. Partly as a result of these concerns, there was pressure from developing countries to have the next round of negotiations be a "development" round. The emphasis on the development nature of the subsequent negotiation round proved to be integral to the argumentation of Brazil in the *Cotton* dispute and WTO agricultural negotiations as well as the evolution of the *C-4* countries and their Cotton Initiative. These issues are crucial in the analytical development of Parts 2 and 3 of this book.

In addition to Brazil's participation in the G15, it was also a Member of the Cairns Group,[296] formed at the time of the Uruguay Round and active in the

---

295 Chairman's Summary, G-15 Ministerial Communique, G-15 Ministerial Meeting (Bangalore, India) in Preparation for the third Ministerial Conference of WTO at Seattle (August 17–18, 1999).

296 The name of the group is derived from the place in which it held its inaugural meeting in August of 1986: Cairns, Northern Queensland, Australia. It was at that time that "ministers

preparation and progress of the Uruguay and Doha Rounds. The Cairns Group was also extremely concerned with the Agriculture Agreement and the elimination of subsidies. It is comprised of nineteen (19) countries[297] that make up over twenty-five (25) percent of the world's agricultural exports. In 1998, the Cairns Group published its Vision Statement recognizing the need to recommence agricultural negotiations pursuant to the Uruguay Round's Agreement on Agriculture. Of particular import, were the three pillars of agricultural negotiations: export subsidies, market access, and domestic support.[298] Prior to this, Brazil hosted the Group in Rio de Janeiro, in June of 1997, to prepare strategies and positions for all key areas of agriculture deemed as needing reform.[299] Brazil's involvement in the Cairns Group was the means for it to become a major player. The Cairns Group played an important role in the Uruguay Round, in "keeping the negotiations on track;"[300] however, its influence waned when it eventually "acquiesced without protest to a deal between the United States and the EC for a very modest outcome in agriculture."[301] This coincided with Brazil's role in the Uruguay negotiations.

After the Uruguay Round, Brazil's role evolved from one of acquiescence to more insistent calls for reform. This is illustrated by a series of statements that illuminated its changing position on trade relations and liberalization. For example, Brazil's Minister for External Relations, Mr. Luiz Felip Lampreia, articulated Brazil's concern about the newly created WTO and urged full implementation and continued agricultural negotiations per the Uruguay Round at the Singapore Ministerial Conference in December of 1996. Specifically, he stated

agreed to form an alliance to ensure that agricultural trade issues would be given a high priority in the Multilateral Trade Negotiations."

297 Members of the Cairns Group includes: Argentina, Australia, Bolivia, Brazil, Canada, Chile, Colombia, Costa Rica, Guatemala, Indonesia, Malaysia, New Zealand, Pakistan, Paraguay, Peru, Philippines, South Africa, Thailand, and Uruguay.
298 Cairns Group Statement, "Cairns Group Vision for the WTO Agriculture Negotiations: Completing the Task," (3 April 1998), <http://www.cairnsgroup.org/vision_statement.html> last visited 10 June 2010.
299 Cairns Group, "Cairns Group Milestones," <http://wwww.cairnsgroup.org/milestones.html> last visited 10 June 2010.
300 As John H. Jackson mentioned in his world trade primer, *The World Trading System: Law and Policy of International Economic Relations*, the Cairns Group "mounted an almost do or die effort to make sure that the Uruguay Round would finally succeed in bringing agriculture under the trading rule system."Jackson, J., *The World Trading System: Law and Policy of International Economic Relations, Second Edition*, MIT Press, © 1997, pp.314.
301 Hoda, A., and Gulati, A., *WTO Negotiations on Agriculture and Developing Countries*, International Food Policy research Institute, Johns Hopkins University Press, Baltimore, © 2007, pp. 189–190, 211.

"A truly meaningful trade liberalization process must necessarily contemplate stronger disciplines to reduce subsidies..."[302] Later, during the Ministerial Conference in Seattle, Washington in 1999, he articulated his warnings concerning the trends he recognized after the Uruguay Round in light of moving toward the commencement of another formal round of negotiations by stating, "We all know that the world is no level playing field, but it is imperative that, at the very least, all players can trust that there are rules which apply to all alike, rules which are not written to protect the strong from their own weaknesses and to prevent the weak from taking advantage of their own strengths."[303]

At the time of the completion of the Uruguay Round, Brazil was also engaged in several regional trade agreement negotiations.[304] Most notable among these is the Free Trade Area of the Americas negotiations, started in 1994.[305] The intent of the establishment of the FTAA was to eliminate or reduce trade barriers between all countries in the Americas, except Cuba. To this end, Brazil proposed to resolve a number of agricultural subsidy issues through regional negotiation. However, Brazil learned that the US was unwilling to agree to address subsidy problems in a region-specific approach, declaring agriculture "off limits in FTAA negotiations."[306] Rather, the US articulated that agriculture must be addressed in a multi-region, multilateral forum. As a result, FTAA negotiations froze on the sides of the US and Brazil. A division between Brazil (leading developing countries) and the US (representing the developed countries) resulted and the FTAA has yet to come to fruition.[307] A comprehensive

---

302 Lampreia, L.F., "Brazil: Statement by H.D. Mr. Luiz Felipe Lampreia," WTO, Ministerial Conference, Singapore (9 December 1996) WT/MIN(96)/ST/8, p. 2.

303 Dr. Luiz Felip Lampreia, "Statement of 1 December, 1999, to the Third Ministerial Meeting of the World Trade Organization of the WTO in Seattle," Brazil, Minister of Foreign Affairs as found in, Rich, P., *Latin America: Its Future in the Global Economy*, New York, NY, © 2002, p. 17.

304 For a paper assessing the impact of these agreements as well as the Uruguay Round agreements, *see*, Teixeira, E., Valverde, S., "Impacts of Mercosul, NAFTA and WTO Round Agreements on the Economies of Argentina, Brazil and Chile," Research Report, UFV, Vicosa, MG., Brazil, (1999) <http://monash.edu.au/policy/conf/1Teixeira.pdf> last visited 13 June, 2010.

305 The FTAA was supposed to serve as an extension of the North American Free Trade Agreement (NAFTA).

306 Cason, J., "Resisting Free Trade: Brazil and the FTAA," Paper presented at the annual meeting of the International Studies Association, 48th Convention, Hilton Chicago, Chicago, IL USA (28 February 2007).

307 As will be discussed in greater detail in Part 3, there is a strong tie between the DDA and FTAA negotiations.

trade agreement stemming from FTAA is not expected to be reached in the foreseeable future, especially in light of the Doha Development Round.

Involvement in collaborative associations among developing nations and experiences with regional trade developments, seen in negotiations such as the FTAA, played a significant role in preparing Brazil for its participation in the current Doha negotiations and the new dispute settlement mechanism of the World Trade Organization. Brazil's role in the Doha Development Round, its participation in the establishment of a new and highly influential coalition in Cancún, and litigating its agricultural interests through the *Cotton* dispute, stands as an example of the progress developing countries have been able to make as the WTO continues to be shaped. As a precursor to the analysis of Brazil's litigation of the *Cotton* dispute, it is important to understand the developments and strategies leading up to the case.

By the time of the initiation of the *Cotton* dispute, Brazil, like many developing countries, had implemented domestic policies for the dramatic liberalization of trade, pursuant to the Uruguay Round and its Agreement on Agriculture. As classical economic theory predicted, the policies increased Brazil's international trade. However, as a result, Brazilian farmers were exposed to the downward biases the determination of global cotton prices caused, in large part, by the non-WTO compliant subsidies on the part of the United States. These domestic reform policies stemmed, to a large extent, from the efforts of agricultural and trade-related industry groups within Brazil.

Beginning in the early 1990s, Brazilian agriculture lobbying organizations such as the Sociedade Rural Brasileira (Brazilian Rural Society), the country's oldest and most prestigious agricultural lobby group and FUNDEPEC Fundo de Desenvolvimento da Pecuaria de São Paulo increased their involvement in agricultural and political efforts to have Brazil more fully integrate within the greater world economy. As mentioned, *supra*, Brazil only began recognizing trade as a potential engine for growth in the 1980s and the results were starting to pay off by the 1990s. However, Brazil's experience with playing a peripheral role in the Uruguay Round negotiations and its realization of the bargaining power asymmetries between Brazil and the US and EU[308] left them in a position where new approaches to the multilateral trading regime were needed to more fully gain from the greater global economy. At this time, the Brazilian Foreign Relations Ministry began "advocating for stronger positions in trade

---

308   Brazil realized that, although it had less bargaining power than the developed countries but was, comparatively, in a far superior position than the C-4 countries.

negotiations."[309] Emphasizing the importance of participating in the design and enforcement of the WTO's rules-based system, Pedro de Camargo Neto, Brazil's Secretary of Production and Trade of the Ministry of Agriculture at the initiation of the *Cotton* dispute, stated, "From now on, no back steps. From now on, the next round will give me progress."[310] In his position at the Ministry of Agriculture, de Camargo Neto was responsible for agriculture negotiations at the WTO, FTAA, MERSOSUR – European Union and helped arrange the initial consultations between Brazil and the US regarding the *Cotton* case and the EU regarding the *Sugar* case, finally bringing both cases within the dispute settlement system of the WTO.[311]

Parts 2 and 3 of this book describe and analyze the strategic choices made, the economic and political factors considered, and the outcomes reached as a result of Brazil and the C-4 choosing to test the legislative and litigation mechanisms of the World Trade Organization as developing countries and thereby increasing their participation in an organization whose membership is aimed at:

> Recognizing that their relations in the field of trade and economic endeavour should be conducted with a view to raising standards of living, ensuring full employment and a large and steadily growing volume of real income and effective demand, and expanding the production of and trade in goods and services, while allowing for the optimal use of the world's resources in accordance with the objective of sustainable development, seeking both to protect and preserve the environment and to enhance the means for doing so in a manner consistent with their respective needs and concerns at different levels of economic development,
>
> Recognizing further that there is need for positive efforts designed to ensure that developing countries, and especially the least developed among them, secure a share in the growth in international trade commensurate with the needs of their economic development,
>
> Being desirous of contributing to these objectives by entering into reciprocal and mutually advantageous arrangements directed to the

---

309 Goldberg, R., Lawrence, R., Milligan, J.K., "Brazil's WTO Cotton Case: Negotiation through Litigation," Harvard Business School, N9-905-405 (September 2004), p. 3.
310 Goldberg, R., Lawrence, R., Milligan, J.K., "Brazil's WTO Cotton Case: Negotiation through Litigation," Harvard Business School, N9-905-405 (September 2004), p. 3.
311 Goldberg, R., Lawrence, R., Milligan, J.K., "Brazil's WTO Cotton Case: Negotiation through Litigation," Harvard Business School, N9-905-405 (September 2004), p. 3.

substantial reduction of tariffs and other barriers to trade and to the elimination of discriminatory treatment in international trade relations,

Resolved, therefore, to develop an integrated, more viable and durable multilateral trading system encompassing the General Agreement on Tariffs and Trade, the results of past trade liberalization efforts, and all of the results of the Uruguay Round of Multilateral Trade Negotiations,

Determined to preserve the basic principles and to further the objectives underlying this multilateral trading system,

"Agree...[312]

...to provide for substantial progressive reductions in agricultural support and protection sustained over an agreed period of time, resulting in correcting and preventing restrictions and distortions in world agricultural markets."[313]

3.5 Summary of Part 1

Part 1 of this book focused on providing an overview of the economic and political backdrop of the *Cotton* case. To do so, Chapter 1 reviewed the development of the world trade in cotton. The differing nature of cotton versus other agricultural commodities was highlighted, as was the relative cost structure of cotton production in developed versus developing economies. It was shown that the United States, in spite of its relatively high production costs of cotton, has maintained export dominance for a long period. Chapter 2 reviewed the types of support programs enjoyed by domestic producers and exporters of US cotton and posited that the ability of the US to achieve and maintain its dominant position in global cotton markets is primarily due to these programs. The subsidy-based global market power of the United States in cotton reflects fundamental asymmetries between the developed and developing cotton-producing countries. Chapter 3 reviewed the political and economic environment that led to these asymmetries and showed that these asymmetries persisted even after the Uruguay Round provisions of the *Agreement on Agriculture* and *Agreement on Subsidies and Countervailing Duties* provided, for the first time, a legal basis to limit such subsidies. Given the concerns on the

---

[312] WTO, "Marrakesh Agreement Establishing the World Trade Organization," The Legal Texts: The Results of the Uruguay Round of Multilateral Trade Negotiations, Cambridge University Press, © 1999.

[313] WTO, "Agreement on Agriculture," The Legal Texts: The Results of the Uruguay Round of Multilateral Trade Negotiations, Cambridge University Press, © 1999, p. 33.

part of cotton producing countries, principally Brazil and the *C-4* nations, about the lack of implementation of the Uruguay agreements as well as their economic and political disadvantages, there was virtually no progress in limiting the magnitude of agricultural subsidies used to sustain and increase production and export market share by the United States. Given that, no WTO Member had assembled the evidentiary, economic, and legal basis to challenge the subsidy-caused asymmetries in many agricultural markets prior to the *Cotton* challenge, new strategies were called for on the part of the developing nations. These, along with a jurisprudential review of the *Cotton* case, are the subjects of Part 2 of this book.

PART 2

Anatomy of the US-Upland Cotton *Dispute and Its Jurisprudential Impact on Agricultural Subsidies under* WTO *Rules*

∴

In the fall of 2002, Brazil requested consultations with the US in the WTO to challenge the types of support programs employed by the US to subsidize domestic upland cotton producers, the amounts spent on these programs, and their effects on global markets. As part of the Dispute Settlement process, each party filed thousands of pages of legal briefs, exhibits, written statements, economic analyses and answers to panel and appellate body questions. A key question is why Brazil chose to commit considerable resources to undertake this legal challenge within the WTO rather than continue to pursue solely its interests in agricultural subsidy reform through bilateral or multilateral negotiations.

As discussed herein, Brazil recognized the inter-relatedness of litigation to negotiations at the WTO. Specifically, Brazil chose to further negotiate trading terms through litigation. To that end, the examination of Brazil's choice to litigate their interests before the WTO establishes a basis for the conclusions set forth in Part 3 regarding the link between the dispute settlement and negotiation mechanisms of the WTO. Further, an assessment of the methodology employed by Brazil provides an effective roadmap for how to choose 'winning' cases and, more specifically, how to effectively discipline trade distorting agricultural subsidies through the DSU of the World Trade Organization. The described compilation of factors involved in the pre-litigation strategy phase (including, *inter alia*, an assessment of the various political, economic factors and expertise needed) were derived from a series of interviews, which took place over the course of three (3) years, in Washington, D.C. and Geneva and Bern, Switzerland. Relevant government delegates, NGOs, scholars, WTO law practitioners involved in the dispute, and Members of the WTO Secretariat as well as representatives from related international organizations were consulted. Telephone interviews were also conducted with government officials, academicians, WTO trade attorneys, and policymakers directly and indirectly involved in the *Cotton* dispute from Geneva, Switzerland and Boise, Idaho USA.

A primary aim of this section of the book is to provide a comprehensive analysis of the *Cotton* dispute, from it conception through the dispute settlement process, as well as its effects on the expanding jurisprudential fabric of WTO trade law. To that end, the text analyzes the *ex ante* considerations and strategy development of the parties involved, then describes the proceedings and rulings of the dispute settlement mechanism of the WTO by following the *Cotton* dispute through the Understanding of Dispute Settlement (DSU). Further, it explores the significance of the case and related developments in relation to the principles, structure and processes of the WTO and the greater multilateral trading system. These are considered in the context of the involvement of Benin and Chad and the lessons learned from their third party participation. Specifically, the cases of Benin and Chad are analyzed to determine the efficacy of the dispute settlement system as it relates to least developed countries. While the dualistic nature of the case as it relates to agricultural negotiations will be discussed, both in terms of Brazil as well as Chad and Benin, a more complete analysis of the *Cotton* case as it relates to the legislative function of the WTO will be conducted in Part 3 of this book.

CHAPTER 4

Origins of Brazil's *US-Upland Cotton*

Part 2 of this book provides a detailed description of the dispute settlement process of the WTO as it unfolded in the five *Cotton* dispute settlement decisions and offers a broader view of the setting, strategies, and implications of the approach taken by the complainant and third parties. It does so in order to elucidate the groundbreaking nature of the case in terms of WTO jurisprudence under the WTO *Agreement on Subsidies and Countervailing Duties (SCM)* and the *Agreement on Agriculture* (AoA) as well as the effects of the case in the political sphere of the multilateral negotiation setting of the Doha Development Round.

The origins of the Cotton dispute are described in Chapter 4, with attention to the factors considered and strategies employed by Brazil in its decision to challenge the agricultural subsidy regimes of the US and the EU through the dispute settlement mechanism of the WTO. This background is especially pertinent in light of the fact that both the US and the EU cases involved several issues of first impression. The strategies employed in the case, including the argumentation and use of experts, establish a clear practitioner's and evidentiary roadmap for future successful challenges to agricultural and other forms of trade-distorting subsidies. The reports and decisions of the WTO Panel, the Appellate Body, and the Arbitrators created a body of jurisprudence that not only clarified the legal nature of a number of subsidy-related issues, but also provides direction for future challenges in terms of how countries formulate future domestic policies and the extent and manner of engagement by developing and least developed countries in the dispute settlement system of the WTO.

4.1 Brazil's Strategic Goals and Relationship with EC Sugar Challenge

After the Uruguay Round, Brazil recognized the need to become more actively involved in negotiations on agriculture (a key issue for Brazilian interests) once they were recommended pursuant to Article 20 of the Agreement on Agriculture.[314] At the time, effects from the Asian Financial Crisis were still being absorbed. One such effect was declining world prices of many commodities,

---

314 This was developed in Part 1 of this book.

inter alia, soybeans, sugar, and cotton. It was also during this time that domestic reform programs were being implemented in Brazil and several developing countries to further liberalize trade. These measures included implementing more stringent IP regimes, liberalizing trade in services, and reducing tariffs in industrial goods. Brazil's realization that their efforts were not being reciprocated in the developed world, as proscribed by the Uruguay Round, created a situation of simultaneous increased resentment toward the US and EU for their continuance of non-WTO compliant agricultural support policies and increased commitment on the part of Brazil to pursue its interests via dispute settlement within the WTO system. This multilateral, rules-based dispute settlement system, with potential penalties for non-compliance, is differentiated from the established negotiations-based process in which there is little incentive for parties to modify existing policies beneficial to politically influential domestic interest groups. While there are risks that adverse rulings within the dispute settlement system may have long-term consequences by setting precedence, the potential benefits of favorable rulings include an increased probability of meaningful and long lasting change.

In terms of the potential effects of Brazil's choice of initiating the dispute resolution process at the WTO, Brazil, like any litigant, had to weigh the various impacts of the litigation on the legislative function of the WTO – in particular its leverage in future multilateral negotiations against the US and EU on reforming agricultural support programs. Three principal questions loomed. First, would the initiation of dispute settlement at the WTO put Brazil in a better or worse negotiating position with its developed country trading partners? Second, what would the impact of the litigation be on enhancing Brazil's ability to put together a coalition of other Members seeking agricultural subsidy reform? And third, related to the first two questions, what is the likely impact of Brazil's pursuit of WTO dispute resolution on potential co-complainants, particularly Africa? Would the litigation bolster the legitimacy of their complaint about the damaging effects of agricultural subsidies on developing country producers and exporters, and bring greater worldwide pressure to bear on the US? Brazil had to assess whether litigating was in the interest of those potential co-complainants.

The link between dispute settlement and negotiations in the WTO: In determining whether and to what extent there was a link between the dispute settlement and legislation mechanisms of the WTO, Brazil had to consider the nature of the institution as well as the dispute settlement – negotiation history leading up to the *Cotton* dispute. Generally, it was understood that the WTO is a political institution, with a history of being predominately a forum to facilitate multilateral negotiations. This was well-established during the GATT era, especially in terms of domestic agricultural regimes being brought for the first time under the multilateral framework during the Uruguay Round. The results of the Uruguay Round negotiations included the establishment of the dispute settlement mechanism. In other words, the political process of the GATT created the legal framework of the WTO and the rules to be followed when nations are to pursue their interests within the WTO dispute settlement process. The political process of the GATT also determined the commencement and subject matter for future multilateral negotiations by requiring that agricultural negotiations were to continue, pursuant to Article 20 of the AoA. By doing so, it is seen that the political and legal processes are tied to each other in that the political process established the legal process and the rules of the legal process determine the conduct and subject matter of future political negotiations. The interplay of the political and legal interactions in a multilateral system means that neither the political process nor the legal framework can be considered in isolation.

Prior to the Cotton dispute, the *Oilseeds* cases[315] from the GATT period are emblematic of the link between trade disputes and negotiations[316] and that disputes directly impact the ability for parties to reach successful negotiated outcomes. Throughout the latter part of the 1980s, and during the Uruguay Round, a 'subsidies war' was fought between the EU (EEC at the time) and the US in an attempt for each to maintain their desired share of the world oilseeds market, including soybeans. Given high levels of surpluses in each country, export subsidies were provided to dump those surpluses on the world market, which severely depressed market prices. The *Oilseeds* disputes were non-violation cases, in which the EU cut tariffs only to impose subsidies with precisely the identical amount of protection for EU soybean producers. In

---

315   GATT, "European Economic Community – Payments and Subsidies Paid to Processors and producers of Oilseeds and Related Animal-Feed Proteins," *Report of the Panel adopted on 25 January 1990*, L/6627-37S/86, (14 December 1989); GATT, "Follow-Up on the Panel Report EEC-Oilseeds," *Report of the Members of the Original Oilseeds Panel*, DS28/R-39S/91 (31 March 1992).

316   The link between trade disputes, relations, and negotiations is well – recognized by scholars and practitioners, and their interconnectedness will be given considerable attention in Part 3 of this book. For an introductory analysis, *see*, Weekes, J., "The External Dynamics of the Dispute Settlement Understanding: Its Impact on Trade Relations and Trade Negotiations, An Initial Analysis," Sidley Austin (23 May 2004), presented at the *Conference on International Trade and Dispute Settlement* in Montevideo on 15 April 2004. (Paper is on file with author). John M. Weekes is a Senior Policy Adviser with Sidley Austin in Geneva, Switzerland. Prior to his affiliation with the firm, he was Canada's Ambassador to the WTO from 1995–1999.

retaliation, toward the end of 1992, the US imposed hundreds of millions of dollars worth of punitive tariffs on the EU. Talks were specifically held to address, in unison, the oilseeds issues and the agricultural dimension of the Uruguay Round.[317] The case entailed the link between The Dillon Round and various concessions given in the early 1960s and the GATT Articles. More specifically, the US argued that the EC subsidies effectively undermined an earlier tariff concession on oilseeds, causing harm to American soybean producers.[318] The Panel found in both cases that the EU's oilseeds-processing subsidies were GATT illegal.

There was a recognized direct link between these pre-WTO disputes under the GATT rules and their effect on the Uruguay Round bilateral negotiations between the EU and the US.[319] In fact, it was only through litigation that agricultural negotiations of the Uruguay Round were eventually concluded in that this litigation was instrumental in allowing negotiations between the EU and US to be completed – resulting in the long awaited resolution referred to as the Blair House Accord. Prior to the Accord, the Director General (DG) of the GATT

---

317   See, Josling, T., "Agricultural Trade Issues in Transatlantic Trade Relations," *The World Economy*, Vol. 16, Issue 5, (1993), pp. 553–573.

318   EEC – *Oilseeds I*: "In these circumstances, the partners of the Community in the successive renegotiations under *Article XXIV:6* could legitimately assume, in the absence of any indications to the contrary, that the offer to continue a tariff commitment by the Community was an offer not to change the balance of concessions previously attained. The Panel noted that nothing in the material submitted to it indicated that the Community had made it clear to its negotiating partners that the withdrawal and reinstitution of the tariff concessions for oilseeds as part of the withdrawal of the whole of the Community Schedule meant that the Community was seeking a new balance of concessions with respect to these items. There is in particular no evidence that the Community, in the context of these negotiations, offered to compensate its negotiating partners for any impairment of the tariff concessions through production subsidies or that it accepted compensatory tariff withdrawals by its negotiating partners to take into account any such impairment. The balance of concessions negotiated in 1962 in respect of oilseeds was thus not altered in the successive *Article XXIV:6* negotiations. The Panel therefore found that the benefits accruing to the United States under the oilseed tariff concessions resulting from the *Article XXIV:6* negotiations of 1986/87 include the protection of reasonable expectations the United States had when these concessions were initially negotiated in 1962." Panel Report on EC – *Oilseeds I*, para. 146, quoted in *Panel Report on Japan – Film*, para. 10.67. As found on the WTO website, "General Agreement on Trade and Tariffs 1994," at <http://www.wto.org/english/res_e/booksp_e/analytic_index_e/gatt1994_08_e.htm#fnt940> last visited 1 July 2010.

319   See, Josling, T., "Agricultural Trade Issues in Transatlantic Trade Relations," *The World Economy*, Vol. 16, Issue 5, (1993), pp. 553–573.

at the time, Arthur Dunkel, drafted a proposed Agreement on Agriculture, now known as part of the Dunkel Draft.[320] In addition, it is important to note that, after the Blair House Accord, representatives of Brazil, Argentina, India, and others urged the EU to conclude these negotiations and proposed the Argentine Proposal.[321] Though this proposal was ultimately unsuccessful, it was recognized that it would have improved conditions in developing countries growing the relevant crops.[322] After Dunkel's tenure, Peter Sutherland became the next DG and aggressively pursued bringing the two parties of the *Oilseeds* cases together and completing the Uruguay Round. The link between the disputes, both of which had exposed the distorting effects of agricultural subsidies on the world market, and negotiations was evident. In fact it was Sutherland who stated, "If the Europeans and the Americans had gotten their act together, this agreement would have been sewn up a long time ago. It's time that was said bluntly, so I'm saying it."[323]

It was this agreement – based on the Dunkel Draft – that finally allowed for a resolution to be reached and the Uruguay Round to be concluded, in line with the concurrent settlement of the US $2 billion *Oilseeds* panel case providing the US the leverage to make the deal in negotiations. It was recognized that the methodology and level of EU subsidies were clearly out of line with economic relations standards and needed to be disciplined. The Commission was, therefore, willing to discipline their subsidy programs, because it was evident that the Member states were in egregious violation. Therefore, the role of the *Oilseeds* cases as a forum to highlight the issue and means to affect the negotiations was critical. Given these lessons learned from the *Oilseeds* cases and that the majority of disputes submitted to GATT concerned agriculture, Brazil could be confident there was sufficient international support that could be

---

320 The Dunkel Draft included a 'Peace Clause,' which later became a key preliminary issue of the *Cotton* case. It was an effective cease-fire on subsidy disputes, for a set duration, and is recognized as having been the *fait accompli* of the EC/US at the close of the Uruguay Round. *See*, Dunkel Draft Final Act of December 1991, MTN.TNC/W/FA, Section L, Part A. The Peace Clause will be discussed in greater detail in Part 3 of this book.

321 The National Oilseeds Processors Association (NOPA) of the US called for *inter alia* other trade distorting subsidies and artificial incentives for production, processing, transportation, and export of oilseeds and oilseeds products. For these concessions, the US would acquiesce to import duties on oilseed products.

322 Stewart, T., *The GATT Uruguay Round: A negotiating History (1986–1992)*, Deventer; Boston: Kluwer Law and Taxation Publishers, © 1993.

323 Interpaks Digest, "The GATT Agriculture Agreement – A Time to Face Market Forces," Vol. 2., No. 1, (Spring 1994), p. 3. This quote first appeared in the *Journal of Commerce*, 19 July 1993.

garnered in the negotiations and third party submissions if a public dispute was brought. Therefore, the increased transparency of having the *Oilseeds* cases brought through a public forum was an example for Brazil in developing its own strategic approach to the Doha Round negotiations. The next assessment Brazil needed to make was whether the link between the dispute settlement process and legislative mechanism would result in a positive or negative outcome.

Would the link create a positive or negative outcome for Brazil? Prior to litigating the *Cotton* dispute, Brazil considered the perceived and actual risks it was taking in initiating a dispute against the US. Drawing from its experience with the *Oilseeds* cases in allowing it to use a settlement in their favor as leverage in negotiations, Brazil considered whether bringing a similar case involving a highly politically charged commodity would effectuate a similar result. Given the degree to which agricultural subsidies are politically driven, they are particularly unpredictable and left to the whims of changing political interests. In this light, Brazil recognized that litigation was an alternative to negotiation and that it might be an effective supplement to the traditional approach of negotiating terms. Given the relationship between dispute resolution and negotiations, Brazil had reason to believe that litigation coupled with negotiation might be a viable strategy to realize meaningful change in the agricultural subsidy regimes in the US and EU.[324]

In considering a litigation option to develop its negotiation strategy, Brazil had considerable experience in the WTO Dispute Settlement system by 2002.[325] In the early stages of the formation of the WTO, Brazil established an office to manage dispute settlement activity[326] as well as created an efficient network of communication between this office, housed in Brasilia, its embassy in Washington, D.C., and Brazil's Permanent Mission to the WTO in Geneva, Switzerland. Further, trade policy formulation no longer became solely developed within the traditional government bureaucracy framework; rather, Brazil

---

324   These assessments were derived and conclusions reached from interviews with scholars and international trade attorneys, and were confirmed by Brazilian government representatives.

325   Brazil is recognized as one of, if not the, most successful dispute settlement participates of the WTO. For an extensive analysis of how Brazil mobilized legal capacity in preparation of and in response to the evolving WTO dispute settlement mechanism, *see*, Shaffer, G., Sanchez, M., and Rosenberg, B., "The Trials of Winning at the WTO: What Lies Behind Brazil's Success," *Cornell International Law Journal*, (Summer 2008), pp. 383–501, p. 459.

326   Davey, W., "The WTO Dispute Settlement System: The First Ten Years," *Journal of International Economic Law*, 8(1), 17–50, doi:10.1093/jielaw/jgi003, p. 41.

chose to coordinate with private firms and work directly with industry.[327] As a result, within the first ten (10) years of the WTO's dispute settlement history (1995–2005), Brazil had initiated *inter alia Cotton* as well as eighteen (18) additional disputes and been the respondent in eight (8) cases. As a result, Brazil was recognized as the developing country having used the system the most.[328] In fact, in 2001, Brazil was the most active WTO complainant.[329] The three (3) disputes Brazil was involved in against the US, prior to *Cotton*, targeted gasoline standards, the *Offset* case involving the Byrd Amendment, and steel safeguards.[330] In each of these cases, Brazil received positive indications of the efficacy of the dispute settlement process. Important to note is that the panel report of the *Offset* case was published two (2) weeks prior to the initiation of *Cotton* (and *Sugar*) and that the results were encouraging, especially in light of the panel's strong recommendation for the US to repeal the contested domestic measures in the case.[331] Further, in regards to the EU, Brazil had brought cases involving poultry imports, preferential treatment of Brazilian coffee, and antidumping duties on tubes and pipe fittings prior to the *Sugar* dispute.[332] The results of these experiences were settlement, prevalence on some issues, and the continuation on others. Therefore, Brazil was familiar with the dispute settlement process and was strategically established to bring disputes through the WTO at the time of *Cotton* and *Sugar*.

At the time of initiating the dispute, however, it is reasonable to assume Brazil was faced with uncertainty about the outcome, and needed to consider a

---

327 Shaffer, G., Sanchez, M., and Rosenberg, B., "The Trials of Winning at the WTO: What Lies behind Brazil's Success," *Cornell International Law Journal*, (Summer 2008), pp. 383–501.

328 Davey, W., "The WTO Dispute Settlement System: The First Ten Years," *Journal of International Economic Law*, 8(1), 17–50, doi:10.1093/jielaw/jgi003, p. 41.

329 Shaffer, G., Sanchez, M., and Rosenberg, B., "The Trials of Winning at the WTO: What Lies behind Brazil's Success," *Cornell International Law Journal*, (Summer 2008), p. 417.

330 *Gasoline* (DS4), *Offset Act* [Byrd Amendment] (DS217), and *Steel Safeguards* (DS259). Davey, W., "The WTO Dispute Settlement System: The First Ten Years," *Journal of International Economic Law*, 8(1), 17–50, doi:10.1093/jielaw/jgi003, p. 41.

331 The Panel report concluded: "Although there could potentially be a number of ways in which the United States could bring the CDSOA into conformity, we find it difficult to conceive of any method which would be more appropriate and/or effective than the repeal of the CDSOA measure. For this reason, we suggest that the United States bring the CDSOA into conformity by repealing the CDSOA." *United States-Continued Dumping and Subsidy Offset Act of 2000, WT/DS217/R, WT/DS234/R, (16 September 2002)*.

332 *Poultry* (DS69), *Soluble Coffee* (DS154 &209), *and Tube or Pipe Fittings* (DS219). Davey, W., "The WTO Dispute Settlement System: The First Ten Years," *Journal of International Economic Law*, 8(1), 17–50, doi:10.1093/jielaw/jgi003, p. 42.

variety of risks in initiating a dispute.[333] For one, though it was known that the US subsidized their cotton sector and to a seemingly high degree, it was unknown how the Agreements on Agriculture and Subsidies and Countervailing Measures would be interpreted and applied to the US programs. While the objective amount of US cotton subsidization was huge, and the dominant export position of the United States suggested the potential for very large price impacts on the world market, the WTO actionable subsidy disciplines and the "peace clause" were untested and, therefore, presented unknown challenges. Second, Brazil could reasonably be uncertain about how the dispute would affect trade relations with the US and the EU if Brazil were to bring disputes against both countries. Along those lines, a risk to be assessed was whether a dispute would 'freeze' negotiations on the issue of the commodity and perhaps other agricultural interests. If a dispute were initiated, would the US be less likely to concede on certain points in negotiations because such concessions and admissions would harm their interests in the DSB process? In addition, there was concern about the timing of an increased role of the DSB within the WTO as a result of its involvement with this case and the potential for an adverse ruling against the US given that ongoing negotiations had yet to be concluded.[334] In the end, by initiating the dispute, Brazil indicated to its trading partners and the United States and the European Union that it was determined that the benefits outweighed the risks. Before initiating WTO litigation, the weighing of risks and the logistics of bringing the disputes needed to be resolved within Brazil, an agricultural crop chose, as well as a team built to employ its strategy.

---

333 The following analysis on the *ex ante* considerations focuses on the US, exclusively, given the resources and information provided during interviews. However, the link between the US and EC challenges was confirmed.

334 There is extensive debate on what is the proper role of the DSB in the WTO. Given a fundamental shift has occurred through the addition of a legal mechanism to the institution, many question whether a more 'legalized' system is better. For example, Joseph Weiler critiques the shift from a negotiation to litigation framework of the WTO, emphasizing the necessity to prevent the system from becoming a 'rule of lawyers' as opposed to simply a system that is built on the 'rule of law.' He sets out the fact that there are now more lawyers meaning that there might be more litigation, and challenges whether that is a positive development. The fact that government and law firms are the only participants of the dispute settlement process is also problematic, given the particular interests and needs they represent. *See*, generally "The Rule of Lawyers and the Ethos of Diplomats: Reflections on the Internal and External Legitimacy of WTO Dispute Settlement," in *Efficiency, Equity, and Legitimacy: The Multilateral Trading System at the Millennium* (R. Porter et al., Brookings Institution Press, 2001).

From a logistics standpoint, Brazil would need to expend considerable resources if it were to pursue the second avenue of litigation within the WTO and the net benefits of litigation, both politically and economically, needed to be clarified. Persuading Brazil that dispute settlement was a worthy strategy took some doing. In order to achieve their aims, an interesting strategy was employed. Internally, representatives of the Brazilian Ministry of Agriculture[335] garnered support from domestic farmers and proposed the action to Brazil's Council of Foreign Trade (CAMEX). CAMEX consists of four of the most influential ministers on matters of trade: the Ministers of Finance, Industry & Trade, Agriculture, and Foreign Relations as well as the Chief of Staff of the President. Initially, there was concern that the connection between litigation and negotiation, unknown at the time, might be negative. There was also apprehension about the timing of the initiation of the dispute and the potential outcome, specifically whether there was sufficient evidence. However, the decision was made to move forward.[336]

At the commencement of the *Cotton* and *Sugar* disputes, the intent of Brazil was to begin placing pressure on the US and EU in the negotiations by enforcing the Agreements on Agriculture and Subsidies and Countervailing Measure through the dispute settlement process. By better defining and disciplining agricultural subsidies in the DSU, the hope was that this would place the US in a position where they could not refute the illegality of their programs or their effects on other Members of the multilateral trading system within the negotiations. At the time the disputes were initiated, the EU was, as it had been at the end of the Uruguay Round, viewed as the "bad guy of agricultural subsidies" in the international trading environment. However, as will be discussed in Part 3, this perception changed dramatically as a result of the *Cotton* and *Sugar* cases and the EU's decision to reform their policies on single farm payments and to implement the recommended provisions of its loss in the *Sugar* dispute. These developments also had the effect of making the US more defensive in the Doha round of negotiations, especially when the National Cotton Council, and other US Farm Organizations feeling threatened by the broad scope of the *Cotton* decision, increased their involvement in those negotiations.

In conducting interviews in the Summer of 2009, representatives from Brazil, Australia, and developing countries, scholars, and Members of the WTO secretariat confirmed that, despite the initial negative reaction by the US,

---

335   Principally, Pedro de Camargo Neto.
336   Confirmed by personal interviews with Brazilian government representatives and involved attorneys.

Brazil's approach was strategically successful given the interconnectivity between the DSU and negotiation system. However, it should be emphasized that, at the time of the dispute, this linkage was not fully established and the *Cotton* dispute played a significant role in further illustrating the point that negotiations are directly affected as a result of what transpires in the WTO's process for dispute resolution. It is now commonly accepted that the connection exists and the strategy is one prudent to employ. For example, as Hilton Zunckel, noted months after the Appellate Body ruling in 2004:

> ...The most immediate solution for a WTO Member aggrieved by agricultural subsidies is to tackle these head on via dispute settlement in the WTO. Dispute settlement gives Members the option of taking ownership of agricultural reform in the sense that a dispute can be initiated and pursued unilaterally without the necessary, but time consuming, consensus building process required by the wider milieu of the Doha Development Agenda negotiations. While tackling the subsidies immediately, this action also has the strategic advantage of bringing pressure to bear on the pace and extent of the negotiation process itself.

In addition to assessing the effects of pursuing dispute resolution in terms of its own position, Brazil also had to consider the effects of litigating its case in the WTO on potential co-complainants, especially the C-4 countries. Again, at the time of the initiation of the dispute, these effects were unknown and had to be evaluated. The nature of these effects are examined herein from the perspective of Brazil, in terms of its risk assessment on what the connection between the dispute and negotiations processes might be for potential co-complainants.[337]

Building a Coalition to Support Case and Increase Negotiation Leverage: An important question Brazil had to consider prior to initiation of the dispute was how to build a coalition in order to garner support for their dispute and increase their leverage in the related negotiations. To that extent, Brazil had to consider potential co-complainants and what their willingness to participate might be, given their interests and perspectives.[338] This was a particularly

---

337   This analysis of the connection between dispute settlement and negotiations from the perspectives of Brazil and the C-4 countries is examined in the context of the legal proceedings of the case in Part 3 of this book.

338   There were cultural as well as political and economic forces to be evaluated. Culturally, it is important to note that litigation is perceived differently across nations. In Brazil, diplomacy is built on arbitration. However, in some cultures litigation is often viewed as an act

important consideration, given the WTO was still relatively new at the time of the initiation of the *Cotton* dispute. Brazil had systemic and economic interests for bringing the *Cotton* dispute. It hoped to impact how the panel would develop a guide for how trade-distorting agricultural subsidies would be disciplined and that providing testimony from some of the most affected LDCs would help establish a roadmap for agricultural negotiations with regards to some of the consequences of such domestic regimes on developing and least developed countries. Therefore, it was key to Brazil to find a way to integrate the LDCs in the dispute settlement process.

Specifically, Brazil's strategy in the dispute process was to include the West Africans as co-complainants. While representatives from Brazil's Ministry of Agriculture were the drivers of this strategy, Brazilian foreign policy dictated that the Ministry of Agriculture could not directly initiate coordination with Africa. Further, representatives of the Ministry of Foreign Relations were not supportive of pursuing dispute resolution and preferred to pursue the route of negotiations. This was both for the logistical and political concerns about potential US and EU responses, as set forth above, as well as political concerns about the potential effects of any perceived Brazil-West African litigation coalition on greater trade relations. There were real concerns about how the US might perceive involvement by Africa in the case, especially as co-complainants. In the end, Ministry of Agriculture representatives acquired the support of NGOs help to determine the level of support that might be forthcoming from potential African co-complainants. One NGO, Oxfam, was highly supportive of the case and became the go between link of Brazil and the West Africans once it was determined that the African LDCs would be supportive of Brazil's litigation strategy.

The determination that support from the West African countries would be forthcoming was important for Brazil's decision to move ahead with litigation at the WTO. In a CAMEX meeting in September of 2002, after several months of meetings and data collection, the Minister of Finance joined with the Ministry of Agriculture to support the proposed litigation and CAMEX voted to move forward. In addition to the considerations described above, another motivating factor was the impending change in administration in Brazil. Some Ministers were concerned that, unless action was soon taken, there could be significant delay in any future progress if they waited until after the new administration took office. Soon after the CAMEX vote in favor of initiating

of hostility. In Asia v. South America v. EU v. China litigation can be perceived as acts of war. The considerations and limitations of LDC involvement (or non-involvement) in the *Cotton* case is described in Chapter 6 of this book.

dispute resolution, the Secretary of Production and Trade with the Brazilian Ministry of Agriculture, Pedro de Camargo Neto, flew to Geneva, Switzerland where he filed the requests for consultations with the US and EU, which resulted in the *US-Cotton* and *EC-Sugar* cases, respectively.

Identified Primary Objectives: In light of these considerations, Brazil's resulting strategy focused on setting WTO legal precedent in terms of disciplining the subsidy regimes of the US and EU. It hoped that the resulting rulings, by 'going on the books,' would limit the options of the US and EU, by applying what disciplines the DSB had available to them. This was particularly important, given the timing of the dispute coincided with increased usage and monies being committed to several of the programs, especially Step 2 and the export credit guarantee subsidy programs (GSM 102 and GSM 103). On the other hand, Brazil also wished to have the dispute further advance long-term interests through negotiations.[339] As mentioned before, one of the concerns was whether the US would be less willing to make certain commitments or concessions in negotiations in fear of similar future litigation. As one trade expert commented, "the US never expected to be disciplined under the AoA and SCM the way they were." Another important objective was the political effect of litigation on Brazil's potential future role in the WTO. It was hoped that this move would facilitate Brazil's emergence as a political power in the WTO and that, ultimately, the dispute would increase Brazil's ability to influence multilateral negotiations. The timing of the dispute fell just after the commencement of the Doha Development Agenda and prior to the Cancun Ministerial Conference, both of which highlighted agriculture and developing country needs in the next round of WTO negotiations. By using its newfound power stemming from its dispute settlement action, Brazil helped to create and influence the G-20 coalition in the Doha Development Round.

Finally, when Brazil chose to litigate, it did so realizing that it was in a 'win/win' situation. If they lost in the dispute, it would simply take the ruling to the negotiations as evidence that stronger disciplines were needed as well as greater reform of the AoA. However, if Brazil won (as it did) in the dispute, it would be able to take the findings into the negotiations and press the US and

---

[339] In researching this subject, the only quote found that does not support this argument is the following: "While noting that both the cotton case and Brazil's challenge against the EC sugar regime were not initiated with the aim of impacting WTO talks. Brazil's ambassador to the WTO, Luiz Felipe de Seixas Correa, said that without these cases, the EC and US 'would never change their policies.'" International Centre for Trade and Sustainable Development (ICTSD), "WTO Panels Confirm Victory for Brazil in Cotton, Sugar Cases," *Bridges Weekly Trade News Digest*, Vol. 8, No. 30, (15 September 2004).

EC for greater policy change. At the end of the day, it gave Brazil tremendous confidence and leverage.

Why Brazil Chose to Challenge US Cotton and EC Sugar: Once the decision to pursue litigation in the WTO was made, Brazil had to choose the commodity upon which it would build its case. Sugar was an easy choice for the dispute against the EU[340] and, initially, soybeans were the preferred commodity against the US, given the economic value of soybean production in Brazil.[341] However, Brazil's initial intent to initiate a soybean case against the US was affected by changing market conditions. An increase in the price of soybeans triggered a reduction of subsidies by the US to its soybean sector. This reduced the likelihood that significant price distortions resulting from US subsidies would be determined in the soybean market. Consequently, Brazil explored the potential of alternative crops. Although cotton constituted a significantly smaller portion of agricultural production in Brazil than soybeans,[342] Brazil was considering an expansion of its cotton production as part of a larger strategy to boost its textile industry. In addition, cotton prices were expected to continue their ongoing price declines and, as a result, thereby increasing the amounts of US subsidies and their effects on global markets. It was, therefore, determined that bringing a case against US cotton subsidies would more likely be successful. Thus, although cotton was not a significant trade interest for Brazil, it was determined that this commodity would be a good initial step in a larger strategy of dismantling US subsidy regimes such as countercyclical and marketing loan programs, for other crops such as soybeans and export credit guarantee (ECG) programs for beef and poultry, in future agricultural negotiations. Therefore, Brazil adopted the approach to highlight *Cotton* as emblematic of illegal, trade distorting subsidy regimes of the US via a public determination by the DSU so as to pressure the US in less transparent negotiations on other commodities of more economic importance to Brazil. In order to influence the negotiations on other commodities, it was hoped that a legal ruling in the *Cotton* case would help Brazil garner more global support and that the *Cotton* dispute would help them in more broad-scale negotiations. This has proven to be the case and that, in terms of garnering global support, it became clear that cotton was the best case that Brazil had against the US. The global effects of US cotton subsidies are severe and the case explicitly highlighted the level of support that the US government gives to an uncompetitive sector. Further, it

---

340   Cite – explain how determined this, few statistics.
341   Over eighteen (18) million acres of soybeans were in production at the time.
342   At the time of the initiation of the dispute, only two (2) million acres were used in Brazil for cotton production.

illuminated the consequences of US subsidy programs, in both economic and ethical terms, the least developed countries in West Africa.

On September 27, 2002, the same day that it requested consultations in the WTO regarding US cotton subsidies, Brazil, in collaboration with Australia and Thailand, requested consultations on the Common Organization for Sugar (CMO), as set forth as Council Regulation 1260/2001, with the European Communities to review the EC sugar policy and legal regimes for sugar and products that contain sugar.[343] The primary objection by Brazil, the world largest sugar producer in the world, was that the subsidies provided by the EC[344] in order to subsidize its domestic producers and to bolster exports, were in violation of several provisions of the WTO, including that the amounts were above its reduction commitment levels. The subsidies guaranteed EC producers a high price for sugar, within certain production quotas.[345] In legal terms, the EC offered less favorable treatment to imported sugar in violation of Article III:4 of the GATT 1994, which requires foreign products to be treated similarly to domestic products. Further, under the Agreement on Agriculture, the EC was: providing illegal export subsidies, not in conformity with their Member Schedules; were not reducing their subsidies in accordance with the AoA; making prohibited payments on the exportation of agricultural products financed by virtue of governmental action; and generally deemed to be circumventing EC subsidy reduction commitments.

The *Sugar* panel found that the EC had acted inconsistently with its obligations of the AoA, by providing export subsidies, in excess of the commitments made in its Member Schedule. Further, it was found that the EC had contravened its WTO commitments by subsidizing the re-export of ACP/India quota sugar, by not showing it in its reduction commitments and by exceeding permitted level of subsidized exports. The Appellate Body upheld the Panel findings. Specifically, the contested measures of the EC's sugar regime were found to be inconsistent with the Agreement on Agriculture. The exports of EC surplus cotton (C sugar) and sugar equivalent to ACP/Indian imports were illegally cross-subsidized with in-quota sugar (A and B sugar).[346]

---

343 The case was designated and referenced as DS 265, DS 266, and DS 283, *EC-Sugar Subsidies*, within the dispute settlement process of the WTO.

344 At the time of the dispute, the EC was the world's second largest exporters in the world, thanks to the government intervention.

345 The CMO categorized sugar production quotas as A, B, and C sugars. The former two were fell under the regulation; however, C sugar was ineligible for price support and was required to be exported.

346 European Commission, "General Overview of Active WTO Dispute Settlement Cases Involving the EC as Complainant or Defendant and of Active Cases under the Trade Barriers Regulation," Brussels, (14 March 2007), p. 8.

Following an appeal, which affirmed the Panel's findings, the European Union ultimately decided to make major reforms to its sugar regime. The EC ceased to export 2.8 million tons of sugar, a new domestic reform would be undertaken, and Brazil was granted the right to export ten (10) percent (%) more sugar. Most importantly to one of the main theses of this book is that the EC reformed their domestic policies by implementing Council Regulation No. 318/2006 to align their regime with the recommendations and rulings of the DSU.[347] As indicated on the EC's website, in the last entry on the dispute in 2007, "since then, the parties have been engaged in discussions on the effects of the sugar reform's implementation and on the evolution of the world sugar market."[348]

Like *Cotton*, onlookers were pleased with Brazil's success. Oxfam called the WTO's decision "a triumph for developing countries."[349] Despite concerns about the effects of the changes on the ACP states relating to favorable EC sugar quotas under the Sugar Protocol of the Cotonou Agreement, Gregor Kreuzhuber, the EC spokesperson on agriculture at the time, projected that the changes would significantly reduce "EU sugar exports and export refunds, abolish intervention, reduce EU production and the internal sugar price."[350]

This section has examined the *ex ante* perceived risks and rewards involved with Brazil's decision to pursue dispute litigation in the WTO. In addition to considering whether there might be a link between its litigation decision and its ongoing and future multilateral negotiations on agricultural policy reform and whether that link might be positive or negative. Brazil also had to consider how to build a coalition when bringing the dispute in order to attract potential co-complainants, especially critical African Members. To that end, Brazil assessed the possible impacts of its litigation actions on potential co-complainants given that participation by countries such as the cotton producing nations of Africa could aid in Brazil's garnering widespread support for disciplining the agricultural subsidy regimes of developed nations. Successful litigation would set precedence for disciplinary actions and would also have

---

347 This development as well as other policy changes undertaken by the EU are discussed in Part 3 of this book.
348 European Commission, "General Overview of Active WTO Dispute Settlement Cases Involving the EC as Complainant or Defendant and of Active Cases under the Trade Barriers Regulation," Brussels, (14 March 2007), p. 8.
349 BBC News, "WTO Raps EU over Sugar Subsidies," (4 August 2004) <http://news.bbc.co.uk/go/pr/fr/-/2/hi/business/3536710.stm> last visited 21 June 2010.
350 International Centre for Trade and Sustainable Development (ICTSD), "WTO Panels Confirm Victory for Brazil in Cotton, Sugar Cases," Bridges Weekly Trade News Digest, Vol. 8, No. 30, (15 September 2004), p. 2.

the likely effect of bolstering reform efforts on other commodities. In the end, Brazil chose to initiate proceedings against the US for its cotton subsidy programs and the EC for its sugar subsidies.

4.2   Strong Evidentiary Basis for Brazil's Challenge

There was a strong evidentiary basis for Brazil's challenge that propelled the initiation of the dispute, though it developed from unexpected beginnings. Initially, as discussed in Section 4.1, Brazil had intended to bring a soybeans dispute against the US, attacking its agricultural subsidies programs, using the soybean subsidies to elucidate the harm the US was causing to Brazilian farmers. However, at the moment a soybeans case was to be initiated, the prices for soybeans began to rise dramatically, undermining the evidence upon which Brazil's arguments were to be based. However, at an opportune period in early 2002, Brazil found a commodity whose evidence was irrefutable – cotton. At the same time, economists at the World Bank, Oxfam, and the International Cotton Advisory Committee (ICAC) became concerned about plummeting cotton prices and their impact on African competitors. A conference was held and attended by a variety of representatives from NGOs, developing and LDC governments, as well as US representatives from the NCC. The fact that prices were plummeting on the world cotton market and international concern was being expressed was perceived as being extremely advantageous to Brazil in terms of being able to bring a case that might give traction to development-based agricultural negotiations.

In terms of building the case, evidence was plentiful and studies – whether conducted by US government agencies, NGOs, or Brazil's economists – seemed to reach similar conclusions. Econometric simulation findings were being published from the ICAC, the World Bank, IMF and Oxfam economists that illustrated the direct link between the US subsidies and their price suppressing effects on the trade of cotton. There were numerous USDA studies that were conducted by the US's Economic Research Services as well as findings by non-governmental agencies (including the World Bank, International Monetary Fund, Oxfam, the OECD, and International Cotton Advisory Committee) that US cotton production and exportation is dependent upon significant US subsidization of cotton.[351] Further, even the NCC confirmed the significant degree

---

351   WTO, "Request for Consultations by Brazil," WT/DS267/1/G/L/571/G/SCM/D49/1G/AG/GEN/54, (3 October 2002), p. 3; *United States – Subsidies on Upland Cotton,* WT/DS267, First Submission of Brazil, (24 June 2003), p. 7.

of dependence of the cotton sector on government support.[352] Even the USDA's own economists concluded that for the US to remain competitive at the international level, under current production methods, some form of government intervention must take place.

Historically, this has been achieved through the distribution of massive subsidies, in particular marketing loan program, crop insurance, Step 2 and counter-cyclical payments, export credit guarantees, among others. Economists concur that subsidies that increase cotton production negatively affect international trade of cotton in the short run as it impacts the price of the commodity. In the case of the US, not only is there subsidization of cotton for domestic consumption, but for the exportation of the commodity. In the marketing year 2001, the US dominated the exports in cotton, accounting for nearly forty (40) percent of total world exports. In this situation, of extreme overproduction bolstered by export subsidies, the world market price-setting effects are thereby amplified and damaging to cotton producing countries, especially those in the developing world.

To demonstrate the effects of US cotton subsidies on world markets, the litigation team employed by Brazil, led by Scott Anderson, collaborated with Professor Dan Sumner (with some assistance from Bruce Babcock) to develop an econometric simulation model that was adapted directly from one used by the US Congress to assess the production, price and trade effects of US agricultural policy – the FAPRI model developed by the University of Missouri and Iowa State University.[353] The model's findings, used by Brazil as foundational to its case, included the fact that between the MY 1998–1999 and 2001–2002, cotton prices were precipitously declining by forty (40) percent (%) as government subsidies were increasing dramatically. Within an eighteen-month period, the value of the cotton market decreased from thirty-five (35) billion US dollars to twenty (20) billion US dollars. Prices reached a low of twenty-nine (29) cents a pound, one-third the value it had been three (3) years prior. The econometric studies used by Brazil, and supported by studies by ICAC, World

---

352 Brazil's opening statement in their first submission to the original panel began with the quote, "The Delta needs cotton farmers, and they can't exist without subsidies," by Kenneth B. Hood, Chairman of the National Cotton Council of America. Thurow, R. and Kilman, S., "US Subsidies Create Cotton Glut That Hurts Foreign Cotton Farms," The Wall Street Journal, (26 June 2002), as Exhibit Bra-3, p. A1.

353 More specifically, Professor Sumner's findings regarding the effects of the largest US subsidy program, the marketing loan subsidies, was confirmed by the USDA's leading economists in separate studies commissioned by the US Congress.

Bank, IMF, and USDA,[354] showed that, at the same time, the US was subsidizing at a record value of three (3) billion US dollars, not including direct payments and crop insurance. In response to the low price environment, the US implemented 'emergency' measures for their cotton producers. In sum, it was estimated that US cotton producers received payments valued between $1.9 billion and $3.9 billion during this period and clear evidence of a breach of the commitments the US had made during the Uruguay Round and established by the Agreement on Agriculture and Subsidies and Countervailing Measures agreement of the WTO.

The evidentiary argument, therefore, was the fact that US cotton subsidies equaled one-fifth of the value of the entire global trade of cotton (valued at $20 billion). In running his model, Professor Sumner found that, if no US subsidies had been provided, world cotton prices received by Brazilian and African producers, among others, would have increased, on average, by 6.5 cents per pound, or 12.6 percent (%), during this 1999–2002 period. Therefore, the conclusion that US governmental intervention was trade distorting was clear and the challenge was evidentially well based.

In addition to the effects on world markets, the degree of economic inefficiency associated with the US cotton support programs was also demonstrated. One statement offered as evidence in the case summarizes the argument: "US upland cotton subsidies have created an Alice in Wonderland world in which rational economic theory does not exist."[355] The reference here is to the trend of US cotton production and export levels during the pre-dispute period which run contrary to the principles of economic efficiency. Two key factors present at the time are key to the argument. First, US cotton producers had experienced some of the highest production costs in the world. Second, the US dollar had appreciated to its highest level for some time. Economic principles predict that a rational policy response to these market conditions, with high-cost producers with a high-valued currency, would be for producers to decrease their cotton production. However, this was not the case. At the time Brazil commenced consultations with the US, regarding their cotton subsidies, Brazil produced evidence that US cotton production had significantly grown from fourteen (14) to over twenty (20) million tons in the 2001 marketing year.[356]

---

354 Although the exact amount of production and price effects varied, every economist publishing results on US cotton subsidies found significant levels of production, export and price effects.

355 *US-Upland Cotton*, DS-267, Statement by the Government of Brazil in Consultations, 3 December 2002.

356 *US-Upland Cotton*, DS-267, Statement by the Government of Brazil in Consultations, 3 December 2002, p. 2.

Relatively, cotton exports increased from twenty-five (25) to thirty-eight (38) of world share.[357] Both developments were occurring within the greater trend of steadily increased production during the several preceding years. Given these factors and the reality that the price of cotton on the world market had been cut in half, it became evident that US competitiveness had been created through the use of massive US subsidies. The practical result of such farm subsidies was the stabilization of revenue to US cotton farmers. Whereas domestic producers in competing countries were more exposed to the volatility of the cash crop, US cotton farmers were insulated from adverse market effects by high levels of government support. Therefore, with the initiation of the dispute, a warning shot was made to the US with regards to its 2002 Farm Bill as well as its position on agriculture within the Doha Round.

The three preceding sections established: Brazil's determination to litigate as opposed to solely negotiate Brazilian agricultural interests at the WTO was a 'win-win' decision; that the Brazilians could be confident that the ethical dimensions of its arguments, bolstered by third party African testimony, could impact negotiations; and that their was an adequate factual basis to bring the dispute. However, in order to ensure that the case was properly procedurally and substantively litigated at the WTO, especially given the complexity and breadth of the challenge, Brazil needed to marshal the requisite economic and legal expertise. As described, *infra*, Brazil did this masterfully.

4.3   Legal and Economic Assistance to Brazil

> From a simple cost-benefit analysis, the political gains for Brazil from its investment in WTO-related expertise and the broader diffusion of this expertise outside the government have been considerable…Brazil's approach has been brilliantly inexpensive.[358]

The formation and litigation of the *Cotton* case illuminates the trade law environment of the WTO as well as necessary components and expertise needed to effectively bring a case before the WTO. Specifically, *Cotton* is especially meaningful because it required a variety of actors and experts to participate in the

---

357   *US-Upland Cotton*, DS-267, Statement by the Government of Brazil in Consultations, 3 December 2002.

358   Shaffer, G., Sanchez, M., and Rosenberg, B., "The Trials of Winning at the WTO: What Lies Behind Brazil's Success," *Cornell International Law Journal*, (Summer 2008), 41 CNLILJ 383, p. 481.

process. From large-multinational law firms to government and academicians, the complexity of and number of interests represented were precedent-setting. This section, detailing the strategies and resources employed by Brazil, supplements the greater portions of this book that analyze the merits of the *Cotton* dispute. The proffered analysis contributes to the expanding literature on how Members use the dispute settlement mechanism of the WTO, and the recognized trends by governments to engage the private sector when developing trade policy and securing and protecting their interests within the multilateral trading environment.[359] Brazil has played a leading role among WTO Members in dispute settlement participation, especially as innovators of how to engage the private sector and build legal capacity within their country.[360]

The *Cotton* dispute was uniquely and, ultimately, successfully litigated before the WTO as a result of a number of exceptional experts. Among those were members of the government litigation team of Brazil who initiated the dispute. Brazil's government litigation expertise was comprised of a number of key players. Most notable was professional diplomat and attorney-by training, Roberto Azevedo, who coordinated the *Cotton* dispute and was the key expert for Brazil in the original proceedings. Luiz Inácio Lula da Silva, President of Brazil at the time of the dispute, was in support of pressing Brazil's agricultural interests through its Permanent Mission to the WTO. The Chief of Brazil's mission was Roberto Azevedo. Azevedo's achievements in his diplomat postings[361] as well as work on the *Cotton* dispute earned him the position of Ambassador to the WTO for Brazil. For the compliance proceedings, Luciano Mazza and Marcus Romalho were the most notable players of the internal legal team of Brazil,[362] with Mr. Mazza arguing most of the compliance case before the 21.5 panel and AB proceedings. Further, Brazil utilized the office they had established, in its

---

359 *See*, Shaffer, G., Sanchez, M., and Rosenberg, B., "The Trials of Winning at the WTO: What Lies Behind Brazil's Success," *Cornell International Law Journal*, (Summer 2008), 41 CNLILJ 383.

360 For an extensive analysis of how Brazil has made national adjustments and built public-private coalitions to further its interests in the WTO, *see*, Shaffer, G., Sanchez, M., and Rosenberg, B., "The Trials of Winning at the WTO: What Lies Behind Brazil's Success," *Cornell International Law Journal*, (Summer 2008), 41 CNLILJ 383.

361 Prior to his posting with the Permanent Mission of Brazil to the WTO, Ambassador Azevedo served in Washington, DC, Moscow, Hong Kong, and Poland, and Houston. During this diplomatic career he received honors from Brazil, including the Order Rio Branco, Commander's; Order Rio Branco, Grã Cruz and Naval and Army Order of Merit. Outside of Brazil he was decorated by Poland, Spain, France, Mexico and Malta.

362 It should be noted that Ambassador Azevedo and Marcus Ramalho are not lawyers, but rather legal experts. Their specialization and competency have been recognized in the WTO legal community as substantial.

capital of Brasilia, to coordinate WTO disputes. Therefore, in terms of expertise as well as organizational development, Brazil was internally prepared to challenge the well established and resourced US (and EU).

Externally, in late 2001, Brazil chose to hire outside counsel.[363] Specifically, it hired the top international trade US-based law firm, Sidley Austin Brown & Woods[364] (Sidley) to begin strategizing how they might defend their agricultural interests within the WTO. The relationship between Sidley and Brazil had previously been established in the *Brazil-Canada Aircraft* (DS70) and *Desiccated Coconuts* (DS22) cases. Scott Andersen,[365] Manager of the Sidley office in Geneva and a seasoned international trade attorney, with experience as Legal Advisor to the US Mission to the WTO and US International Trade Commission, became the lead counsel and began organizing a team to litigate a potential trade dispute against the US, regarding its agricultural subsidy regimes. In his role, Mr. Andersen first contacted Dan Sumner, an agricultural economist, professor and the director of Agricultural Issues Center at University of California in Davis, and requested that he provide an evaluation of US farm legislation and, later, testify as an expert witness for Brazil.

Professor Sumner was a recognized expert in the area of US agricultural subsidies and programs and his application of econometric modeling to agricultural trade issues. At a meeting in California, Dr. Sumner interviewed Mr. Andersen and agreed that the case by the Sidley legal team were compelling. Dr. Sumner's expertise on USDA support programs was derived from his previous work experience as Assistant Secretary for Economics at the USDA and as a regular expert for the US International Trade Commission (USITC), various commodity groups, the Secretary of Agriculture on NAFTA and GATT negotiations and the 1990 Farm Bill.[366] His contributions were recognized by the American Agricultural Economics Association in 1995.

However, Professor Sumner's involvement in the case created controversy and dismay among agricultural interest groups in the US and, as a result of his

---

363   Although there was debate during the formative years of the WTO dispute settlement mechanism, on the appropriateness of having outside counsel represent governments in the WTO, it is widely recognized that this issue is settled and increased competition within the private sphere has been a beneficial development. *See*, Bronckers, M. and Jackson, J. "Editorial Comment: Outside Counsel in the WTO Dispute Processes," as found in Bronkers, M. and Horlick, G. *WTO Jurisprudence and Policy: Practitioners' Perspectives*, Cameron May (2004), pp. 59–64.
364   For more information, *see*, http://www.sidley.com/internationaltrade/.
365   For more information, *see*, http://www.sidley.com/andersen_scott/.
366   The USITC is a quasi-judicial federal agency that provides expertise on trade matters to Congress and the Executive branch.

participation in *Cotton*, his ties to a number of industry affiliations and governmental consulting positions were severed. The fact that an American economist[367] from a public university in one of the largest cotton producing and most highly subsidized states in the country was providing the expertise in opposition to the US left a number of those in the US agriculture industry with impressions of being "dumbfounded, disappointed and shocked."[368] As one industry representative summarized,

> What concerns me is that someone involved with the university of California system who is intimately involved in setting national US farm policy can so easily sell his services to a foreign government. To me it is a clear and obvious conflict of interest. It really surprises me that there is not a system of checks and balances for this type of activity within a university that was built on the backs of California and American agriculture.
> MIKE FREY Chairman of the California Wheat Commission[369]

Throughout the dispute, leaders of the Californian cotton sector and others protested Sumner's, taking their grievance to the respective Dean of UC Davis as well as lobbying to have funds removed from the university in protest of Sumner's participation in the case.[370] Like Mr. Frey, agricultural groups, even those not attached to cotton production, had extraordinarily harsh responses to the participation of Dr. Sumner, including attempts to have him removed from his position at UC Davis. The logic of their concern, as extrapolated from similar statements as above, can be summarized as such: given UC Davis is a public university and therefore taxes (from farmers) were being paid to him, a conflict of interest was created by having him participate in a legal dispute against the US. Although Dr. Sumner was not removed from his position at UC Davis, he did resign from his position with the USDA Agriculture Policy Advisory Committee and invitations to conferences were withdrawn. Charlie Hoppin,

---

367 The fact that a US law firm was providing legal services is also applicable. However, given the international presence of the firm and history of similar representation, was not perceived as egregious as experts from 'within' being used.

368 Cline, H., "Farm Groups Shocked at UC Economist's Testimony in WTO Dispute," *Western Farm Press*, (2 September 2003).

369 Cline, H., "Farm Groups Shocked at UC Economist's Testimony in WTO Dispute," *Western Farm Press*, (2 September 2003).

370 Cline, H., "Brazil Poised to be Major Cotton Player," *Western Farm Press*, (7 January 2004).

Chairman of the California Rice Industry Association was quoted in the press as having said, "I would be afraid to use him again. And I would think many segments of agriculture who now work with the university would start to become reluctant to work with the university that would allow someone to testify for a foreign government against US farm policy."[371] Further, critics of Dr. Sumner's involvement disagreed with his approach in collecting and analyzing the necessary data. Embroiled in the row was Professor Bruce Babcock of Iowa State University. As director of the Centre for Agricultural and Rural Development, Dr. Sumner coordinated with him on Food and Agricultural Policy Research Institute baseline projects. In response, and as submitted by Brazil in its exhibits during the original proceedings,[372] Deputy Chief Economist of the USDA, Joseph W. Glauber expressed serious concerns about the relationship between Dr. Sumner and Prof. Babcock. Some of the tensions that were present are evident in the following email from Bruce Babcock to Joseph Glauber presented as evidence in the dispute proceedings:

> I believe that you are aware of a letter I received from Dan Sumner in October, 2003 concerning a request by the United States for electronic copies of the actual model used for the FAPRI November 2002 baseline and for the various scenarios analyzed by Dan in the Brazil cotton matter.
>
> My reply to Dan (which, again, I believe that you have seen) state that there is no self-contained, operable FAPRI baseline model. There is a set of stand-alone spreadsheets that are linked with the active participation of analysts. I agreed to help Dan consider various adaptations and scenarios with regards to cotton. I did not agree to send him all the various model parts. Nor are we willing to provide such material to Brazil.
>
> Now I understand from Dan that the United States continues to express concerns that Brazil has not provided full access to the FAPRI equations and parameters used in the process conducting analysis with Dan. But Brazil has never had the model components and, as I just noted, I am not prepared to give Brazil full access to all models and equations that we use. I thought I had addressed this issue with my offer to work with the United States in running cotton scenarios. Evidently there remains some confusion on this point.

---

371 Cline, H., "Farm Groups Shocked at UC Economist's Testimony in WTO Dispute," *Western Farm Press*, (2 September 2003).

372 *US-Upland Cotton*, Brazil's First Submission to the Panel, WT/DS267, (24 June 2003), Exhibit Bra-346.

Because of these concern, I am attaching an electronic copy of an Excel Workbook that contains all the U.S. domestic crops equations used to develop the November 2002 FAPRI baseline. These equations were used to develop the November 2002 FAPRI baseline. These equations were used in preparing analysis with Dan for his study of the effects of U.S. cotton subsidies.

I am sending you this material with the understanding that it is for the use by the United States and should not be shared with Brazil or other parties....

I am sending this material in the name of transparency and in the hope that this will put to rest any question about integrity. I continue to be sincere in my offer of being willing to run scenarios.

......

Proponents of the WTO and its dispute settlement process recognized Prof. Sumner's involvement as well as many of the resultant dynamics of the case as 'an academic freedom fight.'[373]

Another interesting dimension of strategy formulation and execution throughout the *Cotton* case was the involvement of least developed countries (LDC) in the dispute, for the first time in WTO history. The participation of LDCs brought in a number of important contributors to the case, including a number of NGOs, another prominent law firm, White & Case,[374] and the Advisory Centre for WTO Law (ACWL).[375] Specifically, pro bono legal assistance was provided to

---

[373] In terms of proving the effects of the export credit guarantees (GSM 102 and 103), the counterfactual analysis was conducted by Professor Aunderam (Finance) from NYU and Professor Matthews from Trinity College, Dublin.

[374] For more information, *see*, http://www.whitecase.com/bmcgivern/. Brendan McGivern and Daniel Crosby were two of the attorneys representing Benin and Chad in the original proceedings. Daniel Crosby is not with Budin & Partners in Geneva, http://www.budin.ch/en/3.asp?page=news.

[375] The ACWL provides legal support to developing and least developed countries throughout the dispute settlement process of the WTO, whether as complainants, respondents and/or third parties. It is jointly administered and funded by several developed and developing countries through the Endowment Fund. Fees to Members are charged according to Annex IV of the Agreement Establishing the ACWL. As stated on its website, "The Advisory Centre on WTO Law (ACWL) is a Geneva-based intergovernmental organisation that was established in 2001 to provide legal advice on WTO law, support in WTO dispute settlement proceedings and training in WTO law to developing countries and least developed countries ("LDCs"). The ACWL's basic mission is to ensure that these Members of the WTO have a full understanding of their rights and obligations under WTO law and an

third parties, Chad and Benin, by the law firm White & Case, by Brendan McGivern and Daniel Crosby, both legal experts of WTO dispute settlement. During the compliance proceedings, Chad was represented by the ACWL and Benin chose not to remain as a third party. Throughout the proceedings, Brazil and its counsel coordinated with White &Case in their representation of Chad and Benin. Further, some collaboration was done between Sidley and the ACWL behind the scenes as it represented Chad in the later stages of the case.

The fees associated with the case for Brazil totaled an estimated three (3) million US dollars. Two-thirds of the costs, prior to the original panel, were paid by Brazil's cotton producers association, Associação Brasileira dos Produtores de Algodão (ABRAPA). The remaining costs incurred throughout the remaining five (5) years of litigation were paid by the Government of Brazil.[376] It may be drawn from these facts as well as the known resistance government officials expressed when first encouraged to bring the case by Pedro de Camargo Neto, Secretary of Production and Trade with the Brazilian Ministry of Agriculture, that an agreement had been reached whereby, if the first findings were in Brazil's favor, the government would fully back the industry. However, if the tactic of bringing a dispute against the US did not prove positive, the Brazilian government's involvement would be reduced and the burden of continuing the case would fall primarily on the Brazilian cotton industry.

The approach the US used to defend its cotton subsidy regimes varied significantly from the strategy and resources, from legal council to veteran experts on agriculture, used in the dispute settlement process for *Cotton* by Brazil. Though the NCC hired counsel to represent them on some matters, this assistance was not significantly recognized. This was due to some extent to the fact that it was not an international trade attorney, but rather an American attorney previously counsel to the NCC, with no relevant WTO litigation expertise. The NCC to a great extent relied on and assumed that the USTR would represent them.[377] Beyond the few domestic attorneys and their own staff working closely with the USTR team, the most notable player was Juan Millan from the Office of General Counsel of the USTR. Juan Millan as well as the USDA's Joseph Glauber,[378] led the US defense team. Further, NCC

---

equal opportunity to defend their interests in WTO dispute settlement proceedings." *See*, http://www.acwl.ch/e/index.html.

376 These statistics and agreements were confirmed through a number of personal interviews with individuals involved in the dispute knowledgeable on such matters.

377 This was in general accordance with most WTO cases. For example, Australia and the EC do not use outside counsel; whereas China does and the US does only to a slight extent.

378 As described *supra*, Joseph Glauber was the Deputy Chief Economist of the USDA.

Vice President for Economic and Policy Analysis, Gary Adams, assisted to some extent in preparation for some of the hearings. However, it is well recognized that the resources devoted by the US paled in comparison to the number and experience level of attorneys and economists working on the case for Brazil. This comparison does not undermine the quality or merits of each party's case. Speaking with representatives and experts involved in the dispute, the US was viewed as a formidable opponent. Further, it should be noted that considerable resources were expended by the US. The following is an institutional analysis conducted to highlight how the approach of Brazil (and Benin and Chad) differed from that of the US, as well as a means to indicate to developing and least developed countries various examples of how to engage in WTO dispute settlement.

The overall criticism of the US strategy was that the USTR was too small in terms of the relatively few individuals working a wide variety of cases, including the *Cotton* case, and too big in terms of the size of the agency. The size of the agency and the necessity of its coordinating with other large bureaucratic entities in the US government, such as the US Department of Commerce and other relevant agencies, made the process extremely inefficient. The few USTR attorneys representing the US in the litigation were well-respected, however, their expertise and training was limited.[379] Juan Millan was the only recognized key WTO player with the requisite experience. Further, it is well known that there is rather high turnover in the USTR and therefore, experience is regularly lost from the organization. Finally, the USTR is required to simultaneously address a number of cases whereas, the Brazilian litigation team and its experts were able to devote time and resources to the *Cotton* case almost exclusively.

The ability by Brazil to bring focused resources to bear on the case was enhanced after the original proceedings when the Sidley team expanded in response to the positive initial rulings. In interviewing several individuals from various sides of the case, it is apparent that, at the same time, the resources employed by the US were even less effective during the appeals process whereas Brazil had economists and lawyers producing and packaging the necessary evidence. Compared to the legal and expert witness services provided by the law firms and inter-governmental agencies for Brazil, the level of expertise employed by the US seemed to be lacking. Even the LDC third parties were able to be well represented and have substantive submissions despite the absence of permanent or well-staffed missions to the

---

379 The international trade and political training of many USTR attorneys consists of two years at diplomacy academy.

WTO in Geneva.[380] Therefore, in terms of an evaluation of the expertise of the case, it is apparent that many lessons can be learned from the strategies employed by Brazil and the third parties and the impact these strategies had on the case.[381] Both political and legal roadmaps have now been drawn for WTO dispute resolution, in terms of experts and resources needed to successfully bring a dispute at the WTO and new norms established in terms of what participants should be involved, the requisite levels of expertise, and the cross-national representation aspect of their involvement. Further, as will be further discussed in Parts Two and Three, the gains are significant. As Gregory Shaffer found, "Brazil would not have won the strategically important U.S. Cotton and EC-Sugar cases without outside agribusiness and law firm support, and it would not have had the statistical analysis which empowered it in its negotiations over new agricultural rules as leader of the G-20 and a members of a new G-4, consisting of the United States, the European Union, Brazil, and India, in the Doha Round."[382]

4.4 Novel Legal and Evidentiary Issues

The *Cotton* dispute will stand as "one of the most definitive pieces of jurisprudence in WTO law in the arena of agricultural trade."[383] There were a number of novel legal and evidentiary issues involved in the *Cotton* dispute. The Dispute Settlement Body (DSB) of the WTO had yet to rule on the vast majority of provisions of the relevant agriculture texts first presented in the *Cotton* dispute. The rulings were key to better defining the connectivity of the Agreement on Agriculture (AoA) and the agreement on Subsidies and Countervailing Measures (SCM), as they relate to subsidy regimes for agricultural products.[384] The following are the many "firsts" that distinguish *Cotton* from any preceding

---

380 Chad does not have a permanent mission to the WTO. Benin does have such a mission, but its resources are limited.
381 More detailed analyses of the various strategies and what developing countries as well as international trade attorneys can learn from the process are included throughout the remainder of this book.
382 Shaffer, G., Sanchez, M., and Rosenberg, B., "The Trials of Winning at the WTO: What Lies Behind Brazil's Success," *Cornell International Law Journal*, (Summer 2008), p. 481.
383 Zunckel, H., "Cottoning on to United States Upland Cotton in Africa," Tralac Trade Brief, Agri Conference, (September 2004), p. 2. The study was presented at the tralac conference "Critical Issues in Agricultural Trade in the African Context," in Stellenbosch, South Africa on 30 September, 2004.
384 A description of these relevant WTO agreements are included in Section 5.2 of Part 2.

case, and will be important and considered in any subsequent related WTO disputes. They are these characteristics that make *Cotton* one of the seminal cases of the WTO.

Cotton was the first dispute in the history of the WTO that addressed *domestic* agricultural subsidies. In addition, it was the first challenge under the WTO subsidies and agricultural rules for US *export* subsidies specifically directed at agricultural products, including local content "Step 2"[385] export price refund subsidies and export credit guarantees (ECGs). The dispute was also the first (and most likely only) "peace clause" challenge.[386] Further, it is the first WTO dispute to test the meaning of the "green box,"[387] under the *Agreement of Agriculture*. Specifically, a determination on the scope of the green box would clarify the extent to which subsidies can be used to give farmers the flexibility to plant various crops and how these can be challenged as trade-distorting subsidies. It further clarified the issue of the connectivity between current production levels and crop subsidization as a basis for being challenged under WTO law. Further, the dispute settlement body (DSB) of the WTO had not yet applied WTO rules to "actionable" subsidies causing "serious prejudice" to agricultural products. This is a particularly important factor of the *Cotton* dispute that will provide guidance to other non-subsidizing and developing (and LDC) countries to successfully challenge agricultural subsidies in future disputes. In addition, the determinations made in the final phase of Arbitration provided significant guidance on the quantitative effects of such subsidy regimes on a developing country market. Further, the Arbitration ruling on the *Cotton* dispute was important because it reflected the acceptance of the use of econometric models as useful evidentiary tools in conducting analyses of subsidy effects. This serves as the original foreshadowing of the advisory role the WTO Economics Division will have on similar future disputes.

The novelty of the legal issues and complexity of the US subsidy regime resulted in highly complex and lengthy submissions to the panels and AB of

---

385 The US Step 2 program was a subsidy unique to cotton. It was designed to provide a constant demand for uncompetitive US cotton. To this end, the US paid domestic users and exporters of US cotton the difference between the lower world market price and higher domestic price. Therefore, it allowed cotton exporters to buy high-priced US cotton and sell it at a much lower price on the world market.

386 The "Peace Clause" exempts domestic agricultural subsidies from challenge during the first nine years of the WTO, 1 January 1995–31 December 2003, if the amount of support after 1995 remains no greater than the support provided in 1992.

387 "Green box" is the working name of domestic support measures falling within the provisions of Annex 2 of the WTO Agreement on Agriculture.

the WTO. The following two chapters of this book set forth the details of *Cotton* as it progressed through the complete dispute settlement system of the WTO, its effect on the jurisprudence of WTO law, and then analyzes the significance of Benin and Chad as LDC third parties to the dispute.[388]

---

388 The novelty and significance of the *Cotton* dispute transcends the dispute settlement process of the WTO. As relates to the theses presented in Parts Three and Four of this book, the *Cotton* dispute has precedential effects in that the size and effects of the challenged subsidies create moral suasion on the parts of other WTO Members that can use the ethical basis of the dispute in WTO negotiations. Further, *Cotton* has established notoriety in the multilateral trading system as a case that illuminates the relationship between litigation and negotiation in the WTO. Finally, it will be historically recognized as a key factor considered by the US in reforming its domestic agricultural subsidy regimes. For organizational purposes, these novelties of the dispute are not discussed in Part 2, covering the anatomy of the dispute.

CHAPTER 5

WTO Dispute Settlement: Case Study on *US-Upland Cotton*

The strong evidentiary, economic, and ethical rationales supporting Brazil's challenge to US cotton subsidies were set forth in Chapter 4. Yet prior to the new 1995 WTO rules in the Agreement on Agriculture and the SCM Agreement – and an exemption from the "peace clause" prohibiting such challenges until 2004 – there was no viable legal option to challenge such subsidies. The old GATT disciplines provided no feasible basis to challenge domestic or export subsidies provided by developed countries that distorted world commodity markets. Further, the dispute settlement procedures of the GATT offered no mandatory requirement to reduce or eliminate subsidies by the losing Member.

Chapter 5 describes and emphasizes the importance of the addition of a binding, rules-based dispute settlement procedure mechanism within the design of the World Trade Organization. It further describes how Brazil used that system and new subsidy disciplines to challenge United States trade-distorting and prohibited export agricultural subsidies. The chapter summarizes the rulings of the five sets of *Cotton* decisions, explicating each stage of the dispute settlement process of the WTO. It sets forth the five rulings in the context of the US subsidy programs and the particular WTO disciplines at issue in the dispute. In addition, it demonstrates how developing country Members can use the WTO dispute settlement system to defend their rights to trade without facing suppressed prices and distorted market share from subsidized competition. The successful outcome of the dispute, as elucidated in Chapter 6, demonstrates how such disputes create important precedent for similar future cases. Further, as argued in Part 3, the cumulative effect of these *Cotton* decisions represents an important step in a long effort to eliminate highly trade-distorting and politically sensitive subsidies. The *Cotton* dispute is of great significance as it illuminates the efficacy of the World Trade Organization, sets distinctive and meaningful precedence for its dispute settlement mechanism, and indicates the ability of its Members to constructively use trade rules.

5.1   WTO Dispute Settlement Overview

The current dispute settlement mechanism of the WTO evolved through the almost fifty (50) years of GATT and was officially established as part of the WTO system created during the Uruguay Round. WTO jurisprudence is recognized international law, fully integrated into the treaty system.[389] It represents an essential component of the rules-based design of the international institution established to facilitate global economic activity through negotiations and dispute settlement. Pursuant to Article 3.2 of the DSU, a dispute settlement process was formalized with the goal of adding greater security and predictability to the multilateral trading system by having a means by which to settle and enforce disputes.[390] The rules and procedures pertaining to the mechanism are set forth in Annex 2 of the Understanding on Rules and Procedures Governing Dispute Settlement (Dispute Settlement Understanding, DSU). Its scope covers the DSU as well as extends to the WTO (Marrakesh) Agreement, GATT 1994, and the multilateral agreements.

The original provisions for the dispute settlement process are contained in Article XXII of the GATT 1947 and XXIII of GATT 1994. The four primary principles of the GATT were: most-favored nation treatment, reciprocity, transparency, and tariff binding and reduction. In the GATT era, complaints alleging legal violations of the GATT were submitted to a panel, which issued a report upon request. The parties involved could then either accept or reject the rulings by consensus. The process was informal and consensus was difficult to reach in the early years, but became somewhat more formalized with increased legal interpretations given by independent panel experts and the evidence provided. There was an evolution within the GATT system that contributed to the formation of the Dispute Settlement Body (DSB) of the WTO. As discussed in Chapter 3, these provisions were changed and significantly enhanced in the Uruguay Round. However, they remain applicable to the dispute process in that they contain some of the procedural and substantive preconditions for commencing a dispute at the WTO. It is important to emphasize that the Uruguay Round was the first time Members were able to negotiate an agreement reforming and establishing the dispute settlement system. The system is a rules-based one, with procedural instructions and timetables for completing a dispute. The greatest alteration from the earlier dispute settlement provisions of the GATT is the

---

389 For extensive analysis on and description of how international economic law works and is incorporated at the domestic level, *see*, Jackson, J., *The Jurisprudence of GATT & the WTO: Insights on Treaty Law and Economic Relations*, © Cambridge University Press, (2000).

390 Annex 2, *Understanding on Rules and Procedures Governing the Settlement of Disputes*, Article 3.2 as found in the WTO's "The Legal Texts: The Results of the Uruguay Round of Multilateral Trade Negotiations," Cambridge University Press, © 1999, p. 355.

integration of a mechanism by which disputes can be resolved and findings enforced.[391]

This chapter details the *Cotton* dispute at each stage of the dispute settlement process. Generally, the following is included as a 'snap shot' of those stages. In WTO dispute settlement, the process begins by one party requesting consultations about a specified matter with another Member. If an agreement cannot be reached during this compulsory stage, proceedings commence. The first proceedings require the parties to submit their arguments and evidence to a 'panel' for review. A 'panel' is a three-person body that functions as an initial trier of fact. The 'Appellate Body' (AB) in the WTO is a standing body that is available, upon request by one of the litigating parties, to review questions of law raised by the panel decisions. In the *Cotton* dispute, there were separate panel and AB proceedings for both the "original" proceedings determining Brazil's original complaint covering the period 2003–2005 and the 2006–2008 "compliance" proceedings in which Brazil challenged the WTO-consistency of the implementation actions taken by the US of the original panel and AB rulings. A final phase was the 2008–2009 Arbitrator proceedings, in which the amount and type of suspension of concessions by Brazil against the US was determined. This phase is referred to as the "Arbitrator" decisions.[392]

5.2   Relevant WTO Agreements: AoA and SCM Agreements

Brazil's decision to challenge the US subsidy regimes through the legal mechanism of the WTO helped define the disciplines for agricultural products, under the two relevant WTO agreements: the Agreement on Agriculture (AoA) and the Agreement on Subsidies and Countervailing Measures (SCM). As mentioned, *supra*, there were several issues needing juridical interpretation, which are considered among the novelties of the dispute.[393] It was the first time domestic agricultural subsidies had been disciplined under these agreements. Along this same line, the SCM had not been applied to agricultural disciplines in the history of the WTO and the 'peace clause' of the AoA had never been considered in

---

391   It the timetable is strictly followed (e.g. no extensions requested/granted), a dispute can be settled within a year or fifteen (15) months if the case is appealed.

392   For a more detailed overview of the dispute settlement process of the WTO, *See*, "A Handbook on the WTO Dispute Settlement System," World Trade Organization, Cambridge University Press (2004), pp. 21–24.

393   For more detailed discussions on the novelty of the dispute, *See*, Andersen, S., and Taylor, M., "Brazil's WTO Challenge to US Cotton Subsidies: The Road to Effective Disciplines of Agricultural Subsidies," *Business Law Brief*, American University, Washington College of Law, Fall/Winter (2009–2010), pp. 2–10; Steinberg, R.H.,

conjunction with the SCM agreement to determine whether it barred claims brought under the latter. Further, the extent to which decoupled support can be considered 'green box' subsidies had not been determined. In addition, the question of whether export credit guarantees were excluded under agricultural export subsidy disciplines was also a key juridical aspect of the dispute.

In interpreting and applying the various agreements through the dispute settlement process, it is important to first understand the applicable sources of law of the system as well as the interpretation guidelines followed by the adjudicating bodies. First, the Marrakesh Agreement Establishing the WTO[394] is part of the greater international legal system, incorporated through Article 38(1) of the Statute of the International Court of Justice.[395] The WTO Agreement in conjunction with its annexed agreements is the relevant source of law for WTO dispute resolution. As mentioned, *supra*, the Understanding on Rules and Procedures Governing the Settlement of Disputes (DSU) sets forth the scope and methodology for bringing and adjudicating a WTO dispute.[396] As Palmeter and Mavroidis explain, "the fundamental source of law in the WTO is therefore the texts of the relevant covered agreements themselves. All legal analysis begins there."[397] Further, as explained, *infra*, pursuant to WTO jurisprudence, strict textual interpretation is required. This jurisprudence, established through the resolution of disputes and as embodied in the rulings,[398] is secondary to the textual interpretation of the agreements. The significance of case precedence should not be understated.

The relevant interpretation guidelines for WTO agreements are drawn from several provisions. The WTO Agreement is the dominating legal text. This is established in two places. First, under Article XVI: 3 of the WTO (Marrakesh)

---

394   Agreement Establishing the World Tade Organization, 15 April 1994, in Final Act Embodying the Results of the Uruguay Round of Multilateral Trade Negotiations, Marrakesh, 15 April 1994, and 33 ILM 1144 (1994).

395   Palmeter, D., and Mavroidis, P., "The WTO Legal System: Sources of Law," *The American Journal of International Law*, Vol. 92, No. 3, (July 1998), pp. 398–413.

396   Agreement Establishing the World Tade Organization, 15 April 1994, in Final Act Embodying the Results of the Uruguay Round of Multilateral Trade Negotiations, Marrakesh, 15 April 1994, and 33 ILM 1144 (1994) and specifically, the Understanding on Rules and Procedures Governing the Settlement of Disputes, 33 ILM at 1226.

397   Palmeter, D., and Mavroidis, P., "The WTO Legal System: Sources of Law," *The American Journal of International Law*, Vol. 92, No. 3, (July 1998), p. 398.

398   Rulings from the GATT do not hold as great of weight as WTO rulings; however, they are used frequently to assist in the interpretation of provisions of agreements. See, Palmeter, D., and Mavroidis, P., "The WTO Legal System: Sources of Law," *The American Journal of International Law*, Vol. 92, No. 3, (July 1998), pp. 400–404, for a detailed analysis of to what extent and how the AB has used GATT decisions.

Agreement, it is set forth that, "in the event of a conflict between a provision of this Agreement and provision of any of the Multilateral Trade Agreements, the provision of this Agreement shall prevail to the extent of the conflict."[399] Second, the General Interpretative Note to Annex IA contains similar language stating that as between the GATT 1994 Agreement and the WTO Agreement, the latter prevails. Generally, it is recognized that there is a narrow interpretation of conflict and a cumulative application of Agreements in AB jurisprudence.[400] Beyond these interpretation guidelines, it is important to note that there are conflicting positions[401] on whether customary international law approaches should be taken by the DSB in interpreting the WTO rules. For example, Joost Pauwelyn argues that the AB should consider other rules of interpretation in international law (e.g., pursuant to Article 31(3)(c) of the Vienna Convention[402] on the Law of Treaties).[403] This dimension of the WTO law has yet to fully evolve and is the source of great attention by scholars and practitioners.[404] However, the basic guidelines outlined, *supra*, were the primary rules of interpretation employed throughout the various proceedings of *Cotton*. In terms of the provisions used by Brazil in its WTO challenge, a much greater analysis will be provided herein. The following are introductory overviews to the two primary agreements involved in the *Cotton* dispute, their relevant parts and aims, and the connection between the two is drawn.

The Agreement on Agriculture (AoA): Placed just after the GATT 1994 and Marrakesh Agreement in the WTO *Legal Texts*, the Agreement on Agriculture was one of the most significant achievements of the Uruguay Round.[405] It is recognized as an important step towards reducing trade distortions in the agriculture sector as well as an initial step towards creating an equitable system through negotiations. This was especially true given the "special" nature of agriculture within the WTO

---

399 WTO, *The Legal Texts: The Results of the Uruguay Round of Multilateral Trade Negotiations*, Cambridge University Press, © 1999, p. 14.

400 Personal notes from discussion on the topic of WTO law interpretation with Professor Thomas Cottier. Bern, Switzerland, (November 2007).

401 "Comment: Interpreting the WTO Agreements – A Commentary on Professor Pauwelyn's Approach," Meltzer FTP, (7 December 2004), p. 917. http://students.law.umich.edu/mjil/article-pdfs/v25n4-meltzer.pdf.

402 Vienna Convention on the Law of Treaties, Jan. 27, 1980, art. 31(3)(c), 1155 U.N.T.S. 331.

403 *See,* generally, Pauwelyn, J., *Conflict of Norms in Public International Law: How WTO Law Relates to Other Rules of International Law,* Cambridge University Press, © 2003.

404 *See,* also, Qureshi., A., *Interpreting WTO Agreements: Problems and Perspectives*, Cambridge University Press, © 2006.

405 For a more detailed history, *see*, Desta, G., *The Law of International Trade in Agricultural Products: From GATT to the WTO Agreement on Agriculture*, Kluwer Law International, Norwell, MA, © 2002.

system. Though countries had touted the strategic needs to be self-sufficient in agricultural production, carry on social and cultural traditions of farming, as well as the modern rationales of stabilizing prices for consumers and producers, the creation of the AoA represented an acknowledgement, at the international level, of the need for disciplines in the area of agriculture so that such measures did not distort markets.[406] In order to fit within the GATT/WTO framework, at a minimum, agricultural policies needed to reflect the three basic tenants of the organization: most-favored nation (Article I), national treatment (Article III), and a general prohibition on trade restrictions (Article XI).[407] However, given the 'special' nature of agriculture, the last principle was exempted from the GATT, primarily at the request of the US and EU. When the Agreement on Agriculture was incorporated into the WTO system, limitations of the AoA were recognized and, under Article 20 of the URAA, negotiations were required to recommence after the completion of the Uruguay Round. Therefore, as the Preamble of the AoA states, the agreement was nominally "a basis for initiating a progress of reform."[408]

The primary aims of the AoA are to increase market access as well as reduce trade-distorting subsidies. Members to the WTO committed to implement the provisions of the AoA within a six (6) year period, beginning in 1995.[409] Further, Members agreed to continue efforts to negotiate and undertake reform in the agricultural sector. Agriculture-related issues are handled by the Agriculture

---

406   The development of and issues addressed in the AoA were discussed with Guest Lecturer and international trade attorney, Bernhard O'Connor, in the Masters in International Law and Economics (MILE) program at the World Trade Institute in Bern, Switzerland, in February of 2005.

407   Most favored nation means that, if a WTO Member cannot grant special treatment to another Member, unless all other Members receive reciprocal treatment. Therefore, the 'most favored nation' is equally treated to all other Members. National treatment requires a WTO Member to treat all other Members of the WTO the same treatment as they do their domestic firms. Therefore, all foreign firms are treated like domestic firms. A general prohibition on imposing trade restrictions requires that countries do not create domestic policies that that unduly burdening trade from one Member to the next. This principle encompasses the idea that to maximize the benefits of trade, globally, countries should be able to employ their comparative advantage without trade-distorting measures being applied that restrict or prohibit trade. These principles are discussed in greater detail in Part 3 of this book.

408   Personal Notes, O'Connor, B., "Agriculture in the WTO," *Lecture*, Masters in International Law and Economics (MILE) Program, World Trade Institute in Bern, Switzerland, (February 2005). *Agreement on Agriculture, The Legal Texts:The Results of the Uruguay Round of Multilateral Trade Negotiations*, World Trade Organization, Cambridge University Press© 1999, p. 33.

409   Therefore, in relation to the *Cotton* dispute, the US had committed to making requisite adjustments by 2001. The phase in period for developing countries was ten (10) years. *See*, Article 1(f) of the *Agreement on Agriculture*.

Committee of the WTO, which reports to the Goods Council. Documentation is officially recorded in annual reports and included in the Goods Council and Secretariat's summary reports.

The legal interpretation of the AoA cannot be understood in isolation; rather, it must be considered with the adjacent Country Schedule, under GATT Article II, that outlines the exact tariffs, market access quotas and subsidy limits and reductions committed to by the Members.[410] The three pillars of agricultural trade (market access, domestic support, and export competition) are reflected in the organization of the *Agreement on Agriculture*.[411] The scope of application of the *Agreement on Agriculture* encompasses all basic agricultural products as well as the products that derive from them as defined in Annex 1 of the AoA, with reference to the Harmonized System of product classification (Chapters 1–24).[412]

The first pillar, market access, sets forth the right of exporters to access foreign markets. Market access is a legal term referring to government-imposed conditions under which a product may enter a market and be released for free circulation within that country.[413] For market access, the AoA converted all non-tariff border (NTB) measures into tariffs.[414] Further, countries were obligated to domestically consume a particular percentage of agricultural imports.[415]

---

410 There has been criticism about the detached approach of not having the Country Schedule integrated into the Agreement on Agriculture. One important point to note, the Schedule is legally subordinate to the provisions of the GATT and "floats free and its terms become more important than the Agreement." For a more detailed discussion, *see*, O'Connor, B., "The Structure of the Agreement on Agriculture," as found in *Agriculture in WTO Law*, Cameron May, © 2005, pp. 83–89 (excerpt from p. 85).

411 Within the *Agreement on Agriculture*, Articles 4 and 5 cover market access; Articles 6 and 7, and Annexes 2–4 cover domestic support; and Articles 8–12 cover export competition. Other provisions cover such topics, *inter alia*, as the Peace Clause, Special and Differential Treatment.

412 Fish and fish products, forestry products and some specific products, which come from the soil, are excluded from the AoA. Personal Notes, O'Connor, B., "Agriculture in the WTO," *Lecture*, Masters in International Law and Economics (MILE) Program, World Trade Institute in Bern, Switzerland, (February 2005).

413 Personal Notes, O'Connor, B., "Agriculture in the WTO," *Lecture*, Masters in International Law and Economics (MILE) Program, World Trade Institute in Bern, Switzerland, (February 2005). *See* also, O'Connor, B., "The Structure of the Agreement on Agriculture," as found in *Agriculture in WTO Law*, Cameron May, © 2005, pp. 83–89.

414 This is done by taking the difference between the average domestic price and the average world price.

415 For more information on the development of the 'market access' pillar of the *Agreement on Agriculture*, under the Uruguay Round, *see,* Croome, J., *Reshaping the World Trading*

The second pillar, domestic support, allows governments to subsidize domestic producers in derogation from the SCM agreement (discussed, *infra*), but also disciplines and calls for a reduction in all subsidies.[416] Domestic support commitments are expressed in terms of Total Aggregate Measurement of Support and "Annual and Final Bound Commitment Levels."[417] Domestic support is categorized into three boxes: amber, green and blue. The amber box refers to measures that are not prohibited, but subject to reduction commitments. General disciplines for domestic support under the amber box are set forth in Article 7 of the AoA, and calculated in various ways. The term *de minimis* refers to support not exceeding five (5) percent (%) of a Member's total value of production of the product (Article 3 & 6 for reduction commitments, *de minimis*). Annex 3 sets forth the means to quantify trade-distorting support, Aggregate Measurement of Support (AMS), which is the "size of annual transfers provided for a specific agricultural product in favor of the producers of that product."[418] When AMS cannot be used, an Equivalent Measurement of Support (EMS) is used as required under Annex 4. Provisions in this pillar as well as the following second pillar were used heavily by Brazil to challenge US subsidy regimes.

Next, green box measures are governmental measures considered economically neutral without significant trade distortive effects on production. There is not a limitation on the amount or type of support under this category. There are two requirements for domestic support programs to be able to be categorized as 'green box' subsidies. First, the support must be provided through a publicly funded rather than privately or consumer-based program.[419] Second, the support cannot have the effect of providing price support to producers.[420] Examples of exempted domestic support measures include: domestic food aid programs, relief from natural disasters, and the most commonly used form – direct payments.[421] Important to note is the fact that all support not categorized in the green box must be included in agricultural support calculated by AMS, product-by-product.

Finally, "blue box" domestic support is a derivative of the latter whereby certain direct payments are allowed, without any spending limitation, to production-minimizing programs tied to Members' reduction commitments

---

    System: A History of the Uruguay Round, World Trade Organization, Geneva, © 1995; Desta, G., *The Law of International Trade in Agricultural Products: From GATT to the WTO Agreement on Agriculture*, Kluwer Law International, Norwell, MA, © 2002.

416 Domestic support was a novel category with no derivation in GATT.
417 *Agreement on Agriculture,* Article 6 (1).
418 Annex 3, *Agreement on Agriculture.*
419 Annex 2(1)(a), *Agreement on Agriculture.*
420 Annex 2(1)(b), *Agreement on Agriculture.*
421 Annex 2, *Agreement on Agriculture.*

under the AoA.[422] In order to qualify as blue box support, payments must be made directly from the government budget to the producers. Further, they must be made conditioned upon some form of a production-limiting requirement.[423] The rationale behind this allowance is that giving farmers money for *not* producing is better than giving them money *to* produce. It is required, under 18.2 of the AoA, that these payments, as well as all domestic support given by governments to producers, be disclosed to the WTO Committee on Agriculture as part of the Members' notification obligations.[424]

The final pillar of the AoA, export competition, addresses the reduction of export subsidies in accordance with Country Schedules under Article 9 of the AoA.[425] There is an extensive list of identified export subsidies. Given the trade-distorting nature of such subsidies, an 'anti-circumvention' provision was included in order to dissuade Members from circumventing their export subsidy commitments.[426] Similar to the other pillars of the AoA, notification is required by WTO Members of their volume of subsidized (and un-subsidized) exports and their expenditures on export subsidies by commodity, as specified in their country schedules.[427] This process ensures that Members are compliant with their commitments under the AoA.

In terms of other provisions of the AoA, the most important 'other provision' is the "peace clause" as set forth in Article 13. Entitled, "due restraint," the peace clause was a temporary (until January 2004) conditional provision that

---

422 Article 6.5, Agreement on Agriculture. Blair House Accord link.

423 A number of other exemptions are also included, under 6.2 of the AoA, for agricultural and rural development in developing countries. Given this book is primarily focused on US programs deemed WTO illegal under the AoA, this portion of the Agreement is not provided in detail. It should be noted that the preamble of the AoA specifically provides for special and differential treatment to developing countries and recognizes the especially precarious position of LDCs and net food-importing developing countries with regard to their security of food supply. The latter is not relevant to this book given cotton is a non-edible commodity. However the importance of agriculture (and adverse effects of trade-distorting subsidies by developed countries) to such Members is paramount.

424 Article 18.2, *Agreement on Agriculture* reads, "The review process shall be undertaken on the basis of notifications submitted by Members in relation to such matters and at such intervals as shall be determined as well as on the basis of such documentation as the Secretariat may be requested to prepare in order to facilitate the review process."

425 Export competition will also be discussed in the following section on the Agreement on Subsidies and Countervailing Measures, given their interconnectivity with regards to agricultural disciplines under the WTO.

426 Articles 10 and 18 of the *Agreement on Agriculture*. The former received considerable judicial review in *US-FSC*.

427 Articles 10 (anti-circumvention) and 18 (implementation of commitments review).

established special rules regarding legal actions brought in relation to agricultural subsidies. In effect, legal actions against domestic agricultural subsidy schemes were not to be brought unless Members violated their set commitments.[428] To that end, the peace clause obviated litigation. This was one of the preliminary issues needing to be determined by the original panel of the *Cotton* dispute.

In the case where disputes arise, involving provisions of the Agreement on Agriculture, the general dispute settlement procedures apply, in accordance with Article 19 of the AoA. And pursuant to Article 21, the GATT and other agreements listed in Annex 1A of the WTO Agreement shall be applied subject to the provisions of the Agreement on Agriculture. Therefore, if a conflict arises between the AoA and another agreement, the AoA takes precedence, provided certain elements are present. This was established by the *EC-Bananas* Panel, which found, "...it is clear from Article 21.1 that the provision of the Agreement on Agriculture prevail over GATT and other Annex 1A agreements. But there must be a provision of the Agreement on Agriculture that is relevant in order for this priority provision to apply. It is not the case that Article 21.1 of the Agreement on Agriculture means that no GATT/WTO rules apply to trade in agricultural products unless they are explicitly incorporated into the Agreement on Agriculture."[429]

The Agreement on Subsidies and Countervailing Measures (SCM): This is linked to the AoA for purposes of establishing what a 'subsidy' is and whether and how it can be disciplined under WTO law.[430] One requisite link between the AoA and SCM is the fact that the definition of subsidy is not contained in the Agreement on Agriculture. Thus, panels and the AB must rely on the SCM. Generally, the SCM broadly defines a subsidy as a financial contribution from the government, which confers a benefit on the recipient.[431] Melaku Geboye Desta distinguishes a subsidy from a "government support programme that is equally available to all spheres of the economy." Desta explains that such a program is not a subsidy *per se* given that

---

[428] Surpassing set commitments was not anticipated, given Members set their commitment rather high in order to ensure compliance. This is one of the reasons several critics of the URAA argue that the agreement was rather weak.

[429] Panel Report, *EC-Bananas III (US)*, WT/DS27/R/USA, para. 7.121.

[430] Important to note is the fact that, in WTO history, there was a shift away from tariffs under the GATT towards an increase in subsidies. Therefore, it can argued that the role of the SCM agreement, especially as applied to the AoA plays a significant role in disciplining the newly favored trade-distorting measures.

[431] For a more detailed description, *see*, Halverson Cross, K., "King Cotton, Developing Countries and the 'Peace Clause': The WTO's *US Cotton Subsidies* Decision," *Journal of International Economic Law*, Vol. 9, No. 1, (30 January 2006), p. 163 and O'Connor, B., "The Agreement on Agriculture and Dispute Settlement," © Cameron May, 2005, p. 113.

it is not trade distortive.[432] However, as soon as a 'specific' "enterprise or industry or group of enterprises or industries" becomes the recipient(s) of support, the subsidy is deemed 'unfair' and disciplines are employed.[433] The legal effect of specificity is that it determines whether an action can be brought regarding the measure before the WTO. In other words, specificity is a prerequisite for finding that a subsidy exists, under Parts II, III, and V of the SCM.[434] If this prerequisite is not met, then they are deemed non-actionable and fall under Part IV of the SCM.[435] In order to distinguish the various subsidies, under the SCM, subsidies are often categorized by the 'traffic light' metaphor to distinguish which are actionable under WTO law. The titles designated are: non-actionable (green), actionable (amber) and prohibited (red).[436] For the *Cotton* dispute, this was particularly important in terms of distinguishing which subsidies were actionable in a WTO dispute settlement context as well as the two types that are *strictly prohibited* (export and import substitution subsidies). As Karen Halverson Cross summarized, "whenever a government confers a financial benefit to a specific group of producers, such benefit will amount to a subsidy that may be challenged by another WTO Member if that subsidy caused 'serious prejudice' to its interests."[437] This means that, even if a subsidy is not prohibited, if it causes 'serious prejudice' it may still be actionable and is, therefore, countervailable.[438] The practical effect of the SCM is that it allows the panel to request that the Member withdraw the measure causing 'serious prejudice.'[439]

In terms of the final pillar of the AoA, export competition, agricultural export subsidies in the forms of, *inter alia*, cash payments and marketing

---

432 Desta, M., *The Law of International Trade in Agricultural Products: from GATT 1947 to the WTO Agreement on Agriculture,* © Kluwer Law International, (2002), p. 170.

433 Desta, M., *The Law of International Trade in Agricultural Products: from GATT 1947 to the WTO Agreement on Agriculture,* © Kluwer Law International, (2002), p. 170. Further, as included and confirmed, for a greater analysis on "specificity," *see,* Palmeter, D., Agriculture and Trade Regulation: Selected Issues in the Application of U.S. Antidumping and Countervailing Duty Laws," *Journal of World Trade,* Vol. 23, No. 1, (1989), pp. 62–63.

434 Desta, M., *The Law of International Trade in Agricultural Products: from GATT 1947 to the WTO Agreement on Agriculture,* © Kluwer Law International, (2002), pp. 170–171.

435 Desta, M., *The Law of International Trade in Agricultural Products: from GATT 1947 to the WTO Agreement on Agriculture,* © Kluwer Law International, (2002), pp. 170–171.

436 Desta, M., *The Law of International Trade in Agricultural Products: from GATT 1947 to the WTO Agreement on Agriculture,* © Kluwer Law International, (2002), p. 171.

437 Halverson Cross, K., "King Cotton, Developing Countries and the 'Peace Clause': The WTO's *US Cotton Subsidies* Decision," *Journal of International Economic Law,* Vol. 9, No. 1, (30 January 2006), p. 163.

438 Halverson Cross, K., "King Cotton, Developing Countries and the 'Peace Clause': The WTO's *US Cotton Subsidies* Decision," *Journal of International Economic Law,* Vol. 9, No. 1, (30 January 2006), p. 163.

439 Significant analysis is conducted, *infra,* on the legal issue of serious prejudice.

subsidies, are disciplined under the WTO. WTO case law prescribes that in order to determine whether an export support measure constitutes a subsidy, the judicial body must use the term subsidy as defined in Part I of the SCM agreement.[440] Therein, as stated above, a subsidy is defined as a financial contribution by a government or public entity within the territory of the WTO Member, given in the form of an income or price support (as set forth in Article XVI of GATT 1994), which confers a benefit.[441] The most significant use of the SCM agreement in the *Cotton* dispute is the fact that it set forth what constitutes these prohibited (export) subsidies, actionable (serious prejudice and adverse effect claims), as well as non-actionable subsides that were allowed. Finally, it includes a caveat establishing its connection to the AoA.

The remainder of this chapter is a description of the legal proceedings of the *Cotton* dispute. It explores the legal rulings at each stage and provides a significantly more detailed analysis of the AoA and SCM and their relevant provisions. The analysis of the dispute was primarily derived from the official reports published by the panels, AB, and Arbitrators as well as relevant exhibits. In addition, understanding and further analysis was gained from interviews with several of the key attorneys working on the dispute, Members of the WTO Secretariat, governmental representatives, and a review of leading scholarly discussion on the content and relevancy of the *Cotton* dispute.[442] Prior to

---

440 *Canada-Dairy*, WT/DS103/AB/R, WT/DS/113/AB/R and adopted 27 October 1999, para. 85.
441 Part 1 of the SCM.
442 A sampling of resources include *inter alia*: Womach, J., "Cotton Production and Support in the United States," CRS Report for Congress, RL32442, (24 June 2004); Sumner, D., "The Impacts of US Cotton Subsidies on Cotton Prices and Quantities: Simulation Analysis for the WTO Dispute," Condensed and Edited version of Annex I presented to the WTO cotton dispute Panel in September 2003; Sapir, A., and Trachtman, J., "Subsidization, Price Suppression, and Expertise: Causation and Precision in Upland Cotton," © American Law Institute (2008); Schnepf, R. "Background on the US-Brazil WTO Cotton Subsidy Dispute," CRS Report for Congress, RL32571, (11 July 2005); Schnepf, R., "Brazil's WTO Case Against the US Cotton Program: A Brief Overview," CRS Report for Congress, RS22187, (17 March 2009); Sumner, D., "US Farm Programs and African Cotton," International Policy Council on Food & Agricultural Trade, IPC Issue Brief 22 (February 2007); Halverson Cross, K., "King Cotton, Developing Countries and the 'Peace Clause': The WTO's *US Cotton Subsidies* Decision," *Journal of International Economic Law*, Vol. 9, No. 1, © Oxford University Press, (2006), pp. 149–195; Steinberg, R., "US-Subsidies on Upland Cotton," *The American Journal of International Law*, Vol. 99, No. 4 (October 2005), pp. 852–861; Davey, W., "*United States-Subsidies on Upland Cotton* Recourse to Article 21.5 by Brazil WT/DS267/AB/RW," Agenda Item 8 (3 June 2009); Zunkel, H., "Cottoning on to United States Upland Cotton in Africa," Tralac Trade Brief, Agri Conference 2004 (September 2004); Thompson, R., "The US Farm Bill and the Doha Negotiations: On Parallel Tracks or a Collision Course?" International Policy Council Food & Agricultural Trade, Issue Brief 15 (September 2005).

U.S.-Upland Cotton, DS267 Timeline (2002–2010)

Date	Event
27 September 2002	Brazil requests consultations with the US.
October 2002-January 2003	Brazil and US hold three consultations, ultimately unsuccessful.
7 February 2003	Brazil requests establishment of a dispute panel; vetoed by US.
18 March 2003	Brazil again requests establishment of a panel; DSB grants.
19 May 2003	Appointment of panelists by WTO Director General.
22 July 2003	First meeting with DSB panel; Peace clause issue reviewed separately.
September 2003	Panel reversed earlier decision; issues to be reviewed together.
17 November 2003	Panel requests and is granted extension for its review.
26 April 2004	Panel releases confidential interim report to two parties.
10 May 2004	Deadline for comments by parties to be submitted to panel.
18 June 2004	Panel's final confidential report released to parties.
8 September 2004	Final report delivered to WTO's DSB, and made public.
18 October 2004	US notified WTO of intention to appeal fourteen issues of report.
16 November 2004	Third party submissions and/or intention to provide testimony filed.
10 December 2004	Parties agree to extension of AB's final report to 3 March 2005.
3 March 2005	AB issues report, upholding most of panel's earlier rulings.
21 March 2005	DSB adopts AB and panel reports, initiating compliance deadlines.
20 April 2005	US announces will implement recommendation and rulings of DSB.
1 July 2005	AB deadline for US removal of prohibited subsidies expires.
4 July 2005	Brazil requests WTO authorization to impose retaliatory measures.
5 July 2005	US objects amount of Brazil's proposed sanctions; requests arbitration.
14 July 2005	DSB assigns original panel as arbitrator for prohibited subsidies issue.
17 August 2005	Brazil and US agree to temporarily suspend arbitration.
1 September 2005	Deadline for US removal of prejudicial effects expires.
6 October 2005	Brazil requests authorization to impose retaliatory measures.

17 October 2005	US objects to amount of proposed sanctions; requests arbitration.
18 October 2005	DSB assigns arbitration role to original panel for prejudicial effects.
21 November 2005	Brazil and US agree to suspend arbitration for actionable subsidies.
24 July 2006	Doha Round negotiations suspended indefinitely.
1 August 2006	Step 2 cotton program eliminated in US.
18 August 2006	Brazil requests formation of a compliance panel for 3 March AB ruling.
28 September 2006	DSB agrees to establish compliance panel.
25 October 2006	Compliance panel members announced.
9 January 2007	Compliance panel extends deadline for ruling.
27 July 2007	Compliance panel issues confidential interim ruling to two parties.
15 October 2007	Compliance panel releases confidential final report to parties.
18 December 2007	Rulings of compliance panel released to public; US not in compliance.
12 February 2008	US notifies intention to appeal compliance panel rulings.
2 June 2008	AB issues its report upholding most of compliance panel's rulings.
18 June 2008	US Farm Bill enacted; GSM-103 eliminated and cap on GSM-102 fees.
25 June 2008	DSB adopts compliance panel and AB reports.
25 August 2008	Brazil asks chair of DSB panel to resume arbitration proceedings.
1 October 2008	Brazil and US agree on arbitration panelists.
9 December 2008	US submission in arbitration proceedings.
13 January 2009	Brazil submission in arbitration proceedings.
31 August 2009	Arbitrator releases decision in two parts; rule on Brazil's requests.
19 November 2009	DSB grants Brazil authorization to impost countermeasures against US.
21 December 2009	Brazil announces authorization to retaliate and cross-retaliate.
8 March 2010	Brazil announces final list of products for retaliatory and countermeasures.
20 April 2010	Memorandum of Understanding entered into; US to compensate Brazil.
18 June 2010	Brazil and US agree on Framework regarding dispute.

detailing the various phases of the case, the following timetable is provided as a brief overview and description of what transpired in *Cotton* as it relates to the dispute settlement mechanism of the WTO.

Cotton Market Developments at Time of Brazil's US-Upland Cotton *Challenge (1999–2002 Reference Period)*

High levels of U.S. production despite record low prices:
- Cotton prices plunged in 1999, 2001, and 2002, with prices hitting record lows in the spring of 2002 at 29 cents per pound – far below the 20 year average price of 72 cents per pound.
- U.S. production of cotton increased during the 1998–2001 period from 13.1 million aces in 1998–99 to 14.6 million acres in 1999/2000, increasing again to 15.3 million acres in 2000/1, and to 15.5 million acres in 2001/2. With record low prices, U.S. production reached the second highest level ever in 2001/2.

Record high levels of U.S. exports – declining 3rd countries exports:
- U.S. cotton export market share increased from 17 percent in 1998/9 to 42 percent in 2002/3. Other far more efficient and lower-cost producers, such as Brazil, were not able to increase their market share during the same period. This increase in U.S. world market share took place as the world market share of low-cost West African producers plunged from 15 percent to 11 percent in the same period.
- U.S. exports more than doubled even though the value of the U.S. dollar increasing by 154 percent against the basket of currencies of other world producers of cotton, such as the Brazilian and African producers. This is directly contrary to economic theory which suggests that, as U.S. products priced in dollars become more expensive, the competitiveness of cheaper foreign products increases. In fact, because of the U.S. subsidies, the opposite occurred.
- Brazilian and African cotton producers have costs of production that are less than half of those of the average U.S. producer. Among major cotton exporters, the United States was the only country to consistently export at prices well-below their costs of production.

Losses suffered by Brazilian and African Producers due to the effects of the U.S. subsidies:
- During 1999–2002, Brazilian cotton farmers lost $478 million in revenues from cotton prices that were suppressed through the effects of the U.S. subsidies.

- According to Professor Nicholas Minot of the International Food Policy Research Institute in Washington, D.C., the effect of low world cotton prices (in part through subsidy-enhanced overproduction in the United States) was to push approximately 90,000 Benin cotton farmers below the poverty line in 2001/2.
- The World Bank, IMF and OXFAM also estimated significant negative impacts on African economies from the effects of the U.S. subsidies.

5.3 Consultation

"Consultation" is a formal process under Article 4 of the Dispute Settlement Understanding (DSU) that allows for WTO Members to engage in bilateral (or multiple-party) discussions in Geneva prior to launching a formal complaint to establish a WTO Panel. These consultations can be an important means for settling disputes – roughly one-third of disputes do not proceed past the consultation phase.[443] As confidential proceedings, the discussions in the consultations can include proposals for resolving disputes that are without prejudice to the parties' positions that could be taken in later formal WTO dispute settlement.[444] Consultations can also be an important basis for disputing countries to exchange factual information and views regarding the strength of the legal bases for any future formal complaints. Particularly in relation to agricultural subsidies, the SCM and AoA set forth rights for Members challenging subsidies to request consultations as well. Submissions under these agreements are required to be in writing, identifying the measures at issue and the legal basis of the complaint.[445] Further, WTO jurisprudence requires a "statement of available evidence" demonstrating the existence and nature of the subsidies being challenged.[446]

In the fall of 2002, Brazil initiated dispute settlement by requesting consultations with the United States, under Article 4 of the DSU as well as Articles 4,

---

[443] "Understanding the WTO: Settling Disputes, A Unique Contribution," World Trade Organization <www.wto.org/english/thewto_e/whatis_e/tif_e/displ_e.htm> last visited, 28 June 2010.

[444] Art. 4.6 of the DSU.

[445] Article 4.4 of the DSU.

[446] *See*, Desta, M., *The Law of International Trade in Agricultural Products: from GATT 1947 to the WTO Agreement on Agriculture*, © Kluwer Law International, (2002), pp. 184–188 for a discussion on the precedent established on what is required of parties to request consultations on agricultural subsidies. Specifically Desta includes an analysis of the FSC and *Australian Leather* rulings, regarding what must be submitted as well as the timeframe in which it should be completed.

7, and 30 of the SCM, Article 19 of the AoA (applying Articles XXII and XXIII of GATT 1994).[447] The dispute was brought at a time when there was a noticeable increase in cotton production in the US and record high subsidies tied to record low world cotton prices.[448] In its formal consultation request, Brazil claimed that US cotton subsidies were causing serious prejudice in the form of significant price suppression in the world cotton market. Brazil claimed that its cotton producers were suffering significant revenue losses due to the effects of what they believed were the result of high and WTO illegal subsidization by the US.[449] Brazil also claimed that US agricultural exports were WTO non-compliant because of subsidies given to support production as well as heavily subsidized lending practices through the US export credit guarantee program.[450] Brazil alleged that such measures were inconsistent with particular United States obligations under the *SCM and Agriculture Agreements*, and the *GATT 1995*.[451] The United States did not agree with these claims and no resolution was reached during any of the three consultation meetings, held throughout December of 2002 and into January of 2003. Therefore, no agreement was reached between Brazil and the United States during the preliminary consultation process.

---

447   World Trade Organization, WT/DS267/1, dated 27 September 2002 and included in record 3 October, 2002.
448   Cotton prices plunged in 1999, 2001, and 2002, with prices hitting record lows in the spring of 2002 at 29 cents per pound – far below the 20 year average price of 72 cents per pound. U.S. production of cotton increased during the 1998–2001 period from 13.1 million aces in 1998–99 to 14.6 million acres in 1999/2000, increasing again to 15.3 million acres in 2000/1, and to 15.5 million acres in 2001/2. With record low prices, U.S. production reached the second highest level ever in 2001/2. *See*, generally, Daniel A. Sumner, *A Quantitative Simulation Analysis of the Impacts of US Cotton* (unpublished paper, on file with the Department of Agricultural and Resource Economics, University of California, Davis, available at http://www.fao.org/es/esc/common/ecg/306/en/sumner.pdf).
449   During 1999–2002, Brazilian cotton farmers lost $478 million in revenues from cotton prices that were suppressed through the effects of the U.S. subsidies.
450   *Ibid*, 4. Specifically, the provisions challenged were "export subsidies, exporter assistance, export credit guarantees, export and market access enhancement to facilitate the export of US upland cotton provided under the Agricultural Trade Act of 1978, as amended, and other measures such as the GSM-102, GSM-103, and SCGP programs, and the Step 1 and Step 2 certificate programs, among others."
451   Specifically, Articles 4.1, 7.1 and 30 of the *Agreement on Subsidies and Countervailing Measures*, Article 19 of the *Agreement on Agriculture*, and Article XXII of GATT 1994. *Ibid*, 4.

5.4 Original Panel Proceedings

Under Articles 8 of the DSU and 4.4 of the SCM, matters under consultation that are unable to be resolved within thirty (30) days may be referred to the DSB for the establishment of a panel. Specifically, "well-qualified governmental and/or non-governmental"[452] individuals are selected from one of the indicative lists[453] or rosters kept by the DSU of potential panelists. Panelists become the preliminary triers of fact. In reviewing the challenged measures, they are allowed to rely on additional experts, under Article 4.5 of the SCM, referred to as the Permanent Group of Experts (PGE) to determine whether there is a prohibited subsidy involved.[454]

Upon the conclusion of the consultation process, Brazil[455] requested a panel be established for the *Cotton* dispute, World Trade Dispute Settlement 267 (WT/DS267), on February 6, 2003.[456] On March 18, 2003 the Panel was established pursuant to Article 8 of the DSU.[457] The composition of a panel is made up of experts in the field of international economic law and trade.[458] Since Brazil and US were unable to agree on the composition of the Panel, the Director-General composed the Panel.[459] In this case, the Panel was comprised of Mr. Dariusz Rosati, the Chair of the Panel and an economist and former

---

452   Article 8.1 DSU.
453   Article 8.4 DSU.
454   The PGE was established under Article 24 of the SCM. There is not a corresponding or similar provision in the DSU.
455   Third parties to the World Trade DS267 included: Argentina, Australia, Benin, Canada, Chad, China, Chinese Taipei, European Communities, India, New Zealand, Pakistan, Paraguay, Venezuela, Japan, and Thailand. *Ibid*, 4.
456   Brazil requested the establishment of the panel pursuant to Article 6 of the DSU, Article XXIII:2 of GATT 1994, Article 19 of the AoA, and Articles 4.4, 7.4, and 30 of the SCM. *See*, WT/DS267/7.
457   As the first panel proceedings in this dispute, they are referred to as the 'original' panel proceedings.
458   For a discussion on the structure of panels, *see*, Ehlermann, C., "Six Years on the Bench of the 'World Trade Court': Some Personal Experiences as Member of the Appellate Body of the World Trade Organization," as found in Bronkers, M. and Horlick, G., *WTO Jurisprudence and Policy: Practitioners' Perspectives*, © Cameron May, (2004), pp. 13–59; specifically pp. 37–44.
459   Brazil specifically requested that the DG compose the Panel. This request was made on the 9 of May. Ten (10) days later, the DG announced the composition of the Panel. *See*, WT/DS267/15 as found in *US-Upland Cotton*, First Submission of Brazil, 24 June 2003, p. 10, WT/DS267.

Foreign Minister for Poland; Mr. Mario Matus, a member of Chili's Foreign Ministry; and Mr. Daniel Moulis, a private sector lawyer from Australia with a specialization in international trade.

Further, pursuant to Article 10 of the DSU, the following Members became third parties to the dispute: Argentina, Australia, Benin, Canada, Chad, China, Chinese Taipei, EC, India, New Zealand, Pakistan, Paraguay, and Venezuela. Under the DSU Article 10.3, third party rights included the right to be involved in the initial stage of the proceedings by participating in the first substantive meeting,[460] receiving and responding to initial briefs and timelines, and an invitation to submit any written comments they had about the initial stage of the original panel proceedings.[461] It should be noted that where a panel deems that a third party has a substantial interest in a matter, it may use its discretion to allow third parties to have enhanced rights.[462] Effectively, this allows *inter alia* third parties to attend the entire first and second substantive meetings. Though the EU's requests for enhanced third party rights were denied, the Panel did emphasize that it would "enable them to participate, as necessary and appropriate, in any second session of the first substantive meeting in a full and meaningful fashion."[463] The EU, New Zealand, Australia, Benin and Chad meaningfully participated throughout the dispute as reflected in the number of submissions, much of which the Panel incorporated into its *Panel Report*.[464] Further, participation by Benin and Chad were given particular attention by the Panel.[465]

Pursuant to the DSU, the panelists were given six (6) months to gather the requisite information and hold hearings prior to the issuance of their report.[466]

---

460 The EC specifically requested the right to be able to see and obtain copies of the oral statement of the main parties at the first substantive meeting and provide views of the Panel to the third parties. *Panel Report*, para. 7.11.

461 Para. 7.3.

462 *AB Report, US-1916 Act*, paras. 149–150.

463 *Panel Report*, paras. 7.11–7.13.

464 For citation purposes, all analysis and findings derived from the final panel report will be cited as such: *Panel Report*, para. xxx. All remaining references to other decisions will be fully cited.

465 *Panel Report*, para. 7.54.

466 Article 12.8 of the DSU. Though there is some flexibility to the time limits of the panels, Article 12.9 of the DSU stipulates that, "in no case should the period from the establishment of the panel to the submission of the report to the Members exceed nine months." In the case of prohibited subsidy cases brought under the SCM Agreement, there is a ninety (90) days time limit with no additional time allowances.

Given the complexity of the case, however, the deadline was extended and the resulting Panel report was lengthier and more detailed as compared to standard WTO decisions. The first meeting between Brazil and the US was held in July 2003. The initial decision was for the Panel to produce separate reports on an issue-by-issue basis. However, in September of 2003, it reversed its decision and chose to issue a combined report focusing on Brazil's prohibited subsidy and serious prejudice claims, and the 'peace clause' issue raised by the US that refuted the validity of Brazil's challenge. In reviewing and applying several US subsidies[467] to the relevant WTO agreements, the Panel determined the following, organized by legal issue[468]:

Order of Analysis of Relevant WTO Agreements: It is important to note the procedural issue determination by the Panel prior to analyzing the Peace Clause and substantive findings from the original Panel proceedings.[469] In analyzing the relevant WTO Agreements and their connectivity, the Panel determined that the appropriate order of analysis would be the AoA, SCM, and GATT Article XVI. This lays important precedence for future disputes as it sets forth the relationship between the agreements in relation to the Peace Clause as well as the appropriate order of analysis.[470] As the Panel stipulated, the

---

467   The various subsidies and their related legislation and regulations were: *Marketing loan/ Loan deficiency* (Sections 1201(a)–(b), 1202(a)(6), 1202(b)(6), 1204(b), 1205(a)(1), 1205(b), 1205(c)(1), 1608 of the FSRI Act of 2002 and 7 USC 7286 or Section 166 of the FAIR Act of 1996 as amended, and 7 CFR 1427.22); *User marketing Step 2* (Section 1207(a) of the FSRI Act of 2002 and 7 CFR 1427.103, 7 CFR 1427.104(a)(1) and (2), 7 CFR 1427.105(a) and 7 CFR 1427.108(d)), *Direct payments* (Section 1103(a)–(d)(1) of the FSRI Act of 2002 and 7 CFR 1412.502), *Counter-cyclical payments* (Section 1104(a)–(f)(1) of the FSRI Act of 2002 and 7 CFR 1412.503), *Crop insurance* (Sections 508(a)(8), 508(b)(1), 508(b)(2)(A)(ii), 508(b)(3), 508(e) and 508(k) and 516 of "the ARP Act of 2000), *Export credit guarantee* (7 USC 5622, in particular, 7 USC 5622(a)(1) and (b), and 7 CFR 1493 which established and main the GSM 102, GSM 103, and SCGP programmes), and *ETI Act of 2000* (ETI Act of 2000, in particular, Section 3, which Brazil asserted inserted new Sections 114, 941, and 943 in the United States Internal Revenue Code). This list of provisions can be referenced in the *Panel Report* at paragraph 7.250.

468   There were several additional procedural issues considered by the original Panel; however, for purposes of this book, only the key procedural issue of the order of analysis and Peace clause are discussed in detail.

469   There were additional procedural claims brought in the original panel proceeding. However, these matters did not directly fall into the scope of the thesis of this book and are not, therefore, addressed.

470   This issue was earlier addressed in the section discussing the *Agreement on Agriculture* above wherein it states that in relation to other WTO agreements, the AoA is prioritized.

"web of cross-references discloses a scheme according to which an analysis of the same measures under the *Agreement on Agriculture*, the SCM *Agreement* and Article XVI of the GATT *1994* concerning export subsidies for agricultural products and, at least during the implementation period for the purposes of Article 13, allegedly actionable subsidies for agricultural products, should be examined first under the *Agreement on Agriculture*."[471] Therefore, the Panel decision better clarified the complex legal relationship between the agreements and proffered an approach for how to analyze interrelated subjects and provisions in the area of agricultural subsidies.[472]

Peace Clause: A preliminary threshold legal issue for Brazil's claims of serious prejudice was the so-called Peace Clause issue, i.e., whether the level of domestic support for upland cotton during 1999–2002, provided through eight (8) measures and the legislative and regulatory provisions facilitating payments under five (5) of those measures,[473] exceeded the level of cotton support in 1992.[474] As described, *supra*, the Peace Clause was included in the AoA as an agreement by Members to exercise "due restraint" in bringing claims

---

471 *Panel Report*, paras. 7.254–264.

472 Brazil first claimed that the measures and export subsidies challenged were not exempt from action based on Articles 13(b)(ii) and 13(c)(ii), respectively, of the *Agreement on Agriculture*. Therefore, Brazil claimed that the US domestic measures identified were inconsistent with the following provisions of the WTO agreements. Specifically: export subsidy provisions of Articles 3.3, 8, 9.1 and 10.1 of the *Agreement on Agriculture;* prohibited subsidies provisions of Articles 3.1(a) and (b) and 3.2 of the SCM *Agreement;* the actionable subsidies provisions of Articles 5(c) and 6.3(c) and (d) of the SCM *Agreement;* the subsidies provisions of paragraphs 1 and 3 of Article XVI of the GATT *1994;* and the national treatment provision of Article III:4 of the GATT *1994*. These claims and their related WTO agreement provisions were extrapolated from paragraphs 7.251 and 7.252 of the *Panel Report*.

473 These included: marketing loan payments (ML), user marketing (Step 2) payments paid to domestic users; production flexibility contract payments; direct payments (DP); counter-cyclical payments (CCP); crop insurance payments; cottonseed payments; and the legislative and regulatory provisions providing payment for the ML, Step 2, DP, CCP, and crop insurance. *See, Panel Report*, para. 7.337.

474 The relevant "peace clause" to Brazil's serious prejudice claims are set out in the "Due Restraint" provisions of Article 13(b) of the *Agreement on Agriculture*. They provide, in relevant part: "*domestic support measures that conform fully to the provisions of Article 6 of this Agreement including direct payments that conform to the requirements of paragraph 5 thereof, as reflected in each Member's Schedule, as well as domestic support within de minimis levels and in conformity with paragraph 2 of Article 6, shall be:* (ii) *exempt from actions based on…Articles 5 and 6 of the Subsidies Agreement….*"

related to agricultural subsidies until after the implementation period, which ended in 31 December 2003.[475] In other words, generally, the Peace Clause prevented WTO Members from bringing WTO cases challenging agricultural subsidies between 1995 until December 31, 2003 so long as certain conditions exist.[476] Further, this exemption from litigation was limited to export subsidies that otherwise conform to the AoA, green box measures, and domestic support that also otherwise complies with the AoA (so long as it does not exceed the commitments established during MY 1992).[477] Brazil's challenge, which began in September 2002, was the first time that any WTO Member demonstrated that the Peace Clause did not bar a challenge because the requisite conditions did not apply. Brazil requested (and the third parties of Argentina, Australia, Benin, China, and India supported) that the Panel find a violation under Article 13 of the AoA, that peace clause was "in the nature of an affirmative defence."[478] However, the US argued[479] and Panel found, that the Peace Clause was not an affirmative defense, but rather a threshold procedural issue, for which the burden of proof rested on Brazil to show that the contested measures are inconsistent and do not satisfy the requisite Article 13 conditions.[480] Brazil was able to accomplish this successfully,[481] as described below.

There were three (3) relevant aspects to the Peace Clause under the agricultural pillars of domestic support and export subsidies. The Peace Clause applied to all three domestic support boxes. In the first instance, the Peace Clause prohibited Members from challenging any green box subsidies during the implementation period. Therefore, Members were able to grant an unlimited number of recognized non- (or nominally) trade distortive subsidies, which were not subject to reduction commitments. In order to be categorized as

---

475   This was the second dispute invoking the peace clause of Article 13 of the AoA. The first it was brought was in the *Brazil-Desiccated Coconut* dispute, WT/DS22.

476   The primary conditions are set forth in the chapeaux of paragraphs (a) and (b) and an additional condition in the proviso in subparagraphs (ii) and (iii) of paragraph (b).

477   Halverson Cross, K., "King Cotton, Developing Countries and the 'Peace Clause': The WTO's *US Cotton Subsidies* Decision," *Journal of International Economic Law*, Vol. 9, Issue 1, (30 January 2006), p. 165.

478   *Panel Report*, para. 7.265.

479   United States' first written submission, paras. 38–41; *Panel Report*, para. 7.266.

480   *Panel Report*, para. 7.285.

481   *Panel Report*, para. 7.286, "....the Panel is of the view that Brazil has succeeded in discharging the burden to show that certain measures at issue do not satisfy the conditions in Article 13...."

such, the subsidies had to be completely decoupled from current production levels of any specific crop.[482] In the case of *Cotton*, Brazil challenged those programs the US claimed were safely held within the green box. Specifically, the direct payments under the 2002 Farm Bill and the production flexibility contract payments under the 1996 Farm Bill were challenged green box subsidies.[483] The rationale for Brazil challenging the designation of the green box subsidies was the legal effect that, if it was proven that they were improperly designated, then those subsidies could be included in determining whether serious prejudice had been caused to Brazil.[484] To that end Brazil argued that they were not green box protected, because they were not decoupled from production, as required under Annex 2 of the Agreement on Agriculture.[485]

There were several issues regarding the Peace Clause analysis of the green box as set forth in Article 13(b)(ii) of the AoA. Specifically, the US disagreed on the characterization of Production Flexibility Contract ("PFC") and Direct Payments to U.S. farmers as non-green box subsidies.[486] They argued that both subsidy schemes are contingent upon historical production of cotton. Paragraphs 6(a) and 6(b) of Annex 2 of the AoA set out the criteria for green box subsidies.[487] Further, the US argued that payments were given to producers holding 'base acreage,' regardless of whether those producers presently grow cotton.[488] In addition, payments are provided without cotton price contingency; rather, payments are established by historical production. However, Brazil argued that, despite these characteristics, these US subsidies were in violation of paragraphs 6(a) and 6(b) of Annex 2 of the AoA "because they permitted updating of base acres from the PFC programme."[489] Article 6(a) reads, "decoupled income support eligibility for such payments shall be determined by clearly-defined criteria such as income, status as a producer or landowner, factor use or production level in a defined and fixed base period." Brazil contested the latter part of the provision, arguing that green box payments

---

482   *Panel Report*, para. 7.364–7.366.
483   *Panel Report*, para. 7.358.
484   The serious prejudice claim is discussed in significant detail, *infra*.
485   Brazil's first written submission, para. 198; *Panel Report*, para. 7.358.
486   United States' first written submission, paras. 55–57; *Panel Report*, para. 7.360.
487   Agreement on Agriculture, Annex 2, Article 6(a) and (b), *The Legal Texts: The Results of the Uruguay Round of Multilateral Trade Negotiations*, World Trade Organization, Cambridge University Press, (c) 1999, p. 50.
488   United States' first written submission, paras. 55–57; *Panel Report*, para. 7.360.
489   Brazil's first written submission, paras. 176–180 and response to Panel Question No. 19; *Panel Report*, para. 7.389.

must be based on a defined and fixed base period.[490] Further, pursuant to paragraph 6(b), green box payments cannot be dependent upon the type of production undertaken in any year after the base period. In the case of US production flexibility and direct payments, both were conditioned on farmers not engaging in the production of fruits and vegetables, melons, tree nuts or wild rice on land for which such payments are received.[491] The underlying economic principle is that payments conditioned upon production (or non production) are trade distortive. Annex 2 allows for unlimited non-trade distortive subsidies, under the green box provisions, so long as they are not coupled as described. Therefore, Brazil was able to argue that the prohibition on growing certain proscribed *inter alia* fruits and vegetables violated the provision, under the green box criteria, and was therefore trade distortive.[492] The Panel found that "PFC payments, DP payment, and the legislative and regulatory provisions that provide for the planting flexibility limitations in the DP programme, do not fully conform with paragraph 6(b) of Annex 2 of the *Agreement on Agriculture*."[493]

However, it was argued, and eventually found by the Panel, that the US Direct Payment program simply continued PFC Payments under a different name. It permitted farmers to update the amount of their eligible acreage to reflect increased production of cotton in 1998–2001.[494] This update establishes a new "fixed" base period contrary to the requirements of the green box. In effect, by updating base periods re-links Direct Payments to production in the period immediately preceding the 2002 U.S. Farm Bill. It was argued that this re-linking of payments also creates the expectation of further base updates that provide incentives for farmers to keep producing the program crops in view of increased Direct Payments following the next base update.[495] This meant that Direct Payments were not fully decoupled and had production and trade-distorting effects.

In sum, Brazil argued that none of the domestic U.S. subsidies challenged by Brazil in this dispute were properly within the green box and must be included within the subsidies counted for purposes of the 1992 comparison.[496] Given

---

490 Brazil's first written submission, paras. 176–180 and response to Panel Question No. 19; *Panel Report*, para. 7.389.
491 *Panel Report*, paras. 7.376–382.
492 *Panel Report*, paras. 7.383–385.
493 *Panel Report*, para. 7.388.
494 *Panel Report*, para. 7.397.
495 Brazil's first written submission, para. 185; *Panel Report*, 7.402.
496 *Panel Report*, para. 7.413–7.414.

the U.S. provided support in each year between 1999–2002 well in excess of 1992 the Panel determined that it could consider Brazil's prohibited and actionable subsidy claims under the *Subsidies Agreement*.[497]

In presenting their positions, the parties disagreed on the methodology employed to compare domestic support to individual commodities in 1992 with other years.[498] Brazil and all third parties argued that budgetary outlays, or actual expenditures, for domestic non-green box subsidies should be counted as supporting the production of cotton.[499] The US argued that calculations under the Peace Clause are undertaken using the 'rate of support,' not budgetary outlays.[500] Therefore, the US requested the panel to consider the 'target price' of 72.9 cents per pound in 1992[501] as compared to the 52.35 cents per pound for marketing loan payments.[502] Further, the US argued that only subsidies requiring production of a particular commodity may be compared to the 1992 figure.[503] In applying either legal test, Brazil was able to demonstrate that US expenditures for cotton in the MY 1999–2002 were considerably higher than they were in 1992.[504] Brazil proved that the 1992 $2.1 billion cap the US agreed not to exceed in their Uruguay Commitments were exceeded by $3.5 billion in 1999, $2.3 billion in 2000, $4.1 billion in 2001, and $3.1 billion in 2002. Further, it was shown, based on expenditures per unit of production, that support in 1999–2002 (29–44 cents per pound) exceeded the 1992 levels of support (28 cents per pound). Therefore, the Panel found that the US had exceeded its commitments and that the domestic support measures were not exempt from challenges by Brazil based on paragraph 1 of Article XVI of the GATT 1994 or Articles 5 and 6 of the SCM.[505]

As a result, the original Panel determined that the amount of support for each year between 1999–2002 exceeded the 1992 level and, therefore, that the

---

497 *Panel Report*, para. 7.415 and 7.608.
498 *Panel Report*, paras. 7.445, and 7.641–644.
499 Brazil's response to Panel Question No. 59; *Panel Report*, para. 7.539.
500 United States' rebuttal submission, paras. 121–126.
501 United States' further rebuttal submission, para. 91; *Panel Report,* para. 7.603.
502 *Panel Report*, paras. 7.542 and 7.600.
503 United States' 3 March 2004 comments, para. 14, second bullet; *Panel Report*, paras. 7.459–460, 7.462–463; United States' rebuttal submission, para. 83, comments on Brazil's response to Panel Question No. 258 and its 11 February 2004 comments, paras. 7–14; United States' rebuttal submission, paras. 76 and 79; United States' comments on Brazil's response to Panel Question No. 258; United States' closing statement at second substantive meeting, para. 25.
504 *Panel Report*, paras. 7.599–607.
505 *Panel Report*, para. 7.608.

US cotton subsidies did not benefit from Peace Clause exemption but, rather, was subject to Brazil's serious prejudice challenge.[506] Specifically, the Panel found that the production flexibility contract and direct payments (and the legislative and regulatory provisions establishing them) are not green box measures and did not conform with paragraph 6(b) of Annex 2 of the AoA.[507] Second, with regards to Article 13(b)(ii), the Panel found that the US programs grant support in excess of its MY 1992 commitments, and therefore were not exempt from challenge based on paragraph 1 of the Article XVI of the GATT 1994 or Articles 5 and 6 of the SCM Agreement.[508] Therefore, Brazil was able to bring two types of claims: (1) the "serious prejudice" claim, which argued that the combination of the seven (7) US subsidies caused significant price suppression in the world and allowed the US to subsume an inequitable share of the cotton market and (2) the prohibited subsidy claims against Step 2 and export credit guarantee subsidies.

Scholars and practitioners have recognized that the original Panel ruling on the Peace Clause has brought needed clarity to its relationship with the AoA, GATT 1994 and the SCM.[509] As Desta summarized, "Thanks to the Panel's analysis on the relationship between the AoA and those other covered agreements within the WTO, it is now clear beyond doubt that as long as countries do not respect their AoA obligations, the Peace Clause affords them absolutely no protection whatsoever. Moreover, to the extent countries respect their obligations under the AoA, their measures remain secure from challenge based on other agreements."[510] Furthermore, significant literature has been contributed about what vulnerabilities now exist in domestic subsidy regimes given that the Peace Clause has now expired.[511] Again, Desta argues that the expiry of the

---

506   This is true whether one looks at total support in monetary terms, at monetary support per unit of production, or at the rate of support suggested by the United States (but adjusted for certain program features that affect the "effective" rate of support per unit of production).

507   *Panel Report*, paras. 7.413–414.

508   *Panel Report*, para. 7.608.

509   Desta, M., "The Integration of Agriculture into WTO Disciplines," as found in O'Conner, B., *Agriculture in WTO Law*, © Cameron May, (2005), pp. 38–40.

510   Desta, M., "The Integration of Agriculture into WTO Disciplines," as found in O'Conner, B., *Agriculture in WTO Law*, © Cameron May, (2005), p. 40.

511   Chambovey, D., "How the Expiry of the Peace Clause (Article 13 of the WTO Agreement on Agriculture) Might Alter Disciplines on Agricultural Subsidies in the WTO Framework," *Journal of World Trade*, Vol. 36 No. 2 (2002), pp. 305–352; Steinberg, R. and Josling, T., "When the Peace Ends: The Vulnerability of EC and US Agricultural Subsidies to WTO Legal Challenge," *Journal of International Economic Law*, Vol. 6 (June 2003), p. 369; and

Peace clause does not change the view presented in the quote, *infra*.[512] Whether another Peace Clause will be included in the next Agreement on Agriculture is yet to be determined. Given the positions of the US and EC, and in light of this ruling, it is rather certain that it will be considerably different than what was negotiated during the Uruguay Round. Finally, Desta concludes:

> I am of the view that the role of the Peace Clause has always been more political rather than legal and, strictly speaking, the expiry of the Peace Clause could not make much legal difference. Ultimately the question will be one of how to reconcile two agreements that impose incompatible obligations on the same subject. In such circumstances, it is clearly provided under AoA Article 21, and reaffirmed by the *US-Upland Cotton* Panel that the AoA provisions will prevail over those of the SCM Agreement or GATT. It thus follows that the Peace Clause is not concerned about measure that violate the AoA; there is no peace in the face of violation.[513]

Export Subsidies Challenge, Export Credit Guarantees and Step 2 Payments to Domestic Users and Exporters of Cotton: As discussed in the 'Order of Analysis' section, the Panel chose to first assess the alleged export measures challenged by Brazil in their relation to the AoA, before analyzing them under the SCM or GATT 1994.[514] It should therefore be read in the following discussion that the original Panel chose to always first consider the AoA as the primary provision when conducting legal analysis.

Export Credit Guarantees: While generally referred to as the *Cotton* case, a crucial aspect of the dispute involved a challenge to US export credit guarantee programs facilitating the export of a wide variety of US agricultural products. The overall negative impacts of these programs on world agricultural markets are roughly comparable to those stemming from the trade-distorting impact of US domestic subsidies for cotton. Brazil challenged three major export credit

---

Halverson Cross, K., "King Cotton, Developing Countries and the 'Peace Clause': The WTO's *US Cotton Subsidies* Decision," *Journal of International Economic Law*, Vol. 9, Issue 1, (30 January 2006).

512 Desta, M., "The Integration of Agriculture into WTO Disciplines," as found in O'Conner, B., *Agriculture in WTO Law*, © Cameron May, (2005), p. 40.

513 Desta, M., "The Integration of Agriculture into WTO Disciplines," as found in O'Conner, B., *Agriculture in WTO Law*, © Cameron May, (2005), p. 40. This issue will be given greater treatment in Part 3 of this book.

514 *Panel Report*, paras. 7.654–677.

guarantees provided by the Commodity Credit Corporation (CCC).[515] Under these three programs, the CCC extends guarantees to support an average of approximately $4 billion per year in agricultural exports.[516] When challenged by Brazil in 2003, CCC guarantees were available for terms of up to 10 years (this was later lowered to three years), and the US took the position that export credit guarantee programs were allowed under WTO rules.[517] The *Cotton* dispute clarified that export credit guarantees that are export subsidies are not exempt from the AoA, but rather the anti-circumvention provision of the AoA requires them to be assessed as part of a Member's scheduled commitments.[518]

CCC regulations make clear that its guarantees are to be used in situations where, without a CCC guarantee, a foreign buyer of US agricultural exports could not secure financing on the market. From the perspective of a bank, the CCC guarantee, which effectively lends the US government's credit rating to the buyer, makes financing risk free. Thereby, the CCC guarantee makes an impossible sale possible. As made evident by Brazil's challenge, CCC guarantees confer benefits that cannot be secured on the market and are used only in such situations where the foreign importer *could not* secure financing by other means. Further, they are uniquely designed for commodity transactions and are not available on the market. This means that, unlike market-oriented instruments, the fees offered do not vary according to the underlying risk to the borrower.[519]

Brazil challenged the CCC export credit guarantee programs under Articles 9.1(a) and 10[520] of the WTO *Agreement on Agriculture* and Article 3.1(a) of the *SCM Agreement*. Brazil demonstrated and the Panel found that the CCC programs constitute export subsidies that circumvent the United States' export subsidy commitments under the Agriculture Agreement.[521] This involved several legal steps:

---

[515] These were the General Sales Manager 102 (GSM-102), General Sales Manager 103 (GSM 103), and Supplier Credit Guarantee (SCGP) programs.

[516] In total, US legislation provides $5.5 billion in export credit guarantees annually. *See, Panel Report*, para. 7.239, citing 7 USC §5622(g).

[517] Given the *Cotton* rulings, it is anticipated that the US will take a considerably different position with regards to export credit guarantees and export subsidy commitments in the Doha negotiations.

[518] Kireeva, I., and O'Connor, B., "The Agreement on Agriculture and Dispute Settlement," as found in O'Connor, B., *Agriculture in WTO Law*, © Cameron May, (2005), p. 125.

[519] Further, the fees are subject to a one (1) percent statutory cap.

[520] Article 10.1 covers any subsidy not listed in Article 9.1 wherein is listed a number of defined export subsidies. *See, Panel Report*, 7.794–796.

[521] Referring to Article 10.2 of the Agriculture Agreement, the United States argued that agricultural export credit guarantees are not subject to WTO rules altogether. Brazil, however,

First, Brazil demonstrated, and the Panel found, that the CCC programs[522] constitute *per se* export subsidies,[523] in violation of Article 10.1 of the AoA,[524] because premium rates for CCC guarantees are inadequate to cover the long-term operating costs and payout losses of the CCC programs.[525] This was deemed to "lead to circumvention of the United States export subsidy commitments."[526] The Panel found that costs and losses of the program outpaced premiums collected under a variety of approaches, including cash-basis accounting and "net-present value" accounting. It determined that it was appropriate to assess the programs from the 'long-term' period requested by Brazil.[527] Looking at 'past performance' over the period 1993–2002, operating costs and losses for the CCC programs outpaced revenue by more than $1 billion using cash-basis accounting.[528] Therefore, it was determined that the programs are "run at a net cost to the United States government."[529]

Second, under the AoA, export subsidies are not *per se* prohibited if they remain within the reduction commitments of a Member.[530] Therefore, the Panel had to determine whether the US export credit guarantees were exempt

---

demonstrated and the Panel found that Article 10.2 only calls upon WTO Members to undertake to negotiate specific disciplines on export credit guarantees; the provision does not, in the interim, exempt those guarantees from the general disciplines on export subsidies included in the Agriculture Agreement and in the Subsidies Agreement. On appeal, two of the three Members of the Appellate Body Division affirmed, one dissenting in agreeing the arguments of the United States. *See* Appellate Body Report, *U.S.-Upland Cotton,* paras 605–628 (majority decision) and paras 631–641 (dissenting opinion).

522 These include: Section 1207(a) of the FSRI Act of 2002 providing for user marketing (Step 2) payments to exporters and export credit guarantees under the GSM 102, GSM 103 and SCGP programs. Brazil also challenged the *ETI Act of 2000*, which is discussed herein. In short, Brazil was successful on the first two claims, but was found not to have established a prima facie case of inconsistency of the ETI Act of 2000.

523 *Panel Report*, paras. 7.867–869. It should be noted that, pursuant to WTO law, a Member cannot challenge another Member's measure(s) *per se* unless the measure(s) "mandate a violation of the WTO Agreement." *US-Upland Cotton,* First Submission of Brazil, (24 June 2003), p. 99.

524 *Panel Report*, para. 7.875.

525 *Panel Report*, paras. 7.804–807.

526 *Panel Report*, paras. 7.892–896.

527 *Panel Report*, paras. 7.831–35.

528 *Panel Report*, paras. 7.842–856.

529 *Panel Report*, paras. 7.842–856.

530 This issue was discussed in detail, *supra*.

from Article 10.1. In *US – FSC*,[531] the Appellate Body in that case concluded that agricultural export subsidies cannot be provided for agricultural products that have not been "scheduled" by a WTO Member.[532] For "unscheduled" products such as, in the case of the United States, cotton and soybeans, no export subsidies can be provided.[533] Specifically, in its assessment of the FSC scheme, the Appellate Body found that "Article 10.1 prevents the application of export subsidies which 'results in, or which threatens to lead to, circumvention' of that prohibition."[534] The US argued this point pursuant to Article 10.2 of the AoA, which provides that "Members undertake to work toward the development of internationally agreed disciplines to govern the provision of export credits, export credit guarantees or insurance programmes and, after agreement on such disciplines, to provide export credits, export credit guarantees or insurance programmes only in conformity therewith."[535] However, the Panel rejected this argument by the US. Rather, Brazil demonstrated, and the Panel found, that the CCC programs circumvent the United States' export subsidy commitments as no US law allows the CCC to control the flow of the guarantees per market conditions or whether adverse effects to other Members occurs.[536]

In addition, Members that claim any quantity exported in excess of their reduction commitment level is not subsidized, pursuant to Article 10.3 and

---

531 *US-FSC* involved a 1984 tax scheme, which had replace its predecessor, the Domestic International Sales Corporation (DISC). The latter had been held to be an illegal export subsidy by a GATT panel in 1976 GATT Panel Report *United States Tax Legislation* (DISC), L/4422-23S/98, adopted in December 1981. Under the 1984 scheme, the EC complained that the FSC scheme was inconsistent with US obligations under the SCM by granting subsidies on the basis of preferential use of domestic rather than foreign imported goods. Further, claims under the AoA were used to argue that the US was granting export subsidies to agricultural goods in excess of its reduction commitments.

532 *US-FSC*, para. 152, WT/DS108/AB/R.

533 *US-FSC*, para. 152, WT/DS108/AB/R: "As regards *scheduled* products, when the specific reduction commitment levels have been reached, the *limited authorization* to provide export subsidies as listed in Article 9.1 is transformed, effectively into a *prohibition* against the provision of those subsidies...." Further, in paras. 146–147, "Under the second clause of Article 3.3, Members have committed *not* to provide *any* export subsidies, *listed in Article 9.1*, with respect to *unscheduled* agricultural products. This clause clearly also involves 'export subsidy commitments' within the meaning of Article 10.1....." Therefore, "the term 'export subsidy commitments' has a wider reach that covers commitments and obligations relating to *both* scheduled and unscheduled agricultural products."

534 Appellate Body Report, *US-FSC*, WT/DS108/AB/R, para. 150.

535 Article 10.2, *Agreement on Agriculture*.

536 *Panel Report*, para. 7.901.

must prove that no export subsidy has been granted, whether it is listed or not in Article 9. The first case establishing this was *Canada-Dairy*, which determined that the complaining Member becomes relieved of its burden to establish the prima facie case provided the Member has established the quantitative part of the claim (i.e. that the Member is exporting more than its commitment level).[537] The standard was further reduced to allow the complaining Member not to have to present evidence, if the responding Member were to fail to meet this legal burden of proof. Therefore, with regards to the anti-circumvention provision of Article 10.3 of the AoA, the complaining Member need only show that the exports exceeded the respondent's commitment levels. This was the standard used in the *Cotton* dispute.

Finally, having found a violation of the *Agriculture Agreement*, the Panel ruled, based on the same evidence, a violation of the prohibited export subsidy provisions of the SCM *Agreement*.[538] The Panel's reasoning can be summarized in the following:

> To the extent that the United States export credit guarantee programmes at issue – GSM 102, GSM 103 and SCGP – do not conform fully to these provisions in Part V of the *Agreement on Agriculture* and do not benefit from the exemption from actions provided by Article 13(c)(ii) of the *Agreement on Agriculture*, they are also export subsidies prohibited by Article 3.1(a) for the reasons we have already given.[539]

Further, given the export subsidies were found to be in violation of Article 3.1(a), they were also deemed to be in violation of Article 3.2. Therefore, since the CCC export credit guarantee programs constitute prohibited export subsidies for other commodities, including unscheduled products and rice, the United States was required, under Article 4.7 of the SCM Agreement, to withdraw them without delay. The Panel set a deadline for withdrawal by 1 July 2005 at the latest – that deadline has never been met.

Step 2 Challenge: A key component of Brazil's challenge was the US's Step 2 program for domestic cotton producers.[540] The US Step 2 program was a subsidy

---

537 AB Report, *Canada-Dairy* (21.5(*II*)), Second Recourse to Article 21.5 of the DSU by New Zealand and United States, WT/DS103AB/RW2 and WT/DS113AB/RW2, adopted 20 December 2002, para. 75.
538 *Panel Report*, paras. 7.946–948.
539 *Panel Report*, paras. 7.946–948.
540 1207(a) of the FSRI Act of 2002 provided the Step 2 marketing loan payments to exporters of upland cotton.

unique to cotton. Designed to provide a constant demand for uncompetitive US cotton, the US government paid domestic users and exporters of US cotton the difference between the lower world market price and the higher US domestic price. As a practical matter, the subsidy enabled US exporters of cotton to buy high-priced US cotton in the United States and sell it at a lower price on the export markets. Similarly, the US Step 2 program enabled US textile mills to buy higher-priced US cotton, which carried the eligibility to receive Step 2 payments, instead of otherwise lower-priced imported cotton, which is not eligible for Step 2 support.

Brazil challenged the program as *per se* import substitution subsidies on two grounds and the Panel upheld both claims. Generally, Brazil argued that because the US had not scheduled export subsidy commitments for cotton in the AoA, it was not allowed to provide any subsidies to assist with the exportation of the commodity as a result.[541] More specifically, under Article 3.1(b) and 3.2 of the *SCM Agreement,* subsidies that are contingent upon export or contingent upon use of local content are prohibited. The US Step 2 payments to cotton are contingent upon proof of export of US cotton by an eligible exporter or contingent upon proof of use of US cotton by a US textile producer.[542] Thus, one part of the program entails an export contingency, while the other part of the program contains a local content contingency. Therefore, the Panel found that both Step 2 payments to exports and Step 2 payments to US textile mills are prohibited subsidies.[543]

The United States recognized that the Step 2 payments were subsidies, but argued, "that Section 1207(a) of the FSRI Act of 2002 – providing for payments to exporters *and* domestic users – is not an export subsidy listed in Article 9.1(a) of the *Agreement on Agriculture* and, in the alternative, not an export subsidy in circumvention of its obligation not to confer an export subsidy with respect to upland cotton contrary to Article 10.1."[544] Thus, the US argued that Step 2 payments are neither export nor local content subsidies, but rather paid on the "use" of US cotton.[545] In essence, the US had devised a legal scheme whereby they tried to merge two WTO inconsistent measures, export and import substitution subsidies, into one legal provision in order to make them effectively permitted.[546] The Panel emphatically rejected this argument,

---

541   *Panel Report,* para. 7.678.
542   *Panel Report,* para. 7.1019.
543   *Panel Report,* para. 7.1098.
544   *Panel Report,* para. 7.684.
545   *Panel Report,* para. 7.685.
546   *Panel Report,* para. 7.741.

emphasizing that "two wrongs cannot make a right."[547] Furthermore, the United States argued that, under the AoA, subsidies to processors of an agricultural good (that also benefit producers) are subject to reduction commitments for domestic support.[548] Under the US argument, local content subsidies – as a subgroup of subsidies to processors – could, therefore, not possibly be prohibited under the *Subsidies Agreement*.[549] However, as the Panel emphasized, WTO rules apply always cumulatively, unless there is a conflict.[550] The Panel found that there is no such conflict between the rules on subsidies to processors under the AoA and the prohibition of local content subsidies under the *Subsidies Agreement* because not all subsidies to processors need necessarily be local content subsidies. It follows that Step 2 payments to domestic users are prohibited under the *Subsidies Agreement*.[551] The Panel, therefore, found that both Step 2 payments to exporters of US cotton (export subsidy) and Step 2 payments to US users of US cotton (local content subsidy) are prohibited subsidies under 3.1(b) of the WTO *Subsidies Agreement* and, as a result, inconsistent with Article 3.2.[552] As the Panel concluded "…Step 2 payments to exporters is inconsistent with Article 3.1(a), it is, consequently, also inconsistent with Article 3.2 of the SCM Agreement."[553]

Additional 3.1(a) and 3.2 Claims: Further, it should be noted that Brazil brought two additional claims against the US, regarding (1) the *FSC Repeal and ETI Act* as a means of establishing that the challenged CCC programs threatened to circumvent US export subsidy obligations and (2) Articles XVI:1 and XVI:3 of the GATT 1994 to argue that the export and actionable subsidies in the relevant marketing years cause serious prejudice by allowing the US to subsume more than an equitable share of world exports.[554] In the former case, Brazil submitted that the same measure in the *FSC Repeal and Extraterritorial Income Act of 2000*, providing export subsidies were similarly inconsistent with Articles 3.3, 8 and 10 of the AoA as well as Article 3.1(a) and 3.2 of the SCM. The Panel deviated from the Appellate Body's test established in *US – FSC* and did

---

547 *Panel Report*, para. 7.741. Further, in line with this reasoning, the Panel warned against allowing Members to allow export-contingent subsidies with prohibited subsidies to avoid disciplines by Article 3.1(a) and (b) of the SCM. *See, Panel Report*, para. 7.756.
548 *Panel Report*, paras. 7.1022–1024.
549 *Panel Report*, paras. 7.684–687.
550 *Panel Report*, para. 7.700.
551 The Appellate Body similarly found that local content subsidies for agricultural products were not carved out of the disciplines of the SCM *Agreement*.
552 *Panel Report*, paras. 7.1097–1098.
553 *Panel Report*, para. 7.761.
554 *Panel Report*, paras. 7.955, 7.991–993.

not find a threat of circumvention. Rather, the Panel found that "the panel and Appellate Body reports in that dispute cannot be taken as providing a final resolution to the part of the matter before us concerning the ETI Act of 2000."[555] Further, the Panel stipulated that "no direct transposition or incorporation of the panel and Appellate Body findings and conclusion would, in any event, be appropriate on the basis of the evidence and argumentation submitted in this dispute." In other words, the Panel found that Brazil had not met the requisite burden of proof by submitting the necessary "direct evidence" to the Panel on the matter.[556] Consequently, it chose not to examine Brazil's claims based on the provisions. In the latter case, the Panel limited its review, finding, "Article XVI:3 applied only to export subsidies as that term is now defined in the *Agreement on Agriculture* and the *SCM Agreement*."[557] In brief, the definition of export subsidy did not exist prior to the AoA and SCM agreements and, as a result, a GATT finding of an absent provision would be unnecessary. As a result, the Panel chose not to examine the Articles XVI:1 and XVI:3 claims.[558]

World Market Suppression and 'Serious Prejudice': Consequent to the Panel's 'peace clause' determination, the Panel proceeded to examine Brazil's claims that the collective effects of the various domestic support payments caused significant price suppression in the world market in violation of Articles 5, 6, and 7 of Part III of the *SCM Agreement*. First, the Panel undertook extensive analysis to determine whether the measures being challenged by Brazil were 'actionable subsidies' for purposes of Part III of the SCM. In order to do so, the Panel had to first review the measures to determine if they met the requisite criteria under Articles 1 and 2 of the SCM. In terms of Article 1, by applying the definition of a subsidy as a financial contribution by a government agency that confers a benefit on the recipient, the Panel was able to find that the measures in question constituted subsidies pursuant to Articles 1.1(a)(1)(i) and 1.1(b).[559]

The US did not contest that the Step 2 payments, marketing loan program payments, crop insurance payments and cottonseed payments were subsidies; however, it did contest the production flexibility contract, direct payment, marketing loan assistance, and counter-cyclical payments. With regards to the latter, the Panel found that those payments were indeed 'financial contributions' in the form of 'grants' within the meaning of Article 1.1(a)(1)(i).[560]

---

555 *Panel Report*, paras. 7.892–896 and 7.966–967.
556 *Panel Report*, paras. 7.949, 7.957–959.
557 *Panel Report*, paras. 7.1016–1017.
558 *Panel Report*, paras. 7.1016–1017.
559 *Panel Report*, paras. 7.1114–1118.
560 *Panel Report*, paras. 7.1114–1118.

Therefore, for purposes of the SCM Agreement, the measures were deemed subsidies under Articles 1.1(a) and (b).[561] As required by Article 1.2, for the purposes of Part III of the SCM, the second analysis was a determination of whether the measures were 'specific' subsidies. Brazil argued that, because the programs targeted – exclusively – 'discrete segments' of the US economy, it had met the second criteria of specificity.[562] Despite some argumentation by the US to the contrary, the Panel agreed with Brazil, finding: "all of the subsidies at issue – i.e. user marketing (Step 2) payments to domestic users and exporters; marketing loan programme payments; PFC payment; MLA payments; DP payments; CCP payments; crop insurance payments and cottonseed payments – are 'specific' within the meaning of Article(s) 2.1a and/or 2.3 of the *SCM Agreement.*"[563]

Given the Panel's conclusions that the measures were actionable subsidies,[564] two serious prejudice claims were made: one for the 'present' serious prejudice realized at the time as well as the continuous 'threat' of serious prejudice in the future. Specifically, these claims are made pursuant to Article 5 of the SCM entitled "Adverse Effect." Brazil's argument and evidence can be summarized as follows: the US cotton subsidies increased and maintained uncompetitive high-cost US cotton production, increased US exports and the US export market share and depressed and suppressed world cotton prices, to the detriment of Brazil and to third party markets. The effect was 'serious prejudice' in the form of significantly decreased revenue and investment opportunities for Brazilian producers. Further, in terms of increasing US exports and market share, Brazil argued that the US used massive subsidies to gain an inequitable share of the world market. Consequently, Brazil argued that the US was in violation of Articles 5(c),[565] 6.3(c),[566] and 6.3(d)[567] of the SCM and Article XVI of GATT.[568]

---

561 *Panel Report,* para. 7.1120.
562 *Panel Report,* para. 7.1122.
563 *Panel Report,* para. 7.1154.
564 As noted by the Panel, "Actionable" subsidies are covered in Articles 5, 6, and 7 of the SCM.
565 As "serious prejudice to the interests of another Member." *Panel Report,* para 7.1109.
566 As serious prejudice in relation to 5(c) where significant price suppression is found. *Panel Report,* para 7.1109.
567 As "significant price undercutting by the subsidized product as compared with the price of a like product of another Member in the same market or significant price suppression, price depression or lost sales in the same market." *Panel Report,* paras. 7.1156–1158.
568 As noted by the Panel, "serious prejudice to the interests of another Member" is used in the SCM as it is used in paragraph 1 of Article XVI of GATT 1994, and includes threat of serious prejudice. Greater analysis of this issue is provided, *infra*.

Demonstrating the causal link[569] between massive US subsidies was an intensely factual exercise involving a wide variety of evidence and econometric modelling[570] submitted in opposition to US argumentation that other factors constituted price suppression.[571] In order to argue that overproduction of cotton in the US, facilitated through the application of massive US subsidies, was creating adverse effects on cotton producers around the world, Brazil submitted evidence from the US Department of Agriculture (USDA) which demonstrated that the US cotton producers would have lost money from the production of cotton absent higher levels of subsidies.[572] US cotton farmers were facing production costs seventy-seven (77) percent higher than their returns from marketing their cotton. Further, Brazil relied on testimony of US agricultural policy expert, Professor Daniel Sumner,[573] developed from evidence created on the Food and Agricultural Policy Research Institute (FAPRI) model, well known and used by the US Congress and US Department of

---

[569] This was one of the primary issues the Panel recognized in assessing Brazil's serious prejudice claim. *See, Panel Report*, paras. 7.1347–7.1356.

[570] The findings of Professor Sumner may be found in Exhibits BRA-105, 275, 279, 280, 313–315, 325, 326, 342–346, and 396 as well as US-56.

[571] The US criticized Brazil "for not identifying the 'subsidized product for each of the types of subsidies from which it claims serious prejudice.'" *Panel Report*, prars. 7.1159–1163. However, the Panel did not find that Brazil was under an obligation to specifically quantify the subsidies, produce evidence of the precise extent to which the US subsidies 'passed through' to the exporter, or that "certain subsidies that are allegedly not directly tied to current production of upland cotton would need to be allocated over total production on a recipient's farm." In essence, the Panel found no need for Brazil to specifically quantify the subsidies. *Panel Report*, paras. 7.1179–1190. Further, the US also tries to argue that other factors more greatly contributed to price suppression, including: competition with synthetic fibers, internal shift from textile production to export markets, strength of the US dollar, China's subsidized cotton, and other factors *inter alia* planting decisions being made based on boll weevil eradication and GM crop production. *See, Panel Report*, paras. 7.1358–7.1363 where the Panel assesses each claim, individually. As determined, these factors paled in comparison to the level and nature of US cotton subsidies.

[572] USDA data showed that, during the period of MY 1997–2002, US cotton farmers would have lost a total of $872 for each acre of upland cotton planted.

[573] The Panel considered the role of econometric modeling results used by Brazil. *See, Panel Report*, paras. 7.1202–7.1209. For background information on and a description of the involvement of Professor Sumner, *see*, Section 4 of this book. In addition, the Panel also considered the role of studies conducted by other organizations/academic institutions. *See, Panel Report*, paras. 7.1210–1215 wherein footnote 1329 sets forth the studies most relied upon by the Panel.

Agriculture, and significant additional evidence. Specifically, Sumner was also able to prove that though the world price of cotton was precipitously declining and the cost of cotton production had increased during the relevant period. It was proven that these trends were occurring at a time when there was a rapid appreciation of the US dollar against other world currencies (including cotton competitors), which would have resulted in the US being in an even less competitive position. However, the US not only maintained but actually increased their cotton exports despite these unfavourable economic conditions. In order to illustrate the incongruity of what was occurring, Sumner also provided projections on what would have been the conditions absent such massive subsidies. Sumner testified that during the MY 1999–2002, US cotton production would have been 28.7 percent lower and exports should have fallen 41.2 percent.[574] Relatively, world prices for cotton would have been 6.5 cents per pound or 12.6 percent higher absent the effects of massive subsidies by the US.[575] Significant attention was given to the "role of econometric modelling results used by Brazil"[576] and the "role of studies by other organizations/academic institutions."[577] In doing so, the Panel determined that it would use the evidence provided by Brazil and attribute evidentiary weight to it.[578] This was a significant ruling in that it set precedent on the amount, sources and quality of evidence relied on by panels in similar cases as well as defined an ever-increasing role of the Economics Division of the WTO dispute settlement process. Further, as discussed in Chapter 6, the fact that the Panel considered evidence from other sources, including Oxfam, meant that the adverse effects of Benin and Chad were significantly regarded in Brazil's claims.[579]

---

574 Brazil's further written submission, para. 183; *Panel Report*, para. 7.1202. As indicated in footnote 1323, Professor Sumner "participated in the first and resumed sessions of the first substantive meeting as well as in the second substantive meeting with the Panel."

575 Brazil's further written submission, para. 183; *Panel Report*, para. 7.1202.

576 *Panel Report*, paras. 7.1202–7.1209.

577 *Panel Report*, paras. 7.1210–1215.

578 *Panel Report*, paras. 7.1205. Specifically, as indicated in footnote 1327, the Panel 'took note of' Professor Sumner's simulations that estimated the cumulative effects of the subsidies, for MY 1999–2002, to approximately be: "a 28 per cent increase in United States upland cotton acreage; a 29 per cent increase in United States production, a 41 per cent increase in United States exports and a 12.6 per cent decrease in world price (A-Index). In terms of relative magnitude, from subsidies with largest to smallest effect: 1. Marketing loan/LDP; 2. User marketing (Step 2) payments; 3. Crop insurance payments; 4. CCP payment; 5. DP payments." This evidence was used extensively by Brazil to substantiate its serious prejudice claim.

579 Footnote 1330 of the *Panel Report*: According to Benin and Chad, the Oxfam report – using data from the International Cotton Advisory Committee – estimates that in 2001 alone,

Actionable Subsidies & Brazil's Claims of "Present" Serious Prejudice: Under Article 5(c) of the SCM, Members are not to cause adverse effects by seriously prejudicing the interests of another Member. As argued by the parties, Article 6.3(d) of the SCM stipulates that 'serious prejudice' occurs where (1) a Member increases its market share over the previous three (3) year average and (2) if the increase follows a consistent trend, to the detriment of other WTO Members.[580] Brazil was able to prove that both of these conditions were met, and the US did not contest the substantive portion of the argument. Rather, the US chose to contest the definition of "world market share."[581] Specifically, it argued that world consumption is defined as a Member's domestic consumption plus exports divided by world consumption.[582] By applying this calculation, exports would be counted twice, leading to inflated world market shares and a total world market share in excess of one hundred (100) percent. This was deemed a conceptual error.[583] Brazil also offered an alternative interpretation of "world market share," which was also not accepted by the Panel.[584] As such, the Panel

---

sub-Saharan exporters lost $302 million as a direct consequence of United States cotton subsidies. The Report further notes that Benin's actual cotton export earnings in 2001/02 were $124 million. However, had United States subsidies been withdrawn, Benin's export earnings are estimated to have been $157 million. Therefore, the value lost to Benin as a result of United States subsidies was $33 million. Chad's cotton export earnings in 2001/02 were $63 million, although in the absence of United States subsidies, Chad would have earned $79 million, thus reflecting a loss of $16 million. For the period from 1999/2000 to 2001/2002, Oxfam estimates a total cumulative loss of export earnings of $61 million for Benin and $28 million for Chad. Benin and Chad agree with Oxfam when it emphasizes, "the small size of several West African economies and their high levels of dependence on cotton inevitably magnify the adverse effects of United States subsidies. For several countries, US policy has generated what can only be described as a major economic shock." *See,* Benin and Chad's written submission to the resumed session of the first substantive meeting, paras. 19–21. Further, *see, Panel Report,* para. 7.1400 for treatment by the Panel of Benin and Chad's request to have their adverse effects considered. *See,* Benin and Chad's response to Panel third party Question Nos. 44 and 55.

580 *Panel Report,* para. 7.1417.
581 United States' further written submission, paras. 97 and 99, and footnote 52; *Panel Report,* para. 701425.
582 United States' further written submission, paras. 97 and 99, and footnote 52; *Panel Report,* para. 701425.
583 *Panel Report,* para. 7.1436.
584 Brazil's further written submission, para. 265; *Panel Report,* paras. 7.1424 and 7.1435. Specifically, Brazil argued that the phrase "world market share" of the SCM should be interpreted to mean a Member's share of the world export market.

found that Brazil had "not established a prima facie case of violation of Article 6.3(d) or Article 5(c) of the SCM Agreement."[585]

Further, Brazil argued that the US violated 6.3(c) of the SCM by suppressing cotton prices around the world.[586] Basic economic analysis demonstrated that by increasing US supply, price for cotton was reduced. Given the global integration of cotton markets, most of which are influenced by US production and export levels, overproduction severely and adversely affected those markets. As a result, adverse effects were realized by the producers in the affected markets, especially the livelihoods of poor farmers in Africa, Central Asia, and Latin America. Due to the price-suppressing effects of US actions, incomes of cotton producers in these countries are reduced by usurping opportunities by these producers to earn hundreds of millions of US dollars over the years assessed.[587] These effects were recognized and given evidentiary weight, but the Panel did not base its decision on the serious prejudice alleged by the third parties.[588] As the Panel concluded, it took "full account of the interest of *all* Members – including those of least-developed Members – in these dispute settlement proceedings in accordance with the rights and obligations provided for in Part III of the SCM Agreement."[589]

---

585   *Panel Report*, para. 7.1465.
586   Brazil's further written submission, paras. 83–89; *Panel Report*, para. 7.1253.
587   For example, Footnote 1330 of the *Panel Report*: "According to Benin and Chad, the Oxfam report – using data from the International Cotton Advisory Committee – estimates that in 2001 alone, sub-Saharan exporters lost $302 million as a direct consequence of United States cotton subsidies." The Report further notes that Benin's actual cotton export earnings in 2001/02 were $124 million. However, had United States subsidies been withdrawn, Benin's export earnings are estimated to have been $157 million. Therefore, the value lost to Benin as a result of United States subsidies was $33 million. Chad's cotton export earnings in 2001/02 were $63 million, although in the absence of United States subsidies, Chad would have earned $79 million, thus reflecting a loss of $16 million. For the period from 1999/2000 to 2001/2002, Oxfam estimates a total cumulative loss of export earnings of $61 million for Benin and $28 million for Chad. Benin and Chad agree with Oxfam when it emphasizes, "the small size of several West African economies and their high levels of dependence on cotton inevitably magnify the adverse effects of United States subsidies. For several countries, US policy has generated what can only be described as a major economic shock." *See,* Benin and Chad's written submission to the resumed session of the first substantive meeting, paras. 19–21.
588   *Panel Report*, paras. 7.1414–1415.
589   *Panel Report*, paras. 7.1414–1415.

Of course, probably the most important evidence is the nature, design, and magnitude of the subsidies themselves.[590] The largest and most trade-distorting domestic subsidy is the US Marketing Loan program, which guarantees farmers revenue of 52 cents per pound of cotton production.[591] If prices are below that level, the US government will pay the difference.[592] In addition, the US offers counter-cyclical payments that provide additional disbursements based on a target price of 72.4 cents per pound.[593] Furthermore, the United States offers its farmers heavily subsidized Crop Insurance policies that insure US cotton farmers against losses from adverse weather conditions, diseases and low prices.[594] Also, the US government pays US cotton farmers non-price triggered Direct Payment income support of 6.67 cents per pound of historic production.[595] Finally, the domestic Step-2 subsidies paid domestic textile users of US cotton the difference between the higher US domestic price and the lower world market price for cotton, thereby effectively increasing demand for US cotton from US textile producers. To that same end, the US offers export credit guarantees to support the export of cotton. This benefits US exporters in that it provides financing for the import of cotton, effectively increasing the demand for US cotton by subsidizing foreign consumers, many of which would be unable to secure financing for their purchases through other means. As mentioned, *supra*, on the export side, the USDA, through the Commodity Credit Corporation (CCC), provides subsidies by financing the exportation of cotton (and other commodities) through export credit guarantee programs. The most significant and challenged programs were the GSM 102, GSM 103 and Supplier Credit Guarantee Programme (SCGP) programs.[596] Brazil argued that

---

590 For a greater description of the challenged US subsidy programs, *see*, Chapter 2 of this book.

591 *Panel Report*, paras. 7.1205. Specifically, as indicated in footnote 1327, Sumner's simulations estimated the cumulative effects of the subsidies, for MY 1999–2002, to approximately be: "a 28 per cent increase in United States upland cotton acreage; a 29 per cent increase in United States production, a 41 per cent increase in United States exports and a 12.6 per cent decrease in world price (A-Index). In terms of relative magnitude, from subsidies with largest to smallest effect: 1. Marketing loan/LDP; 2. User marketing (Step 2) payments; 3. Crop insurance payments; 4. CCP payment; 5. DP payments."

592 In relation to the economic analysis, *supra*, the Marketing Loan program was shown to have suppressed US prices by over thirty (30) percent.

593 *Panel Report*, paras. 7.223–7.226.

594 *Panel Report*, paras. 7.227–7.232.

595 *Panel Report*, paras. 7.218–7.222.

596 *Panel Report*, paras. 7.236–7.244.

the collective effect of all these programs to benefit US cotton farmers was to substantially isolate them from market price effects by covering their costs of production and sustaining very high levels of production and exportation of cotton that otherwise would have been planted to other crops or to no crops at all.

In its argumentation, the US primarily focused on the effects of the US direct and countercyclical payments, arguing that the subsidies did not depend on current production and were therefore not in violation because, by having no production effects, were non-distortive. Brazil counter argued that US cotton producers would have lost over $300 per acre of cotton planted during the specified time period[597] and showed that these US subsidy programs were essential to covering production costs for US producers. By enabling large numbers of cotton growers to produce cotton that, absent the subsidies, would have been uneconomic, the US increased its cotton production and raised its global market share, as estimated by the USDA, from twenty four (24) percent to forty-two (42) percent from 1999 to 2002 and projected that this trend would increase in the future.[598]

Finally, Brazil argued that US subsidies violated GATT Article XVI because the US used WTO inconsistent means to gain an inequitable share of the world market.[599] As stated, *supra*, the US was able to effectively increase their twenty-four (24) percent market share to forty-two (42) between 1999 and 2002. The application of subsidies was in essence the purchasing of market share at the expense of cotton producers in developing and least developing countries. However, the Panel chose "in light of our findings of inconsistency with Articles 5(c) and 6.3(c) of the *SCM Agreement*, and for these reasons, we see no need for an additional examination of 'serious prejudice' for the purposes of Article XVI:1 of the *GATT 1994*."[600] In essence, the Panel determined that its findings of price suppression for marketing loan program, user marketing (Step 2), MLA and CCP payments were sufficient as well as its related determination, under Article XVI:3 of GATT that the US had obtained an "inequitable share of world export trade" with regards to export subsidies.

---

597 *Panel Report*, paras. 7.1353–7.1355. Further, relying on Exhibit BRA-109, the Panel found "that United States upland cotton producers rely on United States government subsidies to cover their production costs." *See*, BRA-109, 2001 then-Chairman of the National Cotton Council before the US House Agriculture Committee.
598 *Panel Report*, para. 7.1351, 7.1283.
599 *Panel Report*, para. 7.1466.
600 *Panel Report*, para. 7.1476.

Threat of Serious Prejudice: A similar legal analysis was conducted under Articles 5(c) and 6.3(c) and (d) of the SCM as well as Articles XVI:1 and XVI:3 of the GATT 1994, wherein it prohibits not only present adverse effects but the use of subsidies in a manner that *threatens* to cause adverse effects. In making this argument, parties must demonstrate the likelihood for potential future harm. Article 5(c) of the SCM sets forth tests for determining the threat to serious prejudice. Brazil argued that the Panel should find the US subsidies at issue threaten to cause serious prejudice.[601] First, Brazil argued that five (5) of the subsidies in the 2002 US Farm Bill are mandatory and, second, the new measures under the 2002 Farm Bill are similar to the previous measures challenged, which are required to continue for the perceived duration from 2003–2007. Third, the nature of the subsidies challenged is evidence of 'threat.'[602] The programs under the 2002 Farm Bill, specifically those identified above as well as the export credit guarantee programs (discussed, *infra*), cause a threat of adverse effects in the form of serious prejudice to the interests of Brazil. Substantively, these include (1) significant price suppression (2) a further increased US world market share and (3) a continued inequitable US share of the world export trade. Fourth, in determining future projections, Brazil argued that, given the gap between cost of production and market returns established earlier, the revenue guaranteed by the US programs would incentivize farmers to continue to produce cotton, if not increase their production. In other words, absent US subsidies, farmers would not choose to produce cotton. Fifth, given this incentive, it could be projected that levels of exports would remain high from the US and price-suppression effects would continue to cause adverse effects in Members' markets, even if world prices were to fluctuate.[603] Brazil was able to establish that cotton production in the US would continue at a high rate in future marketing years and there would be continued price-suppressing effects on world cotton prices from massive US subsidies. Brazil relied on the evidence provided to establish its arguments on current adverse effects, and to demonstrate that serious prejudice occurred in the past.

The 2002 Farm Bill increased the level of support to cotton producers by reintroducing an artificially high cotton target price, increasing Step 2 payments, and increasing the marketing loan rate for the crop. Per the evidence provided by Brazil, it was shown that the price levels at the time and projected price levels indicated that the Marketing Loan and counter-cyclical payments

---

601 *Panel Report*, para. 7.1478.
602 *Panel Report*, para. 7.1480.
603 Direct Payment payments, crop insurance and export credit guarantees are not impacted by market price fluctuations.

would be made throughout the duration of the 2002 Farm Bill. These were characterized as entitlement programs, mandating that subsidies be given, regardless of the effects on trading partners. In these projections, supported by *inter alia* USDA reports and US Senators' statement, it was deemed that there was a threat of serious prejudice for the future years. Under WTO law, Brazil argued that the Panel could find the subsidies as non-compliant with commitments made by the US. If the subsidies caused serious prejudice, it was argued that no US provisions stem from, or would otherwise control, the flow of US cotton subsidies.[604] As argued, Brazil asked the Panel to consider in relation to the SCM and GATT provisions whether, along with the issue of mandated payments, there were effective limits to the volume of production, exports, or US budgetary expenditures related to cotton.[605] In order to establish this argumentation, Brazil again relied on evidence derived from the USDA and FAPRI model. Finally, Brazil argued that increasing reliance by US cotton producers on export sales would enhance the price suppressing effects of the subsidies, given US exports will be directly in competition with other non-US producers. Brazil emphasized the especially adverse harm of the Step 2 payments and export credit guarantees in making this argument.

The primary US defense was that the test Brazil used to argue "threat of" serious prejudice was incorrect.[606] Further, the US argued that prices were high at that time, triggering few price-triggered subsidy payments. As a result, the production-enhancing effect of the US subsidies did not rise to the level of causing adverse effects under Articles 5 and 6 of the SCM. Therefore, no theoretical threat was clearly foreseen and there was no 'imminent' likelihood of future serious prejudice, given the current market conditions.[607] In developing its argument, the US relied on Article 15.7 of the SCM that sets forth the injury standard applicable.[608] This argument was refuted by Brazil on the basis that the SCM does not require 'imminence' and the challenge was redirected to emphasize that the subsidies are built into the US agricultural policy regime, incentivizing overproduction and cut off investment and non-US production.[609] In other words, Brazil argued that the mere existence of the programs being challenged constituted a structural element of the global trade of cotton that effectively prevented investment in cotton production by non-US players

---

604   *Panel Report*, para. 7.891.
605   *Panel Report*, para. 7.1479.
606   *Panel Report*, para. 7.1481.
607   *Panel Report*, para. 7.1481 and footnote 1548 on p. 341.
608   *Panel Report*, para. 7.1481 and footnote 1548 on p. 341.
609   *Panel Report*, paras. 7.1498 and 7.1502–1503.

by promoting US overproduction and consequently suppressing world market prices. By providing a revenue safety net for US producers, US subsidies maintained and enhanced the trade distorting effects of US cotton overproduction. Further, and significant to the threat of serious prejudice claim, was the permanency of the US measures. It was stressed that the US government could not stop the flow of these subsidies under the framework that existed in the 2002 Farm Bill. Therefore, no US law could control or allow Congress to intervene when prices fall or once US subsidies cause serious prejudice to other cotton-producing WTO Members.

Findings: On the matter of Brazil's 'threat of' serious prejudice, the Panel determined that serious prejudice included the concept of threat[610] and therefore, given its present serious prejudice rulings, the US already had an obligation to remove the non-compliant measures. Similar rulings were found with regards to Brazil's SCM Articles 5(c) and 6.3(d) claims.[611] A summation of both the present and threat of serious prejudice rulings are herein offered.

In sum, with regards to the Panel's serious prejudice findings, the following should be noted. The Panel found that three (3) of the price-contingent subsidies – the marketing loan, the counter-cyclical (and the predecessor market loss assistance subsidies), and the domestic Step-2 subsidies – collectively caused significant price suppression in the world market during the reference period of 1999–2002.[612] However, the Panel declined to include direct payment, crop insurance, and cottonseed subsidies in the pool of subsidies that it found to cause significant price suppression because of their "non-price contingent nature" and the Panel's view that these measures "are more directed at income support." Accordingly, the Panel held that "this combination attenuates the nexus between these subsidies with the subsidized product and the single effects-related variable – world price – [and] are of a different nature, and thus effect, than the other (price-contingent) subsidies..."[613]

In making its determination that the US subsidies caused significant price suppression in the world cotton market, the Panel made a number of key factual findings. First, the Panel found that there is an integrated world market for cotton that is impacted by cotton supply and demand factors around the world

---

610   *Panel Report*, para. 7.1487–7.1495.
611   *Panel Report*, paras. 7.1494–7.1503.
612   However, the Panel ultimately found that it was unable to find a clear causal link to Brazil's particular price suppression. As discussed in Section XX below, this finding highlights the need to focus on the particular nature and effect of various subsidies in relation to the type of serious prejudice being challenged.
613   *Panel Report*, para. 7.1307.

and that the world market is integrated by a global price discovery mechanism that impacts cotton prices worldwide.[614]

Second, the Panel found that the United States was a major player in the world cotton market,[615] being the largest exporter of cotton, with a roughly 40 percent market share, and the second largest producer of cotton, accounting for roughly 20 percent of world production. The importance of the United States for the world cotton market also means that supply effects in the United States have a major impact on the world market. Indeed, the evidence showed that US cotton subsidies increased the US supply of cotton at the same time that prices fell.[616]

Third, the Panel analyzed the nature of the US subsidies at issue in this case and found that the US Marketing Loan program, the Step 2 payments and the Counter-Cyclical Payments caused significant price suppression in the world market by enhancing and maintaining high-cost US cotton production.[617] In particular, such US cotton production increased significantly at a time of falling cotton prices. The Panel found that this was only possible due to the nature of the price-triggered US Marketing Loan and Counter-Cyclical Payments providing increased support at times of falling cotton prices.[618] The Panel found that without these subsidies, the average US farmer would not have been able to produce cotton.[619] Further, Brazil argued that, by enabling producers to produce at a profit when, absent the price-contingent and non-price contingent subsidies, such production would be uneconomic in many instances, such subsidies contribute to US production levels and are necessarily tied to global price suppression and serious prejudice. The Panel declined to aggregate programs not contingent on price with those price contingent subsidies, but found that price suppression had occurred within the meaning of Article 6.3(c) of the SCM in line with the reasoning proffered, *supra*.[620]

Thus, the evidence showed that, during 1999–2002, US subsidies played a crucial role in maintaining and expanding US cotton production, increasing US cotton exports and suppressing cotton prices around the world.[621] However, the Panel did not make a finding on the exact level of production and trade

---

614   *Panel Report*, paras. 7.1230–7.1274.
615   *Panel Report*, paras. 7.1281–7.1285, 7.1348.
616   *Panel Report*, para. 7.1351.
617   *Panel Report*, paras. 7.1289–7.1295, 7.1349.
618   *Panel Report*, paras. 7.1286–7.1288, and 7.1290–7.1307.
619   *Panel Report*, paras. 7.1347–7.1355.
620   *Panel Report*, paras. 7.1290–1307.
621   *Panel Report*, para. 7.1296.

effects that caused significant price suppression, even though Brazil presented a number of studies that quantitatively demonstrated these effects.[622]

Brazil, as well as the participating African third parties, also produced evidence showing that the price-suppressing effects of the US cotton subsidies cost Brazilian and other third country cotton producers hundreds of millions of US dollars over the previous years.[623] Countries most affected by the low cotton prices include Brazil, but also least developed counties in West Africa, among them Mali, Benin, and Chad. The Panel took the evidence into consideration in determining serious prejudice, but did not base its decision on the harm caused.[624]

The two legal issues the Panel first identified were (1) pursuant to footnote 13 of the SCM Agreement, to what extent does serious prejudice include threat of serious prejudice and (2) pursuant to Article XVI:1 of the GATT 1994, what is the meaning of "...serious prejudice to the interests of any other Member is caused *or* threatened by any such subsidization?"[625] In terms of the "threat" of serious prejudice, the Panel found that "serious prejudice *includes* a threat of serious prejudice" as cited in the legal provision.[626] The Panel used this reasoning to confirm the second determination, which was as follows:

> We believe that 'threat' of serious prejudice refers to something distinct from serious prejudice. However, in terms of the rising continuum of seriously prejudicing another Member's interests, that ascends from a "threat" of "serious prejudice" up to "serious prejudice," we see "serious prejudice" as necessarily *including* the concept of a "threat" and *exceeding* the presence of a "threat" for purposes of answering the relevant inquiry.

To that end the Panel determined that a finding of either serious prejudice, threat of serious prejudice, or both could appropriately trigger Article 7 SCM remedies.[627] In other words, there is an identical understanding under both the SCM Article 5(c) and paragraph 1 of Article XVI of GATT 1994 that serious prejudice includes threat of serious prejudice. The Panel then applied this

---

622 *Panel Report*, paras. 7.1179–7.1190. Further, the Panel specifically noted that there was no need to quantify the amount, but recognized that the information is available. *See, Panel Report*, para. 7.1300 at Section VII:D and footnote 895 indicating the initial FAPRI results then subsequent USDA submissions of the relevant numbers by Brazil.
623 *Panel Report*, para. 7.1400.
624 *Panel Report*, para. 7.1415.
625 *Panel Report*, paras. and 7.1487–7.1503.
626 *Panel Report*, para. 7.1493.
627 *Panel Report*, paras. 7.1494–7.1495.

legal analysis to the evidence presented and found that the measures in question caused "present" serious prejudice. Therefore, the US was already required to take steps to implement those rulings. Further, the Panel noted that it was not necessary for it to examine all legal claims, but rather, only those that would resolve the matter in issue.[628] As pertaining to Brazil's "threat" of serious prejudice claim, the Panel chose not to address the claims, stating:

> the basket of measure in question may be so significantly transformed or manifestly different from the measures that are currently in question that it is not necessary or appropriate to address Brazil's claims of threat of serious prejudice under Articles 5(c) and 6.3(c) of the SCM Agreement.[629]

It is important to note that in both cases of actual and threatened serious prejudice, the Panel found that Brazil had erroneously relied on an incorrect interpretation of the phrase "world market share" of the SCM. Therefore, the Panel ruled that Brazil had not established a prima facie case.[630] In other words, the Panel chose not to consider the world effects. Rather, its rulings covered 'Brazil only' effects. This is a significant lesson learned for third parties that, unless they are co-complainants, the Panel will not consider (and consequently give a remedy) for the effects suffered to their markets. However, as mentioned, *supra*, it is noteworthy that the evidence and arguments made by third parties were considered and weighed significantly in determining whether and to what degree price suppression was taking place.[631] Further, as noted above, the Panel ultimately found that it was unable to find a clear causal link to Brazil's particular price suppression. This finding highlights the need to focus on the particular nature and effect of various subsidies in relation to the type of serious prejudice being challenged.

In conclusion, the Panel in the original proceedings found that the Peace Clause is not an affirmative defense, but that Brazil's claims were not barred because the production flexibility contract and direct payments, as well as the legislative and regulatory provisions that establish and maintain them, do not satisfy the conditions of Article 13 of the Agreement on Agriculture.[632] In a similar line of reasoning, the Panel found that the volume and nature of the

---

628 *Panel Report*, para. 7.1510.
629 *Panel Report*, paras. 7.1498–1503.
630 *Panel Report*, para. 7.1504.
631 *Panel Report*, para. 7.1415.
632 *Panel Report*, paras. 8.1(a)–(b).

measures in question in the case exceeded the requisite conditions of the Agreement on Agriculture, making them non-exempt from Brazil's challenges based on paragraph 1 of Article XVI of the GATT 1994 or Articles 5 and 6 of the SCM.[633] The Panel made several rulings regarding export credit guarantees. Generally, with regards to ECGs on cotton and other commodities not listed in the US schedule of export subsidy commitments, and for rice, are *per se* subsidies that circumvent US export subsidy commitments under the Agreement on Agriculture.[634] With regards to unscheduled products not supported by the programs under review, the Panel found that circumvention was not found.[635] Further, the Panel found that the Step 2 payments to US cotton users and exporters were import substitution subsidies prohibited by Articles 3.1(b) and 3.2 of the SCM.[636] These are not exempt from the Peace Clause, and are deemed inconsistent with US obligations, prohibited under both the AoA and SCM agreements.[637] Finally, the Panel ruled that the price-contingent subsidies programs caused significant price suppression in the world market for cotton during the relevant years. Consequently, this price suppression caused serious prejudice to Brazil.[638] To that end, the Panel found that the US had "nullified or impaired benefits accruing to Brazil" and recommended the US to eliminate the prohibited subsidies, Step 2 and export credit guarantees by July 2005, and remove the adverse effects of or withdraw the remaining subsidies by September 2005.[639] As stated by the Panel:

> We recommend...the United States bring its measures...into conformity with the *Agreement on Agriculture;* withdraw the prohibited subsidies... without delay...[and]...upon adoption of this report, the United States is under an obligation to 'take appropriate steps to remove the adverse effects or...withdraw the subsidy.'[640]

In response to the decision, the US communicated its intention to comply with the recommendations and rulings of the Panel at a DSB meeting on 20 April, 2005. Specifically, the US emphasized that it wished to take measures to ensure that its WTO obligations were met and had commenced assessing how it might

---

633 *Panel Report*, para. 8.1(c).
634 *Panel Report*, para. 8.1(d)(i).
635 *Panel Report*, para. 8.1(d)(ii).
636 *Panel Report*, paras. 8.1(e)–(f).
637 *Panel Report*, paras. 8.1(e)–(f).
638 *Panel Report*, para. 8.1(g).
639 *Panel Report*, paras. 8.2–8.3.
640 *Panel Report*, para. 8.3(d).

do so.[641] The US relayed that it would need a reasonable period of time to achieve this aim.[642]

5.5 Appellate Body Proceedings

Within the dispute settlement mechanism of the WTO, once a final panel report has been issued, it may either be submitted to the DSB to be considered for adoption[643] or parties may lodge an appeal[644] to the Appellate Body.[645] The Appellate Body is recognized as "the most innovative aspect of the Understanding on Dispute Settlement."[646] Unlike panels, the Appellate Body is a permanent body within the WTO, established under Article 17.1 of the DSU and three (3) of its seven (7) members sit as a division to review decisions. If an appeal is lodged, Article 17.6 restricts the review to "issues of law covered in the panel report and legal interpretations developed by the panel."[647] The appeal process begins only after the appellate simultaneously notifies the DSB and Appellate Body of its decision to do so.[648] The right of appeal is reserved to the

---

641 "Subsidies on Upland Cotton," USTR website: <http://www.ustr.gov/trade-topics/enforcement/dispute-settlement-proceedings/wto-dispute-settlement/subsidies-upland-cott> last accessed 2 August, 2010.
642 "Subsidies on Upland Cotton," USTR website: <http://www.ustr.gov/trade-topics/enforcement/dispute-settlement-proceedings/wto-dispute-settlement/subsidies-upland-cott> last accessed 2 August, 2010.
643 Article 16 of the DSU. The adoption process works thus: the final panel report is submitted to the DSB for review, and is adopted within sixty (60) days of its issuance. This is an automatic process that occurs unless the DSB reaches a negative consensus not to do so. For a more detailed explanation, *see*, Desta, M.G., *The Law of International Trade in Agricultural Products: from GATT 1947 to the WTO Agreement on Agriculture*, Kluwer Law International, Dordrecht, The Netherlands, © 2002, pp. 188–192.
644 Article 17.4 of the DSU.
645 Desta, M.G., *The Law of International Trade in Agricultural Products: from GATT 1947 to the WTO Agreement on Agriculture*, Kluwer Law International, Dordrecht, The Netherlands, © 2002, pp. 188–192.
646 Lowenfeld, A., *International Economic Law*, Second Ed., © Oxford University Press, (2008), p. 178.
647 For an overview of the role and functioning of the Appellate Body, *See*, Lowenfeld, A., *International Economic Law*, Second Ed., © Oxford University Press, (2008), pp. 178–184 and Van den Bossche, P., *The Law and Policy of the World Trade Organization*, Second Ed., © Cambridge University Press, (2008), pp. 288–298.
648 Article 16.4 of the DSU and Rule 20(1) of the Working Procedures. The Notice of Appeal, or any Cross-appeals (required to be submitted within twelve (12) days and titled Notice of Other Appeal) become official WT/DS documents.

parties of the dispute, and third parties may not lodge an appeal without either the complainant or respondent. However, if an appeal is lodged, third parties are able to submit statements independently from the primary parties to the dispute. Generally, the Appellate Body is required to issue its decision within sixty (60) days (ninety (90) days by exception) from the date of receipt of a party's "intent to appeal."[649] In subsidy cases involving the SCM, the deadlines are shortened to thirty (30) and sixty (60) days, by exception.

In *Cotton*, the United States chose to appeal most of the key findings of the original Panel and Brazil challenged an other of the findings in a cross-appeal. Of the Appellate Body at the time of the appeals, Merit E. Janow, Luiz Olavo Baptista and A.V. Ganesan were arbitrarily chosen to review the Panel's decision. Due to the complexity of the case, the ninety (90) day deadline was extended.[650] Similar to the procedures of the panel stage, several of the third parties chose to make submissions to the AB, independent of Brazil and the US, throughout the appellate process.[651]

Specifically, the US challenged the AoA findings of Articles 6.3(c), 9.1(a), 10.1 and 10.2, 13(a) and (b) and the SCM findings under Article 3.1(a) and (b).[652] Further, the US chose to appeal the findings regarding the terms of reference and the application of burden of proof chosen by the Panel for the SCM. Brazil, in its cross-appeal, challenged the Panel's findings under Article 10.1 of the AoA, GATT Article XVI and Article 6.3 of the SCM, the findings on the ETI Act, the Panel's decision to exercise judicial economy during the interim review, and the ruling on Brazil's export credit guarantees as export subsidies claim pursuant to Articles 1.1 and 3.1(a) of the SCM. The Appellate Body rejected all of the US issues under appeal, largely on the same basis as the Panel, but changed the reasoning somewhat in some important ways.

Peace Clause: The Appellate Body affirmed all of the Panel's "peace clause" determinations as pertaining to both the green box and non-green box claims.

---

649   Article 17.5 of the DSU and Desta, M.G., *The Law of International Trade in Agricultural Products: from GATT 1947 to the WTO Agreement on Agriculture*, Kluwer Law International, Dordrecht, The Netherlands, © 2002, pp. 188–192.

650   In the consultations, the AB determined that given the complexity of the case as well as logistical issues (e.g. translation services and case load), the deadline would need to be extended.

651   Arguments from the following third parties were included in the AB Report: Argentina, Australia, Benin & Chad, Canada, China, EU, India, New Zealand, and the Separate Customs Territory of Taiwan, Penghu, Kinmen and Matsu. *See, Appellate Body Report*, paras. 194–248, or pp. 67–84.

652   There were additional procedural claims brought in the original appeal. However, these matters did not directly fall into the scope of the thesis of this book and are not, therefore, addressed.

First, the Appellate Body reviewed the US claim that certain of its measures, specifically the planting flexibility contract payments, direct payments, and the regulatory provisions supporting them, were in compliance with Annex 2 of the AoA as proper green box domestic support measures that did not distort trade or production, and were therefore sheltered from challenge under 13(a) of the AoA.[653] However, the Appellate Body did not agree with the US argumentation and, instead, upheld the Panel's finding that conditioning payments to producers on their compliance with planting flexibility limitations with certain products, while maintaining flexibility to produce certain other products, was correctly interpreted to mean that the payments were related to the type of production undertaken after the base period. Therefore, pursuant to paragraph 6(b) of Annex 2 of the AoA, the flexibility contract and direct payments were not "decoupled income support."[654] As a result, they are not green box measures exempt from US reduction commitments and could be properly challenged by Brazil as support measures "covered by the chapeau to paragraph (b) of Article 13, and are to be taken into account in the analysis of that provision."[655] In reviewing the planting flexibility limitations claim,[656] the AB noted that the Panel found that the planting flexibility limitations in the case "significantly constrain" production decisions. However, per paragraph 1 of Annex 2, setting forth domestic support rules for green box measures, the AB found that the case did not present a situation where such limitations had "no, or at most minimal" trade-distorting or production effects per the "fundamental requirement"[657] of green box measures.[658]

In making this determination, the Appellate Body undertook extensive analysis of Paragraph 6, setting forth the requisite elements of decoupled income support to determine whether the United States' measures were direct

---

653 *Appellate Body Report*, paras. 313–315. Further, it should be noted, as the AB found, "Accordingly, domestic support that conforms fully to the provisions of Annex 2 – that is 'green box' support, which is exempt from the domestic support reduction obligations of the *Agreement on Agriculture* – is also exempt, during the implementation period, from actions based on Article XVI of GATT 1994 and the actionable subsidies provisions of Part III of the *SCM Agreement*." *Appellate Body Report*, para. 319.

654 *Appellate Body Report*, para. 342.

655 *Appellate Body Report*, paras. 341–342.

656 Article 13(a) of the AoA.

657 *Appellate Body Report*, para. 333, "The second sentence of paragraph 1 provides that, "[a]ccordingly," green box measures must conform to the basic criteria stated in that sentence, "plus" the policy-specific criteria and conditions set out in the remaining paragraphs of Annex 2, including those in paragraph 6."

658 *Appellate Body Report*, paras. 333–334.

payments entitled to exemption from reduction commitments. In reviewing each subparagraph, the Appellate Body established that: eligibility for decoupled income support must fall within "clearly-defined criteria" in a "defined and fixed base period;" be completely severed from the payments and type and volume of production in that base period as well as prices and factors of production employed after that base period.[659] Most importantly, the AB emphasized that "no production shall be required in order to receive... payments."[660] In reviewing the United States' production flexibility contract and direct payment measures, the issue concerned the "partial exclusion combining planting flexibility and payments with the reduction or elimination of the payments when the excluded crops are produced, while providing payments even when no crops are produced at all."[661] The issue of whether the choice of crops planted affected payments under the production flexibility contract or direct payment programs was not contested. Instead, the US claimed that payments under these programs are not "related to" the type of production proscribed by paragraph 6(b).[662] The AB chose to apply the Panel's broad ordinary meaning of the term "related to," encompassing both positive and negative associations to the requisite elements of paragraph 6, instead of the more limited interpretation of the term requested by the United States to narrow the scope to only positive connections, in order to meet the objective of the provision to decouple payments from production decisions.[663] Further, the AB ruled that a distinction exists between paragraphs 6(b) and (e), where in the latter case, there is an explicit reference to a positive requirement to produce.[664] The reasoning proffered was:

---

659   *Appellate Body Report*, para. 321.
660   *Appellate Body Report*, para. 321.
661   *Appellate Body Report*, para. 322.
662   *Appellate Body Report*, para. 323.
663   *Appellate Body Report*, para. 324–325.
664   *Appellate Body Report*, para. 327–328. Specifically, the AB analyzed: "The United States seems to argue that the Panel's interpretation of the relationship between paragraphs 6(b) and 6(e) would subsume paragraph 6(e) within the scope of paragraph 6(b), thereby rendering it redundant. In our view, however, paragraph 6(e) continues to serve a purpose distinct from that of paragraph 6(b). It highlights a different aspect of decoupling income support. In prohibiting Members from making green-box measures contingent on production, paragraph 6(e) implies that Members are allowed, in principle, to require no production at all. Accordingly, payments conditioned on a total ban on any production may qualify as decoupled income support under paragraph 6(e). Even assuming that payments contingent on a total production ban could be seen to relate the amount of the payment to the *volume* of production within the meaning of paragraph 6(b) – the volume

We agree with the Panel that a partial exclusion of some crops from payments has the potential to channel production towards the production of crops that remain eligible for payments. In contrast to a total production ban, the channelling of production that may follow from a partial exclusion of some crops from payments will have *positive* production effects as regards crops eligible for payments. The extent of this will depend on the scope of the exclusion. We note in this regard that the Panel found, as a matter of fact, that planting flexibility limitations at issue in this case "significantly constrain production choices available to PFC and DP payment recipients and effectively eliminate a significant proportion of them." The fact that farmers may continue to receive payments if they produce nothing at all does not detract from this assessment because, according to the Panel, it is not the option preferred by the "overwhelming majority" of farmers, who continue to produce some type of permitted crop. In the light of these findings by the Panel, we are unable to agree with the United States' argument that the planting flexibility limitations only negatively affect the production of crops that are excluded.[665]

The Appellate Body found further support for its interpretation provided in paragraph 11 of Annex 2. Specifically, the AB emphasized that several subparagraphs of 11 are similarly written as paragraph 6.[666] In reliance on the drafters'

---

of production being nil – giving meaning and effect to both paragraphs 6(b) and 6(e) suggests a reading of paragraph 6(b) that would not disallow a total ban on any production. In addressing the United States' argument on this point, we recall that the measures at issue in this appeal do not provide for payments contingent on a *total ban* on production of *any* crops. The measures at issue here combine payments and planting flexibility in respect of certain covered crops with the reduction or elimination of such payments when certain other excluded crops are produced. The United States argues that, if paragraph 6(e) means that a Member may require a producer not to produce a particular product, 'it would not make sense to then prohibit a Member, under paragraph 6(b), from making the amount of payment contingent on fulfilling that requirement.' However, in our view, the mere fact that under paragraph 6(e) '[n]o production shall be required in order to receive such payments' does not mean that a partial exclusion of certain crops from payments, coupled with production flexibility regarding other crops, must be consistent with paragraph 6(b)."

665 *Appellate Body Report*, para. 329.
666 Specifically, the AB stated, "Indeed, like paragraph 6(b), paragraph 11(b) requires that the 'amount of…payments…shall not be related to…the type or volume of production… undertaken by the producer in any year after the base period.' However, unlike paragraph 6(b), paragraph 11(b) ends with the phrase 'other than as provided for under criterion (e) below.' Criterion 11(e) specifically envisages that 'payments shall not mandate or in any

intention, the AB found that such similarity in the drafting of the language clearly established that the ordinary meaning encompassed both positive and negative connections "between the amount of payments under a program and the type of production undertaken."[667] Finally, the AB upheld the Panel finding that paragraph 6(b) "would not prevent a WTO Member from making illegal the production of certain crops" stressing that paragraph 6 refers to the production of exclusively lawful crops.[668] As such, the Appellate Body upheld the Panel's finding that the measures were not properly decoupled and therefore not sheltered under the Peace Clause.

Next, the Appellate Body reviewed the United States' claim that its non-green box domestic support measures did not "grant support to a specific commodity in excess of that decided during the 1992 marketing year," thereby making the measures non-exempt under the Peace Clause. As the AB set forth, "Subparagraph (ii) to Article 13(b) exempts non-green box domestic support measures described in the chapeau from actions based on Article XVI:1 of GATT 1994 and Articles 5 and 6 of the *SCM Agreement*. This exemption is, however, subject to a proviso and is thus made conditional upon a requirement that 'such measures do not grant support to a specific commodity in excess of that decided during the 1992 marketing year.'" Therefore, the AB emphasized that appellate review in the dispute focused on "the interpretation and application of this proviso to certain United States domestic support measures."[669] First, the AB applied the similar interpretative analysis as the Panel, regarding specificity. However, although the AB findings resulted in a similar ruling, the analysis varied to some degree. Where the Panel found that upland cotton was a specific commodity granted support under the US programs,[670] the Panel had described the ordinary meaning for the term "specific" differently from the AB,[671] requiring that the commodity be clearly identified and the link between

---

way designate the agricultural products to be produced by the recipients except to require them not to produce a particular product.'" *Appellate Body Report*, para. 335.
667 *Appellate Body Report,* para. 336.
668 *Appellate Body Report*, paras. 331–340.
669 *Appellate Body Report*, para. 347.
670 *Appellate Body Report*, para. 361.
671 "We believe, however, that the terms of this definition do not exhaust the scope of measures that may grant 'support to a specific commodity.' We note in this regard that the Panel looked, in applying its test, to factors such as eligibility criteria and payment rates, as well as the relationship between payments and current market prices of the commodity in question. In our view, the Panel was correct to consider such matters, as the requisite link between a measure granting support and a specific commodity may be discerned not just from an explicit specification of the commodity in the text of a measure, as the

the measure and commodity granted support discernable.[672] To that end, the AB stated, "thus, it is not sufficient that a commodity happens to benefit from support, or that support ends up flowing to that commodity by mere coincidence. Rather, the phrase 'such measures' granting 'support to a specific commodity' implies a discernible link between the support-conferring measure and the particular commodity to which support is granted."[673] Further, the AB found that the US argument on the issue was flawed in that it failed to broaden the scope of the relevant Article 13(b)(ii) provision beyond the "product-specific support" stipulation of Article 1 and Annex 3. It dictated that the term could be clarified by reference to the chapeau of Article 13(b)[674] as it identifies the relevant categories of support measures.[675] Therefore, the Appellate Body found that there was no relevant distinction between product and non-product specific support for Article 6 amber box support subject to reduction commitments, measures within *de minimis* levels under the chapeau, blue box support in accordance with Article 6.5 or the development box support of Article 6.2, for purposes of which the AMS calculation has little practical relevance.[676] Therefore, the AB agreed with the Panel that the proviso allows measures in the chapeau to qualify and be analyzed provided there was a "discernible link between the measure and commodity."[677] This differed from the United States' position that would not have allowed such measures (except product-specific amber box support) to be considered.[678] Therefore, in applying Article 13(b)(ii), the AB had to assess whether the non-green box domestic support measures during the implementation period exceeded the support

---

Panel's test – on its face – seems to imply, but also from an analysis of factors such as the characteristics, structure or design of that measure." *Appellate Body Report*, para. 363.

672   *Appellate Body Report*, para. 362. The AB stated that "the Panel described the ordinary meaning of the term 'specific' as 'clearly or explicitly defined; precise; exact; definite' and as 'specially or peculiarly pertaining to a particular thing or person, or a class of these; peculiar (*to*).'"

673   *Appellate Body Report*, para. 362.

674   "…domestic support measures that conform fully to the provisions of Article 6 of this Agreement including direct payments that conform to the requirements of paragraph 5 thereof, as reflected in each Member's Schedule, as well as domestic support within *de minimis* levels and in conformity with paragraph 2 of Article 6…"

675   *Appellate Body Report*, para. 367.

676   The only type of domestic support clearly excluded from support covered by Article 13(b) is green box support, which does not need to conform with the provisions of Article 6, but rather must conform with the provisions of Annex 2. Green box support, however, qualifies for the exemption from actions provided by Article 13(a).

677   *Appellate Body Report*, para. 368.

678   *Appellate Body Report*, para. 368.

granted to upland cotton in the 1992 marketing year.[679] The AB applied a two-part test: (1) whether the non-green box measure conferred support on a specific commodity (here, upland cotton) and (2) whether there was the requisite discernible link between the US measure and the commodity.[680] With regards to the latter analysis, the AB stated:

> Such a discernible link may be evident where a measure explicitly defines a specific commodity as one to which it bestows support. Such a link might also be ascertained, as a matter of fact, from the characteristics, structure or design of the measure under examination. Conversely, support that does not actually flow to a commodity or support that flows to a commodity by coincidence rather than by the inherent design of the measure cannot be regarded as falling within the ambit of the term "support to a specific commodity."[681]

Although the AB ultimately agreed with the Panel's findings, it did not support Brazil's methodology by which the support was calculated. In applying Article 13(b)(ii) to the challenged measures, the AB first reviewed whether the Panel applied the correct calculation methodology to determine whether support was granted and a discernible link present. Upon review, the AB agreed with the United States that the appropriate calculation under Article 13(b)(ii) should be limited to "payments with respect to upland cotton base acres corresponding to physical acres actually planted with upland cotton" – thereby rejecting the calculation methodology of Brazil.[682] Despite the arguments presented by Brazil with regards to the fruits and vegetables exception, the AB emphasized that the Panel findings were limited to historical base acres payments to producers, and – in line with US argumentation – a link to which, current production could not be extended.[683] Although the AB agreed with this point, it did state that "express reference in the legislation to continued production of upland cotton does not mean that the payments do not grant support to upland cotton...because a link between the four measures at issue and the continued production of upland cotton is discernible from the characteristics, structure and operation of those measures."[684] However, the AB found

---

679 *Appellate Body Report*, para. 371.
680 *Appellate Body Report*, para. 372.
681 *Appellate Body Report*, para. 372.
682 *Appellate Body Report*, para. 375.
683 *Appellate Body Report*, para. 380.
684 *Appellate Body Report*, para. 378.

that the alternative calculation method, the "cotton to cotton" methodology, was appropriate. This methodology allocated, "for each planted acre of upland cotton, payments associated with one upland cotton base acre."[685] Given that this methodology limits the calculation for purposes of Article 13(b)(ii) to base acres that correspond to physical acres actually planted with the crop, it was the preferred methodology to establish the link between the payments and US measures.[686] The Appellate Body concluded,

> We do not, therefore, accept the methodology submitted by Brazil that included, in the Article 13(b)(ii) calculation, payments with respect to both cotton and non-cotton base acres flowing to current production of upland cotton. We believe that only the "cotton to cotton" methodology, included by the Panel in "Attachment to Section VII:D" to its Report as an "appropriate" alternative calculation, sufficiently demonstrates a discernible link between payments under base acre dependent measures (related to upland cotton) and upland cotton.[687]

Further, the AB rejected that the subparagraph of Article 13(b) requires that the calculation methodology must be based solely on those factors that the government can control, relying on a statement by the original Panel.[688] In doing so, the AB distinguished Article 13(b)(ii) terms "grant" and "decided," rejecting the argument that the term "grant" must be read to mean "decided" when determining the 1992 benchmark level of support.[689] The AB further rejected the argument that "unpredictability of producer decisions under planting flexibility rules, *per se*, could modify the specific requirements set out in the proviso to Article 13(b)(ii)". The existence of such unpredictability cannot be a ground to alter the basis of comparison under the proviso to Article 13(b)(ii) from what is actually "grant[ed]" in the implementation period to what is only "decided."[690] Therefore, the AB concluded that "payments with respect to upland cotton base acres to producers currently growing upland

---

685   *Appellate Body Report*, para. 377.
686   *Appellate Body Report*, para. 377.
687   *Appellate Body Report*, para. 380.
688   *Appellate Body Report*, para. 381. Specifically, the Panel had found, "[If] the proviso [to Article 13(b)(ii)] focused on where support was spent due to reasons beyond the control of the government, such as producer decisions on what to produce within a programme, it would introduce a major element of unpredictability into Article 13, and render it extremely difficult to ensure compliance." *Panel Report*, para. 7.487.
689   *Appellate Body Report*, para. 382.
690   *Appellate Body Report*, para. 383.

cotton under the production flexibility contract, market loss assistance, direct payment and counter-cyclical payment measures, calculated in accordance with the 'cotton to cotton' methodology, are support granted to the specific commodity upland cotton in the sense of Article 13(b)(ii) of the Agreement on Agriculture."[691]

Having determined the proper calculation methodology when applying Article 13(b)(ii), the AB next addressed the US appeal regarding the calculation methodology for establishing the value of the price-based payments. Therefore, according to subparagraph (b), the Appellate Body – finding that no guidance was specifically given on how to calculate the support, and considering the fact that neither party challenged how the Panel determined to calculate support – followed a similar approach.[692] The AB identified that paragraph 10 of Annex 3 provides that non-exempt direct payments may be measured using either price gap methodology or budgetary outlay methodology. Although the Panel chose to rely upon actual budgetary outlays, it also included calculations according to price gap methodology as well.[693] In the end, the AB found it unnecessary to choose between the two approaches, given the application of either of the calculation methodologies to the measures at issue resulted in findings that the US had exceed its 1992 marketing year commitments.[694]

Serious Prejudice: The Appellate Body also upheld all "significant price suppression serious prejudice" legal and factual findings that were challenged by the US comprehensive appeal.[695] In reviewing the serious prejudice claims, it followed a similar analysis to the Panel. A preliminary assessment was made whether the Panel had correctly ruled that, in order to find significant price suppression, it must be in the same market. Specifically, the United States refuted the Panel's decision, in line with Brazil's position, that, in order to determine the effect of the subsidy and whether it falls within the meaning of

---

[691] *Appellate Body Report*, para. 384.
[692] It should be noted, "In addressing this issue, we – like the Panel – note that Article 13(b)(ii) gives no specific guidance regarding *how* the 'support' that measures granted in the implementation period or that was decided during the 1992 marketing year should be calculated. The Panel therefore turned to the broader context of the *Agreement on Agriculture* and chose to 'apply the principles of AMS methodology' in accordance with Annex 3 of the *Agreement on Agriculture*, with certain modifications. We observe that, on appeal, neither of the participants, nor indeed any of the third participants that addressed this issue, suggested that the Panel erred in seeking guidance for its calculations in the principles set out in Annex 3." *Appellate Body Report*, para. 388.
[693] *Appellate Body Report*, paras. 388–389.
[694] *Appellate Body Report*, para. 390.
[695] *Appellate Body Report,* paras. 310–496.

Article 6.3(c) of the SCM Agreement, the world market rather than the domestic market of the Member should be considered. Brazil had submitted, specifically, that the relevant market for the case was the world market, including: Brazil, the United States and forty (40) third country markets to which Brazil exports its cotton.[696] Both Brazil and the US interpreted Article 6.3(c) of the SCM Agreement extremely differently. Brazil applied a broad definition, which included any market, whereas the United States requested a narrow market be defined and limited to only those markets where Brazil and the US compete. In applying a broader definition, the US argued that the findings of the Panel were, therefore, inconsistent and erroneous.[697] The AB accepted the Panel's definition of the ordinary meaning of the word "market"[698] and clarified that the product and its trade limited the scope of what constitutes a market as opposed to the definition.[699] Rather, the qualifying language of Article 6.3(c) is the requirement that the effect be in the "same" market.[700] Although other provisions limit the geographic scope of market, the AB agreed with the Panel that 6.3(c) does not explicitly do so, purposefully. "Thus, the ordinary meaning of the word "market" in Article 6.3(c), when read in the context of the other paragraphs of Article 6.3, neither requires nor excludes the possibility of a national market or a world market."[701] The definition of "same market" was found to require that the products be similar and be in competition with one another[702] in a definable market, and "not necessarily sold at the same time and in the same place or country." Therefore, the scope could be a "world market." Therefore, the AB had to construct its own interpretation of this issue, since it was not clearly defined, and ruled – in the case of upland cotton: "If a world market exists for the product in question, Article 6.3(c) does not exclude the possibility of this 'world market' being the 'same market' for the purposes

---

696 *Appellate Body Report*, para. 400.
697 *Appellate Body Report*, para. 402.
698 The Panel described the ordinary meaning of the word "market" as:"a place...with a demand for a commodity or service (*The New Shorter Oxford English Dictionary*, (1993).)"; "a geographical area of demand for commodities or services"; "the area of economic activity in which buyers and sellers come together and the forces of supply and demand affect prices (*Merriam-Webster Dictionary online*.)."
699 *Appellate Body Report*, para. 405.
700 These effects in the same market include: "significant price undercutting," "significant price suppression, price depression [and] lost sales."
701 *Appellate Body Report*, para. 406.
702 The AB pointed out that "determining the area of competition between two products, may depend on several factors such as the nature of the product, the homogeneity of the conditions of competition, and transport costs." *Appellate Body Report*, para. 408.

of a significant price suppression analysis under that Article."[703] To that end, the Panel's decision to consider the "world market" was not incorrect and the AB was "not persuaded by the United States' arguments that the Panel erred with respect to whether United States and Brazilian upland cotton were 'in the same market' according to Article 6.3(c)."[704]

Further, the AB determined that the Panel was correct to rely on the A-Index in assessing the price of upland cotton in the general world market.[705] In sum, the AB ruled,

> ...the Panel found that the A-Index adequately reflected prices in the world market for upland cotton. The Panel also found that "developments in the world upland cotton price would inevitably affect prices" wherever Brazilian and United States upland cotton compete, "due to the nature of the world prices in question and the nature of the world upland cotton market, and the relative proportion of that market enjoyed by the United States and Brazil." It was not necessary, in these circumstances, for the Panel to proceed to a separate analysis of the prices of Brazilian upland cotton in the world market.[706]

Therefore, the AB rejected the US claim that the Panel had erred in its Article 6.3(c) price suppression analysis by failing to examine Brazilian upland cotton prices in its "world market" analysis.[707]

Next, the AB had to determine the central question of whether there was price suppression in the relevant market.[708] Although it did not agree with the Panel's decision to apply the term "price suppression" to both instances of price suppression and price depression, since Article 6.3(c) considered them

---

703 *Appellate Body Report*, para. 408.
704 *Appellate Body Report*, para. 414.
705 *Appellate Body Report*, para. 416.
706 *Appellate Body Report*, para. 417.
707 *Appellate Body Report*, para. 418.
708 *Panel Report*, para. 7.1277..."*Price suppression*" refers to the situation where "prices" – in terms of the "amount of money set for sale of upland cotton" or the "value or worth" of upland cotton – either are prevented or inhibited from rising (i.e. they do not increase when they otherwise would have) or they do actually increase, but the increase is less than it otherwise would have been. *Price depression* refers to the situation where "prices" are pressed down, or reduced. (In the remainder of our analysis, we use the term "price suppression" to refer both to an actual decline (which otherwise would not have declined, or would have done so to a lesser degree) and an increase in prices (which otherwise would have increased to a greater degree). (emphasis added)).

differently, it accepted the definition as correct in its ordinary meaning "when read in conjunction with the French and Spanish versions of Article 6.3(c), as required by Article 33(3) of the *Vienna Convention on the Law of Treaties* (the '*Vienna Convention*')."[709] Further, while not ultimately found to be legally relevant, Brazil and the participating African third parties demonstrated that the price-suppressing effects of the U.S. cotton subsidies cost Brazilian and other third country cotton producers hundreds of millions of U.S. dollars over the past years. Countries most affected by the low cotton prices include Brazil as well as least developed counties in West Africa, including Mali, Benin, and Chad. The AB also found that a specific methodology for determining significant price suppression is not proscribed by Article 6.3(c) and that it did not disagree with the Panel's approach.[710]

In doing so, the AB had to review the sequencing analysis the Panel applied in determining whether the effect of a subsidy is significant price suppression. Again, the AB found little guidance offered expressly in the relevant provision. However, it did note that the Panel's approach was not precluded under the provision and that it did not find any legal error in the approach. This approach was to first determine whether price suppression exists and then, if so, to "examine whether significant price suppression is the effect of the subsidy."[711] The AB did not find a problem with the Panel's decision to therefore separate the issues of price suppression from the effects of the subsidies, though it recognized additional considerations.[712] These included: "(a) the relative magnitude of the United States' production and exports in the world upland cotton market; (b) general price trends; and (c) the nature of the subsidies at issue, and in particular, whether or not the nature of these subsidies is such as to have discernible price suppressive effects."[713] Not only did the AB find these factors to be relevant, but it did not oppose the fact that some of the factors

---

709 *Appellate Body Report*, para. 424.
710 *Appellate Body Report*, para. 427.
711 *Appellate Body Report*, para. 431.
712 *Appellate Body Report*, para. 432. Specifically, the AB noted, "For instance, in its significant price suppression analysis, the Panel could have addressed purely price developments in the world market for upland cotton, such as whether prices fell significantly during the period under examination or whether prices were significantly lower during that period than other periods. Then, in its 'effects' analysis, the Panel could have addressed causal factors related to the nature of the subsidies, their relationship to prices, their magnitude, and their impact on production and exports. In this causal analysis, the Panel could also have addressed factors other than the challenged subsidies that may have been suppressing the prices in question."
713 *Appellate Body Report*, para. 434.

were also considered in the second part of the analysis regarding the effect of the subsidy.[714] Finally, the AB found that in applying this analysis where some cross-over occurs, it is appropriate given that a finding of price suppression requires an analysis of the challenged subsidies and prices in the world market. "Therefore, the fact that the Panel may have addressed some of the same or similar factors in its reasoning as to significant price suppression and its reasoning as to 'effects' is not necessarily wrong."[715]

In its review of the second part of the price suppression analysis, the "effect of the subsidy," the Appellate Body reviewed whether the requisite "causal link" between the challenged subsidies and significant price suppression existed – in other words, whether the subsidies caused price suppression pursuant to Articles 5(c) and 6.3(c) in Part III of the SCM Agreement.[716] The AB recognized that the Panel has some discretion in how it determined the effect of the subsidy,[717] and emphasized that the Panel was correct in considering additional alleged causal factors to ensure that the challenged subsidies were the actual cause[718] of the price suppression.[719] In its final assessment, the AB recognized the extensive and "voluminous" evidential record the Panel, as the initial "triers of fact," collected and reviewed in making its decision.[720] Although there was substantial evidence reviewed, the AB did comment that the Panel could have proffered a greater explanation of its analysis, but that the reasoning provided coupled with evidence on record was not erroneous for its causation analysis.[721] Finally, the AB deviated from the Panel decision with regards to its finding that the correlation between the US subsidies and significant price suppression was sufficient.[722] However, it ultimately agreed with the Panel's approach in applying a long-term analysis to determine the causal link and find that the subsidies provided by the US to its cotton producers allowed them to sell the commodity at a lower price than that necessary to cover their costs of production.[723]

---

714   *Appellate Body Report*, para. 434.
715   *Appellate Body Report*, para. 433.
716   *Appellate Body Report*, para. 435.
717   *Appellate Body Report*, para. 436.
718   The Appellate Body emphasized that the analysis should not be one of causation to determine "injury," as distinguished in the *Anti-Dumping Agreement* and Part V of the SCM Agreement. *Appellate Body Report*, para. 438.
719   *Appellate Body Report*, para. 437.
720   *Appellate Body Report*, para. 458.
721   *Appellate Body Report*, para. 458.
722   *Appellate Body Report*, para. 451.
723   *Appellate Body Report*, para. 453.

The AB also rejected US argumentation regarding the quantification of the amount of subsidies that the Panel had conducted. In terms of the magnitude of subsidies, the AB first pointed out that Article 6.3(c) does not explicitly require the Panel to quantify the amount of the subsidy being challenged. Alternatively, the Panel must ultimately determine whether there was serious prejudice. In doing so, an assessment of the magnitude of subsidies is beneficial to making that determination. As the AB stated, "All other things being equal, the smaller the subsidy for a given product, the smaller the degree to which it will affect the costs or revenue of the recipient, and the smaller its likely impact on the prices charged by the recipient for the product. However, the size of a subsidy is only one of the factors that may be relevant to the determination of the effects of a challenged subsidy. A panel needs to assess the effect of the subsidy taking into account all relevant factors."[724] In its analysis, the AB confirmed that the Panel was correct to focus its analysis on whether the payment(s) was a "specific" subsidy, rather than quantifying the amount of the "benefit" conferred as required by Articles 1 and 2 of the *SCM Agreement*.[725] In sum, the AB determined:

> The provisions of the *SCM Agreement* regarding quantification of subsidies reveal that the methodological approaches to quantification may be quite different, depending on the context and purpose of quantification. The absence of any indication in Article 6.3(c) as to whether one of these methods, or any other method, should be used suggests to us that no such precise quantification was envisaged as a necessary prerequisite for a panel's analysis under Article 6.3(c).[726]

Therefore, the AB ruled that there was not a mandate for the Panel to precisely quantify the subsidies "in order to determine their effect under Article 6.3(c)."[727] Instead, Article 6.3(c) in relation to Article 6.8 and Annex V dictated that the Panel was correct in assessing the magnitude of the subsidy and its relation to the commodity's price in the relevant market when analyzing whether the effect of a subsidy is significant price suppression.[728] Ruling that

---

724   *Appellate Body Report*, para. 461.
725   *Appellate Body Report*, para. 462. Further, the AB analyzed various agreements and similarly concluded that there was not an explicit requirement to quantify the effects. *Appellate Body Report*, para. 463–464.
726   *Appellate Body Report*, para. 465.
727   *Appellate Body Report*, para. 466.
728   Further, the AB did not find a "pass-through" analysis was necessary as was requested by the United States. Specifically, it held, "Therefore, the need for a 'pass-through' analysis under Part V of the *SCM Agreement* is not critical for an assessment of significant price

"a precise, definitive quantification of the subsidy is not required,"[729] the AB concluded that the Panel had not erred in its assessment of the magnitude of subsidies.[730]

Next, the AB addressed the US claim that the panel had erred in finding, with regards to assessing the effect of the subsidy over time "that the payments need not be allocated to the marketing year to which they relate" and making a finding of present serious prejudice related to past recurring subsidy payments, in the absence of a finding "that the past recurring subsidy payments at issue (that is, those from marketing years 1999–2001) had continuing effects at the time of panel establishment."[731] Determining that Article 6.3(c) of the *SCM Agreement* covers both "recurring" and "non-recurring" subsidies, the AB did not find that an assessment of the effect of the subsidies was limited to a particular period of time.[732] The Appellate Body read Article 6.3(c) to require that the "effect" and not "accounting" of the subsidy was required in determining whether the effect of the subsidy may continue beyond the year in which it was paid.[733] It concluded that, in considering the issue in the context of Part III of the *SCM Agreement* as well as in relation to Article 6.4, it is correct to determine the effect beyond the relevant marketing year.[734] Therefore, the AB concluded,

> For these reasons, we are not persuaded by the United States' contention that the effect of annually paid subsidies must be "allocated" or "expensed" solely to the year in which they are paid and that, therefore, the effect of such subsidies cannot be significant price suppression in any subsequent year. We do not agree with the proposition that, if subsidies are paid annually, their effects are also necessarily extinguished annually.[735]

The AB, having upheld the Panel's decision that the effect of the price-contingent subsidies was significant price suppression within the meaning of Article 6.3(c) of the *SCM Agreement*, turned to the final analysis to determine if the

---

suppression under Article 6.3(c) in Part III of the *SCM Agreement*." Rather, the subsidy need only be "properly identified for purposes of significant price suppression under Article 6.3(c) of the *SCM Agreement*." *Appellate Body Report*, para. 471–472.

729 *Appellate Body Report*, para. 467.
730 *Appellate Body Report*, para. 473.
731 *Appellate Body Report*, para. 422.
732 *Appellate Body Report*, para. 475.
733 *Appellate Body Report*, para. 476.
734 *Appellate Body Report*, para. 477–478.
735 *Appellate Body Report*, para. 482.

Panel's determination that the US had caused adverse effects in the form of serious prejudice, contrary to Article 5(c) of the same agreement. Two rationales had been set forth by the Panel for finding significant price suppression and that the price suppression had caused serious prejudice to Brazil pursuant to Article 5(c).[736] Given neither party appealed the determination, under either rationale offered, the AB stated that the relevant findings in paragraphs 7.1390 and 7.1391 would stand "without endorsement or rejection by the Appellate Body."[737]

In conclusion, with regards to the interpretation of Article 6.3(c) by the Panel, the AB found, "the United States has not persuaded us that the Panel committed a legal error in interpreting the relevant legal requirements of Article 6.3(c) or in applying its interpretation to the facts of this case." Finding that the Panel had "set out the findings of fact, the applicability of relevant provisions, and the basic rationale behind this finding, as required by Article 12.7 of the DSU,"[738] the AB determined that "the effect of marketing loan program payments, Step 2 payment, market loss assistance payments, and counter-cyclical payments is significant price suppression within the meaning of Article 6.3(c) of the SCM Agreement."[739]

In reviewing the serious prejudice claim, the Appellate Body chose to employ judicial economy on the issue of whether the Panel had properly interpreted the phrase "world market share" for purposed of Article 6.3(d) of the SCM Agreement.[740] Specifically, Brazil's Appellant's submission had noted its disagreement with the original Panel's finding that only price-contingent subsidies – but not Direct Payment, Crop Insurance, and Cottonseed payments – could be found to contribute to significant price suppression. In affirming the Panel's reliance on only the price-contingent subsidies, the Appellate Body made the following statement: "We do not exclude the possibility that challenged subsidies that are not 'price-contingent' (to use the Panel's term) could have some effect on production and exports and contribute to price suppression."[741] This statement suggests that the Appellate Body may be receptive to the collective effect of subsidies "contributing to" *production* – such as crop insurance and direct payments – even if those subsidies are not linked to prices, and implies that future serious prejudice challenges to agricultural

---

736   *Appellate Body Report*, para. 486.
737   *Appellate Body Report*, para. 488.
738   *Appellate Body Report*, para. 496.
739   *Appellate Body Report*, para. 496.
740   *Appellate Body Report*, para. 496.
741   *Appellate Body Report*, note 589.

subsidies should not shy away from including non-price contingent subsidies in the mix of subsidies to be challenged. To the extent that the collective effect of both price-contingent and non-price-contingent subsidies cover an average farm's total cost of production and provide it with a profit, there is no logical reason why such subsidies should not be seen to "contribute" to production – and be causally linked to varying degrees with various forms of serious prejudice – including in the form of significant price suppression in the world market.

Legal Findings on Import Substitution Subsidies and Export Subsidies – Step 2 Payments: The Appellate Body affirmed in all respects the original panel's Step-2 findings challenged by the United States that both Step 2 payments to exporters of U.S. cotton (export subsidy) and Step 2 payments to U.S. users of U.S. cotton (local content subsidy) are prohibited subsidies under the WTO *Subsidies Agreement*. Specifically, Brazil challenged the program on two grounds: that Step 2 payments were (1) import substitution subsidies inconsistent with Article 3.1(b) of the SCM and (2) export subsidies within the meaning of Article 9.1(a) of the AoA and Article 3.1(a) of the SCM. The Panel upheld both claims finding violations of 3.1(a) and 3.2 of the *SCM Agreement*. Given the timing of the adoption of the Appellate Body report, the panel's six month deadline for implementation meant that the United States had until 1 July 2005 to withdraw these prohibited subsidies.

Prior to setting forth the legal findings of the AB with regards to the US' Step 2 program, it is important to note that, in making its determinations, the Appellate Body more clearly defined the relationship between the AoA and the SCM Agreement. Specifically, the AB agreed with the Panel that Article 21.1 could apply to the three situations proffered by the Panel, namely:

> ...where, for example, the domestic support provisions of the *Agreement on Agriculture* would prevail in the event that an explicit carve-out or exemption from the disciplines in Article 3.1(b) of the *SCM Agreement* existed in the *text* of the *Agreement on Agriculture*. Another situation would be where it would be impossible for a Member to comply with its domestic support obligations under the *Agreement on Agriculture* and the Article 3.1(b) prohibition simultaneously. Another situation might be where there is an explicit authorization in the text of the *Agreement on Agriculture* that would authorize a measure that, in the absence of such an express authorization, would be prohibited by Article 3.1(b) of the *SCM Agreement*.[742]

---

742   *Panel Report*, para. 7.1038. (original emphasis).

Further, the Appellate Body determined that Article 21.1 allows for the provisions of the GATT 1994 and multilateral trade agreement in Annex 1A to apply, unless the AoA has "specific provisions dealing specifically with the same matter."[743] To that end, the AB had to determine whether both the AoA and SCM Agreement had specific provisions that covered subsidies that required preferential use of domestic goods over imported goods.[744] In its analysis, the AB first analyzed the Step 2 payment subsidies. In doing so it considered whether they were measures designed to benefit producers of cotton and directed at agricultural processors, as the United States argued in line with the meaning of Article 6.3 and paragraph 7 of Annex 3 of the AoA. Specifically, the US argued that although users of the cotton receive the challenged payments, the benefit is actually conferred on the producers of US upland cotton.[745] As the AB stated, "We thus turn to the issue raised by the United States' appeal, that is, whether Article 6.3 and paragraph 7 of Annex 3 of the *Agreement on Agriculture* are 'specific provisions dealing specifically with the same matter' as Article 3.1(b) of the *SCM Agreement*, namely, subsidies contingent upon the use of domestic over imported goods."[746] The AB did not agree with US argumentation,[747] but rather found that "paragraph 7 of Annex 3 and Article 6.3 of the AoA do not deal specifically with the same matter as Article 3.1(b) of the SCM Agreement, that is, subsidies contingent upon the use of domestic over imported goods."[748] The effect of this AB determination is that it sets forth a clear guideline to Members that they may provide subsidies "directed at agricultural processor that benefit producers of a basic agricultural commodity in accordance with the *Agreement on Agriculture*, as long as such subsidies do not include an import substitution component."[749] Therefore, in terms of the domestic measures compliance with WTO commitments, a Member will be

---

743 *Appellate Body Report,* para. 532.
744 *Appellate Body Report,* para. 533.
745 *Appellate Body Report,* para. 536.
746 *Appellate Body Report,* para. 538.
747 "The United States argues that, if payments to processors that fall within paragraph 7 are not exempted from the prohibition in Article 3.1(b) of the *SCM Agreement*, paragraph 7 would be rendered inutile. According to the United States, if domestic users were allowed to claim Step 2 payments, regardless of the origin of the cotton, this 'would cause the benefit to [domestic] cotton producers to evaporate' and the 'subsidy would be transformed from a subsidy "in favor of agricultural producers" to a simple input subsidy.' Rather than 'a cotton subsidy,' it would become a 'textile subsidy.'" *Appellate Body Report,* para. 542.
748 *Appellate Body Report,* para. 546.
749 *Appellate Body Report,* para. 542.

considered to be in compliance if its current total AMS does not exceed its annual or final bound commitment level specified in its Country Schedule. In line with the Panel, the AB agreed that:

> Article 6.3 does *not* provide that compliance with such "domestic support reduction commitments" shall necessarily be considered to be in compliance with other applicable WTO obligations. Nor does it contain an explicit textual indication that otherwise prohibited measures are necessarily justified by virtue of compliance with the domestic support reduction commitments.[750]

In reviewing the AoA on preferential agreement, the AB did not find a specific provision for subsidies that have an import substitution component; however, such subsidies were found to be specifically covered by Article 3.1(b) of the *SCM Agreement*.[751] In determining whether it was appropriate to apply the SCM provision, the AB noted that both agreements (AoA and SCM) are part of the WTO Agreement and should be read "harmoniously."[752] Therefore, the AB ruled that "the introductory language of the chapeau[753] makes it clear that the AoA prevails over Article 3 of the *SCM Agreement*, but only to the extent that the former contains an exception."[754] This two-step analysis of reading the AoA and SCM was also applied to the export subsidies analysis, discussed *infra*.[755]

Having established the proper reading of the AoA with the SCM, the AB made the followings determinations with regards to the Step 2 programs.[756] First, under Article 3.1 of the *SCM Agreement*, subsidies that are contingent

---

750   *Appellate Body Report*, para. 545.
751   *Appellate Body Report*, para. 547.
752   *Appellate Body Report*, para. 549. It should be re-emphasized that this is the preferred analysis when the chapeau of Article 3.1(b) does not apply, specifically, where a specific provision is not provided in the AoA.
753   Article 3.1(b) of the *SCM Agreement* provides: Except as provided in the Agreement on Agriculture, the following subsidies, within the meaning of Article 1, shall be prohibited:... (b) subsidies contingent, whether solely or as one of several other conditions, upon the use of domestic over imported goods.
754   *Appellate Body Report*, para. 630.
755   *Appellate Body Report*, para. 570–571.
756   *Appellate Body Report*, para. 537. It should be further noted that the AB decided, in line with the reading of the 3.1(b) in line with the AoA, to "proceed with our examination on the *assumption* that Step 2 payments to domestic users of United States cotton are contemplated by paragraph 7 of Annex 3 of the *Agreement on Agriculture*."

upon export or contingent upon use of local content are prohibited. "...Article 3.1(b) of the SCM Agreement prohibits subsidies that are contingent – that is, 'conditional' – on the use of domestic over imported goods."[757] In line with the interpretative guidelines for reading the AoA and SCM described, *infra*, the AB first determined that although measures could fall within the second sentence of paragraph 7 for their inclusion in the AMS calculation, the AB did not find that if subsidies are deemed import substitution subsides, that they would necessarily be exempt from the explicit prohibition in Article 3.1(b) of the SCM Agreement.[758]

The AB concluded, in rejection of US arguments to the contrary, that, "We agree with the Panel that there is a clear distinction between a provision that requires a Member to include a certain type of payment (or part thereof) in its AMS calculation and one that would authorize subsidies that are contingent on the use of domestic over imported goods."[759] Specifically, the US had again stated its argument that Article 3.1(b) should not have applied (described, *supra*) because of its compliance with Article 6.3 of the AoA. The AB stated, "In sum, we are not persuaded by the United States' submission that the prohibition in Article 3.1(b) of the SCM Agreement is inapplicable to import substitution subsidies provided in connection with products falling under the *Agreement on Agriculture*."[760] Therefore, in line with the analysis provided and regarding the relationship between the AoA and SCM Agreements and as applied to the Step 2 measures, the AB upheld the Panel's finding that "Step 2 payment to domestic users of United States upland cotton, under Section 1207(a) of the FSRI Act of 2002, are subsidies contingent on the use of domestic over imported goods that are inconsistent with" Articles 3.1(b) and 3.2.[761]

The second US claim the AB reviewed was that the Panel had erred in its finding that US Step 2 payments were not *per se* Article 9.1(a) export subsidies listed in the AoA. The US argued that payments were available domestically to exporters and users of upland cotton and, therefore, were not in violation of Articles (a) and 3.2 of the SCM Agreement. In its appeal, the US requested the AB to reverse the Panel's ruling and find that the payments are not "contingent

---

757   *Appellate Body Report*, para. 544.
758   The US had argued that Step 2 payments complied with the US' domestic support reductions pursuant to Article 6.3 of the AoA and, therefore, could not be in violation of Article 3.1(b) of the SCM Agreement. *Appellate Body Report*, paras. 514–525.
759   *Appellate Body Report*, para. 541.
760   *Appellate Body Report*, para. 550.
761   *Appellate Body Report*, para. 551–552.

on export performance."[762] However, the AB upheld – in line with Brazil's position – that the U.S. Step 2 payments to cotton are either contingent upon proof of export of U.S. cotton by an eligible exporter or contingent upon proof of use of U.S. cotton by a U.S. textile producer.[763] Thus, one part of the program entails an export contingency, while the other part of the program contains a local content contingency. Therefore, the Panel found that both Step 2 payments to exports and Step 2 payments the U.S. textile mills are prohibited subsidies. The Appellate Body affirmed these findings:

> In sum, we agree with the Panel's view that Step 2 payments are export-contingent and, therefore, an export subsidy for purposes of Article 9 of the *Agreement on Agriculture* and Article 3.1(a) of the *SCM Agreement*. The statute and regulations pursuant to which Step 2 payments are granted, on their face, condition payments to exporters on exportation. In order to claim payment, an exporter must show proof of exportation. If an exporter does not provide proof of exportation, the exporter will not receive a payment. This is sufficient to establish that Step 2 payments to exporters of United States upland cotton are "conditional upon export performance" or "dependent for their existence on export performance." That domestic users may also be eligible to receive payments under different conditions does not eliminate the fact that an exporter will receive payment only upon proof of exportation.[764]

The United States argued that, because the program entails both contingencies, Step 2 subsidies are neither export nor local content subsidies, but rather paid on the "use, not exportation" of U.S. cotton.[765] The Appellate Body agreed with the Panel's reasoning that the "fact that the subsidy is also available to domestic users...does not 'dissolve' the export-contingent nature of the Step 2 payments to exporters."[766] Further, the AB rejected the US' use of the *Canada-Dairy* dispute to try to argue that the challenged measures were not export subsidies, since they were also available to processors in the domestic

---

762   *Appellate Body Report*, paras. 563–564.
763   *Appellate Body Report*, para. 584.
764   *Appellate Body Report*, para. 582.
765   *Appellate Body Report*, paras. 563–564.
766   *Appellate Body Report*, para. 578. In doing so, the AB agreed with the Panel's reliance on the AB ruling of *US-FSC (Article 21.5-EC)* wherein it was found that the bifurcation of a measure necessarily made it "export-neutral."

market.767 The AB agreed with the Panel's dismissal of the argument, finding that the facts in each case were too dissimilar to apply given the present case required assessment of a measure that clearly distinguished the two recipients and sets forth different contingencies for both. Specifically, the AB noted, "In the case of one set of recipients, eligible exporters, exportation is a necessary condition to receive payment."768 Furthermore, the United States argued that, under the AoA, subsidies to processors of an agricultural good (that also benefit producers) are to be included in the "Aggregate Measurement of Support" and are subject to reduction commitments for domestic support. Under the U.S. argument, local content subsidies – as a subgroup of subsidies to processors – could, therefore, not possibly be prohibited under the *Subsidies Agreement*. However, as the Panel emphasized, and as stated *infra*, WTO rules apply always cumulatively unless there is a conflict. The Panel found that there is no such conflict between the rules on subsidies to processors under the AoA and the prohibition of local content subsidies under the SCM because not all subsidies to processors need necessarily be local content subsidies. It follows that Step 2 payments to domestic users are prohibited under the *SCM Agreement*. The Appellate Body similarly found that local content subsidies for agricultural products were not carved out of the disciplines of the *SCM Agreement*. Therefore, the AB concluded:

> ...we agree with the Panel's view that Step 2 payments are export-contingent and, therefore, an export subsidy for purposes of Article 9 of the *Agreement on Agriculture* and Article 3.1(a) of the *SCM Agreement*. The statue and regulations pursuant to which Step 2 payments are granted, on their face, condition payments to exporters on exportation. In order to claim payment, an exporter must show proof of exportation. If an exporter does not provide proof of exportation, the exporter will not receive a payment. This is sufficient to establish that Step 2 payments to exporters of United States upland cotton are "conditional upon export performance" or "dependent for their existence on export performance." That domestic users may also be eligible to receive payments under different conditions does not eliminate the fact that an exporter will receive payment only upon proof of exportation.769

---

767 United States' appellant's submission, paras. 444–445 (Panel Report, *Canada-Dairy*, para. 7.41 and footnote 496 to para. 7.124).
768 *Appellate Body Report*, para. 581.
769 *Appellate Body Report*, para. 582.

Therefore, the AB found the Step 2 subsidies to fall under Article 9.1(a) of the AoA and be in violation of Article 3.3 and 8 of the AoA.[770] Finally, given the established relationship between the AoA and SCM Agreements, described *infra*, the AB similarly found that the Step 2 payments were export contingent within the meaning of Article 3.1(a) of the SCM Agreement and thus, in violation of Articles 3.1(a) and 3.2.[771]

The eventual elimination by the United States of this subsidy on 1 August 2006 had an important impact on the world cotton market. Brazil's expert Andrew McDonald testified that Step 2 payments to exporters and domestic users of cotton made US cotton the "first choice" low-priced cotton in the world. Exports from other low-cost producers such as Brazil or West African countries are thereby either displaced from the world market or their prices are suppressed. These subsidies also prevented foreign cotton from being imported into the United States because the subsidies lower the effective price of U.S. cotton for U.S. cotton users. In short, the Step 2 program bought increased domestic and export market share for uncompetitive U.S. cotton at the expense of otherwise competitive foreign cotton producers. Indeed, as noted above, the Panel also found this program caused serious prejudice by suppressing cotton prices around the world. Eventually and unfortunately, the United States reinstated the Step 2 subsidy in the 2008 Farm Bill, but eliminated the explicit US cotton "use" contingency. Therefore, although the US temporarily eliminated the program, measures in the 2008 Farm Bill have reinstated the prior effects found by the Panel and AB. Further, as discussed in the following sections, *infra*, Brazil argued that the elimination of Step 2 was less significant than continued non-compliance by the US in not altering or eliminating the Marketing Loan program.

Legal Findings on Import Substitution and Export Subsidies – Export Credit Guarantee Findings: On appeal, the Appellate Body also upheld the original Panel's finding that the three (3) challenged export credit guarantee programs[772] constituted a *per se* export subsidy within the meaning of item (j) of the illustrative list of export subsidies. The first analysis required the AB to review the US appeal that Article 10.2 of the AoA "makes it clear that the export subsidy disciplines in the *Agreement on Agriculture* and the *SCM Agreement* are not applicable to export credit guarantee programs," because the provision "reflects the deferral of disciplines on export credit guarantee programs

---

770 *Appellate Body Report*, para. 583.
771 *Appellate Body Report*, para. 584.
772 These included the GSM 102, GSM 103 and SCGP programs. *Appellate Body Report*, para. 586–589.

contemplated by WTO Members."[773] The US argument continued, stating that "even if the export subsidy disciplines in the SCM Agreement were applicable, its export credit guarantee programs are not prohibited export subsidies under Article 3.1(a) because they do not meet the criteria in item (j) of the Illustrative List of Export Subsidies attached to the SCM Agreement as Annex I, namely that the premiums are inadequate to cover the programs' long-term operating costs and losses."[774]

Consequently, the AB found that the three "export subsidies" programs were correctly found to be in item (j) of the Illustrative List of Export Subsidies. The AB determined that, as such, both the AoA and SCM Agreements applied. Specifically, the AB found that the unscheduled agricultural products and one scheduled product (rice) circumvent the US export subsidy commitments in violation of Article 10.1 of the AoA and Articles 3.1(a) and 3.2 of the SCM Agreement.[775] The AB further recognized that no disciplines had been internationally agreed to, as required under Article 10.2.[776] Further, on the former point, the AB upheld the Panel's finding that Article 10.2 does not define the disciplines for export credit guarantee programs under Article 10.1 so as to exempt them from action under the AoA.[777] As the AB stated,

> We agree with the Panel's view that Article 10.2 does not expressly exclude export credit guarantees from the export subsidy disciplines in Article 10.1 of the *Agreement on Agriculture*. As the Panel observes, were such an exemption intended, it could have been easily achieved by, for example, inserting the words "[n]otwithstanding the provisions of Article 10.1," or other similar language at the beginning of Article 10.2. Article 10.2 does not include express language suggesting that it is intended as an exception, nor does it expressly state that the application of any export subsidy disciplines to export credits or export credit guarantees is "deferred," as the United States suggests. Given that the drafters were aware that subsidized export credit guarantees, export credits and insurance programs could fall within the export subsidy disciplines in the *Agreement on Agriculture* and the SCM *Agreement*, it would be expected that an

---

773   *Appellate Body Report*, para. 590. Article 10.2 of the AoA specifically covers export credit guarantee programs as well as export credits and insurance programs. *Appellate Body Report*, para. 607.
774   *Appellate Body Report*, para. 591.
775   *Appellate Body Report*, para. 592–597.
776   *Appellate Body Report*, para. 607.
777   *Appellate Body Report*, para. 608.

exception would have been clearly provided had this been the drafters' intention.[778]

Finally, the AB agreed with the Panel's finding that the US was erroneous in its argument that Brazil's approach would make meaningless Article 10.2. Instead, the AB found that Brazil's approach was correct in light of the context and meaning of the provision and negotiating history of the AoA.[779] Specifically, the AB relied on paragraph 2 of Article 10 to emphasize that the intention of the drafters was to include an anti-circumvention clause (Article 10.3), reversing the burden of proof when a Member has been found to have exceeded its commitments.[780] The Appellate Body ruled on the burden of proof challenge under Article 10.3 of the *Agriculture Agreement*, finding that "Article 10.3 pursues the aim of preventing circumvention of export subsidy commitments by providing special rules on the reveals of burden of proof where a Member exports an agricultural product in quantities that exceed its reduction commitment level."[781] Where this is the case, the responding Member is "treated as if it has granted WTO-*inconsistent* export subsidies for the excess quantities,

---

778 *Appellate Body Report*, para. 609.
779 *Appellate Body Report*, paras. 611–625. The AB reasoning can be found in the following excerpt: "We agree with the Panel that the meaning of Article 10.2 is clear from the provision's text, in its context and in the light of the object and purpose of the *Agreement on Agriculture*, consistent with Article 31 of the *Vienna Convention*. The Panel did not think it necessary to resort to negotiating history for purposes of its interpretation of Article 10.2. Even if the negotiating history were relevant for our inquiry, we do not find that it supports the United States' position. This is because it does not indicate that the negotiators did not intend to discipline export credit guarantees, export credits and insurance programs *at all*. To the contrary, it shows that negotiators were aware of the need to impose disciplines on export credit guarantees, given their potential as a mechanism for subsidization and for circumvention of the export subsidy commitments under Article 9. Although the negotiating history reveals that the negotiators struggled with this issue, it does not indicate that the disagreement among them related to whether export credit guarantees, export credits and insurance programs were to be disciplined at all. In our view, the negotiating history suggests that the disagreement between the negotiators related to which kinds of specific disciplines were to apply to such measures. The fact that negotiators felt that internationally agreed disciplines were necessary for these three measures also suggests that the disciplines that currently exist in the *Agreement on Agriculture* must apply pending new disciplines because, otherwise, it would mean that subsidized export credit guarantees, export credits, and insurance programs could currently be extended without any limit or consequence." *Appellate Body Report*, para. 623.
780 *Appellate Body Report*, para. 616.
781 *Appellate Body Report*, para. 616.

unless the Member presents adequate evidence to 'establish' the contrary."[782] To that extent, a similar aim is attempted in Article 10.4 to the extent that it disciplines measure where Members circumvent their commitments through food aid transactions.[783] To that end, the AB stated that it was proper to interpret Article 10.2 to mean that its aim was to similarly prevent circumvention by Members. Further, the AB agreed that Article 10.1 contains the disciplines for export subsidies not listed in Article 9.1. The AB explained, "An export credit guarantee that meets the definition of an export subsidy would be covered by Article 10.1 of the *Agreement on Agriculture* because it is not an export subsidy listed in Article 9.1 of that Agreement."[784] The US argued that Article 10.2 simply committed Members to undertake negotiations for the creation of "internationally agreed disciplines"[785] for, *inter alia*, export credit guarantees.[786] The AB did not agree with this interpretation for the reasons stated above. Further, for purposes of the AoA, these programs are not automatically considered export subsidies. Rather, such a characterization of these measures is only appropriate, and such measures can only be disciplined, where there is an "export subsidy component."[787] Further, even if this determination is made, the necessary analysis must be applied. As the AB set forth, in upholding the Panel's decision,

> ...even when export credit guarantees contain an export subsidy component, such an export credit guarantee would not be inconsistent with Article 10.1 of the *Agreement on Agriculture* unless the complaining party demonstrates that it is "applied in a manner which results in, or which threatens to lead to, circumvention of export subsidy commitments." Thus, under the *Agreement on Agriculture*, the complaining party must first demonstrate that an export credit guarantee program constitutes an export subsidy. If it succeeds, it must then demonstrate that such export credit guarantees are applied in a manner that results in, or threatens to lead to, circumvention of the responding party's export subsidy commitments within the meaning of Article 10.1 of the *Agreement on Agriculture*.[788]

---

782   *Appellate Body Report*, para. 616.
783   *Appellate Body Report*, para. 616.
784   *Appellate Body Report*, para. 615.
785   *Appellate Body Report*, para. 615.
786   *Appellate Body Report*, para. 617.
787   *Appellate Body Report*, para. 626.
788   *Appellate Body Report*, para. 626.

Therefore, the AB found, "we do not believe that Article 10.2 of the *Agreement on Agriculture* exempts export credit guarantees, export credits and insurance programs from the export subsidy disciplines in the *Agreement on Agriculture*."[789]

The AB then responded to the US claim that the Panel incorrectly found that the export credit guarantees were subject to Articles 3.1(a) and 3.2 of the SCM Agreement, under the belief that Article 21.1 of the AoA makes 3.1(a) inapplicable to the challenged measures.[790] Specifically, the US analysis was "premised on the proposition that Article 10.2 of the *Agreement on Agriculture* exempts export credit guarantees from the export subsidy disciplines in that Agreement."[791] The AB ruled that the export credit guarantee programs were not exempt from export subsidy disciplines under Article 10.2 of the *Agriculture Agreement*. The AB more clearly defined Article 10.2 and determined that the United States had erroneously interpreted it in light of its commitments. As stated by the Appellate Body:

> We agree with the United States that Article 10.3 of the *Agreement on Agriculture* does not apply to claims brought under the SCM *Agreement*. However, the Panel did not make the error attributed to it by the United States. The Panel made the statement relied on by the United States in the context of its assessment of the United States' export credit guarantee program under the *Agreement on Agriculture*. Although the Panel made use of the criteria set out in item (j) of the Illustrative List of Export Subsidies annexed to the SCM *Agreement* (providing these programs at premium rates inadequate to cover long-term operating costs and losses) it did so as contextual guidance for its analysis under the *Agreement on Agriculture*, and both the United States and Brazil appear to have agreed with the appropriateness of this approach. Thus, the Panel's reference to Article 10.3 did not relate to its assessment of the United States' export credit guarantee programs under the SCM *Agreement*.[792]

The AB found that the US interpretation of Article 10.2 was incorrect and, therefore, rejected the argument.[793]

---

789 *Appellate Body Report*, paras. 626–627.
790 *Appellate Body Report*, paras. 629–630.
791 *Appellate Body Report*, paras. 629–630.
792 *Appellate Body Report*, para. 647.
793 *Appellate Body Report*, para. 630. It should be noted that not all of the AB agreed with this position. In a dissenting opinion, submitted a separate statement arguing that (1)

Therefore, the Appellate Body found, "...according to the United States, 'Article 3 of the SCM Agreement...is subject in its application to Article 21.1 of the *Agreement on Agriculture.*" The United States then argued that, because "export credit guarantees are not subject to the disciplines of export subsidies for purposes of the *Agreement on Agriculture,* Article 21.1 of that Agreement renders Article 3.1(a) of the SCM Agreement inapplicable to such measures"..... "Therefore, because it is premised on an incorrect interpretation of Article 10.2 of the *Agreement on Agriculture,* we reject the United States' argument...."[794]

The next US claim the AB reviewed was that the Panel had not made the necessary factual findings in determining that the CCC provided loan programs with "premium rates inadequate to cover the long-term operating costs and losses of the programs under item (j) of the Illustrative List of Export Subsidies."[795] Although the AB agreed with the US that Article 10.3 of the AoA does not extend to SCM claims, it did not find that the Panel had erred in making its determination and found that both parties had agreed with the approach applied in the Panel's analysis.[796] The AB emphasized that, in making the determination of whether the premiums could cover operating costs and losses, it is necessary to consider the evidence in its entirety "and no one element, in isolation, is determinative."[797] Further, the AB finding confirmed that Brazil had the burden of proof of establishing this issue, despite reference to Article 10.3.[798] In assessing the US argumentation that the Panel had not properly applied the burden of proof, the AB stressed that the Panel's approach was in line with WTO legal precedence of how to allocate burden of proof, essentially by reversing the burden of proof in this instance (explained, *supra*). It is important to note that the AB did disagree with the Panel's approach in extending Article 10.3 to *unscheduled* products.[799] Specifically, the AB explained that,

---

"pursuant to Article 10.2, export credit guarantees, export credits and insurance programs are not currently subject to export subsidy disciplines under the *Agreement on Agriculture,* including the disciplines found in Article 10.1" and (2) that the same programs "provided in connection with agricultural goods are not subject to the prohibition in Article 3.1(a) of the SCM Agreement." *Appellate Body Report,* para. 639. However, the Member prefaced this dissenting opinion with the disclaimer that it was not to be interpreted to mean that he did not agree with all other findings and conclusions of the AB. *Appellate Body Report,* para. 631.

794 *Appellate Body Report,* paras. 629–630.
795 *Appellate Body Report,* para. 658–659.
796 *Appellate Body Report,* para. 647.
797 *Appellate Body Report,* para. 648.
798 *Appellate Body Report,* para. 648.
799 *Appellate Body Report,* para. 652.

in order to make a successful claim, "...the only thing a complainant would have to do to meet its burden of proof when bringing a claim against an *unscheduled* product is to demonstrate that the respondent has exported that product."[800] Applying Article 10.3 in this case would then reverse the burden, and the responding party would have to "demonstrate that it has not provided an export subsidy."[801] The AB found this to be an "extreme result."[802] In distinguishing the two, the AB elucidated,

> In our view, the presumption of subsidization when exported quantities exceed the reduction commitments makes sense in respect of a *scheduled* product because, by including it in its schedule, a WTO Member is reserving for itself the right to apply export subsidies to that product, within the limits in its schedule. In the case of *unscheduled* products, however, such a presumption appears inappropriate. Export subsidies for both unscheduled agricultural products and industrial products are completely prohibited under the *Agreement on Agriculture* and under the *SCM Agreement*, respectively. The Panel's interpretation implies that the burden of proof with regard to the same issue would apply differently, however, under each Agreement: it would be on the respondent under the *Agreement on Agriculture*, while it would be on the complainant under the *SCM Agreement*.[803]

Further, the AB ruled that Brazil needed to make the claim, but with regards to "submissions relating to the cohort re-estimates," the AB agreed with Brazil that where the complaining party can show the trends exist, the responding party then bears the burden to prove they exist.[804] "Accordingly, the isolated statements referred to by the United States do not demonstrate an error by the Panel in the application of the burden of proof."[805] In response to the US argument, Brazil refuted that the US should have brought its claim under Article 11 of the DSU. The AB rejected this argument finding that the US was challenging the Panel's application of item (j) and not requesting a review of the Panel's factual findings. To that extent, the AB found it was proper to so limit its

---

800 *Appellate Body Report*, para. 652.
801 *Appellate Body Report*, para. 652.
802 *Appellate Body Report*, para. 652.
803 *Appellate Body Report*, para. 652.
804 *Appellate Body Report*, para. 656.
805 *Appellate Body Report*, para. 656.

review.[806] Having dismissed Brazil's argument, the AB ruled on the merits of the US allegation, finding that it agreed with the Panel's approach as such:

> ...item (j) calls for an examination of whether the premium rates of the export credit guarantee programme at issue are inadequate to cover the long-term operating costs and losses of the programmes. Beyond that, item (j) does not set forth, or require us to use, any one particular methodological approach nor accounting philosophy in conducting our examination. Nor are we required to quantify precisely the amount by which costs and losses exceeded premiums paid.[807]

Therefore, the AB found that item (j) does not require a trier of fact to choose a calculation methodology and make a precise quantification.[808] Instead, it is sufficient that the assessment focus solely on the inadequacy of the premiums, which can be achieved by determining whether the program is an export subsidy.[809] In conclusion, the AB upheld the Panel's findings that the US export credit guarantee programs were "*per se* export subsidies within the meaning of item (j) of the Illustrative List of Export Subsidies in Annex I of the *SCM Agreement*." Further, the AB found that the programs constituted prohibited 3.1(a) SCM export subsidies.[810] Therefore, the Appellate Body found that the US export credit guarantee programs were in violation of Articles 3.1(a) and 3.2 of the *SCM Agreement*.[811]

---

806   *Appellate Body Report*, para. 663.
807   *Appellate Body Report*, para. 665.
808   *Appellate Body Report*, para. 666.
809   *Appellate Body Report*, para. 666.
810   *Appellate Body Report*, paras. 664–674.
811   Although the Appellate Body upheld the Panel's decision regarding cotton the Appellate Body reversed the Panel's findings relating to pig meat and poultry. However, the Appellate Body indicated it could not complete the analysis on the basis of the record before it. In the later compliance proceeding, Brazil offered proof with respect to pig meat and poultry meat and the compliance panel found that the United States had exceeded its reduction commitments with respect to these two products. Panel Report, *Cotton (21.5)*, Paras. 9.20–27 – Panel found that the claims of Brazil relating to export credit guarantees for exports of pig meat and poultry meat are within the scope of this proceeding under Article 21.5 of the DSU. Para. 14.139–57 – Panel found that the US applied export subsidies in a manner inconsistent with its commitments under the Agriculture and SCM Agreements and, therefore, failed to comply with the DSB recommendations and rulings.

Brazil's Appeal: In turning to Brazil's claims on appeal, the Appellate Body ruled on the issues of "actual" and "threat of" circumvention by the US, under Article 10.1 of the *Agreement on Agriculture*. These analyses were conducted separately. As stated *supra* Article 10.1 is aimed at preventing Members from circumventing their export subsidy commitments.[812] As found earlier in the appeal, the AB set the necessary analysis for finding an Article 10.1 violation. First, the AB found that export programs were not exempt from Article 10.2, but would not automatically be considered "inconsistent with Article 10.1 of the *Agreement on Agriculture* unless the complaining party demonstrates that it is applied in a manner which results in, or which threatens to lead to, circumvention of export subsidy commitments."[813] Therefore, Brazil would be required to first establish that the measure was an export subsidy. Then, it would have to show that it is "applied in a manner that results in, or threatens to lead to, circumvention of the responding party's export subsidy commitments within the meaning of Article 10.1 of the *Agreement on Agriculture*."[814]

In terms of actual circumvention, the AB upheld the Panel's finding that there was actual circumvention for rice and reversed the Panel's finding that actual circumvention had occurred in the case of twelve (12) US scheduled products.[815] Brazil had appealed the claim that no actual circumvention had occurred with regards to "pig meat and poultry meat in 2001."[816] In making its determination, the AB had to first consider whether there were even "sufficient uncontested facts in the record to permit [it] to complete the analysis with respect to the other commodities."[817] Specifically, there was disagreement about the time periods covered in Brazil's claim, each of the parties had varying time periods, and the US and Brazil argued that the use of each one's specific time period supported its claims. The AB concluded "Given the differences between the participants in respect of the data that we would have to examine to determine whether the United States applied export credit guarantees in a manner that results in circumvention of its export subsidy commitments for pig meat."[818] Therefore, in granting Brazil's appeal, the Appellate Body reversed the original panel's finding that Brazil had not established that the application

---

812   *Appellate Body Report*, para. 148.
813   *Appellate Body Report*, para. 626.
814   *Appellate Body Report*, para. 626.
815   *Appellate Body Report*, para. 692.
816   *Appellate Body Report*, para. 681.
817   *Appellate Body Report*, para. 692.
818   *Appellate Body Report*, para. 693.

of export credit guarantees circumvented the U.S. export subsidy commitments for pig meat and poultry meat.[819]

In terms of Brazil's claim that US export credit guarantees to scheduled products other than rice and unscheduled products not covered in the programs are applied in a manner which threatens circumvention under Article 10.1, the Panel rejected Brazil's claim. Therefore, in its presentation to the AB, Brazil appealed the issue on two grounds arguing that the Panel had erred (1) in its interpretation and application of Article 10.1 and (2) in limiting its assessment to only scheduled products other than rice and unsupported unscheduled products, although Brazil had submitted a claim to both scheduled and unscheduled agricultural products eligible to receive export credit guarantees.[820] The AB first reviewed the Panel's definition of 'threat of circumvention' in the context of the ordinary meaning and legal precedence relating to the 10.1 provision of the AoA, finding it to be consistent.[821] However, to the degree that

---

[819] However, the Appellate Body indicated it could not complete the analysis on the basis of the record before it. As it stated, "For the reasons mentioned above, we *reverse* the Panel's finding, in paragraph 7.881 of the Panel Report, that Brazil did not establish actual circumvention in respect of poultry meat and pig meat. Nevertheless, because there are insufficient uncontested facts in the record to enable us to do so, we do not complete the legal analysis to determine whether the United States' export credit guarantees to poultry meat and pig meat have been applied in a manner that 'results in' circumvention of the United States' export subsidy commitments." *Appellate Body Report*, para. 694.

[820] *Appellate Body Report*, paras. 679–680, 696.

[821] In defining 'threat of circumvention,' The Appellate Body has explained that "under Article 10.1, it is not necessary to demonstrate *actual* 'circumvention' of 'export subsidy commitments'." It suffices that "export subsidies" are "applied in a manner which...threatens to lead to circumvention of export subsidy commitments." We note that the ordinary meaning of the term "threaten" includes "[c]onstitute a threat to," "be likely to injure" or "be a source of harm or danger." Article 10.1 is concerned not with injury, but rather with "circumvention." Accordingly, based on its ordinary meaning, the phrase "threaten[] to lead to...circumvention" would imply that the export subsidies are applied in a manner that is "likely to" lead to circumvention of a WTO Member's export subsidy commitments. Furthermore, we observe that the ordinary meaning of the term "threaten" refers to a *likelihood* of something happening; the ordinary meaning of "threaten" does not connote a sense of certainty. *Appellate Body Report*, para. 704. Further, "the concept of 'threat' has been discussed by the Appellate Body within the context of the *Agreement on Safeguards* and the *Anti-Dumping Agreement*. It has explained that 'threat' refers to something that 'has *not* yet occurred, but remains a future event whose actual materialization cannot, in fact, be assured with certainty.' In *US – Line Pipe*, the Appellate Body stated that "there is a continuum that ascends from a 'threat of serious injury' up to the 'serious injury' itself. We emphasize that the Appellate Body's discussion of the concept of 'threat' in previous appeals related to the interpretation of other covered agreements that contain obligations

the Panel found from its interpretation that "an unconditional legal entitlement" was a requirement, the AB did not agree.[822] Further, the AB believed that the Panel 'conflated' the term and could not, therefore, reconcile the ordinary meaning analysis with the interpretations of the Panel.[823] As such, the claim had not been "proven to the required standard."[824] Further, the AB was unwilling to extend its reading of the provision requiring Members to take "anticipatory or precautionary action" as the AB interpreted from Brazil's claim.[825] To that end, the AB stated, "there is no basis in Article 10.1 for requiring WTO Members to take affirmative, precautionary steps to ensure that circumvention of their export subsidy reduction commitments does not occur."[826] In doing so, it found that Brazil's reliance on US – FSC was incorrect and proffered an alternative reading.[827] Generally, the AB found that the Appellate Body in the US-FSC case was describing the measures at issue and did not bar the possibility that a measure not containing the 'legal' and 'discretionary' elements could be found to potentially threaten to lead to circumvention under 10.1 of the AoA.[828] Therefore, the AB modified the Panel's interpretation so as to not require the "unconditional legal entitlement" condition for a threat of circumvention finding.[829]

In applying the modified interpretation, the AB did not find that Brazil had properly established that the US measures were "applied in a manner that threatens to lead to circumvention of the United States' export subsidy commitments in respect of scheduled products other than rice and unscheduled products not supported under the programs."[830] In explaining its decision, the AB found that eligibility of payment is not sufficient and that the US had provided such measures "to *other* unscheduled products or to exports of

---

relating to injury that differ from those relating to circumvention of export subsidy reduction commitments contained in Article 10.1 of the *Agreement on Agriculture*. Our interpretation of 'threat' in Article 10.1 of the *Agreement on Agriculture* is consistent with the Appellate Body's interpretation of the term 'threat' in these other contexts." *Appellate Body Report*, para. 705.

822 *Appellate Body Report*, para. 706.
823 *Appellate Body Report*, para. 706.
824 *Appellate Body Report*, para. 706.
825 *Appellate Body Report*, para. 707.
826 *Appellate Body Report*, para. 707.
827 *Appellate Body Report*, para. 708.
828 *Appellate Body Report*, para. 709.
829 *Appellate Body Report*, para. 710.
830 *Appellate Body Report*, para. 713.

scheduled products in excess of its export subsidy reduction commitments."[831] Therefore, the AB upheld the Panel's decision "albeit for different reasons."[832]

On Brazil's second matter on appeal, it wished to have the AB find that the Panel should have included, in its "threat" of circumvention analysis, "rice (a scheduled product) and unscheduled products supported by the programs (including upland cotton)."[833] However, the AB found that – since the Panel had already established actual circumvention for "scheduled products other than rice and unscheduled products not supported under the programs," the Panel had appropriately exercised judicial economy and had the proper discretion to do so.[834]

Brazil further appealed the Panel's decision to apply judicial economy to Brazil's claim that the ETI Act of 2000 was in violation of WTO obligations under the SCM and AoA in *US-FSC*. Specifically, Brazil argued that the Panel erred in its "interpretation and application of the burden of proof" in rejecting Brazil's claim and that it wished only for the AB to reverse this decision and not make findings on the issue.[835] The US argued – and the AB agreed – that, given the fact that Brazil was not asking for a decision to be made on the issue, the AB did not need to reverse the Panel's conclusion.[836] Similarly, Brazil had appealed the Panel's GATT Article XVI:3 decision to exercise judicial economy as to whether the US had obtained "more than an equitable share of world export trade," which caused serious prejudice. The AB concluded, stating a similar rationale, that this was not a situation where a finding on an issue that would not ultimately become part of a decision was necessary.[837] Therefore, in both situations, the AB concluded that it would neither endorse nor reverse the Panel's decisions.[838]

5.6 DSU Article 21.5 Compliance Proceedings

After the Appellate Body report has been adopted by the DSB, and the reasonable period of time for implementation has commenced, the respondent Member is required to keep the DSB abreast of its efforts to implement the

---

831 *Appellate Body Report*, para. 713.
832 *Appellate Body Report*, para. 714.
833 *Appellate Body Report*, para. 715.
834 *Appellate Body Report*, paras 715–719.
835 *Appellate Body Report*, paras 734, 740, 742.
836 *Appellate Body Report*, paras. 745–748. However, the AB specifically noted that there may be cases where it may be appropriate to make a finding on an issue where a decision would not result.
837 *Appellate Body Report*, para. 761.
838 *Appellate Body Report*, paras 748, 762.

recommendations and rulings, since the DSB keeps the process under surveillance.[839] Given WTO members compose the DSB, it is up to the interested parties to take the initiative to monitor the implementation process.[840] To that end, six (6) months after establishment of the reasonable period of time, the DSB places the issue on its agenda where it remains until the issue has been resolved.[841] At each DSB meeting thereafter, the respondent is required to provide a status report on any progress made for implementation of the recommendations and rulings.[842] Throughout the process, the respondent has the burden of proof to establish that the duration of time lapsed constitutes a "reasonable period of time."

When the parties disagree on whether the respondent has implemented the recommendations and rulings of the Appellate Body, either party may request a panel under Article 21.5 of the DSU.[843] If possible, the DSB will try to have the same panel members that reviewed the dispute in the original proceedings comprise the panel in the compliance proceedings. As established under WTO law, the role of the Compliance Panel is to consider whether, in its totality, the respondent Member has brought its measures into compliance with the rulings and recommendations of the Appellate Body so that it is, therefore, consistent with the relevant WTO agreement(s).[844] If the respondent fails to bring its measure(s) into conformity with its WTO obligations, the complainant can invoke temporary measures as a form of remedy. These measures can be either compensation by the respondent or the suspension of WTO obligations, called 'countermeasures.'[845]

In the *Cotton* dispute, Brazil notified the DSB on 4 July, 2005 that the US had not complied with the rulings and recommendations of the panel and requested that the imposition of appropriate countermeasures be authorized in the areas

---

839   Article 22.8 of the DSU. For a greater discussion, *see*, Van den Bossche, P., *The Law and Policy of the World Trade Organization: Text, Cases and Materials*, Second Edition, © Cambridge University Press (2008), p. 299.

840   WTO Secretariat, *A Handbook on the WTO Dispute Settlement System*, Cambridge University Press, (2007), p. 75.

841   Van den Bossche, P., *The Law and Policy of the World Trade Organization: Text, Cases and Materials*, Second Edition, © Cambridge University Press (2008), p. 299.

842   Van den Bossche, P., *The Law and Policy of the World Trade Organization: Text, Cases and Materials*, Second Edition, © Cambridge University Press (2008), p. 299.

843   WTO Secretariat, *A Handbook on the WTO Dispute Settlement System*, Cambridge University Press, (2007), p. 79.

844   WTO Secretariat, *A Handbook on the WTO Dispute Settlement System*, Cambridge University Press, (2007), p. 80.

845   WTO Secretariat, *A Handbook on the WTO Dispute Settlement System*, Cambridge University Press, (2007), p. 80.

of intellectual property rights (TRIPS) and services (GATS).[846] The following day, the US and Brazil circulated to the DSB a "sequencing" agreement between them of further procedures in this dispute. This was a necessary WTO dispute settlement procedure developed to address the "sequencing" issue. This issue refers to one of the glitches of the dispute settlement system – the fact that the timeframes of the requisite compliance proceedings (in situations where parties disagree as to whether implementation has occurred) and the authorization for the suspension of concessions, under 22.6, are incompatible.[847] Members have addressed this issue through the use of sequencing agreements. Therefore, in line with this scenario, the US objected to the countermeasures requested in the *Cotton* sequencing agreement and the matter was referred to arbitration under Article 22.6 of the WTO Dispute Settlement Understanding (DSU).[848] However, the US and Brazil agreed to suspend the arbitration until the DSB adopted a Compliance Panel report finding that the US has not taken adequate measures to comply with the DSB's original recommendations.[849] Further, the arbitrator was directed to resume work upon Brazil's request.[850]

---

846   *US-Upland Cotton*, WT/DS267/21 (4 July 2005) and, generally, Article 4.10 of the SCM Agreement. Typically, sanctions should be imposed in the same sector as that in which violation was found, pursuant to 22.3(a); however, if impracticable or ineffective, 22.3(b) allows for exceptional application of sanctions in a different sector, but under the same agreement(s). If that is also not effective or practical, 22.3(c) allows for cross-retaliation whereby a Member can suspend concessions in other sectors in alternative agreements. In the case of *Cotton*, Brazil requested suspension of obligations under 22.3(c). This issue will be discussed in greater detail in Section 5.8 of this chapter.

847   Van den Bossche, P., *The Law and Policy of the World Trade Organization: Text, Cases and Materials*, Second Edition, © Cambridge University Press (2008), pp. 306–307.

848   "Understanding between Brazil and the United States Regarding Procedures under Articles 21 and 22 of the DSU and Article 4 of the SCM Agreement," *US-Upland Cotton*, WT/DS267/22 (5 July 2005), at para. 10.

849   Some caution is recommended to Members entering into a sequencing agreement. First, a sequencing arrangement can compromise the suspending Member's potential rights as it can render unenforceable delayed implementation of the rulings and recommendation of the DSB beyond the proscribed reasonable period of time by a responding Member. Second, suspending action may deprive the suspending Member of retaliatory rights in relation to harm caused by the continued use of WTO-inconsistent measures after the expiry of the reasonable period of time until the conclusion of the arbitration and the authorization of suspension by the DSB. This issue is further addressed in Section 5.8 of this book.

850   "Understanding between Brazil and the United States Regarding Procedures under Articles 21 and 22 of the DSU and Article 4 of the SCM Agreement," *US-Upland Cotton*, WT/DS267/22 (5 July 2005), at para. 10.

It should be noted that, at the time of the sequencing agreement, it has been speculated that the parties had anticipated a conclusion to the Doha Round by the end of 2006 as well as amendments be made to the 2007 Farm Bill to reflect the rulings and recommendations of the original proceedings or, at least, the new US Doha Round agriculture commitments.[851] By the end of 2006, however, it was evident neither of these outcomes would transpire given the collapse of the July 2006 talks.[852] Eventually, a Compliance Panel was requested on 18 August, 2006 under 21.5 of the DSU. The matter was initially referred to the original panel on 28 September, 2006. However, it was not possible for the original panel to review the matter and a new panel was established on 25 October, 2007, consisting of Mr. Eduardo Perez Motta (Chairperson),[853] Mr. Mario Matus, and Mr. Ho-Young Ahn.[854]

In initiating "Article 21.5"[855] compliance proceedings, Brazil challenged the US claims that it had fully complied with the decisions of the original panel

---

[851] *See,* Halverson Cross, K., "WTO Appellate Body Upholds Compliance Panel's Findings in *Cotton Subsidies* Dispute," American Society of International Law, Volume 12, Issue 19 (16 September 2008). *See,* <http://www.asil.org/insights080916.cfm> last accessed 3 August, 2010.

[852] "Doha Development Trade Round Collapse, 2006," *Global Issues*: (28 July 2006) at <http://www.globalissues.org/article/663/wto-doha-development-trade-round-collapse-2006> last accessed 3 August, 2010.

[853] The only carryover in the *Cotton* dispute was that Mr. Eduardo Perez Motta was acting Chairperson in both the compliance panel proceedings as well as the 22.6 arbitration proceedings.

[854] Although the compliance panel ultimately decided not to make a finding on the matter, it should be noted that the propriety of the panel's composition was at issue in the compliance proceedings. Specifically, the US had objected to the initial composition of the panel because two of the three proposed panelists were nationals from third party countries in the dispute. Brazil and the EU agreed that challenging panelist participation on this basis would set an "unattractive precedent" and allow parties to always object where similar situations arise. Rather, the determination is to be left to the WTO Director-General. *Compliance Panel,* paras. 8.27–8.28, Pages A-59-63.

[855] This is Article 21.5 of the *DSU*. It provides, in relevant part: "Where there is disagreement as to the existence or consistency with a covered agreement of measures taken to comply with the recommendations and rulings such dispute shall be decided through recourse to these dispute settlement procedures, including wherever possible resort to the original panel." In an unprecedented tactical maneuver, the United States objected to having two of the original panelists from Australia and Poland be compliance panelists because of their links to third parties – an objection the United States had not previously asserted before the original panel. Thus, in practice, the parties presented their argumentation to the Article 21.5 compliance panel that did not have the entire benefit of the steep learning

and the Appellate Body.[856] At the time the Compliance Panel was formed, the United States had repealed the Step 2 program, as of 1 August 2006, and modified some of the challenged export credit guarantee programs.[857] However, two of the most damaging subsidy regimes, the marketing loan and counter-cyclical payments, continued unchanged and effectiveness of the changes to the export guarantee programs remained in question. As a result, Brazil argued that the United States continued to be in violation of WTO rules by failing to bring the relevant measures into compliance with the DSB's recommendations and rulings. Specifically, Brazil alleged continued violations of Articles 3.1(a), 3.2, 5(c), 6.3(c) and (d) of the SCM Agreement and Articles 10.1 and 8 of the AoA.[858]

The interim report was issued on 27 July, 2007 and the final report was issued on 15 October, 2007 and circulated 18 December, 2007.[859] With regards to the marketing loan and counter-cyclical payments, the Compliance Panel found that these payments to cotton producers resulted in continued and significant suppression of global cotton prices, thereby resulting in "present" serious prejudice to Brazilian cotton producers. This, the panel noted, amounted to a failure on the part of the US to comply with the rulings of the DSB. With regard to the changes to the US export guarantee programs, the Compliance Panel found that, despite the changes to the fee structure, described *infra*, the export credit guarantees issued after July, 2005 amounted to an export subsidy. Further, the report maintained that the program, in effect, abrogated US export subsidy commitments under the AoA for a variety of commodities, including unscheduled products, described supra, and for poultry and pig meat as well as rice.[860]

The following are brief descriptions of the major rulings of the Compliance Panel. Additional and considerable attention is given to the issue of compliance in the following section, which sets forth the AB review of the Compliance Panel. Further, Chapters 8 and 9 provide a detailed analysis of compliance with WTO decisions, especially with regards to the US. These analyses focus on the implementation limitations of Members at the domestic level and the

---

curve of the original panel process. This was another factor in the length of the compliance proceedings.

856   *US-Upland Cotton,* Recourse to Article 21.5 of the DSU by Brazil, WT/DS267/RW, herein referred to as "*Compliance Panel.*"
857   *Compliance Panel*, paras. 2.1–2.14, 3.1–3.16.
858   *Compliance Panel*, paras.
859   *US-Upland Cotton*, Compliance Panel, WT/DS267/RW.
860   In the compliance proceeding, Brazil offered proof with respect to pig meat and poultry meat and the compliance panel found that the United States had exceeded its reduction commitments with respect to these two products.

systemic consequential effects needing to be considered by Members when deciding whether to bring domestic measures into compliance with international obligations.

Serious Prejudice: U.S. Jurisdictional Serious Prejudice Defense: A principal US defense of Brazil's serious-prejudice claims was its preliminary objection to the Compliance Panel's jurisdiction, arguing that certain claims by Brazil were outside the scope of Article 21.5 proceedings.[861] The US argument raised a fundamental question about the viability of challenges under the *SCM Agreement* to *annual recurring* subsidy schemes – such as the marketing loan, direct payment, crop insurance, and counter-cyclical subsidies provided by the United States and similar annual payments made by the European Communities. The United States claimed that annual payments under the marketing loan and counter-cyclical programs made after the implementation period (post September 21, 2005) could not be within the Compliance Panel's jurisdiction because the only subsidy payments for which the United States had to remove the adverse effects were those made during the period 1999–2002.[862] Without any new subsidy payments to consider, the US argued, Brazil could not prove that there was present serious prejudice in 2005–2006 from the new basket of price contingent subsidies. Arguing for use of a rigid distinction between "as such" challenges to subsidy *programs* and "as applied" challenges to annual subsidy *payments*, the United States asserted that Brazil had failed to establish that the marketing loan and counter-cyclical subsidy *programs* "as such" violated the *SCM Agreement*.[863]

The Compliance Panel rejected what would have resulted in a wholesale elimination of any implementation obligation of the United States.[864] The Panel found that "a Member does not take appropriate steps to remove adverse effects of a subsidy if it continues to provide payments under the same conditions and criteria as the original subsidy in a manner that causes adverse

---

861 *Compliance Panel*, paras. 9.9, 9.28–9.30, and 9.72–9.73. In its assessment of the scope of the proceedings, the compliance Panel also considered the claim by Brazil that it should make a finding on the 'adverse effects' Brazil suffered from the time period of 22 September 2005-31 July 2006 as a result of the US having not implemented measures to remove them or withdraw the programs under the 2002 Farm Bill during that time. The US refuted the request and compliance Panel agreed that it was inappropriate to do so. *Compliance Panel*, paras. 9.56–9.71.
862 *Compliance Panel*, paras. 9.72–9.73.
863 It is, of course, quite difficult to demonstrate in an "as such" argument that a particular subsidy program will *always* cause serious prejudice. In any particular year, prices may be so high that no subsidy payments will be made.
864 *Compliance Panel*, para. 9.81.

effects."[865] The Panel noted Brazil had not challenged the subsidy programs on an "as such" basis, and therefore held there was no basis for the US preliminary objection. The core basis for the Panel's ruling was its agreement with Brazil that it "was difficult to divorce a payment of a subsidy from the program or legal provision pursuant to which the subsidy is provided."[866]

Having resolved the crucial jurisdictional issue,[867] the Compliance Panel then addressed Brazil's claim that the effect of the new "basket" of marketing loan and counter-cyclical subsidies caused present serious prejudice, *inter alia*, in the form of significant price suppression in the world cotton market. Specifically, in its submissions to the Compliance Panel, Brazil claimed, *inter alia*, that the eventual elimination of the Step 2 subsidy was insufficient to eliminate the significant global price suppression.[868] Brazil was required to essentially re-argue the case that it had put before the original panel but to update it for a new reference period (2005–2006) and examine the effects of marketing loans and countercyclical payments, but not Step 2 subsidies which had been eliminated on 1 August 2006.

In practice, Brazil presented evidence and argumentation that relied heavily on the prior evidentiary findings of the original panel. It claimed and demonstrated that during the reference period of 2005–2006, the combination of the marketing loan and counter-cyclical subsidies caused significant price suppression in the world market.[869] Therefore, the US caused present serious prejudice under Article 5(c) as a result of this price suppression, in violation of 6.3(c) and due to the US' increased market share in violation of Article 6.3(d).[870] The US defense that there was no longer any significant price suppression in the world market was extremely difficult to sustain because so many of the key factors relied on by the original panel had not changed to any significant degree.

The Compliance Panel applied a similar analysis to that completed in the original proceedings to make its determinations. First, the Compliance Panel

---

865　*Compliance Panel*, para. 9.79.
866　*Compliance Panel*, para. 9.52.
867　There were additional procedural claims, including matters dealing with the status of Chad as an LDC, a request for information from the US, a request to open the panel hearing to the public, the late filing of submissions by the US, the propriety of the compliance Panel's composition (discussed, *supra*), and an additional terms of reference issue. These matters did not directly fall into the scope of the thesis of this book are not, therefore, addressed.
868　*Compliance Panel*, para. 10.1.
869　*Compliance Panel*, paras. 10.223–10.225, 10.228.
870　*Compliance Panel*, para. 10.1.

set forth the relevant provisions of Article 5(c) and 6.3(c) of the *SCM Agreement*. Second, it considered a number of interpretive issues related to these provisions. Third, the Compliance Panel considered a number of factors to determine whether the price suppression was 'significant.'

Of note, the Compliance Panel found that there were no material changes to the nature, object, effect, or magnitude of the US marketing loan[871] or counter-cyclical subsidies[872] which continued during the 2005–2006 period at levels at least as high as those of the 1999–2002 period.[873] The fact that the *magnitude of the subsidies*[874] had not significantly changed, since the original proceedings were concluded, allowed the US to maintain its "substantial proportionate influence" on the world market.[875] Further, the *"structure, design and operation"*[876] of the programs being considered (marketing loan and counter-cyclical payments) resulted in continued price suppression.[877] Based on considerable new evidence concerning the operation of these subsidies, the Compliance Panel found that the marketing loan and counter-cyclical subsidies continued to significantly affect the planting decisions of upland cotton farmers and as well as "the level of US upland cotton acreage and production as a result of their mandatory and price-contingent nature and their revenue-stabilizing effect" that can "insulate" revenues of US upland cotton producers when prices are low.[878] However, the Compliance Panel did find that the degree of insulation was less than during the 1999–2002 period.[879] The Compliance Panel also considered both Brazilian and US argumentation on whether, and what degree, US producers were insulated from market conditions and the relation of the subsidies to planting decisions. Though the Compliance Panel agreed with the US that the "degree of insulation is less when expected cotton prices are above their intervention levels," it also noted that "the stable US share of world production and exports does not mean an absence of insulation of US producers from market price signals."[880] A similar

---

871   *Compliance Panel,* paras. 10.75–10.83 (marketing loans).
872   *Compliance Panel,* paras. 10.90–10.103 (counter-cyclical subsides).
873   *Compliance Panel, Cotton 21.5* paras.
874   *Compliance Panel,* paras. 10.108–10.111.
875   *Compliance Panel,* paras. 10.52–10.58.
876   Specifically, the compliance Panel emphasized that the programs "as a result of their mandatory and price-contingent nature and their revenue-stabilizing effect" influence US cotton production. *Compliance Panel,* para. 10.104.
877   *Compliance Panel,* paras. 10.61–10.70.
878   *Compliance Panel,* paras. 10.82 and 10.103–10.104.
879   *Compliance Panel,* para. 101.127.
880   *Compliance Panel,* paras. 10.125–10.127.

inquiry was completed in consideration of Brazil's "discernible temporal coincidence" claim by the Compliance Panel with the finding that, though the effect of the subsidies was more difficult to determine than in the original proceedings, it could find price suppression within the meaning of Article 6.3(c).[881] Further, the Compliance Panel agreed with Brazil that the significant gap between production costs and market revenue, considered "in conjunction with the magnitude" of subsidies, properly supported Brazil's claim that, absent the programs, many US cotton producers would not be able to grow upland cotton because it would not be economically viable.[882] In conclusion, the Compliance Panel found that "without these subsidies the level of US upland cotton acreage and production would likely be significantly lower."[883]

Similarly, while the Compliance Panel found that the importance of the subsidies in covering the total costs of production during the 2005–2006 period diminished somewhat compared with the 1999–2002 period, it still found that "there exists a significant gap between the total costs of production of US upland cotton producers and their market revenue."[884] The Compliance Panel relied heavily on that gap in finding that the "gap between costs and revenue, when analyzed in conjunction with the magnitude of the marketing loan and counter-cyclical subsidies and their importance as a share of the revenue of US cotton producers, supports the proposition that the marketing loan and counter-cyclical payments are an important factor affecting the economic viability of US upland cotton farming."[885]

It is noteworthy that, during the 2005–2006 period, there were no significant changes in the the world cotton market or in world cotton prices The Compliance Panel found that the United States continued to maintain a very high world market share of exports of roughly 40 percent[886] and share of total world production of roughly 20 percent which led the Compliance Panel to find that the United States continued to exercise a predominate proportionate influence on prices in the world market for upland cotton.[887] The Compliance Panel also found, on the disagreement by the parties on the proper use of econometric modeling, that the issue was essentially irrelevant given the fact that whether the FAPRI or ATPSM parameter values were used, price suppression

---

881 *Compliance Panel*, para. 10.146.
882 *Compliance Panel*, para. 10.196.
883 *Compliance Panel*, para. 10104.
884 *Compliance Panel*, para. 10.196.
885 *Compliance Panel*, para. 10.196.
886 *Compliance Panel*, para. 10.56.
887 *Compliance Panel*, para. 10.58.

was found.[888] Nor did the Compliance Panel accept the US arguments that China's increasing impact on world prices as the world's largest producer, as well as largest importer of upland cotton, meant that US subsidies and resulting production and exports no longer had a substantial proportionate influence on world prices.[889] In consideration of the final price suppression analysis, the Compliance Panel dismissed the US argument that market factors, like the role of China in the global trade of cotton, were not considered in assessing the effects of the marketing loan and counter-cyclical payments. Rather, the Compliance Panel stated that, although China may play a significant role, its role "does not diminish the significance of the impact of US subsidies on the world price for upland cotton as a result of their effect on US supply to the world market."[890]

The Compliance Panel agreed with the United States that the elimination of the Step 2 subsidy appeared to have a negative effect on US export performance.[891] The panel found this to be consistent with the effects stemming from removing payments that subsidize exports, a finding also consistent with Brazil's economic simulation model results.[892] However, the Compliance Panel also found, based on US Congressional Budget Office projections, that the elimination of Step 2 subsidy would increase counter-cyclical payments and only slightly reduce marketing loan payments. Thus, the panel found that the effect of eliminating Step 2 subsidies would likely be small and did not diminish the price suppressing effects of the marketing loan and counter-cyclical subsidies.[893] Therefore, it agreed with Brazil that the elimination of Step 2 subsidies did not significantly affect the price suppression effect of the marketing loan and counter-cyclical payments provided by the US to its upland cotton producers.

A significant new finding by the Compliance Panel related to how annual recurring subsidies impact the *long-term* economic viability of US upland cotton farming. Thus, the Compliance Panel stated:

> It is clear to us that whether production of a particular product is higher than would have been the case in the absence of a subsidy is often a critical issue in establishing whether the effect of the subsidy is significant

---

888   *Compliance Panel*, paras. 10.221–10.222.
889   *Compliance Panel*, para. 10.234.
890   *Compliance Panel*, paras. 10.240.10.243.
891   *Compliance Panel*, para. 10231.
892   *Compliance Panel*, para. 10231.
893   *Compliance Panel*, para. 10.239.

price suppression. However, nothing in the text of Article 6 suggests that this can only be examined from a short-term perspective. In our view, the type of effect of a subsidy on production relevant to the analysis under Article 6.3(c) can also be demonstrated on the basis of a longer-term perspective that focuses on how the subsidy affects decisions of producers to enter or exit a given industry. The Panel considers, in this regard, that the evidence on the record, notably the evidence regarding the role of marketing loan and counter-cyclical payments in covering the difference between the market revenue of US upland cotton producers and their costs of production, supports the view that these subsidies have a long-term impact on acreage and production of upland cotton affecting decisions of US cotton farmers to enter or exist cotton farming.[894]

This "longer-term" perspective finding by the Compliance Panel, which was not disturbed on appeal, provides an important tool to assess the causal link between subsidies and the existence of serious prejudice. This is because the magnitude of these subsidies can fluctuate greatly from year-to-year. If only a "short-term" perspective of a few years is taken when prices were high and price-contingent subsides were low, then it would be much more difficult to demonstrate a viable claim. But this long-term methodology endorsed by the *Cotton* Compliance Panel suggests that annual recurring subsidies paid to farmers historically can have long-term effects well into the future. Thus, future challenges to such subsidies should employ this longer-term approach.

Another important ruling by the Compliance Panel, consistent with its longer-term approach, is that it did not find significant the absence of any temporal link between lower world prices and the payment of marketing loan and counter-cyclical subsidies. The Compliance Panel found that world prices had increased generally from the lows of MY 2001–2002.[895] The Compliance Panel concluded that "[t]he fact that recent years have not witnessed the sharp decline in the world market price for upland cotton that occurred during the period considered by the original panel does not necessarily mean that there is currently no price suppression within the meaning of Article 6.3(c) of the *SCM Agreement*."[896] The Compliance Panel's finding on this point, when read in conjunction with its "long-term" approach to examining the effects of subsidies, suggests that future challenges to annual recurring agricultural subsidies need not demonstrate any temporal link between market prices and the

---

894   *Compliance Panel*, para. 10.83.
895   *Compliance Panel*, para. 10.135.
896   *Compliance Panel*, para. 10.146.

provision of subsidies. This is particularly the case where such subsidies have been provided for decades, as with the United States and the European Communities, and where the finding of a temporal point in which subsidies have not distorted the market would be difficult to obtain.

In conclusion, the Compliance Panel found that the US had violated its Article 7.8 obligations under the *SCM Agreement* because it had failed to bring two (2) of its measures into compliance. As a result, the US had caused present serious prejudice to the interests of Brazil within the meaning of Article 5(c) and 6.3(c) of the *SCM Agreement* "...in that the effect of marketing loan payments and counter-cyclical payments provided to US upland cotton producers pursuant to the FSRI Act of 2002 is significant price suppression within the meaning of Article 6.3(c) of the *SCM Agreement* in the world market for upland cotton constituting 'present' serious prejudice to the interests of Brazil within the meaning of Article 5(c)."[897] Therefore, the US had failed to comply with its Article 7.8 obligations under the *SCM Agreement* by not removing the adverse effects or withdrawing the two (2) programs.[898]

Export Credit Guarantees: The rulings of the original Panel, as affirmed by the Appellate Body, granted the United States six months – until July 1, 2006 – to eliminate the prohibited Step-2 and ECG subsidies. The USDA announced on 30 June 2005 that, as of July 1, 2005, it would no longer accept applications for payment guarantees under the GSM 103 program. On February 1, 2006, the US Congress adopted legislation repealing the Step 2 subsidy program for upland cotton as of 1 August 2006. With respect to the ECG GSM programs, the USDA, by October 2005, ceased issuing export credit guarantees under two of its three programs and announced that the CCC would henceforth adopt a new fee schedule for the remaining program, GSM 102. Under the new schedule, fees were increased and fees were allegedly varied with country risk, repayment term (tenor) and repayment frequency (annual or semi-annual). Further, countries were classified in eight risk categories (0–7) with countries in the riskiest categories (7) no longer eligible. Finally, in October 2005, the United States ceased issuing export credit guarantees under the SCGP. Before the Compliance Panel, the United States argued that it had withdrawn the GSM 103 and the SCGP programs, and that export credit guarantees under the revised GSM 102 program made it consistent with WTO obligations.

---

897 *Compliance Panel*, paras. 10.256–1.257.
898 *Compliance Panel*, paras. 10.256–1.257.

Brazil argued that the measures taken to comply by the United States with respect to the GSM 102 export credit guarantee program[899] were insufficient to comply with Articles 10.1 and 8 of the *Agreement on Agriculture*, as well as Articles 3.1(a) and 3.2 of the *SCM Agreement*. Specifically, Brazil returned to its circumvention claims from the original proceedings that argued that the continued GSM 102 export credit guarantees for rice, pig and poultry meat, were prohibited subsidies being used in a manner that resulted in circumvention of US commitments under the AoA.[900] In reliance of the Panel and AB findings[901] on the issue in the context of item (j) of the Illustrative List, the Compliance Panel completed its own analysis of the program as applied to the two (2) relevant AoA provisions with additional submitted evidence,[902] and ultimately agreed that the GSM 102 program constituted export subsidies under Article 10.1 of the AoA.[903] Further, the Compliance Panel then similarly assessed the analyses of the original Panel and AB to determine whether the export subsidies circumvented US commitments. The Compliance Panel relied on evidence offered by Brazil demonstrating the quantity of exports of unscheduled and scheduled products in the form of export credit guarantees, given the cessation of the implementation period (1 July, 2005). In first assessing the unscheduled products, the Compliance Panel found that the US had essentially "committed itself to providing no export subsidies," because it had not specified any reduction commitments.[904] Therefore, the Compliance Panel found that circumvention resulted for the relevant unscheduled products.[905] With regards to the scheduled products (rice, pig and poultry meat), the Compliance Panel remarked on the original panel and AB concerns about the varying schedules of the US and Brazil in trying to quantify commitments.

The ultimate conclusions of the Compliance Panel did not differ from the original proceedings and expressed agreement with Brazil's claim of circumvention based on the basic premise that export subsidies (in the form of export

---

899   "The GSM 102 programme guarantees credit extended by a US private bank...to approved foreign banks...for purchases of US agricultural exports by foreign buyers. The guarantee...is triggered by a default on the part of the foreign bank. The US exporter...submits a notice of default to the CCC and the CCC pays the claim..." *Compliance Panel*, para. 14.15.
900   *Compliance Panel*, para. 14.2, 14.40.
901   These findings differed to the extent that the Panel did not find violation with respect to exports of pig meat and poultry meat; however, the AB reversed this decision but did not complete the analysis. *Compliance Panel*, para. 14.10.
902   *Compliance Panel*, paras. 14.43–14.131.
903   *Compliance Panel*, para. 14.133–14.134.
904   *Compliance Panel*, para. 14.139–14.140.
905   *Compliance Panel*, paras. 14.139–14.140.

credit guarantees) exceeded US commitments for the three scheduled products.[906] Therefore, pursuant to Articles 8 and 10.1 of the AoA, the US was found to have not brought its measure into compliance with the DSB recommendations and rulings.[907] As a result, the Compliance Panel further found that, since the US was acting inconsistently with the AoA, it was not protected from actions under the SCM Agreement. Specifically, Brazil argued and the Compliance Panel found that the scheduled and unscheduled products, as export subsidies exceeding the reduction commitments of the US in violation of the AoA, were similarly in violation of Article 3.1(a) and 3.2 of the SCM Agreement.[908] Therefore, the Compliance Panel found that, in both regards, the US had failed to comply with the DSB recommendations and rulings.[909]

In conclusion, having found the US to be in violation with its obligations of the relevant WTO agreements and were in non-compliance with DSB recommendations and rulings, the Compliance Panel noted that the earlier decisions remained "operative."[910] The US decided to appeal the matter to the AB.

5.7 Appellate Body Proceedings under Article 21.5

Though an express right to appeal is not explicitly proscribed under Article 21.5 of the DSU, the Appellate Body's acceptance of the aircraft-subsidy cases established a precedent that 21.5 panel findings may be appealed.[911] Therefore, in practice, Members have essentially identical rights to Appellate Body review of a compliance panel ruling, pursuant to 16.4 of the DSU, as they do for original panel rulings.[912] Further, Members have the similar requirements, under Rule 20(1), of filing a Notice of Appeal with the Appellate Body as well as notifying, in writing, the DSB of its decision to appeal a panel's decision.[913] To that

---

906   *Compliance Panel,* paras. 14.147–14.148.
907   *Compliance Panel,* paras. 14.149–14.150.
908   *Compliance Panel,* para. 14.153.
909   *Compliance Panel,* paras. 14.153–14.157.
910   *Compliance Panel,* para. 15.2.
911   See, *Canada-Aircraft* (WT/DS70/AB/RW) and *Brazil-Aircraft* (WT/DS46/AB/RW) wherein both 21.5 panel rulings were appealed to the Appellate Body.
912   Wolfrum, R., Stoll, P., and Kaiser, K., *WTO Institutions and Dispute Settlement,* Max Planck Commentaries on World Trade Law, Max Planck Institute for Comparative Public Law and International Law, Martinus Nijhoff Publishers, (2006), p. 516.
913   Article 16.4 states that the appeal process commences when "a party to the dispute formally notifies the DSB of its decision to appeal." Specifically, Rule 20(2)(a)–(d) requires that a Member include the title of the report under appeal, the name and address of the

extent, if a Member disagrees with the determinations of a compliance panel, a Member can appeal the decision to the Appellate Body for review, limited to issues of law.[914]

On 12 February 2008 the United States filed a Notice of Appeal[915] and twelve (12) days later, pursuant to Rule 23 of the Working Procedures, Brazil filed a DSU Articles 16.4 and 17 Notice of Other Appeal in order to cross appeal.[916] The three (3) Appellate Body Members chosen to hear the dispute were Mr. Luiz Olavo Baptista (Presiding member), Ms. Jennifer Hillman, and Mr. David Unterhalter. On appeal, the United States claimed that the Compliance Panel had erroneously ruled that the marketing loan, counter-cyclical payments, and export credit guarantees were measures inconsistent with the SCM and *Agriculture* Agreements. Further, Brazil, concerned that the Appellate Body might reverse specific Panel findings, filed a Notice of Other Appeal in which it conditionally appealed those decisions.[917]

The litigation in the 2007–2008 compliance proceedings regarding Brazil's claims of serious prejudice and prohibited export subsidies was undertaken under the *legal* interpretations that were settled by the original Panel. However, the parties essentially litigated *de novo* many of the fact-based issues that had been addressed before the original Panel. This was due to the fact the measures at issue before the Compliance Panel[918] were "new" and different measures (or combination of previous measures) in view of the changes made by the United States during the implementation period. Thus, Brazil's serious prejudice claims involved the issue of whether a new combination of subsidies,

---

appellate, as well as identify the alleged errors of law and "legal interpretations developed by the panel."

914 It should be noted that, although there is a right to appeal at the WTO, there is no right for the AB to remand the matter back to the panel level. This has been recognized as a weakness of the DSB. *See*, Pauwelyn, J., "Appeal Without Remand: A Design Flaw in WTO Dispute Settlement and How to Fix It," International Centre for Trade and Sustainable Development, last accessed at http://ictsd.org/i/publications/11655/on 1 August, 2010.

915 Notification of an Appeal by the US, Recourse to Article 21.5 of the DSU by Brazil, WT/DS267/33 (19 February 2008).

916 Notice of Other Appeal by Brazil, Recourse to Article 21.5 of the DSU by Brazil, WT/DS267/34 (29 February 2008).

917 Given none of the earlier panel findings were reversed, the AB did not address the conditional appeals.

918 "Compliance Panel" simply refers to the Panel of the compliance proceedings. For clarity purposes of this book, these titles have been proscribed by the author to distinguish between the DSU bodies of the original and 21.5 compliance proceedings. Similarly, the Appellate Body for the compliance proceedings is referred to as the compliance Appellate Body.

consisting only of marketing loan and counter-cyclical subsidies (not Step-2 subsidies), caused serious prejudice in a new reference period – 2005–2006 (as opposed to the 1999–2002 reference period examined by the original Panel). Similarly, the changes to the revised GSM 102 program, coupled with a new reference period to determine if the long-term costs of the program were covered by fees, meant that both Brazil and the United States presented considerable new evidence on the export subsidy claims. Thus, what should have been a relatively rapid compliance process took well over a year to complete, given the length of the parties' submissions and the extent of the new evidence presented to the Compliance Panel.

US Jurisdictional Defense: The final Compliance Appellate Body report for the 21.5 proceedings was issued on 2 June, 2008. In the report, the Compliance AB upheld the Compliance Panel's conclusions on the US' export credit guarantees and Brazil's serious prejudice claim. However, prior to addressing these substantive findings, the Compliance AB made several determinations in reviewing the Compliance Panel's findings on the procedural issue of the scope of compliance proceedings. A central focus of the US appeal was this finding by the Compliance Panel.

In response to US argumentation, a number of third parties agreed with Brazil regarding the effect of the rigid US distinction between "payments" and "programs."[919] In rejecting the US appeal, the Compliance Appellate Body stated that "[w]e have some difficulty accepting the notion that a subsidy program and the payments provided under that program can be assessed separately [because] while the payments may cause adverse effects, the amount of the payments, beneficiaries and the terms and conditions of eligibility will be provided in the subsidy program or legislation authorizing those payments."[920]

The Compliance Appellate Body then noted that the US position would make the WTO subsidy disciplines "meaningless" for annual recurring subsidies.[921] It found as follows:

> [I]n the case of recurring annual payments, the obligation [to implement] is of a continuous nature, extending beyond subsidies granted in the past...and would extend to payments 'maintained' by the respondent Member beyond the time period examined by the panel for purposes of determining the existence of serious prejudice, as long as those payments

---

919 *Compliance AB*, paras. 155–184, including: Argentina, Australia, Canada, Chad, the EU, Japan, and New Zealand.
920 *Compliance AB*, para. 234.
921 *Compliance AB*, para. 238.

continue to have adverse effects... Similarly, a Member would not comply with [its implementation obligations] if it leaves an actionable subsidy in place, either entirely or partially, or replaces that subsidy with another actionable subsidy... [The] option of removing the adverse effects cannot be read as allowing a Member to continue to cause adverse effects by maintaining the subsidies that were found to have resulted in adverse effects.[922]

The Compliance Appellate Body also agreed with the arguments of Brazil and many third parties that the effect of the US argument "would seriously undermin[e] the disciplines contained in Articles 5 and 6 of the *SCM Agreement*" and is inconsistent with the objectives of a "prompt settlement" and "prompt compliance" by WTO Members maintaining measures found to be WTO inconsistent.[923] The Australian delegation, chaired by Ms. Elisabeth Bowes of its Permanent Mission to the WTO, played a critical role in defending the disciplines.[924] The compliance AB specifically cited,

As Australia notes, such panel findings would essentially be declaratory in nature, because there would be no impact on subsidies granted or maintained after the panel made its finding. The complaining Member would have to initiate another dispute to obtain relief with respect to payments made after the period examined by the panel, even if those subsidies are recurring payments or otherwise of the same nature as those found to have resulted in adverse effects. Even if the complaining Member were to succeed in its claims a second time, the subsidizing Member could provide further subsidies after the second panel's ruling, and the complaining Member would have to initiate yet another dispute, and this cycle could continue. As Brazil and several of the third participants have warned, the inability of a complaining Member to obtain relief against subsidies that result in adverse effects to its interests would seriously undermine the disciplines contained in Articles 5 and 6 of the *SCM Agreement*.

This was an extremely important decision by the Compliance Appellate Body to maintain the viability of future challenges to agricultural subsidies. Rejection of the artificial distinction between subsidy "payments" and subsidy

---

922 *Compliance AB*, paras 237–238.
923 *Compliance AB*, paras. 245–246.
924 *Compliance AB*, paras. 246–248.

"programs" means that future challenges of annual recurring agricultural subsidies will simply be focused on the "subsidies" – not annual subsidies isolated from the "program" or legislation creating such subsidies. In practice, it means that future serious prejudice challenges to annual recurring subsidies can result in enforceable obligations to eliminate *future* and *ongoing* subsidies well beyond the reference period used by the original Panel to determine the existence of adverse effects.[925] Therefore, adverse effects claims need not be limited to the recurring subsidies provided only during the time period of the original Panel challenge.

As noted, Brazil had originally claimed that the subsidies provided during the 1999–2002 period caused serious prejudice. The US tried to limit the findings to those dates. However, in the compliance appeal, Brazil claimed that the new subsidies continued to cause serious prejudice during the period 2005–2006. The US defended them by saying that only the lingering effects of 1999–2002 subsidies were properly within the jurisdiction of the compliance 21.5 Panel. However, this Appellate Body ruling is a definitive rejection of the US' attempt to "gut" the disciplines.

For future 21.5 proceedings concerning disciplining agricultural subsidies under the *Agriculture* and *SCM Agreements*, the following can be certain: First, the Compliance AB found that compliance review bodies are not limited to the exact measures taken to comply with the DSB's recommendations and rulings. Of course, if a complainant fails to prevail on one of its claims in the original proceeding state, it may not re-litigate that claim with regards to an unchanged measure. Specifically, the Compliance AB found that Brazil's export guarantees for pig and poultry meat claims had not been resolved on the merits (the original AB had chosen not to complete the analysis) and could therefore be considered within the scope of the Article 21.5 proceedings.[926] Further, the US argued that its marketing loan and counter-cyclical payments were outside the scope of Article 21.5 of the DSU, because the original proceedings were limited to subsidies granted within the 1999–2002 marketing years.[927] However, the Compliance AB rejected this finding and ruled that payments made *after* September 2005 were within the scope of the Article 21.5 proceedings.[928] Further, to the extent that such payments were provided under

---

[925] Please note that this holding by the Appellate Body is limited to annually recurring subsidies, not to past subsidies for which there are no longer any new financial contributions being made.
[926] *Compliance AB*, para. 213.
[927] *Compliance AB*, paras. 217, 220–221.
[928] *Compliance AB*, para. 249.

the same conditions and criteria as in the original proceedings, the Compliance AB ruled that it was proper for the US to be subject to Article 21.5 review and the DSU recommendations. The Compliance AB's rationale was based on a reading of the *SCM Agreement* wherein it states that – where a Member has caused adverse effects – it must remove those effects or withdraw the measure. Again, as stated *supra*, if the Compliance AB would have accepted the US position, any future wronged complainant would be deprived of that remedy and be forced to bring new proceedings to challenge the same WTO-inconsistent subsidies for the only reason that they were applied after a preliminary determination by the triers of fact.

Brazil's Export Subsidy Claims against GSM -102: With respect to the export credit guarantees issued under the revised GSM 102 program after 1 July 2005, the Compliance Panel found that the United States had failed to comply with the DSB recommendations and rulings by acting inconsistently with Articles 10.1 and 8 of the *Agreement on Agriculture* and Article 3.1(a) and 3.2 of the *SCM Agreement*:

> Regarding GSM 102 export credit guarantees issued after 1 July 2005 the United States acts inconsistently with Article 10.1 of the *Agreement on Agriculture* by applying export subsidies in a manner which results in the circumvention of US export subsidy commitments with respect to certain unscheduled products and certain scheduled products, and as a result acts inconsistently with Article 8 of the *Agreement on Agriculture*. Regarding GSM 102 export credit guarantees issued after 1 July 2005 the United States also acts inconsistently with Article 3.1(a) and 3.2 of the *SCM Agreement* by providing export subsidies to unscheduled products and by providing export subsidies to scheduled products in excess of the commitments of the United States under the *Agreement on Agriculture*. By acting inconsistently with Articles 10.1 and 8 of the *Agreement on Agriculture* and Article 3.1(a) and 3.2 of the *SCM Agreement* the United States has failed to comply with the DSB recommendations and rulings. Specifically, the United States has failed to bring its measures into conformity with the *Agreement on Agriculture* and has failed 'to withdraw the subsidy without delay.'[929]

The Compliance Panel concluded, "to the extent that the measures taken by the United States to comply with the recommendations and rulings adopted by the DSB in the original proceeding are inconsistent with the obligations of

---

929 *Compliance Panel*, para. 15.1(c).

the United States under the covered agreements, these recommendations and rulings remain operative."[930]

As mentioned, *supra*, the Compliance Appellate Body rejected the US appeal of the Compliance Panel's finding that GSM-102 measures applying to pig meat and poultry meat were not properly within the Panel's jurisdiction. The Compliance Appellate Body agreed with the Compliance Panel that the revised GSM-102 measure included coverage of pig meat and poultry meat. Further, it found that Brazil should not be barred from challenging the application to pig meat and poultry meat because it had pursued such claims before the original Panel, whose ruling rejecting Brazil's claims was overturned by the original Appellate Body. On appeal, the Appellate Body had upheld the original Panel's finding that the export credit guarantee programs constituted a *per se* export subsidy within the meaning of item (j) of the illustrative list of export subsidies, and a violation of Articles 3.1(a) and 3.2 of the SCM Agreement. In granting Brazil's appeal, the original Appellate Body reversed the original Panel's finding that Brazil had not established that the application of export credit guarantees circumvented the US export subsidy commitments for pig meat and poultry meat.[931]

Regarding the US challenge to the Compliance Panel's findings that the revised GSM-102 program continued to constitute a prohibited export subsidy, the Compliance Appellate Body examined first the quantitative evidence as to whether the long-term operating costs and losses of the program indicated whether it would operate at a loss, thereby constituting an export subsidy. It then examined the qualitative evidence, which the Compliance Panel used to demonstrate that the structure, design and operation of the GSM-102 supports the conclusion that it operates at a loss. In its assessment of the quantitative evidence, the Compliance Appellate Body first articulated as a new legal standard of review that, when Panels function as the initial trier of facts, they must have "provided reasoned and adequate explanations and coherent reasoning."[932] It then applied that new standard to find that the Compliance Panel had improperly accepted Brazil's quantitative evidence while rejecting

---

930   *Compliance Panel*, para. 15.2.

931   However, the Appellate Body indicated it could not complete the analysis on the basis of the record before it. In the later compliance proceeding, Brazil offered proof with respect to pig meat and poultry meat and the compliance Panel found that the United States had exceeded its reduction commitments with respect to these two products.

932   *Compliance AB*, note 618. A discussion of this new standard of review is beyond the scope of this analysis of the Cotton decisions. However, this new standard of review applied in the context of appeals under Article 11 of the DSU, provides a more definitive basis to focus challenges to a panel's reasoning and how it may deal with conflicting evidence in its analysis.

the same type of quantitative evidence submitted by the United States without providing a reasoned or coherent explanation.

Having found that the Compliance Panel had committed error in accepting Brazil's quantitative evidence, the compliance Appellate Body examined the quantitative evidence in the record but concluded that such data support two plausible conclusions, i.e., that the revised GSM 102 program was profitable, or that it was making losses.[933] The Compliance Appellate Body then turned to the qualitative evidence and found that the Compliance Panel had correctly concluded that this evidence supported the conclusion that the GSM 102 program was designed to operate at a loss.[934] Based on this finding, the Compliance Appellate Body affirmed the overall conclusion that the revised GSM-102 program violated Article 3.1(a) and 3.2 of the *SCM Agreement* and Articles 8 and 10.1 of the *Agreement on Agriculture*.[935] By providing export credit guarantees for unscheduled products (including upland cotton) and three (3) scheduled products (rice, poultry meat and pig meat) in a matter that resulted in US subsidy commitments, the US had failed to bring itself into conformity with the DSB's recommendations and rulings of the original proceedings and to withdraw the subsides "without delay."[936]

Brazil's Serious Prejudice Claims: On appeal, the compliance Appellate Body affirmed all of the major serious prejudice related findings and reasoning of the Compliance Panel, which had been challenged by the United States. In doing so, it provided some useful guidance for future panels in assessing serious prejudice claims.

First, the Compliance Appellate Body endorsed the use of econometric modeling and other quantitative techniques to "provide a framework to analyze the relationship between subsidies, other factors, and price movements."[937] It criticized the Panel for not examining in detail the parameters of the competing economic models presented by Brazil and the United States[938] as follows:

---

933   *Compliance Panel*, para. 321.
934   *Compliance Panel*, paras. 322–323.
935   It should be noted that while not reflected in either the compliance panel or the Appellate Body report, Brazil presented considerable argumentation and evidence demonstrating that the ECG was an export subsidy.
936   *Compliance AB*, para. 448.
937   *Compliance AB*, para. 356.
938   The original Appellate Body had also criticized the original Panel for failing to conduct an extensive analysis of the complex facts and economic arguments arising in the dispute. *Compliance AB*, para. 458.

Because the examination of price suppression necessarily involves an analysis of what would have been the case in the absence of an intervening event, modeling exercises are likely to be an important analytical tool that a panel should scrutinize. The relative complexity of a model and its parameters is not a reason for a panel to remain agnostic about them. Like other categories of evidence, a panel should reach conclusions with respect to the probative value it accords to economic simulations or models presented to it. This kind of assessment falls within the panel's authority as the initial trier of facts in a serious prejudice case... [T]he Panel could have gone further in its evaluation and comparative analysis of the economic simulations and the particular parameters used.[939]

As discussed in Section 5.8 below, the Arbitrators in the Article 22.6 proceeding appear to have adhered to the compliance Appellate Body's suggestions when they examined carefully the parameters used by the parties and accepted Brazil's simulation model and its parameters in making its findings. Future challenges to agricultural subsidies will certainly involve econometric modeling to resolve the *but for* counterfactual questions. In view of this relatively strong suggestion from the compliance Appellate Body, the resolution of these counterfactual issues will require both the parties and panels to use and understand the benefits – and limitations – of such models.

A second important finding by the compliance Appellate Body for future serious prejudice challenges of agricultural subsidies is its clarifications regarding the rigor of the causal link required between the effects of the subsidies and the particular form of serious prejudice set out in Article 6.3(c). The compliance Appellate Body held as follows:

> [T]he 'but for' test would be too rigorous if it required the subsidy to be the *only cause* of the price suppression. Instead, the 'but for' test should determine that price suppression is the effect of the subsidy and that there is a 'genuine and substantial relationship of cause and effect.'

Had the Compliance Appellate Body found that the effects of subsidies must be *the only* cause of prices not being as high as they otherwise might be, this would have put a very difficult burden on complaining parties. The explicit

---

[939] *Compliance AB*, paras 357–358.

establishment that it is not fatal if there are other factors influencing prices is a helpful clarification in this and in future cases.[940]

Third, the Compliance Appellate Body affirmed the Compliance Panel's reliance on prior factual findings related to the challenged subsidies and to market structure and conditions. It found that the challenged US subsidies indeed insulated cotton producers from market signals, despite the elimination of the Step 2 program. For market insulation, the Compliance AB added to its previous decisions in emphasizing that a Compliance Panel proceeding is part of a "continuum of events" and confirmed that "it was appropriate for the Panel to have relied on the findings from the original proceedings unless 'any change in the underlying evidence in the record' would have justified departing from them."[941] The fact that the evidence was weighed differently did not constitute an error by the Compliance Panel and that, further, the analysis was essential to establishing the present serious prejudice claim.[942] This holding will be very useful for complaining parties, allowing them to be free from the necessity of having to reprove and re-establish all of the key facts in a compliance proceeding. This restraint on new factual findings in compliance proceedings is useful for protecting the findings of the original Panel's that had found serious prejudice.

Finally, like the Compliance Panel, the Compliance Appellate Body confirmed the importance of assessing the long-term effects of annual, recurring subsidies. It stated: "In our view, the effect of a subsidy on production can also be assessed on the basis of a long-term perspective that focuses on how the subsidy affects decisions of producers to enter or exist a given industry."[943] And significantly, the Compliance Appellate Body noted the Compliance Panel's finding that "the role of marketing loan and counter-cyclical payments in covering the difference between the market revenue of [United States] upland cotton producers and their costs of production, supports the view that these subsidies have a long-term impact on acreage and production of upland

---

940 It should be noted that the original Appellate Body indicated "it would be difficult to make a judgment on significant price suppression without taking into account the effect of the subsidies." *Compliance AB*, para. 433. Thus, the "but for" test arguably could require that the only cause of the relevant price suppression is the effect of the subsidies. Prices may well fluctuate up and down for various reasons. But it is only that portion of the restraint on price movements (which objectively can go either up or down) that is linked to the effects of the subsidies that is relevant.

941 *Compliance AB*, para. 386.

942 *Compliance AB,* paras. 386–404.

943 *Compliance AB*, para. 392.

cotton by affecting decisions of [United States] cotton farmers to enter or exit cotton farming."[944]

This "long term" approach focusing on "exiting" cotton farming should be read in the context that non-price contingent agricultural subsidies, such as direct payments and crop insurance subsidies, do assist farmers in covering their total costs of production. Thus, based on the explicit reasoning of the Compliance Panel and the Compliance Appellate Body, there is no rational reason why such non-price contingent subsidies should not also be deemed to *contribute* to the farmer's decision to "exit" or "enter" the farming of cotton – or any other agricultural commodity. If so, then such subsidies should be included within the pool of subsidies for which subsidizing Members causing serious prejudice must take steps to remove their adverse effects or withdraw the subsidies.

The Compliance Panel and Compliance AB, having rejected the jurisdictional defenses of the US and having upheld Brazil's export credit guarantee and serious prejudice claims,[945] triggered Brazil's right, pursuant to its original sequencing agreement with the United States,[946] to pursue authorization to impose retaliatory measures. To that end, in August of 2008, Brazil requested that the reopening of arbitration proceedings commence.[947]

5.8   Arbitration Proceedings under Article 22.6

Pursuant to 22.2 of the DSU, in the event that a respondent Member fails to implement the recommendations and rulings of the DSB within the reasonable period of time allotted, the complainant Member may request to enter into negotiations with the respondent for appropriate compensation.[948] If, within twenty (20) days of the expiry of the reasonable implementation period, satisfactory compensation is not agreed upon, the complainant may request authorization to retaliate against the respondent. If authorization is given and

---

944 *Compliance AB*, para. 392.
945 *Compliance AB*, paras. 448–449.
946 "Understanding between Brazil and the United States Regarding Procedures under Articles 21 and 22 of the DSU and Article 4 of the SCM Agreement," *US-Upland Cotton*, WT/DS267/22 (5 July 2005).
947 Communication from Brazil, *US-Upland Cotton*, WT/DS267/38, WT/DS267/39, (15 October 2008).
948 Van den Bossche, P., *The Law and Policy of the World Trade Organization: Text, Cases and Materials*, © Cambridge University Press, Second Edition, (2008), pp. 305–306.

the respondent objects to the level of suspension,[949] the dispute may be referred to arbitration before the DSB takes the decision, under Article 22.6 of the DSU.[950] Arbitrators may be comprised of the same panel members who initially reviewed the matter or a new arbitrator can be appointed by the WTO's Director-General (DG). It is important to note that arbitration results are not appealable, and the results are binding for the parties.[951]

In *Cotton*, the Arbitrator was constructed on 1 October 2008[952] and consisted of Mr. Eduardo Perez-Motta (Chairperson), Mr. Alan Matthews, and Mr. Daniel Moulis. The final decisions were not circulated until almost a year later on 31 August 2009. This was precedential given the DSU states that the arbitration process should be completed within sixty (60) days, or within a "reasonable period of time." The extension was again due to the complexity of the case and extensive evidence required. It can be reasonably asserted that the *Cotton* arbitration is the most complex and analytically demanding of any that has come before the WTO. The level of empirical evidence and economic analysis required to determine the amount of damages and retaliatory measures were arguably unprecedented. Similar to the *EC-Bananas III* case, the DSB desired to "avoid future disagreements between the parties."[953] Further, and to emphasize the point above, the results are final and therefore, allowing arbitrators adequate time is particularly important.

Arbitration under Article 22.6 of the DSU focused on the amount and type of countermeasures Brazil now has the authority to adopt. To that end, in the Article 22.6 proceedings, the Arbitrators issued two separate reports on August

---

[949] It should be noted that arbitration proceedings may also be commenced, under Article 21.3 of the DSU, when there is an issue regarding the "reasonable period of time for implementation."

[950] WTO Secretariat, *A Handbook on the WTO Dispute Settlement System*, © Cambridge University Press, (2004), p. 24.

[951] However, as noted, arbitration results can be enforced through Articles 21 and 22 of the DSU.WTO Secretariat, *A Handbook on the WTO Dispute Settlement System*, © Cambridge University Press, (2004), pp. 24–25.

[952] It should be noted, as explained *supra* that Brazil had already pursued arbitration in 2005 and requested countermeasures twice at that time. First, in July, Brazil requested countermeasures when the compliance period ended for prohibited subsidies (WT/DS267/21 – 5 July 2005). Second, in October, Brazil requested countermeasures when the compliance period ended for subsidies that caused serious prejudice (WT/DS267/26 – 7 October 2005). However, do to the sequencing agreement entered into with the US, the parties chose to suspend the work of the arbitrator until there was a confirmation on the claims by the compliance Panel (and compliance AB).

[953] Van den Bossche, P., *The Law and Policy of the World Trade Organization: Text, Cases and Materials*, © Cambridge University Press, Second Edition, (2008), pp. 305–306.

31, 2009 – one under Article 4.11 of the *SCM Agreement* relating to the calculation of the amount and type of suspension of concessions related to Brazil's prohibited export subsidy claims against US export credit guarantee (GSM-102) program and another report under Article 7.10 of the *SCM Agreement* relating to the calculation of the amount and type of suspension of concessions regarding Brazil's serious prejudice claims. Therefore, the first decision addressed the prohibited subsidies at issue[954] and the second decision addressed the actionable subsidies at issue.[955] Some of the following analysis is conducted on each separate claim, but given that a number of issues in front of the Arbitrator were relevant in both decisions, a collective analysis is included as well. For the purposes of describing the *Cotton* decisions, therefore, these two (2) reports are treated as one decision.

After the six-year *Cotton* battle, the WTO arbitrator[956] granted Brazil the right to retaliate against U.S. trade in goods and intellectual property rights in amounts that may well reach more than $800 million.[957] The Arbitrator's calculation of what are effectively "trade damages" followed an earlier United States refusal to eliminate billions of US dollars in annual highly trade-distorting "domestic" subsidies sustaining the world's largest exporter of cotton. The Arbitrators calculated additional amounts of trade damages from the U.S. refusal to stop providing prohibited export subsidies supporting the export of a wide variety of agricultural products. The decision recognizes Brazil's right to retaliate on US-origin goods and authorizes cross retaliation in IPRs and services, conditioned upon the US exceeding an adjustable minimum amount of imports of US goods. The *Cotton* case is the first WTO Dispute Settlement to address retaliation in response to actionable subsidies.[958] Further, the level of retaliation in the *Cotton* case is the second highest amount in the history of the WTO, and the Arbitrator broke new ground in terms of the types and levels of retaliation and cross-retaliation allowed in response to non-compliance of mandated reforms of prohibited subsidies.

---

954 These included: GSM 102, GSM 103, and SCGP export guarantee programs and other unscheduled agricultural products supported under the programs; one scheduled product – rice; and Section 1207(a) of the FSRI Act of 2002.
955 These included: marketing loan program payments, Step 2 payments, market loss assistance payments and countercyclical payments.
956 For convenience, this discussion uses the convention of referring to the three members of the WTO Arbitration panel as the Arbitrator.
957 In a meeting on 19 November 2009, the DSB formally authorized Brazil to impose the Arbitrators' countermeasures.
958 The Arbitrator's decisions also address prohibited subsidies.

In sum, the Arbitrator authorized an upfront payment of US$295 million and two levels of countermeasures that Brazil can now impose against the US as (1) a fixed amount of $147.3 annually for cotton payments and (2) an annual amount for the GSM-102 program that would vary, based on the US usage of the program ($147.4 based on MY2006).[959] Further, cross-sectoral countermeasures against US IPRs and Services, under the WTO *TRIPS* and *GATS Agreements*, respectively, may be imposed to the extent that Brazil applies total countermeasures in excess of a determinable threshold. Varying annually, the threshold for 2006 was $400 million and presently estimated at approximately $560 million.[960]

As an introductory note, it should be stated that, in assessing these levels of retaliatory measures, the Arbitrator included only the effects of prohibited US cotton support programs on Brazil, rather than include a wider consideration of trade effects on other countries. In doing so, the Arbitrators deviated from the previously established approach to arbitration, thus making the issue of precedence questionable (discussed, *infra*). Summations of the Arbitrators' Article 4.11 and Article 7.10 legal findings are set forth as follows:

> *Export Credit Guarantee Countermeasures Findings, under Article 4.11 of the SCM Agreement*: Brazil first requested a proposed level of countermeasures for prohibited subsidies involving Step 2 payments made in the most recently concluded marketing year and "the total of exporter applications received under GSM 102, GSM 103 and SCGP for the most recent concluded fiscal year."[961] However, in its methodology paper,[962] Brazil limited its request to a one-time payment in relation to the Step 2 payments after the period for compliance and before the program's repeal (US$350 million), and countermeasures proportionate to the annual amount of prohibited GSM 102 export credit guarantees issued for export transactions involving unscheduled products, rice, pig meat and poultry meat (US$1.294 billion).[963]

---

959 It should be noted that Brazil had requested approximately US$3 BILLION, under its prohibited subsidy claim and US$1.4 BILLION, under its actionable subsidy claim. The Arbitrators granted US$147.3 and US$147.4 million, respectively.

960 Therefore, of the $820 million in countermeasures, Brazil could impose at present, approximately $260 million in the IPRs and services sectors.

961 *4.11 Arbitration*, para. 2.5.

962 *4.11 Arbitration*, paras. 2.6, 3.2.

963 *4.11 Arbitration*, paras. 2.1–2.6.

On the issue of Step 2 payments made, Brazil requested that countermeasures be determined for the thirteen (13) months after the ninety (90)-day implementation period from (1 July 2005 to 30 July 2006), arguing that the granting of such "one-time" countermeasures would be appropriate to ensure conformity by respondents by the end of the allotted implementation period and to compensate for damages incurred by Brazil during that period.[964] Specifically, when Brazil first made its request for countermeasures in 2005, the US Step 2 program remained in effect. As discussed, *supra*, Brazil and the US had entered into a sequencing agreement, wherein it was agreed that Brazil would not request countermeasures until a 21.5 Compliance review had been completed. However, by the time the Compliance Panel was established under Article 21.5 of the DSU, the US had repealed this measure. In that review, therefore, the Panel declined to make a ruling by the end of the implementation period that the US had failed to withdraw the subsidy as recommended by the DSB.[965] Although acknowledging that the US had not withdrawn the measure in a timely manner, the Arbitrator ruled that a multilateral finding within the timeframe was a prerequisite to being able to be granted such an "exceptional remedy."[966]

This raises an important issue for future dispute resolution involving sequencing agreements and the possible remedies complainants may lose by entering into such arrangements, especially in light of the fact that delays involved in WTO dispute resolution can be considerable. In the *Cotton* case, the delay between the expiry of the implementation period and the authorization of countermeasures exceeded four years.[967] This delay was the result of several developments. As mentioned, Brazil and the US entered into a sequencing agreement under which Brazil agreed to suspend arbitration until the completion of a 21.5 compliance review. The compliance review process took over two (2) and a half (1/2) years to complete, a significantly longer time frame than had been anticipated by the DSU. Additionally, the arbitration process took over a year to complete, far exceeding the 60 (sixty) days originally anticipated and specified by the DSU. These factors resulted in a four (4) year delay period, during which time the US continued to provide those subsidies deemed to be WTO-inconsistent in the earlier *Cotton* proceedings. In the *Cotton* arbitration, it was determined that Brazil's right to countermeasures arose at the end of the

---

964   *4.11 Arbitration*, paras. 3.20–3.21.
965   *Panel Report*, para. 9.71 and *4.11 Arbitration*, para. 3.20.
966   *4.11 Arbitration*, para. 3.38.
967   The reasonable period of time ended on 21 September 2005 and the authorization of countermeasures was given to Brazil by the DSB on 19 November 2009.

implementation period and that, consequently, Brazil's right lapsed when the US withdrew the subsidy sometime after the end of the period.[968] Therefore, the Arbitrator declined to authorize this element of Brazil's claim and ruled that "there was no legal basis" for Brazil to seek countermeasures in relation to the absence of compliance by the US prior to the repealed program.[969] The Arbitrator reasoned,

> In light of our determinations above that countermeasures are a temporary remedy available only where compliance has not been achieved and with a view to inducing such compliance, and that full implementation is preferred to the suspension of concessions or other obligations, we do not consider that there would be a legitimate basis to such countermeasures as requested by Brazil in relation to past payments made until the repeal of Step 2, in the absence of a multilateral determination of non-compliance in relation to such payments and independently of any continuing situation of non-compliance.[970]

Therefore, Step 2 payments for MY 2005 were dismissed on the grounds that they were, in other words, retroactive damages.

With regards to the GSM 102 transactions in Fiscal Year (FY) 2006, the Arbitrator deemed "appropriate"[971] and awarded countermeasures of US$147.4 million, and proposed a simple formula for updating the level of countermeasures,[972]

---

[968] *4.11 Arbitration*, para. 3.62.

[969] *4.11 Arbitration*, paras. 3.1–3.15, 3.62, and 3.64.

[970] *4.11 Arbitration*, para. 3.50.

[971] In determining appropriateness, the Arbitrator considered the identical footnotes in Articles 4.10 and 4.11, which read, "this expression is not meant to allow countermeasures that are disproportionate in light of the fact that the subsidies dealt with under these provisions are prohibited." *SCM Agreement*, as cited and interpreted by the Arbitrator at paras. 4.27–4.33. Interpretation of the adjective 'appropriate' was given considerable further attention in paras. 4.44–4.48 and the level of countermeasures were ultimately lowered based on the Arbitrator's interpretation of the term in the context of footnote 9 of the SCM, so as to ensure that the remedy provided was not excessive. *Arbitration*, paras. 4.114–4.115.

[972] 4.11 Arbitration, *Annex 4. The arbitrator offered the following formula to calculate the amount of countermeasures that Brazil is authorized to take on an annual basis:*

$CM_{t+1} = \alpha(GSM_t^B) + \beta(share_t)(GSM_t^{NB})$

where:

CM_{t+1} is the amount of countermeasures in year $t + 1$ that Brazil is authorized to apply;

GSM_t^B is the transaction value secured by GSM 102 export credit guarantees in fiscal year t obtained by *Brazilian obligors*;

based on export credit guarantee (ECG) amounts to Brazil and other GSM recipients.[973] According to the proscribed formula,[974] countermeasure calculations depend, *inter alia,* on the transaction value secured by GSM 102 and its distribution among classes of obligors. Two features are key to the calculation. The first is the degree of interest rate subsidization offered to foreign obligors.[975] This is essentially the difference between the discounted financing terms offered under the GSM program and the terms that those obligors could have obtained in non-subsidized loan markets ("IRS" subsidy). For characterization purposes, this is considered the amount of the GSM 102 subsidy. The second key element is the "additionality"[976] benefits from the program.[977]

> GSM_t^{NB} is the transaction value secured by GSM 102 export credit guarantees in fiscal year t obtained by *non-Brazilian obligors*;
>
> $share_t$ is Brazil's share of world exports of GSM 102 products in calendar year t;
>
> α is the parameter that relates the transaction value secured by GSM 102 export credit guarantees obtained by Brazilian obligors to their trade-distorting impact on Brazil; and,
>
> β is the parameter that relates the transaction value secured by GSM 102 export credit guarantees obtained by non-Brazilian obligors to their trade-distorting impact on Brazil (apportioned to Brazil's share of world exports of GSM 102 products).
>
> This formula requires the annual updating of only three figures: the transaction value secured by Brazilian obligors in any given calendar year (GSM_t^B), the transaction value secured by non-Brazilian obligors (GSM_t^{NB}), and Brazil's share of world exports in GSM 102 products in the same year ($share_t$). Additionally, the Arbitrator accepted the Ohlin formula and other measures. *4.11 Arbitration,* para. 4.232. For an overview of the use of the parameters of the Ohlin formula in the determination of the magnitude of export guarantees subsidization, see, "Agriculture and trade liberalization: extending the Uruguay Round Agreement," Organization for Economic Co-operation and Development, OECD, (2002), especially pp. 137–139.

973 Initially, Brazil had applied its calculation methodology and argued that the "appropriate" annual countermeasures should be valued at US$1.55 billion. *4.11 Arbitration,* paras. 4.6–4.7.

974 In start of the arbitration proceedings, the Arbitrator had requested clarification as to whether Brazil wished to have a fixed amount of annual countermeasures for prohibited subsidies be granted or a variable amount. Brazil clarified that it was requesting a formula (its formula) be applied for the determination of the appropriate countermeasures. In response, the US stated that a fixed amount was the typical approach, but that previous arbitrators had chosen a formula. The Arbitrator decided to apply the formula approach. *4.11 Arbitration,* paras. 4.3–4.5.

975 *4.11 Arbitration,* paras. 4.6.

976 Additionality was divided into 'full' and 'marginal' additionality. The former refers to "sales to non-creditworthy foreign obligors that simply otherwise would not have been possible" and the latter refers to "sales to creditworthy borrowers where the IRS acts like a sales discount to foreign obligors." *4.11 Arbitration,* para. 4.182.

977 *4.11 Arbitration,* paras. 4.6.

These are the "benefits" reaped by US producers from increased exports due to the ECG program relative to what those exports would have been absent the program. For characterization purposes, this was considered the element that reflects the subsidy's trade effects. Both of these elements, interest rate subsidization and additionality benefits, were used by the Arbitrator to allocate Brazil's share of the trade damages to the cotton market.[978] It is important to note that the Arbitrator distinguished between the trade-distorting impacts of the ECG program in the Brazilian domestic market, the direct impacts, and the impacts in other markets, the "third-country" market impacts.[979] As a result, in determining the amount of trade damages to the Brazilian market, the Arbitrator accounted for the effects of GSM 102-supported trades involving Brazilian obligors within the Brazilian market. In terms of third-country effects, the Arbitrator used Brazil's share of exports to global markets affected by GSM 102 transactions. However, in order to estimate *Brazil's* damages resulting from US prohibited subsidies in the form of ECGs, the Arbitrator held that "the amount of additionality and the IRS must be apportioned to Brazil's share of the market."[980] To that end, the Arbitrator calculated this share for the world market, but found that no apportionment was necessary for the Brazilian domestic market.[981] With regards to the interest rate subsidy and the two types of additionality (full and marginal), the Arbitrator found that Brazilian producers and consumers suffered US$25.27 million, US$80.8 million, and US$41.3 million, respectively.[982] Therefore, in total, the Arbitrator found that the GSM 102 transactions in FY 2006 were deemed to result in an appropriate level of countermeasures in the amount of US$147.4 million.[983] In order to ensure US cooperation with Brazil so that Brazil could properly assess its future retaliatory rights, the Arbitrator determined that "[the] United States shall provide the most recent fiscal year data on GSM 102 transactions."[984] Further, the Arbitrator also decided that the formula can be applied to three scheduled products (pig meat, poultry meat and rice) to the extent that the export subsidies provided to volumes of exports of the products are in excess of US reduction commitments. For the calculation of the corresponding deduction, the

---

978   *4.11 Arbitration*, paras. 4.178–4.181.
979   *4.11 Arbitration*, paras. 4.184–4.202.
980   *4.11 Arbitration*, para. 4.199.
981   *4.11 Arbitration*, paras. 4.199–4.202.
982   *4.11 Arbitration*, paras. 4.208–4.244, Annex 1; paras. 4.245–255, Annex 2; and 4.256–277, Annex 3.
983   *4.11 Arbitration*, paras. 4.277–4.278, Annex 4.
984   *4.11 Arbitration*, Annex 4, para. 5.

Arbitrator determined that "[the] United States shall provide the most recent data on US export prices of the scheduled products."[985]

There was considerable analysis conducted on Brazil's "benefits" calculation approach and the US' "net cost to government" approach. In the end, the Arbitrator rejected the US approach and ruled that it did not find that the elements were cumulatively "benefits," but agreed with Brazil that it's calculation could be used given the "nature and legal status of those guarantees."[986] The US argued that the amount of the countermeasures awarded to Brazil should be limited to the net cost of the program to the US government of providing the ECG program. The US argument was based on its interpretation of item (j) of Annex I to the SCM Agreement that ECG programs that breakeven in terms of net benefits should be considered to provide no subsidy, regardless of any benefits to producers stemming from such programs. The Arbitrator rejected both arguments and found that countermeasures should not be gauged solely in terms of the net cost of providing such programs and that "as a matter of law, it is possible that an item (j)-consistent export credit guarantee programme might still be found to confer a 'benefit.'"[987] The Arbitrator continued, "Brazil would be entitled to continue to apply countermeasures until the full benefit of the GSM 102 programme has been withdrawn."[988] The Arbitrator determined that the benefits derived from the program were substantial and estimated that, in FY 2006, US$997 million in ECGs caused an estimated US$750 million in worldwide damages. Damages to Brazil consisted of the direct impacts, described *supra*, on domestic producers and exporters stemming from the transactions of Brazilian GSM obligors, and the third-country impacts to Brazilian exporters, with an estimated twelve (12) percent of the global export market.[989]

Further, countermeasures for the GSM 102 part are to be updated every year.[990] A preliminary calculation performed for the Brazilian Ambassador's press conference revealed that for MY 2007, 2008 and 2009, there were countermeasures of $112, $373, and $672 million, respectively. The fact that the

---

985   *4.11 Arbitration*, Annex 4, para. 6. As communicated to the DSB, Brazil intends to apply the Arbitrator's formula on the basis of 2009 data. To that end, it informed the DSB that it requested the requisite information (GSM 102 data from fiscal year 2009 and data on export prices for the three listed commodities) from the US and expected the US to comply with the Arbitrator's decision.
986   *4.11 Arbitration*, paras. 4.127–4.172 and para. 4.173.
987   *4.11 Arbitration*, para 4.161.
988   *4.11 Arbitration*, para 4.162.
989   *4.11 Arbitration*, paras. 4.208–4.244, Annex 1 and paras. 4.256–4.277, Annex 3.
990   *4.11 Arbitration*, paras. 4.277–4.278, Annex 4.

Arbitrator allowed Brazil to update the amount of injury suffered from the effects of the ECGs is especially significant, given the 2008 Financial Crisis. As a result of the credit crisis, the US is now using ECGs to a much higher degree (see table at the end of Section 5.8). This will allow Brazil to claim that the total amount of the projected retaliation for 2009 will be in the range of US$650 million in ECGs. Combined with the *Cotton* adverse effects findings (*discussed, infra*), the total level of retaliatory measures will equal approximately US$800 million.

On a related matter, Brazil now has a right to cross-retaliate against US IPR interests (also discussed, *infra*) after the total adverse effects and export subsidy ECG amounts reach around US$400 million.[991] Given the total for 2009 will reach approximately US$800 million, half of Brazil's right to retaliate will be against IPR interests of the US. This will certainly upset the relevant US interest groups and should give Brazil significant additional leverage at the WTO and in bilateral negotiations with the US on the issue of cotton.[992] Practitioners and scholars interviewed noted that this was a surprising aspect of the *Cotton* Arbitrator's decision. This was a positive development for Brazil, who was not granted countermeasures based on "world effects" and could not have otherwise economically justified imposing retaliation based on goods, since it would have caused more harm to its own consumers, by affecting needed goods, than the value of retaliation. As Brazil included in its communications to the DSB, "Brazil welcomes the Arbitrators' recognition of the difficulties faced by our country if it only had the option to apply countermeasures on imports of U.S. goods. The Arbitrators determined that only a limited subset of the overall U.S. imports into Brazil could be subject to countermeasures without resulting in unreasonable costs on the Brazilian economy and its consumers."

Serious Prejudice Countermeasures in relations to Marketing Loan/Counter-Cyclical Payments, under Article 7.10 of the SCM Agreement: The Arbitrator awarded a fixed annual amount of countermeasures of US$147.3 million, which it deemed to be "the amount of countermeasures that are commensurate with the degree and nature of the adverse effects" of the US marketing loan and counter-cyclical payments.[993] The amount was based on the following elements: "Brazil-only" effects (approximately 5% of the world exports), not taking into account any "significance threshold," and as MY 2005 as the

---

991   *4.11 & 7.10 Arbitrations,* paras. 5.230–5.234, 6.5.
992   The issues of leverage and US compliance, as well as a description of the eventual Framework entered into between the US and Brazil are described in Part 3 of this book.
993   *7.10 Arbitration,* paras. 4.193–4.195, Annex 2.

reference period. The Arbitrator wholly adopted the Sumner econometric model, used in earlier proceedings, as well as Brazil's short-term elasticities and the counter-cyclical payment "coupling factor,"[994] with Brazil's futures market price regression to derive price expectations.[995]

Based on the Sumner Model, the Arbitrator found that the marketing loan and counter-cyclical subsidies caused 9.38 percent price suppression in the world market, accounting to overall effects of US$2.905 billion, of which US$2.38 billion are based on sales value effects and US$521.5 million were based on reduced production effects.[996] The Arbitrator obtained its amount of countermeasures based on Brazil's share of total cotton production in the world (5.1 percent).[997]

There are several important aspects of the Arbitrator's decision that are relevant to future challenges to agricultural subsidies. First, and as noted in the introduction of this section of the book, a key aspect of the Arbitrator's decision was to find that the amount of appropriate suspension of concessions for Brazil was limited to the impact on Brazil of the price suppression resulting from the granting of marketing loan and counter-cyclical payments on the world market.[998] Therefore, in calculating the world minus the US, there was 92,689k of cotton produced. Brazil had argued that it was entitled to suspend concessions of more than one (1) billion because it claimed that the serious prejudice determination was significant price suppression of the world market – not significant price suppression for only those transactions involving Brazil. Brazil's share of the world cotton market was roughly five (5) percent in the reference period used to calculate countermeasures. Nevertheless, the Arbitrator stated that Brazil could continue to impose $147.3 million per year for as long as the United States does not eliminate the marketing loan and counter-cyclical subsidies or remove all of the significant price suppression in the world market:

---

994 The coupling factor indicates "the degree of production incentive that a particular programme has on US cotton farmers relative to revenue from the market." *7.10 Arbitration*, para. 4.164.

995 The use of futures market prices as a basis for the model of price expectations was the subject of some debate. Producers make planting decisions relatively early in the year based on their expectations of what prices will prevail in the following December, when most cotton is marketed. The Arbitrator determined that the fitted futures price "better represents farmers' expectation of the price of cotton." *7.10 Arbitration*, paras. 4.179–4.192.

996 *7.10 Arbitration*, paras. 4.193–3.195.

997 *7.10 Arbitration*, paras. 4.193–3.195.

998 *7.10 Arbitration*, para. 4.92.

> The fact that the remedies available to Brazil must be commensurate with the degree and nature of the adverse effects in relation to its own interests does not alter the scope of what the United States might be required to do in order to remove such adverse effects. In particular, it does not modify the fact that the source of the adverse effects determined to exist in this case is the existence of 'significant price suppression' on the *world* market, and this is what the United States must address in removing the adverse effects at issue.[999]

This is an important part of the decision because it means that Brazil can continue to retaliate against the United States until the subsidies are eliminated or *all* their world-wide adverse effects removed.[1000] It should be emphasized that there is no right to appeal decisions of the Arbitrator under WTO rules. For this reason, there is a relatively weak precedential effect of this, or any other Arbitrator's decision on future Arbitrators. Strong arguments exist and have been expressed that the special rules of Article 7.9 and Article 7.10 of the *SCM Agreement* should be given a meaning separate and distinct from the normal rules of Article 22.6 of the *DSU*. While the Arbitrators in *Cotton* did not take an expansive view of interests of the original panel's determination regarding the serious prejudice found to exist – significant price suppression in the world market – this would not preclude arguments to future arbitrators asking them to take a different position.

Nevertheless, an important tactical lesson to be learned from *Cotton* for future challenges to agricultural subsidies is to combine as many complaining parties with the largest possible share of world production or world exports, in order to create the requisite "critical implementation mass" to pressure non-complying Members.[1001] For example, China, Brazil, and India – who

---

999   *7.10 Arbitrator's Report,* para. 4.90.
1000 In conducting interviews, it was found that this is recognized as a small amount and more of a victory for the US and its cotton interest group, the National Cotton Council (NCC). Compared to the approximate two (2) billion US dollars a year the government provides its upland cotton producers in marketing loan and counter-cyclical subsidies, the level of countermeasures awarded Brazil was rather miniscule. However, the sheer fact that the negative decision remains on the books should remain an irritant to the US cotton industry and government as a reminder that it has not implemented the rules and recommendations of the *Cotton* dispute. This issue is discussed in greater detail in Part 3 of this book.
1001 In calculating adverse effects, in MY 2005, production consisted of the following: Brazil (4,700 k 480lb bales), India (19,050), China (28,400), US (28,890), and world (116,579).

collectively total more than half of all world cotton production.[1002] The combined adverse effects to these countries could have amounted to US$1,634,559,538 as estimated by their market share of the total adverse effects of US$2,905,190,586 as established by the Arbitrator.[1003] If these three (3) G-20 Members had joined forces to challenge significant world-wide price suppression caused by U.S. upland cotton subsidies, under the Panel's methodology, the total amount of retaliation under the Arbitrator's formula would have been significantly higher.[1004] The United States would still have the obligation to remove all of the significant price suppression, but considering the higher number, instead of $147.3 million, as an arguably greater incentive to eliminate its WTO-inconsistent conduct.

A second important aspect of the Arbitrator's 22.6 decision is the fact that the Arbitrator accepted the Sumner Model for Brazil and the parameters used in calculating the price effects of the US subsidies. This was especially important for Brazil given the contention over the appropriate economic model to use during the original 21.5 Panel proceedings, as described in the sections *supra*. For future disputes, the Arbitrators have sanctioned the use of the Sumner Model and similar analyses that, as a result, will make bringing similar claims, arguing the viability of the economic model and modeling parameters before the WTO much easier.[1005] The endorsement of the Sumner Model should also be considered in light of the fact that WTO Economic Division played a major advisory role in the Arbitrator's decision. The economic experts in this Division will continue to play an important advisory role in any future WTO challenges to agricultural subsidies. Thus, similar models and parameters as those employed by Professor Sumner can be successfully used to provide credible estimates of the quantity of price effects, production effects, and export effects of subsidies in future disputes.

Therefore, the highly transparent treatment and the ultimate endorsement of such models represents a fairly unique employment of economic analysis by WTO decision-makers and foreshadows the important advisory role played by the WTO Economic Division in any future WTO challenges to agricultural

---

1002 Together, in MY 2005, Brazil, India and China had 56.3% of the rest-of-world production (i.e. world production minus US production).
1003 *See*, earlier footnotes. The arbitrator established the total adverse effects of US$2,905,190,586. That total multiplied by the 56.3% attributed to Brazil, India and China equals US$1,634,559,538.
1004 This was achieved in the *Byrd Amendment* and *Steel Safeguard* cases where, in each, several parties joined as co-complainants to place additional pressure on the US in implementation. The strategy employed proved successful in both cases.
1005 *7.10 Arbitration*, paras. 4.120–4.193.

subsidies. In bringing future disputes, Members should be prepared to engage with the Arbitrator at an extremely high level of fluency on economic modeling issues, especially during arbitration proceedings where the use of economic experts is crucial for the determination of economic damages and appropriate retaliatory rights.[1006] Specifically, the Arbitrator's acceptance of the economic model used by Professor Daniel Sumner along with the various elasticity parameters used with this model means that the use of economic modeling will likely increase in importance in future cases. It is useful to recall the Appellate Body's multiple suggestions in both of its *Cotton* decisions that such models can be useful evidentiary tools in conducting a necessary *but for* analysis of subsidy effects.[1007] The transparent discussion of the analytical details of the model and its various parameters and the ultimate endorsement of its use over the objection of the United States represents a fairly unique application of this economic tool by any WTO decision-maker.

Another important aspect was the Arbitrators' endorsement of the use of short-term analysis in its GSM 102 determinations.[1008] The Arbitrator rejected the US arguments for the use of long-term elasticity estimates and analysis[1009] in assessing the value of eliminating the subsidies and, instead, endorsed the use of a shorter-term analysis in which market adjustments can be captured and adjustment costs can be incorporated.[1010] The rationale for adopting the shorter-term approach was that the Arbitrator determined that the alternative approach would underestimate the adverse effects caused by the continued use of prohibited and actionable subsidies by the US, especially the adjustment costs on producers in the rest of the world.[1011] In practice, the Arbitrator's endorsement of Brazil's use of the shorter-term analysis and short-term

---

1006 Arbitrators have themselves been included given their reputations as renowned research economists. Specifically, in the *Cotton* Arbitrations, one of the arbitrators chosen, Alan Matthews, is a professor of agricultural policy and economics at Trinity College in London, UK.

1007 *7.10 Arbitration*, paras. 4.120–4.192.

1008 This adoption should not be confused with the Arbitrator's endorsement of the 'long-term' analysis for the serious prejudice claim.

1009 *7.10 Arbitration*, paras. 4.135–4.146.

1010 *7.10 Arbitration*, paras. 4.144–4.147.

1011 This was similarly determined for the *4.11 Arbitration* with regards to the calculation of adverse effects for the GSM 102 program. In doing so, the Arbitrator deviated from legally similar cases involving prohibited export subsidies. Specifically, these include: *Brazil-Aircraft*, *US-FSC*, and *Canada-Aircraft*.

elasticity estimates will be useful for future challenges regarding the effects of agricultural subsidies.

Duplicitous Findings for 4.11 and 7.10 Arbitrations: The first Arbitration decision applicable to both arbitration decisions was the Article 22.3 of the DSU determination on the ability of Brazil to cross-retaliate in the form of suspending its concessions not solely on goods, but also under the *TRIPS Agreement* and *GATS*.[1012] This effectively allows Brazil to be able to implement countermeasures in alternative areas that would cause less harm to their domestic economy and impose retaliation in sectors of the US economy that would increase the probability of the US taking steps to comply with the DSB's recommendations and rulings.

In examining Brazil's request for cross-retaliation authorization, the Arbitrator first had to determine the preliminary threshold issue of whether and, if so, to what extent, Articles 4.10 and 7.9 of the *SCM Agreement*, as "special or additional rules" under Appendix 2 of the DSU, displace the legal standard included in Article 22.3 of the DSU. As the Arbitrator stated,

> we must clarify whether the special or additional rules of [Articles 4 and 7] of the *SCM Agreement* constitute the entirety of the applicable rules relating to the type and level or countermeasures that may be authorized in relation to prohibited [and actionable] subsidies, or whether the principles and procedures of Article 22.3 of the DSU and these provisions may be read as complementing each other in defining the rules applicable to the suspension of concessions or other obligations in relation to prohibited [and actionable] subsidies.[1013]

Specifically, the US brought a 22.7 claim under the DSU that the "principles and procedures of Article 22.3 had not been followed" and requested the Arbitrator to examine that issue. However, Articles 4.10 and 7.9 did not require such an examination. Therefore, the Arbitrator was obliged to determine whether a conflict or incompatibility between the two provisions existed, as well as compared to Article 22.3, in which case the "special or additional rules" of Articles 4.10 and 7.9 would prevail.[1014] The Arbitrator determined that a conflict would only exist if the terms "appropriate countermeasures" and "countermeasures commensurate with the degree and nature of the adverse effects" "are interpreted to define not only the permissible level of countermeasures…, but also

---

1012 *4.11 & 7.10 Arbitrations*, paras. 5.61–5.64.
1013 *4.11 & 7.10 Arbitrations*, para. 5.18.
1014 *4.11 & 7.10 Arbitrations*, para. 5.23.

the type of countermeasures that may be authorized, so that the principles and procedures of Article 22.3 of the DSU would be inoperative...."[1015]

In the Arbitrator's view, Articles 4.10 and 7.9 did not treat the types of countermeasures with enough precision to create a conflict between those provisions and Article 22.3. Further, the Arbitrator stated that "it is not clear that the terms [of Articles 4.10 and 7.9] provide any guidance as to the type of countermeasures that may be authorized."[1016] Also, given "the level of detail in which the matter of cross-sectoral retaliation is addressed in the DSU, one would have expected the drafters of the SCM Agreement to provide express guidance to this effect, if they had intended to address differently the question of the type of permissible countermeasures, as well as their level."[1017] Given this, the Arbitrator decided that its purview under 4.11 and 7.9 "relates to the determination of the level of countermeasures" rather than the validity of cross-sectoral retaliation in general, which is contained, rather, in Articles 22.6 and 22.3 of the DSU.[1018]

In conducting its analysis, the Arbitrator examined the governing rules set forth in Article 22.3 of the DSU as well as considered Brazil's argumentation based on WTO jurisprudence.[1019] With regards to the latter, the Arbitrator deviated from the "effectiveness" standard set in *EC – Bananas III (Ecuador) (Article 22.6 – EC)*, which ruled that a consideration by the complainant of the sector that was "least harmful to itself" was sufficient to be consistent with the applicable rules and principles of the DSU.[1020] In the *Cotton* case, the Arbitrator took a different position, viewing the "effectiveness" criterion as pertaining to

---

1015   *4.11 & 7.10 Arbitrations*, para. 5.24.
1016   *4.11 & 7.10 Arbitrations*, para. 5.25.
1017   *4.11 & 7.10 Arbitrations*, para. 5.26.
1018   *4.11 & 7.10 Arbitrations*, para. 5.27.
1019   The standard established in the *EC-Bananas III* (Ecuador) arbitration proceedings (at paragraph 69), required an assessment of the following four (4) issues: (1) whether suspension of concessions in the sector in which violations were found is "not practicable or effect," within the meaning of Article 22.3(c); (2) whether "circumstances are serious enough" to seek suspension under another sector and another covered agreement than those in which violations by the US were found in the Article 21.5 proceedings, within the meaning of Article 22.3(c); (3) whether the trade in the relevant sector, and the "importance of such trade" to the complainant, were taken into account, within the meaning of Article 22.3(d)(i); and, (4) whether "broader economic elements" related to nullification or impairment and the "broader economic consequences" of the requested suspension were taken into account, within the meaning of Article 22.3(d)(ii).
1020   Brazil's Methodology Paper, para. 143. *See*, Brazil's written submission, para. 511. *EC-Bananas III (Ecuador) (Article 22.6 – EC)*, para. 72.

the effectiveness of suspension in the same sector as that of the original violation "rather than an assessment of the relative effectiveness of such suspension, as compared to suspension in another sector or agreement."[1021] The Arbitrator in *Cotton* stated that "[w]e do not share the view of the arbitrator on *EC – Bananas III (Ecuador) (Article 22.6 – EC)* that a consideration by the complaining party of the sector or agreement in which suspension would be 'least harmful' to itself would necessarily be pertinent."[1022] The Arbitrator further stated that "the procedures and principles under Article 22.3 do not entitle a complaining party to freely choose *the most* effective sector or agreement under which to seek suspension."[1023] Instead, according to the Arbitrator, they allow the complaining party "to move out of the same sector or same agreement, where it considers that suspension *in that sector or agreement* is not 'practicable or effective [original emphasis].'"[1024] Nevertheless, the Arbitrator in the *Cotton* case noted that "where the complaining party would cause itself disproportionate harm, such that it would in fact be unable to use the authorization, there would be a basis for concluding that such suspension would not be 'effective.'"[1025] The Arbitrator further determined that, in order to comply with Article 22.3(c), the prevailing party need only have concluded that suspension in the sector in which the violation was found would be *either* impracticable or ineffective and that both conditions do not necessarily need to apply.[1026]

In sum, in the *EC – Bananas III* case, it was determined that, under Article 22.3(c), the prevailing party seeking suspension in an alternative sector need not consider whether suspension in the alternative sector is practicable and effective.[1027] Instead, the burden of establishing that same-sectoral suspension is both effective and practicable lies with the party challenging the application.[1028] In the *Cotton* case, on the other hand, the Arbitrator found that there is sufficient "flexibility" in the process of assessing the relevant conditions in a given case to allow a complainant to invoke considerations other than those set forth in Article 22.3(d).[1029]

1021 *4.11 & 7.10 Arbitrations*, para. 5.78.
1022 *4.11 & 7.10 Arbitrations*, para. 5.78.
1023 *4.11 & 7.10 Arbitrations*, para. 5.78.
1024 *4.11 & 7.10 Arbitrations*, para. 5.78.
1025 *4.11 & 7.10 Arbitrations*, para. 5.79. *See also* Decision by the Arbitrator, *EC – Bananas III (Ecuador)*, para. 73.
1026 *4.11 & 7.10 Arbitrations*, para. 5.70.
1027 Decision by the Arbitrator, *EC – Bananas III (Ecuador)*, para. 77.
1028 Decision by the Arbitrator, *EC – Bananas III (Ecuador)*, para. 78.
1029 *4.11 & 7.10 Arbitrations*, para. 5.84.

Further, in assessing the practicability of Brazil cross-retaliating, the Arbitrator considered many factors in order to reason to its final determination of how Brazil would implement its decision. First, although the Arbitrator recognized that the relationship between Brazil and the US was imbalanced – with the total value of Brazil's imports of US goods amounting to a far greater share of total Brazilian imports than of total US goods exports – it claimed that it was insufficient to make countermeasures in the goods sector "not practicable or effective." Rather, the Arbitrator required a more detailed assessment of the nature of the imports at issue.[1030] First, the Arbitrator divided US goods that Brazil imports into sub-categories (examples). In considering the effects of countermeasures to particular categories, the Arbitrator found that certain categories were impractical and ineffective to apply countermeasures, because of the consequential harm to Brazilian producers' supply chains and the fact that it would be difficult for Brazil to find alternative suppliers.[1031] One category, consumer goods, received particular analysis.[1032] Here, the Arbitrator considered whether countermeasures to particular goods would require Brazil to incur "serious and unreasonable costs." In making this determination, the Arbitrator assessed how available substitutes were to Brazil. In the end, the Arbitrator assigned a twenty (20) percent benchmark to be applied to determine, in particular categories of goods, how easily Brazil could find substitute suppliers.[1033] In several cases, Brazil was able to demonstrate that several categories far exceeded the Arbitrator's benchmark, and therefore proved that finding alternative sources of supply would entail serious and unreasonable costs. In these cases, the Arbitrator determined that applying countermeasures would be impracticable and ineffective.[1034] In applying its twenty (2) percent

---

1030 *4.11 & 7.10 Arbitrations*, paras. 5.139–5.141.

1031 *4.11 & 7.10 Arbitrations*, paras. 5.149–5.153.

1032 *4.11 & 7.10 Arbitrations*, paras. 5.176–5.178. For example, with regards to books and goods for the automotive sector, the Arbitrator found that Brazil could determine that countermeasures in those sub-categories would not be practicable or effective. However, the Arbitrator found that substitute suppliers were available for medical products, food, and arms.

1033 *4.11 & 7.10 Arbitrations*, para. 5.181. The Arbitrator specifically noted that "while there is no exact mathematical precision to this determination, we consider that, for the purposes of our assessment in these proceedings, a US share of imports of 20 per cent constitutes a reasonable threshold by which to estimate the extent to which Brazil may be able to find alternative sources of supply for these three remaining categories of consumer goods imports."

1034 *4.11 & 7.10 Arbitrations*, paras. 5.179–5.183. With regards to the twenty (20) percent benchmark, the arbitrators noted that they were "not intending to signal that this is

benchmark to the share of US imports for the proscribed categories, the Arbitrator found that "Brazil would still have at its disposal imports of other consumer goods from the United States amounting to a total value of at least US$409.7 million from which to suspend concessions or other obligations."[1035] Therefore, a threshold of US$409.7 was fixed, to be updated annually.[1036] Beyond that threshold, Brazil would then be able to apply authorized countermeasures outside of the goods sector.[1037]

Further, in making its determinations, the Arbitrator considered particular characteristics of the prohibited and actionable subsidies at issue to establish whether they legitimately contributed to creating "serious enough" circumstances to warrant cross-retaliation. Specifically, the Arbitrator concluded that Brazil correctly determined that the "circumstances [were] serious enough," noting that the "specific design and structure of the subsidies at issue, as they have been maintained over a significant period of time, is such as to have created an artificial and persisting competitive advantage for US producers over all other operators, and that this has a significant trade-distorting impact" on the US and world market for affected products.[1038] Second, the Arbitrator concluded that it was "beyond the scope of this enquiry" to take into account, in assessing whether the circumstances are "serious enough," what the US termed the "potentially devastating consequences" of countermeasures under the TRIPS Agreement.[1039] Ultimately, the Arbitrators authorized cross-retaliation

---

the appropriate percentage to use in this kind of analysis in all cases." *4.11 & 7.10 Arbitrations*, para. 5.181.

1035 Particularly noteworthy is the fact that the twenty (20) percent benchmark is not found in the DSU and no explanation is offered as to why the number was chosen by the Arbitrator. For future cases, it is clear that this number is not the required benchmark as the Arbitrator emphasized, recognizing ability to find substitute sources varies from Member to Member "[i]n applying a benchmark of 20 per cent, this Arbitrator is not intending to signal that this is the appropriate percentage to use in this kind of analysis in all cases." *4.11 & 7.10 Arbitrations*, para. 5.181.

1036 *4.11 & 7.10 Arbitrations*, paras. 5.183–5.185.

1037 Further, the Arbitrator found "the preference of a Member for a particular type of countermeasure, because it would constitute a more powerful form of persuasion in a political sense, is not a relevant consideration." However, it did recognize and note that – in particular cases- the application of countermeasures or suspension of concessions could be significant enough to cause inflationary impacts. Those were situations needing to be considered. *4.11 & 7.10 Arbitrations*, para. 5.195.

1038 *4.11 Arbitration*, para. 5.219. The Arbitrator further noted that, given the timing of the decision coincided with the credit crisis, it could be expected that the already-recognized trade-distorting effects would be amplified. *4.11 & 7.10 Arbitrations*, paras. 5.217–5.221.

1039 *4.11 Arbitration*, para. 5.224.

wherever a certain annual threshold of US goods exported to Brazil is exceeded.[1040] For MY 2006, the threshold is estimated at roughly US$400 million.

This was an extremely important ruling for Brazil, giving them a particularly delicate pressure point to use in negotiations with the US. IPRs retaliatory rights may provide Brazil an opportunity for developing countries to increase their leverage considerably. Given Brazil's robust generic pharmaceutical industry, it is now in a position to take advantage of a lifting of patent rights (only one of the forms of retaliation that Brazil could take). In essence, it would allow domestic drug makers to manufacture copies of US pharmaceuticals that are still under patent protection. This is a preferred retaliatory measure that would not harm their domestic consumers as would have been the case in retaliating in goods. This could further enhance Brazil's capacity to provide its population with lower-cost medicines by abrogating patent rights. To that extent, this may achieve a more balanced outcome – US cotton farmers receive benefits, while Brazilian consumers receive needed pharmaceuticals at lower prices. Of course, in the long run, such an outcome would discourage the development of drugs for developing country medical diseases (e.g. malaria, sleeping sickness, and TB). Therefore, the better result would be to eliminate US marketing loan and counter-cyclical subsidies for upland cotton and replace them with less trade-distorting subsidies.

Next, as discussed in both analyses above, under WTO law, trade effects can be used to measure trade damages, but this approach was not supported by either the US or Brazil during the arbitration. Further, although Brazil measured "benefits" (discussed *supra*) the Arbitrator did not agree, but did ultimately apply Brazil's methodology to calculate "trade damages."[1041] For the US, this was a welcomed deviation from previous cases,[1042] including the *Canada-Aircraft* decision. The US supported the Arbitrator's "appropriateness" standard to retrofit Brazil's approach.[1043] From that perspective, the US has subsequently expressed concerns regarding the fact that, if the US had

---

1040 *4.11 & 7.10 Arbitrations*, para. 5.201. Only two Arbitration decisions granted this right, prior to *Cotton*, in the *Bananas* and *Internet Gambling* disputes. However, this is the first time that a developing country is recognized as having the effective wherewithal to be able to capitalize on such retaliatory rights.

1041 *4.11 Arbitration*, paras. 4.139–4.153, and 4.165–4.171.

1042 Some practitioners and scholars found this to be a good development, since the Arbitrator found that it has an obligation *vis-à-vis* to the text of the Agreement, and not *vis-à-vis* previous disputes. The Arbitrator did take into consideration previous disputes, but explained his deviation.

1043 *7.10 Arbitration*, paras. 4.193–195, Annex 2.

discharged its burden of proof, why then did the Arbitrator accept Brazil's calculation methodology (discussed, *infra*)?[1044] Rather, from the US perspective, the Arbitrator should have developed its own analysis.[1045] This issue may have significant effects for future 4.10 arbitrations. It has been proffered that a proper approach might be to advance a methodology that is both accurate and addresses the Arbitrator's need for flexibility and data. This would differ from the present approach, which is to have complainants offer a plethora of data, from which the Arbitrator picks and chooses at his discretion.[1046]

In measuring these adverse effects, it should be also noted that – as discussed in the sections above – the Arbitrator's decision to assess their long-term effects will be critical as was found to be considerable in the *Cotton* dispute. The Arbitrator explained that, by adopting Brazil's short-term counterfactual (and its elasticity estimates), the measurement of adverse effects of the challenged US measures would have been underestimated, especially the adjustment costs to other world producers. This marked the first time an arbitrator was charged with calculating countermeasures that are "commensurate with...the adverse effects determined to exist," under Article 7.9 of the SCM Agreement. This decision is not a set precedence for future actionable subsidy cases. Noteworthy is the fact that the *Cotton* dispute involved a specific type of adverse effects. Specifically, Brazil claimed "significant price suppression in the same market" in its serious prejudice claim, under Article 6.3(c) of the SCM Agreement. It remains unknown how a future Arbitrator would interpret and apply the other provisions of the subparagraphs of Article 6.3 or Article 5 mandates, involving "injury to domestic industry" or the "nullification or impairment of benefits."

Finally, implementation in many WTO disputes occurs not always due to the threat of retaliation. Another pressure point is the absolute size of the effects of the WTO-illegality. For example, in the case of cotton, the quantification of the total effects of the significant price suppression totaled $2.905 billion in a representative year Marketing Year 2005.[1047] This is a huge amount by any measure. In view of the ongoing Doha Round negotiations concerning

---

1044 Juan Millan, Cotton Roundtable Discussion, The Graduate Institute (HEI), Geneva, 22 September 2009.
1045 Juan Millan, Cotton Roundtable Discussion, The Graduate Institute (HEI), Geneva, 22 September 2009.
1046 Juan Millan, Cotton Roundtable Discussion, The Graduate Institute (HEI), Geneva, 22 September 2009.
1047 *7.10 Arbitration*, para. 4.193.

reductions in trade-distorting domestic subsidies and the elimination of export subsidies altogether (discussed in the following section), another key aspect of the *Cotton* Arbitration is its findings quantifying the amount of adverse market effects of the U.S. subsidies. The size of such effects can create *moral suasion* and generate international outrage at the impact of such illegality, particularly on developing and least developed countries.[1048]

For example, Australia[1049] expressed its indignation at the U.S.' continued non-compliance in a statement submitted to the Dispute Settlement Body (DSB) of the WTO, after the publication of the Arbitrator's decision.[1050] The statement supported the significant findings of the Arbitrator, including findings that farmers outside the U.S. suffered over $17 billion in damages from 1999–2005 as a result of U.S. WTO-illegal subsidies. In addition, Australia projected that those farmers will continue to suffer similar damages under the 2008 Farm Bill, and further emphasized the fact that the *Cotton* decisions only reflect a few of the subsidies available to the agricultural sector in the U.S.[1051] Australia also stressed the point that a suspension of concessions or obligations is no substitution for full implementation of the recommendations as a means of bringing the U.S. into compliance with its WTO commitments.[1052]

1048 As discussed, *infra*, after the publication of the Arbitrator's decision, Australia submitted a formal statement to the Dispute Settlement Body of the WTO. The statement included the following quote from the Cairns Group's July 20th, 2008 Communiqué: "major subsidizers have provided...trade distorting support – effectively denying the opportunity for others, including low income producers in developing countries, to enter the market." Statement of Australia, "*United States – Subsidies on Upland Cotton: Reports of the Arbitrator*," (25 September 2009). This is explicit recognition by the 19-member Cairns Group of the global adverse effect U.S. subsidies has on producers in developing countries.

1049 To note: Australia was an active third party to the *Cotton* dispute.

1050 Statement of Australia, "*United States – Subsidies on Upland Cotton: Reports of the Arbitrator*," (25 September 2009), p. 1. Important to note is the citation from the Arbitrator's decision, quoted in the statement by Australia, which reads in part: "[T]he specific design and structure of the subsidies at issue, as they have been maintained over a significant period of time, is such as to have created an artificial and persisting competitive advantage for U.S. producers over all other operators....[T]his has a significant trade-distorting impact, not just on the U.S. domestic market, but on the world market in these products." Again, this is explicit recognition by the Arbitrator (and Australia) of the global adverse effect U.S. subsidies has on the world market.

1051 Statement of Australia, "*United States – Subsidies on Upland Cotton: Reports of the Arbitrator*," (25 September 2009), p. 2.

1052 Statement of Australia, "*United States – Subsidies on Upland Cotton: Reports of the Arbitrator*," (25 September 2009), p. 2.

The statement concluded with a call on the US to "implement the rulings and recommendations of the DSB in this long-running dispute without further delay."[1053] Analyses on the issue of compliance, and additional considerations such as *inter alia* the role of other US interests (IPR and Services sectors) at stake, are conducted in Part 3 of this book.

Again, of particular import to the thesis of this book, was the adverse effects determination of $2.9 billion of trade damage to the rest of the world.[1054] Although the Arbitrator chose to calculate countermeasures, considering "Brazil-only effects," the inclusion of the total world effects analysis and final determination[1055] can be used by Brazil and the Cotton 4 (C-4) in the Doha negotiations as will be discussed in Chapter 7 of this book. Therefore, although the arbitrators interpreted the WTO rules to mean that only loss to the complaining party can be considered in authorizing countermeasures, the fact that the arbitrators delineated a specific amount of damages to the world can still be used by smaller economies like the C-4 trying to effectuate agricultural policy change in larger economies like the US.

It is a well-recognized fact that the WTO has limited power to enforce its decisions. However, it also appreciated that an adverse decision can, in fact, allow winning Members to take the moral high ground and "shame" countries into compliance. WTO rulings have frequently become the basis for bilateral or multilateral negotiations that result in policy changes at the domestic level.[1056] This issue is discussed in Part 3 of this book, in relation to compliance considerations and the use of the *Cotton* dispute by Brazil to negotiate with the US in the Doha Round as well as, specifically, the issue of *Cotton* ruling.

1053 Statement of Australia, "*United States – Subsidies on Upland Cotton: Reports of the Arbitrator*," (25 September 2009), p. 2.
1054 *7.10 Arbitration,* para. 4.193.
1055 Noteworthy is the fact that this had not been done in the earlier *Cotton* decisions. By giving Brazil a delineated amount, it can now take it and apply pressure to the US and other Members in the negotiations.
1056 A recent example was China's decision to eliminate, effective, 1September 2009, the discriminatory twenty-five (25) percent tax it had been imposing on imported auto parts, whenever the imported parts were incorporated into a final assembled vehicle that failed to meet certain local content requirements. China's announcement comes after a WTO dispute settlement panel and AB ruling that the charges were contrary to WTO rules. WTD Trade Alert, "China to Eliminate Extra Tariffs on Auto Parts," *Washing Trade Daily* (28 August 2009) at <http://www.washingtontradedaily.com/> last accessed 5 August 2010.

In conclusion, the Arbitrators' decision can be summarized as having awarded US$147.3 million in annual fixed countermeasures, and a variable US$147.4 for US use of the GSM 102 program. Both awards are based on "Brazil-only effects."[1057] The Arbitrator did not take into account a significance threshold, and the adoption of reference period used was MY 2005. Encouragingly, the Arbitrator practically adopted Brazil's methodology in all points.[1058] The Arbitrators endorsed Dan Sumner's model, the short-term elasticities, coupling factor for the counter-cyclical payments, and futures market price regression to derive price expectations. In applying these calculation mechanisms, the Arbitrator determined that the marketing loan and counter-cyclical subsidies caused 9.38 percent price suppression in the world market, amounting to overall adverse effects of $2.905 billion, of which $2.384 billion are based on sales value effects and $521.5 million based on reduced production effects.[1059] The Arbitrator obtained its amount of countermeasures based on Brazil's share of total cotton production in the world (5.1 percent).[1060] With respect to cumulation of countermeasures for past years, the report did not include any findings. The only reference to cumulation concerned the cumulation of annual amounts from the two arbitration decisions.[1061] Therefore, Brazil's total award for 2006 is approximately US$300 million, but can balloon to US$820 million within the next three (3) years, if the US continues to be non-compliant. Further, after suspending concessions on US$400 million in goods, Brazil now has the right to cross-retaliate on US intellectual property rights and services.[1062]

1057 In interviewing several attorneys and government officials, the only significantly upsetting ruling was the 'Brazil-only effects' determination.
1058 In various parts of its decisions, the Arbitrator explicitly mentioned that Brazil's methodology and measures of damage were "appropriate."
1059 *4.11 Arbitration*, paras. 4.193–4.195, Annex 2.
1060 *4.11 Arbitration*, paras. 4.193–4.195.
1061 *4.11/7.10 Arbitration*, paras. 5.100–5.101, 5.103, and 6.1, 6.5.
1062 It is important to note that there are varying ways that Brazil can achieve this. Brazil would not necessarily have to cease trade in US$400 million but could, for example, impose slightly higher tariffs on trade worth that value, before then being able to argue it met the threshold and could then challenge IPRs. This would place the US is a difficult position to argue that Brazil would have to increase its tariffs and effectively stop trade in goods, before being able to proceed.

Summary of Arbitration Findings

Prohibited Subsidies

WTO Arbitrator found that the US had granted prohibited export credit guarantees under its GSM 102 program, causing adverse effects various agricultural markets, in the following:

- Fiscal Year 2006: $997 million in ECGs, causing $750 million dollars worth of harm.
- Fiscal Year 2007:$835 million in ECGs, causing $640 million dollars worth of harm.
- Fiscal Year 2008:$2.3 billion in ECGs, causing $1.81 billion dollars worth of harm.
- Fiscal Year 2009:$4.28 billion in ECGs, causing $3.28 billion dollars worth of harm.

The WTO Arbitrator awarded Brazil the right to retaliate in the amount of $147.4 million based on 2006 data, and – reflecting Brazil's initial calculations – $112 million based on 2007 data, $373 million based on 2008 data and $672 million based on 2009 data.

Adverse Effects from US Marketing Loan Subsidies and Counter-Cyclical Payments

WTO Arbitrator found that $2.1 billion in US marketing loan subsidies and counter-cyclical payment in Marketing Year 2005 cause annual worldwide effects of $2.9 billion.

Over the four-year period since Marketing Year 2005, that amounts to total effects on the world cotton market of $11.6 billion.

The WTO Arbitrator emphasized that the US could bring itself into WTO-compliance only by removing the entirety of the significant price suppression in the world market – i.e., the total amount of annual price effects of $2.9 billion.

The WTO Arbitrator awarded Brazil the right to retaliate in the amount of $147.3 million, annually.

Total Retaliation Amounts

- $819 million based on 2009 data
- $520 million based on 2008 data
- $260 million based on 2007 data

CHAPTER 6

US-Upland Cotton: Key Legal Findings as Precedent for Future WTO Dispute Challenges to Agricultural Subsidies and Lessons Learned from the Involvement of Least Developed Countries

This chapter examines the key legal proceedings and findings of the *Cotton* dispute with particular attention to the original panel rulings and subsequent decisions of the appellate body and arbitrator with regards to the various forms of US cotton support programs. The combined legal findings of the case have created a body of law that is key to an understanding of both the current dispute settlement process and, by way of the set of legal precedence stemming from the case, its possible future development. In addition to contributing to an understanding of the dispute mechanism of the WTO, the analysis herein also demonstrates how the strategies employed in the case can inform strategies for furthering objectives in both the litigation and political environments.

In addition to an analysis of the key findings of the case, the chapter examines the role of least developed countries in the dispute process, focusing on the pivotal role of Chad and Benin as third parties. A number of recognized barriers to full participation by LDCs are discussed and lessons drawn from the strategies employed by Chad and Benin to circumvent some of these barriers. Not only did their participation affect the findings of serious prejudice in the case, it enhanced the negotiating position of least developed and developing nations, particularly the African Members of the WTO and Brazil, in the multilateral political venue of the Doha Development Round. The benefits derived from their participation more generally illustrates the gains from greater LDC participation in the WTO dispute system in terms of furthering the interests of least developed and developing nations as well as a more favorable evolution of the jurisprudence of the system.

6.1 Key Legal Findings

This section of the book extrapolates from Chapter 5 the seven (7) key legal findings of the *Cotton* dispute and sets forth, in brief, the significance each had on the jurisprudence of the WTO dispute settlement system. Those issues identified as primarily important are the following: serious prejudice and the peace clause; local content subsidies; export credit guarantee subsidies; green box direct payments; arbitration determinations; and retaliation. These rulings set juridical precedence that will directly impact negotiations on these provisions of the AoA and SCM agreements within the current negotiations context as well as be considered by WTO Members in the formulation of future domestic agricultural policies. Parts of this section served as the basis of an article co-authored by the author of this book and Scott Andersen of Sidley Austin's Geneva office.[1063]

The Peace Clause: A key preliminary threshold legal topic for Brazil's serious prejudice claim (discussed, *infra*) was the so-called 'peace clause' issue, i.e. whether the U.S. had exceeded their 1992 domestic support levels during each year of the 1999–2002 reference period.[1064] This provision was included as a means to conclude the Uruguay Round negotiations so that the disputes (specifically, regarding the *Oilseeds* panels rulings that EC subsidy policies were GATT illegal) and the associated negotiations *impasse* on domestic subsidy regimes would cease. Effectively, Article 13 required that parties exercise "due restraint" when challenging Members on agricultural subsidies until 2004. In the meantime, negotiations on agriculture were set to recommence, and it was anticipated that the issue would be successfully addressed at that time.

It was found by the panel of the original proceedings that the US had indeed exceeded their domestic support levels and Brazil was, therefore, not barred from bringing the claim. This determination is significant in that it interpreted the scope and efficacy of the peace clause. Also, the expiration of the peace clause in 2004 means that complaining parties can challenge the collective effects of any form of subsidy to establish serious prejudice – even subsidies falling within the green box.[1065] Nor do complaining Members need be concerned with establishing that current levels of subsidization are greater than

---

1063 Further, much of the accompanied analysis is derived from communications with Scott Andersen, the primary attorney representing Brazil and orchestrating the case through the dispute settlement mechanism. The author believed it was critical to interview in order to glean an understanding of the practical effects of the *Cotton* dispute from the perspective of a seasoned WTO attorney.
1064 Andersen, S., and Taylor, M., "Brazil's WTO Challenge to U.S. Cotton Subsidies: the Road to Effective Disciplines of Agricultural Subsidies," *Business Law Brief*, Washington College of Law, American University, (Fall 2009), p. 9 at footnote 13.
1065 Andersen, S., and Taylor, M., "Brazil's WTO Challenge to U.S. Cotton Subsidies: the Road to Effective Disciplines of Agricultural Subsidies," *Business Law Brief*, Washington College of Law, American University, (Fall 2009), p. 5.

historic levels of subsidization for particular product at issue.[1066] Further, it is now being debated whether another peace clause will result from the Doha negotiations. Given the unexpected outcome of the *Cotton* dispute for the US, in relation to the peace clause, it is predicted that if another peace clause is negotiated, it will vary significantly from the one inserted in the Uruguay Round's Agreement on Agriculture.[1067]

Serious Prejudice: The panel and AB found that US domestic support measures caused significant price suppression in the world cotton market during the relevant years and, therefore, caused serious prejudice to the cotton interests of Brazil. Of primary importance, these were the first and only WTO decisions applying the WTO rules to actionable subsidies causing serious prejudice to agricultural products. It was also one of two WTO decisions where the use of a domestic subsidy was proven to cause serious prejudice.[1068] The WTO *SCM Agreement* only prohibits a relatively narrow range of subsides[1069] – all other subsidies are permitted to be granted if they do not cause various forms of serious prejudice to other WTO Members.[1070] Therefore, the fact that several US subsidies were found to be prohibited is critical to future agricultural subsidy claims brought before the WTO.

A major focus of Brazil's claims were that the collective effects of eight (8) different subsidies supporting the production, use and export of U.S. upland cotton caused significant price suppression in the world market and serious prejudice in violation of Article 6.3(c) of the *SCM Agreement*.[1071] The original

---

1066 Andersen, S., and Taylor, M., "Brazil's WTO Challenge to U.S. Cotton Subsidies: the Road to Effective Disciplines of Agricultural Subsidies," *Business Law Brief*, Washington College of Law, American University, (Fall 2009), p. 5. Brazil was forced to expend a considerable amount of resources in the original proceedings to eventually succeed in securing vitally important data to allow the establishment of a peace clause violation.

1067 This conclusion was confirmed by several practitioners, Members of the WTO secretariat, and negotiators through interviews conducted in Geneva, Switzerland in the Summer of 2009.

1068 The other case was *Indonesia-Certain Measures Affecting the Automobile Industry*, WT/DS54/R, WT/DS55/R, WT/DS59/R, WT/DS64/R, adopted 23 July 1998.

1069 These include prohibited export subsidies and prohibited local content subsidies as set forth in Article 3.1(a) and (b) of the *SCM Agreement*.

1070 These various forms of "adverse effects" are set out in Articles 5 and 6 of the SCM. They include significant price suppression and depression, significant lost sales, significant price undercutting, displacement or impedance of market share of exports and imports in third country markets, an increase in the world market share of production, and material injury to the domestic industry of another Member.

1071 It should be noted that a key preliminary threshold legal issue for Brazil's serious prejudice claim was the so-called 'peace clause' issue, i.e. whether the U.S. had exceeded their

panel examined Brazil's primary claim and found that four (4) of the price-contingent subsidies – the marketing loan, the counter-cyclical payments (and the predecessor market loss assistance subsidies), and the domestic Step-2 subsidies[1072] – collectively caused significant price suppression in the world market during the reference period of 1999–2002.[1073]

In response to the original panel and Appellate Body rulings, the United States eliminated the Step 2 subsidy but did not make any changes to the price-contingent marketing loan or counter-cyclical subsidies. Despite the fact that these remaining two price-contingent subsidies constituted the bulk of the subsidies examined by the original panel, the United States argued their effects were not sufficient to cause significant price suppression in the world market. Accordingly, Brazil commenced compliance proceedings in the fall of 2006 claiming that the United States had not complied with the requirement to withdraw the marketing loan and counter-cyclical subsidy programs or otherwise removed the adverse effects of those subsidies.

Brazil claimed that the effect of the new "basket" of marketing loan and counter-cyclical subsidies caused present serious prejudice, *inter alia*,[1074] in the form of significant price suppression. The compliance panel found that there were no material changes to the nature, object, effect, or magnitude of the U.S. marketing loan[1075] or counter-cyclical subsidies[1076] which continued during the 2005–2006 period, and that these programs paid the same, if not higher, levels than during the 1999–2002 period.[1077] Further, based on considerable new evidence concerning the operation of these subsidies during the new reference period of 2005–2006, the compliance panel

---

1992 domestic support levels during each year of the 1999–2002 reference period. This was found and Brazil was, therefore, not barred from bringing the claim. The peace clause expired in 2004.

1072 A discussion of the Step 2 program is set forth, *infra*.

1073 *Panel Report*, paras. 7.1290–7.1304. However, the panel ultimately found that it was unable to find a clear causal link to Brazil's particular price suppression for the non-price contingent subsidies, i.e., Direct Payment, Production Flexibility Contract Payments, Crop Insurance, and Cottonseed Payments. *Panel Report*, paras. 7.1305–7.1307. This aspect of the original panel's decision regarding non-price contingent subsidies and *dicta* from the original Appellate Body is discussed, *infra*.

1074 In *U.S. – Upland Cotton*, the panel had ruled that "the United States upland cotton producers would not have been economically capable of remaining in the production of upland cotton had it not been for the United States subsidies." *Panel Report*, paras. 7.1353–7.1354.

1075 21.5 *Panel Report*, paras. 10.75–10.83 (marketing loans).

1076 21.5 *Panel Report*, paras. 10.90–10.103 (counter-cyclical subsidies).

1077 21.5 *Panel Report*, para. 10.110.

found that the marketing loan and countercyclical subsidies continued to impact significantly the planting decisions of upland cotton farmers and affect the "level of U.S. upland cotton acreage and production as a result of their mandatory and price-contingent nature and their revenue-stabilizing effect" and "insulate" revenues of U.S. upland cotton producers when prices are low.[1078] The panel's causation finding also emphasized that it was appropriate to assess the effects of subsidies by examining the longer term impact on farmers entering or existing the production of cotton, and in covering their total costs of production. In conclusion, the compliance panel found that "without these subsidies the level of U.S. upland cotton acreage and production would likely be significantly lower."[1079]

On appeal, the Appellate Body affirmed all of the major serious prejudice-related findings and reasoning of the compliance panel, which had been challenged by the United States.[1080] In particular, the Appellate Body agreed with the compliance panel's rejection of a U.S. jurisdictional argument that would have excluded from the compliance proceedings any subsidy payments made after 2002. The effect of its decision was that the United States was required to make eliminate or otherwise make significant changes to the marketing loan and counter-cyclical program legislation.[1081] In addition, the Appellate Body endorsed the use of economic modeling and other quantitative techniques to "provide a framework to analyze the relationship between subsidies, other factors, and price movements."[1082] It criticized the panel for not examining in detail the parameters of the competing economic models presented by Brazil and the United States[1083] and for not going far enough in its comparative analysis of these models. Finally, the Appellate Body clarified that the effect of subsidies need not be the only cause of price suppression. This is a pragmatic acknowledgement that there will be other factors impacting the movement of

---

1078 *21.5 Panel Report*, paras. 10.82 and 10.103–10.104.
1079 *21.5 Panel Report*, para. 10.104.
1080 *21.5 AB Report*, paras. 324–446.
1081 *21.5 AB Report*, paras. 233–249.
1082 *21.5 AB Report*, para. 356. For more on this, *See*, Sumner, Daniel A., "A Quantitative Simulation Analysis of the Impacts of U.S. Cotton Subsidies on Cotton Prices and Quantities," Department of Agriculture and Resource Economics., University of California, Davis. Available online at http://www.mre.gov.br/portugues/ministerio/sitios_secretaria/cgc/analisequantitativa.pdf.
1083 The original Appellate Body had also criticized the original panel for failing to conduct an extensive analysis of the complex facts and economic arguments arising in the dispute. *AB Report*, para. 458.

prices and that a significant price suppression claim may be maintained even if there are other factors influencing world prices.[1084]

Lessons Learned from Serious Prejudice Claim: A close review of the briefing and evidence used in Brazil's litigation of its serious prejudice-related claims in the various *Cotton* proceedings demonstrates how document-intensive and expert-intensive a task it is to quantify the effects of subsidies and otherwise establish the causal link to serious prejudice in agricultural commodity markets. There is no doubt that future challenges will require a similar resource-intensive effort to establish causation. Nevertheless, for the reasons set forth, *infra*, it will be considerably easier for future complaining party litigants to plan and successfully prosecute their serious prejudice challenges because of the lessons learned from the *Cotton* decisions.

First, the numerous legal interpretations by the five *Cotton* decisions of the SCM *Agreement* and the *Agreement on Agriculture* have clarified issues such as the existence of a world market, the ability to use any form of subsidy to establish serious prejudice (prohibited export and local content subsidies, expired subsidies with continuing effects, green box subsidies), and the meaning of significant price suppression and how it can be demonstrated causally.

Second, the *Cotton* compliance panel and Appellate Body confirmed that the adverse effects of annually recurring agricultural subsidies can be analyzed using a long-term approach.[1085] Such an analysis would assess whether the collective effect of a number of years of annually recurring subsidies contribute to farmers entering or exiting the production of the crop in question. This is a very important because claims based only on short-term (one or two years)

[1084] It should be noted that the original Appellate Body indicated "it would be difficult to make a judgment on significant price suppression without taking into account the effect of the subsidies." *AB Report*, para. 433. Thus, the "but for" test arguably could require that the only cause of the relevant price suppression is the effect of the subsidies. Prices may well fluctuate up and down for various reasons. But it is only that portion of the restraint on price movements (which objectively can go either up or down) that is linked to the effects of the subsidies that is relevant.

[1085] *Compliance Panel*, para. 10.83 ("In our view, the type of effect of a subsidy on production relevant to the analysis under Article 6.3(c) can also be demonstrated on the basis of a longer-term perspective that focuses on how the subsidy affects decisions of producers to enter or to exit a given industry.") para. 10.176 ("Thus, it appears to us that the effect of the marketing loan and counter-cyclical payments on cotton farmers' production decisions could be best assessed on the basis of data covering the lifetime of the Act.... This period of time is of sufficient length to require a medium to long-term analysis.")*See also 21.5 AB Report, supra* note 27, at para. 422.

effects can easily collapse during the WTO proceedings if the level of subsidies contracts significantly (through increases in commodity prices). This rationale is particularly useful for challenges to subsidies for crops such as rice or cotton that demand specialized equipment and where certain land is only economically viable (with subsidies) to grow a single or a limited number of crops. By contrast, the long-term causation analysis may be less useful for claims involving subsidies for commodities where it is relatively easy to shift from one crop to many other crops.

Third, the compliance panel rejected U.S. arguments that the absence of any temporal link between the lower world prices and the payment of marketing loan and counter-cyclical subsidies meant that the subsidies could not cause price suppression.[1086] The compliance panel's finding on this point, when read in conjunction with its "long-term" approach to examining the effects of subsidies, suggests that future challenges to annual recurring agricultural subsidies need not demonstrate any temporal link between market prices and the provision of subsidies. This appropriately limited an obvious defense in situations where subsidies have been provided for decades (as with the U.S. and EU.) and where it would thus be difficult to identify a temporal point in which subsidies have not distorted the market.

Fourth, while the original panel found that non-price contingent subsidies (direct payments and crop insurance) did not cause significant price suppression, dicta from the Appellate Body suggested that non-price contingent subsidies could contribute to price suppression and other forms of serious prejudice.[1087] In addition, the rationale behind the use of a long-term effects analysis is whether the combined effect of the challenged subsidies provides revenue support to farmers that maintain them in the business of farming the

---

1086   *See Panel Report, supra* note 4, at para. 10.146.
1087   Brazil's Appellant's submission noted its disagreement with the original panel's finding that only price-contingent subsidies – but not Direct Payment, Crop Insurance, and Cottonseed payments – could be found to contribute to significant price suppression. In affirming the panel's reliance on only the "price-contingent" subsidies, the Appellate Body made the following statement: "We do not exclude the possibility that challenged subsidies that are not 'price-contingent' (to use the panel's term) could have some effect on production and exports and contribute to price suppression." ABR *Cotton 21.5, supra* note 27, para. 450, n. 589. This statement suggests that the Appellate Body may be receptive to the collective effect of subsidies "contributing to" *production* – such as crop insurance and direct payments – even if those subsidies are not linked to prices and implies that future serious prejudice challenges to agricultural subsidies should not shy away from including non-price contingent subsidies in the mix of subsidies to be challenged.

commodity in question.[1088] Non-price contingent subsidies that contribute to covering the costs of production or increasing the wealth of a farmer through facilitating the purchase of land or equipment can have a very similar effect on sustaining production as a price-contingent subsidy.

Fifth, the Arbitrators confirmed the viability and utility of particular types of econometric models[1089] to assess the effects of subsidies. Similarly, the Appellate Body in each of its *Cotton* decisions criticized the panels for not explaining how it had taken the particular models into account, and for failing to evaluate and compare the parameters used by such models.[1090] The use of such models is crucial given the counterfactual nature of the entire serious prejudice question, i.e. whether, but for the subsidies, world prices would have been higher. Future complaining parties can adopt and adapt as necessary these models in preparing future challenges. This will significantly facilitate the defense of such models.[1091]

Sixth, the *Cotton* decisions highlighted the utility of a claim of price suppression in challenging such subsidies. Unlike a claim of price *depression*, there is no requirement for a complaining party to explain what may be very wide swings in commodity prices during the reference period examined. In the various *Cotton* proceedings, the U.S. had the near impossible task of trying to demonstrate that other market factors (such as China and India's role in

---

1088 *21.5 Panel Report*, para. 10.83 ("In our view, the type of effect of a subsidy on production relevant to the analysis under Article 6.3(c) can also be demonstrated on the basis of a longer-term perspective that focuses on how the subsidy affects decisions of producers to enter or to exit a given industry.") para. 10.176 ("Thus, it appears to us that the effect of the marketing loan and counter-cyclical payments on cotton farmers' production decisions could be best assessed on the basis of data covering the lifetime of the Act.... This period of time is of sufficient length to require a medium to long-term analysis.")

1089 In this case, models were generated and testimony given by Dr. Daniel Sumner of the University of California, Davis.

1090 *AB Report*, para. 448 ("We note that the Panel indicated expressly that it had taken the models in question into account. It would have been helpful had the Panel revealed how it used these models in examining the question of third country responses."); *21.5 AB Report*, para. 348 ("While the Panel appropriately examined the model, the parameters used by each party, and the arguments made by the parties, and noted the different results generated by the simulations conducted by each party, the Panel could have gone further in its evaluation and comparative analysis of the economic simulations and the particular parameters used.").

1091 By contrast, a significant portion of Brazil's briefing before the *Cotton* panels and Arbitrator was focused on justifying its econometric model and the various price and elasticity parameters used by that model.

world markets) somehow eliminated any price suppressing effects of the U.S. subsidies. However, whether the demand or supply of Chinese cotton (or even subsidies to Chinese producers) may have caused prices to fall was properly treated as irrelevant by all panels and Appellate Body decisions. By contrast, it would be relatively easy for a defending subsidizing Member to defend against a price *depression* claim by demonstrating that many non-subsidy factors caused prices to fall. Similarly, a claim of price *undercutting* would require proof that in particular transactions the actual prices of the subsidizing Member were lower than the prices of the complaining Member's producers. This requires evidence that could be very difficult to obtain and would generally be highly confidential.

Seventh, the compliance panel and Appellate Body's decision rejecting the distinction between subsidy payments and subsidy programs will make it much easier for those Members challenging subsidies to secure implementation by the challenged subsidizing Member. Complaining Members now need only establish the existence of serious prejudice during a reference period by the effects of subsidies. A positive finding of serious prejudice will mean that the losing subsidizing Member will have to make changes to the subsidy program or legislation and not simply claim that the effects of the subsidies granted during the reference period no longer cause serious prejudice.

Finally, an important tactical lesson to be learned from the *Cotton* Arbitration decision is that the focus of the damages is only upon the serious prejudicial effects suffered by a complaining party and it would be beneficial to combine as many complaining parties with the largest possible share of world production or world exports. For example, if China, Brazil, and India – who collectively total more than fifty percent of world cotton production – had joined forces to challenge U.S. upland cotton subsidies, the total amount of retaliation allowed under the Arbitrator's formula would have been far in excess of $1 billion. As a result, the United States would still have the obligation to remove all of the significant price suppression, but it would also have an arguably greater incentive to eliminate its WTO-inconsistent conduct.

In sum, the collective effect of these *Cotton* decisions will considerably aid complaining parties in future disputes. That is not to say that it will be easy to establish the causal link between the subsidies and particular market effects that rise to the level of serious prejudice. Such cases will always be evidence and expert-intensive and require considerable resources and expertise to litigate successfully. However, the clarifications provided by all five of the *Cotton* decisions will allow the structuring and prosecution of the case in a more efficient and less-resource intensive manner than Brazil was forced to endure as the first Member to challenge these subsidies.

Local Content Subsidies: These were the first WTO decisions examining local content (import substitution) subsidies to processors of basic agricultural products as well as export subsidies for agricultural products contingent upon the export of U.S. agricultural products (cotton under the Step 2 program[1092]). The *SCM Agreement* prohibits subsidies granted contingent upon the use of local products, such as U.S. grown cotton, or upon the export of products, such as U.S. cotton. Brazil successfully fought off a number of U.S. arguments in demonstrating that the "Step 2" local content and Step-2 export refund subsidies, which were *de jure* contingent either on the use or export of U.S. cotton in violation of Article 3.1 of the *SCM Agreement*. Though the US argued that the Step 2 payments were distributed according to 'use' of US cotton, and were thus neither an export nor local content subsidy, the original panel and the Appellate Body affirmed Brazil's challenge. The significance of the rulings on local content subsidies is that there is no ambiguity as to whether the SCM Agreement is applicable to agricultural subsidies and the practical outcome that the United States eventually eliminated the Step 2 program in 2006. This may be considered proof of the recognition by the US that the domestic measure was inconsistent. Further, it sends a strong signal to other Members, who might have or consider implementing such a measure.

For example, both the U.S. and the E.U. presently provide subsidies to processors of agricultural goods contingent *de jure* or *de facto* on the use of "local" (U.S. or E.U.) agricultural products. The *Cotton* decisions confirmed that such local content subsidies (in the form of the Step 2 subsidies to U.S. mill users of U.S. cotton) are covered by the WTO subsidies disciplines. This will likely impact a range of agricultural subsidies. For example, the E.U. provides local content subsidies to E.U. purchasers or users of E.U.-produced skimmed milk, skimmed milk powder, cream, butter and concentrated butter.[1093] The E.U.

1092 The U.S. Step 2 program was a subsidy unique to cotton. Designed to provide a constant demand for uncompetitive U.S. cotton, the U.S. government paid domestic users and exporters of U.S. cotton the difference between the lower world market price and the higher U.S. domestic price. As a practical matter, the subsidy enabled U.S. exporters of cotton to buy high-priced U.S. cotton in the United States and sell it at a lower price on the export markets. Similarly, the U.S. Step 2 program enabled U.S. textile mills to buy higher-priced U.S. cotton, which carries the eligibility to receive Step 2 payments, instead of otherwise lower-priced imported cotton that is not eligible for Step 2 support.

1093 *See*, Commission Regulation 1234/2007, Establishing a Common Organization of Agricultural Markets and on Specific Provisions for Certain Agricultural Products, 2007 O.J. (L 299). A number of provisions of the Single CMO Regulation expose the EC to potential local content subsidy claims. They include EC intervention purchases of butter and skimmed milk powder, id. art. 15,16, EC storage subsidies for storage of butter, id. art.

also provides subsidies to purchasers or users of butter and skimmed milk powder contingent upon these products being produced in the E.U.[1094] Similarly, the U.S. sugar program requires the U.S. Government to make sugar marketing loan payments[1095] to sugar processors contingent on the use of domestic U.S. sugar over imported goods.[1096] Under the *Cotton* decision rationale, all of these forms of local content subsidies are contingent on the use of domestic over imported goods, in violation of Article 3.1(b) of the SCM Agreement.

Export Credit Guarantee Subsidies: Another key finding by the panel and AB was that export credit guarantee subsidies to exporters of cotton and other commodities, through the GSM 102, GSM 103, and Supplier Credit Guarantee Program (SCGP) programs were found not to be exempt from AoA export subsidy rules and constitute prohibited export subsidies pursuant to Annex I, Paragraph (j) of the SCM. As required under the provision, the panel and AB found that the rates given through the programs could not "cover the long-term operating costs and losses."[1097] Therefore, the anti-circumvention provision of Article 10.1 of the AoA applied per the argumentation of Brazil. The significance of the ruling is the fact that there is precedence that allows for the application of Article 10.1 and not Article 10.2, which specifically exempts export credit guarantee subsidies. The US had argued for the application of Article 10.2, claiming that the intention was for ECGs to be negotiated in the future. The panel cited the Vienna Convention as well as investigated the drafting history of the AoA to determine that ECGs were not exempt from the AoA export subsidy rules.[1098]

28(a)(ii)–(iii), and EC disposal subsidies to the extent they are paid to processors of EC dairy products and not paid on the export of such products, id. Recitals 43, 60; art. 99–101 (describing measures found in Recitals 43 and 60).

1094 *See*, e.g., id. art. 7, 10(1)(e), 10(1)(f), 100(1) (providing provisions specifically indicating if milk or milk products are produced or originated "in the community").

1095 Federal Agriculture Improvement and Reform Act of 1996, 7 U.S.C. § 7272 (2008).

1096 Agricultural Adjustment Act of 1938, 7 U.S.C. § 1359aa (2008). Similar to a local content requirement, the current U.S. sugar program in the 2008 Farm Act contains a requirement that the size of the overall marketing allotment equal 85 percent of U.S. human consumption of sugar. Id. This constitutes a minimum use requirement for domestic sugar, in violation of Article III of GATT 1994. See id. § 1359bb.

1097 Panel Report, *US-Upland Cotton*, WT/DS267/R, para 7.800.

1098 Halverson Cross, K., "King Cotton, Developing Countries and the 'Peace Clause': The WTO's US Cotton Subsidies Decision," *Journal of International Economic Law*, Vol. 9, No. 1, (30 January 2006), p. 174. It should be noted that there was a dissenting opinion on this

Further, the ECG subsidies were found to be prohibited subsidies because their value exceeded the levels set forth in the US Country Schedule for export subsidies. This was proven for cotton as well as other commodities.[1099] Therefore, the ruling is of particular import since these programs can be challenged by a variety of commodities in future disputes. It is expected that the US will have to change their position regarding ECGs in the present negotiations as a result of *Cotton*.[1100] It is already apparent, as set forth in the Framework (discussed *infra*) negotiated between the US and Brazil, that the US is reevaluating a number of its export credit guarantee programs as a result of the dispute.

Green Box Direct Payments: These were the first WTO decisions clarifying WTO rules relating to a special category of "domestic support" favoring agricultural producers for which Members need not reduce the level of their agricultural subsidies, (i.e., commonly referred to as the "green box").[1101] The panel, and as affirmed by the Appellate Body,[1102] found that U.S. Direct Payments to farmers (who historically farmed cotton on a particular farm) do not meet the criteria

---

issue at the appellate stage. *See*, Halverson Cross at p. 185 and AB Report, *US-Upland Cotton*, WT/DS267/AB/R, adopted 21 March 2005, paras. 631–641.

1099 The requisite showing that there was a violation was proven using the commodity of rice. *See*, Halverson Cross, K., "King Cotton, Developing Countries and the 'Peace Clause': The WTO's US Cotton Subsidies Decision," *Journal of International Economic Law*, Vol. 9, No. 1, (30 January 2006), p. 174.

1100 Halverson Cross, K., "King Cotton, Developing Countries and the 'Peace Clause': The WTO's US Cotton Subsidies Decision," *Journal of International Economic Law*, Vol. 9, No. 1, (30 January 2006), p. 175.

1101 The "green box" is the working name given to the domestic support measures falling within the provisions of Annex 2 of the *Agreement on Agriculture*.

1102 In WTO dispute settlement proceedings, a "panel" is a three-person body that functions as the initial trier of fact. The "Appellate Body" in the WTO is a standing body that is available, upon request by one of the litigating parties, to review questions of law raised by the panel decisions. In the *Cotton* case, there were separate panel and AB proceedings for both the "original" proceedings determining Brazil's original complaint covering the period 2003–2005 and the 2006–2008 "compliance" proceedings in which Brazil challenged the WTO-consistency of the implementation actions taken by the United States of the original panel and Appellate Body rulings. A final phase was the 2008–2009 Arbitrator proceedings in which the amount and type of suspension of concessions by Brazil against the United States was determined. This phase is referred to as the "Arbitrator" decisions. The authors have chosen to distinguish the panels and Appellate Body reports by denoting each body with a descriptor of the proceeding to which we refer (i.e. 'original panel' refers to the panel in the original proceeding). For a more detailed overview, *See*, "A Handbook on the WTO Dispute Settlement System," World Trade Organization. Cambridge University Press (2004), pp. 21–24.

specified in paragraph 6(b) of Annex 2 of the *Agreement on Agriculture*.[1103] In the context of the dispute, this decision meant that the United States could not invoke the peace clause as a defense to Brazil's serious prejudice challenges. And more broadly, the decision means that billions in Direct Payments must be included in the U.S. obligation to reduce its overall levels of trade-distorting support ("Total AMS"). In practice, this will require the United States to eliminate the fruits and vegetables exception to the Direct Payment program or make real cuts in its trade-distorting agricultural subsidies in order to be WTO-consistent.

Arbitration Determinations: Brazil's landmark challenge crossed a possibly final threshold in the six-year battle on August 31, 2009. In light of the continued U.S. failure to implement, three WTO Arbitrators granted Brazil the right to retaliate against U.S. trade in goods, services, and intellectual property rights in amounts that may well reach $800 million.[1104] The Arbitrators' calculation of what are effectively "trade damages" followed an earlier United States refusal to eliminate billions in annual highly trade-distorting "domestic" subsidies sustaining the world's largest exporter of cotton.[1105] Like the four previous WTO panel and Appellate Body reports finding in favor of Brazil's claims against these U.S. subsidies over the period 2004–2008, this new Arbitrator report provides new precedents on several novel legal issues that are relevant to future challenges to agricultural subsidies.

First, a key aspect of the Arbitrator's decision was to find that the amount of appropriate suspension of concessions for Brazil was limited to the impact on Brazil of the price suppression in the world market resulting from the granting of marketing loan and counter-cyclical payments.[1106] Brazil had argued that it was entitled to suspend concessions of more than one billion U.S. dollars because the adverse effects determined to exist by the original panel was

---

1103   This was based on the finding that such farmers could not receive the Direct Payments if they grew fruits and vegetables. The original panel as affirmed by the Appellate Body rejected US arguments that Direct Payment subsidies were "decoupled" from current production as required by Annex 2, paragraph 6(b) because of this "fruit and vegetable" prohibition. *See* Panel Report, *U.S.-Upland Cotton*, paras. 7.364–7.388.

1104   This estimated amount as declared publicly by Brazil reflects both the annual amount calculated for serious prejudice as well as the export credit guarantee amount, which fluctuates on an annual basis.

1105   The Arbitrators also calculated simultaneously additional amounts of trade damages from the U.S. refusal to stop providing prohibited export credit guarantee subsidies supporting the export of billions in U.S. agricultural exports covering a wide variety of agricultural products.

1106   Arbitrator's Report, *Cotton 7.10*, para. 4.92.

significant price suppression in the world market price – not significant price suppression for only those transactions involving Brazil. Brazil's share of the world cotton market was roughly five percent in the reference period used to calculate countermeasures. The Arbitrator valued the damage for which Brazil could continue to impose "countermeasures" of $147.3 million per year for as long as the United States does not eliminate the marketing loan and counter-cyclical subsidies or remove all of the $2.905 billion in annual price suppression experienced by non-US cotton producers in the world market. This is an important part of the decision because it means that Brazil can continue to retaliate against the United States until the marketing loan and counter-cyclical subsidies are eliminated or *all* their worldwide adverse effects removed.[1107]

Another important aspect of the decision was the Arbitrator's acceptance of the use of economic models as useful evidentiary tools in conducing a necessary *but for* analysis of subsidy effects. The transparent use and ultimate endorsement of such models represents a fairly unique use of this economic tool by WTO decision-makers and foreshadows the important advisory role of the WTO Economics Division in any future WTO challenges to agricultural subsidies.

Finally, in view of the ongoing Doha Round negotiations concerning reductions in trade-distorting domestic subsidies and the elimination of export subsidies altogether, another key aspect of the *Cotton* Arbitration is its findings quantifying the amount of adverse market effects of the U.S. subsidies. For example, in the case of the marketing loan and counter-cyclical subsidies for only cotton, the Arbitrator found that the total effects of the significant price suppression totaled $2.905 billion in a representative year Marketing Year 2005. These are huge amounts by any measure. The size of such effects can create *moral suasion* and generate international outrage at the impact of such illegality, particularly on developing and least developed countries.[1108] An analysis

---

1107 It should be emphasized that there is no right to appeal decisions of the Arbitrator under WTO rules. For this reason, there is a relatively weak precedential effect of this, or any other Arbitrator's decision on future Arbitrators. While the Arbitrators in *Cotton* did not take an expansive view of interests of the original panel's determination regarding the serious prejudice found to exist – significant price suppression in the world market – this would not preclude arguments to future arbitrators asking them to take a different position.

1108 As discussed, *infra*, after the publication of the Arbitrator's decision, Australia submitted a formal statement to the Dispute Settlement Body of the WTO. The statement included the following quote from the Cairns Group's July 20th, 2008 Communiqué: "major subsidizers have provided...trade distorting support – effectively denying the opportunity for others, including low income producers in developing countries, to enter the market."

of future potential claims is appropriate, especially given the fact that such domestic subsidy regimes remain and international condemnation of the negative impacts on the trade and development of many developing country agricultural producers continues.

Retaliation: Though Brazil was granted retaliatory rights, pursuant to the 22.6 Arbitration proceedings discussed *supra*, it ultimately chose to postpone the determined retaliatory sanctions against the US. Rather, on June 17 2010 Brazilian ministers and USTR representatives were able to reach a framework on *Cotton*, which compensates Brazilian farmers (and African farmers to a nominal degree through technical assistance) in the value of $147 million a year. Initially, the value of the retaliatory sanctions, granted by the WTO Arbitrators, were set at more than $800 million as well as direct retaliation in the services and IPR sectors. Of primary importance is that the framework does not obviate the US from coming into compliance, pursuant to the WTO rulings. Therefore, the framework should not be considered a permanent solution to the *Cotton* dispute. It is a bilateral decision – allowed by WTO law[1109] – that the two Members reached whereby Brazil will simply postpone imposing the sanctions until the 2012 Farm Bill, at which time Brazil anticipates seeing US policy alterations to their agricultural subsidy regimes. In the meantime, Brazil can end the agreement at any time if the two elements of the Framework are not meeting their intended aims (requiring discourse on reaching a mutually agreed solution[1110] and providing benchmarks for changes to the GSM-102 program[1111]). The effect of this development is that Brazil will not have to retaliate at this time, the Brazilian cotton industry will be compensated out of the established cotton fund at the tune of about $150 million a year,[1112] and through

---

Statement of Australia, "*United States – Subsidies on Upland Cotton: Reports of the Arbitrator*," 25 September 2009.

1109 Retaliatory rights are given to a Member. That Member must then decide whether or not to exercise those rights. This is a key distinction of the WTO system, where the remedies are recommendations for withdrawal of violating measures by the WTO as well as retaliatory rights to the damaged Member.

1110 The Framework sets out a plan for engaging in periodic consultations at least four (4) times a year. These consultations are to continue until October 2012, in line with the timeline of the implementation of the next US Farm Bill.

1111 There is no specific statement of what compliance would entail. The US is expected to keep ECGs below the $5.5 billion cap in the statute. If is exceeds $1.3 billion, it has to raise premiums. The average tenor needs to be kept just over one (1) year.

1112 Considering that the Brazilian cotton industry and government invested $3 million dollars in legal and associated fees to litigate *Cotton*, this is a considerably good return on their investment.

the Framework, it will be able to monitor and provide input on the formulation of the next US Farm Bill. From the perspective of the US, it can continue to subsidize its farmers, has time to alter non-compliant policies, and will have to pay Brazil for that time.

There are two legal implications relevant to the 22.6 Arbitration proceedings and Brazil's right to retaliate. First, with regards to the suspension of Article 22.6 Agreements, Members who agree to suspend Article 22.6 *DSU* proceedings to conduct Article 21.5 proceedings, should do so only if with the understanding that such agreement will not suspend the obligation of the Member to ensure that its measures fully comply with the rulings and recommendations of the DSB. In other words, the suspension agreement should make it clear that if the Article 21.5 Panel finds that a Member has not fully complied with the rulings and recommendations of the DSB, that it shall be subject to suspension of concessions at any level to be determined by an Arbitrator from the date of the end of the reasonable period of time.

Members who maintain WTO-illegal measures are granted a reasonable period of time to make changes to those measures but, at the end of that reasonable period of time, they are not entitled to maintain any illegal WTO measures without facing retaliation. The AB in *Japan-Zeroing*, DS 322, emphasized the critical importance of the meaning of the endpoint of the reasonable period of time. The rationale of this decision suggests that the implementation obligation is not tolled by the existence of Article 21.5 proceedings. To reason otherwise would be to grant the non-implementing Member an extended reasonable period of time – a period that is nowhere to be found in the DSU.

However, the Arbitrators in Cotton 22.6, Article 7.9, ignored and implicitly rejected a request by Brazil to use the end of the reasonable period of time as the period in which to begin the tabulation of the amount of suspension of concessions that Brazil could impose against the United States. Instead, it found that "Brazil may request authorization from the DSB to suspend concessions or other obligations under the Agreements on trade in goods in Annex 1A, at a level not to exceed the value of US$147.3 million annually."[1113] As a practical matter, this meant that Brazil was only entitled to take countermeasures tabulated on an annual amount *after* 31 August 2009. However, the end of the reasonable period of time for the United States to implement the original rulings and recommendations as adopted by the DSB – and which remained in force at the time the Arbitrators issued their decision – was 21 September 2005 – almost four years before. This meant that Brazil effectively "lost" during the "suspensions" of the Article 22.6 proceedings, roughly $600 million.

1113 Arbitrator's Report, *Cotton Article 7.9 of the SCM Agreement*, para. 6.5(a).

A second consideration regarding the 22.6 Arbitration proceedings, is the consideration that the decisions of Arbitrators in the WTO are not *per se* 'precedent.' The decisions of both *Cotton* Arbitrators confirmed again the wisdom of not treating such decisions as "precedent" that are binding or even useful for future Arbitrators. There are good reasons for such a conclusion. First, there is no right of appeal. Arbitrators are free to reason and interpret WTO provisions, such as Articles 4 and 7 of the *SCM Agreement* as they see fit without regard to previous panel or Appellate Body jurisprudence. Second, there is no participation of third parties who could have brought horizontal concerns into play and offered alternative interpretations for the Arbitrators to consider. And third, there is no adoption of the Arbitrator's reports by the Dispute Settlement Body. The absence of such adoption could limit the comments that Members could make with respect to the Arbitrator's decisions. Normally, the adoption of panel and Appellate Body reports creates the opportunity for Members to widely discuss the merits and demerits of these decisions.

It is noteworthy that the decisions of the *Cotton* Arbitrators are not consistent with some of the key findings of prior Arbitrators. For example, the Arbitrators in *Cotton* refused to apply the magnitude of subsidy principles used in two precedential cases, *Canada Aircraft* and the *FSC*.[1114] Further, the Arbitrator's decision to examine "Brazil-only" effects is contrary to the decisions of the Arbitrator in *FSC* in which the EU was entitled to suspend concessions related to the full amount of the benefits of the *FSC* subsidy.[1115] The upshot of these fairly significant differences suggests that Arbitrators do not, in any significant manner, feel bound by the decisions of prior Arbitrators. It is suggested, therefore, that where appropriate, Members litigating Article 22.6 proceedings should point out the factors detailed about which reinforce the absence of any precedent effect of prior Arbitrator's decisions. This will leave them free to present interpretations of WTO provisions and to present methodologies without regard to the interpretations offered by previous Arbitrators. Accordingly, litigants in future Article 7.9 proceedings should freely reject the decisions of the *Cotton* Arbitrators in finding a "Brazil-only" effects. Similarly, the Arbitrator's failure to impart any different meaning to Articles 7.9 apart from normal Article 22.6 nullification or impairment calculations appears to be inconsistent with the "special and additional" status of those provisions.

Combined, these legal findings have created and/or further defined a body of law that is essential to the development of the dispute settlement mechanism

---

1114 *Canada*-Aircraft (WT/DS70/AB/R) and *US-FSC* (WT/DS108/AB/RW).
1115 *US-FSC* (WT/DS108/AB/RW).

of the WTO. The legal issues and their identified significance discussed, *supra*, were issues of first impression by the DSB. As such, they set the legal precedence that stands as definitive law to be referenced by negotiators as well as considered by policymakers at the domestic level. In addition to these precedential implications, the *Cotton* case also illustrates how successful policy strategies can further a nations interests in both the litigation and political environments. As described in the following section, the role of LDCs, specifically Chad and Benin, affected the findings of serious prejudice in the dispute settlement process as well as served to enhance the negotiating position of Brazil and the African countries in the political arena of the Doha Round.

6.2 Lessons from the Involvement of Chad and Benin

Within the ever-expanding membership of the WTO, developing and least developed countries (LDCs) constitute an overwhelming majority. However, the interests of those Members have yet to be fully integrated into the structure of the system or expressed through involvement by a great number of WTO Members. This void is often dismissed as solely stemming from weak economic and political positioning within the global trading system. However, the principles of the WTO reach beyond these limitations to encourage Member participation and the fair consideration of the interests of all Members. To that end, developments have been undertaken to achieve these goals. The *Cotton* dispute and Cotton Initiative are the two most significant examples of the need for progress to be made in the "development" round to more meaningfully include the developing world in the WTO.

This section of Part 2 of this book analyzes the least developed country participation in the *Cotton* dispute. The section is included to proffer explanations for why there was not greater participation by LDCs in the dispute as well as to argue that many of the hesitations by LDCs for not wishing to participate were alleviated by the eventual outcome of the case and by the experiences stemming from Benin and Chad's participation in *Cotton*.

LDC Involvement in the WTO Dispute Settlement Mechanism: Why is it important that LDCs, like many African Members,[1116] become more involved in the dispute settlement system of the WTO? In addressing this question, it is

---

1116 This section concentrates on LDC involvement from African countries, given its relevancy to the *Cotton* dispute; however, the concerns posed are also applicable to other LDCs.

important to remember that, in order to provide predictability and stability in the world-trading environment, a rules-based dispute settlement system was created to ensure the enforcement of those mutually agreed upon rules.[1117] The dispute system of the WTO has been used more heavily than other international legal systems, including its predecessor the GATT and the International Court of Justice.[1118] However, the predominance of developed nations' use of the system relative to that of developing countries is troublesome. The fact that dispute settlement activity is concentrated in developed and a handful of developing countries is irregular and poses the question whether the dispute settlement system is effectively being utilized. This was particularly acute at the time of the *Cotton* dispute, when there was a perceivable absence of LDC involvement in the system. The fact that there has been a recognizable increased use of the system since *Cotton* means that its outcome provided added incentives for developing and LDC countries to successfully engage in the system. Therefore, the credibility of the system, in terms of access and use, has improved to some degree, but continues to be a source of consideration.

Given that the dispute settlement process is still in the relatively early stage of development, there remain opportunities for significant progress and improvement.[1119] Progress is needed in terms of structural reforms of the litigation mechanism, in terms of its functionality as well as improving the jurisprudence of the system. By not participating in dispute settlement, African countries consequently do not have their development interests reflected in the interpretations of panelists and the AB, nor are the obligations most affecting them incorporated into rulings. If the WTO is to remain a sustainable institution, reflecting the interests of all of its Members, then all types of Members should be involved, especially those less politically and economically advantaged,

---

1117 For a detailed understanding of the significance of Africa's involvement, specifically, in the dispute settlement mechanism of the WTO in terms of the predictability and sustainability of the institution, *see*, Mosoti, V., "Africa in the First Decade of WTO Dispute Settlement," *Journal of International Economic Law*, Vol. 9, Issue 2, (11 May 2006), pp. 427–453.

1118 McRae, D., "What is the Future of WTO Dispute Settlement?" *Journal of International Economic Law*, Vol. 7(1) 3, (2004), p. 9.

1119 For a greater analysis of the currently recognized limitations of the WTO dispute settlement mechanism as they affect LDC and other small Members, *see*, Pauwelyn, J., "Appeal without Demand: A Design Flaw in WTO Dispute Settlement and How to Fix It," © International Centre for Trade and Sustainable Development (ICTSD), Dispute Settlement and Legal Aspects of International Trade, Issue Paper No. 1 (June 2007).

which constitute over a third of the WTO membership.[1120] Beyond the dispute settlement mechanism, African participants can further develop WTO jurisprudence, which can be used to clarify negotiating positions.[1121] Even more expansive, by contributing to and more directly influencing the dispute settlement process, developing and LDC Members can help move the WTO from a primarily power-based system to a rules-based system. This would enable developing and LDC Members to help shift the WTO so that it remains more consistent with the goal of universal applicability for all Members, regardless of their stage of economic development.

Why is participation from African Members low? A number of limitations have been identified regarding the participation of LDCs in WTO dispute settlement.[1122] These include: inadequate retaliatory relief, lack of expertise and resources and other internal barriers, and fears of political and economic pressures.[1123] The first two of these factors can be considered market-oriented because they arise from economic or structural factors while the last factor is essentially political in nature.

A key second market-oriented rationale for the lack of LDC involvement centers on the retaliation mechanisms. As noted by Chad Bown and Bernard Hoekman, the current retaliation-as-remedy approach is not feasible given the economic and political conditions of LDCs.[1124] Specifically, "they lack the capacity to impose the large political-economic welfare losses on potential

---

[1120] See, Mosoti, V., "Africa in the First Decade of WTO Dispute Settlement," *Journal of International Economic Law*, Vol. 9, Issue 2, (11 May 2006), pp. 427–453.

[1121] Manduna, C., "Daring to Dispute: Are there shifting trends in African participation in WTO dispute settlement," TRALAC Trade Brief, No. 3 (June 2005).

[1122] For extended analyses on the constraints of the dispute settlement system, in terms of LDC involvement, See, Nottage, H., "Developing Countries in the WTO Dispute Settlement System," Global Economic Governance Program, Working Paper, GEG Working Paper 2009/47, (January 2009); Shaffer, G., "Weaknesses and proposed improvements to the WTO Dispute Settlement System: an economic and market-oriented view," *WTO at 10: A Look at the Appellate Body* conference, Sao Paulo, Brazil, 15–17 May, 2005, (13 May 2005); Bown, C. and McCulloch, R., "Developing Countries, Dispute Settlement, and the Advisory Centre on WTO Law," Stanford Seminar, JEL No. F13; and Bown, C., *Self-Enforcing Trade: Developing Countries and WTO Dispute Settlement*, The Brookings Institution, Washington, D.C, © 2009.

[1123] Nottage, H., "Developing Countries in the WTO Dispute Settlement System," Global Economic Governance Program, Working Paper, GEG Working Paper 2009/47, (January 2009).

[1124] Bown, C. and Hoekman, B., "WTO Dispute Settlement and the Missing Developing Country Cases: Engaging the Private Sector," *Journal of International Economic Law*, Vol. 8, Issue 4, Oxford University Press, © 2005, pp. 861–890.

respondent countries that would generate the internal political pressure in those countries that may be a necessary element to induce compliance with adverse DSU rulings."[1125] In a conference on the topic of economically small Members of the WTO and their ability to effectively retaliate against non-complying parties, government representatives and academicians discussed the limitations of the present retaliation-as-remedy approach.[1126] Pamela Coke-Hamilton of the Inter-American Development Bank discussed how the WTO is not insulated from the political and economic asymmetries of the Members and, as a result the limited power small states have in the WTO.[1127] Beyond the costs of access issue discussed, *infra*, Coke-Hamilton emphasized the fact that – especially where the US is the largest trading partner with another country – that country is unlikely to retaliate, even if given the right.[1128] A representative from Burkina Faso testified on this point, exclaiming that as of 2007 significant work had been accomplished, but that there was still no recognizable outcome from the *Cotton* dispute in the country, and production continues to decline. His description of the WTO negotiations was that it was a 'race' that everyone is allowed to enter, but that the participants already know who wins the race.

1125 Bown, C. and Hoekman, B., "WTO Dispute Settlement and the Missing Developing Country Cases: Engaging the Private Sector," *Journal of International Economic Law*, Vol. 8, Issue 4, Oxford University Press, © 2005, p. 863.

1126 "Small States in WTO Dispute Settlement," Conference, King & Spalding, Washington, DC, (25 March 2009), accessed online. As described online, "WTO Members whose economies are small and developing have not taken full advantage of the WTO's Dispute Settlement system. In those instances where they bring a challenge, it can be difficult to enforce their rights, as recently illustrated in United States – Measures Affecting the Cross-Border Supply of Gambling and Betting Services. Join us for a panel discussion that seeks to inquire why these nations are not active users of the dispute settlement system, and what actions could be taken to increase their participation. Panelists: Andrea Marie Brown, Executive Director, Anti-dumping and Subsidies Commission Kingston, Jamaica; Mark Mendel, Mendel-Blumenfeld LLP, Argued on behalf of Antigua in Gambling; Joost Pauwelyn, Senior Advisory, King &Spalding and Professor of International Law at the Graduate Institute of International Studies in Geneva, Switzerland; Cosponsored by the American Society of International Law and American Bar Association International Trade Committee."

1127 "Small States in WTO Dispute Settlement," Conference, King & Spalding, Washington, DC, (25 March 2009), accessed online.

1128 Ms. Hamilton discussed these points in relation to the *Bananas* cases and *Gambling* case where the smaller states 'won' on paper, but where retaliatory action was not taken by them given the factors discussed here.

...trade sanctions – in essence the only legal remedy available at the WTO – may (sometimes) work for powerful complainants, it is unlikely to work for smaller players. On the contrary, rather than putting pressure on the violating country, when a small player retaliates it is more likely to harm *its own* economy (higher input and consumer prices) as well as *its own* political interests (think of the risk of being cut-off from foreign assistance).[1129]

Alternative views were also discussed as well as solutions proffered. From a more positive position, retaliation requires of course that 'losing' countries do not comply with adverse DSU rulings, and may have been a legitimate fear of retaliation as was found in the *Cotton* case. However, a recent study by Bruce Wilson, Director of the Legal Affairs Division of the WTO, found that, overall, there is considerable compliance by WTO Members faced with recommendations by the DSU.[1130] Joost Pauwelyn stresses that the threat of retaliation is more important than the actual act of retaliating. Given the high reputation costs, as Bruce Wilson found, parties are likely to comply. As Pauwelyn wrote, "Given these deficiencies, one may ask why WTO Members still comply with 90 per cent of WTO rulings and, in particular, developing countries have rarely faced the problem of non-implementation. The answer is most likely that it is not the *legal* remedies, nor the *economic* pressure exerted by trade sanctions that induces countries to behave. Rather, it is the *political* pressure of peer review, example-setting and shunning *internationally*, at WTO meetings, and the *domestic* political pressure, from both sectors harmed by the original violation (steel consumers) and those threatened by retaliation (orange growers), that pushes countries to eventually step in line."[1131] Mark Mendel of Mendel-Blumenfeld LLP argued that, especially in disputes where the US is the violating party, the 'biggest weapon in the arsenal' is the US' reputation, integrity of the system and its commitment to it.[1132]

In deviation from the barriers recognized for non-entry by LDC and small states, Pauwelyn (and the ACWL) argues that the capacity to retaliate is not a

---

1129 Pauwelyn, J., "WTO Victory on Steel Hides Deficiencies," *JURIST Legal Intelligence*, (23 January 2004), http://jurist.law.pitt.edu/forum/Pauwelyn1.php.
1130 Wilson, B., "Compliance by WTO Members with Adverse WTO Dispute Settlement Rulings," *Journal of International Economic Law*, Vol. 10, Issue 2, (2007), p. 397.
1131 Pauwelyn, J., "WTO Victory on Steel Hides Deficiencies," *JURIST Legal Intelligence*, (23 January 2004), http://jurist.law.pitt.edu/forum/Pauwelyn1.php.
1132 "Small States in WTO Dispute Settlement," Conference, King & Spalding, Washington, DC, (25 March 2009), accessed online.

significant factor in gaining compliance.[1133] If small[1134] states were to retaliate there are identified effective means for doing so. The guidelines Pauwelyn sets forth are to (1) minimize harm to one's own country and (2) try to maximize harm on the violating country. Though this is difficult, given many of the products are in one's own country, targeting a few politically sensitive goods that are not of great importance to the retaliator's economy can effectuate compliance. What is most important in this scenario is to "pick products that send a political message to the violator."[1135] In the alternative, where products are deemed of significant value, creating a list of more products at lower levels, or targeting intellectual property rights (IPRs) can be effective.[1136]

The retaliatory framework described above can be considered a market-oriented impediment to greater LDC participation that is essentially external in nature. The types of internal market-oriented barriers to greater LDC participation are also important to consider. Lack of expertise and resources is one of the primary prohibiting factors for LDC involvement. LDCs are small-scale participants in relevant agricultural markets and, as a result, are forced to behave as price takers in these markets. Without the ability to impose a markup on their sales of affected commodities or generate significant profits, LDCs do not have the requisite financial resources to initiate or sustain the costly dispute settlement process.[1137] As discussed below, one of the main policy recommendations made by scholars in this area involve mechanisms for reducing costs of litigation for LDCs.

Lack of domestic procedures and expertise required for identifying, quantifying, and articulating (often referred to as 'naming, blaming, and claiming')[1138]

1133 "Small States in WTO Dispute Settlement," Conference, King & Spalding, Washington, DC, (25 March 2009), accessed online. This view is also held by the Advisory Centre on WTO Law (ACWL) as learned from communications.

1134 Pauwelyn does not limit small states to those that are 'economically small,' but can also include price-setting countries. He emphasized that it is not the level of development, but market size that matters. "Small States in WTO Dispute Settlement," Conference, King & Spalding, Washington, DC, (25 March 2009), accessed online.

1135 "Small States in WTO Dispute Settlement," Conference, King & Spalding, Washington, DC, (25 March 2009), accessed online.

1136 "Small States in WTO Dispute Settlement," Conference, King & Spalding, Washington, DC, (25 March 2009), accessed online.

1137 Bown, C. and Hoekman, B., "WTO Dispute Settlement and the Missing Developing Country Cases: Engaging the Private Sector," *Journal of International Economic Law*, Vol. 8, Issue 4, Oxford University Press, © 2005, p. 863.

1138 *See*, Felstiner, Wl *et al.*, "The Emergence and Transformation of Disputes: Naming, Blaming and Claiming," 15 *Law & Society Review*, (1980–81), p. 631; Shaffer, G., "The

the adverse domestic impacts of external market effects are not present in most LDCs.[1139] Before any dispute resolution process can begin, a Member has to first recognize that an injury is occurring. Members also have to indentify the cause of the damage and the responsible parties. In addition, they must have the ability to mobilize and coordinate the requisite resources to assess and quantify the damage being experienced and to pursue the dispute resolution process. Industry infrastructure such as trade associations and lobbying organizations are common in developed economies and serve many of these functions. Even developing nations often have industry organizations that not only identify that their interests are being harmed, but also bring pressure to pursue the DSU process and marshal resources to support the case, as is evident from the role of industry participation on the part of Brazil in the *Cotton* case.[1140] These resources, however, are too often absent in least developed economies and, consequently, contribute to their inability to bring a complaint to the WTO.[1141] As noted by Amin Alavi, in a review of the literature on African countries' participation in the WTO's dispute settlement mechanism (DSM), "the main problem identified is that the DSM (and the WTO) has become too technically complex and demanding for most developing nations to use effectively in the absence of adequate assistance."[1142]

In addition to the economic, market-oriented factors, *supra*, there are political factors that deter LDC involvement in WTO dispute settlement. Predominantly, there is a fear by LDCs of retaliation by respondents in the form of the reduction or elimination of various forms of support. For example, LDCs are often dependant upon developed potential respondents for foreign aid, development assistance, debt relief, and preferential market access. Therefore,

---

Challenges of WTO Law: Strategies for Developing Country Adaptation," *World Trade Review* Vol.5, Issue 2, (2006), p. 179; and Nottage, H., "Developing Countries in the WTO Dispute Settlement System," Global Economic Governance Program, Working Paper, GEG Working Paper 2009/47, (January 2009).

1139 Shaffer, G., "The Challenges of WTO Law, Strategies for Developing Country Adaptation," *World Trade Review*, Vol. 5, Issue 2, (2006), p. 185.

1140 As mentioned in Chapter 4, Brazil has a three pillar approach to engaging in WTO dispute resolution: a WTO dispute settlement division in Brasilia, coordination between the division and their WTO permanent mission in Geneva, and organized relations in the private sector. *See*, Shaffer, G., "The Challenges of WTO Law: Strategies for Developing Country Adaptation," *World Trade Review*, Vol. 5, Issue 2, (2006), p. 183.

1141 *See*, Horn, H., Nordstrom, H., and Mavroidis, P., "Is the Use of the WTO Dispute Settlement System Biased?" *CEPR Discussion Paper* 2340 (1999), p. 13.

1142 Amin, A., "African Countries and the WTO's Dispute Settlement Mechanism," *Development Policy Review*, Vol. 25, No. 2, (2007), p. 28.

the sheer vulnerability of the LDCs and their related concerns over the withdrawal of support strongly dissuade them from initiating WTO disputes. Although there is little empirical evidence of a direct tie between bringing WTO disputes and retaliation outside of the WTO through bilateral aid withdrawal, the connection is recognized by several scholars[1143] and this perception by LDCs is confirmed through the interviews conducted for the completion of this book.

It is important to note that the factors elucidated here for the lack of LDC involvement, both economic and political, are all interdependent. The fact that most LDCs are small producers contributes to their lack of market power and ability to bear the costs of WTO litigation. It also contributes to the lack of internal domestic infrastructure to support litigation efforts as well as the inability of LDCs to effectively retaliate and discipline larger economies that are pursuing damaging and WTO-illegal agricultural support programs.

How is it possible to increase LDC participation? Given that litigation costs, both in the formulation and execution of a WTO dispute, are prohibitive to LDCs, this issue is of utmost importance to address. An initial step in this direction was the creation of the Advisory Centre on WTO Law (ACWL). This was the first attempt to augment the dispute settlement process of the WTO with the aim of increasing developing and LDC involvement.[1144] The ACWL is an intergovernmental organization established at the commencement of the Doha Development Round as a means to provide legal support on the legal agreements reached in the Uruguay Round, supply representation through the dispute settlement process, and train Members about the substance and procedure of the dispute settlement mechanism of the WTO. The Centre and the services provided by it are not part of the WTO; rather, it is a separate entity, funded by its Members.[1145] The creation of the ACWL has been recognized as an important initial step that has since been followed by the resources provided by the United Nations Centre on Trade & Development (UNCTAD) and the WTO to develop training programs in WTO dispute settlement.[1146] However,

---

1143 Shaffer, G., "The Challenges of WTO Law, Strategies for Developing Country Adaptation," *World Trade Review*, (2006), p. 193, at footnote 66 and as set forth in, Nottage, H., "Developing Countries in the WTO Dispute Settlement System," Global Economic Governance Program, Working Paper, GEG Working Paper 2009/47, (January 2009).

1144 Bown, C., *Self-Enforcing Trade: Developing Countries and WTO Dispute Settlement*, The Brookings Institution, Washington, D.C, © 2009, p. 145.

1145 Agreement Establishing the Advisory Centre on WTO Law, www.acwl.ch/e/about/basic_documents.html.

1146 Shaffer, G., "The Challenges of WTO Law: Strategies for Developing Country Adaptation," *World Trade Review*, Vol. 5, Issue 2, (2006), p. 183.

as noted by Bown and McCulloch "the availability of low-cost ACWL services has not been enough to expand the set of developing countries that undertake litigation under the DSU to enforce their foreign market access rights."[1147] In this vein, scholars recommend that greater involvement by the private sector in supporting LDCs is critical to increase LDC participation.[1148] Specifically, Bown and Hoekman argued that actual cost reduction for LDCs across the system is preferred to implementing reforms aimed at reducing costs, and suggested that viable avenues to pursue include inducing greater support from "legal service centres, the private sector, NGOs, development organizations, international trade litigators, economists, consumer groups, and even law schools to improve poor country access to lower cost legal assistance."[1149] In their study, they described the value added to such sectors by their participation in WTO litigation and emphasized the need to coordinate efforts among these groups in order to provide adequate assistance to LDCs. As described *infra*, *Cotton* was an excellent example of both the involvement by a sampling of these groups as well as their coordination.

Lambert Botha of the Trade Law Centre of South Africa (TRALAC), stresses that the primary means to mobilize industry, in hopes of increasing African LDC participation at the multilateral level, is through trade associations.[1150] Specifically, he emphasized the need to create more and stronger forums between industry and government. Coordination at this level would help move Members from a short-medium to long-term view as they formulate trade policies and reorganize themselves internally. Further, such synchronization should better facilitate and disseminate communications regarding what is developing within the WTO that might impact industry. Further, discussions at this level allow participants to assess what cannot be achieved bilaterally. For example, he recommended that a framework needs to be established to set the playing field for market access and preferential treatment, which must be effectuated at the multilateral level. This is an example of the shift away from topics reserved for governments that did not affect industry prior, to topics that

---

1147 Bown, C. and McCulloch, R., "Developing Countries, Dispute Settlement, and the Advisory Centre on WTO Law." 2009, p. 28 xxx.
1148 Bown, C. and Hoekman, B., "WTO Dispute Settlement and the Missing Developing Country Cases: Engaging the Private Sector," *Journal of International Economic Law*, Vol. 8, Issue 4, Oxford University Press, © 2005, pp. 861–890.
1149 Bown, C. and Hoekman, B., "WTO Dispute Settlement and the Missing Developing Country Cases: Engaging the Private Sector," *Journal of International Economic Law*, Vol. 8, Issue 4, Oxford University Press, © 2005, p. 864.
1150 Personal phone interview, Summer 2009, Geneva, Switzerland.

directly impact them at present. After the conceptual alteration is achieved, participation in dispute settlement at the WTO can be actualized. As a result, internal capacity is built within local groups and the requisite skills transferred. There are several institutions looking into this exact issue and co-operations trying to organize themselves by obtaining data on trading partners as well as trying to minimize trade facilitation and address historical barriers, such as corruption as the borders.[1151]

Beyond cost barriers, there are two perceived difficulties with integrating least develop countries (LDCs) within the WTO. One is the need for opportunities for participation to be structurally incorporated within the system. The second is a shortage of interest in increased participation by LDCs in both the dispute settlement process and the legislative functions of the organization due to a lack of understanding of the potential benefits to be gained from such participation. One solution proffered for structurally incorporating more LDCs within the system (and reducing costs for them as well) is the inclusion of a small claims procedure in the DSU.[1152] The general concept would be to create an international mechanism, similar to domestic small claims courts that would allow lesser developed countries to bring disputes on legal bases already ruled upon by the DSB and to offer alternative remedies other than retaliatory relief (e.g. compensation). A full discussion of this proposal was developed in 2007 by the Chief Economist on the National Board of Trade in Sweden, Hakan Nordstrom, and Gregory Shaffer of the University of Wisconsin School of Law. It is important to note that there are tremendous political and legal barriers recognized in implementing such a system, though the economic justifications are supported, and aims of greater participation by LDCs could feasibly be

---

1151 WTO African Members are taking steps at present to coordinate industry and government as well as participate in government-government co-operations. Examples of cotton-specific associations include African Cotton & Textile Industries Federation (ACTIF), Cotton South Africa (Cotton SA), and Tanzania Cotton Board (TCB), as well as more broadly-focused associations of the Common Market for Eastern and Southern Africa (COMESA), Eastern and Southern African Business Organization (ESABO), South African Development Community (SADC), the Sachel and Southern African Enterprise Network (SAEN), and the Southern and West African Enterprise Network (SAEN and WAEN). These are distinguished from national, regional or multilateral associations, or the many associations that are located in the US or EU for the promotion of trade and investment between them and Africa.

1152 Nordstrom, H., and Shaffer, G., "Access to Justice in the World Trade Organization: The Case for a Small Claims Procedure, A Preliminary Analysis," ICTSD Project on Dispute Settlement, Issue Paper No. 2, (June 2007).

met.[1153] Of value, however, is the fact that such proposals are being considered[1154] and evaluations by the private and public sectors are being made regarding the fairness and efficacy of the dispute settlement process in terms of LDCs and small states, generally, in the WTO.[1155]

Another structural adjustment for future consideration is the inclusion of representatives from LDCs in the Appellate Body[1156] or African nations involved in the dispute settlement of the WTO Secretariat. At present, there has been limited representation by Africans as panelists.[1157] Undertaking such a structural adjustment would not only encourage participation by LDCs, but would also allow for greater capacity building for Africa so that expertise can be developed and retained in the LDCs.

In terms of boosting LDC participation, recognition of the gains from their involvement in a rules-based system needs to be communicated to LDCs. The early development of the WTO was strongly shaped by political forces and by the preference on the part of developed Members to negotiate as oppose to litigate. Traditionally, developed parties chose to use their power to effectuate desired results. However, this is not a viable strategy for LDCs with limited political and economic power to move negotiations. More recent developments within the WTO system are more amenable to developing and LDCs to further their interests through litigation *via* the DSU, the aim of which is to evaluate trade issues among parties in a *milieu* in which decisions are made more objectively and on a more level playing field. However, in discussing this solution with interviewees, one limitation recognized was how to measure the output of participation of LDCs in the dispute settlement process in order to

---

1153 Nordstrom, H., and Shaffer, G., "Access to Justice in the World Trade Organization: The Case for a Small Claims Procedure, A Preliminary Analysis," ICTSD Project on Dispute Settlement, Issue Paper No. 2, (June 2007).

1154 Another proposal offered by Pamela Coke-Hamilton was a cross-retaliation remedy, whereby larger countries could receive (or buy) retaliatory rights from smaller countries. "Small States in WTO Dispute Settlement," Conference, King & Spalding, Washington, DC, (25 March 2009), accessed online.

1155 For example, *see*, Pauwelyn, J., "Appeal without Demand: A Design Flaw in WTO Dispute Settlement and How to Fix It," © International Centre for Trade and Sustainable Development (ICTSD), Dispute Settlement and Legal Aspects of International Trade, Issue Paper No. 1 (June 2007); Alavi, A., "African Countries and the WTO's Dispute Settlement Mechanism," *Development Policy Review*, Vol. 25, Issue 1(2007), pp. 25–42.

1156 To date, there has only been one Egyptian national that has served as an Appellate Body member.

1157 Manduna, C., "Daring to Dispute: Are there shifting trends in African participation in WTO dispute settlement," TRALAC Trade Brief, No. 3 (June 2005), p. 4.

'sell' what benefits are being realized at the multilateral level. This is especially critical in terms of expanding industry involvement as discussed, *supra*.

In conclusion, LDC involvement in the legal process of the WTO has been limited in the past. LDCs have traditionally only been involved in the dispute settlement process as third parties and, as a result, the decision by some Members of the C-4 (Benin and Chad) to limit their participation to this role was not out of the ordinary. Indeed, there have been benefits for LDCs from 'free-riding' in the system as third parties and could be a viable strategy to continue to employ in some cases. However, an important outcome from the *Cotton* case is that the gains from active LDC participation were made more visible and will thereby serve as an incentive for an increased role by LDCs in future cases.

As a result of *Cotton*, the importance of early and active participation as third parties to enhance the political and negotiating power of LDCs is apparent. For example, early participation by African third parties significantly heightened the profile of their cotton interests within the WTO, dramatically increased global awareness and interest in their plight, and increased transparency of the effects of agricultural support programs generally. All of these added significantly to the ability of African countries to more successfully negotiate their interests, focus attention on developing nations, and make cotton a key element of the Doha Development Round. Further, in addition to these types of political gains, the potential for financial compensatory gains for LDCs by even more active engagement in dispute settlement proceedings as co-complainants are highlighted by the *Cotton* case. A number of these considerations and lessons learned are set forth in the following sections, including: seminal nature of *Cotton*, implications for political standing of parties, impact of third party submissions, political concerns and consequences, as well as remedies provided to LDCs.

Seminal Nature as LDC Case: Though it remains that no African least developed country (LDC) has yet to participate in the dispute settlement mechanism of the WTO as either complainant or respondent, *Cotton* is a seminal case within the WTO legal system because it was the first time that LDC African countries participated in a dispute concerning trade in agriculture.[1158]

1158 Through the *Cotton* original and compliance proceedings, it remained that though some developing countries initiated a number of cases (almost half against other developing countries), no African LDCs had initiated a dispute. Participation can be described in the following: South Africa was involved in two (2) and Egypt four (4) cases as respondent parties at the time of *Cotton*. Nigeria and Zimbabwe were involved in one (1) dispute each, Senegal in two (2), Tanzania and Malawi in three (3), and Mauratius in five (5) disputes.

In addition to *EC-Sugar*, *Cotton* is recognized as one of the two most important cases concerning trade in agriculture. African LDC involvement uniquely characterized the Cotton case as a development dispute and has become recognized as a case in which the interests of African LDCs rose to the fore despite their participation as third parties rather than co-complainants or respondents. In short, the public perception of the *Cotton* case is strongly tied to the plight of African LDCs.

The participation by Benin and Chad[1159] in *Cotton* as third parties and nine (9) sugar-exporting African countries in *Sugar*, albeit limited, was significant.[1160,1161] In the case of *Cotton*, the participation was key to establishing the serious prejudice claim that US subsidies were causing adverse effects on the world market as well as developing ethical arguments to be used in the political environment of WTO negotiations. *Sugar* was demonstrably different from the *Cotton* case because the African countries involved were defending a perceived challenge against their preferential access to the EU market and, unlike in *Cotton*, industry provided significant assistance to the third parties. Therefore, the African, Caribbean, and Pacific Group of States (ACP) worked with the respondents in order to try to protect their interests and received considerable support from the EC and EC sugar industry.[1162] This was also the case with the *Bananas* disputes, where the Africans were yet again brought in to defend a challenged EC regime, to ensure that their interests were represented.[1163]

Another significant difference is that, *ex post* one can argue that in the case of *Cotton* the African LDCs could have been co-complainants; whereas, in the *Sugar* case, this is not applicable, because the ACP countries were on the responding side. Further, it was highly unlikely that Brazil would bring a

---

See, Alavi, A., "African Countries and the WTO's Dispute Settlement Mechanism," Development Policy Review, Vol. 25, Issue 1 (2007), p. 27.

1159 Though several African countries are affected by US subsidy regime, *inter alia* Senegal, Mali, Burkina Faso, and Togo, only Chad and Benin chose to participate.

1160 There were twenty-one (21) third parties in *EC-Sugar*, almost half of which were African countries. They included, *inter alia*: Côte d'Ivoire, Guyana, Kenya, Madagascar, Malawi, Mauritius, Swaziland, and Tanzania.

1161 There have been five (5) disputes, which have included African countries, three (3) of those have been as Members of the ACP group.

1162 Support was provided *via* the Cotonou Agreement assistance program, which gave funds to the ACP sugar producers to hire the services of a private law firm. Manduna, C., "Daring to Dispute: Are there shifting trends in African participation in WTO dispute settlement," TRALAC Trade Brief, No. 3 (June 2005), p. 8.

1163 Manduna, C., "Daring to Dispute: Are there shifting trends in African participation in WTO dispute settlement," TRALAC Trade Brief, No. 3 (June 2005), p. 3.

dispute against a LDC in the *Sugar* case both because the Africans' interests were not consequential to Brazil's claim and, probably more importantly, such a move would have been politically unacceptable.

The differences between the *Sugar* and *Cotton* cases are also illustrative of the likelihood of compliance resulting from a dispute settlement case. In the *Sugar* case, it is important to note that the EU complied with the rulings of the DSB and at a much quicker rate than did the US in the *Cotton* case.[1164] One factor accounting for this difference stems from the nature of the political body required to implement compliance measures and whether such implementation requires administrative or legislative action. As the Director of the WTO's Legal Affairs Division, Bruce Wilson emphasized that compliance is determinant upon this factor.[1165] "It is noticeable, if not unsurprising, that compliance has been more rapid where the WTO violations can be corrected through administrative action as opposed to legislative action." This was explained as consequential given the legislative process of altering national statutes can take a significantly longer period, given more complicated processes and political dynamics, than executive action.[1166] The increased likelihood that required changes would be made by the administrative body of the EU in the Sugar case, rather than through legislative action in the *Cotton* case, may be partially responsible for increased African participation in the *Sugar* dispute. In the wake of the *Cotton* decisions, however, there is likely wider recognition on the part of LDCs that cases against trade-distorting agricultural subsidies can be successfully litigated.[1167] Further, in the wake of *Cotton*, there is now much less information asymmetry and increased transparency regarding how the rules are to be interpreted, and a new precedent set for how agricultural subsidies will be disciplined in the future. Overall, it is recognized that, in both cases, "the recent involvement of African countries in two very complex disputes, requiring a combination of technical analysis, the use of experts; political endeavours and pursuing solutions through the Doha negotiations, is cause for

---

1164 The compliance issue of *Cotton* is given considerable attention in Chapter 10 of this book, in terms of the need to and difficulties of bringing the US' domestic subsidy regime into compliance with the WTO rulings.

1165 Wilson, B., "Compliance by WTO Members with Adverse WTO Dispute Settlement Rulings: The Record to Date," *Journal of International Economic Law*, Vol. 10, Issue 2, (11 May 2007), p. 397.

1166 Wilson, B., "Compliance by WTO Members with Adverse WTO Dispute Settlement Rulings: The Record to Date," *Journal of International Economic Law*, Vol. 10, Issue 2, (11 May 2007), p. 399.

1167 Historically, there were few appeals cases, since most cases are settled.

some optimism that African countries can participate meaningfully in WTO dispute settlement."[1168]

Impact of Third Party Submissions: In general terms, WTO Member countries can have their interests protected through the DSU by participating as either a complainant, a co-complainant, or a third party. As mentioned *supra*, no African LDC had participated in the DSU in a role other than a third party. In the *Cotton* case, the DSB established a Panel in March 2003, pursuant to Brazil's request. Several other WTO Members reserved their third-party rights at the time with Benin and Chad joining as third parties shortly thereafter.[1169] Of all the African producing countries, only Benin and Chad joined the dispute.

By joining as third parties, Benin and Chad reserved the right to have their interests heard and to incorporate the impacts of the US cotton support regime on their economies into the findings of the Panel and Appellate Body. In the original proceedings, Benin and Chad submitted evidence about the extent to which their countries were adversely impacted by the trade-distorting subsidy regimes of the US. In its original submission to the Panel at the first session of the first meeting of the Panel, for example, Benin presented evidence about the effects of the US subsidy programs and made the case that they threaten the entire existence of their domestic cotton industry.[1170] Benin and Chad later made a joint submission to the first meeting of the Panel that succinctly detailed the state of the cotton sector in each country and presented evidence about the serious prejudice nature of the effects of US subsidies. Benin, which has a permanent mission in Geneva, presented the bulk of the evidence from sources such as the International Monetary Fund, the United Nations Development Program, and a detailed study by the International Food Policy Research Institute, which supplied one of its research fellows to Benin's delegation.[1171] Chad does not have a permanent mission in Geneva, but submitted a detailed statement by the President of African Cotton Association. Their evidence was credible and the assistance provided them *pro bono* by the coordinated efforts

---

1168 Manduna, C., "Daring to Dispute: Are there shifting trends in African participation in WTO dispute settlement," TRALAC Trade Brief, No. 3 (June 2005), p. 5.

1169 The third parties in the dispute were Argentina, Canada, China, Chinese Taipei, the EU, India, Pakistan, Australia, New Zealand, Paraguay, Venezuela, Benin, and Chad.

1170 Upland Cotton: Report of the Panel United States Upland Cotton WT/DS 267, Annex B-5, para. 19.

1171 Minot, N. and L. Daniels. 2002. Impact of Global Cotton Markets on Rural Poverty in Benin. IFPRI, Washington DC: November, 2002. See also Goreaux, L. Prejudice Caused by Industrialised Countries Subsidies to Cotton Sectors in Western and Central Africa. Background document to the submission made by Benin, Burkina Faso, Chad and Mali to the WTO (TN/AG/GEN/4). WTO, Geneva: June 2003.

of a private law, Oxfam, the ACWL, and others detailed above, greatly added to the efficacy of their arguments. The complexity and magnitude of the evidence required was precedential. To that end, it should be noted that – even in light of such demanding conditions – Benin and Chad were able to gather the requisite expertise to compete against the US before the WTO. This was accomplished without the support of a recognizable African lobby or organized industry.

Benin and Chad joined as third parties under Article 10.2 of the DSU, which states that "third parties shall have an opportunity to be heard by the panel and to make written submissions to the panel. These submissions shall also be given to the parties to the dispute and shall be reflected in the panel report."[1172] The evidence submitted by third parties, including Benin and Chad, was reflected in the report of the Panel and the evidence provided by Benin and Chad was significant in demonstrating the adverse effects of US upland cotton subsidies.[1173] Indeed, the Panel found that the significant price suppression resulting from US cotton support measures constituted serious prejudice, but it limited its ruling of serious prejudice to Brazilian upland cotton producers. In line with Article 10.1 of the DSU, which states that the "interests of the parties to a dispute and those of other Members under a covered agreement at issue in the dispute shall be fully taken into account during the panel process," Brazil argued that others, particularly Benin and Chad, had also suffered serious prejudice. However, the US argued, with the support of the EU, that only the effects on Brazilian producers were relevant and that only the interests of Brazil, as the complainant, were to be considered. While Benin and Chad submitted that Article 24.1 of the DSU[1174] allows for their interests to be considered as least developed countries, the Panel found that Article 7 of the SCM

1172 Understanding on Rules and Procedures Governing the Settlement of Disputes, Article 10, Annex 2 of the WTO Agreement, *The Legal Texts: The Results of the Uruguay Round of Multilateral Trade Negotiations*, World Trade Organization, © Cambridge University Press, (1999), p. 362.

1173 *Panel Report*, para. 7.54. In this section of the *Report*, the Panel indicated the level of involvement by the two parties as well as the arguments it used in its rulings. These can be found in paras. 7.267, 7.990, 7.1211, 7.1233, and 7.1400.

1174 Article 24.1 of the DSU states: "At all stages of the determination of the causes of a dispute and of dispute settlement procedures involving a least-developed country Member, particular consideration shall be given to the special situation of least-developed country Members." Understanding on Rules and Procedures Governing the Settlement of Disputes, Article 24, Annex 2 of the WTO Agreement, *The Legal Texts: The Results of the Uruguay Round of Multilateral Trade Negotiations*, World Trade Organization, © Cambridge University Press, (1999), p. 373.

Agreement sets forth the necessary steps for WTO Members to bring their interests into consideration by the dispute settlement process as complainants and that the serious prejudice to be examined by the Panel is that suffered by the complaining Member. Thus, the evidence submitted by Benin and Chad was used in support of the argument that serious prejudice had occurred to Brazil.

Chad and Benin's decision to join the *Cotton* case as third parties imposed some burden on them in terms of the resources expended to gather and bring their evidence to the dispute settlement process. However, the resource demands on them would have been much greater if they had joined as co-complainants. The effect of the Panel's decision to limit the finding of serious prejudice to Brazil, as the complainant in the dispute, was to eliminate Chad and Benin from any future retaliatory measures. However, their evidence presented demonstrated the extent of the damage caused by the price suppression stemming from the US upland cotton support regime. As discussed in the next section, this proved to be of paramount importance in the furtherance of their interests, and indeed the interests of developing and LDCs generally, in the Doha Round. Indeed, the LDC involvement in *Cotton* provides is a model for why, when and how developing countries should bring or participate in a WTO dispute.

Lessons Learned from LDC Involvement. The dispute settlement process is a risky and sometimes lengthy process that can involve considerable expense and yield uncertain outcomes. Before bringing a dispute, an assessment of what can be obtained by LDCs in negotiations, bilateral agreements, and economic partnership agreements must be undertaken in order to determine what cannot be achieved bilaterally or through multilateral negotiations. In the wake of the *Cotton* case, some of the key issues involved with making such assessments have been brought into sharper focus.

One consideration centers on the institutional capacity of LDCs in terms of domestic expertise and industry support. The coordination between NGOs, the ACWL, and representatives from Benin and Chad in the *Cotton* case demonstrates how requisite skills can be transferred to LDCs. Further, *Cotton* also demonstrates the importance of domestic trade associations and industry groups in mobilizing resources and encouraging government participation in the dispute settlement process. Many of the previous achievements in terms of technical assistance resulting from bilateral negotiations are reserved for governments and often do not benefit industry directly. While it is often difficult to measure the gains from LDC participation in the dispute settlement process, one key lesson learned from *Cotton*, is that such gains can be substantive to both domestic industry and governmental interests. For example, Brazil's participation as a complainant in *Cotton* required an expenditure of approximately three (3) million US dollars in legal and associated fees over the course of the dispute and eventually yielded a nearly $150 million dollar annual settlement, and perhaps a long term US cotton subsidy reform that could benefit Brazil and other developing and LDCs into the future. From the perspective of industry interests, these types of advancements cannot be achieved bilaterally or without a multilateral litigation framework. As noted by Shaffer, *et al.*, Brazil's participation as a complainant in the dispute settlement of the WTO demonstrates that increasing the level of LDC participation will allow such nations to more efficiently use their limited resources.[1175]

While the 'Brazil only' ruling on retaliatory sanctions denied similar long-term gains to Chad and Benin, their participation as third parties and their evidentiary support of the price suppression and serious prejudice caused by US cotton support programs yielded demonstrable benefits. Although not specifically mentioned in the original November 2001 Declaration of the Doha Ministerial Conference, cotton subsidies soon became a key issue. Chad and Benin, joined by the other C-4 countries of Burkina Faso and Mali wrote to the WTO DG Supachai in April 2003 with the Sectoral Initiative in Favour of Cotton. This Initiative was presented by Burkina Faso's President to the Trade Negotiations Committee in June 2003 and the proposal was discussed during the Agriculture Committee's Special Sessions in July 2003.[1176]

On the first day of the Fifth WTO Ministerial Conference in Cancun in September 2003, cotton became central to the negotiations on agriculture with the Cotton Initiative.[1177] Similar to the evidence presented during the initial stages of the dispute settlement process, Benin, Chad and the other C-4 countries described the damage caused to their respective economies by the cotton subsidy programs of the developed countries. The C-4's Cotton Initiative called for the elimination of such cotton subsidies and for compensation paid to the C-4 countries while the subsidies continued. It is interesting to note that WTO-DG Supachai chose to directly address the issue at Cancun to underscore the importance of the issue and remarked that while he did not "usually intervene in debates like this," he noted that the issue was important and observed that the C-4 were not asking for special treatment, but for a solution based on a fair

---

1175   *See*, Shaffer, G., Sanchez, M., and Rosenberg, B., "The Trials of Winning at the WTO: What Lies Behind Brazil's Success," *Cornell International Law Journal*, (Summer 2008), 41 CNLILJ 383, p. 484.
1176   *See*, WTO document TN/AG/GEN/4.
1177   The Cotton Proposal is found in the Ministerial Conference documents *WT/MIN(03)/W/2* and *WT/MIN(03)/W/2/Add.1*.

multilateral trading system."[1178] At the Meeting of African Union (AU) Trade Ministers in Cancun, WTO-DG Supachai acknowledged:

> It is also partly through the efforts of African and other developing countries that development issues are at the heart of the Doha Agenda. Moreover because of your efforts LDC's issues have been given priority attention in the negotiations and Members have been encouraged to adopt autonomous measures such as AGOA and the Everything But Arms initiative. Recently Benin, Burkina Faso, Chad and Mali presented a sectoral initiative on cotton, which has generated a great deal of support. It has succeeded in focusing the attention of the international community on the harmful effects of trade-distorting subsidies across the board on agriculture. The Cancún meeting is an opportunity to make progress on this issue.[1179]

By effectively demonstrating the adverse effects of the cotton support policies of developed countries on African LDCs through the dispute resolution process and through the Cotton Initiative, the *Cotton* case further emphasizes the importance of dispute settlement for the negotiating process by raising the political standing and negotiating power of economically disadvantaged nations in multilateral negotiations. This argument is further developed in the following chapter.

6.3 Summary of Part 2

Part 2 included a detailed anatomy of the *Cotton* dispute and emphasized the importance of its precedence, from the perspective of what it contributed to WTO jurisprudence for the future implications of the rulings on WTO Members. These implications will affect how countries formulate future domestic policies and the extent and manner of engagement by developing and least developed countries in the dispute settlement system of the WTO. Chapter 4 covered the origins of the dispute, discussing the factors considered and strategies

---

[1178] WTO News "Day 1: Conference kicks off with 'facilitators' named and cotton debated," http://www.wto.org/english/thewto_e/minist_e/min03_e/min03_10sept_e.htm.

[1179] WTO News: Speeches – DG Supachai Panitchpakdi, *Remarks by Dr. Supachai Panitchpakdi Director-General World Trade Organization*, Meeting of African Union (AU) Trade Ministers, Cancún, 9 September 2003, http://www.wto.org/english/news_e/spsp_e/spsp17_e.htm.

employed by Brazil in deciding to challenge US and EU subsidy regimes at the WTO, especially considering that both cases involved several issues of first impression.

Chapter 5 described the five (5) *Cotton* proceedings as the case moved through the WTO dispute settlement system. The complexity of the challenge as well as the thoroughness of its assessment through each available review mechanism of the WTO establishes *Cotton* among the ranks of precedential WTO disputes. *Cotton* is now recognized as a particularly important case study on the dispute settlement process of the WTO. To that end, the WTO litigation mechanism was discussed as applied to the *Cotton* dispute.

Chapter 6 identified the key legal findings of the dispute and analyzed the significance of Benin and Chad's involvement in *Cotton*. It was shown that a number of recognized barriers to full participation by LDCs were successfully circumvented by Benin and Chad. Further, their success as engaged third parties is emblematic of increasing LDC involvement as well as illustrates the necessity for LDCs to participate in the system so that they might better protect their interests and contribute to the evolution of the WTO dispute settlement mechanism and its jurisprudence.

These chapters constituted the legal analysis portion of this book, fully considering the system, players, and effects of the dispute settlement mechanism of the WTO. Their contents were built upon the economic and political backdrop described in Part 1. In Part 3, the legal analysis will be applied to the political framework of the WTO to determine if, how and to what extent legalization of the institution has impacted the legislative mechanism of the WTO as well as Members at the domestic level. The primary inquiry is whether these linkages exist and whether bringing a legal challenge at the WTO effectively (and efficiently) furthers Members' interests within negotiations and in the world-trading environment.

PART 3

Relevance of the US-Upland Cotton *Dispute on the* WTO's *Legislative Mechanism, Agricultural Subsidy Programs of* WTO *Members at Domestic Level, and Sustainability of the World Trade Organization*

∴

> Litigation in the area of agricultural subsidies and trade policies is helping the ongoing process of policy and trade reform.
> TIMOTHY JOSLING

∴

Part 3 first sets forth two (2) case studies on the issue of cotton within the WTO. The first is on Brazil as a Member choosing to *litigate* its interests through the dispute settlement process of the WTO. The second is on the C-4 – a group of four African LDCs who chose to *negotiate* their interests through the political process of the WTO. Separately, they describe the two divergent mechanisms of the multilateral trading system. Further, an assessment of each mechanism illuminates the strengths and weakness of the varying approaches Members can take in engaging in the system. As described, Brazil decided to negotiate by litigating; whereas, the C-4 chose to only negotiate or, in the case of Benin and Chad, chose to participate as third parties to the *Cotton* dispute. The primary thesis of Chapter 7 is that the two mechanisms are becoming more and more entwined and that the combination of the two mechanisms is especially powerful in effectuating change within the WTO and at the domestic level. Further, by highlighting each approach, it is hoped that more developing countries and LDCs will choose to employ the Brazilian and C-4 strategies in order to similarly participate in future negotiations and dispute resolution at the WTO.

After analyzing how the *Cotton* dispute was used by Brazil and the C-4 to increase their negotiation leverage and pressure domestic reform of agricultural subsidies, the difficulties of the US in complying with the *Cotton* findings and responding to global outrage and pressure on the cotton issue are discussed in Chapter 8. Generally, domestic reform pressures are set forth. Thereafter, two specific resulting developments are described. First, the most recent US Farm Bill is analyzed. Because this was an underwhelming and disappointing domestic response to the efforts of Brazil and the C-4, explanations are offered in order to gain greater insight into the US political system to determine what barriers remain to Brazil and the C-4 in ensuring US domestic agricultural reform and WTO compliance. Second, the Memorandum of Understanding (MOU) between the US and Brazil (the most recent development in the *Cotton* dispute) is analyzed. The 2008 Farm Bill and US-Brazil MOU are interim outcomes to the cotton issue. The final outcome is anticipated to be the successful completion of the Doha Round and the full implementation by the US of the DSB's rulings and recommendations in the *Cotton* dispute.

Given a final outcome to the cotton issue has not been realized, Chapter 9 argues for forward progress in reaching that objective. Having considered the domestic interests and barriers confronting the US Congress on the issue of cotton in Chapter 8, the final chapter considers what could result if the desired outcomes of implementation and a completion to the Doha Round do not happen. Prior to setting forth the two most extreme consequences – systemic failure to the legislative and litigation mechanisms of the WTO, ethical considerations for why the US should comply with the *Cotton* dispute and responsibly respond to the interests of a significant portion of the WTO Members, are explored. By developing an ethical context from which to consider the potential adverse effects of noncompliance by the US, it is hoped that greater perspective on the breadth and importance of the issue may be gained. This is especially necessary for the twenty thousand US farmers being subsidized to the detriment of US taxpayers, African farmers, and the few billion citizens of the world relying on a system designed to prevent war and facilitate trade for their betterment.

CHAPTER 7

Impact of *US-Upland Cotton's* Legal Precedent on Negotiation Leverage within the Doha Development Agenda of the WTO

The *Cotton* dispute not only established much-needed precedence in WTO law in the area of agricultural subsidies and clarified the *Agriculture* and *SCM Agreement* (and the relationship between the two agreements), it was also a political 'win' to both Brazil and the developing world in the WTO negotiations context. As a result of *Cotton*, agriculture-reliant countries,[1180] particularly those involved in the production of cotton, demonstrated how litigation through the WTO dispute settlement mechanism can be strategically used to further their interests and enhance negotiation leverage in the Doha Development Round.[1181]

This chapter analyzes the link between the *Cotton* dispute and negotiations on cotton and other agricultural products; the importance of cotton within the current negotiation agenda; how Brazil was able to use *Cotton* to leverage itself within the Doha negotiations; and the political wins by least developing countries to establish themselves within the political framework of the WTO. These theses are set forth within two (2) case studies (Brazil and the C-4), both of which build from earlier sections of this book, wherein the economic and political backgrounds of the Members' positions within the global trade of cotton and within the WTO were established. It is argued in this chapter that in both cases, the litigation of cotton interests positively impacted the negotiation positions of Brazil and the C-4, specifically.

1180   A relatively high number of developing countries are net exporters of agricultural products – sixty-three (63) out of a recognized 148. Valdes, A., and McCalla, A., "Where the interests of developing countries converge and diverge," as found in Ingco, M. and Winter, A., *Agriculture and the New Trade Agenda: Creating a Global Trading Environment for Development*, Cambridge University Press, © World Bank (2004), p. 147.

1181   *Cotton* is now used as a case study at the Harvard Business School. *See*, Goldberg, R., Lawrence, R., and Milligan, K., "Brazil's WTO Cotton Case: Negotiation through Litigation," HBS, N9-905-405 (23 September 2004). A copy of the case study was obtained by Professor Ray A. Goldberg by the author. The case study can now be found inthe two (2)-volume set, *see*, Devereaux, C., Lawrence, R., and Watkins, M., *Case Studies in US Trade Negotiation*, Institute for International Economics, © 2006.

What ultimate outcome the *Cotton* dispute will have reflected on the Doha Development Round is unknown as this time, given the Round has not been successfully completed to date.[1182] Therefore, this chapter limits its analysis to the developments and overall impact *Cotton* has had on shaping and influencing the negotiations. The theses set forth, *infra*, have been confirmed through interviews with Members of the WTO Secretariat, scholars and practitioners of WTO law, panel members, negotiators, government representatives, and involved NGOs. A consensus has been reached that there is a direct connection between the legislative and judicial mechanisms of the World Trade Organization.

7.1 Brazil

As discussed in Part 2 of this book, Brazil recognized an opportunity to negotiate its domestic agricultural interests by litigating at the WTO. Specifically, it hoped to move and influence WTO negotiations on agriculture by using litigation as one of its primary tactics.[1183] Prior to *Cotton*, Brazil was becoming more active in the legislative process; however, given negotiations in the area of agriculture had stalled and the effects of falling prices and rising subsidy usage by the US was causing devastating effects on the world market, Brazil chose to employ an alternative strategy and bring the *Cotton* (and *Sugar*) case before the WTO dispute settlement body.[1184] This section specifically sets forth why,

---

[1182] This issue is the focus of Chapter 9 of this book.

[1183] For an overview on agricultural issues in the DDA, *see*, Ingco, M. and Winter, A., *Agriculture and the New Trade Agenda: Creating a Global Trading Environment for Development*, Cambridge University Press, © World Bank (2004). Aggarwal, R., "Dynamics of Agriculture Negotiations in the World Trade Organization," Journal of World Trade, Volume 39 No. 4, (2005), pp. 741–761, Das, D., "The Doha Round of Multilateral Trade Negotiations and Trade in Agriculture," Journal of World Trade, Volume 40 No. 2, (2006), pp. 259–290, and, Honma, M., "Agricultural Issues in the Doha Development Agenda Negotiations," as found in Taniguch, Y *et al.*, *The WTO in the Twenty-first Century: Dispute Settlement, Negotiations, and Regionalism in Asia*, Cambridge University Press, (2007), pp. 328–340.

[1184] For a background on the decisions made and strategy developed by Brazil, *See*, Chapter 4 of this book. As discussed therein, Brazil was well-primed for engaging in the dispute resolution process of the WTO and had brought several cases before the WTO. *See*, Shaffer, G., Sanchez, M., and Rosenberg, B., "The Trials of Winning at the WTO: What Lies behind Brazil's Success," *Cornell International Law Journal*, (Summer 2008). Further, for an in-depth cost-benefit analysis of WTO dispute resolution, *see*, Javelosa, J. and Schmitz, A, "Cost-Benefit Analysis of a WTO Dispute," University of Florida: Institute of Food and Agricultural Sciences and the International Agricultural Trade and Policy Center, Working

and how, Brazil chose to use the litigation mechanism to move and influence negotiations. Further, it describes how Brazil was able to take the "cotton issue" – a one commodity issue – and move it into the multilateral arena of broader agricultural negotiations.[1185] Finally, the chapter describes how Brazil's use of litigation in the *Cotton* case helped, along with the C-4 countries, establish cotton as the litmus test for the Doha Development Agenda.

Interfacing Dispute Resolution and Negotiation Strategies: The *Cotton* dispute played a pivotal role in the changing dynamics of WTO negotiations. It can be argued that the perspective of the system has changed from a system in which economic and political power was paramount to a system infused with the rule of law through the addition of a more formalized, rules-based dispute resolution mechanism. In other words, the *Cotton* case has helped transform the system in which the 'rule of power' has been moderated by the 'rule of law.' However, the *Cotton* dispute is a particularly interesting case study as it clearly demonstrates the principle that, in this case, law can increase power. In conducting interviews with government representatives and WTO Secretariat Members, it was recognized that this has been a positive development and helps clarify the relationship between the political and legal aspects of the WTO. Generally, it ensures greater predictability and stability in the system to the degree that a set body of rules can be applied in situations where trade disputes arise, as opposed to Members solely wielding power to achieve their aims. More specifically, it can give less powerful Members more leverage and demonstrates how participating in WTO dispute resolution can help 'mitigate disparities in power.'[1186] Brazil's engagement as a developing (albeit economically large) country and, perhaps to a larger extent, the successful[1187] involvement of Benin and Chad, shed light on the concerns regarding the likely political and economic consequences that might result from economically

---

Paper Series (July 2004), WPTC 04–03. Finally, the general economic and political backdrop of the case was thoroughly covered in Part 1.

1185 Specifically, in the case of beef and pork (two extremely important agricultural products to Brazil), Brazil has used its negotiation leverage in the cotton deal to influence the US on negotiations over beef and pork. Given the sensitivity of communications and request for anonymity by interviewees, this Chapter only discusses Brazil's impact on negotiations more generally.

1186 Weekes, J., "The External Dynamics of the Dispute Settlement Understanding: Its Impact on Trade Relations and Trade Negotiations – An Initial Analysis." The paper was given to the author by Mr. John Weekes and subsequently supported by a personal interview in August of 2009.

1187 The term 'successful' is assigned here to emphasize that the numerous barriers to LDC involvement and concerns over whether adverse political consequence would result were proven to be surmountable in the former and unnecessary in the latter.

small countries challenges to developed country domestic policies.[1188] However, it should be emphasized that the system is a politically-based system, supported by the rule of law. Enforcing legal rulings and recommendations of the DSB requires both law and politics. Given that the foundation of the WTO system and the interests represented therein are derived from industry and national interests, interest groups – political in nature and function – are strong drivers of the system.

Further, the actual interplay between law and politics is incorporated into the processes and structure of the WTO.[1189] Sequentially, litigation can only occur after the completion of negotiations and the adoption of the resulting rules. However, litigation can influence future negotiations in that the legal interpretation of a provision by a WTO legal body that was previously negotiated can impact how Members will negotiate terms on that matter. Structurally, on the legal side, the rules are used by the legal bodies such as the Dispute Settlement Body, Panels, and Appellate Body while, on the political side, the negotiations direct the political bodies and requisite functions of bodies such as the General Council, Trade Negotiations Committees, and Ministerials. Both avenues – political and legal – are aimed at the common objective of creating an "open, rules-based trade system to provide an environment for mutually-beneficial trade."[1190] Direct cross-over between the legal and

---

1188 Such examples of positive outcomes resulting from developing country involvement in dispute settlement include: the *EU-Sugar* case, where – as a result of the dispute – the EU stopped exporting four (4) million WTO-illegal tons of sugar into the world. As a result, the world market price of sugar has increased and a lower EU market share has resulted. This has translated into jobs in affected developing countries. Further, Brazil's win on the *Chicken Poultry* case created about $3 billion in additional exports from Brazil. As a result, workers in Brazilian poultry operations and smaller operations no doubt have realized increased incomes. Further, this has translated into an increased tax base of Brazil, which helps President Lula's income distribution programs for the urban and rural poor. Finally, the elimination of anti-dumping duties or illegal safeguard measures for steel and agricultural goods in the SU and EU through successful WTO challenges open markets that were previously closed to developing countries. Peru's successful *Sardines* challenge to the EU allowed their exports to be shipped and marketed into the EU, using the generic term "sardines." As a result, it could be speculated that fewer poor Peruvians are working on these sardine boats whose families are dependent upon open markets.

1189 For an excellent description of these relationships and to see the figure from which this analysis was derived, *see*, Josling, T., *et al.*, "Implications of WTO Litigation for the WTO Agricultural Negotiations," International Food & Agricultural Trade Policy Council, IPC Issue Brief 19, (March 2006), p. 3.

1190 Josling, T., *et al.*, "Implications of WTO Litigation for the WTO Agricultural Negotiations," International Food & Agricultural Trade Policy Council, IPC Issue Brief 19, (March 2006), p. 3.

political dimensions of the WTO occur because of the fact that the negotiations design the articles and agreements, which are then used to structure the negotiations and because there is a distinct connection between the political and legal bodies of the WTO. While each performs separate tasks, the decisions and operations of each directly impact the other. As derived from interviews, the WTO dispute settlement process is never a purely legal procedure – working with negotiators is an absolute must.[1191] Therefore, it should be recognized that the political and legal aspects of the WTO are inseparable. As John M. Weekes noted on the topic, "dispute resolution, the management of trade relations, and trade negotiations need to be clearly seen as part of a coherent integrated process."[1192]

In this light, Brazil's choice to bring the *Cotton* dispute is reflective of a growing trend in the WTO of Members litigating claims in order to exert pressure on other Members to effectuate change in the responding Member's domestic policies[1193] and to affect multilateral negotiations. In considering the effects of this trend, Timothy Josling *et al.* warned, "[at] best a healthy tension between the litigation and negotiation processes of the WTO may lead to more informed and precise negotiated outcomes. At worst such confrontations run the danger of eroding the political support for the WTO and weaken the trade regime."[1194] In the case of *Cotton*, it can be argued that Brazil brought the dispute responsibly. First, agriculture has long been a difficult area of WTO negotiations (*see*, Chapter 3) and progress – although mandated by the URAA – had not been made on more fully liberalizing trade in agricultural products. A contributing source of impediments to significant trade liberalization is that the

---

1191 Personal interviews with members of the WTO Secretariat, government representatives, three individuals from the iDEAS Centre, and attorneys working on the case.

1192 Weekes, J., "The External Dynamics of the Dispute Settlement Understanding: Its Impact on Trade Relations and Trade Negotiations – An Initial Analysis." The paper was given to the author by Mr. John Weekes and subsequently supported by a personal interview in August of 2009. Mr. Weekes has been engaged in trade policy matters since 1971, was the former Canadian Ambassador to the WTO (1995–1999), and is now Senior International Trade Policy Adviser with the law firm of Sidley Austin.

1193 Although there are only three (3) primary agricultural subsidy cases that have been litigated at the WTO (*US-Cotton, EU-Sugar,* and *Canada-Dairy*), over twenty-three (23) cases involving agricultural products have been initiated and resulted in the establishment of a Panel. Further, the three agricultural subsidy cases are recognized as having "the most significance for rule changes through negotiations." Josling, T., *et al.*, "Implications of WTO Litigation for the WTO Agricultural Negotiations," International Food & Agricultural Trade Policy Council, IPC Issue Brief 19, (March 2006). p. 6.

1194 Josling, T., *et al.*, "Implications of WTO Litigation for the WTO Agricultural Negotiations," International Food & Agricultural Trade Policy Council, IPC Issue Brief 19, (March 2006).

commitments made during the Uruguay Round were uncertain.[1195] In the case of *Cotton*, consider the number of novel issues that had not been clarified, including issues regarding the Peace Clause, the categorization of subsidies, the question of whether export credit guarantees were prohibited export subsidies, and the proper assessment of serious prejudice, *et al.* John Weekes confirmed that *Cotton* "will obviously have a direct bearing on [these] key aspects of the agriculture negotiations."[1196] Therefore, for both legal and political reasons, the initiation of a dispute was of strategic importance to Brazil in order to further its interests in the international trade arena.[1197]

The Case of Cotton *in* WTO *Negotiations:* The significance of *Cotton* is not only the jurisprudence it contributed to the dispute settlement mechanism, but also the impact its findings have had, and will continue to have, on the perceptions about negotiations and the potential behavior of negotiators.[1198] Although the starting point of this understanding is to determine how the findings in the case interpreted the WTO rules (set forth in Chapter 5) considering the effects of the dispute on negotiations is critical as it explains why Members choose to litigate at the WTO. As described in Part 1, there was a strong *economic* rationale for Brazil bringing the *Cotton* dispute. However, it cannot be dismissed that – given the timing of the dispute within the context of the Doha negotiations – Brazil did not consider the impact of its decision to litigate on the political process. As Pedro de Camargo Neto noted in 2006 at an international conference on the issue of cotton, "agricultural trade rules should never have been left behind in international agreements in the first place. The only reason it took more than half a century to include agriculture in the multilateral trading system was that developed countries preferred to ignore the broader consequences of their domestic policies. They could afford

---

1195 For a discussion on agriculture in the Uruguay Round, *see*, Tangermann, S., "Has the Uruguay Round Agreement on Agriculture Worked Well?" International Agricultural Trade Research Consortium (IATRC), Working Paper #01-1, (October 2001). Further, for an overview of this issue, *see*, Chapter 3 of this book.

1196 This was also confirmed by attorneys working on the case, members of the WTO Secretariat, and government representatives from Brazil and Australia.

1197 In addition, there was an ethical rationale for the commencement of the dispute, in the fact that the most developed nation in the world was knowingly maintaining subsidies that economically destroyed more competitive cotton producing countries in some of the least developed countries in the world. This topic is reserved for further discussion until Chapter 9 of this book.

1198 For excellent insights into WTO negotiations, *see*, Jawara, F. and Kwa, A., *Behind the Scenes at the WTO: the Real World of International Trade Negotiations: Lessons of Cancun*, Zed Books, London, (2004).

to postpone the political difficulties that adjustments would bring at home." Even those skeptical of the benefits of challenging the US in the *Cotton* case acknowledge its importance in moving domestic policy reform forward. For example, a 2004 press release stated that, "[w]hile noting that both the cotton case and Brazil's challenge against the EC sugar regime were not initiated with the aim of impacting WTO talks, Brazil's ambassador to the WTO, Luiz Felipe de Seixas Correa, said that without these cases, the EC and US 'would never change their policies.'"[1199] Therefore, even this statement recognized the necessity of Brazil to bring the cases, in order to move the positions of the EC (EU) and US on domestic agricultural subsidies. As argued in this book, although agriculture was eventually brought under the multilateral system, *Cotton* was a key element required to make it no longer possible for the US to postpone making necessary domestic policy adjustments.

Finally, with regards to the interconnectivity of the dispute settlement and negotiation processes of the WTO, it can be argued that one of the primary assumptions by Members in bringing a dispute is the idea that they will be able to use the findings in the negotiations context. Particularly given the fact that there is no immediate implementation and no damages for past harm for a winning Member, there must be an applicable payoff for Members to engage in the process. In assessing this issue, it is recognized that political leverage is the only immediate deliverable of a WTO dispute. There is considerable value in the ability of a Member to use a negative ruling in order to bring world opinion and moral suasion to bear to induce the losing Member to implement the recommendations and rulings of the DSB, to concede on the matter, or to take a more favorable position in negotiations. Further, it signals to other Members not to implement domestic policy measures similar to those that have been challenged and ultimately found to be WTO inconsistent. In the negotiation context, these 'other' Members are put on notice by the DSB of what are (or are not) desirable negotiating positions.

Whether, how and to what extent Brazil was able to use the political gains from the legal process can be determined by looking at what was achieved. In sum, it is argued herein that in taking a more offensive position in the negotiations through the initiation of the *Cotton* dispute, Brazil changed significantly and forever the negotiation dynamics of the WTO. It gave Brazil a credible seat at the table and confidence to more aggressively pursue its interests. This was one of the eventual outcomes of Brazil bringing the case. At the time of its

---

1199 International Centre for Trade and Sustainable Development (ICTSD), "WTO Panels Confirm Victory for Brazil in Cotton, Sugar Cases," *Bridges Weekly Trade News Digest*, Vol. 8, No. 30, (15 September 2004).

initiation, however, it should be kept in mind that there was, in essence, a ticking clock in that the effects the US cotton subsidy programs, particularly the Step 2 and ECG programs, were getting worse – both in terms of the extent to which the programs were being used and the amount of funds being spent on the programs by the US.[1200]

More generally, given that the subsidy programs challenged by Brazil were used by the US for other commodities as well, a cotton victory was also a victory for reform policies pertaining to those products. By bringing the Cotton case, Brazil sought to clarify[1201] the commitments made by the US in the Uruguay Round and the process by which Members categorize subsidies (e.g. Green Box) and to make clear to the world community, via the dispute, that the US had not been playing by the very rules that it had been instrumental in designing at the multilateral level. This was an appropriate usage of the dispute settlement system by Brazil. As paragraph 2 of Article 3 of the DSU states, with regards to the role of the dispute settlement mechanism of the WTO, [the DSM] "serves to preserve the rights and obligations of Members under the covered agreements, and to *clarify* the existing provisions of those agreements." [emphasis added]. Further, it educated the world on the devastating effects of the measures the US maintained, in violation of the principles and rules of the WTO system.[1202] As discussed in Chapter 8 of this book, the *Cotton* decisions should not only help Members agree to greater reductions to subsidies through WTO negotiations on agriculture, but should help build a momentum in the US for subsidy reform. Further, *Cotton* created greater transparency and clarification of what Members agreed to in the Uruguay Round and, as a result, it is anticipated that Members will likely consider more carefully their positions and future agreements in the Doha Development Round.

A similar 'awareness creating effect' that *Cotton* had on the negotiations was that Brazil was able to expand how Members approached agricultural negotiations from a national point of view to a more comprehensive one. Although one of the preliminary drivers of bringing the *Cotton* dispute was to further the

---

1200 These programs were powerful tools in that US farmers and commodity exporters participating in the programs benefitted by being shielded from experiencing the adverse effects of tight credit conditions to which other Members were exposed.

1201 As John Weekes pointed out, there are several provisions within the Punta del Este Declaration that specifically call for the clarification by Members. One such interpretation of the role of the DSU and its impact on negotiations, is that it helps clarify the rule previously negotiated as well as those issues being negotiated.

1202 *See*, Anderson, K., *et al.*, "Impact of Global Trade and Subsidy Policies on Developing Country Trade," *Journal of World Trade*, Vol. 40 No. 5, (2006), pp. 945–968. This subject is also reserved for further discussion until Chapter 9 as well.

national interests of Brazil, the ruling of the case emphasized the interconnectivity and broader effects of WTO-inconsistent national policies on global agricultural trade. By increasing the awareness among WTO Members of these possible economic consequences, made more concrete via legal determinations, countries are more likely to approach negotiations with a broader view of their positions, in contrast to the approach based on a more narrowly focused self-interest that has characterized countries' positions taken in the past. This result further developed and strengthened the relationship between the political aspect of the WTO, operating through diplomacy, and the WTO's legal aspect, functioning through the rule of law. Specifically, as will be described here, this shift in thinking enabled countries that were historically unable to agree on agricultural issues, due to conventional, nation-specific perspectives, to create the strongest agricultural alliance in the world by forming the G20.

In 2002, given the context of the Doha negotiations, the US' reaction to the initiation of *Cotton* was one of annoyed frustration. As Josling summarized, "[at] first, many in the US (and in Europe) saw the act of bringing the case as an unhelpful complication to the negotiation process."[1203] The Doha Declaration mandated negotiations on agriculture, emphasizing that reform in agricultural trade would remain central to the success of the next WTO round of negotiations.[1204] To that end, the Declaration required that modalities[1205] on Agriculture be agreed on by 31 March of 2003. In order to achieve this deadline, Stuart Harbinson,[1206] Chair of the Agriculture Negotiation Committee, with

---

1203 Josling, T., *et al.*, "Implications of WTO Litigation for the WTO Agricultural Negotiations," International Food & Agricultural Trade Policy Council, IPC Issue Brief 19, (March 2006), p. 18.

1204 Two phases of negotiations were completed prior to the formal commencement of the Doha Development Agenda. From early 2000 through March 2001, six (6) special sessions were completed where a number of proposals were submitted and discussed. Thereafter, from March 2001 through March 2002, more informal talks were undertaken where Members presented off-the-record 'non-papers.' In both phases, Brazil participated. Further, it should be noted that pursuant to Article 20 of the URAA, negotiations on agriculture were required to recommence shortly after the completion of the Uruguay Round.

1205 Modalities are targets (including numerical targets) for achieving the objectives set forth in the Doha Ministerial Declaration. For agriculture, the modalities cover: tariffs, subsidies, market access, and domestic subsidies. For a discussion on the creation of agricultural modalities, *see*, Shanahan, P., "WTO DDA Negotiations on Agriculture: Framework for Establishing Modalities," Tralac – Agri Conference (30 September 2004), given in Stellenbosch. Paper on file with author.

1206 Stewart Harbinson was the Permanent Representative of Hong Kong.

little input by Members,[1207] produced a text that was criticized and ultimately rejected.[1208] This was the first attempt at reaching a compromise for the requisite modalities. Although the US and Cairns Group[1209] were willing to work from the text, the EU (who proposed an alternative text) was recognized as the ultimate driver in rejecting the 'Harbinson Text.'[1210] As described in Chapter 3 the Cairns Group was the primary agriculture-oriented negotiating group, established during the Uruguay Round, and the only organized agriculture-focused negotiating group at the commencement of the Doha negotiations.[1211] However, the primacy of the Cairns Group was about to change with the formation of the G20. Although Brazil was a member of the Cairns Group, it maintained what could be described as only a moderate leadership position. Brazil eventually determined that it was best for it to take an 'autonomous position' in the agricultural negotiations.[1212] This shift was described by two scholars as follows:

> Since [the Uruguay Round], although the group has been unrelenting as a forceful advocate of agricultural trade liberalization, it has not really lived up to its potential to develop into a third force in the WTO negotiations. In fact, by the time the Fifth Ministerial Meeting of the WTO was held at Cancun in September 2003, that role seemed to have passed on to

---

1207 The only meaningful submission was by the EU, which submitted its text on 16 December 2002. This was.

1208 In the text, the three areas, or 'pillars,' of negotiation were identified: market access, domestic support, and export competition.

1209 As mentioned *supra*, Brazil was a member of the Cairns group, an association of several developing and three (3) developed countries whose commonality is their competitiveness as agricultural exporters.

1210 The text was circulated to Members on 12 February 2003 and was entitled, "First Draft of Modalities for the Further Commitments." *See*, WTO, TN/AG/W/1/Rev. 1 (18 March 2003). For a detailed analysis of the Harbinson Text, *see*, Bjornskov, C. and Lind, K., "Underlying Policies in the WTO, the Harbinson Proposal and the Modalities Agreement," *Revue Economique*, Vol. 56., No. 6, (November 2005), pp. 1385–1412.

1211 Jawara, F. and Kwa, A., *Behind the Scenes at the WTO: the Real World of International Trade Negotiations: Lessons of Cancun*, Zed Books, London, (2004), introduction and pp. 22–24.

1212 It was recognized that the Cairns Group had 'gone soft' in the negotiations. *See*, Jawara, F. and Kwa, A., *Behind the Scenes at the WTO: the Real World of International Trade Negotiations: Lessons of Cancun*, Zed Books, London, (2004) and Veiga, P., "Brazil and the G20 Group of Developing Countries," as found in Gallagher, P. *et al.*, *Managing the Challenges of WTO Participation: 45 Case Studies*, Cambridge University Press, (December 2005), p. 111.

the Group of 20 developing countries (G20), some of whose leading members belonged to the Cairns Group.[1213]

Therefore, it was not until some developing countries of the Cairns Group united and rejected the EU-US Text on agricultural modalities at the Ministerial Conference (MC) in Cancun, Mexico in September 2003, that Brazil became a recognized leader in multilateral agricultural negotiations. Not only was Brazil's leadership created on the platform of the *Cotton* dispute issues, Brazil employed a similar public-private partnership approach to capacity-building for organizing the G20 coalition as it had in structuring its litigation strategy (*See*, Chapter 4). As Pedro da Motto Veiga commented, "[one] of the more interesting features of the decision-making process leading to the establishment of the G20 was that it involved intensive interaction between public and private domestic actors and between these actors and external players. Even more interestingly, the domestic and external dynamics became more and more interconnected as the G20 was set up and became a relevant player in agricultural negotiations at the WTO." Another key to Brazil and the G20's success was that it welcomed collaboration with other negotiating groups as well. As a result, it was able to gain wide support and respect among several coalitions and effectuate positive influence on those groups as well (discussed, *infra*).

Cancun, although a failure in some regards, was a success for Brazil in that it proved to be the genesis of the G20 and was markedly the first example of how Brazil used its *Cotton* dispute strategy to increase its leverage in negotiating groups and influence WTO negotiations. In the same way that the US and EU were being challenged in the dispute settlement mechanism, it became apparent that both superpowers were also being challenged in negotiations as well. As Josling states, "The ability of the transatlantic partners to determine how far and fast to move on agriculture was being challenged by countries whose economic potential was becoming realized. Bargaining 'in the shadow of the law' is not comfortable for politicians, who see their room for compromise constrained by legal interpretations of political negotiations."[1214] It is clear, therefore, that the litigation of the *Cotton* dispute not only reduced the ability of economically powerful nations from pursuing their own interests unilaterally,

---

1213 Hoda, A., and Ashok, G., *WTO Negotiations on Agriculture and Developing Countries*, The Johns Hopkins University Press, (2007), p. 189.

1214 Josling, T., *et al.*, "Implications of WTO Litigation for the WTO Agricultural Negotiations," International Food & Agricultural Trade Policy Council, IPC Issue Brief 19, (March 2006), p. 18.

it also increased the importance of agriculture as a focal issue in multilateral negotiations and raised the profile of the developing world on these issues.

The newly-established Group of 20 (G20),[1215] formed as a negotiating coalition to further a 'Southern' agricultural agenda in multilateral *fora*, pressed the US and EU for greater market access and subsidy reduction in response to their polarizing 'joint text.' Brazil (along with its two emerging economic partners, India and South Africa) were leaders in this effort.[1216] Having signed the Brasilia Declaration months prior to Cancun, Brazil brought together the three (3) countries in order to advance the liberalization and reform of agriculture in the developed world and further development in developing countries, and the concept of the G20 began to form.[1217] The first G20 accomplishment was the draft framework proposal that Brazil and India developed, which quickly gained the support of other developing countries, among them China, South Africa, Indonesia, the Philippines, and Argentina. Although ultimately unsuccessful because the US and EU were unwilling to offer meaningful concessions,[1218] this was the first attempt by Brazil, in its emerging leadership role, to bring the cotton issue into agricultural negotiations as an example of non-compliance by the US. Specifically, through the G20, Brazil pushed to have issues *inter alia* the elimination of export and domestic support schemes (two of the primary challenges in *Cotton*) included in the negotiation agenda.[1219]

During this process, two important changes in the political landscape developed that proved to be not only challenging but also instructive to the strategic pursuit of the interests of Brazil and other developing countries. The first was on the formation of South-South coalition building. Building a sound interest group to represent a variant position to that of the Northern agenda was critical. However, in creating this division, it may be considered that it may have ultimately added to the discordant tone of the Cancun Ministerial Conference

---

1215 At the time, the G20 consisted of: Argentina, Bolivia, Brazil, Chile, China, Colombia, Costa Rica, Cuba, Ecuador, El Salvador, Guatemala, India, Mexico, Pakistan, Paraguay, Peru, the Philippines, South Africa, Thailand, and Venezuela.

1216 Stiglitz, J. and Charlton, A., *Fair Trade For All: How Trade Can Promote Development*, © Oxford University Press, 2005, p. 63.

1217 Amorim, C. "Statement to the 60th Session of the UN General Assembly," 17 September 2005.

1218 Further, although the US was active in these negotiations and put forward proposals for liberalizing agriculture, it should not be overlooked that, domestically, the US had just increased its own trade-distorting support to farmers through the passage of the 2002 Farm Bill.

1219 Veigá, P., "Brazil and the G20 Group of Developing Countries," as found in Gallagher, P. *et al.*, *Managing the Challenges of WTO Participation: 45 Case Studies*, Cambridge University Press, (December 2005), p. 109.

(MC) and led to the widely-held view that the Cancun MC was considered a failure because of an impasse between North–south negotiations.[1220] However, the strategic validity of Brazil's decision to build coalition capacity and its ability to bring Members who traditionally were in opposition to one another in the agricultural negotiations at the WTO should not be discounted. In line with Brazil's changing foreign economic policies, it chose to build its G20 coalition. In doing so, it used the platform to propel itself into the subsequently-formed Five-Interested Parties (FIP) group (discussed, *infra*),[1221] comprised of the five most influential players in agricultural negotiations representing both North and South agendas.

The second change in the ongoing political dynamics was the power shift that was occurring within the WTO in which, instead of the traditional approach of having the greatest economic powers set the rules, the developing world was organizing and speaking out about concerns over the WTO negotiations. Thus, the US-EU proposal for the agricultural modalities was rejected by the South, predominately comprised of developing countries.[1222] Therefore, by bringing together public-private partnerships and Members whose agricultural interests were previously in opposition, Brazil was able to successfully form the G20 and begin "untying the agricultural knot in the multilateral negotiations."[1223]

Since the WTO Doha Round of negotiations was characterized as the 'development' round, it was recognized that agriculture – the most significant area of trade for most developing countries – would be the focus of the Cancun MC, and talks in that area would set the atmosphere for other negotiations. To that end, when the agricultural talks collapsed, the Cancun MC failed. This has been a continued pattern in the last seven (7) years. Further, in some regards, the Cancun MC failure catalyzed certain countries (notably, Brazil) into increasing their leadership roles and moving forward with the interests of the G20. After Cancun, the G20 re-engaged and ignited cooperation by hosting negotiations in Brasilia, Brazil in December of 2003. Among the guests invited, was Pascal Lamy, the then-Commissioner of the EU and future Director General

---

1220 For a brief history on US-Brazil trade relations, prior to Cancun, *see*, Schott, J., "US-Brazil Trade Relations in a New Era," Institute for International Economics, (2003).

1221 The FIP group is also referred to as the Non-Group-5 or NG-5.

1222 This development challenged the criticism many have regarding developing country membership in the WTO and the questionable benefits from and involvement in the negotiation processes. *See*, Jones, K., *Who's Afraid of the WTO?*, Oxford University Press, (2004), pp. 147–166.

1223 Veiga, P., "Brazil and the G20 Group of Developing Countries," as found in Gallagher, P. et al., *Managing the Challenges of WTO Participation: 45 Case Studies*, Cambridge University Press, (December 2005), p. 111.

of the WTO. Further, as a result of the negotiations in Brasilia, the tone changed from one of reproach, to constructive dialogue.

By the following summer, the 2004 July Framework was concluded, which focused *inter alia* on agriculture (and cotton, specifically).[1224] Leading up to the July Framework, Brazil was one (1) of the five (5)[1225] countries invited by the US to begin agricultural negotiations.[1226] The group, referred to as the Five-Interested Parties (FIP) met in the months preceding the end of July and "formally replace the Quad...as the decision-making core."[1227] Important to emphasize is the timing of the formation of FIP, the subsequent talks and eventual resulting text setting forth, *inter alia*, a commitment to the elimination of export subsidies and significant reductions in domestic support. It is important to note that, at this time, the *Cotton* dispute was already well under way and that the original Panel reports were publically available and the confidential final Appellate Body report was available to two (2) of the five (5) Members of FIP. It is highly likely that the preliminary *Cotton* outcomes influenced talks during this time. Further, the timing coincided with the Cotton Initiative having placed cotton separately within the agricultural negotiations. Therefore, at the time of the *Cotton* proceedings, cotton was specifically being negotiated between the US and Brazil as part of the FIP talks. The lack of transparency of the FIP negotiations, the source of a great deal of criticism, can partly be explained by the fact that Brazil and the US were litigating one of the few issues being negotiated in the talks.

Although unclear at the time the *Cotton* and *Sugar* disputes were initiated, by 2004 the connection between dispute resolution and WTO negotiations was recognized. Given the final original ruling on the merits of *Cotton* were already out[1228] and, in anticipation of the preliminary AB ruling in the *Sugar* case, it was speculated in an August 6, 2004 article that: "If the preliminary ruling is upheld by the WTO in September, it could strengthen the hand of developing

---

1224 Officially the July Framework was adopted by the General Council on 1 August 2004 as WT/L/579. For a concise overview of the Framework, *see*, Josling, T., "The WTO Agricultural Negotiations: Progress and Prospects," Choices: The Magazine for food, farm and resource issues, Publication of the American Agricultural Economics Association, 2nd Quarter, 20(2) (2005).

1225 The other Members included the EU, Australia, and India.

1226 Further, the month before (June), Brazil hosted conferences to discuss development concerns – particularly the UNCTAD conference held 13–18 of June at which the WTO DG Supachai Panitchpakdi was a participant.

1227 Wilkinson, R., "Ghost of a Chance: ACUNS in Hong Kong," Academic Council on the United Nations System, *Informational Memorandum* 65 (2006), p. 2.

1228 *See*, "Dispute Settlement – Cotton Dispute Ends in Comprehensive Victory for Brazil," International Centre for Trade and Sustainable Development (ICTSD), News and Analysis, Volume 12 No. 4, (August 2008).

nations as they hammer out the details of a deal reached last weekend in Geneva, where the trade body's 147 Members agreed to a negotiating framework to reduce farm subsidies in the rich nations by as much as 20 percent and cut import tariffs on everything from corn to soybeans."[1229] Therefore, the link between the two mechanisms of the WTO as well as the effect the ruling might have on other commodities was evident. Further, the fact that a favorable ruling could instill the confidence in other Members to bring similar disputes was a real concern. This placed additional pressure on the US. As the article continued to explain, "The decision could also trigger a fresh wave of complaints at the WTO, which had already ruled in favor of Brazil in late June in a landmark case against the billions of dollars in annual subsidies that the United States pays cotton farmers. 'It's going to be very interesting to watch whether Brazil in particular is going to use its legal victories in cotton and now sugar to mount other cases,' said Gary Hufbauer, a senior fellow and trade specialist at the Institute for International Economics in Washington.'"[1230] At present, the success of the Doha Round in reducing subsidies will directly influence the decision of Brazil and other similarly-situated Members.

Brazil continued to play a leading role in the G20 and within the FIPS group[1231] to further its agricultural agenda leading up to the December Hong Kong MC in 2005. In preparation for the Cancun MC, several meetings and mini-ministerials were held. Some positive developments resulted from efforts by the G20 and FIPS/G4 efforts, including the US' offer to cut Amber Box domestic support by sixty (60) percent. However, in the same timeframe, the EU came under pressure for putting forward an undesirable proposal at the Hong Kong MC. Prior to Hong Kong, the new DG – Pascal Lamy – tried to lower expectations and notify Members that the objectives of concluding negotiations on full modalities in Agriculture would not be achieved. Although the overall outcome of the Hong Kong MC and the text produced as a result of the Hong Kong MC were disappointing to many, some positive developments were achieved for LDCs. The C-4 received recognition of their interests in having trade-distorting subsidies eliminated.[1232] Further LDCs succeeded in gaining concession on Duty-Free Quota-Free market access in developed and developing

---

1229 Benson, T., "WTO Rules in Favour of Brazil in Sugar Dispute," *The Financial Express*, (6 August 2004), as originally published in the *New York Times*.

1230 Benson, T., "WTO Rules in Favour of Brazil in Sugar Dispute," *The Financial Express*, (6 August 2004), as originally published in the *New York Times*.

1231 At this time, the group had four Members, amended to be called the G4 or 'Quad,' and later to be expanded to the FIPS Plus.

1232 This issues will be further discussed in the following section, detailing the development of the C-4 in the WTO.

country markets. For Brazil, an end date for the elimination of export subsidies was set. More importantly, although proposals reflecting demands relevant to Brazil, Brazil was able to enhance its leadership position within the WTO by using its position in the G20 to further the interests of other developing and LDC Members (see Brazil – C-4 discussion, below).[1233]

Therefore, not only was Brazil able to strengthen its political stance through the process of litigating its interests in the *Cotton* case, but it was able to enhance the political standing of other Members as well. Prior to the Cancun MC, Benin, Burkina Faso, Mali, and Chad (now recognized as the C-4) submitted a sectoral initiative in favor of cotton to the WTO, which became known as the Cotton Initiative. Specifically, Brazil's litigation approach contributed to the C-4 negotiation strategy in that the group can use the dispute in furthering the Cotton Initiative and negotiations within the context of the resulting Subcommittee on Cotton. The effects could have been further enhanced had C-4 members joined the dispute as co-complainants. As it stands, they are only able to indirectly capitalize on the outcome of the case by virtue of the third party participation by Chad and Benin. Had they joined as co-complainants, the Arbitrator would have measured damages to Brazil and West Africa. This could have further added to their arguments regarding the 'legitimacy of the system' being threatened by the maintenance by the US of WTO-inconsistent subsidies. Therefore, more direct participation might have empowered them as part of the coalition. However, the political gains remain significant. There is now a clear-cut case and widespread understanding of the effects of US subsidies on other cotton-producing economies in the world. Although all of these issues are discussed in detail in the following section, the connection is drawn here to emphasize that an informal coalition between the interests of Brazil and the C-4 helped the LDCs in pushing their cotton agenda through the Cotton Initiative as well as highlight greater development interests within the WTO. Given the present round of negotiations is a 'development' round, this allowed Brazil to contribute to the agenda by arming LDCs with a credible ruling, supported by exceptional evidence, and ultimately endorsed by the DSB, to further their cotton agenda. As such, Brazil further enhanced its leadership position within the WTO.

In the time between the Hong Kong MC and the suspension of the Doha Development Agenda in 2006, Brazil continued to be active in the

---

1233 Recognized assistance was offered between the G20 and the G33 (developing countries), Africa Caribbean Pacific (ACP), least developed countries (LDC), African, Caribbean Community (CARICOM), Cotton-4, and small and vulnerable economies (SVEs).

newly-comprised G6.[1234] In a February 2006 talk on Brazil's trade policy in the Doha Round given by H.E. Clodoaldo Hugueney, Ambassador of Brazil to the WTO, it was clear that agriculture was the aim and that the G20 was the means by which Brazil would ultimately influence the Doha negotiations.[1235] Specifically, he emphasized that the G20 wanted an overall reduction in subsidies as opposed to negotiating how Members can shift their subsidies from box to box under the AoA. These were two (2) core issues that had arisen in the *Cotton* dispute.[1236] Further, it was clear from the questions asked and responses given from representatives from the Press, attendees from various embassies, and academicians that the US 2008 Farm Bill would be an indicator of what was happening and could happen in the agricultural negotiations. Further, there was serious concern about Members' ability to agree to agriculture modalities by the upcoming deadlines.[1237]

In March of 2006, it became clear to the G6 that the EU and US were hardening their positions on negotiation issues, including agriculture. As a result the April 2006 deadline for negotiating agriculture modalities was missed, despite efforts by Pascal Lamy to keep Members engaged. Similar failures resulted in June and July of the same year. By this time, the US and the rest of the world were aware that the AB had upheld the original Panel's decision on *Cotton*. And it was during this time that the US did make progress in modifying its subsidy programs. Specifically, by August the Step 2 program had been effectively repealed. This coincided with the development of a more constrained and protectionist political environment in the US, given that the US Congress was

---

1234 The G6 was comprised of the EU, US, India, Brazil, Australia and Japan. Brazil was also noted to have been active in 2006 at the G20 St Petersburg summit. President Lula da Silva greater engaged at these talks.

1235 "Brazil's Trade Policy in the Doha Round: A Discussion with H.E. Clodoaldo Hugueney, Ambassador of Brazil to the World Trade Organization," Carnegie Endowment for International Peace, Moderator: Sherman Katz, (23 February 2006). The summary used was prepared by a Carnegie Junior Fellow, Vyborny, K., and Intern, Ocheltree, M. (Paper on file with author).

1236 "Brazil's Trade Policy in the Doha Round: A Discussion with H.E. Clodoaldo Hugueney, Ambassador of Brazil to the World Trade Organization," Carnegie Endowment for International Peace, Moderator: Sherman Katz, (23 February 2006). The summary used was prepared by a Carnegie Junior Fellow, Vyborny, K., and Intern, Ocheltree, M. (Paper on file with author).

1237 "Brazil's Trade Policy in the Doha Round: A Discussion with H.E. Clodoaldo Hugueney, Ambassador of Brazil to the World Trade Organization," Carnegie Endowment for International Peace, Moderator: Sherman Katz, (23 February 2006). The summary used was prepared by a Carnegie Junior Fellow, Vyborny, K., and Intern, Ocheltree, M. (Paper on file with author).

facing a mid-term election in the fall. After the suspension of the DDA by Pascal Lamy, indicating the 'dire straits' of the negotiations,[1238] Brazil again tried to reignite negotiations, on behalf of the G20, by holding a Ministerial Meeting in Rio de Janeiro, Brazil on 9–10 September of 2006. The following spring, in 2007, Brazil was again legitimately placed within the core countries developing a plan for setting the negotiations back on track. In a ministerial meeting in Delhi, India in April, the G4 and G6 agreed to complete modalities by June of that same year.

Unfortunately, the talks in Delhi collapsed three (3) days into the five-day meeting. However, this was not entirely a negative outcome as it eventually led to a positive result. Although Brazil (specifically, Foreign Minister Celso Amorim) was perceived as walking out on the Delhi meeting, Brazil refuted the claim by stating that it became clear that the US and EU had not changed their positions. Specifically, the US and EU were unwilling to discuss agriculture issues, but rather wanted to shift the discussion to non-agriculture market access (NAMA) issues. This was unacceptable to Brazil. Therefore, this was yet another example of Brazil exerting its political capital, buttressed by the *Cotton* outcome, to try to push the US to negotiate on the issue. Pascal Lamy then directed the TNC chairs to begin drafting an Agriculture text. The resulting text was considered by Brazil to be, overall, a positive development and served as a building block for further progress on agricultural issues. Therefore, as a representative in the G20, G4 and G6 Brazil was able to successfully exert influence on what would ultimately be included in the text.

At the end of July, the message "No Meetings until Further Notice" flashed onto the screens of the lobby of the WTO.[1239] The Doha mini-Ministerial talks had officially collapsed. It is understood in Geneva circles that although the Special Safeguard Mechanism[1240] was pinpointed as the sticking point of the negotiations, cotton certainly was one of the primary reasons for the collapse.

1238 "Doha Trade Talks: Acrimony and Blame after Collapse of Trade Talks," *Spiegel Online*, (25 July 2006).

1239 The author was present at the WTO when the message was first displayed, after spending a few days in Geneva to follow the talks, engaging delegates, Members of the WTO Secretariat, and onlookers. The WTO Mini-Ministerial in Geneva ran from 22–29 July, 2008. For a description of the developments of the MM, *see*, International Centre for Trade and Sustainable Development, *Bridges Daily Update* Issues 2–11 (22–30 July 2008).

1240 Special safeguards (SSG) are currently found in Article 5 of the AoA. The concept of a new special safeguard mechanism was proposed in the US-EU joint text in Cancun, arguably for the benefit of agriculturally-oriented developing countries. The idea, extent to which they could be applied, and actual structuring of which has remained the focus of heated debate between developed and developing countries.

"In the most widespread view, the United States did not want to face the cotton issue to protect the wealth of a few thousand cotton farms."[1241] Given the US 2008 Farm Bill had just been passed, it left little room for negotiations on the topic. As will be discussed in Chapter 8, the 2008 Farm Bill was widely perceived as a step in the wrong direction in agricultural trade reform and provided the domestic legal basis within the US to continue to provide massive levels of WTO-illegal subsidies. Since the 2008 Farm Bill is expected to remain in effect for at least four (4) years (typical timeframe for Farm Bills), the USTR's representative, Susan Schwab, was unable to offer a subsidy cut greater than what was reflected in the legislation.[1242]

In the past year, Brazil has continued to exercise its leadership role in the 'international economic arena' by using *Cotton* to influence negotiations.[1243] As a result of the outcomes of the *Cotton* case, Brazil's influence and negotiating position in the Doha Round continues to be strengthened at each stage of the proceedings.[1244] Continuing to lead the G20, while maintaining ties to other negotiating coalitions, President Lula of Brazil openly criticized the US, regarding its farm subsidies, at the London G20 Summit in April of 2009. As was reported in the press, "The recent threats made by the CAMEX[1245] and the cotton dispute in general, are now a further step for Brazil to be asserting its leadership and its role as the voice of agricultural exporting and developing countries during recent international negotiations."[1246] In an accounting of some of the most recent meetings at the WTO, it is apparent that the approach to managing the conclusion of the Doha Round is changing. Negotiators from Member countries on agricultural issues are seeking for an expansion of US agricultural modalities to include all of the essential elements of the findings

---

1241 Khor, M., "Why WTO Talks Collapsed," *Global Trends* as published in *The Star Online*, (4 August 2008).
1242 For a full analysis of agricultural negotiations after the 2008 collapse, *see*, Nouel, G.L., "Stocktake of the WTO Agricultural Negotiations after the Failure of the 2008 Talks," European Parliament, Directorate-General for Internal Policies, Brussels (2009).
1243 *See*, Blossier, F., "The WTO Cotton Dispute: How the US is Trying to Escape International Trade Regulation while Brazil Asserts Itself as a Regional Leader," Council on Hemispheric Affairs, (2 June 2010).
1244 *See*, Tollini, H., "Lessons from the Cotton Dispute: A View from Brazilian Industry," International Centre for Trade and Sustainable Development, *Bridges*, Volume 12 No. 6 (December 2008).
1245 As discussed in Chapter 4, CAMEX is the Brazilian Trade Chamber.
1246 *See*, Blossier, F., "The WTO Cotton Dispute: How the US is Trying to Escape International Trade Regulation while Brazil Asserts Itself as a Regional Leader," Council on Hemispheric Affairs, (2 June 2010).

of the *Cotton* case. There is also a perceived increase in the commitment to successfully conclude the Doha Round as well as to strengthen the overall effectiveness of the WTO. At the same time, however, there is ample room for frustration with respect to the divide between the pledges of the G-20 countries to successfully conclude the Round with the lack of progress on specific issues required to make such a conclusion possible. A principal reason for frustration is the inability of the US to make meaningful progress on negotiations while, at the same time, obtaining the requisite Congressional approval. In addition, a perceived lack of commitment on the part of the US stems from the fact that, at this time, the US has neither an ambassador to the WTO in Geneva nor a chief agriculture negotiator. While the US has the potential to be seen as the spoiler in the Doha Round, there remains the possibility that countries with interests on agricultural issues that are aligned with those of the US are willing to have the US assume this role so that their interests can be carried forward while, at the same time, negative public attention is directed primarily at the US. In spite of these setbacks, there remain reasons for hope that the good will expressed for the Obama administration will translate into progress on difficult issues.

On the issue of agriculture, the Chair of the Agriculture Committee and New Zealand WTO Ambassador, David Walker, maintained that negotiations need to be brought to a conclusion. Specifically, he noted that the bilateral negotiations between the US and Brazil, China and India need to deliver in order to achieve this objective.[1247] In reviewing the latest draft agriculture modalities text, however, concern has been expressed that little progress has been made. In light of the arbitration decisions in the *Cotton* case, however, Brazil can begin to apply the *Cotton* decisions and its resulting increased leverage to influence negotiations. Specifically, Brazilian Foreign Minister Celso Amorim stated, "It's not that we want to retaliate, it's just that this authorization gives us negotiating tools that will, we hope, change distorting laws in that and other rich countries."[1248] Therefore, the Arbitrator decision in *Cotton* is not only about the monetary compensation for which a Member can retaliate, it has also given Brazil, the Cairns Group, the G20, and other developing countries increased leverage and the moral high ground in WTO agricultural negotiations.[1249] Further, it was reported in September that the US and Brazil

---

1247 Derived from personal correspondence.
1248 According to the Agence France-Presse and found in the *Washington Trade Daily*, Amorim made this statement to his Indian and South African counterparts shortly after the Arbitrator's award was known.
1249 As of the submission of this book, the G20 had just dropped the Doha target and no ultimate conclusion to the Round had been reached.

are hopeful that a 2010 Doha deal can be reached; however, the EU would like to see a pledge first.[1250] Unfortunately, the G20 recently backed out of the multilateral talks stating that it wanted to focus on bilateral and regional deals.[1251] It is unknown whether this is a strategic political move or the beginning of the end of the Doha Round.

Conclusion: Although litigation is often recognized as a contentious and polarizing undertaking in the context of trade at the multilateral level, it can be a beneficial alternative approach to negotiations. According to John Weekes, "[a]lthough it may appear counterintuitive to a casual observer, resorting to the provisions of the DSU usually has the effect of depoliticizing a dispute. By filing a complaint, a government takes a matter which is often a highly contentious irritant in international relations and turns it into a technical exercise to be argued on its legal merits by advocates from the Members involved."[1252] The decision can then be used in negotiations to help guide and influence how talks on the matter will be addressed and ultimately responded to by Members.

There are additional positive political consequences to dispute resolution. As Josling wrote, "[i]n this instance, the cotton case gave additional motivation for completing the Round. Politicians in developed countries have taken the prospect of a flurry of similar challenges through the WTO on established farm policies seriously. Changes to domestic policy are painful whether as a result of negotiations or litigation. But with litigation forcing the pace of change, the advantages of anticipating future cases by negotiating subsidy and tariff reductions are increased."[1253] In conclusion, Brazil and the United States have significantly vested interests in the Doha Round being successfully concluded. To that end, US-Brazilian relations need considerable attention so that the significant leadership positions of these two Members can be employed to resolve trade issues. As has been pointed out, it is hard to imagine two countries other than the US and Brazil, in the context of a development round, better able to

---

1250 Colitt, R. and Ennis, D., "US, Brazil see 2010 Doha deal; EU wants G20 pledge," *Reuters India*, (18 September 2009).
1251 Ljunggren, D., "G20 Leaders Drop Doha Target, See Smaller Deals," *Reuters*, (26 June 2010).
1252 Weekes, J., "The External Dynamics of the Dispute Settlement Understanding: Its Impact on Trade Relations and Trade Negotiations – An Initial Analysis." The paper was given to the author by Mr. John Weekes and subsequently supported by a personal interview in August of 2009.
1253 Josling, T., *et al.*, "Implications of WTO Litigation for the WTO Agricultural Negotiations," International Food & Agricultural Trade Policy Council, IPC Issue Brief 19, (March 2006), p. 18.

foster the successful completion of the Doha Round.[1254] Until an agricultural agreement – reflecting both North and South agendas – is reached, the future of Doha Round remains bleak. The steps that are being taken to achieve this aim, and analysis about what more needs to be done, are the topics of the following Chapters.

7.2 The C-4, Cotton Initiative and the Creation of the Subcommittee on Cotton

> Brazil was getting hurt by the [US] cotton subsidies, but the African countries were getting destroyed.[1255]
> PEDRO DE CAMARGO

In the Doha Development Agenda (DDA) negotiations, cotton took on a central role because of efforts by Brazilian and African cotton exporters to highlight the importance of cotton to them as well as the devastating impacts of US subsidies on the rural economies of African cotton-producing countries. Though a number of 'Franc Zone' countries produce and are affected by suppressed world cotton prices due to US subsidies, the four countries of Burkina Faso, Benin, Mali, and Chad (Cotton-4, or C-4) organized to promote their cause throughout the negotiations in an unprecedented approach. As described in the previous section, their situation within the international trading system has been illuminated in large part due to the highly publicized *Cotton* dispute and the formation of the Cotton Initiative, which resulted in the separation of cotton from the greater agricultural talks, and into the WTO's Subcommittee on Cotton. Despite the small share of cotton trade in the total trading scheme, the response (or lack thereof) to the efforts of the Cotton Initiative – symbolic of the difficulties experienced in integrating the concerns of developing countries into the WTO system – has been a primary reason for

---

1254 For a discussion on recognized leadership challenges for WTO Member, specifically the Brazil, *see*, Deere, C., "WTO Leadership Challenges in 2009," International Centre for Trade and Sustainable Development: News and Analysis, Volume 12 No. 6, (January 2009). The most pertinent need applicable to this section is the fact that the article calls for *inter alia* Brazil and the US to continue to engage and encourage participation in negotiations by developing countries. Although coalition-building has proven useful, it was emphasized that the Member need to continue participating at the multilateral level.

1255 Becker, E. and Benson, T., "Brazil's Road to Victory over US Cotton," *The New York Times*, (4 May 2004).

the delays, dislocations, breakdowns, and impasses of DDA negotiations.[1256] Despite the significant attention to cotton and its high profile in the negotiations, the issue of cotton has not been resolved. As a result, cotton is now considered the litmus test for the Doha Development Round.

The 'Cotton Issue' was developed within the framework of the WTO, first in 2002 when Brazil initiated the *Cotton* dispute and, subsequently, in 2003 when the C-4 demonstrated that US cotton subsidies were causing trade-distortion in the form of declining world cotton prices and consequential reduction in export revenues.[1257] Global cotton output was valued at an estimated US$25–30 billion at the time and the US was subsidizing its cotton producers on average US$3 billion, annually. Given that cotton is a key export commodity for the C-4 countries, the deleterious effects of the subsidies were raised in the multilateral forum of the WTO as a means to improve conditions in the cotton sectors of these countries by attempting to reduce the subsidies before they caused even more destruction to these economies. Although Brazil and the C-4 were each attempting to combat the effects of US subsidies, their approaches differed. As John Baffes remarked, "[e]ven though the subsidies affect all non-subsidizing, cotton-producing countries, only Brazil and the C-4 chose to bring a case to the WTO and, despite the fact that both fought the same subsidies, they chose different paths."[1258] Although the C-4 as a whole chose the traditional approach of negotiating its interests through the WTO legislative mechanism, two of them chose to participate additionally as third parties to the *Cotton* dispute. This section is a case study on the C-4 and is devoted to describing how these LDCs were able to successfully engage in WTO negotiations and carve out a significant position within the Doha 'Development' Agenda using the political process.[1259] Although the process has been tumultuous and a successful resolution has not been reached, significant lessons have been learned in the process. Further, it is recognized that significant reform is expected if the DDA is going to accomplish its stated goal of being a development round. Further, the role of dispute settlement, specifically *Cotton*, and its impact on the efficacy of a coalition is significant. In some cases, the

---

1256 *See*, "Agriculture: the Heart of the Doha Round" in Newfarmer, R., *Trade, Doha, and Development: A Window Into the Issues*, The World Bank, (2006), pp. 77–139.

1257 "African Countries Take Plight of Cotton Farmers to WTO," International Centre for Trade and Sustainable Development (ICTSD), *Bridges*, Volume 3, No. 10, (2 June 2003).

1258 Baffes, J., "Learning from the Cotton Problem: Settling Trade Disputes," International Economic Bulletin, (June 2010).

1259 For an overview of trade and development within the Doha Round, *see*, Newfarmer, R., *Trade, Doha, and Development: A Window Into the Issues*, The World Bank, (2006).

litigation process can now be argued to be a precondition to establishing 'winning' coalitions.

Key Players in the Cotton Initiative: At the outset, it is important to note the various players involved in framing the cotton agenda and whose participation was arguably the key for Brazil and the C-4 in successfully obtaining favorable findings by the DSB as well as the creation of the cotton Sub-Committee to specifically address the issue, turning cotton into the litmus test of Doha. The C-4 countries were organized and assisted by a Swiss NGO – the iDEAS Centre,[1260] armed with credible studies conducted by the well-regarded international NGOs of Oxfam[1261] and the Hewlett Endowment/Cato Institute.[1262] Simultaneously, two of the four Members were being offered pro

---

[1260] Not only was the iDEAS Centre the organizing force behind the Cotton Initiative in the WTO, it was instrumental in educating and facilitating discussions on the issue with a variety of interest groups. For example, it has participated in and/or supported several conferences such as its "Can Negotiations on Agriculture Deliver Pro-development Reforms? The Case of West African Cotton," on 17 June in the WTO.

As stated on its website, "iDEAS Centre is an independent, non-profit organization dedicated to helping low-income countries to integrate into the world trading system – in a way that supports their national poverty reduction and economic development efforts. The Centre offers practical, results-oriented advisory services and executes projects aimed at strengthening the capacities of developing/transition country governments to shape both their domestic economic policies as well as the international policies that affect them. The overall goal of the Centre's projects is to empower low-income countries:

"by using their WTO membership (or accession process) in a way that promotes their country's sustainable human development; deepening their understanding of development challenges and linkages with trade and WTO rules; and improving policy coherence;

by participating more effectively in international trade forums and negotiations and by harnessing the free market forces and rules of a liberal world trade system to achieve poverty alleviation and economic growth."

Through its projects supporting developing country participation in the WTO and facilitating the integration of development-related concerns into industrial country positions, the Centre wants to contribute to international discussions on WTO institutional reforms and to encourage global cooperation for "win-win" solutions on the trade and development interface." *Visit*, http://www.ideascentre.ch/.

[1261] As found on its website, "Oxfam is an international confederation of 14 organizations working together in 99 countries and with partners and allies around the world to find lasting solutions to poverty and injustice. We work directly with communities and we seek to influence the powerful to ensure that poor people can improve their lives and livelihoods and have a say in decisions that affect them." *Visit*, http://www.oxfam.org/en/about.

[1262] Of particular import, as found on its website, "Global Development – Examining the Effects of U.S. Farm Policy: The Global Development Program awarded $7,444,000 in

bono services from high profile international law firms and additional assistance by the Advisory Centre on WTO Law in the *Cotton* dispute. It was a pioneering effort for the good of Benin and Chad, and is now an excellent example for LDCs of how to mobilize the necessary specialized resources and the media in order to increase their visibility and credibility at the WTO. Such "mobilization of public opinion and the media is essential."[1263] The use of private counsel translated into increased effectiveness of their presentations. Their submissions were substantive. Most importantly, the information exchange between the two processes, litigation and negotiation, was critical and substantially moved the cotton agenda forward in the Doha negotiations. As discussed in Chapter 4, Benin and Chad's involvement was precedential and important as an indicator of a number of misapprehensions about LDC participation in WTO dispute settlement. Further, the participation of these two Members provided important guidance on how to access and utilize a variety of resources available to LDCs. The two players, Chad and Benin, were provided the necessary resources to be able to quantify and articulate the cotton issue to the world and proved to be the greatest capacity-building strategy for the C-4 (and Brazil).

With regards to the cotton issue and the various players involved in prioritizing it within the negotiations and, at the same time, increasing global awareness, scholars and observers of the WTO have raised the question of the role of the media and NGOs in the *Cotton* dispute on the potential for US implementation of reforms. One significant impact these players had on the dispute, as well as on-going negotiations, is that they were able to effectively

---

grants, including support for research on global trade and for organizations helping to increase Americans' knowledge of international development issues. A $201,000 grant to the Cato Institute, a Washington, DC think tank, will fund a research project on how U.S. farm policy for important commodities – sugar, rice, dairy, and cotton – affect the world's poorest producers and consumers. The Global Development Program also made grants to several media organizations devoted to bringing information about development issues to a wide audience, including a $2,000,000 grant to the Independent Television Service. The grant will support the International Media Development Fund, an initiative of the Independent Television Service, which helps independent producers from other countries create documentaries on compelling international stories for American audiences." *Visit,* http://www.hewlett.org/news/hewlett-foundation-announces-67-63-million-in-new-grants.

1263 Imboden, N. and Nivet-Claeys, A., "Cotton and the LDCs in the WTO: Negotiations and Litigation, Two Sides of the Same Coin." Given to the author by Anne-Sophie Nivet Claeys of the iDEAS Centre, August 2009. [original in French; translated by Warwick Wilkins, revised by Nicole Antonietti.].

communicate to a wide audience, from international trade practitioners to the layman, the effects US subsidies are having on other areas of the world. However, many critics have noted that the resulting or even outright outrage garnered is not sufficient to effect significant alteration of US policies. The question of these broader implications on the likelihood of reform will be explored in the following chapter. For the purposes of this case study, the focus is an analysis of the strategies, efforts and developments on the part of the C-4 countries. To that end, a brief description of the Cotton Initiative and its resulting Sub-Committee on Cotton are first set forth. Following these descriptions is an analysis of the interplay between the *Cotton* dispute and the Cotton Initiative. As will be illustrated, participation in both venues – political and legal – was critical to the advancement of cotton in the Doha Development Agenda.

The process of centralizing cotton, in the context of the development agenda of the Doha Round, may be summarized in the following timeline:

Cotton in the WTO negotiations timeline

30 April 2003	C-4 first writes WTO DG Supachai, submitting the Cotton Initiative
10 June 2003	President Blaise Compaoré of Burkina Faso presents Cotton Initiative to the TNC
1, 18 July 2003	Agricultural Committee considers Cotton Initiative during Special Session
10–14 Sept. 2003	Cotton Initiative is integrated as paragraph of Draft Cancun Ministerial Text, but not part of Agricultural Framework
2 August 2004	Cotton is integrated into the Agricultural Framework, part of July Package
	Issue will be dealt with "ambitiously, expeditiously, and specifically"
19 November 2004	Subcommittee is formed

Cotton Initiative: It is difficult to overstate the importance of cotton for many developing countries, especially those least developed in Africa. It is also difficult to overstate the deleterious effects of depressed cotton prices on the economies of these LDCs. In testimony given to the original Panel by Benin and Chad, for example, a study by the International Food Policy Research Institute was presented that estimated the direct correlation between depressed cotton prices and rural poverty in Benin and Chad.[1264] The findings in the *Cotton* case demonstrated that some of the damage suffered by LDCs due to world cotton price suppression is caused by the domestic cotton support policies of developed nations, particularly the US.

The global awareness of these issues, increased as a result of the early findings in the *Cotton* dispute, was further heightened in April, 2003 when the C-4 countries of Chad, Benin, Burkina Faso, and Mali submitted to the WTO Director General the "Sectoral Initiative in Favour of Cotton" (the Cotton Initiative, or CI) to be included in the Doha Development Round.[1265] The Cotton Initiative described the importance of cotton production and trade to several African countries and the role that cotton production and trade plays in their economic and social development and poverty reduction programs. The CI also stated that several African countries have undertaken reform measures aimed at improving quality and competitiveness[1266] by several African countries, but that the effect of these reforms have been largely negated by the continuation of cotton support measures by certain Members. Further, the Initiative described the damage being done to African cotton producing and exporting nations by the cotton support policies of developed countries.

Of particular importance in the Cotton Initiative is the twofold request by the C-4 countries calling for (1) the elimination of cotton support measures that distort global cotton prices and (2) monetary compensation be paid to the C-4 countries to cover the economic losses these countries suffer while these support programs remain in place. This latter request is especially noteworthy in that, with this proposal, the C-4 "entered uncharted territory" as this was the first time that direct compensation was requested for the damages from trade practices that are contrary to the rules and principles of the WTO, "rather than the typical remedy of authorizing countermeasures."[1267] The precedential nature of the request for compensation raised several legal issues.[1268] In addition, it raised issues regarding the role of donor countries from which compensation would be forthcoming, including whether the compensation should

---

1264 Minot, Nicholas.
1265 TN/AG/GEN/4 of 16 May 2003.
1266 TN/AG/SCC/GEN/2 of 22 April, 2005.
1267 Baffes, J., "Learning from the Cotton Problem: Settling Trade Disputes," International Economic Bulletin, (June 2010).
1268 *See*, "Legal Issues in Relation to Financial Compensation under the Cotton Initiative," International Lawyers and Economists Against Poverty (ILEAP), Negotiation Advisory Brief No. 3 (January 2004).

be paid as development assistance or in some other form and what agency should be in charge of its collection and distribution.[1269] Although the compensation issue loomed large at the time of the submission of the CI to the WTO, it should be kept in mind that it was viewed as a temporary measure, to be in effect only as long as the WTO-inconsistent subsidies remained in place. As stated by Mr. Samuel Amehou, Benin's WTO Ambassador to Geneva, stated, "Compensation is in fact only a stop-gap solution in relation to the benefits that will flow from the restoration of the free market."[1270]

Shortly after the Cotton Initiative was submitted to the WTO DG, President Blaise Compaoré of Burkina Faso presented the Initiative to the Trade Negotiations Committee (TNC), in June 2004. This high-profile presentation helped to frame the Initiative in terms of the fight against poverty.[1271] This, along with the strength of the evidence on the negative impacts of WTO-inconsistent cotton support policies on LDCs, garnered worldwide attention and broad support for the Cotton Initiative and the plight of African LDCs. As Mr. Amadou Toumani Toure, President of the Republic of Mali, stated, "Our demand is simple: apply free trade rules not only to those products that are of interest to the rich and powerful, but also to those products where poor countries have a proven comparative advantage."[1272]

The widespread attention of the importance of cotton as a development issue raised its profile at the September 2003 Cancun MC, as discussed *infra*, and the proposal became a Cancun MC document,[1273] with the intent of seeking a decision on the Cotton Initiative as an agenda item.[1274] During the Cancun MC, Members disagreed about whether to maintain the independence of the issues contained in the CI or whether cotton should be part of a larger discussion centered on the three pillars of the agriculture negotiations (market

---

1269 For a detailed analysis of this issue, see Osakwe, D., "The Role of Donors and Lessons from Implementing the Mandate on Cotton Development Assistance," International Conference on Cotton at "The Next Steps for Africa," Woodrow Wilson Center, Washington DC, (26 October 2006).

1270 iDEAS Centre literature, distributed to author.

1271 Imboden, N. and Nivet-Claeys, A., "Cotton and the LDCs in the WTO: Negotiations and Litigation, Two Sides of the Same Coin." Given to the author by Anne-Sophie Nivet Claeys of the iDEAS Centre, August 2009. [original in French; translated by Warwick Wilkins, revised by Nicole Antonietti.].

1272 iDEAS Centre literature, distributed to author.

1273 WT/MIN(03)/W/2 and Add. 1, September, 2003.

1274 Titled "Poverty Reduction: Sectoral Initiative in Favour of Cotton – Joint Proposal by Benin, Burkina Faso, Chad and Mali."

access, domestic support, and export subsidies).[1275] By the end of the failed Cancun MC, no real negotiations on the Cotton Initiative had taken place and, as discussed in Section 3.2, the view is widely held that the cotton issue is one of the principal causes for the overall failure of the Cancun MC.

Following the breakdown of negotiations in Cancun, the focus of the debate regarding the Cotton Initiative was on how to include it into the agenda of the Doha Development Round. The United States and other, principally developed, countries pressed for the inclusion of cotton in the general negotiations on agriculture. The C-4 countries resisted this inclusion and pressed for its separate treatment, expressing concern that the integration of cotton into the overall agriculture negotiations would dilute its importance and decrease the chances for meaningful progress. Following the session of the WTO General Council from 27 July to 1 August, 2004, the C-4 eventually yielded to the pressure for the inclusion of cotton into the overall negotiations on agriculture only after the WTO General Council stressed the importance of cotton and included the now-famous pledge to address cotton "ambitiously, expeditiously, and specifically"[1276] within the negotiations on agriculture and "to work on all trade-distorting policies affecting the sector in all three pillars of market access, domestic support, and export competition."[1277]

The struggle over the inclusion of cotton within broader agricultural negotiation versus its treatment as a separate sector raises the broader issue of sectoral versus systemic treatment of negotiations on agriculture. The pressure by the C-4 for a sectoral approach was precedential. It can be argued that with the submission of the Cotton Initiative, the C-4 and other developing countries were looking for immediate sectoral remedies for cotton support programs while, at the same time, seeking a systemic solution to the general problem of subsidy programs for a broad range of agricultural commodities.[1278] Although

---

1275 World Trade Organization, "Agriculture Negotiations: Backgrounder. The Issues, and Where We are Now." Updated 1 December, 2004.
1276 Para. 1(b), WT/L/579 of 2 August 2004 (the July Package document).
1277 Para. 4, WT/L/579 of 2 August 2004 (the July Package document).
1278 Scholars are now considering the advisability of a sectoral approach versus other approaches to multilateral trade negotiations. For example, in the context of increasing the probability of success in the Doha Negotiations, see Perez del Castillo, C. *et al.*, "The Doha Round and Alternative Options for Creating a Fair and Market-Oriented Agricultural Trade System," International Food & Agricultural Trade Policy Council, IPC Position Paper, Trade negotiations Policy Series, (November 2009). For an overview of the issues and dynamics of developing economies in the Doha Round negotiations, see, Das, D., The Doha Round of Multilateral Trade Negotiations, Palgrave Macmillan, New York, (2005), pp. 87–112.

negotiating mandates in a sectoral approach are likely to be more focused and, as a result be easier to successfully negotiate, they also may be less ambitious and bypass more important and economically meaningful reforms. Further, the gains in one sector would not be generally applicable to other sectors, nor be applicable to non-participants in sectoral-specific agreements. This is especially important in negotiations on trade-related subsidies. Non-participation in sectoral negotiations by Members with WTO-inconsistent policies in that sector will decrease the likelihood of successful resolution and reductions of those policies.

A method to increase the effectiveness and applicability of sectoral negotiations is to ensure participation by all WTO Members without regard to their individual offensive or defensive concerns of the sectoral concerns under negotiation. In this light, it is interesting to note that, in accordance with the text of the July Package, the Committee on Agriculture, Special Session agreed to the establishment of the Sub-Committee on Cotton on 19 November 2004 with the charge to focus on cotton as a separate and specific issue in the talks on agriculture.[1279] While acknowledging the special importance of the issue to particular Members, the meetings of the Sub-Committee were deemed to be open to all Members, Observer Governments, and international organizations that have observer status in the Special Session of the Committee on Agriculture, to which the Sub-Committee was assigned to periodically report.

The July Package recognized the need to pursue "coherence between trade and development aspects of the cotton issue" and this coherence is a major topic for treatment by the Sub-Committee.[1280] The inclusion of these topics and the recognition that they are linked is important for the interests of the C-4 and other LDC and developing nations reliant on cotton production and exportation. Under issues related to trade are negotiations on the crucial and difficult topics of trade barriers, domestic support and export subsidies. Under the development-related aspects are instructions for the Secretariat and the WTO Director General and Member countries to work with international organizations, such as the IMF, FAO, World Bank, and International Trade Centre, non-governmental organizations, and other members of the development community to facilitate economic development for developing country Members.

1279 Its terms of reference and work program are set out in document TN/AG/13 of 26 November 2004 and TN/AG/SSC/1 of 29 March 2005.

1280 Coherence between trade and development aspects of the cotton issue would be pursued as set out in the text of the July Package (Annex A, paragraph 5 of the July Package: document WT/L/579 of 2 August 2004).

Cotton & Cotton Initiative Interplay: The most significant effect the Cotton Initiative had on the *Cotton* dispute, and vice versa, was the framing of the dispute as a development issue with particular import as an African issue.[1281] This allowed Brazil to use the starkest example of the adverse effects of US subsidies in its argumentation. Further, the transference of the issues raised in the *Cotton* case to ongoing negotiations was made easier for the Africans because it was framed as a dispute involving development issues of particular relevance to the Doha agenda. The direct result was the placement of cotton squarely[1282] within the agenda of the Doha Development Round and, simultaneously, 'on the books' in WTO jurisprudence. Typically, disputes are initiated because: (1) a Member's policy is suspected of violating WTO rules[1283] (2) there is a reasonable economic interest in engaging at the WTO[1284] and (3) the political interest at the international level to litigate against another Member is great enough to warrant the potential political price of doing so.[1285] The precedential approach in the *Cotton* dispute was that all three of these factors existed. They were considered as part of the perspective of the C-4 and were explicitly framed as such by Brazil. Consequently, global attention was drawn to both the dispute process with the participation by Benin and Chad[1286] and, at the same time, the ongoing multilateral negotiations milieu as the C-4

1281 For an interesting read about cotton and its significance as a development issue, *see*, Baffes, J. "Cotton and Developing Countries: Implications for Development," as found in Newfarmer, R., *Trade, Doha, and Development: A Window Into the Issues*, The World Bank, (2006), pp. 119–138.

1282 Prior to the 'Sectoral Initiative in Favour of Cotton," cotton did not appear in the Doha Declaration. However, after the Cancun Ministerial Conference in 2003, it appeared as a separate and important agenda item. *See*, Imboden, N. and Nivet-Claeys, A., "Cotton and the LDCs in the WTO: Negotiations and Litigation, Two Sides of the Same Coin." Given to the author by Anne-Sophie Nivet Claeys of the iDEAS Centre, August 2009. [original in French; translated by Warwick Wilkins, revised by Nicole Antonietti.] Paper on file with author.

1283 In an interview with Hans Jakob, who worked at the iDEAS Centre for over two years, it was mentioned that this is never enough to incentivize a Member to initiate a dispute.

1284 As discussed in Chapter 4, there is almost always a well-funded and organized lobby that makes this determination and moves the play in this direction.

1285 This three (3) step approach was developed from a number of interviews with WTO litigators, one academician, and two Members of the WTO Secretariat.

1286 As confirmed in several interviews, a significant reason the other two Members of the C-4 did not join in the dispute was due to the political fear factor. Further, the historical norms of the system were that negotiations are more politically acceptable to legally challenging another Member. Noteworthy is the fact that, initially, over twenty (20) countries were approached in hopes that more would join the dispute and Cotton Initiative.

quickly became the poster child of the Doha Development Round. It can be reasonably argued that the result of this visibility is that cotton has remained as the only tangible element of the 'development' aspect of the current Doha Round. Divergent views have been expressed in terms of the reasons why this might be the case. While some argue that the goal and objective of prioritizing development issues were too lofty, most participants interviewed during the research for this study expressed the view that, instead, the goal and efforts to keep the focus on development were long overdue. To that end, and in that conceptual framework, the fact that the world could see, in both the legal and political realms of the WTO, the shortcomings of the system and dire need for reform, particularly with regards to agricultural subsidies, was supreme. The following is an analysis of two approaches and the interplay between the two.

Prior to the Cancun MC (described in Section 7.1), the *Cotton* dispute and the Cotton Initiative were moving in unison, as is made clear by a comparison of the *Cotton* and *C-I* timetables given above. However, after the Cancun failure, the DSB was required to move forward, separately, from the political process and begin making determinations on the very issues being addressed in the negotiations (perhaps most importantly, the Peace Clause and export subsidies). To that extent, the *Cotton* dispute had a particularly significant influence on how the cotton issue would be handled in the separately conducted negotiations. Some criticism of the effects of the separation of the litigation and negotiation processes has been offered with the claim that the US found a loophole that arose because of the divergent paths pursued by Brazil and the C-4 and the fact that the dispute ended before the negotiations. Specifically, the US has not implemented measures mandated by the dispute process, explicitly stating that it is waiting to first learn the final results of the Doha negotiations. This is an unusual strategy by the US, with the potential to compromise the dispute process, given there is not a provision in the DSU that allows for a Member to delay implementation because of an ongoing round of negotiations. Such a decision can create negative precedence and threaten the dispute settlement system, as will be discussed in greater detail in the following chapter. In addition, as Nicolas Imboden and Anne-Sophie Nivet-Claeys of the iDEAS Centre wrote, "…the coexistence of the two approaches made it possible for the US to try to "sell" the same thing twice over: to agree to something as a concession in negotiations that they are in any case obliged to implement following the dispute settlement, but have still not carried out. This was particularly the case for the export subsidies, which the United States have not yet completely eliminated despite several legal rulings, and which are set down in the negotiations as a concession with an implementation date extending beyond that imposed upon the US."[1287] Finally, noteworthy is the fact that, in all proceedings in the dispute, the parties referenced the negotiations, clearly linking the two processes. Both processes continued to move along and evolve. The ultimate query was whether, eventually, legal precedent would work in the negotiations and/or whether the Cotton Initiative could effectuate change at the domestic level.

Benin and Chad reported to the Panel that their position in the dispute was the same as their position in the negotiations.[1288] There were two messages they were conveying in the Doha Round and both were articulated in *Cotton:* (1) the importance of cotton in their countries and (2) that cotton as a product within the multilateral system was important. While these two messages were conveyed through the Cotton Initiative and within the cotton negotiations[1289] there was anticipation that similar arguments will be adapted for similar commodities for other markets in future disputes and negotiations.

In terms of the importance of cotton to their economies, Benin and Chad supplied extensive evidence on the value of cotton exports.[1290] For example, as listed in the Panel report in the original proceedings, "in their joint submission, Benin and Chad extensively explained the situation of the cotton sector in

---

1287 Imboden, N. and Nivet-Claeys, A., "Cotton and the LDCs in the WTO: Negotiations and Litigation, Two Sides of the Same Coin," paper given to author by Anne-Sophie Nivet Claeys of the iDEAS Centre. [original in French; translated by Warwick Wilkins, revised by Nicole Antonietti].

1288 As Chadian trade minister Youssouf Abbassalah reported to the news, "African trade ministers favor dialogue to resolve the dispute over subsidies." "African Trade Ministers Urge End to US Cotton Subsidies," VOANews.com, Washington (26 October 2006).

1289 Further, The information was dispersed at the WTO and international conferences were established to develop dialogue and an exchange of positions in order for solutions to be proffered. In these environs, the Doha Round and the *Cotton* dispute were given considerable attention.

1290 Pursuant to WTO law, Brazil had the burden to produce the economic evidence required to establish harm. Benin and Chad were involved to show support and to increase its negotiation leverage and global position in the Doha Round. Brazil explained the situation in Benin and/or Chad in its further submission dated 9 September 2003 (executive summary included as Annex E item 1) at paragraph 1; in its answers dated 27 October 2003 to questions from the Panel at paragraphs 61, 121, 159 (see Annex I item 5); in Exhibit BRA-294, and in its further rebuttal submission dated 18 November 2003 (executive summary included as Annex G item 1) at paragraph 87. Numerous exhibits also pertain to the cotton sectors in Benin and/or Chad, in particular, Exhibit BRA-15, an OXFAM briefing paper, Exhibits BRA-264 through BRA-268 and BRA-294. The US referred to the submission of Benin in its response dated 11 August 2003 to the Panel's Questions at paragraph 26 (see Annex I item 2).

their respective countries."[1291] Specifically, in Benin, cotton accounts for 29 percent of total employment and in Chad it accounts for 10 percent of total employment.[1292] Further, as offered in Chapter 1, "the reliance of these countries on the export of cotton as a means of economic development is evidenced by the degree to which cotton comprises total exports: approximately sixty-five (65) (70) percent of exports for Benin, forty (40) percent for Mail, and forty-five (45) to seventy one (71) percent for Burkina Faso.[1293] Given their reliance on exporting cotton, it is evident why three of the four *C-4* counties, Burkina Faso, Mali and Benin, lobbied for the establishment of the *Subcommittee on Cotton* within the WTO Doha Development negotiations. These countries, along with Cameroon, Central African Republic, Cote d'Ivoire, Senegal, Togo, and Niger comprise the 'Franc Zone,' which is only second to the United States as a leading exporter of cotton."[1294] In addition, an estimated fifteen (15) million people in West and Central Africa rely on the production of cotton as their main source of income.[1295]

The issue of cotton's importance extends beyond the production of cotton to the consequential effects of income and food security. "...[c]otton has been considered a success in central and West Africa, improving the standards of living for small farmers by increasing access to basic needs and schooling. Cotton cultivation has also contributed positively to the overall agricultural sector, translating into benefits for grain and dairy production. In fact, the cotton industry is responsible for the great majority of job creation in C-4

1291 *Panel Report*, para. 7.54.
1292 Shui, S., "Importance of Cotton Production and Trade and Strategies to Enhance Cotton's Contribution to Economy and Food Security in Africa." FAO Commodity and Trade Division, In WTO African Regional Workshop on Cotton, 23–24 March 2004, WTO Document WT/L/587. Alston, J., Sumner, D., Brunke, H., "Impacts of Reductions in US Cotton Subsidies on West African Cotton Producers," Oxfam America (2007), p. 2.
1293 Gillson, I., Poulton, Co., Balcombe, K., and Page, S., "Understanding the Impact of Cotton Subsidies on Developing Countries," Working Paper (May, 2004), p. 7. <http://www.odi.org.uk/resources/download/3608.pdf> last visited 2 June, 2010.
1294 Meyer, L., MacDonald, S., and Foreman, L., "Cotton Backgrounder," USDA Outlook Report from the Economic Research Service, (March, 2007), World Agricultural Supply and Demand Estimates, WAOB, USDA statistics from 2004–2006 period.
1295 Minister Choguel Kokala Maiga, Trade Minister of Mali at "The Next Steps for Africa: A Report of an International Conference on Cotton," held on 26 October 2006 and hosted by the International Food & Agricultural Trade Policy Council, The Woodrow Wilson International Center for Scholars, and the iDEAS Centre.

 It should be further noted that over 300 million people rely on the cotton industry for employment, many of whom reside in poor, rural areas of developing countries. Benin and Chad are among a much large group of damaged countries.

countries. Cotton also plays an important role in building and strengthening regional integration and synergies. In short cotton is the essence of a virtuous cycle of economic and social development in West and Central Africa."[1296] As indicated by this quote, Benin and Chad are not the only countries similarly situated. Generally, more than two thirds of the total volume of cotton in the world is produced in developing countries. Production had decreased by nearly 50% during the past 4 years (ICAC). As a result of the significance of cotton to a great portion of WTO Members, the C-4's WTO initiative, although "established due to the importance of cotton to the economic and social health of Benin, Chad, Burkina Faso, and Mali"[1297] is of substantial importance to the greater membership of the WTO. Given this economic backdrop, "...distortive subsidies for cotton producers in developed countries pose an external problem for impoverished economies that are dependent on cotton as a major source of livelihood."[1298] As stated in literature from the iDEAS Centre,

> Cotton is one of the few products through which the countries of West and Central Africa can benefit from the world trading system. With their submission on cotton, they are not asking for grants, loans or exceptions. They are merely calling for the respect of the basic principles of the WTO, in other words, for fair competition and equitable trade. The WTO cannot overlook a distortion of this nature in the cotton market. Especially in the light of the "Doha Development Agenda," the commitments made in favour of disadvantaged Members must not be forgotten.[1299]

As developed in Part 1 of this book, no WTO Members were more harmed by the massive US trade-distorting subsidies than African LDCs. In *Cotton*, Benin and Chad offered into evidence studies showing the direct and indirect effects US cotton subsidies were having on their markets. Consequently, the benefits

---

1296 Minister Choguel Kokala Maiga, Trade Minister of Mali at "The Next Steps for Africa: A Report of an International Conference on Cotton," held on 26 October 2006 and hosted by the International Food & Agricultural Trade Policy Council, The Woodrow Wilson International Center for Scholars, and the iDEAS Centre.
1297 Ambassador Malloum Bamanga Abbas, the permanent representative of Chad in Geneva, at "The Next Steps for Africa: A Report of an International Conference on Cotton," held on 26 October 2006 and hosted by the International Food & Agricultural Trade Policy Council, The Woodrow Wilson International Center for Scholars, and the iDEAS Centre.
1298 Terry Townsend, Executive Director of International Cotton Advisory Committee at "A US-Africa Dialogue on the Cotton Trade," hosted by the Carnegie Endowment and iDEAS Centre, Washington, D.C. (20 July 2009).
1299 Pamphlets distributed to author upon visits to the iDEAS Centre.

from cotton production in the region were being undercut by US subsidization. This evidence was also used in the negotiations and released through the media to communicate to Members and the global community that change by the US was essential. Further, Benin and Chad articulated the relevance of cotton within the context of the Doha Development Round, emphasizing the fact that the cotton issue was emblematic of the broader issue of the effects of agricultural subsidization in developed countries on developing and least developed Members.

The issues of the *Cotton* case can now be applied to similar commodities that can be stored and by Members who have a similar share of global production traded internationally (for example, corn, sugar, biofuels, and wheat). Addressing the dichotomy between developed and developing country interests was the objective of the Doha Development Round. Generally, it is believed that cotton is the most distorted commodity market in what is already an extremely distorted trade in agricultural products. This is primarily the case, due to massive trade-distorting subsidies granted by developed countries. This was demonstrated in the *Cotton* dispute. The lack of progress on the cotton issue, a clear example of trade-distortion, threatened the confidence in the principal values and workings of the system.[1300]

The clarity of the effects of the cotton support programs by the US on the economies of African LDCs was effectively demonstrated in the Cotton dispute. In the dispute, representation by Benin and Chad consisted of the following: Benin, through its permanent mission in Geneva, was represented by a delegation headed by its Ambassador, which included a research fellow[1301] of the International Food Policy Research Institute, who presented the results of a study entitled "Effect of falling cotton prices on rural poverty in Benin."[1302] Chad, which does not have a permanent mission in Geneva, was represented

---

1300 This concern is addressed to some extent in this section, but given greater consideration in Chapters 8 and 9 of this book.
1301 Mr. Nicholas Minot. See also *infra*, Section VII:G, relating to the involvement of experts as Members of party and third party delegations in these Panel proceedings.
1302 Brazil also submitted a report by Mr. Nicholas Minot and Ms. Lisa Daniels as Exhibit BRA-244. The study found the following, as stated by Brazil:
(1) From January 2001 to May 2002, world cotton prices fell almost 40 percent, from 64 cents per pound to 39 cents per pound [based on A-Index prices]... In addition to stagnant demand, cotton prices have been pushed down by increased government support to cotton growers...
(2) At least in the case of Benin, to the extent that fluctuations in world cotton prices are transmitted to farmers, they will have a significant effect on rural incomes and poverty. The broader implication is that polices that subsidize cotton production in

at the resumed session of the first substantive meeting by a delegation headed by its Brussels-based Ambassador, who presented a detailed statement by the Chairman of the *Société Cotonnière du Tchad* (*"Cotontchad"*) and the *Association Cotonnière Africaine*, Mr. Ibrahim Malloum.

In addition to the representation by these individuals and studies by these organizations, Benin and Chad (and Brazil) were supported by various submissions of compelling studies on the existence of low prices received by African producers, the effects of US studies on the C-4, and the impact those low prices have on income levels in the African LDCs. In terms of studies used, "The ICAC reported that African producers in Benin, Chad, Mali, Cote d'Ivoire received no subsidies between August 1999-July 2003". Brazilian producers received subsidies of only 1–2 cents per pound of cotton produced during 2000–2002 – far less than the 37 cents per pound received, on average, by US producers between 1999–2002. The export market share of US upland cotton increased from 17 percent in 1998–99 to 42 percent in 2000–03. This increase in US world market share took place as the West African producers' world market share plunged from 15 to 11 percent in the same period. Other, far more efficient and lower-cost producers such as Brazil were not able to increase their market share during the same period. According to Professor Nicholas Minot of the International Food Policy Research Institute in Washington, DC, "the effect of the US subsidies in lowering world cotton prices (through overproduction in the US) was to push an approximately ninety-thousand (90,000) Benin cotton farmers below the poverty line in 2001–02." In order to illustrate the disparity of positions, Brazil submitted in para. 191 of the *Further Submission of Brazil* on 9 September 2003: "To put the export effects of this single program [GSM 102] into perspective: the estimated impact of 500,000 bales of exports (representing 109,000 metric tons) – exceeds all of the exports of Cameroon, the Central African Republic, Chad, Cote-D'Ivoire and two-thirds of the exports of Benin, Burkina Faso and Mali in MY 2001."[1303]

In addition, a well-respected study of the stakes for the C-4 found that "in terms of cotton production, trade and economic welfare in Africa..." as well as the potential gains to the C-4 through their Cotton Initiative, Kym Anderson

---

the United States and elsewhere, damping world prices, have an adverse impact on rural poverty in Benin and (by extension) other poor cotton-exporting countries.

1303 Exhibit Bra-208 ("Cotton: World Statistics," ICAC, September 2003, p. 56). The U.S. export credit guarantee effect of an estimated 500,000 bales of increased exports represented 10 percent of all African exports in MY 2001 (Exhibit Bra-41 ("The Future of Federal Farm Commodity Programs (Cotton)," Hearing before the House of Representatives Committee on Agriculture, 15 February 2001, p. 12)).

and Ernesto Valenzuela found, "[f]or Sub-Saharan Africa the potential gains are huge relative to the effects on them of reforming other merchandise trade policies. And they could be more than doubled if that reform provided the cash for farmers to take advantage of the biotechnology revolution and adopt GM cotton varieties. But those potential gains, and the affordability of switching to costly GM seed, depend crucially on the extent to which high-income countries are willing to lower domestic support to their cotton farmers."[1304] Another example of argumentation used by Brazil to highlight the impacts to the two LDC third parties, "[s]uch price suppression is also significant when examined in the context of its impact on Brazilian producers – not to mention producers in least developed countries such as Benin and Chad."[1305]

In addition, Benin and Chad responded to the Panel's Questions on 27 October 2003, arguing for the inclusion of the effects to their economies as well... "In any event, the Panel need not rely exclusively on the presumption set out in DSU Article 3.8, since Benin and Chad have already provided to the Panel detailed evidence about the adverse effects of US subsidies on West and Central Africa. Benin and Chad also note the similarities in language between the SCM Agreement ('adverse effects') and DSU Article 3.8 ('adverse impact'). This reinforces the relevance and applicability of the latter provision."

The involvement of Benin and Chad was given particular attention, in accordance with Article 24.1 of the DSU, and their testimony and submissions were used by the Panel in making its final determinations.[1306] Represented by private legal counsel,[1307] Benin and Chad Benin provided a detailed written submission and presented an oral statement at the first session of the first meeting of the Panel and provided written responses to the Panel's questions following that session. In addition, Benin and Chad made a detailed joint written submission, and presented separate oral statements, at the resumed session of the first meeting of the Panel. They provided joint written responses

---

1304   Anderson, K., and Valenzuela, E., "WTO's Doha Cotton Initiative: A Tale of Two Issues," Centre for Economic Policy Research, Discussion Paper Series, No. 5567, (March 2006). The research was conducted and included in the World Bank's project on "Agricultural Trade Reform and the Doha Development Agenda."
1305   See Exhibit Bra-15 ("Cultivating Poverty: The Impact of US Cotton Subsidies on Africa," Oxfam Briefing Paper 30, 27 September 2002, pp. 2–3); Exhibit Bra-244 ("Impact of Global Cotton Markets on Rural Poverty in Benin," Nicholas Minot and Lisa Daniels, 25 April 2003, pp. 17–27).
1306   Specifically, the Panel referred to the arguments of Benin and Chad at paragraphs of the final report. See, Panel Report, para. 7.54.
1307   White & Case in Geneva, Switzerland. See, https://www.whitecase.com/geneva/.

to the Panel's questions following that session.[1308] As argued in this book, Benin and Chad were not the only beneficiaries of dispute settlement participation. Brazil, the US and other third parties referred to Benin and Chad's situation at various parts of the proceedings.[1309] As set forth by Brazil[1310] and captured in the original Panel report,

> The record shows that the adverse effects suffered by Brazilian producers have also been suffered by producers in Africa. Nicolas Minot testified for Benin at the hearing on 8 October. His econometric analysis focused on the effect of lower upland cotton prices on poverty among Benin cotton farmers. Based on his economic analysis, a ten percent decrease in upland cotton prices drove approximately 83,500 Benin upland cotton farmers below the poverty line.[1311] The evidence that African producers have suffered adverse effects by reason of the effects of the US subsidies confirms and supports the evidence presented by Brazil that it producers are suffering adverse effects as well.[1312]

1308 The further submission submitted on 3 October 2003, and responses to certain of the Panel's Questions, submitted on 27 October 2003. (See Annex E item 4 and Annex J item 14.).

1309 For example, Brazil has explained the situation in Benin and/or Chad in its further submission dated 9 September 2003 (executive summary included as Annex E item 1) at paragraph 1; in its answers dated 27 October 2003 to questions from the Panel at paragraphs 61, 121, 159 (see Annex I item 5); in Exhibit BRA-294, and in its further rebuttal submission dated 18 November 2003 (executive summary included as Annex G item 1) at paragraph 87. Numerous exhibits also pertain to the cotton sectors in Benin and/or Chad, in particular, Exhibit BRA-15, an OXFAM briefing paper, Exhibits BRA-264 through BRA-268 and BRA-294. The United States referred to the submission of Benin in its response dated 11 August 2003 to the Panel's Questions at paragraph 26 (see Annex I item 2).

1310 In its serious prejudice argumentation, Brazil stated that the interests of African countries were also threatened. Specifically, it wrote, "Brazilian upland cotton producers and Brazil are not the only WTO Members suffering serious prejudice by reason of the U.S. subsidies. Upland cotton producers in Africa and several African economies are also seriously prejudiced by the U.S. subsidies on upland cotton." *Further Submission of Brazil*, (9 September 2003).

1311 Benin's 8 October Oral Statement (Statement of Nicolas Minot, para. 24–25) (estimating that a 40 percent reduction in price caused 334,000 people to fall below the poverty line, and indicating that smaller reductions in the cotton price cause roughly proportional changes in income, as shown in Table 3 of his paper attached to Benin's 1 October Further Third Party Submission).

1312 Para. 121.

Brazil also submitted an Oxfam report, "Cultivating Poverty,"[1313] that quantified and assessed cotton prices received by African producers, finding that they had precipitously declined to half of what the countries had been receiving in the mid-1990s. The report also offered an assessment of the effect these prices had on the rural communities of the LDCs. Comparisons were also made, which were illuminating. The following excerpt from Brazil's 9 September *Further Submission* sets forth some of the most dramatic findings,[1314]

Using USDA documents, Oxfam concluded that in MY 2001 the U.S. provides $3.9 billion in subsidies to its 25,000 upland cotton farmers. The Oxfam Report uses the following comparisons to put the size of the U.S. subsidies into perspective:

- **more in subsidies than the entire GDP of Burkina Faso** – a country in which more than two million people depend on cotton production. Over half of these farmers live below the poverty line. Poverty levels among recipients of cotton subsidies in the US are zero.
- **three times more in subsidies than the entire USAID budget for Africa's 500 million people**[1315] [original emphasis]

Finding that African farmers suffered from significant price declines in 2000–2001, Oxfam calculated the impact of U.S. subsidies on the fragile economies of several African countries:

For the region as a whole, the losses amounted to $301m, equivalent to almost one-quarter of what it receives in American aid. Eight cotton-producing countries in West Africa accounted for approximately two-thirds ($191m) of overall losses.

The small size of the countries concerned and their high level of dependence on cotton magnify the effect of US policies. For individual countries, US cotton subsidies led to economic shocks of the following magnitude:

- Burkina Faso lost 1 per cent of GDP and 12 per cent of export earnings
- Mali lost 1.7 per cent of GDP and 8 per cent of export earnings
- Benin lost 1.4 per cent of GDP and 9 per cent of export earnings

---

1313 Exhibit Bra-15 ("Cultivating Poverty: The Impact of US Cotton Subsidies on Africa," Oxfam Briefing Paper 30, 27 September 2002, pp. 2–3. See also page 17–19 for more detailed information) (emphasis in original).

1314 *Further Submission of Brazil*, (9 September 2003).

1315 Exhibit Bra-15 ("Cultivating Poverty: The Impact of US Cotton Subsidies on Africa," Oxfam Briefing Paper 30, 27 September 2002, pp. 2–3. See also page 17–19 for more detailed information)(emphasis in original).

> These losses have generated acute balance-of-payments and domestic budget pressures, and pushed several countries to the brink of renewed debt crisis. The economic losses inflicted by the US cotton subsidy program outweigh the benefits of aid. Mali received $37m in aid in 2001 but lost $43m as a result of the lower earnings. The cotton subsidy programme has also undermined the Heavily Indebted Poor Countries (HIPC) Initiative, costing countries such as Benin, Burkina Faso, and Chad more than they have received in debt relief.[1316] [original emphasis].

Brazil's submission also included the summations of a study commissioned by West and Central African (specifically, the C-4) countries and conducted by Louis Goreux to assess the effects of US, EU, and Chinese subsidies in their region.[1317] As Brazil argued, the study found that those effects total US $250 million lost in net export earnings for the region as a result of suppressed prices.[1318] This evidence was used to further Brazil's argument that US subsidization of its cotton sector suppresses world prices and, consequently, adversely affects cotton producers in African countries.

Further, Brazil included a World Bank Working Paper, "Cotton Sector Strategies in West and Central Africa,"[1319] which emphasized that cotton producers in Africa are competitive on cost factors and could have benefited from its comparative advantage absent US subsidies.[1320] Brazil quoted the study, in which it stated, "few other countries can produce cotton profitably at this price level."[1321] The study emphasized the difficulty African cotton farmers have in switching to other crops in times of cotton price declines.[1322] Therefore, the evidence emphasized the facts that the C-4 were competitive at growing

---

1316 Exhibit Bra-15 ("Cultivating Poverty: The Impact of US Cotton Subsidies on Africa," Oxfam Briefing Paper 30, 27 September 2002, pp. 2–3. See also page 17–19 for more detailed information)(emphasis in original).

1317 Exhibit Bra-264("Prejudice Caused by Industrialized Countries Subsidies to Cotton Sectors in Western and Central Africa," Louis Goreux, June 2003, p. 34).

1318 Exhibit Bra-264("Prejudice Caused by Industrialized Countries Subsidies to Cotton Sectors in Western and Central Africa," Louis Goreux, June 2003, p. 34).

1319 Exhibit Bra-265 ("Cotton Sector Strategies in West and Central Africa," World Bank Policy Research Working Paper 2867, July 2002).

1320 Exhibit Bra-265 ("Cotton Sector Strategies in West and Central Africa," World Bank Policy Research Working Paper 2867, July 2002, p. 12).

1321 Exhibit Bra-265 ("Cotton Sector Strategies in West and Central Africa," World Bank Policy Research Working Paper 2867, July 2002, p. 12).

1322 Exhibit Bra-265 ("Cotton Sector Strategies in West and Central Africa," World Bank Policy Research Working Paper 2867, July 2002, p. 13).

cotton and that, not only were opportunities for it to capitalize on its competitive advantage being obstructed. Further, their comparative advantage in cotton makes it difficult for the C-4 countries to readjust their production when their cotton sectors are harmed.

Finally, Brazil included in its exhibits newspaper articles on the 'publicized' issue of harm to African economies as a result of US subsidies to its upland cotton sector. These were submitted as further evidence that US cotton subsidies were damaging the C-4 and is mentioned here to emphasize the point that the issue was getting significant attention around the world. Some choice quotes from these newspapers, as submitted by Brazil, include the following:

> Burkina Faso's hand picked cotton is the cash crop that permits smallholders farmers to buy fertilizers and invest in the other crops that get rotated on the land. If cotton doesn't sell at a decent price, it affects everything else... That includes Koumbia's little schoolhouse, whose third classroom remains unfinished.[1323]
>
> Cotton is our ticket into the world market. Its production is crucial to economic development in West and Central Africa, as well as to the livelihoods of millions of people there. Cotton accounts for up to 40 percent of export revenues and 10 percent of gross domestic product in our two countries, as well as in Benin and Chad. More than that, cotton is of paramount importance to the social infrastructure of Africa, as well as the maintenance of its rural areas[1324]
>
> Not only is cotton crucial to our economies, it is the sole agricultural product for our countries to trade. Although African cotton is of the highest quality, our production costs are about 50 percent lower than in developed countries even though we rely on manual labor[1325]
>
> In the period from 2001 to 2002, America's 25,000 cotton farmers received more in subsidies – some $3 billion – than the entire economic output of Burkina Faso, where two million people depend on cotton.... Thus, the payments to about 25,000 relatively well-off farmers has the

---

[1323] Exhibit Bra-201 ("The Long Reach of King Cotton," The New York Times, 5 August 2003).

[1324] Exhibit Bra-201 ("Your Farm Subsidies Are Strangling Us," Letter from President Amadou Tourmani Touré of Mali and President Balise Compaoré of Burkina Faso to the The New York Times, 11 July 2003).

[1325] Exhibit Bra-201 ("Your Farm Subsidies Are Strangling Us," Letter from President Amadou Tourmani Touré of Mali and President Balise Compaoré of Burkina Faso to the The New York Times, 11 July 2003).

unintended but nevertheless real effect of impoverishing some 10 million rural people in West and Central Africa.[1326]

These articles, and especially the use of these studies, were persuasive evidence that added to Brazil's position in the *Cotton* dispute. Further, it helped frame the position of the C-4 and communicate that position to the world.

Further, in terms of the premise of this section, the direct reference by Brazil to the Cotton Initiative of Benin, Burkina Faso, Chad and Mali is critical to making the point that the two approaches were simultaneously and harmoniously evolving.[1327] Brazil specifically noted that the C-4 was also using the same studies to demonstrate the effects of US subsidies and, in particular, were arguing the significance of its cotton sector in the negotiations.[1328,1329] As a result of the *Cotton* dispute, the C-4 also obtained a victory in the WTO as they had legal proof that US subsidies were hurting other countries' cotton producers. Although the C-4 did not obtain a right to retaliate, it is well-understood that the C-4 expects the US to reform its regime. The outcome of the dispute gave them the legitimacy to say that they support Brazil and, in return, they receive Brazil's support in the negotiation process. For example, Brazil's specific reference to the C-4's Cotton Initiative strengthened its legal argument which, in turn, multiplied the number and dimensions of the issues addressed, and connected the two mechanisms, dispute resolution and negotiation, to create the greater cotton agenda within the WTO.[1330]

From Litigation to Negotiation: The choice by two of the C-4 to participate in the litigation of *Cotton* was precedential. On the other hand, the choice by the C-4 coalition to negotiate its interests through the WTO was not unusual, but the means were quite extraordinary. First, it is important to consider the choice of litigation as opposed to negotiation. Second, concise snapshots of the developments of the C-4 over the past eight (8) years are described, chronologically.

1326 Exhibit Bra-201 ("Your Farm Subsidies Are Strangling Us," Letter from President Amadou Tourmani Touré of Mali and President Balise Compaoré of Burkina Faso to the The New York Times, 11 July 2003).
1327 Exhibit Bra-266 (TN/AG/GEN/4).
1328 Exhibit Bra-266 (TN/AG/GEN/4, p. 4) citing Exhibit Bra-264 ("Prejudice Caused by Industrialized Countries Subsidies to Cotton Sectors in Western and Central Africa," Louis Goreux, June 2003).
1329 Exhibit Bra-266 (TN/AG/GEN/4, pp. 2-3).
1330 "These four African Members propose to remedy the serious prejudice suffered by them, by a decision to eliminate cotton subsidies within three years and request compensation payments during this implementation period." Exhibit Bra-267 (TN/AG/GEN/6) and Exhibit Bra-268 (WT/GC/W/511).

As mentioned in earlier sections of this book, there were a number of perceived barriers the African LDCs recognized as blocking greater participation in the dispute settlement process. Generally, it is established that the C-4 were specifically interested in cotton and not necessarily the greater subsidy regimes of the US (in contrast to Brazil, which had a number of commodities at risk of greater economic worth). The C-4 had a narrower objective that was trying to be achieved. Further, as described by those working with the C-4, timing was of the essence. Given that a round of WTO negotiations had commenced, the C-4 recognized an opportunity to bypass the lengthy dispute settlement process and to prospectively alter trade policies through the multilateral framework. The option to litigate, if so desired, could be done in the future (as has recently been threatened). The perception was that the litigation process would take substantially longer than the negotiation process. As it turned out, this has not been the case.

Further, if the C-4 were to join Brazil,[1331] its participation could delay proceedings, further prejudicing the Members. As a perhaps more beneficial result, the C-4 participated to a limited degree in the *Cotton* case and was able to develop its own argumentation within the negotiation framework that reflected the intentions and interests of the C-4. This independent and tailored approach could, arguably, have further enhanced its reputation in the WTO.[1332]

An additional factor was that the idea of the permanency of the results of the negotiations was attractive to the C-4. Given WTO disputes are retroactive, and negotiations are proactive, the C-4 decided to focus its resources and energies in the direction of negotiation. It could be argued that Brazil was in a preferential position with regards to the fact that it had sufficient resources to devote to the dispute as well as transfer that 'win' to the negotiations. Further, concerns as to whether an investment in the complex dispute settlement mechanism by inexperienced participants, without any certainty that the US would comply with the rulings and recommendations of the DSU, was unappealing. If the C-4 wished to change the future rules, then taking advantage of the fact that a WTO Round of negotiations – a 'development' round no less – would be more expeditious. In line with this economic consideration, a number of studies were being published on the potential economic benefits

---

1331 Another option would be for the C-4 and Brazilian claims to be merged, as in the first initiator scenario.
1332 Interviews with Nicolas Imboden and Anne-Sophie Nivet-Claeys of the iDEAS Centre, Geneva, Switzerland, Fall 2007-Fall 2009 as well as interviews with WTO attorneys and two Members of the WTO Secretariat in July-August, 2009.

that the C-4 could gain from the completion of a Doha deal.[1333] Therefore, the C-4 chose to challenge subsidies that were "in flagrant contradiction with the international commitments made by the countries applying them"[1334] through the legislative mechanism of the WTO.

There were several leveraging outcomes Brazil and the C-4 acquired by pursuing simultaneous, yet divergent approaches. Publicity of the cotton issue was increased significantly. Further, valuable information was gained about the relative expense of participating in both systems to LDCs. Of particular import was the lesson that many of the requisite resources are available to LDCs at nominal costs. For Brazil and the C-4, it is evident that the return on investment in participation may well significantly exceed the costs. Finally, it was learned that the political and legal mechanisms of the WTO are linked and that both should be considered when developing engagement strategies. Given the *Cotton* dispute and the fact that it was framed as a development case, it instantly became politicized by the underlying economic and political asymmetries (discussed in Part 1). In this context, the vulnerability of the C-4 countries in terms of their relatively dependent relationship with the US can be a barrier to the initiation of a WTO dispute and opposition in negotiations given the 'welfare' position of African LDCs.

In terms of assessing the impact that each development (*Cotton* and the Cotton Initiative) had on the mechanism of the other, some effects are evident. First, the current negotiations are indisputably different as a result of the litigation process. The Peace Clause has expired and, if another one is to be negotiated, it will irrefutably differ from the last, given the US was unable to protect itself in spite of its existence. Further, it is now known that export credit guarantees can be disciplined as export subsidies. Finally, there is now a clear roadmap for countries that wish to bring a serious prejudice claim.

1333   Specifically, it was found that developing countries could potentially gain twice the value of what the US would have to spend in order to comply with the *Cotton* dispute, in comparing the two approaches. *See* Anderson, K. and Valenzuela E., "WTO's Doha Cotton Initiative: How Will It Affect Developing Countries?" The World Bank Group, *Trade Note*, No. 27, (30 March 2006) as found in Imboden, N. and Nivet-Claeys, A., "Cotton and the LDCs in the WTO: Negotiations and Litigation, Two Sides of the Same Coin," paper given to author by Anne-Sophie Nivet Claeys of the iDEAS Centre. [original in French; translated by Warwick Wilkins, revised by Nicole Antonietti].

1334   Imboden, N. and Nivet-Claeys, A., "Cotton and the LDCs in the WTO: Negotiations and Litigation, Two Sides of the Same Coin," paper given to author by Anne-Sophie Nivet Claeys of the iDEAS Centre. [original in French; translated by Warwick Wilkins, revised by Nicole Antonietti]. *See*, Sumner, D., "Boxed in – Conflicts between US farm Policies and WTO obligations," *Trade Policy analysis*, Cato Institute, No. 32, (December 2005), p. 25.

Further, the fact that the C-4 chose the route of negotiation is significant[1335] and raises the issue of how to move forward given the rulings in the *Cotton* case. In a 2006 conference on "The Next Steps for Africa," the importance of the cotton issue and use of the *Cotton* dispute by the C-4 was acknowledged. Specifically, it was stated, "[w]ith agriculture at the center of the impasse in the World Trade Organization's (WTO) Doha Development Round (DDR) of multilateral trade talks, the considerable levels of domestic support provided to agricultural sectors in developed countries continue to be one of the main areas of contention for negotiators. Developing countries dependent on agricultural commodity exports have called on the United States and the European Union to reduce or eliminate significant agricultural subsidies."[1336] Speakers and participants emphasized the need for action on multiple fronts. Their suggestions for 'next steps' in Africa included:

- Resuming and rapidly concluding the Doha Round negotiations;
- Urging the US to reform its cotton subsidies, given that these subsidies do play a major role in lowering the international price of cotton, and adversely affect the incomes and livelihoods of African cotton producers;
- Recognizing that the reform of cotton subsidies can best occur through multilateral negotiations;
- Calling for actions by African governments and the private sector to address competitiveness issues;
- Improving donor coordination, and
- Working toward a better donor-recipient dialogue on cotton.[1337]

Some observers and participants have articulated that the *Cotton* dispute is a piece of history; whereas, the conclusion of the Doha Round would go further than mere implementation of a Panel. In this view, negotiations result in policy reforms and rules and, as a result, exceed the scope of the rulings of the Panel. Brazil recognized this and used the dispute to leverage its negotiating position.

1335 For an overview of the issues and dynamics of the Doha Round negotiations, *see*, Das, D., *The Doha Round of Multilateral Trade Negotiations*, Palgrave Macmillan, New York, (2005).
1336 "The Next Steps for Africa: A Report of an International Conference on Cotton," held on 26 October 2006 and hosted by the International Food & Agricultural Trade Policy Council, The Woodrow Wilson International Center for Scholars, and the iDEAS Centre.
1337 "The Next Steps for Africa: A Report of an International Conference on Cotton," held on 26 October 2006 and hosted by the International Food & Agricultural Trade Policy Council, The Woodrow Wilson International Center for Scholars, and the iDEAS Centre.

The C-4 has similarly taken the approach of using the *Cotton* dispute to build leverage and increase attention to its cause.

In order to assess the progress of the Cotton Initiative, the following observations are offered in line with the discussion of the sections, *supra*, on the developments of the C-I and the Subcommittee on Cotton. As mentioned in the latter section, the cotton issue officially became part of the Agricultural Framework in the WTO in the July 2004 Package. The differential status of cotton was confirmed in the December 2005 Hong Kong Declaration.[1338] The series of proposals by the C-4[1339] were well received and supported by virtually all Members,[1340] including the EU.[1341] The only country to oppose the submissions by the C-4 was the US, which continued to claim that the proposals were antithetical to its interests. At the same time, however, the US failed to offer any counter proposals due, in large part, to domestic pressures by influential lobbying organizations, specifically the National Cotton Council. As a result, the US did not fulfill the Hong Kong directive to treat cotton in an "ambitious, rapid and specific manner."

In 2007, additional work was conducted in the Sub-Committee on Cotton[1342] and eventually a proposal was submitted to the Agricultural Committee by the C-4. In fact, it was the only proposal deemed to conform to the directives of the Hong Kong MC. These directives included the following: the elimination of all cotton export subsidies by developed countries, the granting of duty and

---

1338 For an analysis of what was considerable for LDCs to gain from DDA involvement leading up to Hong Kong, *see*, Ismail, F., "How Can Least-Developed Countries and Other Small, Weak and Vulnerable Economies Also Gain from the Doha Development Agenda on the Road to Hong Kong?" Journal of World Trade, Volume 40 No. 1, (2006), pp. 37–68.

1339 For example, TN/AG/SCC/1 (29 March 2005). *See also*, "African Group Proposes Cotton Distortions Scrapped by September," WTO (29 April 2005), TN/AG/SCC/GEN/2.

1340 "WTO Members Express Some Support for Cotton Proposal," International Centre for Trade and Sustainable Development (ICTSD), (3 May 2006).

1341 *See*, "Mixed Reception for 'Cotton Four' Domestic Support Proposal," WTO, (27 March 2006), TN/AG/SCC/GEN/4 and "Wide Support for Much of 'Cotton Four' Domestic Support Proposal," WTO (28 April 2006).

1342 WTO, "Ouagadougou Declaration on the Sectoral Initiative in Favour of Cotton," Communication from Furkina Faso, (12 January 2007), TN/AG/SCC/GEN/7, WTO, "Director-General's Consultative Framework Mechanism on Cotton," High-Level Session, (16 March 2007), TN/AG/SCC/W/7, WTO, and "High-Level Session on Cotton," Communication from Argentina, (26 March 2007), TN/AG/SCC/GEN/8, and WTO, "Implementation of the Development Assistance Aspects of the Cotton-Related Decisions in the 2004 July Package and Paragraph 12 of the Hong Kong Ministerial Declaration," Item 2C: Coherence Betweeen Trade and Development Aspects: Update on the Development Aspects of Cotton, (14 December 2007), TN/AG/SCC/W/9.

quota-free access by developed nations to LDC cotton exports, and more rapid and aggressive reductions in cotton support programs. Chairman Falconer of the Agriculture Committee specifically noted the efforts by the C-4 to contribute to the progressive movement of the cotton agenda and assist with evolution of agricultural negotiations. Chairman Falconer reminded the Members that "the Cotton-4 proposal remained on the table."[1343] As a result, it seemed that the pathway to negotiations on cotton had been cleared.

2008: The cotton issue did not receive considerable attention at the July 2008 WTO ministerial; however, subsequent consultations among the four main parties concerned (the US, EU, Brazil, and the C-4 countries) have helped build better understanding of the issues and of one another.[1344] However, by the end of 2008, DG Pascal Lamy officially announced that cotton had become the 'litmus test' for Members' commitment to the Doha Development Round[1345] and work between the Director General and the Sub-Committee on Cotton continued.[1346] At the subsequent July ministerial breakdown, Lamy specifically sought answers on *inter alia* the US and EU overall trade-distorting domestic support.[1347]

2009: Finally, in view of the ongoing Doha Round negotiations concerning reductions in trade-distorting domestic subsidies and the elimination of export subsidies altogether, another key aspect of the *Cotton* Arbitration is its findings quantifying the amount of adverse market effects of the U.S. subsidies. For example, in the case of the marketing loan and counter-cyclical subsidies for only cotton, the Arbitrator found that the total effects of the significant price suppression totaled $2.905 billion in a representative year Marketing Year 2005. These are huge amounts by any measure. The size of such effects can create *moral suasion* and generate international outrage at the

---

1343 *See*, WTO, "Implementation of the Development Assistance Aspects of the Cotton-Related Decisions in the 2004 July Package and Paragraph 12 of the Hong Kong Ministerial Declaration," TN/AG/SCC/W/8 (11 July 2007).

1344 Crawford Falconer, former Chair of the WTO Agricultural Negotiations Committee as "A US-Africa Dialogue on the Cotton Trade," sponsored by the Carnegie Endowment and iDEAS Centre, Washington, D.C. (20 July 2009).

1345 Lamy, P. "Cotton is 'litmus test' for development commitment in Doha Round," in a speech at the UNCTAD High Level Multi Stakeholder Meeting on Cotton, Geneva (2 December 2008).

1346 *See*, WTO, "Director-General's Consultative Framework Mechanism on Cotton," Table of Project Proposals by Cotton Proponents, (10 November 2008), WT/CFMC/W/46.

1347 "An Unusual Break Down," *Washington Trade Daily*, Volume 17 No. 155, ©Trade Reports International Group, Maryland, (4 August 2008).

impact of such illegality, particularly on developing and least developed countries.[1348] For example, Australia[1349] expressed its indignation at the US' continued non-compliance in a statement submitted to the Dispute Settlement Body (DSB) of the WTO, after the publication of the Arbitrator's decision.[1350] The statement supported the significant findings of the Arbitrator, including findings that farmers outside the US suffered over US$17 billion in damages from 1999–2005 as a result of US WTO-illegal subsidies.[1351] In addition, Australia projected that those farmers will continue to suffer similar damages under the 2008 Farm Bill.[1352] Further, Australia emphasized the fact that the *Cotton* decisions only reflect a few of the subsidies available to the agricultural sector in the US.[1353] Australia also stressed the point that a suspension of concessions or obligations is no substitution for full implementation of the recommendations as a means of bringing the US into compliance with its WTO commitments.[1354] The statement concluded with a call on the U.S. to "implement the rulings and

---

[1348] As discussed, *infra*, after the publication of the Arbitrator's decision, Australia submitted a formal statement to the Dispute Settlement Body of the WTO. The statement included the following quote from the Cairns Group's July 20th, 2008 Communiqué: "major subsidizers have provided...trade distorting support – effectively denying the opportunity for others, including low income producers in developing countries, to enter the market." Statement of Australia, "*United States – Subsidies on Upland Cotton: Reports of the Arbitrator*," (25 September 2009). This is explicit recognition by the 19-Member Cairns Group of the global adverse effect U.S. subsidies has on producers in developing countries.

[1349] Australia was a third party to the *Cotton* dispute.

[1350] *Ibid.*, p. 1. Important to note is the citation from the Arbitrator's decision, quoted in the statement by Australia, which reads in part: "[T]he specific design and structure of the subsidies at issue, as they have been maintained over a significant period of time, is such as to have created an artificial and persisting competitive advantage for U.S. producers over all other operators.... [T]his has a significant trade-distorting impact, not just on the U.S. domestic market, but on the world market in these products." Again, this is explicit recognition by the Arbitrator (and Australia) of the global adverse effect U.S. subsidies has on the world market.

[1351] Statement of Australia, "*United States – Subsidies on Upland Cotton: Reports of the Arbitrator*," (25 September 2009), p. 2.

[1352] Statement of Australia, "*United States – Subsidies on Upland Cotton: Reports of the Arbitrator*," (25 September 2009), p. 1. Such damages are projected, given no substantial positive changes were made to the 2008 Farm Bill.

[1353] Statement of Australia, "*United States – Subsidies on Upland Cotton: Reports of the Arbitrator*," (25 September 2009). p. 2.

[1354] Statement of Australia, "*United States – Subsidies on Upland Cotton: Reports of the Arbitrator*," (25 September 2009), p. 2.

recommendations of the DSB in this long-running dispute without further delay."[1355]

The cross-retaliation section of the Arbitrator's report is clearly both new and very important in that it could give more strength to the ability of smaller countries like those of the C-4 to secure compliance from larger countries. In the worst case scenario, as reported in December of 2009, "Burkina Faso and other West African cotton producers threatened in Geneva to launch WTO litigation against Washington over the US subsidies, saying 'we cannot wait forever because our entire cotton industry will appear.'"[1356]

The C-4 policies on cotton remain nearly identical to what was first proposed in 2003. Specifically, what the C-4 represents, and continues to request in the negotiations, was summarized last year by His Excellency Mamadou Sanou, Minister of Trade, Entrepreneurship and Handicraft, Burkina Faso, at an international conference "A US-Africa Dialogue on the Cotton Trade." As the Coordinator of the C-4, he outlined the C-4 countries' cotton policies as such:[1357]

- The cotton industry serves an economically and socially critical purpose in the C4 countries by providing income and employment in poor, rural areas.
- Structural aid to enhance the production and marketing of cotton is vital. Short-term aid should be targeted at providing a safety net for producers during years of poor production; however, it should not distort long-term growth.
- Development and structural assistance cannot be a substitute for equitable trading rules and a level playing field in the international cotton market.
- The resolution of an aggressive cotton agreement in the WTO will not only improve the welfare of C4 cotton farmers; it will also demonstrate the ability of smaller economies to join together and have their voices heard.
- The African countries have chosen negotiation rather than litigation to find a solution to their cotton problem. They have made concrete proposals and have obtained an agreement at the Hong Kong ministerial that cotton

---

1355 Statement of Australia, "*United States – Subsidies on Upland Cotton: Reports of the Arbitrator*," (25 September 2009), p. 2.
1356 "Calls Grow to Smash WTO Deal into Digestible Pieces," The New York Times, by Reuters (3 December 2009).
1357 His Excellency Mamadou Sanou, Minister of Trade, Entrepreneurship and Handicraft of Burkina Faso, and Coordinator of the C-4 at "A US-Africa Dialogue on the Cotton Trade," sponsored by the Carnegie Endowment and iDEAS Centre, Washington, D.C. (20 July 2009).

should be treated "ambitiously, expeditiously and specifically." They are still waiting for a response from the United States and the EU.

To that end, it is not a question of what the C-4 needs or hopes to aim from a successful conclusion of the Doha Agenda. What remains is to know what the US needs in order to cooperate at the international level and implement consistent domestic measures at the national level.

Present Situation: As reported in the news, "[a]t present, the Cotton Initiative is still parked. The US is still insisting that the Africans 'give something.' USTR Susan Schwab[1358] even tantalized them in the last meetings, remarking that they 'have the numbers, etc. on cotton....'" Given the many collapses, impasses, and most recent walk out by the G20, the question must be posed whether the Doha Round is overloaded with too many issues? This is quite possible. Given Members chose to negotiate the Doha Round as a 'single undertaking,' all issues (and therefore interests) are considered. Since the WTO requires consensus by its membership, the fact that the "Doha oxcart is so fully loaded" decreases the ability to build consensus in the negotiations.[1359] Therefore, it is reasonable to assume that nothing can be agreed upon everything is agreed upon. "The US and other countries with large cotton subsidies have not yet offered specific cotton proposals. It seems that real negotiations have yet to start. There can be no progress without engagement in concrete negotiations by all parties."[1360]

However, in assessing what issues may be untied from the interwoven interests of Members so that the agenda can be scaled down to some degree,[1361] one conclusion may be reached – cotton is not the issue that can be set aside. If agriculture is the key to the success of the Doha Round, as many scholars and practitioners believe[1362] – only cotton will turn that key. As Nicolas Imboden and Anne-Sophie Nivet-Claeys wrote, "...there will be no Doha without

---

1358 Susan Schwab was the primary USTR negotiator at the time. She was succeeded by the Ron Kirk.
1359 Personal communication, August 2009.
1360 Crawford Falconer, former Chair of the WTO Agricultural Negotiations Committee at "A US-Africa Dialogue on the Cotton Trade," sponsored by the Carnegie Endowment and iDEAS Centre, Washington, D.C. (20 July 2009).
1361 This is not to convey that the negotiations need not remain ambitious. It is understood that, in order for the major Members of the WTO to make gains, a considerable number of areas of the negotiations need to continue.
1362 Anderson, K. and Martin, W., "Agriculture: the Key to Success of the Doha Round," as found in Newfarmer, R., *Trade, Doha, and Development: A Window Into the Issues*, The World Bank, (2006), pp. 77–84.

cotton."[1363] The economic, political, and legal consequences of doing so would be grave. This is the issue of the following two chapters. For now, and in the context of the issues and development addressed in this chapter, it is simply concluded that, in light of the two case studies presented here, a settlement between the US and Brazil, as reflected in the recent Memorandum of Understanding (MOU), is not the desired or acceptable result to the cotton issue for the Doha Development Agenda. African LDCs need relief from the severe negative effects of cotton subsidies, not relatively nominal monetary annual payoffs while subsidies remain in place. As summarized by one scholar on the effect of the MOU on the C-4:

> One can also anticipate the dire consequences of such a fund on sub-Saharan cotton producers. Even if part of the financial pool is destined to flow to them, the voice of the coalition of Benin, Burkina Faso, Chad and Mali was not being heard at all during the WTO negotiations. Thus one of the organization's major problems was revealed: the fact that the voice of the understaffed and inexperienced country delegations tend to be almost a non-factor when it comes to cotton pricing. The problem appears even more catastrophic when one learns through Inter Press Service that, "Studies by international organizations show that the total abolition of U.S. subsidies would increase the world cotton price by 14 percent." According to the charity Oxfam, this would translate into additional revenue that could feed one million more children per year, or pay the school fees of two million children in West Africa.[1364]

It is hoped that the strategy employed by Brazil and the C-4 to retrospectively challenge not only how and to what extent the US *had* been violating its WTO commitments through the legal process, but the prospective precautionary measure of ensuring that greater commitments and stronger disciplines are adopted in the Doha negotiation will work.[1365] Further, the opportunity for

---

1363 Imboden, N. and Nivet-Claeys, A., "Cotton and the LDCs in the WTO: Negotiations and Litigation, Two Sides of the Same Coin," paper given to author by Anne-Sophie Nivet Claeys of the iDEAS Centre. [original in French; translated by Warwick Wilkins, revised by Nicole Antonietti].

1364 Blossier, F., "The WTO Cotton Dispute: How the US is Trying to Escape International Trade Regulation while Brazil Asserts itself as a Regional Leader," *Council on Hemispheric Affairs*, (1 June 2010).

1365 For a brief overview of what is perceived to have developed in the Doha Round, *see*, Bouet, A. and Laborde, D., "Eight Years of Doha Trade Talks: Where Do We Stand?" International Food Policy Research Institute, IFPRI Issue Brief 61 (November 2009).

extensive use of the system by LDCs, as demonstrated by the C-4, should instill confidence in other developing and least developed countries to increase their participation in the system. Barriers to the legal, political, media, and practical support have been consequently taken down by the LDCs. If the Doha Round is not completed, the fact that the progress made by Brazil and the C-4 failed to garner significant gains might further dissuade developing countries and LDCs from participating in the future. A meaningful and expedient conclusion to Doha is that much more important for that reason. If the inequities of the Uruguay Round[1366] are to be remedied and a fairer and improved system is to result, action must be taken in the Doha Round and at the domestic level of developed nations to particularly address the interests of the C-4. As even recognized by US' trade representative to Africa, "Only with reduced trade barriers can we open the world economy and reduce poverty worldwide."[1367]

1366 For an critique on the Uruguay Round and discussion on possibilities of the Doha Round, see, Lal Das, B., *The Current Negotiations in the WTO: Options, Opportunities and Risks for Developing Countries*, Zed Books, London (2005).

1367 USTR for Africa Florizelle Liser at "The Next Steps for Africa: A Report of an International Conference on Cotton," held on 26 October 2006 and hosted by the International Food & Agricultural Trade Policy Council, The Woodrow Wilson International Center for Scholars, and the iDEAS Centre.

CHAPTER 8

Political Limits on Implementation in the United States

The dispute settlement and legislative mechanisms of the WTO differ dramatically from the process of formulating domestic legislation, in terms of the pressures and constraints faced.[1368] As generally known, "all politics are local." Trade politics are no exception. This is an important feature to consider when analyzing why the US has not come into greater compliance and what complexities remain in reforming US agricultural policies. Given the local nature of politics and the especially long history and political entrenchment of the cotton lobby in the US political system, the following questions are important to consider: (1) why should the US alter their farm policies? and (2) what would happen if they do not? Answers to these questions are offered in Chapter 9. First, Chapter 8 describes how some compliance has already taken place and what this might mean in terms of the willingness on the part of the US to come into greater conformity with the rulings and recommendations of the DSB. Although beginning with this more optimistic view, several cautionary points are made in terms of the domestic hurdles that remain. Where possible, suggestions for alternative solutions are proffered as well as the reframing of the issues and the implications for non-action. Though the *Cotton* case has not yet been resolved, this chapter ends on a 'high note' to the extent that it discusses the importance for a successful conclusion to the Doha Development Round and the optimistic signs that bilateral dispute resolution between the US and Brazil is currently taking place, as evidenced by the Memorandum of Understanding and subsequent June Framework recently entered into between the two countries.

1368 For greater analysis on this issue as well as the relationship of WTO and domestic law, *see*, Jackson, J., *The Jurisprudence of GATT & the WTO*, Cambridge University Press, (2000), pp. 195–259 and 367–372. Further, for an assessment of the domestic structures of the US (and EU) in relation to international trade, *see*, Molyneux, C., *Domestic Structures and International Trade: The Unfair Trade Instruments of the United States and European Union*, Hart Publishing, Portland, Oregon, (2001).

8.1 Reform in the US and Its Limitations

'If the United States can go to the moon, which is rather complicated, one would think it could figure out a way, if it wanted, to help its cotton producers, without hurting US farmers in Africa,' Francois Traore, President of Burkina Faso's National Cotton Producers Union.[1369]

After considering the economic and political backdrop of the cotton issue and learning of the patent non-compliance by the US in not conforming its domestic agricultural policies to its international commitments, as established by law, the question must be posed why the US chooses not to alter its domestic law. In short, there are limitations on the ability of the US Government to change its policies given the pressures placed on it by interest groups – a powerful element to the workings of the US political process. However, in comparing the concentrated benefits to a few parties to the more dispersed costs to many, and the potential threat of additional WTO disputes brought against the present subsidy regime,[1370] compliance should be seriously considered. Further, two examples of the willingness by the US to effectuate the needed change are encouraging. The elimination of the US' Step 2 program in reaction to the *Cotton* dispute, as well as the Memorandum of Understanding that was recently entered into between Brazil and US, indicate that compliance is possible. As the quote above indicates, if the US is dedicated to the concept of agricultural reform, agricultural reform in the US will be possible.

To develop this argument, Chapter 8 first describes the US' reactions from the US cotton lobby, the greater agricultural sector, and the US taxpayer to the *Cotton* dispute as well as the greater cotton issue within the context of the Doha Development Agenda.[1371] Next, an explanation based on public choice theory is offered as to why the US subsidy regime has seen only limited reform and, in some aspects, evolved to be an even more trade-distorting threat to the interests of the developing world. Thereafter, an analysis of potential threats the US might face in terms of additional WTO disputes, if it continues to not comply with the rulings and recommendations of the DSB is offered. To that

---

[1369] As submitted by Brazil in its September 2003 *Further Submission*, Exhibit Bra-201 ("The Long Reach of King Cotton," The New York Times, 5 August 2003).
[1370] Further considerations on this issues are set forth in Chapter 9.
[1371] For reading on the poverty and the formulation of trade policy, *see*, Cline, W., *Trade Policy and Global Poverty*, Institute for International Economics, Washington, D.C., (2004).

end, the section concludes with a description of what Brazil and the US have agreed to as an interim conclusion to the *Cotton* dispute.

Pursuant to the DSB rulings and recommendations, there are five implementation options available to the US: "eliminate the subsidy; reduce the subsidy to diminish its adverse effect; revise the program function to reduce the linkage between the subsidy and the adverse effect (aka, decoupling); pay a mutually acceptable compensatory payment to offset the adverse effects of the subsidy; or suffer the consequences of trade retaliation."[1372] The following is a description of reactions by the US to the *Cotton* dispute and the options proscribed.[1373] As set forth in this section, the US has chosen none of these options and has pursued alternative approaches to trying to maintain its subsidy regime while, at the same time, continuing to participate in the WTO system and preserve relations with Brazil.

Reactions by the US: The *Cotton* dispute has caused significant concern among agricultural interest groups of the US, and perhaps in no more significant group than the National Cotton Council (NCC). In blatant contempt for[1374] the Arbitrator's decision, the Chairman of the NCC, Jay Hardwick, commended the USTR on its efforts to protect the cotton sector's national interests in Geneva three months after the decision was circulated, and boldly exclaimed that the C-4 needed to cooperate with the US, by increasing market access for US goods, and to concentrate on its own internal issues.[1375] The NCC, *via* the USTR, is contesting the validity of US participation in the Doha agricultural negotiations by stating that US agriculture cannot "find any benefit to a Doha Round," without first obtaining increased US market access into developing countries.[1376] In other words, the US would like to use its *Cotton* loss as a bargaining chip to negotiate WTO compliance for greater market access, even

---

1372 "Brazil's WTO Case Against the US Cotton Program: A Brief Overview," Congressional Research Service, (29 April 2008).

1373 For an analysis on compliance issues within the WTO system, *see*, Choi, W., "To Comply or Not Comply? – Non-Implementation Problems in the WTO Dispute Settlement System," *Journal of World Trade*, Vol. 41 No. 5, (2007), pp. 1043–1071.

1374 For an excellent primer on the US political process and the role of lobbyists, *see*, Redman, E., *The Dance of Legislation: An Insider's Account of the Workings of the United States Senate*, University of Washington Press, (2001). Further, the following handout is available as an informational reference guide to the various agencies involved in US trade, *see* http://www.itcdc.com/PDFs/abcs-of-dc.pdf.

1375 Nelson, T., "NCC Chairman Commends USTR and Urges African Cooperation," National Cotton Council of America, *News*, (4 December 2009).

1376 Nelson, T., "NCC Chairman Commends USTR and Urges African Cooperation," National Cotton Council of America, *News*, (4 December 2009).

though the US is already obligated by law to implement the DSB's rulings and recommendations (this point is discussed more, *infra*.).[1377]

Further, NCC Vice President Craig Brown noted that price suppression in the world market was actually being caused by Brazil *et al* and that the US and Africa are suffering as a result.[1378] Further, Mr. Brown dismissed the recent threat by the C-4 to bring a similar dispute against the US at the WTO, stating that the group needed to "re-evaluate who is actually distorting world cotton trade and work with the United States as it attempts to (1) help reform the West African cotton production infrastructure; and (2) obtain meaningful market access from the largest cotton users in the world."[1379]

As argued in earlier portions of this book, the *Cotton* decisions extend beyond the US cotton sector. The rulings threaten non-cotton producers who receive similar significant subsidies from the US government. As such, it is reasonable to assume that a "circling the wagon" syndrome has afflicted the greater agricultural sector in the US. Unfortunately, this could have real and adverse effects on progress in the Doha Round, given even greater force will be exerted in the negotiations with the potential for 'freezing' negotiators in all areas of agriculture. Even more adversely consequential is the fact that most of the opposition could be derived from non-exporting agricultural lobby groups who may develop a negative reaction to the WTO and the liberalization of the WTO.

The assumption that this has been transpiring in the US is reasonable, as reflected in the fact that the US seems to be heading in the wrong direction. Specifically, the 2008 Farm Bill (discussed, *infra*, in the context of future potential challenges) has proven more trade distorting than the 2002 Farm Bill,[1380] which was recognized as having undone nearly all the progress made after the Uruguay Round. One exception was compliance by the US in eliminating the Step 2 program in 2006. At the time, partial implementation demonstrated recognition by the US of the need to comply in order to add legitimacy to the system and be perceived as a cooperative player in the Doha negotiations. Further, it is known that resisting implementation is not in the overall interest of the US. There was hope that this was an indication of US willingness to bring

---

1377 For an example of US pro-cotton sentiment, *see*, "Cotton is Key Fabric of High Ground Economy," *Business Images High Ground of Texas*, (27 March 2006).
1378 Nelson, T., "NCC Chairman Commends USTR and Urges African Cooperation," National Cotton Council of America, *News*, (4 December 2009).
1379 Nelson, T., "NCC Chairman Commends USTR and Urges African Cooperation," National Cotton Council of America, *News*, (4 December 2009).
1380 Even in the author's local newspaper, this very issue was addressed. Specifically, *see*, "Cotton Subsidies in '07 Farm Bill Prompt Global Trade Concerns," *Times-News*, Twin Falls, Idaho USA (11 November 2007), E3.

its domestic measures into conformity with the DSB's rulings. However, this program, and its resulting effects, was added back under a different name in the 2008 Farm Bill,[1381] despite significant consternation, alternative proposals, and a Presidential veto.[1382] The US recognized its non-compliance.

A brief by the US Congressional Research Service entitled, "Brazil's WTO Case against the US Cotton Program: A Brief Overview," acknowledges, and explicitly details, the extent to which the US is not in compliance. In the report's description of the 2008 Farm Bill, it is noted that, although the Step 2 program was eliminated and efforts have been made to export credit guarantees,[1383] the Farm Bill does not "address the serious prejudice charge related to price-contingent subsidies. Instead...offer higher levels of price and income support that could potentially aggravate the perception (if not the reality) of "serious prejudice" in the marketplace."[1384] Specifically, the report goes on to describe various parts of the Farm Bill to illuminate its vulnerability to WTO challenge. The Farm Bill would (and did),

- extend current marketing loan provisions and the CCP program;
- raise both loan rates and target prices for several commodities, while only lowering (marginally) the target price for upland cotton; offer producers the choice of revenue-based support options in lieu of CCP (which includes significantly higher per-acre revenue guarantees for cotton than under the current 2002 farm bill);
- change the world price used by USDA to determine cotton marketing loan repayment rates from a Northern European price to a Far Eastern price, which presumably would result in larger payments under the provisions of the program;
- and create a new cotton-user payment of 4 cents per pound. (This payment appears similar to the WTO-illegal Step 2 payment except that cotton from all origins (not just domestic sources) is eligible for the payment. Since the United States imports very little cotton, most payments would still likely go to domestically sources cotton. As a result, this subtle technical loophole

---

1381 "USDA Finalizes Cotton Program to Replace Step 2 Rejected by WTO," *Inside US Trade*, (7 November 2008).

1382 For background reading on the issues and debate leading up to the '2007' Farm Bill, *see*, "Looking Forward: A More Market-Oriented 2007 Farm Act," informa economics: an AGRA informa company, McLean, VA (February 2007).

1383 Significantly, in 2005, the US began to scale back its subsidies. *See*, "West Africa versus the United States on Cotton Subsidies: How, Why and What Next?" *Journal of Modern African Studies*, Vol. 44 No. 2 (2006), pp. 251–274.

1384 "Brazil's WTO Case Against the US Cotton Program: A Brief Overview," Congressional Research Service, (29 April 2008).

might be subject to a WTO challenge if it survives the congressional legislative process and emerges as part of a new farm bill.)[1385]

In addition, the report mentions additional non-compliant features of the Farm Bill and concludes that "this glaring retention of the status quo has important WTO implications, as both Canada and Brazil have recently initiated WTO cases against the United States charging that the United States has exceeded its total AMS limit on several occasion in recent years if direct payments are included in the AMS calculation."[1386] Although ultimately overridden, the adoption of the intended 2007 Farm Bill was not passed until 2008, and after its veto by US President George W. Bush.[1387] In a statement by Agriculture Deputy Secretary Chuck Conner on the President's veto, the following acknowledgements were made:

> The President has stated time and time again that he would not accept a farm bill that fails to reform farm programs at a time when farm income and crop prices are setting records, and he has remained true to his word. It is irresponsible to ask the American taxpayer who is struggling to make ends meet, to subsidize farm couples and those who make more than a million dollars a year. This is bad policy, and unfair.
>
> Unfortunately, this bill continues to support programs that benefit those who do not need it, and because of this, our non-farmers in America are justifiably questioning the rationale and fairness behind farm bills in general.
>
> Yet Congress decided to go in another direction, and sent the President a bill that grossly overspends in typical Washington, DC fashion.[1388]

This is indicative of the power of the agricultural sector in lobbying and the argumentative nature of the farm bill, as well as the growing concern and

---

1385 "Brazil's WTO Case Against the US Cotton Program: A Brief Overview," Congressional Research Service, (29 April 2008).
1386 The report references two additional analyses of these two challenges, CRS Report RS22724 and RL22728. "Brazil's WTO Case Against the US Cotton Program: A Brief Overview," Congressional Research Service, (29 April 2008). It should be noted that although Canada and Brazil began a challenge against the US TAMS based primarily on the peace clause findings of the *Cotton* case, styled as a challenge to 'corn,' higher prices by the time the case was initiated obviated the claim.
1387 Noteworthy is the fact that some of the greatest levels of cotton subsidies go to home state constituents of President Bush, cotton farmers in Texas.
1388 USDA, "Statement by Agriculture Deputy Secretary Chuck Conner on the President's Veto of the Farm Bill," Statement Release No. 0133.08 (21 May 2008).

awareness about the disparities structurally created and fueled by US Farm Bills. Therefore, the 2008 Farm Bill further exacerbated the dynamics and complicated agricultural negotiations at the WTO.[1389]

Why is it the case that agricultural policies in the US are becoming progressively more distortive? One rationale can be attributed to the vastly different approaches and objectives of the US agricultural and trade policies. Although overlap is considerable, it is the case that the two do not adequately coordinate, as evidenced by the conflict between US trade policy and the Farm Bill in 2007,[1390] and particularly demonstrated in the case of cotton. Further, in order to analyze why the US continues to head in the direction of non-reform, it is important to consider what considerations in the past have led to the current farm policy. The present situation for why the US has not taken steps to comply with the WTO is somewhat analogous to the position the US was in when it undid many of the policy changes it had after the Uruguay Round. As Daniel Sumner explained,

> The attempt to limit farm subsidies proved politically unsustainable for several reasons. First, prices really were quite low from 1998 through 2001, and many farmers have faced major losses without additional government support. Second, budget deficits that had been a major factor in limiting farm program support in the 1980s and 1990s were much less of an issue from 1998 through 2001. Finally, the weakened administration in the late 1990s was willing to accommodate farm interests in states from which Senate votes were needed.[1391]

In approaching the question of whether, how and when to implement WTO compliant domestic agricultural policies, the US has indicated that it is waiting for the completion of the Doha Development Round.[1392] John Weekes

---

1389 "New Farm Bill Program Complicates Compliance with US Doha Offer," *Inside US Trade* (23 may 2008).
1390 Krist, W., "Trade Policy and the Farm Bill," Woodrow Wilson International Center for Scholars, [paper adapted 8 August 2007 to reflect 27 July 2007 *Cotton* dispute and passage of House version of '2007' Farm Bill]. As emphasized, greater consistency with US international obligations needed to be incorporated in the '2007'Farm Bill.
1391 *See,* Sumner, D., "Farm Subsidy Tradition and Modern Agricultural Realities," Paper for American Enterprise Institute Project on Agricultural Policy for the 2007 Farm Bill and Beyond <http://aic.ucdavis.edu/research/farmbill07/aeibriefs/20070515_sumnerRationales final.pdf > last visited 30 June 2010.
1392 For related background reading, *see,* MacDonald, S., "The New Agricultural Trade Negotiations: Background and Issues for the US Cotton Sector," Economic Research Service, USDA, Cotton and Wool Situation and Outlook/CWS-2000, (November 2000).

explained why a Member may choose delayed implementation, basing his opinion on his previous tenure as Canada's Ambassador to the WTO.[1393] Specifically, he stated, "One of the reasons for the slow adoption, or the non-adoption, of panel reports during the Uruguay Round was because the governments against whom the findings were made wanted to avoid the difficult challenges of implementing the results. It became apparent that the process of implementation would be facilitated by doing so 'in the context of the conclusion of the Round.' Indeed a number of reports were adopted with exactly that sort of proviso."[1394] In considering the point in the context of the present negotiations, Weekes concluded, "Implementing politically difficult findings is much easier in the context of a larger package of agreements. This is a political reality."[1395] In the case of the US, this is particularly so given that implementation requires the passage of legislation by Congress.[1396] Negotiated results set implementation on a "fast track," while the implementation of "DSB findings require separate action by Congress."[1397] Weekes' perspective aligns with most who recognize that at its basic function, the WTO is a forum for managing trade relations among its Members. Further, in terms of the development of goodwill in the context of Doha negotiations, working closer with Brazil (and, therefore, the G20), it is arguable that the US can further improve its broader standing in the South and with developing countries.[1398] In considering the present Brazil-US situation, the following advice can be applicable,

---

1393 Weekes, J., "The External Dynamics of the Dispute Settlement Understanding: Its Impact on Trade Relations and Trade Negotiations, An Initial Analysis," Sidley Austin (23 May 2004), presented at the *Conference on International Trade and Dispute Settlement* in Montevideo on 15 April 2004. (Paper is on file with author).

1394 The *Oilseeds* dispute is a perfect example.

1395 Weekes, J., "The External Dynamics of the Dispute Settlement Understanding: Its Impact on Trade Relations and Trade Negotiations, An Initial Analysis," Sidley Austin (23 May 2004), presented at the *Conference on International Trade and Dispute Settlement* in Montevideo on 15 April 2004. (Paper is on file with author).

1396 For a greater discussion on the relationship and process of implementing WTO rules in US law, *see*, Barcelo, J., "The Status of WTO Rules in US Law," Cornell Law School: Legal Studies Research Paper Series, No. 06–004 (6 January 2006) available at http://ssrn.com/abstract=887757.

1397 Weekes, J., "The External Dynamics of the Dispute Settlement Understanding: Its Impact on Trade Relations and Trade Negotiations, An Initial Analysis," Sidley Austin (23 May 2004), presented at the *Conference on International Trade and Dispute Settlement* in Montevideo on 15 April 2004. (Paper is on file with author).

1398 In particular, relations with Venezuela, Argentina, Ecuador, and Bolivia have become opponents to US influence.

WTO Members should be thinking of how to use the Round to facilitate completion of the unfinished business of implementation. Of course, it will be necessary to avoid the appearance that somehow WTO Members are "paying" in negotiation for the removal of "illegal" measures. This should not be too difficult. After all it is widely known that the mercantilist rhetoric surrounding trade negotiations is just that – rhetoric. Furthermore governments which have "won" may also find it more advantageous that the findings be implemented through negotiation because they will have a say in how it is done. Implementation of panel findings is a matter in the first instance for the losing party to undertake. As has been seen in several WTO cases such implementation is not always done in a manner that results in compliance.[1399]

Additional reforms that need to be made are the removal of programs that cause serious prejudice and the alteration of the circumstances under which direct payments are made, as determined by the Green Box definition. Further, the US needs to remove all remaining illegal export subsidies. These are changes that are overdue, from the perspective of the dispute process, and are not contingent upon the outcome of the Doha Development Round. Once the Doha Round is completed, the parameters set therein should be used in the formulation of the 2012 Farm Bill. Although still in a speculation phase, where an actual outcome is unknown returning to the fact that at one point there was partial-implementation by the US, gives hope that the lobby is not intractable.[1400]

The *Cotton* case demonstrated the enormous cost of the US cotton support programs, not only to Brazil, the developing world, but to US taxpayers as well. These costs have become more apparent in light of the Arbitrator's decision in the *Cotton* case. Specifically, the media and scholarly attention has been re-mobilized and significant attention has been given to the cotton issue in the US press.[1401] This has further enhanced awareness about the global effects of

---

1399 Weekes, J., "The External Dynamics of the Dispute Settlement Understanding: Its Impact on Trade Relations and Trade Negotiations, An Initial Analysis," Sidley Austin (23 May 2004), presented at the *Conference on International Trade and Dispute Settlement* in Montevideo on 15 April 2004. (Paper is on file with author).

1400 For the most recent US assessment of the cotton issue, *see*, Schnepf, R., "Brazil's WTO Case Against the US Cotton Program," Congressional Research Service, RL 32571, (30 June 2010).

1401 *See*, Bassett, T., "Untangling the Threads: Africa, the United States and the Cotton Controversy," The Illinois International Review, University of Illinois, (July 2008) at http://www.ips.uiuc.edu/ilint/mt/iir/online/2008/07/bassett.html.

US subsidies and their costs to US taxpayers.[1402] Also, the Arbitrator's decision was circulated a few months before it became known that an increase in US cotton exports is expected, with almost all "US cotton headed for the export market."[1403] Further, in light of the latest Memorandum of Understanding (MOU) between the US-Brazil (discussed below), the issue is being increasingly framed as an issue of importance to US taxpayers and not just poor African farmers or Brazilian cotton growers. The increasing awareness of the costs of the programs has caused increased concern and even indignation by the American citizenry.

In the wake of the recent MOU between the US and Brazil,[1404] the increased awareness that US taxpayers will not only have to continue to subsidize US producers, but will be required to pay nearly $150 million annually to Brazilian cotton farmers.[1405] Given the vulnerable economic climate in the US, the news has not been well received in the general community. In considering the situation from the US-Africa perspective, some news coverage has emphasized the fact that Benin and Chad will not meaningfully benefit from the arrangement. An interesting perspective was submitted by Brazil, regarding US-Africa relations, "...Americans would be horrified to learn that all the good

---

1402 See, "Pay to Play in Trade," *FinancialTimes.com*, Comment Editorial (21 June 2010) at http://www.ft.com/cms/s/0/3f038526-7d68-11df-a0f5-00144feabdc0.html, Rauch, J., "Why You're Bribing Brazilian Farmers," *National Journal Magazine*, (29 May 2010), Simoes, C. and Soliani, A., "Brazil Won't Retaliate Against US over Cotton Aid," *Bloomberg Businessweek*, (20 June 2010), Lincicome, S., "The Madness of Cotton; the Feds Want US Taxpayers to Subsidize Brazilian Farmers," *Wall Street Journal*, (21 May 2010), at http://online.wsj.com/article/NA_WSJ_PUB:SB10001424052748703961104575226290221967322.html and "My (and Your) Tax Dollars to Subsidize Brazilian Cotton Farmers Indefinitely," (21 June 2010) at http://lincicome.blogspot.com/2010/06/my-and-your-tax-dollars-to-subsidize.html.

1403 See, *Washington Trade Daily*, 7 December 2009, wherein it quotes USDA Chief Economist Joseph Glauber as having said that "the Agriculture Department is projecting an increase in US cotton exports, with almost all US cotton headed for the export market. The department is estimating exports of 11 million bales out of a crop of 12.6 million bales. My Glauber said the high export level will be a boon, given that domestic use of cotton is at record low levels."

1404 The MOU, agreed to in April 2010, was in effect for 60 days but, during that time, the Framework for providing annual payments was developed.

1405 For reading on why Members choose to settlement, see, Guzman, A., and Simmons, B., "To Settle or Empanel? An Empirical Analysis of Litigation and Settlement at the World Trade Organization," *The Journal of Legal Studies*, Vol. 31 No. 1, Part 2: Rational Choice and International Law, (January 2002), pp. 5205–5235. Although the focus of the article is on the preliminary stage of the dispute settlement process, many of the considerations and rationales provided are also applicable to the final arbitration and implementation phase.

accomplished by dedicated volunteers and millions of dollars in aid is overwhelmed by the havoc wreaked by Washington's bloated cotton subsidies."[1406] Therefore, in addition to the direct costs of funding the subsidy programs and the payments to Brazil specified by the MOU between the US and Brazil, US taxpayers are paying the indirect costs of development aid to Africa and other developing countries to, at least partially, offset the damage done by the subsidies to these countries. In all of these cases, the benefit derived by a few thousand US farmers is to the detriment of to the welfare of many – both domestically and internationally. Especially, in the case of Africa, aid would prove more beneficial absent the cotton subsidy programs because, without the adverse effects of US subsidies, it would allow these countries to increase income and make better use of the aid given. As it stands, one of the tragedies of US cotton subsidies is that well-meaning aid to Africa is undercut.

Public Choice: In light of the negative effects of the US subsidy programs on the US economy and on the economies of Brazil and the developing world, the question arises as to why these programs persist and even expand over time. In economic terms, the net benefits to the US as a whole are negative, as evidenced by facts such as the costs of these cotton support programs exceeding the value of the crop itself, yet the political will to reform the programs is lacking. A ready answer to the question of the political viability of these programs can be found in public choice theory, pioneered by Kenneth Arrow, James Buchanan, Gordon Tullock, and Anthony Downs, among others, approximately fifty years ago.[1407] Public choice theory applies economic principles to the analysis of political behavior. Specifically, public choice adopts the economic model of utility maximization and the principle that human behavior is guided by rational self-interest in which decisions are made on the basis of the benefits and costs of actions to decision-makers.[1408] While rational behavior forms the basis of economic models of the behavior of market participants, public choice presumes that it also guides the behavior of participants in the political realm.

In the political context, public choice theory explains the phenomenon of low levels of interest, knowledge, and participation of voters in the political

---

1406 Exhibit Bra-201 ("The Long Reach of King Cotton," The New York Times, 5 August 2003).

1407 See Arrow, K., *Social Choice and Individual Values*, second ed., Wiley, (1951); Buchanan, J. and Tullock, G., *The Calculus of Consent: Logical Foundations of Constitutional Democracy*, University of Michigan Press, Ann Arbor, MI, (1962); Downs, A., *An Economic Theory of Democrac,*, Harper, New York, (1957).

1408 Note that rational self-interest includes consideration of units larger than the individual, such as the interests of family, friends and community.

process. Political scientists have long noted the low levels of voter turnout in US elections and the low level of knowledge of the issues on the part of the population that votes. Public choice theory explains this on the basis of evaluating the costs and benefits to voters of being informed and voting. Because information is not free, there are costs associated with being informed on the pertinent issues and of voting. The benefits to being an informed voter, on the other hand, are relatively low because, among other things, there is little likelihood that an individual's vote will affect the outcome of an election. Thus, for much of the population, it is rational to be ignorant of the issues at play in elections and to opt out of voting.[1409] Further, the costs of inefficient government programs are generally spread among all taxpayers, so that the costs of such programs to each individual voter are relatively low. In the case of the cotton subsidies, for example, the cost of the programs, while totaling nearly $3billion annually, are spread among millions of US citizens and amount to only about $10 on a per capita basis. As a result, it is not worthwhile for voters to be informed about or work to change such programs even though their net benefits to the economy as a whole are negative.

While the costs of many government programs are spread among a rationally ignorant populace, the benefits of such programs are generally concentrated on a relatively few recipients. In the case of cotton, for example, the huge amounts spent on the support programs are directed to only a few thousand cotton producers in the US and, as a result, the individual benefit to recipients are substantial. It is critical to the interest of these recipients that such programs be maintained and, when possible, increased. Given the rational ignorance on the part of voters and the special interests for affected industry groups, the incentive for politicians to vote in favor of such programs is apparent. By doing so, they direct benefits to special interests that are the recipients of the government's largesse. If, on the other hand, they vote against such programs in order to decrease the inefficiency and costs of these programs to the country as a whole, they risk the ire of virtually the only part of the population that is aware of how the politician votes on the issue. In other words as a result, voting for such programs, despite their inefficiency, will greatly increase both the level of campaign contributions from special interests and the probability of winning re-election. In sum, public choice provides an economic explanation for the political maxim, described *supra*, that "all politics are local."

1409 This is known as 'rational ignorance' on the part of voters. See, for example, Caplan, B., *The Myth of the Rational Voter: Why Democracies Choose Bad Policies*, Princeton, University Press, Princeton, NJ, 2007.

Applying the public choice argument to the political difficulties of reducing or eliminating cotton support programs, it is important to note that cotton is grown in seventeen (17) states in the US. A member of Congress from any of those states will have to continually vote in favor of cotton subsidies for the reasons just described. If cotton programs stood alone in terms of agricultural support programs, it is possible that they would be in the minority and such subsidies could be eliminated. But, cotton support programs are part of nine (9) "program" crops that are grown all over the country, including soybeans, corn, barley, wheat, rice, sorghum, and others. The amounts spent on these program crops is enormous, with soybeans, corn, and cotton accounting for well over fifty (50) percent of total agricultural expenditures at the federal level. As a result, the probability of garnering a majority of lawmakers to vote against such subsidy programs is dramatically reduced.

This dynamic is referred to as the "domestic political impediment" to trade reform. The more widespread the program and the larger the program, the bigger is the impediment to trade reform. There is little difficulty, as a result, in understanding the difficulty faced by negotiators at the multilateral level, such as those participating in the WTO system, to effect meaningful and significant reductions in trade-distorting agricultural support programs, when those programs are so strongly and deeply politically rooted at the domestic level.

Support for US Reform: Given the public choice explanation for the difficulty of subsidy reform, *supra*, it is interesting to recognize that there has been a perceptible shift within the US for agricultural reform. This was also alluded to in part of the analysis above. The costs are now perhaps great enough – especially given cross-sectoral threats in IPR and services, to sufficiently bolster incentive interest groups and US taxpayers to challenge the lobbying efforts of the NCC and greater agricultural sector. In opposition to this 'circling the wagons' phenomenon, some opposition – within the political sphere even – seems to be growing. In response to the news of the Arbitrator's decision, a coalition of four members of the US Congress, both liberal and conservative,[1410] expressed their opposition to the cotton subsidies, stating that the "U.S. cotton program is a barrier to trade and economic growth and must be reformed. In light of this ruling, we urge you to take a strong stance in working to reform these egregious subsidies."[1411] The letter further noted that "it is imperative to

---

1410   They are Republican Representatives Jim Flake of Arizona and Paul Ryan of Wisconsin and Democratic Representatives Ron Kind of Wisconsin and Barney Frank of Massachusetts.
1411   Letter from Reps. Kind, Flake, Frank and Ryan to President Barak Obama, (22 April 2010), p. 1.

restructure the GSM-102 Export Guarantee Program, which fails to cover its operating costs and effectively serves as an illegal export subsidy."[1412] In stating their opposition to the continuation of the cotton subsidies while, at the same time, paying Brazil for cotton-related technical assistance, the letter noted:

> From this ruling, it is clear that our agricultural subsidies are grossly outdated and are quickly becoming a liability for future trade growth. Instead of effectively reforming our programs, we are electing to pay $147.3 million annually to Brazilian agribusiness so that we can continue to pay around $3 billion a year to large U.S. agribusiness. This policy distorts the marketplace and is fiscally irresponsible. By the time we reform the cotton programs in the 2012 farm bill, the U.S. will have spent close to half a billion dollars in 'technical assistance' to Brazilian agribusiness. With the current fiscal environment, we need to focus on reforming our programs so that they responsibly use taxpayer dollars now.[1413]

In the past, it was especially difficult to challenge these interest groups, because of the longstanding tradition of legitimate corruption, where the subsidies actually finance the lobbyists. The US cotton lobby is a classic case where members use the dues from the association in order to obtain subsidies. In the case of the most recent MOU, the lobby proved strong enough to make US taxpayers compensate Brazilian farmers in order to protect US farmers. However, armed with the Arbitrator's decision authorizing Brazil to retaliate in the goods as well as IPR and services sectors, other interest groups are now motivated to protect equally-legitimate interests with coalitions of similar strength to the agricultural sector.

Further, support for domestic reform is not only beginning to take form in the US, but outside the US as well. For example, US' transatlantic counterpart and prior subsidy 'partner in crime,' the EU, was faced with a similar case and has brought its domestic policies into conformity as a result of, and in line with, the agricultural policy overhaul through the Common Agricultural Policy (CAP). Most importantly to one of the main arguments of this book is that the EC reformed their domestic policies by implementing Council Regulation No. 318/2006 in order to align their regime with the

---

1412 Letter from Reps. Kind, Flake, Frank and Ryan to President Barak Obama, (22 April 2010), p. 2.
1413 Letter from Reps. Kind, Flake, Frank and Ryan to President Barak Obama, (22 April 2010), pp 1–2.

recommendations and rulings of the DSU.¹⁴¹⁴ As stated by the EC in 2007, "since then, the parties have been engaged in discussions on the effects of the sugar reform's implementation and on the evolution of the world sugar market."¹⁴¹⁵ Like *Cotton*, onlookers were pleased with Brazil's success in pressing for these reform measures. Oxfam called the WTO's decision "a triumph for developing countries."¹⁴¹⁶ Despite concerns about the effects of the changes on the ACP states relating to favorable EC sugar quotas under the Sugar Protocol of the Cotonou Agreement, Gregor Kreuzhuber, the EC spokesperson on agriculture at the time, projected that the changes would significantly reduce "EU sugar exports and export refunds, abolish intervention, reduce EU production and the internal sugar price."¹⁴¹⁷

Potential Future Challenges: In considering needed reforms to the present 2008 Farm Bill, as well as the formulation of the 2012 Farm Bill, the US should consider the possibility that other Members are presently able to challenge its programs in the WTO.¹⁴¹⁸ This is especially true given the fact that, based on the interpretation of the DSU, no revived Peace Clause will shelter certain of its programs from challenges by other Members. Though a new Peace Clause may be negotiated in the Doha Development Agenda, it is unlikely that more favorable terms will be reached. Further, it would be wise for the US to be proactive and consider the wider objectives of greater market access, as opposed to the limited view of domestic support.¹⁴¹⁹ For example, encouraged by the

---

1414 This development, as well as other policy changes undertaken by the EU, are discussed, *infra*.

1415 European Commission, "General Overview of Active WTO Dispute Settlement Cases Involving the EC as Complainant or Defendant and of Active Cases under the Trade Barriers Regulation," Brussels, (14 March 2007), p. 8.

1416 BBC News, "WTO Raps EU over Sugar Subsidies," (4 August 2004) <http://news.bbc.co.uk/go/pr/fr/-/2/hi/business/3536710.stm> last visited 21 June 2010.

1417 International Centre for Trade and Sustainable Development (ICTSD), "WTO Panels Confirm Victory for Brazil in Cotton, Sugar Cases," Bridges Weekly Trade News Digest, Vol. 8, No. 30, (15 September 2004), p. 2.

1418 *See*, Steinberg, R., and Josling, T., "When the Peace Ends: The Vulnerability of EC and US Agricultural Subsidies to WTO Legal Challenge," *Journal of International Economic Law*, Oxford University Press, Vol. 6, No. 2, (2003), pp. 369–417.

1419 A related question posed has been the issue of to what degree and in what circumstances the WTO should allow for 'opt outs' by Members. In other words, would it be appropriate to allow Member to choose not to comply with the rulings and recommendations of the DSB. In the case of *Cotton*, given the political entrenchment of subsidies and the extreme difficulty it might be for the US administration to change its policies, it has been considered whether this would this be a situation where the US should 'opt out.' Most generally, this approach has been deemed most appropriate in the developing and LDC cases, and

precedent set by the *Cotton* case, Canada filed a complaint against the US corn program in January 2007,[1420] citing many of the same programs that had been found actionable in the *Cotton* case. If the cotton decision is carried over to other commodities, programs such as marketing loan provisions, counter-cyclical payments and direct payments all risk being reclassified as amber box policies that would be subject to reductions.[1421] Close attention to cotton decisions affects future farm legislation and might orient bills in favor of conservative programs – re-orientation of farm policy.[1422] In addition, the following sets forth a few potential future challenges that are foreseeable given current US agricultural policy.

There are a number of potential challenges to US agricultural subsidy programs under WTO subsidy disciplines[1423] that could be based on the strategic roadmap and legal precedent of the *Cotton* dispute. In the United States, these vulnerable subsidy programs, in addition to cotton, include annual domestic support subsidies (marketing loans, counter-cyclical subsidies, crop insurance and most recently, ACRE program subsidies) for crops such as rice, wheat, soybeans, sorghum, and corn. Claims could also be asserted against EC single farm payments – subsidies that are roughly similar to the US Direct Payment subsidies as well as against prohibited local content subsidies provided by the European Communities and the United States to processors of products such as dairy and sugar. In addition, claims could be asserted against

---

not for developed countries. However, it has been considered in the context of the *EC-Beef Hormones* cases.

1420 Schnepf, R., "U.S.-Canada Corn Trade Dispute," Congressional Research Service Report for Congress, http://canada.usembassy.gov/content/can_usa/trade_corn_crs210107.pdf. Again, It should be noted that although Canada and Brazil began a challenge against the US TAMS based primarily on the peace clause findings of the *Cotton* case, styled as a challenge to 'corn,' higher prices by the time the case was initiated obviated the claim.

1421 One approach suggested in assessing the vulnerability of subsidy programs under the current US Farm Bill, required the consideration of the following: "(1) whether the subsidy payment is contingent upon current prices, production, yield, or revenue; (2) whether US world export and production account for a large world share which impacts the world market equilibrium; and (3) the extent to which the subsidies for a product cover a significant percentage of the cost of production." [Personal communication, 8 October, 2009]. For confidentiality considerations, this approach is not analyzed in detail or context here.

1422 Abdelnour, R., Peterson, W., "The WTO Decision on US Cotton Policy," Cornhusker Economics, University of Nebraska – Lincoln Extension, (March, 2007), http://digitalcommons.unl.edu/agecon_cornhusker/308.

1423 This includes claims that could be asserted under Articles 3.1, 5 and 6 of the SCM *Agreement* and the claims under Articles 3, 6, 7, 8, 9 and 10 of the *Agreement on Agriculture*.

export subsidies provided in excess of reduction commitments for such products as sugar. A brief summary of these potential claims is provided, *infra*.

Challenges to US annual recurring domestic support subsidies: The US 2008 Farm Bill[1424] largely maintained, for a number of "program" crops, the same "price-contingent" marketing loan and counter-cyclical subsidies condemned in the *Cotton* decisions. The 2008 Farm Bill also continued the Direct Payment and crop insurance subsidies, and added a new subsidy program (ACRE).[1425] As described in Chapter 5, the original Panel found that Brazil had not sufficiently demonstrated a causal link between the Direct Payment[1426] and crop insurance subsidies[1427] and significant price suppression.[1428] However, by employing the "long-term" causation focus of the *Cotton* Compliance Panel and Appellate Body decisions, it will be possible, under certain market circumstances, to make strong arguments that the collective effect of all of these subsidies – including the non-price contingent subsidies – is to cause serious prejudice in the world or in third country markets in violation of Article 6.3 of the *SCM Agreement*.

The viability of such claims will depend first on whether the prices of the particular commodity being challenged are low enough over the same period of time to create payments of at least a modest amount of marketing loan and counter-cyclical subsidies. Another important factor would be whether the collective amount of the subsidies is necessary to cover at least some portion of the total cost of production. The strength of the claim will be enhanced if the US market share in the market at issue is sufficiently high to impact prices at the global or individual market levels. Historically, commodity prices have fluctuated considerably and, during periods of low prices, there will be much larger US subsidies that can be challenged under the *Cotton* rationale. For example, billions in marketing loan subsidies were provided when prices for soybeans fell in the period 2000–2001, and, similarly, corn prices collapsed in the 2005–2006 period.[1429]

1424 P.L. 110–234.
1425 P.L. 110–234 § 1105.
1426 P.L. 110–234 § 1101–09.
1427 P.L. 110–234 tit. XII.
1428 *See* Babcock, B., "Breaking the Link between Food and Biofuels," 14 Iowa AG Review; Vol. 1. No. 10 (2008), *available* at http://www.card.iastate.edu/iowa_ag_review/summer_08/IAR.pdf. (finding that the pattern of payments for Iowa corn proved "nearly identical to the situation for corn in other states and for wheat and soybeans in all states....[which] suggests that a large proportion of US farmers will find ACRE much more attractive than current commodity programs.").
1429 *See* Press Release, American Soybean Association, American Soybean Association Urges Agriculture Secretary to Maintain Oilseed Loan Rates (19 October 2001) (on file with the

Another important factor would be whether the collective amount of the subsidies is necessary to cover at least some portion of the total cost of production. Indeed, the Congressional Research Service analysis shows that U.S. subsidy programs were essential for US farmers of a number of different commodities to cover their total costs of production.[1430] This crucial fact, coupled with the large US world market share of exports and production of a number of different commodities, suggests that the US will be vulnerable when prices fall for those commodities receiving significant domestic support. On the other hand, it will be more difficult to challenge the U.S. domestic support subsidies if over a 4–5 year period prices have been so high that few price-contingent subsidies were provided.

Challenges to Total Aggregate Measurement of Support: Another result of the *Cotton* case is to increase US vulnerability to challenges under Article 3.2 of the *Agreement on Agriculture* for failing to restrain the total amount of subsidies provided to US domestic agricultural producers to $19.1 billion ("total aggregate measurement of support" or "AMS"). Prior to the *Cotton* dispute, the United States claimed that more than $5 billion in Direct Payments were "green box" subsidies that need not be counted towards its $19.1 billion AMS limit. However, the *Cotton* ruling that such subsidies were *not* green box subsidies (for purposes of the "peace clause" analysis) now means that the United States must include them as part of their total domestic support. The Congressional Research Service,[1431] as well as a WTO challenge by Brazil[1432] and Canada,[1433] provided analysis suggesting that the inclusion of Direct Payments as part of domestic support meant the United States was in violation for a number of years over the past decade of its $19.1 billion AMS limit contrary to Article 3.2 of the *Agreement on Agriculture.* If and when commodity prices fall, the United

---

American Soybean Association), *available at* http://www.soygrowers.com/newsroom/releases/2001%20releases/Loan+RateOct192001.pdf; Alexei Barrionuevo, *Mountains of Corn and a Sea of Farm Subsidies,* N.Y. Times, Nov. 9, 2005, at Business, *available at* http://www.nytimes.com/2005/11/09/business/09harvest.html?_r=1&pagewanted=print.

1430 Schnepf, R., and Womach, J., "Potential Challenges to US Farm Subsidies in the WTO: A Brief Overview," Congressional Research Services (25 October 2006).

1431 *See*, Schnepf, R. and Womach, J., "Potential Challenges to US Farm Subsidies in the WTO: A Brief Overview," Congressional Research Service (25 October 2006).

1432 Request for Consultation by Brazil, *United States – Domestic Support and Export Credit Guarantees for Agricultural Products,* WT/DS365/1 (17 July 2007).

1433 Request for Consultation by Canada, *United States – Subsidies and Other Domestic Support for Corn and Other Agricultural Products,* WT/DS357/1 (11January 2007).

States will again be vulnerable to future challenges regarding their total aggregate measurement of support.[1434]

Challenges to Prohibited Local Content Subsidies: Both the United States and the European Union presently provide subsidies to processors of agricultural goods contingent *de jure* or *de facto* on the use of "local" (US or EU) agricultural products. The *Cotton* decisions confirmed that such local content subsidies (in the form of the Step-2 subsidies to US mill users of US cotton) are covered by the WTO subsidies disciplines. The European Union provides local content subsidies to EU purchasers or users of EU-produced skimmed milk, skimmed milk powder, cream, butter and concentrated butter.[1435] The European Union also provides subsidies to purchasers or users of butter and skimmed milk powder contingent upon these products being produced in the European Union.[1436] Similarly, the US sugar program requires the US Government to make marketing loan payments[1437] contingent on the use of domestic versus imported goods and the US sugar supply management marketing allotments.[1438] Under the *Cotton* decision rationale, all four of these forms of local

---

1434 In addition to Direct Payments, the United States also failed to include within its total aggregate measurement of support other forms of domestic support constituting billions of additional payments. These include "domestic support" in favor of US agriculture in the form of various forms of U.S. farmer tax breaks, disaster payments non-conforming to the provisions of the green box, and irrigation subsidies. When the these omitted additional forms of domestic support, together with Direct Payments, are included, the calculation of U.S. non-exempt support shows persistent U.S. violations of Article 3.2 of the *Agreement on Agriculture*. *See,* Schnepf, R. and Womach, J., "Potential Challenges to US Farm Subsidies in the WTO: A Brief Overview," Congressional Research Service (25 October 2006).

1435 *See,* Commission Regulations 1234/2007, Establishing a Common Organization of Agricultural Markets and on Specific Provisions for Certain Agricultural Products, 2007 O.J. (L299). A number of provisions of the Single CMO Regulation expose the EU to potential local content subsidy claims. They include EU intervention purchases of butter and skimmed milk powder, *id.* art.15, 16, EU storage subsidies for storage of butter, *id.* art. 28(a)(ii)-(iii), and EC disposal subsidies to the extent they are paid to processors of EU dairy products and not paid on the export of such products, *id.* Recitals 43, 60; art.99–101 (describing measures found in Recitals 43 and 60).

1436 *See, e.g., id.* 7, 10(1)(e), 10(1)(f), 100(1) providing provisions specifically indicating if milk or milk products are produced or originated "in the community".

1437 Section 156 of the Federal Agriculture Improvement and Reform Act of 1996, as amended, 7 U.S.C. §7272 (2008).

1438 Section 359 of the Agricultural Adjustment Act of 1938, 7 U.S.C. §1359aa(2008). Similar to a local content requirement, the current US sugar program in the 2008 Farm Act contains a requirement that the size of the overall marketing allotment equal 85 percent of U.S. human consumption of sugar. This constitutes a minimum use requirement for domestic

content subsidies are contingent on the use of domestic over imported goods, in violation of Article 3.1(b) of the *SCM Agreement*.

Challenges to Prohibited Export Subsidies: Finally, the *Cotton* decisions determined that WTO Members cannot provide agricultural export subsidies beyond their reduction commitments for particular products. If they do, then such subsidies can be challenged without going through the considerable complications of establishing trade effects and serious prejudice (as in an *actionable* subsidy claim). This would include, for example, the future provision of export credit guarantees or other forms of export subsidies provided contingent upon the export of various products. This is a significant aspect of the decision because there are only a relatively few number of products for which the United States has the protection of being scheduled (hence allowing them to provide such subsidies). For a large group of products, the United States cannot provide *any* subsidies contingent, *de jure* or *de facto* upon export without being in violation of Article 3.1 of the *SCM Agreement*.[1439] Finally, under the rationale of the parallel *EC Sugar* decision, the operation of a heavily subsidized and Government controlled *domestic* commodity regime, such as the US sugar regime which requires that excess sugar be exported, means that such products can be deemed to benefit from export subsidies in violation of Articles 3.3, 8 and 9.1(c) of the *Agreement on Agriculture*.[1440]

The *Cotton* decisions provide considerable clarity to the Byzantine world of WTO agricultural subsidy disciplines. As the first decisions under the relatively vague and general actionable subsidy rules of the *SCM Agreement*, the decisions offer the analytical and evidentiary tools for government trade officials and their counsel to assess the extent of the negative impact on trade from various forms of subsidies. In the case of domestic cotton subsidies, that

---

sugar, in violation of Article III:5 of GATT 1994. *See* Section 359b(b)(1) of the Agricultural Adjustment Act of 1938, 7 U.S.C. §1359bb.

1439 According to the United States Schedule entitled "Commitments Limiting Subsidization," filed with the WTO, the United States only made export subsidy reduction commitments on the following categories of products: Wheat, coarse grains, rice, vegetable oils, butter, skimmed milk powder, cheese, bovine meat, pigmeat, poultry meat, live dairy cattle, and eggs. In terms of the quantity of the commitments, wheat is by far the largest, followed by skimmed milk powder, course grains, bovine meat, poultry meat, and vegetable oils.

1440 The current US sugar regime requires that any sugar produced in The U.S. sugar program prohibits U.S. processors, under risk of civil penalties, from marketing sugar produced in quantities greater than their marketing allotments. Instead, these processors can either hold the sugar in stocks, sell it for a use other than domestic human consumption, or dispose of it in the export market. *See* Section 359b(d)(2) of the Agricultural Adjustment Act of 1938, as amended by the 2008 Farm Bill.

impact is enormous – $2.9 billion in world-wide price suppressing effects on cotton each year. The *Cotton* decisions, set forth in Chapter 5, also have greatly clarified the prohibited subsidy disciplines and placed very strict limits on the use of export credit guarantees that provide benefits by avoiding severe competitive disadvantages to non-subsidized exporters. The export and local content prohibited subsidy aspects of the decision offer the hope that such highly trade-distorting subsidies can be more easily identified and successfully challenged in the future.

The deleterious effects quantified by the most recent *Cotton* Article 22.6 decisions have the additional significant benefit of supporting the Doha Round negotiating efforts to further limit the amount of trade distorting domestic support programs and to eliminate entirely highly trade distorting export subsidies for agricultural products. These multilateral reform efforts are crucial to ensure long-lasting and comprehensive reform for the forms of agricultural subsidies that have the most severe distorting effects on international trade. The *Cotton* decisions confirmed and established as a *fact* the wide-ranging harm inflicted on many WTO Member agricultural producers who struggle to compete with their heavily subsidized counterparts in world markets. Thus, the WTO *Cotton* decisions compel – and fully support – a successful negotiated multilateral result that will alleviate the severe negative impacts of these highly trade-distorting subsidies. The following is a description of what steps Brazil and the US have taken in order to use the Article 22.6 decision and address the cotton issue within the context of the Doha negotiations and at the domestic level.

8.2   Brazil-US Memorandum of Understanding and June Framework

September 2009-April 2010: With the headline "Brazil Ready to Escalate US Trade Dispute," in the *Financial Times* on 31 August 2009, the world was put on notice that the WTO Arbitrator had granted Brazil's request to implement countermeasures against the US.[1441] Soon it was widely known that Brazil held a US$300 million dollar bargaining chip in both US-Brazilian relations and WTO negotiations (discussed in Chapter 5).[1442] Since that date, the Governments of

---

[1441] Wheatly, J., "Brazil Ready to Escalate US Trade Dispute," *Financial Times*, (31 August 2009), p. 4.

[1442] For an analysis of suspending WTO obligations, from the US experience, *see*, Andersen, S. and Blanchet, J., "The United States' Experience and Practice in Suspending WTO Obligations," in Part IV: The Domestic Politics and Procedures for Implementing Trade

Brazil and the US have strategized as onlookers have wondered what eventual outcome might result in the eight-year trade dispute. The National Cotton Council (NCC) reacted to the ruling by using the media to promote its belief that the Arbitrator had made miscalculations, arguing that cotton is an "industry that's substantially different in 2008 and 2009 than it was in 2005."[1443] In a conference call with reporters, CEO Mark Lange of the NCC explicitly stated that the lobby would begin working with the USTR to bring "the evolving world markets to the attention of the WTO."[1444] Pressure by the NCC was soon evident in the possibility of the USTR requesting the establishment of another compliance panel to confirm that, given these new conditions, the US was no longer violating WTO law.[1445] However, this option was soon abandoned and another strategy developed.

In the days following the Arbitrator's ruling, Brazil began readying its list of items to employ sanctions against. At the same time, Brazil and the US both expressed preferences for negotiation as opposed to retaliation. Foreign Minister Celso Amorim clarified Brazil's goal, "The objective of retaliation in the WTO is not punishment, but getting the infractor country to change its legislation to comply with the rules."[1446] This was true for the US as well. As Ron Kirk of the USTR noted, "My approach is always to prefer diplomacy over more confrontational methods, so we would welcome the opportunity to hear their thoughts as to what they think might constitute a reasonable settlement of this matter." Subsequently, the two met and Mr. Kirk requested Minister Amorim to employ the permitted retaliation 'deliberate[ly] and thoughtful[ly].'[1447] In the same meeting, the US mentioned the possibility of entering into a bilateral trade agreement with Brazil, which Celso Amorim

---

Retaliation of Bown, C and Pauwelyn, J., *The Law, Economics and Politics of Retaliation in WTO Dispute Settlement*, Cambridge University Press, pp. 235–243, (2010). Specifically, as set forth, *infra*, the US preference (like Brazil) is to not have to suspend obligations.

1443 Mark Lange, Chief Executive Officer, on behalf of the National Cotton Council. Campbell, E., "Cotton Council Says WTO Ruling Doesn't Reflect Market," *Bloomberg.com*, (31 August 2009).

1444 Mark Lange, Chief Executive Officer, on behalf of the National Cotton Council. Campbell, E., "Cotton Council Says WTO Ruling Doesn't Reflect Market," *Bloomberg.com*, (31 August 2009).

1445 "USTR under Pressure to Bring Cotton Compliance Panel after Ruling," *Inside US Trade*, (4 September 2009).

1446 Colitt, R., "Brazil Seeks Talks over US Cotton, Eyes Drug Case," *Forbes.com*, (1 September 2009).

1447 "US Official Urges 'Thoughtful' WTO Reprisals by Brazil," *AFP*, (17 September 2009).

considered so long as it was within its MERCUSUR commitments.[1448] In the meantime, developments in the US progressed along a different route as the NCC, as well as other agricultural farm interest groups,[1449] were beginning to promote the earlier-considered compliance panel idea and submitted a request to the USTR to pursue the option. Their concern was that, "if implemented, the WTO decision would cause unwarranted harm to US agricultural producers and US agribusinesses."[1450] In Geneva, the new Chair of the Agricultural Committee, David Walker, held a meeting with Brazil, the US, the EU, and the C-4 to discuss the cotton issue and assess the intentions of the US.[1451] The US responded that it was not in a position to provide numbers on what it might be willing to commit to, until it could assess the overall Doha negotiations.[1452]

By November, Brazil had readied itself for retaliations and the Brazilian Chamber of Foreign Trade (CAMEX)[1453] published its preliminary list of 222 American products for private sector review, some of which, including food, medicine, medical equipment, appliances, cosmetics, and car parts, in addition to cotton, would face proposed tariffs exceeding 100 percent.[1454] In response to the list, USTR Spokeswoman Nefeterius A. McPherson iterated Ron Kirk's initial preference, "We are interested in working with our counterparts in Brazil to identify a solution to this situation without Brazil resorting to countermeasures."[1455] Although Brazil's initial date for the implementation

---

1448 Jeffris, G., "Brazil, US Study Resolution to WTO Cotton Ruling Impasse," WallStreetJournal.com, (17 September 2009). In terms of bilateral settlement, the US has used this approach in the past as a means to work around WTO dispute resolution. For example, in 2006, Uruguay began a case against US rice subsidies. However, the case was not pursued when subsidies declines and the US and Uruguay worked out a deal to give Uruguay more beef access to US market.

1449 Among the groups were the NCC, American Farm Bureau Federation, United Egg Association, and US Grain Council. See, "Agriculture, Farm Groups Send USTR Letter Seeking New WTO Panel on Cotton Program," BNA Newsfeed, (24 September 2009).

1450 "Agriculture, Farm Groups Send USTR Letter Seeking New WTO Panel on Cotton Program," BNA Newsfeed, (24 September 2009).

1451 "US Says No to 'Cotton' – For Now," *Washington Trade Daily*, (27 September 2009).

1452 "US Says No to 'Cotton' – For Now," *Washington Trade Daily*, (27 September 2009).

1453 Mulveny, J., Marques, C., "Brazil May Levy 100% Duties on US Goods in January 2010: Importers Have Short Time to Comment before Retaliation List Finalized," Sandler, Travis & Rosenberg, PA (18 November 2009).

1454 "Brazil Publishes Draft Retaliation List in WTO Cotton Dispute with US," *Inside US Trade*, (9 November 2009).

1455 Sullivan, B., "Brazil Readies Cotton Retaliation Against US," *The Commercial Appeal*, (10 November 2009).

of countermeasures was January 2010, it first delayed the action for one month.[1456]

By February of 2010, Brazil had developed a final list and announced that its WTO-authorized sanctions be applied to US trade totaling US$829.3 million and would consist of tariffs and infringement of intellectually property rights. The latter measures were proposed to include suspensions or limitations on US$270 million worth of patents, copyrights, and trademark on imports as well as temporary measures banning royalty payments. Brazil also proposed a list of US$560 million worth of US goods that would be subject to retaliatory tariffs. Brazil was prepared to retaliate[1457] and the US was eager to negotiate.[1458] At the time, legislation for the Brazilian government to accomplish the IP withdrawal of rights had been drafted and the overall Brazilian sentiment was that it fully expected to have to impose sanctions.[1459] This was also the opinion held by the ICTSD in evaluating US and Brazilian positions[1460] and within days the decree was published in Brazil's federal register, giving authorization to suspend or limit "intellectual property rights locally to imports from the US, and temporary blockage of royalty remittances related to intellectual property."[1461] Soon after, Secretary of State Hilary Clinton visited Brazil and sent two additional high-level officials thereafter as a means to continue to press for a settlement to stave off retaliation beyond the thirty-day timeframe Brazil had chosen. In response, Brazilian President Luiz Inácio Lula da Silva called on the US to bring its domestic policies into conformity, in order for Brazil to not have to implement retaliatory measures.[1462] In addition, US-Brazilian talks regarding greater market access for Brazilian beef, orange juice and ethanol coupled with compensation for the cotton sector were ongoing.[1463] Brazil next chose to

---

1456 "Around the Globe," *Washington Trade Daily*, (15 December 2009).
1457 Ferreira, B. *et al*, "Retaliation Programme Developed Against United States Following WTO Dispute," ILO:Trade & Customs, Brazil (22 January 2010) at www.iloinfo.com.
1458 Colitt, R., "Update 2-US, Brazil Talk to Avoid Brazil Cotton Retaliation," *Forexpros.com*, (4 February 2010).
1459 Dantas, Iuri, "Brazil to Sanction US on Goods, Intellectual Rights (Update 1)," *BusinessWeek.com* (9 February 2010).
1460 "Brazil Ponders Cotton Retaliation," ICTSC, Vol. 14 No. 1, (February 2010).
1461 Good, K., "Trade" *FarmPolicy.com* (15 February 2010). Specifically, it was noted, "Brazil's government Thursday formalized guidelines for an $830 million retaliation against US cotton subsidies granted by a World Trade Organization ruling last year."
1462 Bonds, "Lula: Brazil Urges US to Respect WTO Cotton Ruling," *Reuters.com*, (10 March 2010).
1463 Bonds, "Lula: Brazil Urges US to Respect WTO Cotton Ruling," *Reuters.com*, (10 March 2010).

launch "a process of public consultations" to engage industry, before implementing its countermeasures.[1464] Given the severity of the sanctioned counter measures, it was not surprising that a last minute settlement was reached between the two parties the day before Brazil's retaliation strategy would go into effect.[1465]

April Memorandum of Understanding, then June Framework between Brazil and US: After several delays in implementing the Arbitrator's decision the *Cotton* dispute has reached an interim outcome.[1466] The US was successfully able to forestall Brazil from implementing authorized countermeasures by entering into a Memorandum of Understanding (MOU) with Brazil in April of 2010.[1467] The MOU required the US to establish and provide annual payments of US$147.3 million to a fund to provide technical assistance and capacity building.[1468] The duration of the MOU was set to continue until 2012 (the anticipated time of the passage of the next US Farm Bill) or until a mutually-agreed upon solution to the *Cotton* dispute was reached.[1469] Further, the US agreed to near-term modifications to its GSM 102 program and "to engage with the government of Brazil in technical discussions regarding the operation of the program."[1470] In addition, the US made commitments to publish "a proposed rule that recognizes the Brazilian State of Santa Catarina as being free of certain animal disease, which is an essential step for the official recognition that Brazilian meat exports are disease-free."[1471] The US was given until 21 April to

---

1464 The Press Office of the Brazilian Ministry of External Relations, "US Cotton Dispute – Public Consultations About Measures for the Suspension of Concessions or Obligations vis-à-vis the United States in the Area of Intellectual Property Rights," Brazilian Embassy (15 March 2010).
1465 "US and Brazil Settle Cotton Dispute," *Washington Trade Daily*, (6 April 2010).
1466 Wade, S., "US, Brazil WTO Framework Not Final Solution," *Southeast Farm Press*, (2 July 2010).
1467 "Brazil Delays Cotton Sanction after US Agrees to Near-Term Actions," *WorldTrade\Interactive*, Vol. 17, Issue 69 (7 April 2010).
1468 "US and Brazil Settle Cotton Dispute," *Washington Trade Daily*, (6 April 2010).
1469 "Brazil Delays Cotton Sanction after US Agrees to Near-Term Actions," *WorldTrade\Interactive*, Vol. 17, Issue 69 (7 April 2010).
1470 "US and Brazil Settle Cotton Dispute," *Washington Trade Daily*, (6 April 2010).
1471 Brazilian Ministry of Foreign Relations and the Brazilian Trade Chamber (CAMEX), "MOU-Brazil-US WTO Cotton Dispute," *Press Release*, (20 April 2010). As discussed at an IPC meeting, "Although progress on SPS disputes is of course also welcome, IPC member Carlos Perez del Castillo notes that 'publically linking what should really be a scientific issue of whether a specific state in Brazil is or is not free of certain animal diseases, to a more political agreement such as this one on cotton, is rather unusual.'" "The Cotton Dispute," International Food & Agricultural Trade Policy Council (IPC), IPC Alert,

comply with the MOU, and Brazil agreed not to retaliate for another sixty (60) days by publishing a CAMEX resolution the following day that would delay the imposition of countermeasures.[1472] In essence, the US 'bought time' and temporarily avoided retaliation.[1473]

In recent interviews conducted with involved parties since the Arbitrator's decision was reported, it has become clear that Brazil does not recognize this as a final outcome. Rather, it is another move by Brazil to use its legal win to apply political pressure on the US to reform its domestic measures. The US Farm Bill is expected in 2012. Therefore, this allows the US and Brazil to work together within the WTO negotiations context as well as exert substantial pressure on the US. Further, it compensates Brazilian farmers to some extent. The LDCs are mentioned in the MOU, but it is uncertain to what extent they may actually benefit from the MOU. Although the MOU framework is a settlement to some extent, it is noteworthy that Brazil can end the agreement at any time.

Reactions to the MOU have been mixed. Responses range from "a bad deal is better than no deal" to the previously-described reaction by four (4) members of the House of Representatives in their open letter to President Obama calling for "reform of the United States 'egregious' cotton subsidies"[1474] and stating that the agreed-upon annual payments to Brazilian agribusiness interests and the continuation of cotton subsidies are not "fiscally responsible and WTO compliant."[1475] Further, it may be reasonably assumed that one of the primary reasons why the US is working with Brazil is because of the likelihood that the potentially widespread and significant IPR- related sanctions will mobilize resources in those sectors and provide signals to the NCC that it is not the only effective lobby in Washington. In addition, the US does not want to completely disregard WTO trade policy, and this way they can be perceived as good citizens, while, at the same time, minimizing the costs of non-compliance. In this light, it is important to note that the MOU between Brazil and the US is not

---

FP7NTM/Impact, (8 April 2010) at http://www.ntm-impact.eu/innovaportal/v/406/1/innova.front/ipc_alert:_the_us-br_cotton_dispute_8_april_%6010.

1472 Brazilian Ministry of Foreign Relations and the Brazilian Trade Chamber (CAMEX), "MOU-Brazil-US WTO Cotton Dispute," *Press Release*, (20 April 2010).

1473 "Brazil again Delays Cotton Sanctions after US Meets Three Conditions," Brazilian Ministry of Foreign Relations and the Brazilian Trade Chamber (CAMEX), "MOU-Brazil-US WTO Cotton Dispute," *Press Release*, (20 April 2010).

1474 "Lawmakers Oppose Cotton Payments to Brazil, Call for Subsidy Reform," *WorldTrade\Interactive*, Sandler, Travis & Rosenberg, PA, Vol. 17 Issue 83, (27 April 2010).

1475 "Lawmakers Oppose Cotton Payments to Brazil, Call for Subsidy Reform," *WorldTrade\Interactive*, Sandler, Travis & Rosenberg, PA, Vol. 17 Issue 83, (27 April 2010). The letter was dated 22 April, 2010.

part of the WTO dispute process nor is it strictly WTO-legal. For example, the ECG program continues, in which the fees from obligors are below market rates that would normally prevail and, as a result, continue to constitute WTO non-compliant export subsidies.

After the sixty (60) day deadline, continued negotiations between the countries led the US and Brazil to enter into 'The June Framework.'[1476] The Framework is similar to the MOU with the addition of an agreement by the US to a "substantial" cut in subsidies.[1477] Further, the present Framework similarly includes some development aid from Brazil to African countries. However, the benefits to African LDCs are limited due, primarily, to the fact that they did not participate as co-complainants. However, the Framework does specifically recognize C-4 interests:

> the fund may also be used for activities related to international cooperation in the cotton sector in sub-Saharan Africa, in Mercosur members and associate members, in Haiti, of [in] any other developing country as the parties may agree upon...

Therefore, as it stands, the US will still be overproducing and over-exporting cotton to the world market and, as a result, continue to cause price suppression. However, there will be some modifications to GSM 102.[1478] Also, important to note that the agreement in place at the moment will be renegotiated year-to-year and is not permanent in the sense that the US still has the obligation, under WTO law, to remove the subsidies or the adverse effects. Further, WTO Ambassador Roberto Azevedo emphasized to the press that Brazil retained the right to retaliate at any time "should the negotiations become deadlocked."[1479] The US response to the June Framework is positive.[1480] As Nefeterius McPherson, spokeswoman for USTR stated, "We are pleased with

---

1476   The Framework was signed on 17 June 2010. Simoes, C. and Soliani, A., "Brazil Won't Retaliate Against US Over Cotton Aid (Update2)," *BloombergBusinessweek.com*, (17 June 2010).
1477   Simoes, C. and Soliani, A., "Brazil Won't Retaliate Against US Over Cotton Aid (Update2)," *BloombergBusinessweek.com*, (17 June 2010).
1478   "Brazil to Further Postpone Retaliatory Sanctions Against US in Cotton Dispute," *WorldTrade\Interactive*, Vol. 17 Issue 122 (21 June 21 2010).
1479   Simoes, C. and Soliani, A., "Brazil Won't Retaliate Against US Over Cotton Aid (Update2)," BloombergBusinessweek.com, (17 June 2010).
1480   "US, Brazil Agree on Framework Regarding WTO Cotton Dispute," at USTR website, http://www.ustr.gov/about-us/press-office/press-releases/2010/june/us-brazil-agree-framework-regarding-wto-cotton-disput.

this decision, and look forward to signing the framework soon. We hope to build upon this positive development to forge a stronger bilateral trading relationship with Brazil."[1481] At the domestic level, given the large fund, the Framework and greater global implications of the subsidies, the cotton issue should remain in the media and help effectuate change in the 2012 Farm Bill. Further, it is significant that the IPR sector is now involved and remains vulnerable to retaliation. It cannot be understated that it only took Brasilia and Washington ten (10) days to come to a resolution, after an eight-year battle, as soon as intellectual property rights were threatened.

In terms of the ongoing Doha negotiations, although the governments of the US and Brazil seem to be communicating well, it is safe to assume that the NCC (although ultimately having to agree with the Framework), does not want bilateral negotiations and coordination with the Brazilians at Doha at present. Further, practitioners and analysts speculate that the present South-South coalition paradigm of Brazil in the WTO is a barrier to having meaningful negotiations on cotton and that Brazil, as the recipient of monetary benefits from the US, has a reduced incentive to maintain its leadership in the Doha Round. The danger, in this view, is that cotton's role as the key to the negotiations is now lost.

Practitioners and scholars have commenced reviewing the Framework within the context of the Doha negotiations and in the context of the global ongoing economic downturn. In the first instance, the International Centre for Trade and Sustainable Development (ICTSD) has published a study on the effects of a cotton deal to importing and exporting countries.[1482] As ICTSD reported, "Washington's failure to overhaul its cotton programme has had important implications for cotton farmers in Brazil and other developing countries, according to a recent study conducted by Mario Jales."[1483] Mario Jales released his preliminary results in April of 2010. His study "estimates the price, production and trade effects of reforming cotton subsidies and tariffs under alternative scenarios, with a primary focus on the WTO Doha Round."[1484]

1481 Simoes, C. and Soliani, A., "Brazil Won't Retaliate Against US Over Cotton Aid (Update2)," BloombergBusinessweek.com, (17 June 2010).
1482 Jales, M., "How Would a Trade Deal on Cotton Affect Importing and Exporting Countries?" ICTSD (April 2010).
1483 ICTSD, "Brazil, US Strike 'Framework' Deal in Cotton Dispute," *Bridges Weekly Trade News Digest*, Vol. 14, No. 23 (23 June 2010).
1484 Jales, M., "How Would a Trade Deal on Cotton Affect Importing and Exporting Countries?" ICTSD (April 2010).

It will be interesting to learn whether his projections are proved correct per the June Framework.

Some initial analysis finds that the Framework contains some general principles and procedural issues, such as the requirement of periodic consultations, but lacks specific requirements in terms of subsidy reductions. For example, there are no provisions within the Framework requiring the reduction in counter-cyclical or marketing loan payments. Further, Section II of the Framework purports to address GSM 102 modifications, but there is little indication of specific reduction measures required to achieve compliance other than language about keeping ECG levels significantly below US$5.5 billion, as mandated by the cap, and allowing payments to continue at levels just above US$1 billion without modification. Finally, under Section III: *consultation* discussions (as described, *supra*) is an interesting example of the explicit coordination at the international for developing domestic policies. Brazil's right to provide input, as a result of WTO dispute resolution, is significant. This development cannot be understated as a projection of the direction and influence of the relationship between international and domestic law.

Although these elements of the Framework may lead some observers to conclude that it provides more of a symbolic than actual approach to substantive reforms, given the troubled economic situation at present, and the undesirable effects that increased trade restrictions would have on global trade, this can be considered a positive interim outcome. As International Food & Agricultural Trade Policy Council Chairperson Carlo Trojan stated, "A negotiated compensation settlement is always preferable to trade restrictions, which is after all what countermeasures are. This is especially the case today, when trade flows have finally begun to pick up again after a significant decline caused by the financial crisis, yet the ideal resolution to a WTO dispute is compliance by the guilty party with the panel's findings. While the US has taken some steps to address the underlying policies found to be WTO illegal, it has deferred on the big ticket items – the marketing loans and countercyclical payments."[1485] To that end, the next and final chapter sets forth the ethical and systemic considerations the US should evaluate when formulating its 2012 Farm Bill.

1485 "The Cotton Dispute," International Food & Agricultural Trade Policy Council (IPC), IPC Alert, FP7NTM/Impact, (8 April 2010) at http://www.ntm-impact.eu/innovaportal/v/406/1/innova.front/ipc_alert:_the_us-br_cotton_dispute_8_april_%6010.

CHAPTER 9

Effect of Non-Compliance by the US: Ethical Systematic Considerations

9.1 Ethical Basis for the Cotton Findings and for Future Reform

'America wants us to comprehend the evil posed by violent anti-Western terrorism, and we do,' said President Blaise Compaoré [of Burkina Faso]. 'But we want you to equally concern yourself with the terror posed here by hunger and poverty, a form of terrorism your subsidies are aiding and abetting. If we cannot sell our cotton we will die.'[1486]

The *Cotton* dispute and Cotton initiative involved "ethical" implications of both a successful as well as unsuccessful result. The primary ethical dimensions of *Cotton* involved issues of vertical equity, especially those between developed and least developed countries. At one level, a trade action can be particularly unethical because it is an egregious violation by an economically strong WTO Member against a particularly weak one (Africa). Brazil recognized that this was best illustrated by an LDC, rather than by itself, a stronger developing country. Therefore, Brazil tried to portray its sense of outrage by highlighting the morality of the US violation by including Africa. Though it did so only somewhat, the third party impact was important. Further, this was particularly well illustrated, given the unique nature of cotton as a non-foodstuff commodity produced by very poor African countries. Not many other agricultural products fit that characterization, which made it more difficult for the US to defend its subsidy regime on more acceptable and traditional agriculture protectionist grounds (e.g. food safety). This substantively added to the ethical dimension of the case, because the price suppression effects would be more easily ethically justified with edible commodities imported by LDCs for domestic consumption.

At the system level, establishing a US violation would represent a significant breach of the moral philosophy supporting the greater legal system. Underlying principles requiring not only compliance with the law, but the spirit of the law, were recognized by Brazil as having been violated. Further, comparable to domestic law, the concept of *mens rea*, could be applied to

---

[1486] Exhibit Bra-201 ("The Long Reach of King Cotton," The New York Times, 5 August 2003).

argue that implementing domestic regimes while cognizant of the economic harm done to less developed counties and their being in violation of prescribed law is unethical under an international legal order that recognizes the rule of law, especially a legal order whose principles of most favored nation (MFN) and national treatment (NT) are based in equity, one of the foundational building blocks of ethics.

To highlight some of the ethical dimensions of the US cotton subsidy programs, Brazil sought to include the participation of the Africans at the commencement of the dispute.[1487] This was based on two reasons: (1) the economic impacts were especially severe in Africa where cotton was particularly important representing in some countries the majority of its exports and source of income for hundreds of thousands of farmers and (2) the societal impacts experienced in the affected communities from suppressed world prices as a result of US subsidies were incapable of being justified. Therefore, the ethical considerations were framed in both the terms of equitability of the market share of cotton as well as the more qualitative impacts the severe imbalances had on African nations. Pursuant to WTO rules, Members are not to obtain an inequitable market share especially by means of WTO commitment violations. Further, as discussed in Part 1 of this book, the effects of trade distorting subsidies on competing markets, especially those in developing and least developed countries, is significant. The link between US subsidies and rural welfare in African nations was being studied at the time of the *Cotton* dispute and the outcomes of the research confirmed the link and found grim effects. As discussed in Chapters 4 and 7, the recognition by Brazil that these effects were being severely felt in West African nations was integral to their determination that Brazil's (as well as African) interests would be furthered by having these impacted countries join the dispute as co-complainants.

Though the Africans considered participating as co-complainants, at the time immediately prior to the initiation of the Cotton dispute, US Government agencies were working on aid to Africa through the African Growth & Opportunity Act (AGOA), development assistance and food aid through USAID. Given their limited trade expertise and resources, and uncertainty about the process that they had never been involved in before, resulted in the African countries declining to be co-complainants.[1488] However, the countries of Benin and Chad participated in the dispute as third parties – preferring to

---

1487 This was introduced in Section 4.1.
1488 It is important to note that Brazil did not formally request these countries to be co-complainants as doing so would have been in violation of Brazil's foreign policy and international norms.

pursue a negotiating strategy (with Burkina Faso and Mali) alongside Brazil's litigation strategy. Without the participation of the African countries, albeit limited, the dispute could be perceived, as one interviewee stated, "a group of millionaire cotton growers in the US versus a group of millionaire cotton growers in Brazil." Further, Brazil's choice of cotton as an economic development tool was ethically problematic given that Brazil had been criticized for the rate at which new agricultural production was achieved through deforestation.[1489] Therefore, it could have been difficult for Brazil to take the 'ethical' stance against the US when its own agricultural practices of clear cutting millions of acres a year, were being scrutinized and deemed environmentally unconscionable.[1490] Given these dynamics, the participation of the African cotton producing nations, even limited as third parties, as expressed through their Cotton Initiative, added a significant ethical component to the dispute. As Brazil could be confident of and as was found in the study of *Cotton* in the WTO, ethical issues have an impact on the strategy of parties to disputes, on the Panel, on world opinion putting pressure on the US, and impact on negotiations. Brazil recognized the potential for exploiting the ethical dimension of its case and did so in *Cotton*.

It is important to note the role that ethical considerations can play in multinational agreements on political and economic issues. Indeed, one can argue that these considerations are foundational to these agreements and to the WTO itself. The WTO's predecessor, the GATT was created by the Bretton Woods both to promote economic goals and to incorporate an ethical framework to inform multinational interactions. The economic goals form part of the founding goals of the GATT, stated in the preamble to the GATT, include the raising of living standards, ensuring full employment, promoting a steadily growing volume of real income, and expanding the production and exchange of goods.[1491] In addition, as Thomas Cottier has noted, the institutions created by

---

1489 Brazil's conversion of forest to cropland accounted for an estimated annual average of 7,330 square miles (or 4.7 million acres) of lost forested land between 1996 and 2005. Ljunggren, D., "Brazil Sets Target to Slow Amazon deforestation," *The Guardian*, 3 December 2008.

1490 Deforestation is one of the largest sources of the removal of carbon sequestration capacity. For a greater discussion on agricultural production, deforestation, and environmental consequences in Brazil, see, Morton, D. et al., "Cropland expansion changes deforestation dynamics in the southern Brazilian Amazon," Proceedings of the National Academy of Sciences of the United States of America, (27 July 2006) PNAS, Vol. 103, No. 39, 14637–14641.

1491 General Agreement on Tariffs and Trade Preamble, Oct. 30, 1947, 61 Stat. A3, T.I.A.S. No. 1700, 55 U.N.T.S. 187.

Bretton Woods "sought to contribute to the aspirations of Article 28 of the Universal Declaration."[1492] Indeed, the Preamble to the GATT concludes with noting that the nations entering into this agreement are "desirous of contributing to these objectives by entering into reciprocal and mutually advantageous arrangements directed to the substantial reduction of tariffs and other barriers to trade and to the elimination of discriminatory treatment in international commerce."[1493] The ethical dimensions of intergovernmental relations were made even more explicit at the time of the founding of the WTO as the successor of the GATT. As Cottier notes:

> Fifty years later, the Charter of the World Trade Organization (WTO) amended this goals "allowing for the optimal use of the world's resources in accordance with the objective of sustainable development, seeking both to protect and preserve the environment and to enhance the means for doing so in a manner consistent with their respective needs and concerns at different levels of economic development."[1494]

In addition to these values based upon ethical cosmopolitanism,[1495] the adverse effects of actions by developed nations on poorer countries can be considered in the light of the economic notions of horizontal and vertical equity.[1496] In terms of vertical equity, those nations with higher incomes and levels of economic development should bear a greater economic burden in order to impact the general global welfare than those nations with a lower ability to contribute. In other words, from the vertical position, there is a moral

---

1492 Article 28 states: "Everyone is entitled to a social and international order in which the rights and freedoms set forth in this Declaration can be fully realized." Universal Declaration of Human Rights, G.A. res. 217A (III), U.N. Doc A/810 at 71 (1948).
1493 General Agreement on Tariffs and Trade Preamble, Oct. 30, 1947, 61 Stat. A3, T.I.A.S. No. 1700, 55 U.N.T.S. 187.
1494 Cottier, T., "Cosmopolitan Values in International Economic Law: Myths and Realities." NCCR Trade Working Paper No 2008,22, November 2008, p. 3.
1495 Appiah, K., *Cosmopolitanism: Ethics in a World of Strangers*, W.W. Norton & Co., New York (2006).
1496 As Brazil submitted in its 9 September 2003 *Further Submission*, "This is a case involving basic economic principles of supply and demand. It is a case about too much upland cotton being produced and exported by high-cost U.S. producers. It is about the role played by $12.9 billion in U.S. government payments in increasing and maintaining the world's highest export market share of upland cotton. Given the wide disparity in costs of production and the amount of subsidies provided to U.S. upland cotton producers and their competitors in countries like Argentina, Brazil, Benin and Chad, this case is about equity."

obligation to take into consideration the effects of one's actions. When shaping future agricultural policies, countries must take into account the world as a whole. Horizontal equity refers to the equal treatment of nations with similar levels of economic welfare. In the past, there was a severe disconnect between domestic agricultural and international development policy. The *Cotton* dispute has endeavored to bring the two together. This will have considerable long-term implications. Neither of these equity considerations nor the promotion of fostering equitability across the globe in international relations is explicit in the classical economic view of international trade as being designed to maximize efficiencies by promoting the development of comparative advantages, based, on underlying factor endowments, and market exchange. However, the promotion of greater global economic efficiency is only part of the goals of the post-World War II multinational trading agreements such as the GATT and the WTO and is explicit in the charter statement of the WTO.

The inclusion of least developed countries in the *Cotton* dispute brought both equity considerations to the fore. As discussed and cited, *supra*, Brazil explicitly argued the ethics of the case, in terms of the "equitable share of world export trade" and its inclusion of testimony from West Africans and their plight as competitors with US cotton subsidies. Specifically, Brazil illustrated using undisputed ICAC data that the US share of world exports of cotton more than doubled between 1998 and 2002. This constituted an increase in market share from 18.7 to 39.3 percent. Consequentially, African producers' share decreased from 10.2 to 8.1 percent of world trade. As the submission stated, "if a picture is worth a thousand words, it is this one." It continues in the submission,

> Brazil submits it is not equitable for a heavily subsidized WTO Member to more than double its share of competitive world markets for upland cotton in only five years reflecting a significant contribution of subsidies. And it is not equitable for that Member to do so when its costs of production were double those of the *poorest and neediest producers in the world*.

Therefore, the ethical component of the dispute is closely tied to the effects US subsidies have on the welfare of the relevant cotton producing African countries.

In interviewing several practitioners and scholars, it was found that most were hesitant to consider the *Cotton* dispute as an 'ethics' case. Rather, it was preferred to frame the case as yet another example of a Member's ability to "name and shame" the trade policies of another in light of a favorable DSB ruling. Further criticism focused on perspectives from practitioners and government representatives who found that, although fears of lost reputation can be of great concern to the US, moral suasion and ethics tend to have little impact on US Congress. This was explained in analyzing the congressional districts and determining, overall, that the constituents living in these districts – by and large – are not 'development' people. Further, in asking them to consider resource allocation, it was stressed that they are only marginally impacted. When asked, the issue that an actual number was assigned to the degree of harm being caused, responses tended to merge toward the answer that it clarified the issue, but does not add to the ethical argument of the case. Finally, in addition, many scholars and practitioners preferred to consider the *Cotton* dispute in terms of legitimacy to the WTO as more comparable to 'public value' cases, where the public welfare concerns are at issue, as in the cases of the *Hormones* or *US-Tuna* disputes. To that end, it is argued that economics of international trade should engender social sympathy. This has been applied in other areas, internationally, in terms of trade and the environment; regionally, in terms of FTAs and labor concerns; and domestically, in the US with healthcare and even organizations, such as PETA. In order to reach the identified audiences who would be more accepting of the name/shame approach, and the like, it might be necessary to assess the ethical components of the case more in terms of threatened legitimacy and, therefore, sustainability of the system as provided in the following section. In considering how to use an ethical framework to improve the WTO system, perhaps one should follow Niebuhr's classical wisdom, which provides, "an adequate political morality must do justice to the insights of both moralists and political realists."[1497]

In considering non-compliance by the US, in an ethics context, consideration of how to create greater awareness of the adverse effects of US subsidies on the world, "cotton is a case in point. The U.S. government currently pays its own cotton barons US$3.4 bn in subsidies – a lot more than it gives in aid to the whole of Africa...These subsidies encourage the U.S. cotton industry to overproduce."[1498] Abatement of US subsidies would bring world prices back to competitive levels, and thus raise the incomes of the poor cotton exporters. This would then lead them to sustainable growth. This would be a meaningful contribution to the system. Awareness of the violation and awareness of the harm are two ethical components. Further, understanding of what dramatic impact policy change could have on those who are harming is an issue of

---

1497 Niebuhr, R., *Moral Man & Immoral Society: A Study in Ethics and Politics*, Library of Theological Ethics, Westminster John Knox Press, Louisvill, KY, (2001), p. 233.

1498 Exhibit Bra-201 ("Cottoning on to Unfair Trade," Special Report Famine diary, 15 July 2003, Guardian Unlimited).

ethics. As submitted in the *Cotton* dispute, "US cotton subsidies amount to more than the US spends on aid for Africa. Eliminating cotton subsidies would raise the world cotton price by 26%, which would mean an extra seven cents for every pound of African cotton, enough to lift farming communities out of starvation, educate their children, and pay for healthcare."

Therefore, non-compliance by the US in the *Cotton* dispute can be considered not only to constitute illegal, but unethical behavior in light of the harm caused coupled with knowledge of that harm. This was especially egregious, given the US was aware that cotton was known to be an example where, for certain LDCs, the commodity was the only product in which it held a competitive advantage. It seemed especially unjust that a Member, through the employment of subsidies knowingly and dismissively, destroys the economy of another in violation of rules that it developed. As will be discussed, *infra*, that harm is not only committed against Brazil and the C-4, but the WTO system. As a result, non-compliance permeates and fosters not only dire economic consequences but an unethical culture of 'wrongful obedience.'[1499] As Youssouf Abbassalah, Chadian Trade Minister stated, "the US must find a way to protect their cotton farmers without hurting African farmers. He called it a moral obligation."[1500]

> Die *Suende* ist ein Versinken in das Nichts.
> LON L. FULLER on "The Morality of Law"[1501]

9.2 US Threat to the Legitimacy and Sustainability of the WTO

Despite the constraints described in Chapter 8 and the strength of the domestic interests opposing agricultural reform in the US, a primary reason for the US to bring its agricultural policies into conformity with WTO commitments it to preserve the integrity of a system from which it benefits to a much greater extent than the costs of compliance to the cotton sector. WTO non-compliance by the United States on the cotton issue is a considerable threat to the legitimacy and sustainability of the dispute settlement and legislative mechanisms

---

1499 Rhode, D., *Ethics in Practice: Lawyers' Roles, Responsibilities and Regulation*, Oxford University Press, (2000), pp. 94–122.
1500 "African Trade Ministers Urge End to US Cotton Subsidies," *VOANews.com*, Washington (26 October 2006).
1501 Fuller, L., *The Morality of Law*, Storrs Lectures on Jurisprudence Yale Law School, 1963, Yale University Press, New Haven, (1964).

of the WTO. As Gary Clyde Hufbauer emphasized, "Compliance with dispute settlement resolutions is essential to guarantee the credibility of the system."[1502] Further, non-compliance by the US has simultaneously stalled negotiations on cotton, agricultural products more generally, and – given its central role in the development agenda – a conclusion to the Doha Round. This section includes analyses of the adverse effects of US non-compliance on both facets of the multilateral trading system, calling for recognition by the US of the detrimental consequences to the credibility of the WTO. If compliance does not result, the aims for equity within the Doha Development Agenda may be considered lost and the legitimacy of the system threatened.[1503] If these elements do not survive, there is a great likelihood that the WTO system will not as well.

Dispute Settlement Mechanism: "Effective enforcement of negotiated commitments is a pre-condition for the trading system to work."[1504] The *Cotton* dispute was the largest dollar compensation package in WTO history, but will it solve the long-term subsidy problem? Robert Hudec argued "compliance is the appropriate measure of the outcome of a case."[1505] To that end, in the *Cotton* dispute, current US agricultural programs are not in compliance with their WTO obligations as determined by the findings of the DSU of the WTO and further non-compliance is likely to have severe implications for the legitimacy and ultimate sustainability of the dispute settlement mechanism of the WTO. If Members do not respect the system in which they are a Member, the system itself is in danger of becoming irrelevant. This outcome would be especially egregious in relation to the US, given that the US was instrumental in the design, financing and operations of the organization as well as the primary authors of the rules by which it is asking its fellow Member countries to participate. Further, US non-compliance can be seen as being hypocritical and self-serving given that the US has used the system heavily (94 disputes in

---

1502 Gary Clyde Hufbauer, Senior Fellow at the Peterson Institute for International Economics at "A US-Africa Dialogue on the Cotton Trade," sponsored by the Carnegie Endowment and iDEAS Centre, Washington, D.C. (20 July 2009).

1503 For a more extensive analysis on the credibility of the WTO and assessment of the efficacy of the multilateral trading system, *see*, Porter, R., *et al. Efficiency, Equity, Legitimacy: The Multilateral Trading System at the Millennium*, Brookings Institution, Center for Business and Government, Harvard, University, (2001).

1504 Hoekman, B. and Kostecki, M., *The Political Economy of the World Trading System: The WTO and Beyond*, Third Edition, Oxford University Press, (2009), p. 84.

1505 Hudec, R., *Enforcing International Trade Law: The Evolution fo the Modern GATT Legal System*, Butterworth, New York (1993) as found in Hoekman, B. and Kostecki, M., *The Political Economy of the World Trading System: The WTO and Beyond*, Third Edition, Oxford University Press, (2009), p. 85.

15 years). In cases where the US receives a favorable ruling, as one trade analyst noted, "the U.S. government is quick to laud the decision and demand that the offending party immediately comply."[1506] However, in the *Cotton* dispute, the US has reacted considerably differently.

Although the dispute settlement process is relatively young, the last fifteen (15) years. coupled with almost fifty (50) years of experience with the GATT, has proven that a mechanism for resolving trade disputes at the multilateral level is needed and can be effective. In arriving at this point, one element is an absolute requirement – compliance. As John Jackson projected with regards to the WTO dispute system,

> The WTO as an institution continues to require attention in several respects. First, an important question is whether the new dispute settlement procedures will work effectively. There will indeed be temptations of some member nations, probably the largest, to ignore or undermine the results of dispute settlement procedures when those procedure do not entirely suit their interests. The dispute settlement procedure will lose credibility, and thus will fail in its primary purpose of establishing and maintaining a creditable "rule-oriented" system.[1507]

To this end, the *Cotton* dispute and Cotton Initiative are tests of the commitment by the US to the system, which it was instrumental in designing. This raises the issue of principle versus practice. Is it enough for the US to only engage the system on principle without practicing those principles?

Given the disconnect between domestic political influences, *via* maintained sovereignty and national interest, and international obligations, it is reasonable that noncompliance may often result. In fact, "when entering into an agreement, states hope that both sides will comply, but they also recognize that a violation may occur."[1508] However, and as is especially the case with LDCs, smaller economies are more greatly harmed in cases of non-compliance by Members. This was proven to be especially true in the *Cotton* dispute.

1506 Daniella Markheim is Jay Van Andel Senior Trade Policy Analyst in the Center for International Trade and Economics at The Heritage Foundation. *See*, Markheim, D., "Brazilian Retaliation Against US Trade Violations: A Signal for Reform," The Heritage Foundation (24 February 2010) at http://www.heritage.org/Research/Reports/2010/02/Brazilian-Retaliation-Against-US-Trade-Violations-A-Signal-for-Reform.

1507 Jackson, J., *The Jurisprudence of GATT & the WTO: Insights on Treaty Law and Economic Relations*, © Cambridge University Press, 2000, 411.

1508 Guzman, A., *How International Law Works: A Rational Choice Theory*, Oxford University Press, (2008), p. 78.

One of the primary factors considered by the C-4 (and Benin and Chad, specifically) was to consider whether they could retaliate – given US non-compliance. As shown in the case of cotton, the system relies on a Member's ability to successfully implement countermeasures. LDCs and other developing countries do not possess the requisite leverage or resources to meaningfully retaliate without harming their domestic economy, perhaps to an even more detrimental degree. This distinguished Brazil from the African LDCs. Though the C-4 gained from limited participation *via* Benin and Chad as third parties, it does not have any retaliatory right. In many ways, participation did increase the legitimacy and perceived equitability of the system as the legal 'win' was also a dispute settlement 'win' with regards to LDC participation. The dispute resolution system proved to be a legitimate forum in which LDCs could push for and obtain, fair treatment by economically large Members. These advances in credibility of the system would be eroded by continued non-compliance by the US. As a result, in future cases, the US would experience greater difficulty in trying to pressure an opposing Member in the dispute process into compliance. "The cotton issue really questions the very credibility of the system. If the large developed countries are authorised to disobey the rules, how can developing countries then be required to abide by them?"[1509]

By examining the potential discomfort in making the requisite domestic policy changes compared to the systemic consequences of not making those changes, it is clear that the US needs to comply. In reviewing the past fifteen (15) years of WTO dispute settlement, it can be reasonably argued that this approach has proven successful and a peaceful means for resolving trade disputes between Members. One study by Won-Mog Choi unfortunately concluded that, despite this reality, the US "founder and largest supporter...of the system, has become the most frequent defaulter."[1510] Won-Mog Choi similarly concludes that this is mostly due to the fact that, when it comes to deciding whether to comply or not, the US is "taken captive by the special-interest politics of Congress."[1511] To that end, the US needs to recognize that there is a

---

1509 Imboden, N. and Nivet-Claeys, A., "Cotton and the LDCs in the WTO: Negotiations and Litigation, Two Sides of the Same Coin," paper given to author by Anne-Sophie Nivet Claeys of the iDEAS Centre. [original in French; translated by Warwick Wilkins, revised by Nicole Antonietti].

1510 Choi, W., "To Comply or Not to Comply? Non-Implementation Problems in the WTO Dispute Settlement System," *Journal of World Trade*, Vol. 41 No. 5, (2007), pp. 1043–1071, at 1069–1070.

1511 Choi, W., "To Comply or Not to Comply? Non-Implementation Problems in the WTO Dispute Settlement System," *Journal of World Trade*, Vol. 41 No. 5, (2007), pp. 1043–1071, at 1069–1070.

self-interest to preserving the system, and that continued non-compliance is damaging the system.

Given widespread global support for President Obama, especially among European countries, and the fact that the US Congress is presently controlled by the Democratic party, agricultural policy reform can arguably be more easily achieved than under previous administrations. However, it should be emphasized, as described in Chapter 8, that a Republican president, and former governor of Texas, a large cotton-producing state, George W. Bush vetoed the 2008 Farm Bill. However, in a political environment burdened by the lingering effects of the recent financial crisis and ongoing economic slowdown, climate change, and healthcare reform, it is unlikely that significant political capital will be devoted to the cotton issue and greater agricultural policy. However, with US Taxpayers subsidizing Brazilian farmers and the fiscal scrutiny of federal spending occurring in the present economic climate, the opposite may prove to be true. With efficient media mobilization providing the necessary awareness of the issue, Congress may prioritize other issues beyond agricultural interests and, in the current atmosphere of budgetary constraint, justify significant resource transference from the cotton sector and the interests of the NCC to other segments and needs of the American political landscape. This, coupled with a continued threat by Brazil to the intellectually property and services sectors of the US, may prove the perfect storm for dramatic and substantial changes in cotton policies in specific and agricultural reform in general.

Finally, as described in Chapter 3, Congress abdicated much of its power with regards to trade issues to the USTR, part of the Executive Branch of the US government. This is significant and was done intentionally because Congress was aware that, in such matters requiring collective action at the international level, Congressional constituent interests would effectively 'tie their hands' in negotiations, as predicted by public choice theory described in the previous chapter. However, the influence of special interest lobbying groups, such as the NCC, reaches beyond Congress to the USTR. To that extent, pressure on the USTR must come from other sectors of the economy, and their Congressional supporters, in order for significant reform to be a meaningful possibility.

Another central consideration in assessing the likelihood of reform and the damage of non-compliance is that of the effect of reputation. Andrew Guzman offers insight into reputation as it relates to retaliation and reciprocity in the context of international law.[1512] As Guzman describes, fundamental to how

---

1512 Guzman, A., *How International Law Works: A Rational Choice Theory*, Oxford University Press, (2008), pp. 71–118.

reputation is gained and lost is the issue of compliance.[1513] As stated, "when choosing between violation and compliance, at least one of those actions will generate a change in reputation...the state will comply if the reputational gain from compliance exceeds the increase in nonreputational payoffs available if it violates its commitment."[1514] Therefore, in applying this theory to the cotton issue, it can be argued that the US could gain in reputation by complying, since the expectation at this point is for the US to continue to violate its commitments, given factors such as the entrenchment of the NCC and the significant nonreputational payoffs to actors such as Congressional representatives who ensure the receipt of massive subsidies. However, in assessing the potential reputational gain to the US in complying with the WTO rulings and placing the Doha talks in a position where a conclusion can be reached, there is a high probability of significant gain from compliance. This is especially so, prospectively, when considering the future reputation of the US. "When recent conduct has damaged a state's reputation, the state may set out to rebuild it by complying with international legal rules it otherwise would have been tempted to ignore."[1515] Again, the cotton issue within the WTO is an ideal example. It cannot be understated the international reputational damage the US has suffered as a result of *Cotton*. Therefore, the US should be more open to considering compliance in order to rebuild its reputation. Further, from a systemic perspective, the importance of obligation is key. According to Guzman, "the relative importance of an international legal obligation affects the reputational consequences of violating it."[1516]

In sum, while there are domestic political impediments to meaningful reform of cotton and other commodity subsidies, there are significant costs to a failure to do so and varied types of gains from moving toward WTO compliance. America's refusal to comply with adverse WTO rulings erodes US credibility and influence in the debate shaping globalization and, further, undermines the multilateral trading system. The US cannot afford to incur either trade retaliation or the loss of its leadership position in international economic issues and, further, be perceived as damaging the WTO system that

---

1513 Guzman, A., *How International Law Works: A Rational Choice Theory*, Oxford University Press, (2008), p. 73.

1514 Guzman, A., *How International Law Works: A Rational Choice Theory*, Oxford University Press, (2008), p. 75.

1515 Guzman, A., *How International Law Works: A Rational Choice Theory*, Oxford University Press, (2008), p. 86.

1516 Guzman, A., *How International Law Works: A Rational Choice Theory*, Oxford University Press, (2008), p. 85.

is already weakened by nations' inability to conclude Doha round trade negotiations.

Legislative Mechanism: If a conclusion is reached in the near future in the Doha Round, the changes in a 'Doha Package' could direct the drafting of the 2012 Farm Bill. Therefore, there is increasing urgency that a multilateral solution to the cotton issue be addressed expeditiously. However, it is important to note that whether a conclusion is reached or not in Doha, there are significant gains in economic efficiency to be had from meaningful change to the US domestic agricultural subsidy regime. For example, an application of basic economic principles illustrates that there are long-terms gains to be had by the significant reduction in relatively inefficient cotton production and the consequential transference of resources to more efficient commodities – resulting in an increase in those activities in which the US has a comparative advantage.

One applicable approach to the legislative difficulties of achieving WTO compliance is based on the perspective of Andrew Guzman who analyzed the gains from bilateral versus multilateral agreements and why retaliation and reciprocity are not effective means in the multilateral context. Guzman offered the notion that it is easier, in the multilateral context, for governments to "overcome collective action problems."[1517] By way of explanation, Guzman used cases in which states were trying to address "environmental, human rights, and nuclear arms policies" – issues at least as difficult to resolve as the cotton issue. Applying Guzman's notion of collective action, it is here argued that if poverty and development are the aims of the Doha Round and given that agricultural negotiations will dramatically affect more than two-thirds of the membership of the WTO, should not "multilateral cooperation allow[s] states to act collectively and internalize more fully the costs and benefits of their policy choices?"[1518] Further, in applying his reputational analysis (*supra*)[1519] to the WTO negotiation context, it can be reasonably assumed that – given the Round has now been framed as a development round with the cotton issue as its litmus test – damage to the reputation of the US by not complying with WTO rulings or cooperating in the Round would be significant and potentially insurmountable, at least in the short and medium term. In essence, the reputation of the US would be tarnished if the development aspect of the Round is left

---

1517 Guzman, A., *How International Law Works: A Rational Choice Theory*, Oxford University Press, (2008), p. 64.
1518 Guzman, A., *How International Law Works: A Rational Choice Theory*, Oxford University Press, (2008), p. 65.
1519 Guzman, A., *How International Law Works: A Rational Choice Theory*, Oxford University Press, (2008), pp. 71–118.

unaccomplished due to its non-compliance. Consequently, what the US would lose, Brazil (and the G20) would gain because the resulting isolation and diminution of the reputation and negotiating influence of the US would only strengthen the reputation of Brazil and G20. The creation of the 'Post-American World' described by scholars such as Fareed Zakaria may well come to pass sooner than expected.[1520]

Applicable also to the reputational assessment of the US are the issues of moral suasion and international outrage, discussed earlier in this book. The example given was that of Australia's reaction to the Arbitrator's finding that the total adverse effects realized on the world market as a result of US subsidies totaled US$2.905 billion. This determination contributed to growing resentment by countries such as Australia and New Zealand, who have managed to become competitive in agricultural product trade despite, or, more likely, because of the elimination of agricultural subsidies. Further, and as stated before, the size of the damage done by US subsidies is huge by any measure. Taking this legal finding and applying it to the context of the Doha Round, it is not surprising that continued non-compliance incensed Australia to write to the DSB, after the Arbitrator's decision, condemning the US subsidy practices.[1521] As stated before, the statement supported the significant findings of the Arbitrator, including findings that farmers outside the US suffered over US$17 billion in damages from 1999–2005 as a result of U.S. WTO-illegal subsidies.[1522] In addition, Australia projected that those farmers will continue to suffer similar damages under the 2008 Farm Bill.[1523] Further, Australia emphasized the

---

[1520] Zakaria, F., *The Post-American World*, W.W. Norton & Co., (2008). In his book, Fareed Zakaria describes the growing influence of the BRIC countries and the growing influence of *et al.* Brazil, and shifting of power at the international level.

[1521] Statement of Australia, "United States – Subsidies on Upland Cotton: Reports of the Arbitrator," (25 September 2009), p. 1. Important to note is the citation from the Arbitrator's decision, quoted in the statement by Australia, which reads in part: "[T]he specific design and structure of the subsidies at issue, as they have been maintained over a significant period of time, is such as to have created an artificial and persisting competitive advantage for U.S. producers over all other operators.... [T]his has a significant trade-distorting impact, not just on the U.S. domestic market, but on the world market in these products." Again, this is explicit recognition by the Arbitrator (and Australia) of the global adverse effect U.S. subsidies has on the world market.

[1522] Statement of Australia, "United States – Subsidies on Upland Cotton: Reports of the Arbitrator," (25 September 2009), p. 2.

[1523] Statement of Australia, "United States – Subsidies on Upland Cotton: Reports of the Arbitrator," (25 September 2009), p. 1. Such damages are projected, given no substantial positive changes were made to the 2008 Farm Bill.

fact that the *Cotton* decisions only reflect a few of the subsidies available to the agricultural sector in the US and stressed the point that a suspension of concessions or obligations is no substitution for full implementation of the recommendations as a means of bringing the US into compliance with its WTO commitments.[1524] The statement concluded with a call on the US to "implement the rulings and recommendations of the DSB in this long-running dispute without further delay."[1525] Therefore, considerable reputational damage has already occurred, but this damage could be reversed given US compliance in the near term.

Another example of frustration by Members is the recent decision by the G20 to drop the Doha target and to begin focusing on bilateral and regional trade agreements[1526] instead of continued participation in the multilateral framework. Although Canadian Prime Minister Stephen Harper does not see this as the end to Doha, this is evidence that another, severe impasse has resulted in the Doha negotiations. As Pascal Lamy described the dynamics of negotiations at present to a group of business leaders at the recent G20 Summit in Toronto, Canada, "Although 80 percent of the job is done, negotiators are considering the remaining 20 percent, staring at each other waiting for the other side to move first."[1527] As stated earlier, such a stalemate could have deleterious effects on the sustainability of the multilateral system, which has already seen a proliferation in bilateral and regional trade agreements over the last several years.[1528] Again, there is no better time than now for the US to demonstrate leadership and improve its reputation by committing itself to a strategy of compliance.

The consequences of reputational and other loss are not only felt by the US, but more devastatingly all of the Members relying on the functionality of the multilateral system. This is no more disappointing than in the case of the

---

1524 Statement of Australia, "United States – Subsidies on Upland Cotton: Reports of the Arbitrator," (25 September 2009), p. 2.
1525 Statement of Australia, "United States – Subsidies on Upland Cotton: Reports of the Arbitrator," (25 September 2009), p. 2.
1526 Ljunggren, D., "G20 Leaders Drop Doha Target, See Smaller Deals," *Reuters.com*, (26 June 2010). For a greater discussion on regional trade agreements and the WTO, particularly how they may better accommodate developing countries and other related issues, *see*, Steger, D., *WTO: Redesigning the World Trade Organization for the Twenty-first Century*, Wilfrid Laurier University Press, (2010), specifically Part 6, pp. 363–436.
1527 Ljunggren, D., "G20 Leaders Drop Doha Target, See Smaller Deals," *Reuters.com*, (26 June 2010).
1528 *See*, Steger, D., *WTO: Redesigning the World Trade Organization for the Twenty-first Century*, Wilfrid Laurier University Press, (2010), specifically Part 6, pp. 363–436.

African LDCs and their efforts to engage the system by bringing the Cotton Initiative. As stated by IPC Vice Chairperson Marcel Regunaga, "The cotton initiative, which the Africans were able to incorporate in the Doha Round, unfortunately remains stuck, along with the rest of the Doha negotiations, reminding us that a healthy and evolving multilateral trade system requires *both* negotiations and dispute settlement."[1529]

The overriding purpose of the WTO is to facilitate global economic efficiency, increasing international trade and, by so doing, promote the functionality of the global market. Through the introduction of the Cotton Initiative, supported by their participation in the dispute resolution process, the African LDCs have chosen to more actively participate in multilateral negotiations in the belief that, by so doing, the resulting awareness and reform of damaging subsidies would lead to long-term solutions to chronic price suppression for cotton and deleterious agricultural policies generally. In the view of many, for the continued functioning of the world trading system and credibility of the WTO role, the needs of the weakest Members in that system must be protected and promoted. This is especially true for commodities such as cotton, in which those weakest Members are the very ones with the clearest competitive advantage of production. Rather than suffer from chronic poverty due to distortions of the market caused by self-serving and inefficient policies of richer countries, those weakest Members are entitled to the increased incomes and economic betterment that should stem from their ability to be efficient producers.

These gains for African LDCs and other developing nations will only come about with significant changes to US agricultural policies. In the meantime, the fact that these countries will not benefit from agreements such as the Brazil-US MOU and resulting Framework means that they will benefit only if these types of agreements prod the US into WTO compliance. As stated by Nicolas Imboden, Executive Director of the IDEAS Center, "This situation exemplifies how difficult it is for LDCs to benefit from the dispute settlement process" in that "their scope of action is limited because they lack serious retaliation threats to force the big players into compliance or compensation."[1530] Therefore, the fate of the African cotton initiative depends, to a large extent, on

---

[1529] "The Cotton Dispute," International Food & Agricultural Trade Policy Council (IPC), IPC Alert, FP7NTM/Impact, (8 April 2010) at http://www.ntm-impact.eu/innovaportal/v/406/1/innova.front/ipc_alert:_the_us-br_cotton_dispute_8_april_%6010.

[1530] "The Cotton Dispute," International Food & Agricultural Trade Policy Council (IPC), IPC Alert, FP7NTM/Impact, (8 April 2010) at http://www.ntm-impact.eu/innovaportal/v/406/1/innova.front/ipc_alert:_the_us-br_cotton_dispute_8_april_%6010.

the fate of the greater DDA. Their only other source of hope rests with the potential for gains stemming from any compensation or other legal recourse from the ramifications of the *Cotton* dispute or from bringing similar disputes with more direct involvement than their role as third parties. Absent the potential benefits from litigation, the best hope of LDCs likely rests with the Doha negotiations. Although some recent studies have concluded that the Doha Round as it stands at present would not dramatically alter world trade, generally, a recent study by Antoine Bouet and David Laborde of the International Food Policy Research Institute assessed the scenario of a failed Doha and concluded,

> The failure of a WTO agreement would be a clear sign of international noncooperation; it would launch trade conflicts and litigations (especially between High-Income and Developing Countries) and would be the first unsuccessful Round despite the fact that it is the first Round to focus on development and the first Round launched by the WTO. In a period of economic stagnation, the risk is high that this failure would give WTO members the incentive to pursue non-cooperative strategies via the adoption of protectionist policies. In that case, the loss would be much greater than a mere US$79 billion. This study concludes there would be a potential loss of at least US$1,064 billion in world trade if world leaders were to fail to conclude the Doha Development Round of trade negotiations in the next few weeks and if countries were to implement subsequently protectionist policies, as was observed after the end of the Uruguay Round. Thus, the stakes in Geneva are very high and the July 2008 package appears to be the closest and most promising step toward a global development agenda for a world in turmoil.[1531]

Overall, as outlined above, compliance is virtually a necessary condition not only for the improvement of least developed and developing nations, but also for the maintenance and improvement of the multilateral trading and negotiation system. Compliance should be a prerequisite to participation in the dispute settlement process.[1532] Another solution considered is whether a

---

1531 Bouet, A., and Laborde, D., "The Potential Cost of a Failed Doha Round," International Food Policy Research Institute, IFPRI Issue Brief 56, (December 2008).

1532 An alternative view is that the conditions for reform may be improved when parties may be allowed to 'opt out' of having to implement some adverse rulings. This has been considered by scholars in the context of building into the system a means by which parties may efficiently breach their commitments. However, this has been deemed more appropriate in situations where developing countries or LDCs are involved.

compensatory mechanism should be added to the present remedy of suspending concessions. What is argued here is that violating Members should absolutely not be able to maintain non-compliant measures nor be allowed to use the potential withdrawal of those measures as bargaining chips in negotiations. Although the legal and political mechanisms of the WTO are tied, compliance may be subject to some negotiation, but not as a means to blackmail an entire Round of negotiations. This is the most damaging result of non-compliance by the US in the *Cotton* dispute. The preferred outcome is compliance by the US, which would provide the impetus for the conclusion of the Doha Round and represent a historical marker for the US. The political capital the US could gain in its relations with the South, particularly LDCs, as well as its credibility in a system in which it is immensely invested. This would seem motivation enough for compliance. Finally, as argued in Section 9.1, the US has an ethical obligation to conform its agricultural policies to its international commitments.

9.3 Summary of Part 3

Built upon the economic and political foundations of the *Cotton* dispute as well as the comprehensive description of the five proceedings through which it developed, Part 3 set forth an analysis of the extent to which Brazil and the C-4 have been able to leverage the *Cotton* dispute in Doha negotiations. Though each chose divergent paths, it was learned that both the legislative and dispute mechanisms of the WTO were required to frame and further the interests of cotton-producing Members.

Given no final outcome has been achieved at this time on the cotton issue, and the deleterious effects of US continued violation are being realized, Part 3 of this book provided a number of ethical considerations involved in the *Cotton* dispute as well as set a vertical-horizontal framework of equability, under which to analyze US non-compliance. It is within the proffered context that US non-compliance with its WTO commitments, particularly in terms of the dispute settlement and legislative mechanisms of the multilateral trading system, that it was determined the unethical US behavior stands to threaten the legitimacy and sustainability of the World Trade Organization. Therefore, it was argued that the consequences of not resolving the cotton issue in an ethical and expedient manner will be detrimental not only to Brazil and the C-4, but the greater system and its Members.

Summation of Findings and Conclusion

The WTO's *Cotton* dispute is an excellent case study and indicator of the efficacy of the World Trade Organization, after fifteen (15) years in operation and in the context of the Doha Development Agenda. Due to the dualistic nature of the litigation to both the dispute settlement as well as legislative mechanisms of the WTO, *Cotton* contributes to the novel interwoven interests and processes by which international trade is conducted and managed. The fact that cotton is an essential and historical commodity, grown and traded around the world makes it an important commodity to examine, especially given its production in countries of various economic sizes. It perfectly represents the political imbalances within the trade relations of these nations and as they play out in the international arena. Further, a study on the trade of cotton illustrates classical economic theory, which has been the foundation of trade relations and the development of the WTO system throughout its history. A reduction in tariffs after its predecessor, GATT, seems to be linked to an increase in subsidies. Subsidies are recognized as being highly trade distortive and even moreso in the present trading environment where tariffs are lower than ever before.

The Dispute Settlement Body in the *Cotton* dispute not only ruled on the trade distorting effects, but globally published the degree and effects of the subsidies. In terms of the dispute settlement process, the *Cotton* dispute was the first agricultural subsidies case brought before the WTO and the first case in which LDC countries participated. It is an excellent case from which to learn about the dispute settlement process as it 'made the full loop' and offers a comprehensive understanding of the legal system of the WTO. Finally, it is an aim of this book to bring new analyses of the dispute – specifically, the ethical considerations that should be regarded when implementing domestic policies known to be non-compliant and damaging to economies that depend on commitments made through negotiations.

The primary legal scope of the book is the Agreement on Agriculture (AoA) and Agreement on Subsidies and Countervailing Measures (SCM) as they have been interpreted through the various *Cotton* proceedings of the Understanding on Dispute Settlement (DSU). More specifically, agricultural subsidies (prohibited v. actionable as well as domestic support and export subsidies) are interpreted, Article 13 of the AoA known as the Peace Clause was considered – both the rulings through the *Cotton* proceedings as well as its future application, the legal determination of serious prejudice, and the effectiveness of the remedies provided (specifically, retaliatory measures). Two additional analyses were included: (1) the lessons learned for WTO lawyers, in terms of the strategies executed as well as (2) lessons learned for developing countries engaged in the dispute settlement process of the WTO.

The political scope of the book was the negotiation frameworks developed under the Doha Development Agenda and related negotiations. Specifically, a description of the development of the Cotton Initiative as well as an analysis of its efficacy was included. Agricultural committee negotiations and the participation of external interest groups as well as the formation of internal coalitions will be assessed. Further, the creation of the Subcommittee on Cotton in the Agricultural negotiations was used as a negotiating strategy for issue definition. Within this negotiation analysis were considerations of domestic agricultural support measures, agricultural export subsidies, the determination of schedule of concessions, and agricultural subsidies. The inclusion of a political analysis was used to establish the greater link between the legal and political system of the WTO. Issues such as how litigation can be an effective negotiating tool and how it builds political strength in talks is a key evaluation. In summary, a conclusion was proffered as to what the case means to the negotiation framework.

The domestic scope of this book included the formulation and implementation of policies in line with international commitments. The role and applicability of international law (particularly, treaties) was evaluated. More specifically, the domestic subsidy regimes of the relevant countries (US, EU, Brazil, and C-4 countries) were described. The majority of analysis is focused on US domestic agricultural policy and its most recent Farm Bills. Included was an assessment of how both the legal and political cotton developments in the WTO influenced change in US agricultural policy as well as trade relations between Brazil and the US. The case was a win for Brazil, which propelled its political leadership in the present Doha negotiations and contributed to the rebalancing of powers between the developed and developing nations. From the African perspective, the conclusion of whether its aim of improving its position within the global cotton markets is in unknown at present. However, it is certain that the *Cotton* dispute does establish an effective means and methods by which least developed countries can utilize the WTO system. The message sent to other developing countries as well is positive. A determination of what was expended versus what was gained was included in the book.

Finally, the ethical foundations and considerations pertinent to the *Cotton* dispute were examined. A description of cosmopolitan ethics was applied to international trade, using cotton as the emblem of the development issues currently faced in the WTO. Questions of whether the WTO system and procedures are fair, just and ethical were responded to. It is hoped that this analysis will provide the moral suasion necessary for domestic change in the US as reinforced by the foundational principles committed to by one of the founding and most influential designers of the WTO.

In summary, the *Cotton* dispute added significantly to the jurisprudence of the DSU of the WTO. *Cotton* demonstrates how the WTO dispute settlement can provide support for the legislative function of the WTO. Specifically, this was demonstrated through the formation and utilization of the G-20, the African group and their Cotton Initiative, and both coalitions' collective effect on softening up the US and EU's positions. Further, the role of the media and NGOs as well as the chosen representation and Brazil in the case sets an impressive precedent for how participants can access and utilize the WTO system. The WTO *Cotton* case played a key role in organizing and empowering African cotton countries in the Doha negotiations. Although a change in markets in Brazil has not been realized at this time, the case and the related political developments, have undoubtedly added to Brazil's political weight in bilateral as well as multilateral trade relations. Further, it was established that Brazil won the case. A number of chilling (legal) and multiplier (political) effects result from this outcome. The precedence of the case will be applied to future WTO cases and negotiations as well as considered when Members formulate their domestic policies to make significant changes or not implement new bad policies by different WTO Members. The *Cotton* (and related *Sugar*) disputes were important parts of a process for pushing the world's biggest subsidizer, and the EU, to change the nature of their subsidies to less trade-distorting methods. These included eliminating production support such as US marketing loan subsidies, both domestic support methods as well as moving to eliminate export subsidies such as Step 2. Most importantly, it added *as fact* the effects of the US's cotton program on developing nations, furthering the moral suasion argument that the rate and sheer size of subsidies are unethical and policies should be designed that consider the consequential impacts, in line with an understanding of cosmopolitan ethics. *Cotton* also exposes the limitations of the WTO dispute settlement system for Members, especially least developing countries who only received secondary benefits secured by others. The concern then arises whether any short-term implementation benefits will be received and the long-term benefits are still unrealized. Finally, *Cotton* exposes the resistance of economically large WTO Members, in highly political cases, to implement policy changes at the domestic level.

General References

Allison, G., Zelikow, P., *Essence of Decision: Explaining the Cuban Missile Crisis,* Addison Wesley Longman, New York (1999).
Alverez, J., *International Organizations a Law-Makers,* Oxford University Press, New York (2005).
Arup, C., *The New World Trade Organization Agreements: Globalizing Law through Services and Intellectual Property,* Cambridge University Press, Cambridge (2001).
Anderson, K., "Multilateral Trade Negotiations, European Integration, and Farm Policy, *Economic Policy* (April, 1994), No. 18.
Anderson, S., *Views from the South,* Food First Books, The International Forum on Globalization, Chicago (2000).
Anderson, K., Hoekman, B., *The Global Trading System: Volume I*, I.B. Tauris Publishers, London (2002a).
Anderson, K., Hoekman, B., *The Global Trading System: Volume II*, I.B. Tauris Publishers, London (2002b).
Anderson, K., Hoekman, B., *The Global Trading System: Volume III*, I.B. Tauris Publishers, London (2002c).
Anderson, K., Hoekman, B., *The Global Trading System: Volume IV*, I.B. Tauris Publishers, London (2002d).
Antle, J., *World Agricultural Development and the Future of US Agriculture*, American Enterprise Institute for Public Policy Research, Washington DC (1988).
Appiah, K., *Cosmopolitanism: Ethics in a World of Strangers*, Norton Press (2006).
Appiah, K., *Experiments in Ethics*, Harvard University Press, Cambridge (2008).
Atack, J., Bateman, F., *To Their Own Soil: Agriculture in the Antebellum North*, Iowa State University Press, Ames (1987).
Baffes, John, "The Multilateral Trading System: A US-African Dialogue," Presentation, sponsored by the iDEAS & Carnegie Endowment in Washington, DC (July 20, 2009).
Bassett, T., *The Peasant Cotton Revolution in West Africa*, Cambridge University Press, Cambridge (2001).
Bhagwati, J., *The World Trading System at Risk,* Princeton University press, Princeton (1991).
Bhagwati, J., *Free Trade Today*, Princeton University Press, Princeton (2002).
Bhagwati, J., Panagariya, A., and Srinivasan, T.N., *Lectures on International Trade*, Second Ed., The MIT Press, Cambridge (1998).
Blank, S., *The End of Agriculture in the American Portfolio*, Quorum Books, London (1998).

Blank, S., *The Economic of American Agriculture: Evolution and Global Development*, M. E. Sharpe, London (2008).

Bronckers, M., Horlick, G., *WTO Jurisprudence and Policy Practitioners' Perspectives*, Cameron May Ltd., London (2004).

Brown, C., *Self-Enforcing Trade*, Brookings Institution, Washington DC (2009).

Browne, W., *Private Interests, Public Policy, and American Agriculture*, University Press of Kansas, Lawrence, Kansas, p. 91 (1988, 2007).

Cline, W., *Trade Policy and Global Poverty*, Institute for International Economics and Center for Global Development (2004).

Cohen, D., *Globalization and Its Enemies*, The MIT Press, Cambridge, MA (2006).

Cohn, D., *The Life and times of King Cotton*, Oxford University Press, New York (1956).

Cohn, T., *Governing Global Trade*, Ashgate Publishing, Burlington (2002).

Cottier, T., et al., *Human Rights and International Trade*, Oxford University Press (2005).

Cottier, T., et al., *The Role of the Judge in International Trade Regulation: Experiences and Lessons for the WTO*, University of Michigan Press, World Trade Forum, Vol. 4 (2006).

Das, L., *The Current Negotiations in the WTO: Options, Opportunities and Risks for Developing Countries*, Zed Books, Third World Network, New York (2007).

Das, P., *The Doha Round of Multilateral Trade Negotiations: Arduous Issues and Strategic Responses*, Palgrave Macmillian, New York (2005).

Desta, M., *The Law of International Trade in Agricultural Products*, Kluwer Law International, London (2002).

Devereaux, C., Lawrence, R., Watkins, M., *Case Studies in US Trade Negotiations Vol. 1: Making the Rules*, Institute for International Economics, Washington DC (2006a).

Devereaux, C., Lawrence, R., Watkins, M., *Case Studies in US Trade Negotiations Vol. 2: Resolving Disputes*, Institute for International Economics, Washington DC (2006b).

Devuyst, Y., *The European Union at the Crossroads*, P.I.E – Peter Lang, New York (2003).

Diakosavvas, D., "The Uruguay Round Agreement on Agriculture in Practice: How Open are OECD Markets? Mimeo. *Directorate for Food, Agriculture and Fisheries*. Paris: OECD (2001).

Diakosavvas, D., Guillot, S., "The Uruguay Round Agreement on Agriculture: An Evaluation of Its Implementation in OECD Countries," OECD, Paris, France (April, 2001).

Dixit, A., Norman, V., *Theory of International Trade*, Cambridge University Press, Cambridge (1980).

Eichengreen, B., *Globalizing Capital: A History of the International Monetary System*, Princeton University Press, Princeton (2008).

Eishengreen, B., Wyploz, C., Park, Y., *China, Asia, and the New World Economy*, Oxford University Press, New York (2008).

Feenstra, R., *Advanced International Trade*, Princeton University Press, Princeton (2004).

Fieldhouse, D.K., *The West and the Third World*, Blackwell Publishers, Malden (1999).

Fischer, R., *Latin American and the Global Economy: Export Trade and the Threat of Procetion*, Palgrave Macmillian, New York (2001).

Fite, G., *Cotton Fields No More*, The University Press of Kentucky, Lexington (1984).

Folsom, R., Gordon, M., Spanogle, J. Jr., *International Trade and Investment: In a Nut Shell*, West Publishing Co., St. Paul (1996).

Fratianni, M., Savona, P., Kirton, J., *Sustaining Global Growth*, Ashgate Publishing, Burlington (2003).

Fuller, L., *The Morality of Law*, Yale University Press (1964).

Gardener, B., *US Agricultural Policy: The 1985 Farm Legislation*, American Enterprise Institute for Public Policy Research, Washington DC (1985).

Gardener, B.D., *Plowing Ground in Washington*, Pacific Research Institute for Public Policy, San Francisco (1995).

Goode, W., *Dictionary of Trade Policy Terms*, Cambridge University Press, Cambridge (2007).

Griller, S., *At the Crossroads: The World Trading System and the Doha Round*, Springer (2008).

Guzman, A., *How International Law Works: A Rational Choice Theory*, Oxford University Press (2008).

Hajnal, P., *The G8 System and the G20*, Ashgate Publishing, Burlington (2007).

Hoekman, B., Matoo A., English, P., *Development, Trade, and the WTO: A Handbook*, The World Bank, Washington DC (2002).

Hoekman, B., Olarrega M., *Global Trade and Poor Nations*, Brookings Institution, Washington DC (2007).

Hoekman, B., Kostecki, M., *The Political Economy of the World Trading System: From GATT to WTO*, Oxford University Press, New York (1995).

Hoekman, B., Kostecki, M., *The Political Economy of the World Trading System: The WTO and Beyond*, Third Edition, Oxford University Press, New York (2009).

Hofstede, G., *Cultures and Organizations: Software of the Mind*, McGraw Hill, New York (1997).

Honda, A., Gulati A., *WTO Negotiations on Agriculture and Developing Countries*, Johns Hopkins University Press, Baltimore (2007).

Ingco, M. and Winter, A. *Agriculture and the New Trade Agenda: Creating a Global Trading Environment for Development*, Cambridge University Press, World Bank (2004).

International Trade Centre: Product and Market Development, *Cotton Exporter's Guide*, UNCTAD, WTO OMC, Geneva, WTO/UNCTAD/WTO, ITC/P218.E/PMD/MDS/07-XI (2007).

Irwin, D., Mavroidis, P., Sykes, A., *The Genesis of the GATT*, Cambridge University Press, Cambridge (2008).

Jackson, J., *The World Trading System*, The MIT Press, Cambridge (1997).

Jackson, J., *The Jurisprudence of GATT & the WTO: Insights on Treaty Law and Economic Relations*, Cambridge University Press (2000).

Jacobson, T., Smith, G., *Cotton's Renaissance: A Study in Markey Innovation*, Cambridge University Press, Cambridge (2001).

Jawara, F., Kwa, A., *Behind the Scenes at the WTO: The Real World of International Trade Negations Lessons of Cancun*, Zed Books, London (2003).

Jones, K., *Who's Afraid of the WTO?* Oxford University Press, New York (2004).

Josling, T., Taylor, T., *Banana Wars*, CABI Publishing, Cambridge (2003).

Kaplinsky, R., *Globalization, Poverty and Inequality*, Polity Press, Cambridge (2005).

Krueger, A., *Trade Policies and Developing Nations*, The Brookings Institute, Washington DC (1995).

Krugman, P., Obstfeld, M., *International Economics: Theory and Policy*, Addison Wesley, New York (2003).

Lama, D. (His Holiness the Dalai Lama), *Ethics for the New Millennium*, Riverhead Books, New York (1999).

Low, P., *Trading Free: The GATT and the US Trade Policy*, Twentieth Century Fund Book, New York (1993).

Lowenfeld, A., *International Economic Law*, Oxford University Press, New York (2008).

Lynn, D., Heyck, D., *Surviving Globalization in Three Latin American Communities*, Broadview Press, Ltd., Peterborough (2002).

Mankiw, N., *Principles of Economics*, Thomson, South-Western, Cambridge (2004).

Marin, L., *Food for Thought*, Johns Hopkins University Press, Baltimore (1989).

Maskus, K., *Intellectual Property Rights in the Global Economy*, Institute for International Economics, Washington DC. (2000).

Meyers, M., Ferrarini, B., *Agricultural Exports as Egine of Growth for Developing Countries? A Case Study on International Trade in Tobacco*, Seco and WTI Publikation, Berne (2004).

Messerlin, P., "Measuring the Costs of Protection in Europe: European Commercial Policy in the 2000s," Washing: Institute for International Economics (2001).

Messerlin, P., "Agriculture in the Doha Agenda," The World Bank (August, 2002).

Molyneux, C., *Domestic Structures and International Trade: The Unfair Trade Instruments of the United States and European Union*, Hart Publishing, Studies in European Law and Integration (2001).

Morrison, T., Conway, W., *Kiss, Bow, or Shake Hands: Europe*, Business, Avon (2007).

Najam, A., Halle, M., Melédez-Ortiz, R., *Envisioning a Sustainable Development Agenda for Trade and Environment*, Palgrave Macmillian, New York (2007).

Narasaiah, M., *World Trade Organizations and the Developing Countries*, Discovery Publishing House, New Delhi (2001).

Narlikar, A., *The World Trade Organization: A Very Short Introduction*, Oxford University Press, New York (2005).

Newbery, D., Stiglitz, J., *The Theory of Commodity Price Stabilization*, Clarendon Press, Oxford (1981).

Newfarmer, R., *Trade, Doha, and Development: A Window into the Issues*, The World Bank, Trade Department, Washington DC (2006).

Niebuhr, R., *Moral Man & Immoral Society: A Study in Ethics and Politics*, Westminster John Knox Press, Louisville, KY (2001).

O'Connor, B., *Agriculture in WTO Law*, Cameron May Ltd., London (2005).

Odell, J., *Negotiating Trade: Developing Countries in the WTO and NAFTA*, Cambridge University Press, Cambridge (2006).

OECD, "The Uruguay Round Agreement on Agriculture: An Evaluation of Its Implementation," Paris (2001).

Pasour, E. Jr., Rucker, R., *Plowshares & Pork Barrels*, The Independent Institute, Oakland (2005).

Patterson, D,. Afilalo, A., *The New Global Trading Order: Evolving State and Future Trade*, Cambridge University Press, Cambridge (2008).

Pauwelyn, J., *Conflict of Norms in Public International Law*, Cambridge University Press, Cambridge (2003).

Peláez, C.M., Peláez, C.A., *Government Intervention in Globalization*, Palgrave Macmillian, New York (2008).

Perry, E., *Practical Export Trade Finance*, Dow Jones-Irwin, Homewood (1989).

Porter, P., et al, *Efficiency, Equity, Legitimacy: The Multilateral Trading System at the Millennium*, Brookings Institution Press, Washington, DC (2001).

Pryles, M., Waincymer, J., Davies, M., *International Trade Law*, LBC Information Services, Sydney (1996).

Rajan, G., Zingales, L., *Saving Capitalism from the Capitalists*, Crown Business, New York (2003).

Redman, E., *The Dance of Legislation: An Insider's Account of the Workings of the United States Senate*, University of Washington Press, Seattle and London (2001).

Reinert, E., *Globalization, Economic Development and Inequality: An Alternate Perspective*, New Horizons in Institutional and Evolutionary Economics, Chetlenham (2004).

Rhode, D., *Ethics in Practice: Lawyers' Roles, Responsibilities, and Regulation*, Oxford University Press (2000).

Rich, G., *Latin American: Its Future in the Global Economy*, Palgrave Macmillian, New York (2002).

Rubin, A., *Ethics and Authority in International Law*, Cambridge University Press, Cambridge Studies in International and Comparative Law (1997).

Rugman, A., Boyd, G., *The World Trade Organization in the New Global Economy*, new Horizons in International Business, Chetlenham (2001).

Sampson, G., *The WTO and Sustainable Development*, United Nations University Press, New York (2005).

Schmitz, A., Moss, C., Schmitz, T., Koo, W., *International Agricultural trade Disputes: Case Studies in North America*, University of Calgary Press, Calgary (2005).

Selcher, W., *Brazil in the International System: The Rise of a Middle Power*, Westview Press, Bolder (1981).

Seyoum, B., *Export–import Theory, Practices, and Procedures*, Routledge, New York (2009).

Soros, G., *On Globalization*, Public Affairs, New York (2002).

Steger, D., *WTO: Redesigning the World Trade Organization for the Twenty-first Century*, Wilfrid Laurier University Press (2010).

Stern, R., *U.S. Trade Policies in a Changing World Economy*, The MIT Press, Cambridge (1988).

Starbird, Irving R., United States, Economic Research Service, Department of Agriculture, *The U.S. Cotton Industry* (June 1987).

Stiglitz, J., Charlton, A., *Fair Trade for All: How Trade can promote Development*, Oxford University Press, New York (2005).

Stokey, E., Zeckhauser, R., *A Primer for Policy Analysis*, Norton & Company, New York (1978).

Stubbs, R., Unerhill, G., *Political Economy and the Changing Global Order*, Oxford University Press, New York (2000).

Sumner, D., *Agricultural Policy Reform in the United States*, AEI Press, Washington DC (1995).

Sumner, Daniel A., "U.S. Farm Policy and the White Commodities: Cotton, Rice, Sugar and Milk," International Food & Agricultural Trade Policy Council (Washington, DC: IPC, 2007).

Tabb, W., *Unequal Partners*, The New York Press, New York (2002).

Tangermann, S., "Has the Uruguay Round Agreement on Agriculture Worked Well?" Mimeo, Directorate for Food, Agriculture and Fisheries, Paris: OECD (2001).

Townsend, Terry, Executive Director of the International Cotton Advisory Committee (ICAC), "The Multilateral Trading System: A US-African Dialogue," Presentation, sponsored by the iDEAS & Carnegie Endowment in Washington, DC (July 20, 2009).

Tufte, E., *Data Analysis for Politics and Policy*, Prentice-Hall, London (1974).

Turner, B., *The Statesman's Yearbook: The Politics, Cultures, and Economies of the World: 2007*, 143rd Edition, Palgrave Macmillan (2006).

Tweeten, L., Thompson, S., *Agricultural policy for the 21st Century*, Iowa State Press, Ames (2002).

Van den Bossche, P., *The Law and Policy of the World Trade Organization: Text, Cases, and Materials*, Cambridge University Press, Cambridge (2008).

Wallerstein, I., *Africa and the Modern World*, Africa World Press, Inc. Trenton (1986).

Williams, M., *The Realist Tradition and the Limits of International Relations*, Cambridge University Press, Cambridge Studies in International Relations (2005).

Williamson, R., Glade Jr. W., Schmitt. K., *Latin American-US Economic Integrations*, American Enterprise Institute for Public Policy Research, Washington DC (1974).

Wilson, D., *International Business Transactions: In a Nut Shell*, West Publishing Co., St. Paul (1984).

Womach, Jasper., CSR Report for Congress, *Cotton Production and Support in the United States*, June 24, 2004a.

Womach, J., "Cotton Production and Support in the United States," CRS Report for Congress, Congressional Research Service (2004b).

Woodman, H., *King Cotton and His Retainers*, University of South Carolina Press, Lexington (1968).

World Trade Organization, *The Legal Texts: Results of the Uruguay Round of Multilateral Trade Negotiations*, Cambridge University Press (1994).

World Trade Organization, *WTO Agriculture Negotiations: The Issues, and Where We are Now*, WTO (updated 1 December, 2004).

WTO, *Anlytical Index: Guide to WTO Law and Practice: Volume 1*, Cambridge University Press, World Trade Organization, Cambridge (2007a).

WTO, *Anlytical Index: Guide to WTO Law and Practice: Volume 2*, Cambridge University Press, World Trade Organization, Cambridge (2007b).

WTO, *Appellate Body Repertory of Reports and Awards: 1995–2006*, Compiled by the Appellate Body Secretariat, Cambridge University Press, World Trade Organization, Cambridge (2007c).

WTO Secretariat, *The WTO Dispute Settlement Procedures*, Cambridge University Press, Cambridge (2005).

WTO Secretariat, *A Handbook on the WTO Settlement System,* Cambridge University Press, Cambridge (2007).

WTO Secretariat, *A Handbook on Reading WTO Goods and Services Schedules,* Cambridge University Press, Cambridge (2009).

Zakaria, F., *The Post-American World*, W.W. Norton & Co. (2008).

Zielger, D., *War, Peace, and International Politics*, Addison, Wesley, Longman, Inc., New York (2000).

Index

Actionable subsidies   130, 152, 152n473, 164–166, 166n565, 169, 182n654, 239, 250, 251, 255, 264
Ad valorem (in proportion to worth)   72
Adverse effects   25, 51, 72, 140n423, 143, 161, 166–169, 169
Advisory Centre on WTO Law (intergovernmental) (ACWL)   126n375, 281n1123, 284n1134, 286, 286n1143, 327
African Cotton & Textile Industries Federation (A.C.A.)   288n1152
African Group   349n1340, 405
African Growth & Opportunity Act (AGOA)   386
aggregate measure of support (AMS)   57n193, 70, 139, 186, 189n693, 199, 200, 361, 373
Agreement on Agriculture (AoA-WTO)   2, 68, 68n221, 69, 69n222, 69n225, 69n226, 70n229, 71n232, 72, 72n235, 73, 75, 76, 76n246, 77, 78, 81, 85, 92, 94, 96, 96n313, 103, 107, 116, 120, 129, 130n387, 132, 134, 136, 136n405, 137, 137n409, 138, 138n410, 138n411, 139n415, 139n417, 139n418, 139n419, 139n420, 139n421, 140n422, 140n424, 140n426, 141, 141n431, n408
Agricultural Policy Advisory Committee for Trade   60
Agricultural Risk Protection Act of 2000   48n157
Agricultural Technical Advisory Committee for Trade   60
Alexandria Cotton Exporters Association (ACTIF)   288n1152
Amber Box   70, 139, 186, 317, 371
Andersen, S.   123, 263n1064
anti-dumping   90, 193n719, 212n822, 282n1127, 306n1189
Appellate Body (AB)   134
Appellate Body Report (ABR)   160n522, 161n535, 165, 181n652, 182n654, 182n655, 182n656, 182n657, 182n658, 182n659, 183n660, 183n661, 183n662, 183n663, 183n664, 183n665, 184n666, 184n667, 185n668, 185n669, 185n670, 185n671, 185n672, 185n673, 185n675, 186n678, 186n679, 187n680, 187n681, 187n682, 187n683, 187n684, 187n685, 190n600, 191n701, 191n702, 191n703, 191n704, 191n705, 192n710, 192n711, 192n712, 192n713
Arbitration   4, 112n338, 130, 216, 216n850, 217n854, 237–260, 261, 263, 270, 274, 275, 277, 278, 322, 350, 365n1406
Arbitrator   103, 134, 144, 235, 262, 318, 358, 398
Argentina   8, 89n291, 92n297, 93n304, 107, 149n456, 150, 153, 181n652, 229n920, 290n1170, 314, 314n1126, 349n1343, 388n1497
Australia   7, 8, 16, 18, 22, 73n240, 91n296, 92n296, 111, 116, 127n377, 150, 153, 181n652, 217n856, 229n920, 230, 258, 258n1051, 258n1052, 258n1053, 319n1235, 351, 351n1349, 351n1350, 351n1351, 351n1352, 351n1353, 351n1354, 351n1355, 352n1356, 352n1357, 352n1358, 398, 398n1522, 399n1526
Azevedo, R.   122, 382

Benin   1, 2, 23, 62, 126n374, 147, 262, 305, 365, 386
Blue Box   73, 139, 140, 186
Brazil   1, 7n7, 40, 100, 103–131, 132, 303, 356, 385
Brazilian Chamber of Foreign Trade (CAMEX)   378
Brazilian Cotton Producers Association (ABRAPA)   127
Burkina Faso   2, 23, 24, 26, 27, 62, 282, 291n1160, 293n1173, 296, 297, 318, 324, 329, 330, 330n1275, 336, 337, 339, 342–344, 344n1325, 345, 345n1327, 352, 352n1358, 354, 385, 387

Calcot, Ltd   59, 59n199
California Rice Industry Association   125
Caribbean Community and Common Market   318n1234

INDEX

Carnegie Endowment   13, 13n25, 13n26, 14n27, 319n237, 319n238, 319n1236, 337n1299, 350n1345, 352n1358, 392n1503
Chad   1, 2, 23, 24, 26, 62, 79, 100, 101, 126–129, 129n380, 131, 149n456, 150, 168, 168n580, 170n588, 177, 178, 181n652, 192, 279, 291–298, 305, 318, 324, 338–341, 341n1310, 343–345, 365, 386, 388, 394
Chinatex   52
Commodity Credit Corporation (CCC)   36, 37, 41, 51, 159, 172
Common Agricultural Policy (EC)   54, 75, 80, 156, 159n519, 276n1112, 369, 384
Common Commercial Policy (CCP)   47, 152n474, 166, 168n579, 171n592, 172, 360
Common Market for East and Southern Africa (COMESA)   85
Compliance panel   188n689, 210n812, 215–236, 217n854, 217n855, 217n856, 265–268, 270, 372, 377
Congressional Research Service   10n17, 28, 37n105, 38n112, 47n151, 47n152, 59n201, 69n223, 360, 360n1385, 361n1387, 364n1401, 371n1421, 373, 373n1432, 374, 374n1435
Consultation   147–149, 373n1433, 373n1434, 384
Cotton Board (USA)   56, 57, 57n191, 58, 288n1152
Cotton Council International (USA) (CCI)   57
Cotton Growers Cooperative   26, 27, 30, 32, 33, 59, 172, 338n1303, 365, 387
Cotton Incorporated   56, 58, 58n194
Cotton Initiative   60, 63, 64, 77, 91, 279, 296, 297, 316, 318, 324–355, 385, 387, 393, 400, 404, 405
Cotton South Africa (Cotton SA)   288n1152
Cotton subsidy   21, 31–43, 44–51, 118, 127, 143n442, 198n748, 296, 310, 343, 366, 386
Countermeasure   243, 255n1038
countervailing duties (CVD)   2, 96, 103

Dillon Round   106
Director General (WTO)   106, 238
Direct Payments   43, 46n146, 155, 165, 171, 173n604, 175, 183, 185, 196, 219, 265n1074, 268n1088, 274, 274n1104, 371, 372

Dispute Settlement Body (DSB)   129, 130, 133, 258, 258n1049, 275, 275n1109, 278, 304, 306, 351, 351n1349
Dispute Settlement Understanding (WTO)   105n316, 133, 147, 216, 305n1187, 307n1193, 323n1253, 363n1394, 363n1396, 363n1398, 364n1400
Doha Development Agenda (DDA)   23, 63, 67, 68, 70, 72n234, 73n241, 74–79, 89, 112, 114, 303–355, 357, 370, 392
Doha Development Round   22, 62, 71, 74, 75, 78, 94, 103, 114, 262, 286, 290, 303, 304, 310, 325, 329, 331, 333, 334, 338, 348, 350, 356, 362, 364, 401

Economic Research Service (ERS)   8, 11n19, 18n39, 18n41, 19, 20n47, 24n62, 28n74, 38n110, 39n115, 39n119, 41n123, 79n253, 84n273, 118, 336n1295, 362n1393
Embargo Act and War of 1812   31
Ethical   1, 2, 4, 116, 121, 131n388, 132, 291, 301, 308n1198, 384–405
Euro currency   27
European Community   3, 116, 149n456, 219, 225, 371
European Union   83, 95, 110, 117, 129, 348, 356n1369, 374
Export Credit Guarantee (ECG) Programs   50, 51, 115

Farm Bill   38, 39
Farm Security and Rural Investment Act of 2002   38n113, 40n121, 44n138, 63
Federal Agriculture Improvement and Reform Act of 1996   38n113, 272n1096, 374n1438
Federal Crop Insurance Corporation (FCIC)   36, 48
First Five Year Plan of 1953 (China)   52
Fiscal Year (FY)   240, 242, 242n973, 243n973, 244, 245n986, 261
Food, Agriculture, Conservation, and Trade Act of 1990   38n113
Food and Agricultural Policy Research Institute (FAPRI)   167
Food and Agriculture Act   38
Food and Agriculture Organization of the United Nations (FAO)   23, 24n59, 53n173, 54, 81, 332, 336n1293

Foreign Agricultural Service (FAS)   51n165
Francophone African States   8
free trade agreement (FTA)   90, 93, 93n305, 93n306
Free Trade Area for the Americas (FTAA)   93, 93n305, 93n306, 93n307, 94, 95

General Agreement on Tariffs and Trade (GATT-WTO)   64, 96, 387n1492, 388n1494
General Sales Manager 102 (GSM 102)   51, 159n516
General Sales Manager 103 (GSM 103)   51, 159n516
genetically modified (GM or GMO)   15
genetically modified organism (GMO)   15
Glauber, J.   125, 127, 127n378, 365n1404
G-20 Members   3, 249
Greece   8, 53, 54
Green Box   70, 73, 85, 130, 130n387, 135, 139, 153–157, 181, 182, 182n654, 182n658, 183n665, 185, 186, 186n677, 187, 263, 267, 273, 273n1102, 310, 364, 373, 374n1435
gross domestic product (GDP)   23, 79

Harmonized System of Product Classification   138

iDEAS Centre   307n1192, 326, 326n1261, 327n1264, 330n1271, 330n1272, 330n1273, 333n1283, 336n1296, 337, 337n1297, 337n1298, 337n1299, 338n1300, 346n1333, 347n1334, 353n1361, 354n1364, 355, 392n1503, 394n1510, 1368
India   8, 10, 11, 13n26, 14n27, 29–30, 37, 86, 88, 89n291, 89n292, 91n295, 116, 129, 149n456, 150, 153, 181n652, 248, 248n1002, 249n1003, 249n1004, 293n1170, 314, 316n1226, 319n1235, 320, 323n1251
intellectual property (IP)   216, 239, 260, 274, 284, 379, 380n1465, 383
intellectual property rights(s) (IPRs)   216, 239, 260, 274, 284, 379, 380n1465, 383
intergovernmental organization (IGO)   286
International Bank for Reconstruction and Development (World Bank)   27n72
International Centre for Trade and Sustainable Development (ICTSD)   114n339, 117n350, 228n915, 280n1120, 289n1156, 309n1200, 316n1229, 320n1240, 321n1245, 324n1255, 325n1258, 349n1341, 370n1418, 383
International Cotton Advisory Committee (ICAC)   9, 12, 13n25, 29, 118
International Food Policy Research Institute (IFPRI)   14, 26n68, 26n70, 92n301, 147, 293, 328, 338, 339, 354n1366, 401, 401n1532
International Labour Organization (UN)   379n1458
International Monetary Fund (IMF)   82, 84n271
International Trade Centre UNCTAD/WTO   7n6, 332
International Trade Commission (U.S.)   123
International Trade Organization (ITO)   64n206

least-developed countries (LDC)   24, 71, 349n1339
Loan Deficiency payment (LDP)   20, 39, 40, 45, 46

Mali   2, 23–26, 62, 79, 177, 291n1160, 293n1173, 296, 297, 318, 324, 329, 330, 336n1296, 337n1297, 339, 342, 343, 344n1325, 345, 354, 387
Marketing Year   29, 119, 120, 164, 173, 185, 187, 189, 195, 231, 240, 257, 261, 275, 350
Market Loss Assistance Subsidy Payments   43
McNary-Haugen Bill   35, 35n97
Millan, J.   127, 128, 257n1045, 257n1046, 257n1047
ministerial conference   71n232, 72, 74, 76, 85, 90, 91n295, 92, 93, 93n305, 114, 296, 296n1178, 313, 314, 333n1283
most-favoured-nation (clause, principle or treatment)   386
Multifibre Agreement (GATT 1947)   69n226, 133, 142n432, 142n433, 142n434, 142n435, 142n436, 147n446, 180n644, 181, 650
Multiplier effect   2–4

National Bureau of Economic Research (NBER)   32n83
National Cotton Council of America (NCC)   8n12, 119n352, 358n1376, 358n1377, 359n1379, 359n1380

INDEX 417

National Economic Council (NEC)   60
national treatment (clause or principle)   137, 137n407, 152n473, 286
non-agricultural market access   320
non-governmental organization (NGO)   332
non-tariff barrier (NTB)   69, 89
North American Free Trade Agreement (NAFTA)   93n305

Oilseeds Dispute   105, 363n1395
Organization for Economic Co-operation and Development (OECD)   76, 243n973

Pakistan   8, 11, 92n297, 149n456, 150, 293n1170
Panel   7n7, 43, 100, 103, 133, 262, 304, 363, 387
Peace Clause   107n320, 110, 130, 130n386, 132, 134, 138n411, 140, 141, 141n431, 142n437, 142n438, 143n443, 151, 151n469, 152n475, 153, 153n478, 154, 156, 157, 157n712, 158, 162, 179, 181, 185, 263, 265, 273n1100, 274, 308, 347, 361n1381, 370, 373
Pedro de Camargo   69, 70n228, 95, 111n335, 114, 127, 308
Permanent Group of Experts (PGE)   149
President's Advisory Committee for Trade Policy and Negotiations (ACTPN)   60
Price suppression   25, 26, 30, 44, 69, 143n442, 148, 157, 165, 165n567, 165n568, 167, 168n572, 172, 173, 175, 175n613, 176, 177–179, 189, 190n701, 191–197, 191n709, 220–225, 235, 236, 247–249, 257, 260, 261–265, 264n1071, 268n1088, 269, 270, 274, 275, 295, 296, 340, 350, 359, 382, 385, 400
Production Flexibility Contract payment (PFC)   43, 46–48, 152n474, 154, 265n1074
Public choice   357, 366–368, 395

Republic of China   8, 30
Republic of Uzbekistan   8, 30, 330
Retaliation   106, 216n847, 239, 246, 249, 251, 252, 255, 256, 261, 263, 276, 277, 281–283, 285, 286, 289, 352, 358, 377, 377n1443, 378n1456, 382n1455, 397, 400
(Agreement on) Sanitary and Phytosanitary (Measures) (WTO)   89

Serious prejudice, also 'threat of'   166, 166n569, 173–175, 177, 178
Southern African Development Community (SADC)   86, 288n1152
Southern Common Market (MERCOSUR)   382
Soybean   105, 106, 118, 372
special and differential treatment   68, 69n224, 75, 76, 77, 88, 89, 89n292, 138n411, 140n423
Step 2 subsidies (Program)   49, 171, 175, 201, 203, 220, 223, 229, 265, 271, 374
Sub-Committee on Cotton (WTO)   3, 78, 328, 332, 349, 350
Sugar Dispute   3, 109, 111, 292, 316, 317, 317n1231, 405
Sumner, D.   9, 25, 167, 250, 269, 362
Sumner Model   247, 279
Supplier Credit Guarantee Program (SCGP)   51, 171, 272

Tariff   32, 69–71, 72n234, 78, 89, 106n318, 133, 138, 323
Tariff Bill of 1816   32
Total aggregate measurement of support   139, 373, 374, 374n1435
(Agreement on) Trade-Related Aspects of Intellectual Property Rights (WTO)   78, 216, 255, 261

UN Centre for International Trade Law (UNCITRAL)   392n1506
UN Conference on Trade And Development (UNCTAD)   7n6, 7n8, 7n9, 8n10, 9, 12, 23n57, 90, 286, 316n1227, 350n1346
UN Development Program (UNDP)   44, 57, 293, 326n1263
United Kingdom (UK)   58n197
United Nations (Organization)   7, 12, 23, 53n173, 53n174, 86n278, 286, 293, 316n1228
United States Agency for International Development (USAID)   27, 342, 386
United States Department of Agriculture (USDA)   8, 12, 20, 43, 44
United States International Trade Commission (USITC)   123
United States of America (US or USA)   387n1491

United States Trade Representative, Office of the (USTR) 59
Upland cotton 7–30, 31, 62–97, 100, 103–131, 132–261, 262–298, 303–355, 360
Uruguay Round Agreement on Agriculture (also: AoA) 2, 70n229, 72n235, 76, 76n246, 308n1196
U.S. Code 48n157
U.S. Department of Agriculture (USDA) 38n110, 39n115, 39n118

World Bank 13, 22n52, 23, 23n58, 25, 26, 27n72, 52n169, 52n170, 52n171, 53n172, 53n173, 53n174, 72, 72n237, 78n249, 80n258, 82, 84n271, 118, 147, 304n1184, 325n1257, 332, 347n1334
World market suppression 165
World Trade Organization (WTO) 64, 89, 388

Printed in the United States
By Bookmasters